DEMOCRACY IN AMERICA

DOVER THRIFT EDITIONS

Alexis de Tocqueville

Translated by
Henry Reeve

Edited, with notes, by
Francis Bowen

TWO VOLUMES BOUND AS ONE

DOVER PUBLICATIONS, INC.
MINEOLA, NEW YORK

Bibliographical Note

This Dover edition, first published in 2017, is an unabridged republication of two volumes originally published by Sever and Francis, Cambridge, Massachusetts, in 1863 [Third edition]. The works appear here for the first time as a bound volume.

Sensitive readers should be forewarned that the text in places contains racial and cultural references that may be deemed offensive by modern standards.

International Standard Book Number
ISBN-13: 978-0-486-81559-6
ISBN-10: 0-486-81559-5

Manufactured in the United States by LSC Communications
81559501   2017
www.doverpublications.com

DEMOCRACY IN AMERICA

VOLUME I

PREFACE

THE present publication has been made to conform as nearly as possible to the twelfth edition of the original work, the latest which appeared at Paris under the direct supervision of the author. De Tocqueville appended to this edition, published in 1850, his essay, written three years before, for the Academy of the Moral and Political Sciences, on Democracy in Switzerland; a full report of his remarkable Speech in the Chamber of Deputies predicting the Revolution of 1848 just a month before its occurrence; and a feeling and eloquent Advertisement, addressed to his countrymen, pointing them to the example of the United States, and urging the study of American institutions as affording the most instructive lessons for the organization and conduct of the new French republic. These three additions are here for the first time translated, both because they have an intimate connection with the body of the work, and because they reflect much light upon the character and opinions of the writer towards the close of his life. The first of them is specially interesting to American readers, as it contains an able analysis and criticism of the republican institutions of Switzerland, illustrated by frequent

comparison with the constitutions and laws of the
American republics.

The writer's confidence in the ultimate success
and peaceful establishment of democracy, as the
controlling principle in the government of all
nations, seems to have been not only not impaired,
but strengthened, in the latter part of his life, by
the observations which he continued to make of
the trial that it was undergoing in the United
States, and of the progress and prosperity of this
country in the years subsequent to the first publication of his great work. And if his life had
been spared to witness the terrible ordeal to
which the providence of God is now subjecting
us, it may confidently be believed that this trust
on his part would not have been shaken, even if
he should have been compelled to admit, that the
Federal tie which once bound our large family of
democratic States together would probably never
be reunited. He would clearly have seen, what
most of the politicians of Europe seem at present
incapable of perceiving, that it is not representative democracy, but the Federal principle, which
is now on trial, and that the only question is,
whether any bond is strong enough to hold together a confederacy so populous and extensive
as to form in the aggregate the largest and most
powerful empire that the world has ever known.
He who would attempt to make up his own opinion on this great question can find no better guide
than in the present work. De Tocqueville is the
friend, but by no means the indiscriminate eulo-
gist, of American institutions; and his criticisms,
which are shrewd and searching, ought to be even
more welcome than his commendations, for they
are more instructive. He foresaw, if not the im-

mmence, at least the probability, of the great convulsion which the country is now undergoing ; and there can be no clearer indication of the causes which have at last induced it, than that which was made by this wise and impartial foreigner nearly thirty years ago.

The notes which I have made, though somewhat numerous, are generally very brief. They are notes, and not disquisitions, my object being only to elucidate or correct the text, and not to controvert or supplement it by foisting my own opinions upon the reader's notice. Most of them are only corrections of slight errors on points of detail, such as a stranger who made but a short stay in the country could not be expected to avoid, or notices that some statements now require to be limited or modified, in consequence of the changes that have taken place during the last quarter of a century. An outline sketch of De Tocqueville's life is designed only to satisfy curiosity as to the chief points in his career, without entering into any analysis of his character and labors. Those who seek further information can obtain it from the Memoirs and Correspondence that have recently been published by his life-long friend, M. de Beaumont.

In accepting an invitation to become the editor of this work, I supposed that it would only be necessary for me to translate the new matter that had been appended to the recent editions of the original, and to supply such brief annotations as a careful revision of the text might show to be necessary. It was intended to furnish an exact reprint of the English translation, which passed to a second edition in London, a year ago, under the respectable name of Mr. Henry Reeve. But a

comparison of it with the original was hardly
begun, before I found to my dismay that this
translation was utterly inadequate and untrust-
worthy. As a pretty thorough exposure of its
demerits has recently been made in an English
periodical, where there can be no suspicion of an
unfavorable bias, I can have no scruple in speaking
of it as it deserves. It is generally feeble, inele-
gant, and verbose, and too often obscure and incorrect. On comparing every line of it with the
original, the alterations which were found to be
necessary were so numerous and sweeping, that
perhaps the present edition, of the first volume at
least, might more fitly be called a new translation
than an amended one. The second volume, I
ought to say, is somewhat better done ; as it was
published several years after the appearance of
the first, forming in fact a distinct work, the translator had found time to increase his familiarity
with the French language, and even to make some
progress in his knowledge of English.

This is plain speaking, and I feel bound to vindicate it, by offering some specimens of the translation, both in its primitive and its amended state.
The following extracts are taken almost at random
from the body of the book, and the original is prefixed to facilitate the labor of comparison. The
citations are all from the first volume, and the
references for Mr. Reeve's translation are to the
second London edition, Longmans, 1862.

Des hommes sacrifient à une opinion religieuse leurs amis, leur famille
et leur patrie ; on peut les croire absorbés dans la poursuite de ce bien intel-
lectuel qu'ils sont venus acheter à si haut prix. On les voit cependant re-
chercher d'une ardeur presque égale les richesses matérielles et les jouissances
morales, le ciel dans l'autre monde, le bien-être et la liberté dans celui-ci.
Sous leur main les principes politiques, les lois et les institutions humaines
semblent choses malléables, qui peuvent se tourner et se combiner à volonté.

Devant eux s'abaissent les barrières qui emprisonnaient la société au sein de laquelle ils sont nés ; les vieilles opinions, qui depuis des siècles dirigeaient le monde, s'évanouissent ; une carrière presque sans bornes, un champ sans horizon se découvre : l'esprit humain s'y précipite ; il le parcourt en tous sens ; mais, arrivé aux limites du monde politique, il s'arrête de lui-même ; il dépose en tremblant l'usage de ses plus redoutables facultés ; il abjure le doute ; il renonce au besoin d'innover ; il s'abstient même de soulever le voile du sanctuaire ; il s'incline avec respect devant des vérités qu'il admet sans les discuter. — p. 52.

REEVE'S TRANSLATION.

It might be imagined that men who sacrificed their friends, their family, and their native land to a religious conviction, were absorbed in the pursuit of the intellectual advantages which they purchased at so dear a rate. The energy, however, with which they strove for the acquirement of wealth, moral enjoyment, and the comforts as well as liberties of the world, is scarcely inferior to that with which they devoted themselves to Heaven.

Political principles, and all human laws and institutions were moulded and altered at their pleasure ; the barriers of the society in which they were born were broken down before them ; the old principles which had governed the world for ages were no more ; a path without a term, and a field without an horizon were opened to the exploring and ardent curiosity of man : but at the limits of the political world he checks his researches, he discreetly lays aside the use of his most formidable faculties, he no longer consents to doubt or to innovate, but carefully abstaining from raising the curtain of the sanctuary, he yields with submissive respect to truths which he will not discuss. — p. 33.

REVISED TRANSLATION.

One would think that men who had sacrificed their friends, their family, and their native land to a religious conviction would be wholly absorbed in the pursuit of the treasure which they had just purchased at so high a price. And yet we find them seeking with nearly equal zeal for material wealth and moral good, — for well-being and freedom on earth, and salvation in heaven. They moulded and altered at pleasure all political principles, and all human laws and institutions ; they broke down the barriers of the society in which they were born ; they disregarded the old principles which had governed the world for ages ; a career without bounds, a field without a horizon, was opened before them : they precipitate themselves into it, and traverse it in every direction. But, having reached the limits of the political world, they stop of their own accord, and lay aside with awe the use of their most formidable faculties ; they no longer doubt or innovate ; they abstain from raising even the veil of the sanctuary, and bow with submissive respect before truths which they admit without discussion. — p. 54.

Chez les petites nations, l'œil de la société pénètre partout ; l'esprit d'amélioration descend jusque dans les moindres détails : l'ambition du peuple étant fort tempérée par sa faiblesse, ses efforts et ses ressources se tournent presque entièrement vers son bien-être intérieur, et ne sont point sujets à se dissiper en vaine fumée de gloire. De plus, les facultés de chacun y étant généralement bornées, les désirs le sont également. La médiocrité des fortunes y rend les conditions à peu près égales ; les mœurs y ont une allure simple et paisible. Ainsi, à tout prendre et en faisant état des divers degrés de moralité et de lumière, on rencontre ordinairement chez les petites nations plus d'aisance, de population et de tranquillité que chez les grandes. — p. 190.

REEVE'S TRANSLATION.	REVISED TRANSLATION.
In small nations the scrutiny of society penetrates into every part, and the spirit of improvement enters into the most trifling details ; as the ambition of the people is necessarily checked by its weakness, all the efforts and resources of the citizens are turned to the internal benefit of the community, and are not likely to evaporate in the fleeting breath of glory. The desires of every individual are limited, because extraordinary faculties are rarely to be met with. The gifts of an equal fortune render the various conditions of life uniform ; and the manners of the inhabitants are orderly and simple. Thus, if one estimate the gradations of popular morality and enlightenment, we shall generally find that in small nations there are more persons in easy circumstances, a more numerous population, and a more tranquil state of society, than in great empires. — p. 176.	In small states, the watchfulness of society penetrates into every part, and the spirit of improvement enters into the smallest details ; the ambition of the people being necessarily checked by its weakness, all the efforts and resources of the citizens are turned to the internal well-being of the community, and are not likely to evaporate in the fleeting breath of glory. The powers of every individual being generally limited, his desires are proportionally small. Mediocrity of fortune makes the various conditions of life nearly equal, and the manners of the inhabitants are orderly and simple. Thus, all things considered, and allowance being made for the various degrees of morality and enlightenment, we shall generally find in small nations more ease, population, and tranquillity than in large ones. — p. 202.

On ne rencontrera jamais, quoi qu'on fasse, de véritable puissance parmi les hommes, que dans le concours libre des volontés. Or, il n'y a au monde que le patriotisme, ou la religion, qui puisse faire marcher pendant longtemps vers un même but l'universalité des citoyens.

Il ne dépend pas des lois de ranimer des croyances qui s'éteignent; mais il dépend des lois d'intéresser les hommes aux destinées de leur pays. Il dépend des lois de réveiller et de diriger cet instinct vague de la patrie qui n'abandonne jamais le cœur de l'homme, et, en le liant aux pensées, aux passions, aux habitudes de chaque jour, d'en faire un sentiment réfléchi et durable. Et qu'on ne dise point qu'il est trop tard pour le tenter ; les nations ne vieillissent point de la même manière que les hommes. Chaque génération qui naît dans leur sein est comme un peuple nouveau qui vient s'offrir à la main du législateur. — pp. 113, 114.

REEVE'S TRANSLATION.	REVISED TRANSLATION.
Whatever exertions may be made, no true power can be founded among men which does not depend upon the free union of their inclinations ; and patriotism or religion are the only two motives in the world which can	Do what you may, there is no true power among men except in the free union of their will ; and patriotism or religion are the only two motives in the world which can long urge all the people towards the same end.

permanently direct the whole of a body politic to one end.

Laws cannot succeed in rekindling the ardor of an extinguished faith ; but men may be interested in the fate of their country by the laws. By this influence, the vague impulse of patriotism, which never abandons the human heart, may be directed and revived ; and if it be connected with the thoughts, the passions, and the daily habits of life, it may be consolidated into a durable and rational sentiment. Let it not be said that the time for the experiment is already past ; for the old age of nations is not like the old age of men, and every fresh generation is a new people ready for the care of the legislator. — p. 95.

Laws cannot rekindle an extinguished faith ; but men may be interested by the laws in the fate of their country. It depends upon the laws to awaken and direct the vague impulse of patriotism, which never abandons the human heart ; and if it be connected with the thoughts, the passions, and the daily habits of life, it may be consolidated into a durable and rational sentiment. Let it not be said that it is too late to make the experiment ; for nations do not grow old as men do, and every fresh generation is a new people ready for the care of the legislator. — p. 118.

La commune, prise en masse et par rapport au gouvernement central, n'est qu'un individu comme un autre, auquel s'applique la théorie que je viens d'indiquer.

La liberté communale découle donc, aux États-Unis, du dogme même de la souveraineté du peuple ; toutes les républiques américaines ont plus ou moins reconnu cette indépendance ; mais chez les peuples de la Nouvelle-Angleterre, les circonstances en ont particulièrement favorisé le développement.

Dans cette partie de l'Union, la vie politique a pris naissance au sein même des communes ; on pourrait presque dire qu'à son origine chacune d'elles était une nation indépendante. Lorsque ensuite les rois d'Angleterre réclamèrent leur part de la souveraineté, ils se bornèrent à prendre la puissance centrale. Ils laissèrent la commune dans l'état où ils la trouvèrent ; maintenant les communes de la Nouvelle-Angleterre sont sujettes ; mais dans le principe elles ne l'étaient point ou l'étaient à peine. Elles n'ont donc pas reçu leurs pouvoirs ; ce sont elles au contraire qui semblent s'être dessaisies, en faveur de l'État, d'une portion de leur indépendance : distinction importante, et qui doit rester présente à l'esprit du lecteur.

Les communes ne sont en général soumises à l'État que quand il s'agit d'un intérêt que j'appellerai social, c'est-à-dire qu'elles partagent avec d'autres. Pour tout ce qui n'a rapport qu'à elles seules, les communes sont restées des corps indépendants ; et parmi les habitants de la Nouvelle-Angleterre, il ne s'en rencontre aucun, je pense, qui reconnaisse au gouvernement de l'État le droit d'intervenir dans la direction des intérêts purement communaux.

On voit donc les communes de la Nouvelle-Angleterre vendre et acheter, attaquer et se défendre devant les tribunaux, charger leur budget ou le dégrever, sans qu'aucune autorité administrative quelconque songe à s'y opposer.

Quant aux devoirs sociaux, elles sont tenues d'y satisfaire. Ainsi, l'État a-t-il besoin d'argent, la commune n'est pas libre de lui accorder ou de lui refuser son concours. L'État veut-il ouvrir une route, la commune n'est pas maîtresse de lui fermer son territoire. Fait-il un réglement de police, la commune doit l'exécuter. Veut-il organiser l'instruction sur un plan uniforme dans toute l'étendue du pays, la commune est tenue de créer les écoles voulues par la loi. — pp. 77, 78.

REEVE'S TRANSLATION.	REVISED TRANSLATION.

The township, taken as a whole, and in relation to the government of the country, may be looked upon as an individual to whom the theory I have just alluded to is applied. Municipal independence is therefore a natural consequence of the principle of the sovereignty of the people in the United States : all the American republics recognize it more or less ; but circumstances have peculiarly favored its growth in New England.

In this part of the Union, the impulsion of political activity was given in the townships ; and it may almost be said that each of them originally formed an independent nation. When the kings of England asserted their supremacy, they were contented to assume the central power of the State. The townships of New England remained as they were before ; and although they are now subject to the State, they were at first scarcely dependent upon it. It is important to remember that they have not been invested with privileges, but that they have, on the contrary, forfeited a portion of their independence to the State. The townships are only subordinate to the State in those interests which I shall term *social*, as they are common to all the citizens. They are independent in all that concerns themselves ; and amongst the inhabitants of New England I believe that not a man is to be found who would acknowledge that the State has any right to interfere in their local interests. The towns of New England buy and sell, prosecute or are indicted, augment or diminish their rates, without the slightest opposition on the part of the administrative authority of the State.

They are bound, however, to com-

The township, taken as a whole, and in relation to the central government, is only an individual like any other to whom the theory I have just described is applicable. Municipal independence in the United States is, therefore, a natural consequence of this very principle of the sovereignty of the people. All the American republics recognize it more or less ; but circumstances have peculiarly favored its growth in New England.

In this part of the Union, political life has its origin in the townships ; and it may almost be said that each of them originally formed an independent nation. When the kings of England afterwards asserted their supremacy, they were content to assume the central power of the State. They left the townships where they were before ; and although they are now subject to the State, they were not at first, or were hardly so. They did not receive their powers from the central authority, but, on the contrary, they gave up a portion of their independence to the State. This is an important distinction, and one which the reader must constantly recollect. The townships are generally subordinate to the State only in those interests which I shall term *social*, as they are common to all the others. They are independent in all that concerns themselves alone ; and amongst the inhabitants of New England I believe that not a man is to be found who would acknowledge that the State has any right to interfere in their town affairs. The towns of New England buy and sell, prosecute or are indicted, augment or diminish their rates, and no administrative authority ever thinks of offering any opposition.

ply with the demands of the community. If the State is in need of money, a town can neither give nor withhold the supplies. If the State projects a road, the township cannot refuse to let it cross its territory; if a police regulation is made by the State, it must be enforced by the town. A uniform system of instruction is organized all over the country, and every town is bound to establish the schools which the law ordains. — pp. 60, 61.

There are certain social duties, however, which they are bound to fulfil. If the State is in need of money, a town cannot withhold the supplies; if the State projects a road, the township cannot refuse to let it cross its territory; if a police regulation is made by the State, it must be enforced by the town; if a uniform system of public instruction is enacted, every town is bound to establish the schools which the law ordains. — pp. 80, 81.

D'une autre part, je doute fort qu'un vêtement particulier porte les hommes publics à se respecter eux-mêmes, quand ils ne sont pas naturellement disposés à le faire ; car je ne saurais croire qu'ils aient plus d'égard pour leur habit que pour leur personne.

Quand je vois, parmi nous, certains magistrats brusquer les parties ou leur adresser des bons mots, lever les épaules aux moyens de la défense et sourire avec complaisance à l'énumération des charges, je voudrais qu'on essayât de leur ôter leur robe, afin de découvrir si, se trouvant vêtus comme les simples citoyens, cela ne les rappellerait pas à la dignité naturelle de l'espèce humaine.

Aucun des fonctionnaires publics des États-Unis n'a de costume, mais tous reçoivent un salaire.

Ceci découle, plus naturellement encore que ce qui précède, des principes démocratiques. Une démocratie peut environner de pompe ses magistrats et les couvrir de soie et d'or sans attaquer directement le principe de son existence. De pareils priviléges sont passagers ; ils tiennent à la place, et non à l'homme. Mais établir des fonctions gratuites, c'est créer une classe de fonctionnaires riches et indépendants, c'est former le noyau d'une aristocratie. Si le peuple conserve encore le droit du choix, l'exercice de ce droit a donc des bornes nécessaires.

Quand on voit une république démocratique rendre gratuites les fonctions rétribuées, je crois qu'on peut en conclure qu'elle marche vers la monarchie. Et quand une monarchie commence à rétribuer les fonctions gratuites, c'est la marque assurée qu'on s'avance vers un état despotique ou vers un état républicain. — pp. 245, 246.

REEVE'S TRANSLATION.

On the other hand, it is very doubtful whether a peculiar dress contributes to the respect which public characters ought to have for their own position, at least when they are not otherwise inclined to respect it. When a magistrate (and in France such instances are not rare) indulges his

REVISED TRANSLATION.

On the other hand, it is very doubtful whether a peculiar dress induces public men to respect themselves, when they are not otherwise inclined to do so. When a magistrate (and in France such instances are not rare) snubs the parties before him, or indulges his wit at their expense, or

trivial wit at the expense of the prisoner, or derides the predicament in
which a culprit is placed, it would be
well to deprive him of his robes of
office, to see whether he would recall
some portion of the natural dignity
of mankind when he is reduced to the
apparel of a private citizen.

A democracy may, however, allow
a certain show of magisterial pomp,
and clothe its officers in silks and
gold, without seriously compromising
its principles. Privileges of this kind
are transitory; they belong to the
place, and are distinct from the individual: but if public officers are not
uniformly remunerated by the State,
the public charges must be intrusted
to men of opulence and independence,
who constitute the basis of an aristocracy; and if the people still retains
its right of election, that election can
only be made from a certain class of
citizens.

When a democratic republic renders offices which had formerly been
remunerated, gratuitous, it may safely
be believed that that state is advancing to monarchical institutions; and
when a monarchy begins to remunerate such officers as had hitherto been
unpaid, it is a sure sign that it is
approaching towards a despotic or a
republican form of government. —
pp. 238, 239.

shrugs his shoulders at their pleas of
defence, or smiles complacently as
the charges are enumerated, I should
like to deprive him of his robes of
office, to see whether, when he is reduced to the garb of a private citizen,
he would not recall some portion of
the natural dignity of mankind.

No public officer in the United
States has an official costume, but
every one of them receives a salary.
And this, also, still more naturally
than what precedes, results from democratic principles. A democracy may
allow some magisterial pomp, and
clothe its officers in silks and gold,
without seriously compromising its
principles. Privileges of this kind are
transitory; they belong to the place,
and not to the man: but if public
officers are unpaid, a class of rich
and independent public functionaries
will be created, who will constitute
the basis of an aristocracy; and if
the people still retain their right of
election, the choice can be made only
from a certain class of citizens.

When a democratic republic renders gratuitous offices which had formerly been remunerated, it may safely
be inferred that the state is advancing
towards monarchy. And when a
monarchy begins to remunerate such
officers as had hitherto been unpaid,
it is a sure sign that it is approaching
a despotic or a republican form of
government. — pp. 263, 264.

Ce qu'ils apercevaient d'abord, c'est que le conseil d'Etat, en France,
étant un grand tribunal fixé au centre du royaume, il y avait une sorte de
tyrannie à renvoyer préliminairement devant lui tous les plaignants. —
p. 126.

REEVE'S TRANSLATION.

They were at once led to conclude
that the Conseil d'Etat in France was
a great tribunal, established in the
centre of the kingdom, which exercised a preliminary and somewhat
tyrannical jurisdiction in all political
causes. — p. 108.

REVISED TRANSLATION.

They at once perceived that, the
Council of State in France being a
great tribunal established in the centre of the kingdom, it was a sort of
tyranny to send all complainants before it as a preliminary step. — p. 131.

Les peuples entre eux ne sont que des individus. C'est surtout pour
paraître avec avantage vis-à-vis des étrangers qu'une nation a besoin d'un
gouvernement unique. — pp. 137, 138.

REEVE'S TRANSLATION.

The external relations of a people may be compared to those of private individuals, and they cannot be advantageously maintained without the agency of the single head of a Government. — p. 121.

REVISED TRANSLATION.

The people in themselves are only individuals; and the special reason why they need to be united under one government is, that they may appear to advantage before foreigners. — p. 144.

Il y a des gens en France qui considèrent les institutions républicaines comme l'instrument passager de leur grandeur. Ils mesurent des yeux l'espace immense qui sépare leurs vices et leurs misères de la puissance et des richesses, et ils voudraient entasser des ruines dans cet abîme pour essayer de le combler. Ceux-là sont à la liberté ce que les compagnies franches du moyen âge étaient aux rois; ils font la guerre pour leur propre compte, alors même qu'ils portent ses couleurs : la république vivra toujours assez longtemps pour les tirer de leur bassesse présente. Ce n'est pas à eux que je parle. — p. 356.

REEVE'S TRANSLATION.

There are persons in France who look upon republican institutions as a temporary means of power, of wealth, and distinction ; men who are the *condottieri* of liberty, and who fight for their own advantage, whatever be the colors they wear : it is not to these that I address myself. — p. 364.

REVISED TRANSLATION.

There are persons in France who look upon republican institutions only as a means of obtaining grandeur ; they measure the immense space which separates their vices and misery from power and riches, and they aim to fill up this gulf with ruins, that they may pass over it. These men are the *condottieri* of liberty, and fight for their own advantage, whatever be the colors they wear. The republic will stand long enough, they think, to draw them up out of their present degradation. It is not to these that I address myself. — p. 393.

Perhaps it is not too much to say of a work which has hitherto been before the English and American public only in such a translation as this, that it still remains to be perused by them for the first time in a form in which it can be understood and appreciated. I have bestowed a good deal of labor upon it, in the hope of aiding the circulation of a book of which it has been justly said by the highest living authority on the science of general politics, Mr. John Stuart Mill, that it is

" such as Montesquieu might have written, if to his genius he had superadded good sense, and the lights which mankind have since gained from the experiences of a period in which they may be said to have lived centuries in fifty years." Especially ought it to be generally studied here in the United States, where no thinking man who exercises the privileges of a voter can fail to derive from it profitable information respecting the nature of the institutions under which he lives, together with friendly warnings and wise counsels to aid him in the proper discharge of his political duties.

CAMBRIDGE, August 5, 1862.

AUTHOR'S ADVERTISEMENT

TO THE TWELFTH EDITION.*

HOWEVER sudden and momentous the events which we have just beheld so swiftly accomplished, the author of this book has a right to say that they have not taken him by surprise.† His work was written fifteen years ago, with a mind constantly occupied by a single thought, — that the advent of democracy as a governing power in the world's affairs, universal and irresistible, was at hand. Let it be read over again, and there will be found on every page a solemn warning, that society changes its forms, humanity its condition, and that new destinies are impending. It was stated in the very Introduction of the work, that "the gradual development of the principle of Equality is a providential fact. It has all the chief characteristics of such a fact; it is universal, it is durable, it constantly eludes all human

---

* The twelfth edition of this work appeared at Paris in 1850, and this Advertisement was prefixed to it by De Tocqueville in reference to the French Revolution of 1848. — AM. ED.

† The writer here alludes to a speech which he made in the Chamber of Deputies, on the 27th of January, 1848, just one month before the Revolution was accomplished. He annexed a report of this speech to the twelfth edition of his work, and a translation of it will be found at the end of the second volume. — AM. ED.

interference, and all events as well as all men
contribute to its progress. Would it be wise to
imagine that a social movement, the causes of
which lie so far back, can be checked by the efforts of one generation ? Can it be believed that
the democracy, which has overthrown the feudal
system and vanquished kings, will retreat before
tradesmen and capitalists? Will it stop now that
it is grown so strong and its adversaries so weak?"

He who wrote these lines in the presence of a
monarchy which had been rather confirmed than
shaken by the Revolution of 1830, may now fearlessly ask again the attention of the public to his
work. And he may be permitted to add, that the
present state of affairs gives to his book an immediate interest and a practical utility which it had
not when it was first published. Royalty was then
in power; it has now been overthrown. The institutions of America, which were a subject only
of curiosity to monarchical France, ought to be a
subject of study for republican France. It is not
force alone, but good laws, which give stability to
a new government. After the combatant, comes
the legislator ; the one has pulled down, the
other builds up; each has his office. Though it
is no longer a question whether we shall have a
monarchy or a republic in France, we are yet to
learn whether we shall have a convulsed or a
tranquil republic, — whether it shall be regular
or irregular, pacific or warlike, liberal or oppressive, — a republic which menaces the sacred rights
of property and family, or one which honors and

protects them both. It is a fearful problem, the solution of which concerns not France alone, but the whole civilized world. If we save ourselves, we save at the same time all the nations which surround us. If we perish, we shall cause all of them to perish with us. According as democratic liberty or democratic tyranny is established here, the destiny of the world will be different; and it may be said that this day it depends upon us, whether the republic shall be everywhere finally established, or everywhere finally overthrown.

Now this problem, which among us has but just been proposed for solution, was solved by America more than sixty years ago. The principle of the sovereignty of the people, which we enthroned in France but yesterday, has there held undivided sway for over sixty years. It is there reduced to practice in the most direct, the most unlimited, and the most absolute manner. For sixty years, the people who have made it the common source of all their laws have increased continually in population, in territory, and in opulence; and — consider it well — it is found to have been, during that period, not only the most prosperous, but the most stable, of all the nations of the earth. Whilst all the nations of Europe have been devastated by war or torn by civil discord, the American people alone in the civilized world have remained at peace. Almost all Europe was convulsed by revolutions; America has not had even a revolt.* The republic there has not been

---

* Thank God that this is history, though it is not the present fact. The

the assailant, but the guardian, of all vested rights; the property of individuals has had better guaranties there than in any other country of the world; anarchy has there been as unknown as despotism.

Where else could we find greater causes of hope, or more instructive lessons? Let us look to America, not in order to make a servile copy of the institutions which she has established, but to gain a clearer view of the polity which will be the best for us; let us look there less to find examples than instruction; let us borrow from her the principles, rather than the details, of her laws. The laws of the French republic may be, and ought to be, in many cases, different from those which govern the United States; but the principles on which the American constitutions rest, — those principles of order, of the balance of powers, of true liberty, of deep and sincere respect for right, — are indispensable to all republics; they ought to be common to all; and it may be said beforehand, that wherever they shall not be found, the republic will soon have ceased to exist.

1848.

record of what our country has been, and of what she accomplished during three quarters of a century, is beyond the power even of a gigantic rebellion to blot out. Let only the faint-hearted, on looking into the past, exclaim, with the great Italian,

> " Nessun maggior dolore
> Che ricordarsi del tempo felice
> Nella miseria."

Nobler spirits will say, though the memory of what has been be the only star which shines in the thick darkness that now surrounds us, it shall light us on to mightier efforts, and kindle in our hearts a surer hope of the reappearance of the day, — of a day whose sunshine shall not be broken even by the one dark cloud that dimmed our former prosperity. — AM. ED.

CONTENTS OF VOL. I.

CONTENTS.

CHAPTER VI.

CHAPTER VII.

CHAPTER VIII.

CHAPTER IX.

CHAPTER X.

CHAPTER XI.

CHAPTER XII.

CHAPTER XIII.

INTRODUCTION.

A MONGST the novel objects that attracted my attention during my stay in the United States, nothing struck me more forcibly than the general equality of condition among the people. I readily discovered the prodigious influence which this primary fact exercises on the whole course of society; it gives a peculiar direction to public opinion, and a peculiar tenor to the laws; it imparts new maxims to the governing authorities, and peculiar habits to the governed.

I soon perceived that the influence of this fact extends far beyond the political character and the laws of the country, and that it has no less empire over civil society than over the government; it creates opinions, gives birth to new sentiments, founds novel customs, and modifies whatever it does not produce. The more I advanced in the study of American society, the more I perceived that this equality of condition is the fundamental fact from which all others seem to be derived, and the central point at which all my observations constantly terminated.

I then turned my thoughts to our own hemisphere, and thought that I discerned there something analogous to the spectacle which the New World presented to me. I observed that equality of condition, though it has not there reached the extreme limit which it seems to have attained in the United States, is constantly approaching it; and that the democracy which governs the American communities appears to be rapidly rising into power in Europe.

Hence I conceived the idea of the book which is now before the reader.

It is evident to all alike that a great democratic revolution is going on amongst us; but all do not look at it in the same light. To some it appears to be novel but accidental, and, as such, they hope it may still be checked; to others it seems irresistible, because it is the most uniform, the most ancient, and the most permanent tendency which is to be found in history.

I look back for a moment on the situation of France seven hundred years ago, when the territory was divided amongst a small number of families, who were the owners of the soil and the rulers of the inhabitants; the right of governing descended with the family inheritance from generation to generation; force was the only means by which man could act on man; and landed property was the sole source of power.

Soon, however, the political power of the clergy was founded, and began to increase: the clergy opened their ranks to all classes, to the poor and the rich, the vassal and the lord; through the Church, equality penetrated into the Government, and he who as a serf must have vegetated in perpetual bondage took his place as a priest in the midst of nobles, and not unfrequently above the heads of kings.

The different relations of men with each other became more complicated and numerous as society gradually became more stable and civilized. Hence the want of civil laws was felt; and the ministers of law soon rose from the obscurity of the tribunals and their dusty chambers, to appear at the court of the monarch, by the side of the feudal barons clothed in their ermine and their mail.

Whilst the kings were ruining themselves by their great

enterprises, and the nobles exhausting their resources by private wars, the lower orders were enriching themselves by commerce. The influence of money began to be perceptible in state affairs. The transactions of business opened a new road to power, and the financier rose to a station of political influence in which he was at once flattered and despised.

Gradually the diffusion of intelligence, and the increasing taste for literature and art, caused learning and talent to become a means of government; mental ability led to social power, and the man of letters took a part in the affairs of the state.

The value attached to high birth declined just as fast as new avenues to power were discovered. In the eleventh century, nobility was beyond all price; in the thirteenth, it might be purchased. Nobility was first conferred by gift in 1270; and equality was thus introduced into the government by the aristocracy itself.

In the course of these seven hundred years, it sometimes happened that the nobles, in order to resist the authority of the crown, or to diminish the power of their rivals, granted some political influence to the common people. Or, more frequently, the king permitted the lower orders to have a share in the government, with the intention of depressing the aristocracy.

In France, the kings have always been the most active and the most constant of levellers. When they were strong and ambitious, they spared no pains to raise the people to the level of the nobles; when they were temperate and feeble, they allowed the people to rise above themselves. Some assisted the democracy by their talents, others by their vices. Louis XI. and Louis XIV. reduced all ranks beneath the throne to the same degree of subjection; and, finally, Louis XV. descended, himself and all his court, into the dust.

As soon as land began to be held on any other than a feudal tenure, and personal property in its turn became able to confer influence and power, every discovery in the arts, every improvement in commerce or manufactures, created so many new elements of equality among men. Henceforward every new invention, every new want which it occasioned, and every new desire which craved satisfaction, was a step towards a general levelling. The taste for luxury, the love of war, the empire of fashion, and the most superficial as well as the deepest passions of the human heart, seemed to co-operate to enrich the poor and to impoverish the rich.

From the time when the exercise of the intellect became a source of strength and of wealth, we see that every addition to science, every fresh truth, and every new idea became a germ of power placed within the reach of the people. Poetry, eloquence, and memory, the graces of the mind, the glow of imagination, depth of thought, and all the gifts which Heaven scatters at a venture, turned to the advantage of the democracy; and even when they were in the possession of its adversaries, they still served its cause by throwing into bold relief the natural greatness of man. Its conquests spread, therefore, with those of civilization and knowledge; and literature became an arsenal open to all, where the poor and the weak daily resorted for arms.

In running over the pages of our history for seven hundred years, we shall scarcely find a single great event which has not promoted equality of condition.

The Crusades and the English wars decimated the nobles and divided their possessions: the municipal corporations introduced democratic liberty into the bosom of feudal monarchy; the invention of fire-arms equalized the vassal and the noble on the field of battle; the art of printing opened the same resources to the minds of all classes; the post-office brought knowledge alike to the door of the cottage and to the gate of the palace; and Protestantism proclaimed that all men are alike able to find the road to heaven. The discovery of America opened a thousand new paths to fortune, and led obscure adventurers to wealth and power.

If, beginning with the eleventh century, we examine what has happened in France from one half-century to another, we shall not fail to perceive, at the end of each of these periods, that a twofold revolution has taken place in the state of society. The noble has gone down on the social ladder, and the commoner has gone up; the one descends as the other rises. Every half-century brings them nearer to each other, and they will soon meet.

Nor is this peculiar to France. Whithersoever we turn our eyes, we perceive the same revolution going on throughout the Christian world. The various occurrences of national existence have everywhere turned to the advantage of democracy: all men have aided it by their exertions, both those who have intentionally labored in its cause, and those who have served it unwittingly; those who have fought for it, and those who have declared themselves its opponents, have all been driven along in the same track, have all labored to one end; some ignorantly and some unwillingly, all have been blind instruments in the hands of God.

The gradual development of the principle of equality is, therefore, a Providential fact. It has all the chief characteristics of such a fact: it is universal, it is durable, it constantly eludes all human interference, and all events as well as all men contribute to its progress.

Would it, then, be wise to imagine that a social movement, the causes of which lie so far back, can be checked by the efforts of one generation? Can it be believed that the democracy which has overthrown the feudal system, and vanquished kings, will retreat before tradesmen and capitalists? Will it stop now that it has grown so strong, and its adversaries so weak?

Whither, then, are we tending? No one can say, for terms of comparison already fail us. The conditions of men are more equal in Christian countries at the present day than they have been at any previous time, or in any part of the world; so that the magnitude of what already has been done prevents us from foreseeing what is yet to be accomplished.

The whole book which is here offered to the public has been written under the impression of a kind of religious terror produced in the author's mind by the view of that irresistible revolution which has advanced for centuries in spite of every obstacle, and which is still advancing in the midst of the ruins it has caused.

It is not necessary that God himself should speak in order that we may discover the unquestionable signs of his will. It is enough to ascertain what is the habitual course of nature and the constant tendency of events. I know, without a special revelation, that the planets move in the orbits traced by the Creator's hand.

If the men of our time should be convinced, by attentive observation and sincere reflection, that the gradual and progressive development of social equality is at once the past and the future of their history, this discovery alone would confer the sacred character of a Divine decree upon the change. To attempt to check democracy would be in that case to resist the will of God; and the nations would then be constrained to make the best of the social lot awarded to them by Providence.

The Christian nations of our day seem to me to present a most alarming spectacle; the movement which impels them is already so strong that it cannot be stopped, but it is not yet so rapid that it cannot be guided. Their fate is still in their own hands; yet a little while, and it may be so no longer.

The first of the duties which are at this time imposed upon those who direct our affairs, is to educate the democracy; to renovate, if possible, its religious belief; to purify its morals; to regulate its movements; to substitute by degrees a knowledge of business for its inexperience, and an acquaintance with its true interests for its blind instincts; to adapt its government to time and place, and to make it conform to the occurrences and the men of the times. A new science of politics is needed for a new world.

This, however, is what we think of least; placed in the middle of a rapid stream, we obstinately fix our eyes on the ruins which may still be descried upon the shore we have left, whilst the current hurries us away, and drags us backward toward the gulf.

In no country in Europe has the great social revolution which I have just described made such rapid progress as in France; but it has always advanced without guidance. The heads of the state have made no preparation for it, and it has advanced without their consent or without their knowledge. The most powerful, the most intelligent, and the most moral classes of the nation have never attempted to take hold of it in order to guide it. The democracy has consequently been abandoned to its wild instincts, and it has grown up like those children who have no parental guidance, who receive their education in the public streets, and who are acquainted only with the vices and wretchedness of society. Its existence was seemingly unknown, when suddenly it acquired supreme power. Every one then submitted to its caprices; it was worshipped as the idol of strength; and when afterwards it was enfeebled by its own excesses, the legislator conceived the rash project of destroying it, instead of instructing it and correcting its vices. No attempt was made to fit it to govern, but all were bent on excluding it from the government.

The consequence has been, that the democratic revolution has taken place in the body of society, without that concomitant change in the laws, ideas, customs, and manners, which was necessary to render such a revolution beneficial. Thus we have a democracy, without anything to lessen its vices and bring out its natural advantages; and although we already perceive the evils it brings, we are ignorant of the benefits it may confer.

While the power of the crown, supported by the aristocracy, peaceably governed the nations of Europe, society, in the midst of its wretchedness, had several sources of happiness which can now scarcely be conceived or appreciated. The power of a part of his subjects was an insurmountable barrier to the tyranny of the prince; and the monarch, who felt the almost divine character which he enjoyed in the eyes of the multitude, derived a motive for the just use of his power from the respect which he inspired. The nobles, high as they were placed above the people, could not but take that calm and benevolent interest in their fate which the shepherd feels towards his flock; and without acknowledging the poor as their equals, they watched over the destiny of those whose welfare Providence had intrusted to their care. The people, never having conceived the idea of a social condition different from their own, and never expecting to become equal to their leaders, received benefits from them without discussing their rights. They became attached to them when they were clement and just, and submitted to their exactions without resistance or servility, as to the inevitable visitations of the Deity. Custom and the manners of the time, moreover, had established certain limits to oppression, and put a sort of legal restraint upon violence.

As the noble never suspected that any one would attempt to deprive him of the privileges which he believed to be legitimate, and as the serf looked upon his own inferiority as a consequence of the immutable order of nature, it is easy to imagine that some mutual exchange of good-will took place between two classes so differently gifted by fate. Inequality and wretchedness were then to be found in society; but the souls of neither rank of men were degraded.

Men are not corrupted by the exercise of power, or debased by the habit of obedience; but by the exercise of a power which they believe to be illegitimate, and by obedience to a rule which they consider to be usurped and oppressive.

On the one side were wealth, strength, and leisure, accompanied by the refinements of luxury, the elegance of taste, the pleasures of wit, and the cultivation of the arts; on the other, were labor, clownishness, and ignorance. But in the midst of this coarse and ignorant multitude it was not uncommon to meet with energetic passions, generous sentiments, profound religious convictions, and wild virtues.

The social state thus organized might boast of its stability, its power, and, above all, its glory.

But the scene is now changed. Gradually the distinctions of rank are done away; the barriers which once severed mankind are falling down; property is divided, power is shared by many, the light of intelligence spreads, and the capacities of all classes are equally cultivated. The State becomes democratic, and the empire of democracy is slowly and peaceably introduced into the institutions and the manners of the nation.

I can conceive of a society in which all men would feel an equal love and respect for the laws of which they consider themselves as the authors; in which the authority of the government would be respected as necessary, though not as divine; and in which the loyalty of the subject to the chief magistrate would not be a passion, but a quiet and rational persuasion. Every individual being in the possession of rights which he is sure to retain, a kind of manly confidence and reciprocal courtesy would arise between all classes, alike removed from pride and servility. The people, well acquainted with their own true interests, would understand that, in order to profit by the advantages of society, it is necessary to satisfy its requisitions. The voluntary association of the citizens might then take the place of the individual exertions of the nobles, and the community would be alike protected from anarchy and from oppression.

I admit that, in a democratic state thus constituted, society would not be stationary. But the impulses of the social body might there be regulated and made progressive. If there were less splendor than in the midst of an aristocracy, the contrast of misery would also be less frequent; the pleasures of enjoyment might be less excessive, but those of comfort would be more general; the sciences might be less perfectly cultivated, but ignorance would be less common; the impetuosity of the feelings would be repressed, and the habits of the nation softened; there would be more vices and fewer great crimes.

In the absence of enthusiasm and an ardent faith, great sacrifices may be obtained from the members of a commonwealth by an appeal to their understandings and their experience; each individual will feel the same necessity of union with his fellows to protect his own weakness; and as he knows that he can obtain their help only on condition of helping them, he will readily perceive that his personal interest is identified with the interests of the whole community. The nation, taken as a whole, will be less brilliant, less glorious, and perhaps less strong; but the majority of the citizens will enjoy a greater degree of prosperity, and the people will remain quiet, not because they despair of a change for the better, but because they are conscious that they are well off already.

If all the consequences of this state of things were not good or useful, society would at least have appropriated all such as were useful and good; and having once and for ever renounced the social advantages of aristocracy, mankind would enter into possession of all the benefits which democracy can afford.

But here it may be asked what we have adopted in the place of those institutions, those ideas, and those customs of our forefathers which we have abandoned.

The spell of royalty is broken, but it has not been succeeded by the majesty of the laws. The people have learned to despise all authority, but they still fear it; and fear now extorts more than was formerly paid from reverence and love.

I perceive that we have destroyed those individual powers which were able, single-handed, to cope with tyranny; but it is the government that has inherited the privileges of which families, corporations, and individuals have been deprived; to the power of a small number of persons — which, if it was sometimes oppressive, was often conservative — has succeeded the weakness of the whole community.

The division of property has lessened the distance which separated the rich from the poor; but it would seem that, the nearer they draw to each other, the greater is their mutual hatred, and the more vehement the envy and the dread with which they resist each other's claims to power; the idea of Right does not exist for either party, and Force affords to both the only argument for the present, and the only guaranty for the future.

The poor man retains the prejudices of his forefathers without their faith, and their ignorance without their

virtues; he has adopted the doctrine of self-interest as
the rule of his actions, without understanding the science
which puts it to use; and his selfishness is no less blind
than was formerly his devotedness to others.

If society is tranquil, it is not because it is conscious of
its strength and its well-being, but because it fears its
weakness and its infirmities; a single effort may cost it its
life. Everybody feels the evil, but no one has courage or
energy enough to seek the cure. The desires, the repin-
ings, the sorrows, and the joys of the present time lead to
no visible or permanent result, like the passions of old men,
which terminate in impotence.

We have, then, abandoned whatever advantages the old
state of things afforded, without receiving any compensation from our present condition; we have destroyed an
aristocracy, and we seem inclined to survey its ruins with
complacency, and to fix our abode in the midst of them.

The phenomena which the intellectual world presents
are not less deplorable. The democracy of France, hampered in its course or abandoned to its lawless passions, has
overthrown whatever crossed its path, and has shaken all
that it has not destroyed. Its empire has not been gradually introduced, or peaceably established, but it has constantly advanced in the midst of the disorders and the
agitations of a conflict. In the heat of the struggle, each
partisan is hurried beyond the natural limits of his opinions
by the doctrines and the excesses of his opponents, until he
loses sight of the end of his exertions, and holds a language
which does not express his real sentiments or secret instincts. Hence arises the strange confusion which we are
compelled to witness.

I can recall nothing in history more worthy of sorrow
and pity, than the scenes which are passing under our eyes.
It is as if the natural bond which unites the opinions of
man to his tastes, and his actions to his principles, was

now broken; the sympathy which has always been observed between the feelings and the ideas of mankind appears to be dissolved, and all the laws of moral analogy to be abolished.

Zealous Christians are still found amongst us, whose minds are nurtured on the thoughts which pertain to a future life, and who readily espouse the cause of human liberty as the source of all moral greatness. Christianity, which has declared that all men are equal in the sight of God, will not refuse to acknowledge that all citizens are equal in the eye of the law. But, by a singular concourse of events, religion has been for a time entangled with those institutions which democracy assails; and it is not unfrequently brought to reject the equality which it loves, and to curse that cause of liberty as a foe, whose efforts it might hallow by its alliance.

By the side of these religious men, I discern others whose looks are turned to earth rather than to heaven. These are the partisans of liberty, not only as the source of the noblest virtues, but more especially as the root of all solid advantages; and they sincerely desire to secure its authority, and to impart its blessings to mankind. It is natural that they should hasten to invoke the assistance of religion, for they must know that liberty cannot be established without morality, nor morality without faith. But they have seen religion in the ranks of their adversaries, and they inquire no further; some of them attack it openly, and the remainder are afraid to defend it.

In former ages, slavery was advocated by the venal and slavish-minded, whilst the independent and the warm-hearted were struggling without hope to save the liberties of mankind. But men of high and generous characters are now to be met with, whose opinions are at variance with their inclinations, and who praise that servility which they have themselves never known. Others, on the con-

trary, speak of liberty as if they were able to feel its sanctity and its majesty, and loudly claim for humanity those
rights which they have always refused to acknowledge.

There are virtuous and peaceful individuals whose pure
morality, quiet habits, opulence, and talents fit them to be
the leaders of the surrounding population. Their love of
country is sincere, and they are ready to make the greatest
sacrifices for its welfare. But civilization often finds them
among its opponents; they confound its abuses with its
benefits, and the idea of evil is inseparable in their minds
from that of novelty.

Near these I find others, whose object is to materialize
mankind, to hit upon what is expedient without heeding
what is just, to acquire knowledge without faith, and prosperity apart from virtue; claiming to be the champions of
modern civilization, they place themselves arrogantly at its
head, usurping a place which is abandoned to them, and
of which they are wholly unworthy.

Where are we, then?

The religionists are the enemies of liberty, and the
friends of liberty attack religion; the high-minded and
the noble advocate bondage, and the meanest and most
servile preach independence; honest and enlightened citizens are opposed to all progress, whilst men without patriotism and without principle put themselves forward as the
apostles of civilization and intelligence.

Has such been the fate of the centuries which have preceded our own? and has man always inhabited a world
like the present, where all things are out of their natural
connections, where virtue is without genius, and genius
without honor; where the love of order is confounded
with a taste for oppression, and the holy rites of freedom
with a contempt of law; where the light thrown by conscience on human actions is dim, and where nothing seems
to be any longer forbidden or allowed, honorable or shameful, false or true?

I cannot believe that the Creator made man to leave him in an endless struggle with the intellectual miseries which surround us. God destines a calmer and a more certain future to the communities of Europe. I am ignorant of his designs, but I shall not cease to believe in them because I cannot fathom them, and I had rather mistrust my own capacity than his justice.

There is a country in the world where the great social revolution which I am speaking of seems to have nearly reached its natural limits. It has been effected with ease and quietness; say rather that this country is reaping the fruits of the democratic revolution which we are undergoing, without having had the revolution itself.

The emigrants who colonized the shores of America in the beginning of the seventeenth century somehow separated the democratic principle from all the principles which it had to contend with in the old communities of Europe, and transplanted it alone to the New World. It has there been able to spread in perfect freedom, and peaceably to determine the character of the laws by influencing the manners of the country.

It appears to me beyond a doubt that, sooner or later, we shall arrive, like the Americans, at an almost complete equality of condition. But I do not conclude from this, that we shall ever be necessarily led to draw the same political consequences which the Americans have derived from a similar social organization. I am far from supposing that they have chosen the only form of government which a democracy may adopt; but as the generative cause of laws and manners in the two countries is the same, it is of immense interest for us to know what it has produced in each of them.

It is not, then, merely to satisfy a legitimate curiosity that I have examined America; my wish has been to find there instruction by which we may ourselves profit. Who-

ever should imagine that I have intended to write a pan-
egyric would be strangely mistaken, and on reading this
book, he will perceive that such was not my design: nor
has it been my object to advocate any form of government
in particular, for I am of opinion that absolute excellence
is rarely to be found in any system of laws. I have not
even pretended to judge whether the social revolution,
which I believe to be irresistible, is advantageous or prejudicial to mankind. I have acknowledged this revolution
as a fact already accomplished, or on the eve of its accomplishment; and I have selected the nation, from amongst
those which have undergone it, in which its development
has been the most peaceful and the most complete, in order
to discern its natural consequences, and to find out, if possible, the means of rendering it profitable to mankind. I confess that, in America, I saw more than America; I sought
there the image of democracy itself, with its inclinations,
its character, its prejudices, and its passions, in order to
learn what we have to fear or to hope from its progress.

In the first part of this work, I have attempted to show
the direction given to the laws by the democracy of America, which is abandoned almost without restraint to its
instinctive propensities; and to exhibit the course it prescribes to the government and the influence it exercises on
affairs. I have sought to discover the evils and the advantages which it brings. I have examined the precautions
used by the Americans to direct it, as well as those which
they have not adopted, and I have undertaken to point out
the causes which enable it to govern society. I do not
know whether I have succeeded in making known what I
saw in America, but I am certain that such has been my
sincere desire, and that I have never, knowingly, moulded
facts to ideas, instead of ideas to facts.

Whenever a point could be established by the aid of
written documents, I have had recourse to the original

text, and to the most authentic and approved works.* I have cited my authorities in the notes, and any one may refer to them. Whenever opinions, political customs, or remarks on the manners of the country were concerned, I have endeavored to consult the most enlightened men I met with. If the point in question was important or doubtful, I was not satisfied with one testimony, but I formed my opinion on the evidence of several witnesses. Here the reader must necessarily rely upon my word. I could frequently have quoted names which are either known to him, or which deserve to be so, in proof of what I advance; but I have carefully abstained from this practice. A stranger frequently hears important truths at the fireside of his host, which the latter would perhaps conceal from the ear of friendship; he consoles himself with his guest for the silence to which he is restricted, and the shortness of the traveller's stay takes away all fear of his indiscretion. I carefully noted every conversation of this nature as soon as it occurred, but these notes will never leave my writing-case. I had rather injure the success of my statements than add my name to the list of those strangers who repay the generous hospitality they have received by subsequent chagrin and annoyance.

I am aware that, notwithstanding my care, nothing will be easier than to criticise this book, if any one ever chooses to criticise it.

---

* Legislative and executive documents have been furnished to me with a kindness which I shall always remember with gratitude. Among the American statesmen who have thus helped my researches, I will mention particularly Mr. Edward Livingston, then Secretary of State, afterwards Minister Plenipotentiary at Paris. During my stay at Washington, he was kind enough to give me most of the documents which I possess relating to the Federal Government. Mr. Livingston is one of the few men whose writings cause us to conceive an affection for them, whom we admire and respect even before we come to know them personally, and to whom it is a pleasure to owe a debt of gratitude.

Those readers who may examine it closely will discover, I think, in the whole work, a dominant thought which binds, so to speak, its several parts together. But the diversity of the subjects I have had to treat is exceedingly great, and it will not be difficult to oppose an isolated fact to the body of facts which I cite, or an isolated idea to the body of ideas I put forth. I hope to be read in the spirit which has guided my labors, and that my book may be judged by the general impression it leaves, as I have formed my own judgment not on any single reason, but upon the mass of evidence.

It must not be forgotten that the author who wishes to be understood is obliged to push all his ideas to their utmost theoretical consequences, and often to the verge of what is false or impracticable; for if it be necessary sometimes to depart from the rules of logic in action, such is not the case in discourse, and a man finds it almost as difficult to be inconsistent in his language, as to be consistent in his conduct.

I conclude by myself pointing out what many readers will consider the principal defect of the work. This book is written to favor no particular views, and in composing it, I have entertained no design of serving or attacking any party. I have undertaken, not to see differently from others, but to look further than others, and whilst they are busied for the morrow only, I have turned my thoughts to the whole future.

DEMOCRACY IN AMERICA.

CHAPTER I.

EXTERIOR FORM OF NORTH AMERICA.

North America divided into two vast Regions, one inclining toward the Pole, the other toward the Equator. — Valley of the Mississippi. — Traces found there of the Revolutions of the Globe. — Shore of the Atlantic Ocean, on which the English Colonies were founded. — Different Aspects of North and of South America at the Time of their Discovery. — Forests of North America. — Prairies. — Wandering Tribes of Natives. — Their outward Appearance, Manners, and Languages. — Traces of an unknown People.

NORTH AMERICA presents in its external form certain general features which it is easy to discriminate at the first glance.

A sort of methodical order seems to have regulated the separation of land and water, mountains and valleys. A simple but grand arrangement is discoverable amidst the confusion of objects and the prodigious variety of scenes.

This continent is divided almost equally into two vast regions, one of which is bounded on the north by the Arctic Pole, and by the two great oceans on the east and west. It stretches toward the south, forming a triangle, whose irregular sides meet at length above the great lakes of Canada. The second region begins where the other terminates, and includes all the remainder of the continent. The one slopes gently toward the Pole, the other toward the Equator.

The territory comprehended in the first region descends toward the north with so imperceptible a slope, that it may almost be said to form a plain. Within the bounds of this immense level tract there are neither high mountains nor deep valleys. Streams meander through it irregularly; great rivers intertwine, separate, and meet again, spread into vast marshes, losing all trace of their channels in the labyrinth of waters they have themselves created, and thus at length, after innumerable windings, fall into the Polar seas. The great lakes which bound this first region are not walled in, like most of those in the Old World, between hills and rocks. Their banks are flat, and rise but a few feet above the level of their waters, — each of them thus forming a vast bowl filled to the brim. The slightest change in the structure of the globe would cause their waters to rush either towards the Pole or to the tropical seas.

The second region has a more broken surface, and is better suited for the habitation of man. Two long chains of mountains divide it, from one extreme to the other: the one, named the Alleghany, follows the direction of the shore of the Atlantic Ocean; the other is parallel with the Pacific.

The space which lies between these two chains of mountains contains 1,341,649 square miles.* Its surface is therefore about six times as great as that of France.

This vast territory, however, forms a single valley, one side of which descends from the rounded summits of the Alleghanies, while the other rises in an uninterrupted course to the tops of the Rocky Mountains. At the bottom of the valley flows an immense river, into which the various streams issuing from the mountains fall from all parts. In memory of their native land, the French formerly called this river the St. Louis. The Indians, in

---

* Darby's View of the United States, p. 499.

their pompous language, have named it the Father of Waters, or the Mississippi.

The Mississippi takes its source at the boundary of the two great regions of which I have spoken, not far from the highest point of the table-land where they unite. Near the same spot rises another river [the Red River of the North], which empties itself into the Polar seas. The course of the Mississippi is at first dubious: it winds several times towards the north, whence it rose; and only at length, after having been delayed in lakes and marshes, does it assume its definite direction, and flow slowly onward to the south.

Sometimes quietly gliding along the argillaceous bed which nature has assigned to it, sometimes swollen by freshets, the Mississippi waters over 2,500 miles in its course. At the distance of 1,364 miles from its mouth, this river attains an average depth of fifteen feet; and it is navigated by vessels of 300 tons burden for a course of nearly 500 miles. Fifty-seven large navigable rivers contribute to swell the waters of the Mississippi; amongst others, the Missouri, which traverses a space of 2,500 miles, the Arkansas, 1,300 miles, the Red River, 1,000 miles, the Ohio, 959 miles; four whose course is from 800 to 1,000 miles in length, viz. the Illinois, the St. Peter's, the St. Francis, and the Des Moines; besides a countless multitude of rivulets which unite from all parts their tributary streams.

The valley which is watered by the Mississippi seems to have been created for it alone, and there, like a god of antiquity, the river dispenses both good and evil. Near the stream, nature displays an inexhaustible fertility; in proportion as you recede from its banks, the powers of vegetation languish, the soil becomes poor, and the plants that survive have a sickly growth.* Nowhere have the great

* This statement is exaggerated, or gives a false impression. The fertile

convulsions of the globe left more evident traces than in the valley of the Mississippi. The whole aspect of the country shows the powerful effects of water, both by its fertility and its barrenness. The waters of the primeval ocean accumulated enormous beds of vegetable mould in the valley, which they levelled as they retired. Upon the right bank of the river are found immense plains, as smooth as if the husbandman had passed over them with his roller. As you approach the mountains, the soil becomes more and more unequal and sterile; the ground is, as it were, pierced in a thousand places by primitive rocks, which appear like the bones of a skeleton whose flesh has been consumed by time. The surface of the earth is covered with a granitic sand, and huge, irregular masses of stone, among which a few plants force their growth, and give the appearance of a green field covered with the ruins of a vast edifice. These stones and this sand discover, on examination, a perfect analogy with those which compose the arid and broken summits of the Rocky Mountains. The flood of waters which washed the soil to the bottom of the valley, afterwards carried away portions of the rocks themselves; and these, dashed and bruised against the neighboring cliffs, were left scattered like wrecks at their feet.*

The valley of the Mississippi is, upon the whole, the most magnificent dwelling-place prepared by God for man's abode; and yet it may be said that at present it is but a mighty desert.†

On the eastern side of the Alleghanies, between the base of these mountains and the Atlantic Ocean, there lies

land " near the stream " is often over five hundred miles broad, and only on the western side, and at a greater distance than this, is found a great sterile tract to which this description is applicable. — Am. Ed.

* See Appendix A.

† The population of the valley is now nearly thrice as great as it was when this was written. — Am. Ed.

a long ridge of rocks and sand, which the sea appears to
have left behind as it retired. The mean breadth of this
territory does not exceed one hundred miles; but it is
about nine hundred miles in length. This part of the
American continent has a soil which offers every obstacle
to the husbandman, and its vegetation is scanty and un-
varied.

Upon this inhospitable coast the first united efforts of
human industry were made. This tongue of arid land
was the cradle of those English colonies which were destined one day to become the United States of America.
The centre of power still remains here; whilst in the rear
of it the true elements of the great people to whom the
future control of the continent belongs are gathering almost in secrecy together.

When the Europeans first landed on the shores of the
West Indies, and afterwards on the coast of South America, they thought themselves transported into those fabu-
lous regions of which poets had sung. The sea sparkled
with phosphoric light, and the extraordinary transparency
of its waters discovered to the view of the navigator all
the depths of the abyss.* Here and there appeared little
islands perfumed with odoriferous plants, and resembling
baskets of flowers floating on the tranquil surface of the
ocean. Every object which met the sight, in this enchanting region, seemed prepared to satisfy the wants or
contribute to the pleasures of man. Almost all the trees
were loaded with nourishing fruits, and those which were
useless as food delighted the eye by the brilliancy and
variety of their colors. In groves of fragrant lemon-trees,

---

* Malte Brun tells us (Vol. III. p. 726) that the water of the Caribbean
Sea is so transparent, that corals and fish are discernible at a depth of sixty
fathoms. The ship seemed to float in air, the navigator became giddy as
his eye penetrated through the crystal flood, and beheld submarine gardens,
or beds of shells, or gilded fishes gliding among tufts and thickets of sea-
weed.

wild figs, flowering myrtles, acacias, and oleanders, which were hung with festoons of various climbing-plants, covered with flowers, a multitude of birds unknown in Europe displayed their bright plumage, glittering with purple and azure, and mingled their warbling with the harmony of a world teeming with life and motion.*

Underneath this brilliant exterior, death was concealed. But this fact was not then known, and the air of these climates had so enervating an influence, that man, absorbed by present enjoyment, was rendered regardless of the future.

North America appeared under a very different aspect: there, everything was grave, serious, and solemn; it seemed created to be the domain of intelligence, as the South was that of sensual delight. A turbulent and foggy ocean washed its shores. It was girt round by a belt of granitic rocks, or by wide tracts of sand. The foliage of its woods was dark and gloomy; for they were composed of firs, larches, evergreen oaks, wild olive-trees, and laurels.†

Beyond this outer belt lay the thick shades of the central forests, where the largest trees which are produced in the two hemispheres grow side by side. The plane, the catalpa, the sugar-maple, and the Virginian poplar mingled their branches with those of the oak, the beech, and the lime.

In these, as in the forests of the Old World, destruction was perpetually going on. The ruins of vegetation were heaped upon each other; but there was no laboring hand to remove them, and their decay was not rapid enough to make room for the continual work of reproduction. Climbing plants, grasses, and other herbs forced their way through the mass of dying trees; they crept along their bending trunks, found nourishment in their dusty cavities,

---

* See Appendix B.

† These are not good specimens of the trees on our Atlantic coast. Firs, pines, cypresses, white and live oaks, would have been a better enumeration. — Am. Ed.

and a passage beneath the lifeless bark.   Thus decay gave
its assistance to life, and their respective productions were
mingled together.   The depths of these forests were gloomy
and obscure, and a thousand rivulets, undirected in their
course by human industry, preserved in them a constant
moisture.   It was rare to meet with flowers, wild fruits, or
birds, beneath their shades.   The fall of a tree overthrown
by age, the rushing torrent of a cataract, the lowing of the
buffalo, and the howling of the wind, were the only sounds
which broke the silence of nature.

To the east of the great river, the woods almost disappeared; in their stead were seen prairies of immense
extent.   Whether Nature in her infinite variety had denied
the germs of trees to these fertile plains, or whether they
had once been covered with forests, subsequently destroyed
by the hand of man, is a question which neither tradition
nor scientific research has been able to answer.

These immense deserts were not, however, wholly un-
tenanted by men.   Some wandering tribes had been for
ages scattered among the forest shades or the green pas-
tures of the prairie.   From the mouth of the St. Lawrence
to the Delta of the Mississippi, and from the Atlantic to
the Pacific Ocean, these savages possessed certain points of
resemblance which bore witness of their common origin:
but at the same time, they differed from all other known
races of men;* they were neither white like the Europeans,

* With the progress of discovery, some resemblance has been found to
exist between the physical conformation, the language, and the habits of the
Indians of North America, and those of the Tongous, Mantchous, Moguls,
Tatars, and other wandering tribes of Asia.   The land occupied by these
tribes is not very distant from Behring's Strait; which allows of the supposition, that at a remote period they gave inhabitants to the desert continent
of America.   But this is a point which has not yet been clearly elucidated
by science.   See Malte Brun, Vol. V.; the works of Humboldt; Fischer,
" Conjecture sur l'Origine des Américains "; Adair, " History of the American Indians."

nor yellow like most of the Asiatics, nor black like the negroes. Their skin was reddish brown, their hair long and shining, their lips thin, and their cheekbones very prominent. The languages spoken by the North American tribes were various as far as regarded their words, but they were subject to the same grammatical rules. These rules differed in several points from such as had been observed to govern the origin of language. The idiom of the Americans seemed to be the product of new combinations; and bespoke an effort of the understanding, of which the Indians of our days would be incapable.*

The social state of these tribes differed also in many respects from all that was seen in the Old World. They seem to have multiplied freely in the midst of their deserts, without coming in contact with other races more civilized than their own. Accordingly, they exhibited none of those indistinct, incoherent notions of right and wrong, none of that deep corruption of manners, which is usually joined with ignorance and rudeness among nations who, after advancing to civilization, have relapsed into a state of barbarism. The Indian was indebted to no one but himself; his virtues, his vices, and his prejudices were his own work; he had grown up in the wild independence of his nature.

If, in polished countries, the lowest of the people are rude and uncivil, it is not merely because they are poor and ignorant, but that, being so, they are in daily contact with rich and enlightened men. The sight of their own hard lot and their weakness, which is daily contrasted with the happiness and power of some of their fellow-creatures, excites in their hearts at the same time the sentiments of anger and of fear: the consciousness of their inferiority and their dependence irritates while it humiliates them. This state of mind displays itself in their manners and language;

* See Appendix C.

they are at once insolent and servile. The truth of this is easily proved by observation: the people are more rude in aristocratic countries than elsewhere; in opulent cities than in rural districts. In those places where the rich and powerful are assembled together, the weak and the indigent feel themselves oppressed by their inferior condition. Unable to perceive a single chance of regaining their equality, they give up to despair, and allow themselves to fall below the dignity of human nature.

This unfortunate effect of the disparity of conditions is not observable in savage life: the Indians, although they are ignorant and poor, are equal and free.

When Europeans first came among them, the natives of North America were ignorant of the value of riches, and indifferent to the enjoyments which civilized man procures to himself by their means. Nevertheless there was nothing coarse in their demeanor; they practised an habitual reserve, and a kind of aristocratic politeness.

Mild and hospitable when at peace, though merciless in war beyond any known degree of human ferocity, the Indian would expose himself to die of hunger in order to succor the stranger who asked admittance by night at the door of his hut; yet he could tear in pieces with his hands the still quivering limbs of his prisoner. The famous republics of antiquity never gave examples of more unshaken courage, more haughty spirit, or more intractable love of independence, than were hidden in former times among the wild forests of the New World.* The Europeans pro-

---

* We learn from President Jefferson's "Notes upon Virginia," (p. 148,) that among the Iroquois, when attacked by a superior force, aged men refused to fly, or to survive the destruction of their country; and they braved death like the ancient Romans when their capital was sacked by the Gauls. Further on, (p. 150,) he tells us that there is no example of an Indian, who, having fallen into the hands of his enemies, begged for his life; on the contrary, the captive sought to obtain death at the hands of his conquerors by the use of insult and provocation.

duced no great impression when they landed upon the shores of North America; their presence engendered neither envy nor fear. What influence could they possess over such men as we have described? The Indian could live without wants, suffer without complaint, and pour out his death-song at the stake.* Like all the other members of the great human family, these savages believed in the existence of a better world, and adored, under different names, God, the Creator of the universe. Their notions on the great intellectual truths were in general simple and philosophical. †

Although we have here traced the character of a primitive people, yet it cannot be doubted that another people, more civilized and more advanced in all respects, had preceded it in the same regions.

An obscure tradition which prevailed among the Indians on the borders of the Atlantic, informs us that these very tribes formerly dwelt on the west side of the Mississippi. Along the banks of the Ohio, and throughout the central valley, there are frequently found, at this day, *tumuli* raised by the hands of men. On exploring these heaps of earth to their centre, it is usual to meet with human bones, strange instruments, arms and utensils of all kinds, made of metal, and destined for purposes unknown to the present race.

The Indians of our time are unable to give any information relative to the history of this unknown people. Neither did those who lived three hundred years ago, when America was first discovered, leave any accounts from

* See "Histoire de la Louisiane," by Lepage Dupratz; Charlevoix, "Histoire de la Nouvelle France"; "Lettres du Rev. G. Heckewelder"; "Transactions of the American Philosophical Society," Vol. I.; Jefferson's "Notes on Virginia," pp. 135 – 190. What is said by Jefferson is of especial weight, on account of the personal merit of the writer, of his peculiar position, and of the matter-of-fact age in which he lived.

† See Appendix D.

which even an hypothesis could be formed. Tradition —
that perishable yet ever renewed monument of the pristine
world — throws no light upon the subject. It is an un-
doubted fact, however, that in this part of the globe thousands of our fellow-beings once lived. When they came
hither, what was their origin, their destiny, their history,
when and how they perished, no one can tell.

How strange does it appear that nations have existed,
and afterwards so completely disappeared from the earth
that the memory even of their names is effaced! their languages are lost; their glory is vanished like a sound without an echo; though perhaps there is not one which has
not left behind it some tomb in memory of its passage.
Thus the most durable monument of human labor is that
which recalls the wretchedness and nothingness of man.

Although the vast country which we have been describing was inhabited by many indigenous tribes, it may
justly be said, at the time of its discovery by Europeans,
to have formed one great desert. The Indians occupied,
without possessing it. It is by agricultural labor that man
appropriates the soil, and the early inhabitants of North
America lived by the produce of the chase. Their implacable prejudices, their uncontrolled passions, their vices,
and still more, perhaps, their savage virtues, consigned
them to inevitable destruction. The ruin of these tribes
began from the day when Europeans landed on their
shores: it has proceeded ever since, and we are now witnessing the completion of it. They seem to have been
placed by Providence amidst the riches of the New World
only to enjoy them for a season; they were there merely
to wait till others came. Those coasts, so admirably
adapted for commerce and industry; those wide and deep
rivers; that inexhaustible valley of the Mississippi; the
whole continent, in short, seemed prepared to be the abode
of a great nation yet unborn.

In that land the great experiment was to be made, by civilized man, of the attempt to construct society upon a new basis; and it was there, for the first time, that theories hitherto unknown, or deemed impracticable, were to exhibit a spectacle for which the world had not been prepared by the history of the past.

CHAPTER II.

ORIGIN OF THE ANGLO-AMERICANS, AND IMPORTANCE OF THIS ORIGIN IN RELATION TO THEIR FUTURE CONDITION.

Utility of knowing the Origin of Nations, in order to understand their Social Condition and their Laws. — America the only Country in which the Starting-Point of a great People has been clearly observable. — In what Respects all who emigrated to British America were similar. — In what they differed. — Remark applicable to all the Europeans who established themselves on the Shores of the New World. — Colonization of Virginia. — Colonization of New England. — Original Character of the first Inhabitants of New England. — Their Arrival. — Their first Laws. — Their Social Contract. — Penal Code borrowed from the Hebrew Legislation. — Religious Fervor. — Republican Spirit. — Intimate Union of the Spirit of Religion with the Spirit of Liberty.

AFTER the birth of a human being, his early years are obscurely spent in the toils or pleasures of childhood. As he grows up, the world receives him, when his manhood begins, and he enters into contact with his fellows. He is then studied for the first time, and it is imagined that the germ of the vices and the virtues of his maturer years is then formed.

This, if I am not mistaken, is a great error. We must begin higher up; we must watch the infant·in his mother's arms; we must see the first images which the external world casts upon the dark mirror of his mind, the first occurrences which he witnesses; we must hear the first words which awaken the sleeping powers of thought, and stand by his earliest efforts, — if we would understand the prejudices, the habits, and the passions which will rule his

life. The entire man is, so to speak, to be seen in the cradle of the child.

The growth of nations presents something analogous to
this; they all bear some marks of their origin. The circumstances which accompanied their birth and contributed
to their development affect the whole term of their being.

If we were able to go back to the elements of states, and
to examine the oldest monuments of their history, I doubt
not that we should discover in them the primal cause of
the prejudices, the habits, the ruling passions, and, in short,
of all that constitutes what is called the national character.
We should there find the explanation of certain customs
which now seem at variance with the prevailing manners;
of such laws as conflict with established principles; and of
such incoherent opinions as are here and there to be met
with in society, like those fragments of broken chains
which we sometimes see hanging from the vaults of an old
edifice, and supporting nothing. This might explain the
destinies of certain nations which seem borne on by an unknown force to ends of which they themselves are ignorant. But hitherto facts have been wanting to researches
of this kind: the spirit of inquiry has only come upon
communities in their latter days; and when they at length
contemplated their origin, time had already obscured it,
or ignorance and pride adorned it with truth-concealing
fables.

America is the only country in which it has been possible to witness the natural and tranquil growth of society,
and where the influence exercised on the future condition
of states by their origin is clearly distinguishable.

At the period when the peoples of Europe landed in the
New World, their national characteristics were already
completely formed; each of them had a physiognomy of
its own; and as they had already attained that stage of
civilization at which men are led to study themselves, they

have transmitted to us a faithful picture of their opinions, their manners, and their laws. The men of the sixteenth century are almost as well known to us as our contemporaries. America, consequently, exhibits in the broad light of day the phenomena which the ignorance or rudeness of earlier ages conceals from our researches. Near enough to the time when the states of America were founded, to be accurately acquainted with their elements, and sufficiently removed from that period to judge of some of their results, the men of our own day seem destined to see further than their predecessors into the series of human events. Providence has given us a torch which our forefathers did not possess, and has allowed us to discern fundamental causes in the history of the world which the obscurity of the past concealed from them.

If we carefully examine the social and political state of America, after having studied its history, we shall remain perfectly convinced that not an opinion, not a custom, not a law, I may even say not an event, is upon record which the origin of that people will not explain. The readers of this book will find in the present chapter the germ of all that is to follow, and the key to almost the whole work.

The emigrants who came at different periods to occupy the territory now covered by the American Union differed from each other in many respects; their aim was not the same, and they governed themselves on different principles.

These men had, however, certain features in common, and they were all placed in an analogous situation. The tie of language is, perhaps, the strongest and the most durable that can unite mankind. All the emigrants spoke the same tongue; they were all offsets from the same people. Born in a country which had been agitated for centuries by the struggles of faction, and in which all parties had been obliged in their turn to place themselves under the protection of the laws, their political education had been perfected in this rude school; and they were more conversant with the notions of right, and the principles of true freedom, than the greater part of their European contemporaries. At the period of the first emigrations, the township system, that fruitful germ of free institutions, was deeply rooted in the habits of the English; and with it the doctrine of the sovereignty of the people had been introduced into the bosom of the monarchy of the house of Tudor.

The religious quarrels which have agitated the Christian world were then rife. England had plunged into the new order of things with headlong vehemence. The character of its inhabitants, which had always been sedate and reflective, became argumentative and austere. General information had been increased by intellectual contests, and the mind had received in them a deeper cultivation. Whilst religion was the topic of discussion, the morals of the people became more pure. All these national features are more or less discoverable in the physiognomy of those Englishmen who came to seek a new home on the opposite shores of the Atlantic.

Another remark, to which we shall hereafter have occasion to recur, is applicable not only to the English, but to the French, the Spaniards, and all the Europeans who successively established themselves in the New World. All these European colonies contained the elements, if not the development, of a complete democracy. Two causes led to this result. It may be said generally, that on leaving the mother country the emigrants had, in general, no notion of superiority one over another. The happy and the powerful do not go into exile, and there are no surer guaranties of equality among men than poverty and misfortune. It happened, however, on several occasions, that persons of rank were driven to America by political and religious quarrels. Laws were made to establish a gradation of ranks; but it was soon found that the soil of America was opposed to a territorial aristocracy. To bring that refractory land into cultivation, the constant and interested exertions of the owner himself were necessary; and when the ground was prepared, its produce was found to be insufficient to enrich a proprietor and a farmer at the same time. The land was then naturally broken up into small portions, which the proprietor cultivated for himself. Land is the basis of an aristocracy, which clings to the soil that supports it; for it is not by privileges alone, nor by birth, but by landed property handed down from generation to generation, that an aristocracy is constituted. A nation may present immense fortunes and extreme wretchedness; but unless those fortunes are territorial, there is no true aristocracy, but simply the class of the rich and that of the poor.

All the British colonies had then a great degree of family likeness at the epoch of their settlement. All of them, from their beginning, seemed destined to witness the growth, not of the aristocratic liberty of their mother country, but of that freedom of the middle and lower orders of which the history of the world had as yet furnished no complete example.

In this general uniformity, however, several striking differences were discernible, which it is necessary to point out. Two branches may be distinguished in the great Anglo-American family, which have hitherto grown up without entirely commingling; the one in the South, the other in the North.

Virginia received the first English colony; the emigrants took possession of it in 1607. The idea that mines of gold and silver are the sources of national wealth was at that time singularly prevalent in Europe; a fatal delusion, which has done more to impoverish the European nations who adopted it, and has cost more lives in America, than the united influence of war and bad laws. The men sent to

Virginia* were seekers of gold, adventurers without resources and without character, whose turbulent and restless spirit endangered the infant colony,† and rendered its
progress uncertain. Artisans and agriculturists arrived
afterwards; and, although they were a more moral and
orderly race of men, they were hardly in any respect
above the level of the inferior classes in England.‡ No
lofty views, no spiritual conception, presided over the
foundation of these new settlements. The colony was
scarcely established when slavery was introduced; § this
was the capital fact which was to exercise an immense influence on the character, the laws, and the whole future
of the South. Slavery, as we shall afterwards show, dishonors labor; it introduces idleness into society, and with
idleness, ignorance and pride, luxury and distress. It enervates the powers of the mind, and benumbs the activity
of man. The influence of slavery, united to the English

* The charter granted by the crown of England in 1609 stipulated,
amongst other conditions, that the adventurers should pay to the crown a
fifth of the produce of all gold and silver mines. See Marshall's Life of
Washington, Vol. I. pp. 18 – 66.

† A large portion of the adventurers, says Stith (History of Virginia),
were unprincipled young men of family, whom their parents were glad to
ship off in order to save them from an ignominious fate, discharged servants, fraudulent bankrupts, debauchees, and others of the same class, people more apt to pillage and destroy than to promote the welfare of the
settlement. Seditious leaders easily enticed this band into every kind of
extravagance and excess. See for the history of Virginia the following
works: —

"History of Virginia, from the First Settlements in the Year 1624," by
Smith.

"History of Virginia," by William Stith.

"History of Virginia, from the Earliest Period," by Beverley.

‡ It was not till some time later that a certain number of rich English
capitalists came to establish themselves in the colony.

§ Slavery was introduced about the year 1620, by a Dutch vessel,
which landed twenty negroes on the banks of the James River. See
Chalmers.

character, explains the manners and the social condition of the Southern States.

In the North, the same English character as the ground received totally different colors. Here I may be allowed to enter into some details.

In the English colonies of the North, more generally known as the States of New England,* the two or three main ideas which now constitute the basis of the social theory of the United States were first combined. The principles of New England spread at first to the neighboring States; they then passed successively to the more distant ones; and at last, if I may so speak, they *interpenetrated* the whole confederation. They now extend their influence beyond its limits, over the whole American world. The civilization of New England has been like a beacon lit upon a hill, which, after it has diffused its warmth immediately around it, also tinges the distant horizon with its glow.

The foundation of New England was a novel spectacle, and all the circumstances attending it were singular and original. Nearly all colonies have been first inhabited, either by men without education and without resources, driven by their poverty and their misconduct from the land which gave them birth, or by speculators and adventurers greedy of gain. Some settlements cannot even boast so honorable an origin; St. Domingo was founded by buccaneers; and, at the present day, the criminal courts of England supply the population of Australia.

The settlers who established themselves on the shores of New England all belonged to the more independent classes of their native country. Their union on the soil of Amer-

---

* The States of New England are those situated to the east of the Hudson. They are now six in number:—1. Connecticut; 2. Rhode Island; 3. Massachusetts; 4. New Hampshire; 5. Vermont; 6. Maine. [The last two, as distinct States, are of comparatively recent origin.]

ica at once presented the singular phenomenon of a society
containing neither lords nor common people, and we may
almost say, neither rich nor poor. These men possessed,
in proportion to their number, a greater mass of intelligence than is to be found in any European nation of our
own time. All, perhaps without a single exception, had
received a good education, and many of them were known
in Europe for their talents and their acquirements. The
other colonies had been founded by adventurers without
families; the emigrants of New England brought with
them the best elements of order and morality; they landed
on the desert coast accompanied by their wives and children. But what especially distinguished them from all
others was the aim of their undertaking. They had not
been obliged by necessity to leave their country; the social
position they abandoned was one to be regretted, and their
means of subsistence were certain. Nor did they cross the
Atlantic to improve their situation or to increase their
wealth; it was a purely intellectual craving, which called
them from the comforts of their former homes; and in
facing the inevitable sufferings of exile, their object was
the triumph of an idea.

The emigrants, or, as they deservedly styled themselves,
the Pilgrims, belonged to that English sect the austerity
of whose principles had acquired for them the name of
Puritans. Puritanism was not merely a religious doctrine,
but it corresponded in many points with the most absolute
democratic and republican theories. It was this tendency
which had aroused its most dangerous adversaries. Perse-
cuted by the government of the mother country, and disgusted by the habits of a society which the rigor of their
own principles condemned, the Puritans went forth to seek
some rude and unfrequented part of the world, where they
could live according to their own opinions, and worship
God in freedom.

A few quotations will throw more light upon the spirit of these pious adventurers than all that we can say of them. Nathaniel Morton,* the historian of the first years of the settlement, thus opens his subject : —

"Gentle Reader, — I have for some length of time looked upon it as a duty incumbent especially on the immediate successors of those that have had so large experience of those many memorable and signal demonstrations of God's goodness, viz. the first beginners of this Plantation in New England, to commit to writing his gracious dispensations on that behalf; having so many inducements thereunto, not only otherwise, but so plentifully in the Sacred Scriptures : that so, what we have seen, and what our fathers have told us (Psalm lxxviii. 3, 4), we may not hide from our children, showing to the generations to come the praises of the Lord ; that especially the seed of Abraham his servant, and the children of Jacob his chosen (Psalm cv. 5, 6), may remember his marvellous works in the beginning and progress of the planting of New England, his wonders and the judgments of his mouth ; how that God brought a vine into this wilderness ; that he cast out the heathen, and planted it ; that he made room for it and caused it to take deep root ; and it filled the land (Psalm lxxx. 8, 9). And not only so, but also that he hath guided his people by his strength to his holy habitation, and planted them in the mountain of his inheritance in respect of precious Gospel enjoyments : and that as especially God may have the glory of all unto whom it is most due ; so also some rays of glory may reach the names of those blessed Saints, that were the main instruments and the beginning of this happy enterprise."

It is impossible to read this opening paragraph without an involuntary feeling of religious awe ; it breathes the

* "New England's Memorial," p. 13 (Boston, 1826). See also Hutchinson's History, Vol. II. p. 440.

very savor of Gospel antiquity. The sincerity of the author heightens his power of language. In our eyes, as well as in his own, it was not a mere party of adventurers gone forth to seek their fortune beyond seas, but the germ of a great nation wafted by Providence to a predestined shore.

The author continues, and thus describes the departure of the first pilgrims : —

" So they left that goodly and pleasant city of Leyden,* which had been their resting-place for above eleven years ; but they knew that they were pilgrims and strangers here below, and looked not much on these things, but lifted up their eyes to heaven, their dearest country, where God hath prepared for them a city (Heb. xi. 16), and therein quieted their spirits. When they came to Delfs-Haven they found the ship and all things ready ; and such of their friends as could not come with them followed after them, and sundry came from Amsterdam to see them shipt, and to take their leaves of them. One night was spent with little sleep with the most, but with friendly entertainment and Christian discourse, and other real expressions of true Christian love. The next day they went on board, and their friends with them, where truly doleful was the sight of that sad and mournful parting, to hear what sighs and sobs and prayers did sound amongst them ; what tears did gush from every eye, and pithy speeches pierced each

---

* The emigrants were, for the most part, godly Christians from the northern [central] part of England, who had quitted their native country because they were " studious of reformation, and entered into covenant to walk with one another according to the primitive pattern of the Word of God." They emigrated to Holland, and settled in the city of Leyden in 1610, where they abode, being lovingly respected by the Dutch, for many years : they left it in 1620 for several reasons, the last of which was, that their posterity would in a few generations become Dutch, and so lose their interest in the English nation ; they being desirous rather to enlarge his Majesty's dominions, and to live under their natural prince. — *Translator's Note.*

other's heart, that sundry of the Dutch strangers that stood on the Key as spectators could not refrain from tears. But the tide (which stays for no man) calling them away, that were thus loth to depart, their Reverend Pastor, falling down on his knees, and they all with him, with watery cheeks commended them with most fervent prayers unto the Lord and his blessing; and then with mutual embraces and many tears they took their leaves one of another, which proved to be the last leave to many of them."

The emigrants were about 150 in number, including the women and the children. Their object was to plant a colony on the shores of the Hudson; but after having been driven about for some time in the Atlantic Ocean, they were forced to land on the arid coast of New England, at the spot which is now the town of Plymouth. The rock is still shown on which the pilgrims disembarked.*

"But before we pass on," continues our historian, "let the reader with me make a pause, and seriously consider this poor people's present condition, the more to be raised up to admiration of God's goodness towards them in their preservation: for being now passed the vast ocean, and a sea of troubles before them in expectation, they had now no friends to welcome them, no inns to entertain or refresh them, no houses, or much less towns, to repair unto to seek for succour: and for the season it was winter, and they that know the winters of the country know them to be sharp and violent, subject to cruel and fierce storms, dangerous to travel to known places, much more to search unknown coasts. Besides, what could they see but a hideous and

* This rock has become an object of veneration in the United States. I have seen bits of it carefully preserved in several towns of the Union. Does not this sufficiently show how all human power and greatness are entirely in the soul? Here is a stone which the feet of a few poor fugitives pressed for an instant, and this stone becomes famous; it is treasured by a great nation, a fragment is prized as a relic. But what is become of the doorsteps of a thousand palaces? Who troubles himself about them?

desolate wilderness, full of wilde beasts, and wilde men? and what multitudes of them there were, they then knew not: for which way soever they turned their eyes (save upward to Heaven) they could have but little solace or content in respect of any outward object; for summer being ended, all things stand in appearance with a weather-beaten face, and the whole country, full of woods and thickets, represented a wild and savage hew; if they looked behind them, there was the mighty ocean which they had passed, and was now as a main bar or gulph to separate them from all the civil parts of the world." *

It must not be imagined that the piety of the Puritans was merely speculative, or that it took no cognizance of the course of worldly affairs. Puritanism, as I have already remarked, was scarcely less a political than a religious doctrine. No sooner had the emigrants landed on the barren coast described by Nathaniel Morton, than it was their first care to constitute a society, by subscribing the following Act:—

" In the name of God. Amen. We, whose names are underwritten, the loyal subjects of our dread Sovereign Lord King James, &c. &c., Having undertaken for the glory of God, and advancement of the Christian Faith, and the honour of our King and country, a voyage to plant the first colony in the northern parts of Virginia; Do by these presents solemnly and mutually, in the presence of God and one another, covenant and combine ourselves together into a civil body politick, for our better ordering and preservation, and furtherance of the ends aforesaid: and by

---

* Though the work from which the foregoing extracts are taken appeared under the title of "New England's Memorial," as written by Nathaniel Morton, it was compiled by him chiefly from the manuscripts of William Bradford, who was one of the leaders of the Pilgrims during their stay in Holland, and was elected the governor of their settlement at Plymouth, which office he continued to hold for many years. The language in these extracts is almost entirely that of Bradford. — Am. Ed.

virtue hereof do enact, constitute, and frame such just and equal laws, ordinances, acts, constitutions, and offices, from time to time, as shall be thought most meet and convenient for the general good of the Colony: unto which we promise all due submission and obedience," &c.*

This happened in 1620, and from that time forwards the emigration went on. The religious and political passions which ravaged the British empire during the whole reign of Charles I. drove fresh crowds of sectarians every year to the shores of America. In England, the stronghold of Puritanism continued to be in the middle classes; and it was from the middle classes that most of the emigrants came. The population of New England increased rapidly; and whilst the hierarchy of rank despotically classed the inhabitants of the mother country, the colony approximated more and more the novel spectacle of a community homogeneous in all its parts. A democracy, more perfect than antiquity had dared to dream of, started in full size and panoply from the midst of an ancient feudal society.

The English government was not dissatisfied with a large emigration which removed the elements of fresh discord and further revolutions. On the contrary, it did everything to encourage it, and seemed to have no anxiety about the destiny of those who sought a shelter on the soil of America from the rigor of their laws. It appeared as if New England was a region given up to the dreams of fancy, and the unrestrained experiments of innovators.

The English colonies (and this is one of the main causes of their prosperity) have always enjoyed more internal freedom and more political independence than the colonies

---

* The emigrants who founded the State of Rhode Island in 1638, those who landed at New Haven in 1637, the first settlers in Connecticut in 1639, and the founders of Providence in 1640, began in like manner by drawing up a social contract, which was acceded to by all the interested parties. See Pitkin's History, pp. 42 and 47.

of other nations; and this principle of liberty was nowhere more extensively applied than in the States of New England.

It was generally allowed at that period, that the territories of the New World belonged to that European nation which had been the first to discover them. Nearly the whole coast of North America thus became a British possession towards the end of the sixteenth century. The means used by the English government to people these new domains were of several kinds: the king sometimes appointed a governor of his own choice, who ruled a portion of the New World in the name and under the immediate orders of the crown;* this is the colonial system adopted by the other countries of Europe. Sometimes, grants of certain tracts were made by the crown to an individual or to a company,† in which case all the civil and political power fell into the hands of one or more persons, who, under the inspection and control of the crown, sold the lands and governed the inhabitants. Lastly, a third system consisted in allowing a certain number of emigrants to form themselves into a political society under the protection of the mother country, and to govern themselves in whatever was not contrary to her laws. This mode of colonization, so favorable to liberty, was adopted only in New England.‡

---

* This was the case in the State of New York.

† Maryland, the Carolinas, Pennsylvania, and New Jersey were in this situation. See Pitkin's History, Vol. I. pp. 11 – 31.

‡ See the work entitled "Historical Collection of State Papers and other authentic Documents intended as Materials for an History of the United States of America, by Ebenezer Hazard," (Philadelphia, 1792,) for a great number of documents relating to the commencement of the colonies, which are valuable from their contents and their authenticity: amongst them are the various charters granted by the king of England, and the first acts of the local governments.

See also the analysis of all these charters given by Mr. Story, Judge of

In 1628,* a charter of this kind was granted by Charles I. to the emigrants who went to form the colony of Massachusetts. But, in general, charters were not given to the colonies of New England till their existence had become an established fact. Plymouth, Providence, New Haven, Connecticut, and Rhode Island † were founded without the help, and almost without the knowledge, of the mother country. The new settlers did not derive their powers from the head of the empire, although they did not deny its supremacy; they constituted themselves into a society, and it was not till thirty or forty years afterwards, under Charles II., that their existence was legally recognized by a royal charter.

This frequently renders it difficult, in studying the earliest historical and legislative records of New England, to detect the link which connected the emigrants with the land of their forefathers. They continually exercised the rights of sovereignty; they named their magistrates, concluded peace or declared war, made police regulations, and enacted laws, as if their allegiance was due only to God.‡ Nothing can be more curious, and at the same time more instructive, than the legislation of that period; it is there that the solution of the great social problem which the United States now present to the world is to be found.

the Supreme Court of the United States, in the Introduction to his "Commentaries on the Constitution of the United States." It is proved by these documents, that the principles of representative government and the external forms of political liberty were introduced into all the colonies almost from their origin. These principles were more fully acted upon in the North than in the South, but they existed everywhere.

* See Pitkin's History, p. 35. Also, the "History of the Colony of Massachusetts Bay," by Hutchinson, Vol. I. p. 9.

† See Pitkin's History, pp. 42, 47.

‡ The inhabitants of Massachusetts had deviated from the forms which are preserved in the criminal and civil procedure of England; in 1650, the name of the king was not yet put at the head of the decrees of justice. See Hutchinson, Vol. I. p. 452.

Amongst these documents we shall notice, as especially characteristic, the code of laws promulgated by the little state of Connecticut in 1650.*

The legislators of Connecticut † begin with the penal laws, and, strange to say, they borrow their provisions from the text of Holy Writ.

" Whosoever shall worship any other God than the Lord," says the preamble of the Code, " shall surely be put to death." This is followed by ten or twelve enactments of·the same kind, copied verbatim from the books of Exodus, Leviticus, and Deuteronomy. Blasphemy, sorcery, adultery,‡ and rape were punished with death ; an outrage offered by a son to his parents was to be expiated by the same penalty. The legislation of a rude and half-civilized people was thus applied to an enlightened and moral community. The consequence was, that the punishment of death was never more frequently prescribed by statute, and never more rarely enforced. §

The chief care of the legislators, in this body of penal laws, was the maintenance of orderly conduct and good morals in the community : thus they constantly invaded

* Code of 1650, p. 28 (Hartford, 1830).

† See also in Hutchinson's History, Vol. I. pp. 435, 456, the analysis of the penal code adopted in 1648 by the colony of Massachusetts : this code is drawn up on the same principles as that of Connecticut.

‡ Adultery was also punished with death by the law of Massachusetts : and Hutchinson (Vol. I. p. 441) says that several persons actually suffered for this crime. He quotes a curious anecdote on this subject, of what took place in the year 1663. A married woman had had criminal intercourse with a young man ; her husband died, and she married the lover. Several years had elapsed, when the public began to suspect the previous intercourse of this couple : they were thrown into prison, put upon trial, and very narrowly escaped capital punishment.

§ Except in England, up to the beginning of the present century, where more than one hundred crimes were statutably punishable with death, but not more than one out of a hundred convicted persons were actually executed. — AM. ED.

the domain of conscience, and there was scarcely a sin which was not subject to magisterial censure. The reader is aware of the rigor with which these laws punished rape and adultery; intercourse between unmarried persons was likewise severely repressed. The judge was empowered to inflict either a pecuniary penalty, a whipping, or marriage,* on the misdemeanants; and if the records of the old courts of New Haven may be believed, prosecutions of this kind were not unfrequent. We find a sentence, bearing date the 1st of May, 1660, inflicting a fine and reprimand on a young woman who was accused of using improper language, and of allowing herself to be kissed.† The Code of 1650 abounds in preventive measures. It punishes idleness and drunkenness with severity. ‡ Innkeepers were forbidden to furnish more than a certain quantity of liquor to each consumer; and simple lying, whenever it may be injurious,§ is checked by a fine or a flogging. In other places, the legislator, entirely forgetting the great principles of religious toleration which he had himself demanded in Europe, makes attendance on divine service compulsory,‖ and goes so far as to visit with severe punishment,¶ and even with death, Christians who

---

* Code of 1650, p. 48. It appears sometimes to have happened that the judges inflicted these punishments cumulatively, as is seen in a sentence pronounced in 1643 (New Haven Antiquities, p. 114), by which Margaret Bedford, convicted of loose conduct, was condemned to be whipt, and afterwards to marry Nicolas Jemmings, her accomplice.

† New Haven Antiquities, p. 104. See also Hutchinson's History for several causes equally extraordinary.

‡ Code of 1650, pp. 50, 57.   § Ibid., p. 64.   ‖ Ibid., p. 44.

¶ This was not peculiar to Connecticut. See, for instance, the law which, on the 13th of September, 1644, banished the Anabaptists from Massachusetts. (Historical Collection of State Papers, Vol. I. p. 538.) See also the law against the Quakers, passed on the 14th of October, 1656. "Whereas," says the preamble, "an accursed race of heretics called Quakers has sprung up," etc. The clauses of the statute inflict a heavy fine on all captains of ships who should import Quakers into the country. The Quakers

chose to worship God according to a ritual differing from his own.* Sometimes, indeed, the zeal for regulation induces him to descend to the most frivolous particulars: thus a law is to be found in the same code which prohibits the use of tobacco. † It must not be forgotten that these fantastical and vexatious laws were not imposed by authority, but that they were freely voted by all the persons interested in them, and that the manners of the community were even more austere and puritanical than the laws. In 1649, a solemn association was formed in Boston to check the worldly luxury of long hair. ‡

These errors are no doubt discreditable to human reason; they attest the inferiority of our nature, which is incapable of laying firm hold upon what is true and just, and is often reduced to the alternative of two excesses. In strict connection with this penal legislation, which bears such striking marks of a narrow, sectarian spirit, and of those religious passions which had been warmed by persecution and were still fermenting among the people, a body of political laws is to be found, which, though written two hundred years ago, is still in advance of the liberties of our age.

The general principles which are the groundwork of modern constitutions — principles which, in the seventeenth century, were imperfectly known in Europe, and

who may be found there shall be whipt and imprisoned with hard labor. Those members of the sect who should defend their opinions shall be first fined, then imprisoned, and finally driven out of the province. Historical Collection of State Papers, Vol. I. p. 630.

* By the penal law of Massachusetts [1647] any Catholic priest who should set foot in the colony after having been once driven out of it was liable to capital punishment. [This act had a political rather than an ecclesiastical purpose, and was of a piece with the penal legislation of England at about the same period, and long afterwards, against the Catholics. — Am. Ed.]

† Code of 1650, p. 96.

‡ New England's Memorial, p. 316. See Appendix E.

not completely triumphant even in Great Britain — were all recognized and established by the laws of New England: the intervention of the people in public affairs, the free voting of taxes, the responsibility of the agents of power, personal liberty, and trial by jury, were all positively established without discussion.

These fruitful principles were there applied and developed to an extent such as no nation in Europe has yet ventured to attempt.

In Connecticut the electoral body consisted, from its origin, of the whole number of citizens; and this is readily to be understood,* when we recollect that in this young community there was an almost perfect equality of fortune, and a still greater uniformity of opinions.† In Connecticut, at this period, all the executive functionaries were elected, including the Governor of the State.‡ The citizens above the age of sixteen were obliged to bear arms; they formed a national militia, which appointed its own officers, and was to hold itself at all times in readiness to march for the defence of the country.§

In the laws of Connecticut, as well as in all those of New England, we find the germ and gradual development of that township independence, which is the life and mainspring of American liberty at the present day. The political existence of the majority of the nations of Europe commenced in the superior ranks of society, and was gradually and imperfectly communicated to the different members of the social body. In America, on the contrary,

---

* Constitution of 1638, p. 17.

† In 1641 the General Assembly of Rhode Island unanimously declared that the government of the state was a democracy, and that the power was vested in the body of free citizens, who alone had the right to make the laws and to watch their execution. Code of 1650, p. 70.

‡ Pitkin's History, p. 47.

§ Constitution of 1638, p. 12.

it may be said that the township was organized before the county, the county before the State, the State before the Union.

In New England, townships were completely and definitively constituted as early as 1650. The independence of the township was the nucleus round which the local interests, passions, rights, and duties collected and clung. It gave scope to the activity of a real political life, thoroughly democratic and republican. The colonies still recognized the supremacy of the mother country; monarchy was still the law of the State; but the republic was already established in every township.

The towns named their own magistrates of every kind, rated themselves, and levied their own taxes.* In the New England town, the law of representation was not adopted; but the affairs of the community were discussed, as at Athens, in the market-place, by a general assembly of the citizens.

In studying the laws which were promulgated at this early era of the American republics, it is impossible not to be struck by the remarkable acquaintance with the science of government, and the advanced theory of legislation, which they display. The ideas there formed of the duties of society towards its members are evidently much loftier and more comprehensive than those of European legislators at that time: obligations were there imposed upon it which it elsewhere slighted. In the States of New England, from the first, the condition of the poor was provided for; † strict measures were taken for the maintenance of roads, and surveyors were appointed to attend to them; ‡ records were established in every town, in which the results of public deliberations, and the births, deaths, and marriages of the citizens, were entered; § clerks were directed to

* Code of 1650, p. 80.   † Ibid., p. 78.   ‡ Ibid., p. 49.
§ See Hutchinson's History, Vol. I. p. 455.

keep these records; * officers were charged with the administration of vacant inheritances, and with the arbitration of litigated landmarks; and many others were created, whose chief functions were the maintenance of public order in the community.† The law enters into a thousand various details to anticipate and satisfy a crowd of social wants which are even now very inadequately felt in France.

But it is by the mandates relating to Public Education that the original character of American civilization is at once placed in the clearest light. "It being," says the law, "one chief project of that old deluder, Satan, to keep men from the knowledge of the Scripture by persuading them from the use of tongues, to the end that learning may not be buried in the graves of our forefathers, in church and commonwealth, the Lord assisting our endeavors." ‡ Here follow clauses establishing schools in every township, and obliging the inhabitants, under pain of heavy fines, to support them. Schools of a superior kind were founded in the same manner in the more populous districts. The municipal authorities were bound to enforce the sending of children to school by their parents; they were empowered to inflict fines upon all who refused compliance; and in cases of continued resistance, society assumed the place of the parent, took possession of the child, and deprived the father of those natural rights which he used to so bad a purpose. The reader will undoubtedly have remarked the preamble of these enactments: in America, religion is the road to knowledge, and the observance of the divine laws leads man to civil freedom.

If, after having cast a rapid glance over the state of American society in 1650, we turn to the condition of Europe, and more especially to that of the Continent, at the same period, we cannot fail to be struck with astonish-

---

* Code of 1650, p. 86.　　† Ibid., p. 40.　　‡ Ibid., p. 90.

ment. On the continent of Europe, at the beginning of the seventeenth century, absolute monarchy had everywhere triumphed over the ruins of the oligarchical and feudal liberties of the Middle Ages. Never perhaps were the ideas of right more completely overlooked, than in the midst of the splendor and literature of Europe; never was there less political activity among the people; never were the principles of true freedom less widely circulated; and at that very time, those principles, which were scorned or unknown by the nations of Europe, were proclaimed in the deserts of the New World, and were accepted as the future creed of a great people. The boldest theories of the human mind were reduced to practice by a community so humble, that not a statesman condescended to attend to it; and a system of legislation without a precedent was produced offhand by the natural originality of men's imaginations. In the bosom of this obscure democracy, which had as yet brought forth neither generals, nor philosophers, nor authors, a man might stand up in the face of a free people, and pronounce with general applause the following fine definition of liberty.*

"Concerning liberty, I observe a great mistake in the country about that. There is a twofold liberty, natural (I mean as our nature is now corrupt) and civil or federal. The first is common to man with beasts and other creatures. By this, man, as he stands in relation to man simply, hath liberty to do what he lists; it is a liberty to evil as well as to good. This liberty is incompatible and inconsistent with authority, and cannot endure the least restraint of the most just authority. The exercise and

---

* Mather's "Magnalia Christi Americana," Vol. II. p. 13. This speech was made by Winthrop; he was accused of having committed arbitrary actions during his magistracy, but after having made the speech, of which the above is a fragment, he was acquitted by acclamation, and from that time forwards he was always re-elected Governor of the State. See Marshall. Vol. I. p. 166.

maintaining of this liberty makes men grow more evil, and in time to be worse than brute beasts: *omnes sumus licentiâ deteriores.* This is that great enemy of truth and peace, that wild beast, which all the ordinances of God are bent against, to restrain and subdue it. The other kind of liberty I call civil or federal; it may also be termed moral, in reference to the covenant between God and man, in the moral law, and the politic covenants and constitutions, amongst men themselves. This liberty is the proper end and object of authority, and cannot subsist without it; and it is a liberty to that only which is good, just, and honest. This liberty you are to stand for, with the hazard not only of your goods, but of your lives, if need be. Whatsoever crosseth this, is not authority, but a distemper thereof. This liberty is maintained and exercised in a way of subjection to authority; it is of the same kind of liberty wherewith Christ hath made us free." *

I have said enough to put the character of Anglo-American civilization in its true light. It is the result (and this should be constantly present to the mind) of two distinct elements, which in other places have been in frequent hostility, but which in America have been admirably incorporated and combined with one another. I allude to the spirit of Religion and the spirit of Liberty.

The settlers of New England were at the same time ardent sectarians and daring innovators. Narrow as the limits of some of their religious opinions were, they were free from all political prejudices.

Hence arose two tendencies, distinct but not opposite, which are everywhere discernible in the manners as well as the laws of the country.

* De Tocqueville copied from the "Magnalia" Cotton Mather's imperfect and faulty report of this speech. I have substituted Winthrop's own report of it, as he inserted it at the time in his "Journal," a corrected edition of which has been recently published by Mr. James Savage. — AM. ED.

One would think that men who had sacrificed their friends, their family, and their native land to a religious conviction would be wholly absorbed in the pursuit of the treasure which they had just purchased at so high a price. And yet we find them seeking with nearly equal zeal for material wealth and moral good, — for well-being and freedom on earth, and salvation in heaven. They moulded and altered at pleasure all political principles, and all human laws and institutions; they broke down the barriers of the society in which they were born; they disregarded the old principles which had governed the world for ages; a career without bounds, a field without a horizon, was opened before them: they precipitate themselves into it, and traverse it in every direction. But, having reached the limits of the political world, they stop of their own accord, and lay aside with awe the use of their most formidable faculties; they no longer doubt or innovate; they abstain from raising even the veil of the sanctuary, and bow with submissive respect before truths which they admit without discussion.

Thus, in the moral world, everything is classified, systematized, foreseen, and decided beforehand; in the political world, everything is agitated, disputed, and uncertain. In the one is a passive though a voluntary obedience; in the other, an independence scornful of experience, and jealous of all authority. These two tendencies, apparently so discrepant, are far from conflicting; they advance together, and mutually support each other.

Religion perceives that civil liberty affords a noble exercise to the faculties of man, and that the political world is a field prepared by the Creator for the efforts of mind. Free and powerful in its own sphere, satisfied with the place reserved for it, religion never more surely establishes its empire than when it reigns in the hearts of men unsupported by aught beside its native strength.

Liberty regards religion as its companion in all its battles and its triumphs, — as the cradle of its infancy, and the divine source of its claims. It considers religion as the safeguard of morality, and morality as the best security of law, and the surest pledge of the duration of freedom.*

REASONS OF CERTAIN ANOMALIES WHICH THE LAWS AND CUSTOMS OF THE ANGLO-AMERICANS PRESENT.

Remains of Aristocratic Institutions amidst the most complete Democracy. — Why ? — Careful Distinction to be drawn between what is of Puritanical and what of English Origin.

THE reader is cautioned not to draw too general or too absolute an inference from what has been said. The social condition, the religion, and the manners of the first emigrants undoubtedly exercised an immense influence on the destiny of their new country. Nevertheless, they could not found a state of things originating solely in themselves : no man can entirely shake off the influence of the past ; and the settlers, intentionally or not, mingled habits and notions derived from their education and the traditions of their country with those habits and notions which were exclusively their own. To know and to judge the Anglo-Americans of the present day, it is therefore necessary to distinguish what is of Puritanical and what of English origin.

Laws and customs are frequently to be met with in the United States which contrast strongly with all that surrounds them. These laws seem to be drawn up in a spirit contrary to the prevailing tenor of American legislation ; and these customs are no less opposed to the general tone of society. If the English colonies had been founded in an age of darkness, or if their origin was already lost in the lapse of years, the problem would be insoluble.

I shall quote a single example to illustrate my meaning. The civil and criminal procedure of the Americans has

* See Appendix F.

only two means of action, — committal or bail. The first act of the magistrate is to exact security from the defendant, or, in case of refusal, to incarcerate him: the ground of the accusation and the importance of the charges against him are then discussed.

It is evident that such a legislation is hostile to the poor, and favorable only to the rich. The poor man has not always a security to produce, even in a civil case; and if he is obliged to wait for justice in prison, he is speedily reduced to distress. A wealthy person, on the contrary, always escapes imprisonment in civil cases; nay, more, if he has committed a crime, he may readily elude punishment by breaking his bail. Thus all the penalties of the law are, for him, reduced to fines.* Nothing can be more aristocratic than this system of legislation. Yet in America, it is the poor who make the law, and they usually reserve the greatest advantages of society to themselves. The explanation of the phenomenon is to be found in England; the laws of which I speak are English, and the Americans have retained them, although repugnant to the general tenor of their legislation and the mass of their ideas.

Next to its habits, the thing which a nation is least apt to change is its civil legislation. Civil laws are familiarly known only to lawyers, whose direct interest it is to maintain them as they are, whether good or bad, simply because they themselves are conversant with them. The bulk of the nation is scarcely acquainted with them; it sees their action only in particular cases, can with difficulty detect their tendency, and obeys them without thought.

I have quoted one instance where it would have been easy to adduce many others. The picture of American society has, if I may so speak, a surface-covering of democracy, beneath which the old aristocratic colors sometimes peep out.

* Crimes no doubt exist for which bail is inadmissible, but they are few in number.

CHAPTER III.

SOCIAL CONDITION OF THE ANGLO-AMERICANS.

SOCIAL condition is commonly the result of circumstances, sometimes of laws, oftener still of these two causes united; but when once established, it may justly be considered as itself the source of almost all the laws, the usages, and the ideas which regulate the conduct of nations: whatever it does not produce, it modifies.

If we would become acquainted with the legislation and the manners of a nation, therefore, we must begin by the study of its social condition.

THE STRIKING CHARACTERISTIC OF THE SOCIAL CONDITION OF THE ANGLO-AMERICANS IS ITS ESSENTIAL DEMOCRACY.

The first Emigrants of New England. — Their Equality. — Aristocratic Laws introduced in the South. — Period of the Revolution. — Change in the Laws of Inheritance. — Effects produced by this Change. — Democracy carried to its utmost Limits in the new States of the West. — Equality of Mental Endowments.

MANY important observations suggest themselves upon the social condition of the Anglo-Americans; but there is one which takes precedence of all the rest. The social condition of the Americans is eminently democratic; this was its character at the foundation of the colonies, and it is still more strongly marked at the present day.

I have stated in the preceding chapter that great equality existed among the emigrants who settled on the shores

of New England. Even the germs of aristocracy were
never planted in that part of the Union. The only influence which obtained there was that of intellect; the people
were used to reverence certain names as the emblems of
knowledge and virtue. Some of their fellow-citizens acquired a power over the others which might truly have
been called aristocratic, if it had been capable of transmission from father to son.

This was the state of things to the east of the Hudson:
to the southwest of that river, and as far as the Floridas,
the case was different. In most of the States situated to
the southwest of the Hudson some great English proprietors had settled, who had imported with them aristocratic
principles and the English law of inheritance. I have
explained the reasons why it was impossible ever to establish a powerful aristocracy in America; these reasons
existed with less force to the southwest of the Hudson.
In the South, one man, aided by slaves, could cultivate a
great extent of country; it was therefore common to see
rich landed proprietors. But their influence was not altogether aristocratic, as that term is understood in Europe,
since they possessed no privileges; and the cultivation of
their estates being carried on by slaves, they had no tenants depending on them, and consequently no patronage.
Still, the great proprietors south of the Hudson constituted
a superior class, having ideas and tastes of its own, and
forming the centre of political action. This kind of aristocracy sympathized with the body of the people, whose
passions and interests it easily embraced; but it was too
weak and too short-lived to excite either love or hatred.
This was the class which headed the insurrection in the
South, and furnished the best leaders of the American
Revolution.

At this period, society was shaken to its centre. The
people, in whose name the struggle had taken place, con-

ceived the desire of exercising the authority which it had acquired; its democratic tendencies were awakened; and having thrown off the yoke of the mother country, it aspired to independence of every kind. The influence of individuals gradually ceased to be felt, and custom and law united to produce the same result.

But the law of inheritance was the last step to equality. I am surprised that ancient and modern jurists have not attributed to this law a greater influence on human affairs.*

* I understand by the law of inheritance all those laws whose principal object it is to regulate the distribution of property after the death of its owner. The law of entail is of this number: it certainly prevents the owner from disposing of his possessions before his death; but this is solely with the view of preserving them entire for the heir. The principal object, therefore, of the law of entail, is to regulate the descent of property after the death of its owner: its other provisions are merely means to this end.

[We have had one modern jurist, Daniel Webster, who anticipated De Tocqueville in pointing out the prodigious influence, upon social and political affairs, of laws regulating the tenure and inheritance of property. In his oration delivered at Plymouth, December 22, 1820, Mr. Webster said: "The character of the political institutions of New England was determined by the fundamental laws respecting property." He enumerated the abolition of the right of primogeniture, the curtailment of entails, long trusts, and other processes for fettering and tying up lands, and the facilities offered for the alienation of estates through subjecting them to every species of debt, through public registries and the simplicity of our forms of conveyance, as acts which "*fixed the future frame and form of the government.*" "The consequence of all these causes," he said, "has been a great subdivision of the soil and a great equality of condition, — the true basis, most certainly, of a popular government."

In alluding to the law in France which renders compulsory an equal division of estates on the death of their owners, Mr. Webster ventured to predict that, "if the government do not change the law, the law, in half a century, will change the government; and this change will not be in favor of the power of the crown, as some European writers have supposed, but against it."

This remarkable prophecy, uttered in December, 1820, was fulfilled first by the Revolution of July, 1830, and then, in a still more marked degree, by that of February, 1848. — AM. ED.]

It is true that these laws belong to civil affairs; but they ought, nevertheless, to be placed at the head of all political institutions; for they exercise an incredible influence upon the social state of a people, whilst political laws only show what this state already is. They have, moreover, a sure and uniform manner of operating upon society, affecting, as it were, generations yet unborn. Through their means, man acquires a kind of preternatural power over the future lot of his fellow-creatures. When the legislator has once regulated the law of inheritance, he may rest from his labor. The machine once put in motion will go on for ages, and advance, as if self-guided, towards a point indicated beforehand. When framed in a particular manner, this law unites, draws together, and vests property and power in a few hands; it causes an aristocracy, so to speak, to spring out of the ground. If formed on opposite principles, its action is still more rapid; it divides, distributes, and disperses both property and power. Alarmed by the rapidity of its progress, those who despair of arresting its motion endeavor, at least, to obstruct it by difficulties and impediments. They vainly seek to counteract its effect by contrary efforts; but it shatters and reduces to powder every obstacle, until we can no longer see anything but a moving and impalpable cloud of dust, which signals the coming of the Democracy. When the law of inheritance permits, still more when it decrees, the equal division of a father's property amongst all his children, its effects are of two kinds: it is important to distinguish them from each other, although they tend to the same end.

In virtue of the law of partible inheritance, the death of every proprietor brings about a kind of revolution in the property; not only do his possessions change hands, but their very nature is altered, since they are parcelled into shares, which become smaller and smaller at each division. This is the direct, and as it were the physical, effect of the

law. It follows, then, that, in countries where equality of
inheritance is established by law, property, and especially
landed property, must constantly tend to division into
smaller and smaller parts.   The effects, however, of such
legislation would only be perceptible after a lapse of time,
if the law were abandoned to its own working; for, supposing the family to consist of only two children, (and, in
a country peopled as France is, the average number is not
above three,) these children, sharing amongst them the
fortune of both parents, would not be poorer than their
father or mother.

But the law of equal division exercises its influence not
merely upon the property itself, but it affects the minds of
the heirs, and brings their passions into play.   These indirect consequences tend powerfully to the destruction of
large fortunes, and especially of large domains.

Among nations whose law of descent is founded upon
the right of primogeniture, landed estates often pass from
generation to generation without undergoing division, —
the consequence of which is, that family feeling is to a certain degree incorporated with the estate.   The family represents the estate, the estate the family, — whose name,
together with its origin, its glory, its power, and its virtues, is thus perpetuated in an imperishable memorial of
the past and a sure pledge of the future.

When the equal partition of property is established by
law, the intimate connection is destroyed between family
feeling and the preservation of the paternal estate; the
property ceases to represent the family; for, as it must
inevitably be divided after one or two generations, it has
evidently a constant tendency to diminish, and must in the
end be completely dispersed.   The sons of the great landed proprietor, if they are few in number, or if fortune
befriends them, may indeed entertain the hope of being
as wealthy as their father, but not of possessing the same

property that he did; their riches must be composed of other elements than his. Now, as soon as you divest the land-owner of that interest in the preservation of his estate which he derives from association, from tradition, and from family pride, you may be certain that, sooner or later, he will dispose of it; for there is a strong pecuniary interest in favor of selling, as floating capital produces higher interest than real property, and is more readily available to gratify the passions of the moment.

Great landed estates which have once been divided never come together again; for the small proprietor draws from his land a better revenue, in proportion, than the large owner does from his; and of course, he sells it at a higher rate.* The calculations of gain, therefore, which decide the rich man to sell his domain, will still more powerfully influence him against buying small estates to unite them into a large one.

What is called family pride is often founded upon an illusion of self-love. A man wishes to perpetuate and immortalize himself, as it were, in his great-grandchildren. Where family pride ceases to act, individual selfishness comes into play. When the idea of family becomes vague, indeterminate, and uncertain, a man thinks of his present convenience; he provides for the establishment of his next succeeding generation, and no more. Either a man gives up the idea of perpetuating his family, or at any rate, he seeks to accomplish it by other means than by a landed estate.

Thus, not only does the law of partible inheritance render it difficult for families to preserve their ancestral domains entire, but it deprives them of the inclination to attempt it, and compels them in some measure to co-operate

---

* I do not mean to say that the small proprietor cultivates his land better, but he cultivates it with more ardor and care : so that he makes up by his labor for his want of skill.

with the law in their own extinction. The law of equal
distribution proceeds by two methods : by acting upon
things, it acts upon persons ; by influencing persons, it
affects things. By both these means, the law succeeds in
striking at the root of landed property, and dispersing rapidly both families and fortunes.*

Most certainly it is not for us, Frenchmen of the nineteenth century, who daily witness the political and social
changes which the law of partition is bringing to pass, to
question its influence. It is perpetually conspicuous in our
country, overthrowing the walls of our dwellings, and removing the landmarks of our fields. But although it has
produced great effects in France, much still remains for
it to do. Our recollections, opinions, and habits present
powerful obstacles to its progress.

In the United States, it has nearly completed its work
of destruction, and there we can best study its results.
The English laws concerning the transmission of property
were abolished in almost all the States at the time of the
Revolution. The law of entail was so modified as not materially to interrupt the free circulation of property.† The
first generation having passed away, estates began to be
parcelled out ; and the change became more and more

* Land being the most stable kind of property, we find, from to time,
rich individuals who are disposed to make great sacrifices in order to obtain
it, and who willingly forfeit a considerable part of their income to make sure
of the rest. But these are accidental cases. The preference for landed property is no longer found habitually in any class but among the poor. The
small land-owner, who has less information, less imagination, and fewer passions than the great one, is generally occupied with the desire of increasing
his estate : and it often happens that by inheritance, by marriage, or by the
chances of trade, he is gradually furnished with the means. Thus, to balance
the tendency which leads men to divide their estates, there exists another,
which incites them to add to them. This tendency, which is sufficient to prevent estates from being divided *ad infinitum,* is not strong enough to create
great territorial possessions, certainly not to keep them up in the same family.
† See Appendix G.

rapid with the progress of time. And now, after a lapse
of a little more than sixty years, the aspect of society is
totally altered; the families of the great landed proprietors
are almost all commingled with the general mass. In the
State of New York, which formerly contained many of
these, there are but two who still keep their heads above
the stream; and they must shortly disappear. The sons
of these opulent citizens have become merchants, lawyers,
or physicians. Most of them have lapsed into obscurity.
The last trace of hereditary ranks and distinctions is destroyed, — the law of partition has reduced all to one level.

I do not mean that there is any lack of wealthy individuals in the United States; I know of no country, indeed,
where the love of money has taken stronger hold on the
affections of men, and where a profounder contempt is
expressed for the theory of the permanent equality of
property. But wealth circulates with inconceivable rapidity, and experience shows that it is rare to find two
succeeding generations in the full enjoyment of it.

This picture, which may, perhaps, be thought to be over-
charged, still gives a very imperfect idea of what is taking
place in the new States of the West and Southwest. At
the end of the last century, a few bold adventurers began
to penetrate into the valley of the Mississippi; and the
mass of the population very soon began to move in that
direction: communities unheard of till then suddenly appeared in the desert. States whose names were not in
existence a few years before, claimed their place in the
American Union; and in the Western settlements we may
behold democracy arrived at its utmost limits. In these
States, founded off-hand, and as it were by chance, the
inhabitants are but of yesterday. Scarcely known to one
another, the nearest neighbors are ignorant of each other's
history. In this part of the American continent, therefore,
the population has escaped the influence not only of great

names and great wealth, but even of the natural aristocracy of knowledge and virtue. None are there able to wield that respectable power which men willingly grant to the remembrance of a life spent in doing good before their eyes. The new States of the West are already inhabited; but society has no existence among them.

· It is not only the fortunes of men which are equal in America; even their acquirements partake in some degree of the same uniformity. I do not believe that there is a country in the world where, in proportion to the population, there are so few ignorant, and at the same time so few learned, individuals. Primary instruction is within the reach of everybody; superior instruction is scarcely to be obtained by any.* This is not surprising; it is, in fact, the necessary consequence of what we have advanced above. Almost all the Americans are in easy circumstances, and can, therefore, obtain the first elements of human knowledge.

In America, there are but few wealthy persons; nearly all Americans have to take a profession. Now, every profession requires an apprenticeship. The Americans can devote to general education only the early years of life. At fifteen, they enter upon their calling, and thus their education generally ends at the age when ours begins.†

* This was an exaggerated statement even when De Tocqueville wrote, thirty years ago. But now, in the Atlantic States, through the influence of the Universities and of scientific and literary associations, there are probably, in proportion to the population, as many scholars, men of science, and highly educated men, as in any country of Europe. — Am. Ed.

† Members of what are called the learned professions — law, physic, and divinity — do not usually begin practice in America before they are twenty-two or twenty-three years old. The average age of the graduates of American Colleges is over twenty years, and two or three years after graduation must be devoted to professional studies. Boys become apprentices to the mechanic trades, it is true, at fourteen years; but this is the usual age for the beginning of apprenticeship in England and on the continent of Europe. As

Whatever is done afterwards is with a view to some special and lucrative object; a science is taken up as a matter of business, and the only branch of it which is attended to is such as admits of an immediate practical application.

In America, most of the rich men were formerly poor; most of those who now enjoy leisure were absorbed in business during their youth; the consequence of which is, that, when they might have had a taste for study, they had no time for it, and when the time is at their disposal, they have no longer the inclination.

There is no class, then, in America, in which the taste for intellectual pleasures is transmitted with hereditary fortune and leisure, and by which the labors of the intellect are held in honor. Accordingly, there is an equal want of the desire and the power of application to these objects.

A middling standard is fixed in America for human knowledge. All approach as near to it as they can; some as they rise, others as they descend. Of course, a multitude of persons are to be found who entertain the same number of ideas on religion, history, science, political economy, legislation, and government. The gifts of intellect proceed directly from God, and man cannot prevent their unequal distribution. But it is at least a consequence of what we have just said, that although the capacities of men are different, as the Creator intended they should be, Americans find the means of putting them to use are equal.

In America, the aristocratic element has always been feeble from its birth; and if at the present day it is not actually destroyed, it is at any rate so completely disabled, that we can scarcely assign to it any degree of influence on the course of affairs.

a general rule, children of the poorest parents are not compelled to begin hard labor at so early an age in the United States as in Great Britain. De Tocqueville's statement is confused, because he does not sufficiently indicate which "professions" or "callings" he is speaking of. — AM. ED.

The democratic principle, on the contrary, has gained so much strength by time, by events, and by legislation, as to have become not only predominant, but all-powerful. There is no family or corporate authority, and it is rare to find even the influence of individual character enjoy any durability.

America, then, exhibits in her social state an extraordinary phenomenon. Men are there seen on a greater equality in point of fortune and intellect, or, in other words, more equal in their strength, than in any other country of the world, or in any age of which history has preserved the remembrance.

POLITICAL CONSEQUENCES OF THE SOCIAL CONDITION OF THE ANGLO-AMERICANS.

THE political consequences of such a social condition as this are easily deducible.

It is impossible to believe that equality will not eventually find its way into the political world, as it does everywhere else. To conceive of men remaining forever unequal upon a single point, yet equal on all others, is impossible; they must come in the end to be equal upon all.

Now I know of only two methods of establishing equality in the political world; every citizen must be put in possession of his rights, or rights must be granted to no one. For nations which are arrived at the same stage of social existence as the Anglo-Americans, it is, therefore, very difficult to discover a medium between the sovereignty of all and the absolute power of one man: and it would be vain to deny that the social condition which I have been describing is just as liable to one of these consequences as to the other.

There is, in fact, a manly and lawful passion for equality

which incites men to wish all to be powerful and honored.
This passion tends to elevate the humble to the rank of the
great; but there exists also in the human heart a depraved
taste for equality, which impels the weak to attempt to
lower the powerful to their own level, and reduces men to
prefer equality in slavery to inequality with freedom. Not
that those nations whose social condition is democratic
naturally despise liberty; on the contrary, they have an
instinctive love of it. But liberty is not the chief and
constant object of their desires; equality is their idol: they
make rapid and sudden efforts to obtain liberty, and, if they
miss their aim, resign themselves to their disappointment;
but nothing can satisfy them without equality, and they
would rather perish than lose it.

On the other hand, in a state where the citizens are all
nearly on an equality, it becomes difficult for them to preserve their independence against the aggressions of power.
No one among them being strong enough to engage in the
struggle alone with advantage, nothing but a general combination can protect their liberty. Now, such a union is
not always possible.

From the same social position, then, nations may derive
one or the other of two great political results; these results are extremely different from each other, but they both
proceed from the same cause.

The Anglo-Americans are the first nation who, having
been exposed to this formidable alternative, have been
happy enough to escape the dominion of absolute power.
They have been allowed by their circumstances, their origin, their intelligence, and especially by their morals, to
establish and maintain the sovereignty of the people.

CHAPTER IV.

THE PRINCIPLE OF THE SOVEREIGNTY OF THE PEOPLE IN AMERICA.

It predominates over the whole of Society in America. — Application made of this Principle by the Americans even before their Revolution. — Development given to it by that Revolution. — Gradual and irresistible Extension of the Elective Qualification.

WHENEVER the political laws of the United States are to be discussed, it is with the doctrine of the sovereignty of the people that we must begin.

The principle of the sovereignty of the people, which is always to be found, more or less, at the bottom of almost all human institutions, generally remains there concealed from view. It is obeyed without being recognized, or if for a moment it be brought to light, it is hastily cast back into the gloom of the sanctuary.

" The will of the nation " is one of those phrases which have been most largely abused by the wily and the despotic of every age. Some have seen the expression of it in the purchased suffrages of a few of the satellites of power; others, in the votes of a timid or an interested minority; and some have even discovered it in the silence of a people, on the supposition that the fact of submission established the right to command.

In America, the principle of the sovereignty of the people is not either barren or concealed, as it is with some other nations; it is recognized by the customs and proclaimed by the laws; it spreads freely, and arrives without impediment at its most remote consequences. If there be a country in the world where the doctrine of the sovereignty of the people can be fairly appreciated, where it can be studied in its application to the affairs of society, and where its dangers and its advantages may be judged, that country is assuredly America.

I have already observed that, from their origin, the sovereignty of the people was the fundamental principle of most of the British colonies in America. It was far, however, from then exercising as much influence on the government of society as it now does. Two obstacles — the one external, the other internal — checked its invasive progress.

It could not ostensibly disclose itself in the laws of colonies which were still constrained to obey the mother country; it was therefore obliged to rule secretly in the provincial assemblies, and especially in the townships.

American society at that time was not yet prepared to adopt it with all its consequences. Intelligence in New England, and wealth in the country to the south of the Hudson, (as I have shown in the preceding chapter,) long exercised a sort of aristocratic influence, which tended to keep the exercise of social power in the hands of a few. Not all the public functionaries were chosen by popular vote, nor were all the citizens voters. The electoral franchise was everywhere somewhat restricted, and made dependent on a certain qualification, which was very low in the North, and more considerable in the South.

The American Revolution broke out, and the doctrine of the sovereignty of the people came out of the townships, and took possession of the State. Every class was enlisted in its cause; battles were fought and victories obtained for it; it became the law of laws.

A change almost as rapid was effected in the interior of society, where the law of inheritance completed the abolition of local influences.

As soon as this effect of the laws and of the Revolution became apparent to every eye, victory was irrevocably pronounced in favor of the democratic cause. All power was, in fact, in its hands, and resistance was no longer possible. The higher orders submitted without a murmur and without a struggle to an evil which was thenceforth inevitable. The ordinary fate of falling powers awaited them : each of their members followed his own interest ; and as it was impossible to wring the power from the hands of a people whom they did not detest sufficiently to brave, their only aim was to secure its good-will at any price. The most democratic laws were consequently voted by the very men whose interests they impaired : and thus, although the higher classes did not excite the passions of the people against their order, they themselves accelerated the triumph of the new state of things ; so that, by a singular change, the democratic impulse was found to be most irresistible in the very States where the aristocracy had the firmest hold. The State of Maryland, which had been founded by men of rank, was the first to proclaim universal suffrage, and to introduce the most democratic forms into the whole of its government.

When a nation begins to modify the elective qualification, it may easily be foreseen that, sooner or later, that qualification will be entirely abolished. There is no more invariable rule in the history of society : the further electoral rights are extended, the greater is the need of extending them ; for after each concession the strength of the democracy increases, and its demands increase with its strength. The ambition of those who are below the appointed rate is irritated in exact proportion to the great number of those who are above it. The exception at last becomes the rule, concession follows concession, and no stop can be made short of universal suffrage.*

* See Appendix H.

At the present day the principle of the sovereignty of
the people has acquired, in the United States, all the practical development which the imagination can conceive.
It is unencumbered by those fictions which are thrown
over it in other countries, and it appears in every possible
form, according to the exigency of the occasion. Sometimes the laws are made by the people in a body, as at
Athens; and sometimes its representatives, chosen by universal suffrage, transact business in its name, and under its
immediate supervision.

In some countries, a power exists which, though it is in
a degree foreign to the social body, directs it, and forces it
to pursue a certain track. In others, the ruling force is
divided, being partly within and partly without the ranks
of the people. But nothing of the kind is to be seen in
the United States; there society governs itself for itself.
All power centres in its bosom; and scarcely an individual
is to be met with who would venture to conceive, or, still
less, to express, the idea of seeking it elsewhere. The
nation participates in the making of its laws by the choice
of its legislators, and in the execution of them by the
choice of the agents of the executive government; it may
almost be said to govern itself, so feeble and so restricted
is the share left to the administration, so little do the authorities forget their popular origin and the power from
which they emanate. The people reign in the American
political world as the Deity does in the universe. They
are the cause and the aim of all things; everything comes
from them, and everything is absorbed in them.

CHAPTER V.

NECESSITY OF EXAMINING THE CONDITION OF THE STATES BEFORE THAT OF THE UNION AT LARGE.

IT is proposed to examine, in the following chapter, what is the form of government established in America on the principle of the sovereignty of the people; what are its means of action, its hindrances, its advantages, and its dangers. The first difficulty which presents itself arises from the complex nature of the Constitution of the United States, which consists of two distinct social structures, connected, and, as it were, encased one within the other; two governments, completely separate and almost independent, the one fulfilling the ordinary duties, and responding to the daily and indefinite calls, of a community, the other circumscribed within certain limits, and only exercising an exceptional authority over the general interests of the country. In short, there are twenty-four small sovereign nations, whose agglomeration constitutes the body of the Union. To examine the Union before we have studied the States, would be to adopt a method filled with obstacles. The form of the Federal Government of the United States was the last to be adopted; and it is in fact nothing more than a summary of those republican principles which were current in the whole community before it existed, and independently of its existence. Moreover, the Federal Government is, as I have just observed, the exception; the government of the States is the rule. The author who should attempt to exhibit the picture as a whole, before he had explained its details, would necessarily fall into obscurity and repetition.

The great political principles which now govern American society undoubtedly took their origin and their growth in the State. We must know the State, then, in order to gain a clew to the rest. The States which now compose the American Union all present the same features, as far as regards the external aspect of their institutions. Their political or administrative life is centred in three focuses of action, which may be compared to the different nervous centres which give motion to the human body. The township is the first in order, then the county, and lastly the State.

THE AMERICAN SYSTEM OF TOWNSHIPS.*

Why the Author begins the Examination of the Political Institutions with the Township. — Its Existence in all Nations. — Difficulty of establishing and preserving Municipal Independence. — Its Importance. — Why the Author has selected the Township System of New England as the main Topic of his Discussion.

It is not undesignedly that I begin this subject with the Township. The village or township is the only association which is so perfectly natural, that, wherever a number of men are collected, it seems to constitute itself.

The town or tithing, then, exists in all nations, whatever their laws and customs may be: it is man who makes monarchies and establishes republics, but the township seems to

---

* It is by this periphrasis that I attempt to render the French expressions *Commune* and *Système Communal.* I am not aware that any English word precisely corresponds to the general term of the original. In France, every association of human dwellings forms a *commune,* and every *commune* is governed by a *Maire* and a *Conseil municipal.* In other words, the *mancipium,* or municipal privilege, which belongs, in England, to chartered corporations alone, is alike extended to every *commune* into which the cantons and departments were divided at the Revolution. Thence the different application of

come directly from the hand of God. But although the existence of the township is coeval with that of man, its freedom is an infrequent and fragile thing. A nation can always establish great political assemblies, because it habit ually contains a certain number of individuals fitted by their talents, if not by their habits, for the direction of affairs. The township, on the contrary, is composed of coarser materials, which are less easily fashioned by the legislator. The difficulty of establishing its independence rather augments than diminishes with the increasing intelligence of the people. A highly civilized community can hardly tolerate a local independence, is disgusted at its numerous blunders, and is apt to despair of success before the experiment is completed. Again, the immunities of townships, which have been obtained with so much difficulty, are least of all protected against the encroachments of the supreme power. They are unable to struggle, single-handed, against a strong and enterprising government, and they cannot defend themselves with success unless they are identified with the customs of the nation and supported by public opinion. Thus, until the independence of townships is amalgamated with the manners of a people, it is easily destroyed; and it is only after a long existence in the laws that it can be thus amalgamated. Municipal freedom is not the fruit of human efforts; it is rarely created by others; but is, as it were, secretly self-produced in the midst of a semi-barbarous state of society. The constant action of the laws and the national habits,

the expression, which is general in one country and restricted in the other. In America, the counties of the Northern States are divided into townships, those of the Southern into parishes; besides which, municipal bodies, bearing the name of corporations, exist as cities. I shall apply these several expressions to render the term *commune*. The word "parish," now commonly used in England, belongs exclusively to the ecclesiastical division; it denotes the limits over which a *parson's* (*persona ecclesiæ*, or perhaps *parochianus*) rights extend. — *Translator's Note.*

peculiar circumstances, and, above all, time, may consolidate it; but there is certainly no nation on the continent of Europe which has experienced its advantages. Yet municipal institutions constitute the strength of free nations. Town-meetings are to liberty what primary schools are to science; they bring it within the people's reach, they teach men how to use and how to enjoy it. A nation may establish a free government, but without municipal institutions, it cannot have the spirit of liberty. Transient passions, the interests of an hour, or the chance of circumstances, may create the external forms of independence; but the despotic tendency which has been driven into the interior of the social system, will, sooner or later, reappear on the surface.

To make the reader understand the general principles on which the political organization of the counties and townships in the United States rests, I have thought it expedient to choose one of the States of New England as an example, to examine in detail the mechanism of its constitution, and then to cast a general glance over the rest of the country.

The township and the county are not organized in the same manner in every part of the Union; it is easy to perceive, however, that nearly the same principles have guided the formation of both of them throughout the Union. I am inclined to believe that these principles have been carried further, and have produced greater results, in New England than elsewhere. Consequently, they stand out there in higher relief, and offer greater facilities to the observations of a stranger.

The township institutions of New England form a complete and regular whole; they are old; they have the support of the laws, and the still stronger support of the manners of the community, over which they exercise a prodigious influence. For all these reasons, they deserve our special attention.

LIMITS OF THE TOWNSHIP.

THE township of New England holds a middle place between the *commune* and the *canton* of France. Its average population is from two to three thousand;* so that it is not so large, on the one hand, that the interests of its inhabitants would be likely to conflict, and not so small, on the other, but that men capable of conducting its affairs may always be found among its citizens.

POWERS OF THE TOWNSHIP IN NEW ENGLAND.

The People the Source of all Power in the Township as elsewhere. — Manages its own Affairs. — No Municipal Council. — The greater Part of the Authority vested in the Selectmen. — How the Selectmen act. — Town-Meeting. — Enumeration of the Officers of the Township. — Obligatory and remunerated Functions.

IN the township, as well as everywhere else, the people are the source of power; but nowhere do they exercise their power more immediately. In America, the people form a master who must be obeyed to the utmost limits of possibility.

In New England, the majority act by representatives in conducting the general business of the State. It is necessary that it should be so. But in the townships, where the legislative and administrative action of the government is nearer to the governed, the system of representation is not adopted. There is no municipal council; but the body of voters, after having chosen its magistrates, directs them in everything that exceeds the simple and ordinary execution of the laws of the State.†

---

* In 1830 there were 305 townships in the State of Massachusetts, and 610,014 inhabitants; which gives an average of about 2,000 inhabitants to each township. [Some have over 10,000 inhabitants each, and some have less than 500. — AM. ED.]

† The same rules are not applicable to the cities, which generally have a

This state of things is so contrary to our ideas, and so different from our customs, that I must furnish some examples to make it intelligible.

The public duties in the township are extremely numerous, and minutely divided, as we shall see farther on; but most of the administrative power is vested in a few persons, chosen annually, called " the Selectmen." *

The general laws of the State impose certain duties on the selectmen, which they may fulfil without the authority of their townsmen, but which they can neglect only on their own responsibility. The State law requires them, for instance, to draw up the list of voters in their townships; and if they omit this duty, they are guilty of a misdemeanor. In all the affairs, however, which are voted in town-meeting, the selectmen carry into effect the popular mandate, as in France the Maire executes the decree of the municipal council. They usually act upon their own responsibility, and merely put in practice principles which have been previously recognized by the majority. But if they wish to make any change in the existing state of things, or to undertake any new enterprise, they must refer to the source of their power. If, for instance, a school is to be established, the selectmen call a meeting of the voters on a certain day, at an appointed place. They explain the urgency of the case; they make known the means of satisfying it, the probable expense, and the site which seems to be most favorable. The meeting is con-

mayor, and a corporation divided into two bodies; this, however, is an exception which requires the sanction of a law. — See the Act of the 22d February, 1822, regulating the powers of the city of Boston. It frequently happens that small towns, as well as cities, are subject to a peculiar administration. In 1832, 104 townships in the State of New York were governed in this manner. — *Williams's Register.*

* Three selectmen are appointed in the small townships, and nine in the large ones. — See " The Town Officer," p. 186. See also the Revised Statutes of Massachusetts.

sulted on these several points; it adopts the principle, marks out the site, votes the tax, and confides the execution of its resolution to the selectmen.

The selectmen alone have the right of calling a townmeeting; but they may be required to do so. If ten citizens wish to submit a new project to the assent of the town, they may demand a town-meeting; the selectmen are obliged to comply, and have only the right of presiding at the meeting. These political forms, these social customs, doubtless seem strange to us in France. I do not here undertake to judge them, or to make known the secret causes by which they are produced and maintained. I only describe them.

The selectmen are elected every year, in the month of March or April. The town-meeting chooses at the same time a multitude of other town officers, who are intrusted with important administrative functions. The assessors rate the township; the collectors receive the tax. A constable is appointed to keep the peace, to watch the streets, and to execute the laws; the town clerk records the town votes, orders, and grants. The treasurer keeps the funds. The overseers of the poor perform the difficult task of carrying out the poor-laws. Committee-men are appointed to attend to the schools and public instruction; and the surveyors of highways, who take care of the greater and lesser roads of the township, complete the list of the principal functionaries. But there are other petty officers still; such as the parish-committee, who audit the expenses of public worship; fire-wards, who direct the efforts of the citizens in case of fire; tithing-men, hogreeves, fence-viewers, timber-measurers, and sealers of weights and measures.*

---

* All these magistrates actually exist; their different functions are all detailed in a book called " The Town Officer," by Isaac Goodwin, (Worcester, 1827,) and in the Revised Statutes.

There are, in all, nineteen principal offices in a township. Every inhabitant is constrained, on the pain of being fined, to undertake these different functions; which, however, are almost all paid, in order that the poorer citizens may give time to them without loss.* In general, each official act has its price, and the officers are remunerated in proportion to what they have done.

LIFE IN THE TOWNSHIP.

Every one the best Judge of his own Interest. — Corollary of the Principle of the Sovereignty of the People. — Application of these Doctrines in the Townships of America. — The Township of New England is Sovereign in all that concerns itself alone, and Subject to the State in all other Matters. — Duties of the Township to the State. — In France, the Government lends its Agents to the *Commune*. — In America, it is the reverse.

I HAVE already observed, that the principle of the sovereignty of the people governs the whole political system of the Anglo-Americans. Every page of this book will afford new applications of the same doctrine. In the nations by which the sovereignty of the people is recognized, every individual has an equal share of power, and participates equally in the government of the state. Why, then, does he obey the government, and what are the natural limits of this obedience? Every individual is always supposed to be as well informed, as virtuous, and as strong as any of his fellow-citizens. He obeys the government, not because he is inferior to those who conduct it, or because he is less capable than any other of governing himself; but because he acknowledges the utility of an association with his fellow-men, and he knows that no such association can exist without a regulating force. He is a subject in all

---

* This is an error: most of them are performed gratuitously; and when pay is given, it is so small as to be almost nominal. — AM. ED.

that concerns the duties of citizens to each other; he is free, and responsible to God alone, for all that concerns himself. Hence arises the maxim, that every one is the best and sole judge of his own private interest, and that society has no right to control a man's actions, unless they are prejudicial to the common weal, or unless the common weal demands his help. This doctrine is universally admitted in the United States. I shall hereafter examine the general influence which it exercises on the ordinary actions of life: I am now speaking of the municipal bodies.

The township, taken as a whole, and in relation to the central government, is only an individual, like any other to whom the theory I have just described is applicable. Municipal independence in the United States is, therefore, a natural consequence of this very principle of the sovereignty of the people. All the American republics recognize it more or less; but circumstances have peculiarly favored its growth in New England.

In this part of the Union, political life had its origin in the townships; and it may almost be said that each of them originally formed an independent nation. When the kings of England afterwards asserted their supremacy, they were content to assume the central power of the state. They left the townships where they were before; and although they are now subject to the state, they were not at first, or were hardly so. They did not receive their powers from the central authority, but, on the contrary, they gave up a portion of their independence to the state. This is an important distinction, and one which the reader must constantly recollect. The townships are generally subordinate to the state only in those interests which I shall term *social*, as they are common to all the others. They are independent in all that concerns themselves alone; and amongst the inhabitants of New England, I believe that not a man is to be found who would acknowledge that the state has any right to interfere in their town affairs. The towns of New England buy and sell, prosecute or are indicted, augment or diminish their rates, and no administrative authority ever thinks of offering any opposition.

There are certain social duties, however, which they are bound to fulfil. If the State is in need of money, a town cannot withhold the supplies; if the State projects a road, the township cannot refuse to let it cross its territory; if a police regulation is made by the State, it must be enforced by the town; if a uniform system of public instruction is enacted, every town is bound to establish the schools which the law ordains. When I come to speak of the administration of the laws in the United States, I shall point out how, and by what means, the townships are compelled to obey in these different cases: I here merely show the existence of the obligation. Strict as this obligation is, the government of the State imposes it in principle only, and in its performance the township resumes all its independent rights. Thus, taxes are voted by the State, but they are levied and collected by the township; the establishment of a school is obligatory, but the township builds, pays, and superintends it. In France, the state collector receives the local imposts; in America, the town collector receives the taxes of the State. Thus the French government lends its agents to the *commune;* in America, the township lends its agents to the government. This fact alone shows how widely the two nations differ.

SPIRIT OF THE TOWNSHIPS OF NEW ENGLAND.

How the Township of New England wins the Affections of its Inhabitants.
— Difficulty of creating local Public Spirit in Europe. — The Rights
and Duties of the American Township favorable to it. — Sources of local
Attachment in the United States. — How Town Spirit shows itself in
New England. — Its happy Effects.

IN America, not only do municipal bodies exist, but they
are kept alive and supported, by town spirit. The township of New England possesses two advantages, which
strongly excite the interest of mankind, — namely, independence and authority. Its sphere is limited, indeed; but
within that sphere, its action is unrestrained. This independence alone gives it a real importance, which its extent
and population would not insure.

It is to be remembered, too, that the affections of men
generally turn towards power. Patriotism is not durable
in a conquered nation. The New-Englander is attached
to his township, not so much because he was born in it,
but because it is a free and strong community, of which he
is a member, and which deserves the care spent in managing it. In Europe, the absence of local public spirit is
a frequent subject of regret to those who are in power;
every one agrees that there is no surer guaranty of order
and tranquillity, and yet nothing is more difficult to create.
If the municipal bodies were made powerful and independent, it is feared that they would become too strong, and
expose the state to anarchy. Yet, without power and independence, a town may contain good subjects, but it can
have no active citizens. Another important fact is, that
the township of New England is so constituted as to excite
the warmest of human affections, without arousing the
ambitious passions of the heart of man. The officers of
the county are not elected,* and their authority is very

* This is a mistake; they are chosen by popular vote. — AM. ED.

limited. Even the State is only a second-rate community, whose tranquil and obscure administration offers no inducement sufficient to draw men away from the home of their interests into the turmoil of public affairs. The Federal Government confers power and honor on the men who conduct it; but these individuals can never be very numerous. The high station of the Presidency can only be reached at an advanced period of life; and the other Federal functionaries of a high class are generally men who have been favored by good luck, or have been distinguished in some other career. Such cannot be the permanent aim of the ambitious. But the township, at the centre of the ordinary relations of life, serves as a field for the desire of public esteem, the want of exciting interest, and the taste for authority and popularity; and the passions which commonly embroil society change their character, when they find a vent so near the domestic hearth and the family circle.

In the American townships, power has been disseminated with admirable skill, for the purpose of interesting the greatest possible number of persons in the common weal. Independently of the voters, who are from time to time called into action, the power is divided among innumerable functionaries and officers, who all, in their several spheres, represent the powerful community in whose name they act. The local administration thus affords an unfailing source of profit and interest to a vast number of individuals.

The American system, which divides the local authority among so many citizens, does not scruple to multiply the functions of the town officers. For in the United States, it is believed, and with truth, that patriotism is a kind of devotion which is strengthened by ritual observance. In this manner, the activity of the township is continually perceptible; it is daily manifested in the fulfilment of a duty, or the exercise of a right; and a constant though gentle motion is thus kept up in society, which animates without disturbing it. The American attaches himself to his little community for the same reason that the mountaineer clings to his hills, because the characteristic features of his country are there more distinctly marked; it has a more striking physiognomy.

The existence of the townships of New England is, in general, a happy one. Their government is suited to their tastes, and chosen by themselves. In the midst of the profound peace and general comfort which reign in America, the commotions of municipal life are unfrequent. The conduct of local business is easy. The political education of the people has long been complete; say rather that it was complete, when the people first set foot upon the soil. In New England, no tradition exists of a distinction of ranks; no portion of the community is tempted to oppress the remainder; and the wrongs which may injure isolated individuals are forgotten in the general contentment which prevails. If the government has faults, (and it would no doubt be easy to point out some,) they do not attract notice, for the government really emanates from those it governs, and whether it acts ill or well, this fact casts the protecting spell of a parental. pride over its demerits. Besides, they have nothing wherewith to compare it. England formerly governed the mass of the colonies; but the people was always sovereign in the township, where its rule is not only an ancient, but a primitive state.

The native of New England is attached to his township because it is independent and free: his co-operation in its affairs insures his attachment to its interest; the well-being it affords him secures his affection; and its welfare is the aim of his ambition and of his future exertions. He takes a part in every occurrence in the place; he practises the art of government in the small sphere within his reach; he accustoms himself to those forms without which liberty can only advance by revolutions; he imbibes their spirit;

he acquires a taste for order, comprehends the balance of powers, and collects clear practical notions on the nature of his duties and the extent of his rights.

THE COUNTIES OF NEW ENGLAND.

THE division of the counties in America has considerable analogy with that of the *arrondissements* of France. The limits of both are arbitrarily laid down, and the various districts which they contain have no necessary connection, no common tradition or natural sympathy, no community of existence; their object is simply to facilitate the administration.

The extent of the township was too small to contain a system of judicial institutions; the county, therefore, is the first centre of judicial action. Each county has a court of justice, a sheriff to execute its decrees, and a prison for criminals. There are certain wants which are felt alike by all the townships of a county; it is therefore natural that they should be satisfied by a central authority. In Massachusetts, this authority is vested in the hands of several magistrates, who are appointed by the Governor of the State, with the advice of his council.* The County Commissioners have only a limited and exceptional authority, which is applicable to certain predetermined cases. The State and the townships possess all the power requisite for ordinary public business. The budget of the county is only drawn up by its Commissioners, and is voted by the legislature; there is no assembly which directly or indirectly represents the county. It has, therefore, properly speaking, no political existence.

A twofold tendency may be discerned in most of the

---

* The council of the Governor is an elective body. [The County Commissioners are now elected by popular vote. See Revised Statutes. — AM. ED.]

American constitutions, which impels the legislator to concentrate the legislative, and to divide the executive power.
The township of New England has in itself an indestructi-
ble principle of life; but this distinct existence could only
be fictitiously introduced into the county, where the want
of it has not been felt. All the townships united have but
one representation, which is the State, the centre of all
national authority: beyond the action of the township and
that of the State, it may be said that there is nothing but
individual action.

THE ADMINISTRATION OF GOVERNMENT IN NEW ENGLAND.

Administration not perceived in America. — Why? — The Europeans believe that Liberty is promoted by depriving the Social Authority of some
of its Rights; the Americans, by dividing its Exercise. — Almost all
the Administration confined to the Township, and divided amongst the
Town-Officers. — No Trace of an Administrative Hierarchy perceived,
either in the Township or above it. — The Reason of this. — How it
happens that the Administration of the State is uniform. — Who is empowered to enforce the Obedience of the Township and the County to
the Law. — The Introduction of Judicial Power into the Administration.
— Consequence of the Extension of the Elective Principle to all Functionaries. — The Justice of the Peace in New England. — By whom appointed. — County Officer: insures the Administration of the Townships.
— Court of Sessions. — Its Mode of Action. — Who brings Matters
before this Court for Action. — Right of Inspection and Indictment
parcelled out like the other Administrative Functions. — Informers encouraged by the Division of Fines.

NOTHING is more striking to a European traveller in
the United States, than the absence of what we term the
Government, or the Administration. Written laws exist
in America, and one sees the daily execution of them; but
although everything moves regularly, the mover can nowhere be discovered. The hand which directs the social
machine is invisible. Nevertheless, as all persons must

have recourse to certain grammatical forms, which are the foundation of human language, in order to express their thoughts; so all communities are obliged to secure their existence by submitting to a certain amount of authority, without which they fall into anarchy. This authority may be distributed in several ways, but it must always exist somewhere.

There are two methods of diminishing the force of authority in a nation. The first is to weaken the supreme power in its very principle, by forbidding or preventing society from acting in its own defence under certain circumstances. To weaken authority in this manner is the European way of establishing freedom.

The second manner of diminishing the influence of authority does not consist in stripping society of some of its rights, nor in paralyzing its efforts, but in distributing the exercise of its powers among various hands, and in multiplying functionaries, to each of whom is given the degree of power necessary for him to perform his duty. There may be nations whom this distribution of social powers might lead to anarchy; but in itself, it is not anarchical. The authority thus divided is, indeed, rendered less irresistible and less perilous, but it is not destroyed.

The Revolution of the United States was the result of a mature and reflecting preference of freedom, and not of a vague or ill-defined craving for independence. It contracted no alliance with the turbulent passions of anarchy; but its course was marked, on the contrary, by a love of order and law.

It was never assumed in the United States, that the citizen of a free country has a right to do whatever he pleases; on the contrary, more social obligations were there imposed upon him than anywhere else. No idea was ever entertained of attacking the principle or contesting the rights of society; but the exercise of its authority was divided, in order that the office might be powerful and the officer insignificant, and that the community should be at once regulated and free. In no country in the world does the law hold so absolute a language as in America; and in no country is the right of applying it vested in so many hands. The administrative power in the United States presents nothing either centralized or hierarchical in its constitution ; this accounts for its passing unperceived. The power exists, but its representative is nowhere to be seen.

We have already mentioned, that the independent townships of New England were not under guardianship, but took care of their own private interests ; and the municipal magistrates are the persons who either execute the laws of the State, or see that they are executed.* Besides the general laws, the State sometimes passes general police regulations ; but more commonly, the townships and town officers, conjointly with the justices of the peace, regulate the minor details of social life, according to the necessities of the different localities, and promulgate such orders as concern the health of the community, and the peace as well as morality of the citizens.† Lastly, these town magistrates provide, of their own accord and without any impulse from without, for those unforeseen emergencies which frequently occur in society.‡

---

* See "The Town-Officer," especially at the words SELECTMEN, ASSESSORS, COLLECTORS, SCHOOLS, SURVEYORS OF HIGHWAYS. I take one example in a thousand : the State prohibits travelling on Sunday without good reason; the *tything-men*, who are town-officers, are required to keep watch and to execute the law.

The selectmen draw up the lists of voters for the election of the Governor, and transmit the result of the ballot to the Secretary of the State.

† Thus, for instance, the selectmen authorize the construction of drains, and point out the proper sites for slaughter-houses and other trades which are a nuisance to the neighborhood.

‡ For example, the selectmen, conjointly with the justices of the peace, take measures for the security of the public in case of contagious diseases.

It results from what we have said, that, in the State of Massachusetts, the administrative authority is almost entirely restricted to the township,* and that it is there distributed among a great number of individuals. In the French *commune*, there is properly but one official functionary, — namely, the Maire; and in New England, we have seen that there are nineteen. These nineteen functionaries do not, in general, depend one upon another. The law carefully prescribes a circle of action to each of these magistrates; within that circle, they are all-powerful to perform their functions independently of any other authority. Above the township, scarcely any trace of a hierarchy of official dignities is to be found. It sometimes happens, that the county officers alter a decision of the townships, or town magistrates; † but, in general, the authorities of the county have no right to interfere with the authorities of the township, ‡ except in such matters as concern the county.

The magistrates of the township, as well as those of the

* I say *almost*, for there are many incidents in town-life which are regulated by the justices of peace in their individual capacity, or by an assembly of them in the chief town of the county; thus, licenses are granted by the justices.

† Thus, licenses are granted only to such persons as can produce a certificate of good conduct from the selectmen. If the selectmen refuse to give the certificate, the party may appeal to the justices assembled in the Court of Sessions; and they may grant the license. The townships have the right to make by-laws, and to enforce them by fines, which are fixed by law; but these by-laws must be approved by the Court of Sessions. [In several respects, these laws and customs have been altered by general legislation since the time when De Tocqueville wrote. But I do not think it necessary to specify all these alterations, as generally it is not the principle, but only the details, of the law that have been changed. — AM. ED.]

‡ In Massachusetts the county magistrates are frequently called upon to investigate the acts of the town magistrates; but it will be shown farther on that this investigation is a consequence, not of their administrative, but of their judicial power.

county, are bound, in a small number of predetermined cases, to communicate their acts to the central government.* But the central government is not represented by an agent whose business it is to publish police regulations and ordinances for the execution of the laws, or to keep up a regular communication with the officers of the township and the county, or to inspect their conduct, direct their actions, or reprimand their faults. There is no point which serves as a centre to the radii of the administration.

How, then, can the government be conducted on a uniform plan? and how is the compliance of the counties and their magistrates, or the townships and their officers, enforced? In the New England States, the legislative authority embraces more subjects than it does in France; the legislator penetrates to the very core of the administration; the law descends to minute details; the same enactment prescribes the principle and the method of its application, and thus imposes a multitude of strict and rigorously defined obligations on the secondary bodies and functionaries of the State. The consequence of this is, that, if all the secondary functionaries of the administration conform to the law, society in all its branches proceeds with the greatest uniformity. The difficulty remains, how to compel the secondary bodies and functionaries of the administration to conform to the law. It may be affirmed, in general, that society has only two methods of enforcing the execution of the laws: a discretionary power may be intrusted to one of them of directing all the others, and of removing them in case of disobedience; or the courts of justice may be required to inflict judicial penalties on the offender. But these two methods are not always available.

The right of directing a civil officer presupposes that of

---

* Thus, the town committees of schools are obliged to make an annual report to the Secretary of the State on the condition of the schools.

cashiering him if he does not obey orders, and of rewarding him by promotion if he fulfils his duties with propriety.
But an elected magistrate cannot be cashiered or promoted. All elective functions are inalienable until their term
expires. In fact, the elected magistrate has nothing to
expect or to fear, except from his constituents; and when
all public offices are filled by ballot, there can be no series
of official dignities, because the double right of commanding and of enforcing obedience can never be vested in the
same person, and because the power of issuing an order
can never be joined to that of inflicting a punishment or
bestowing a reward.

The communities, therefore, in which the secondary
functionaries of the government are elected, are perforce
obliged to make great use of judicial penalties as a means
of administration. This is not evident at first sight; for
those in power are apt to look upon the institution of elective functionaries as one concession, and the subjection of
the elected magistrate to the judges of the land as another.
They are equally averse to both these innovations; and as
they are more pressingly solicited to grant the former than
the latter, they accede to the election of the magistrate, and
leave him independent of the judicial power. Nevertheless, the second of these measures is the only thing that
can possibly counterbalance the first; and it will be found
that an elective authority which is not subject to judicial
power will, sooner or later, either elude all control or be
destroyed. The courts of justice are the only possible
medium between the central power and the administrative
bodies; they alone can compel the elected functionary to
obey, without violating the rights of the elector. The
extension of judicial power in the political world ought,
therefore, to be in the exact ratio of the extension of elective power: if these two institutions do not go hand in
hand, the State must fall into anarchy or into servitude.

It has always been remarked that judicial habits do not render men apt to the exercise of administrative authority. The Americans have borrowed from their fathers, the English, the idea of an institution which is unknown upon the continent of Europe: I allude to that of Justices of the Peace.

The Justice of the Peace is a sort of middle term between the magistrate and the man of the world, between the civil officer and the judge. A justice of the peace is a well-informed citizen, though he is not necessarily learned in the law. His office simply obliges him to execute the police regulations of society, a task in which good sense and integrity are of more avail than legal science. The justice introduces into the administration, when he takes part in it, a certain taste for established forms and publicity, which renders him a most unserviceable instrument for despotism; and, on the other hand, he is not a slave of those legal superstitions which render judges unfit members of a government. The Americans have adopted the English system of justices of the peace, depriving it of the aristocratic character which distinguishes it in the mother country. The Governor of Massachusetts appoints a certain number of justices of the peace in every county, whose functions last seven years. He further designates three individuals from the whole body of justices, who form in each county what is called the Court of Sessions.* The justices take a personal share in the public administration; they are sometimes intrusted with administrative functions in conjunction with elected officers; † they sometimes con-

---

* The Court of Sessions no longer exists as such; its functions have been merged in those of the ordinary legal tribunals. — AM. ED.

† Thus, for example, a stranger arrives in a township from a country where a contagious disease prevails, and he falls ill. Two justices of the peace can, with the assent of the selectmen, order the sheriff of the county to remove and take care of him. In general, the justices interfere in all the important acts of the administration, and give them a semi-judicial character.

stitute a tribunal, before which the magistrates summarily prosecute a refractory citizen, or the citizens inform against the abuses of the magistrate. But it is in the Court of Sessions that they exercise their most important functions. This court meets twice a year, in the county town; in Massachusetts, it is empowered to enforce the obedience of most* of the public officers.† It must be observed that, in Massachusetts, the Court of Sessions is at the same time an administrative body, properly so called, and a political tribunal. It has been mentioned that the county is a purely administrative division. The Court of Sessions presides over that small number of affairs which, as they concern several townships, or all the townships of the county in common, cannot be intrusted to any one of them in particular.‡ In all that concerns county business, the duties of the Court of Sessions are purely administrative; and if in its procedure it occasionally introduces judicial forms, it is only with a view to its own information,§ or as a guaranty to those for whom it acts. But when the administration of the township is brought before it, it acts

* I say *most* of them, because certain administrative misdemeanors are brought before the ordinary tribunals. If, for instance, a township refuses to make the necessary expenditure for its schools, or to name a school-committee, it is liable to a heavy fine. But this penalty is pronounced by the Supreme Judicial Court or the Court of Common Pleas.

† In their individual capacity, the Justices of the Peace take a part in the business of the counties and townships. In general, the most important acts of the town can be performed only with the concurrence of some one of them.

‡ These affairs may be brought under the following heads: — 1. The erection of prisons and courts of justice. 2. The county budget, which is afterwards voted by the State legislature. 3. The distribution of the taxes so voted. 4. Grants of certain patents. 5. The laying down and repairs of the county roads. [Most of these acts are now performed by the County Commissioners. — AM. ED.]

§ Thus, when a road is under consideration, almost all difficulties are disposed of by the aid of the jury.

as a judicial body, and only in some few cases as an administrative body.

The first difficulty is, to make the township itself, an almost independent power, obey the general laws of the State. We have stated, that assessors are annually named by the town-meetings to levy the taxes. If a township attempts to evade the payment of the taxes by neglecting to name its assessors, the Court of Sessions condemns it to a heavy fine. The fine is levied on each of the inhabitants; and the sheriff of the county, who is the officer of justice, executes the mandate. Thus, in the United States, government authority, anxious to keep out of sight, hides itself under the forms of a judicial sentence; and its influence is at the same time fortified by that irresistible power which men attribute to the formalities of law.

These proceedings are easy to follow and to understand. The demands made upon a township are, in general, plain and accurately defined; they consist in a simple fact, or in a principle without its application in detail.* But the difficulty begins when it is not the obedience of the township, but that of the town officers, which is to be enforced. All the reprehensible actions which a public functionary can commit are reducible to the following heads. —

He may execute the law without energy or zeal;

He may neglect what the law requires;

He may do what the law forbids.

Only the last two violations of duty can come before a legal tribunal; a positive and appreciable fact is the indis-

---

* There is an indirect method of enforcing the obedience of a township. Suppose that the funds which the law demands for the maintenance of the roads have not been voted; the town surveyor is then authorized, *ex officio*, to levy the supplies. As he is personally responsible to private individuals for the state of the roads, and indictable before the Court of Sessions, he is sure to employ the extraordinary right which the law gives him against the township. Thus, by threatening the officer, the Court of Sessions exacts compliance from the town.

pensable foundation of an action at law. Thus, if the selectmen omit the legal formalities usual at town elections, they may be fined. But when the officer performs his duty unskilfully, or obeys the letter of the law without zeal or energy, he is out of the reach of judicial interference. The Court of Sessions, even when clothed with administrative powers, is in this case unable to enforce a more satisfactory obedience. The fear of removal is the only check to these quasi-offences, and the Court of Sessions does not originate the town authorities; it cannot remove functionaries whom it does not appoint. Moreover, a perpetual supervision would be necessary to convict the officer of negligence or lukewarmness. Now the Court of Sessions sits but twice a year, and then only judges such offences as are brought to its notice. The only security for that active and enlightened obedience, which a court of justice cannot enforce upon public functionaries, lies in the arbitrary removal of them from office. In France, this final security is exercised by the heads of the administration; in America, it is obtained through the principle of election.

Thus, to recapitulate in a few words what I have described: —

If a public officer in New England commits a crime in the exercise of his functions, the ordinary courts of justice are *always* called upon to punish him.

If he commits a fault in his administrative capacity, a purely administrative tribunal is empowered to punish him; and, if the affair is important or urgent, the judge does what the functionary should have done.*

Lastly, if the same individual is guilty of one of those intangible offences which human justice can neither define nor appreciate, he annually appears before a tribunal from

* If, for instance, a township persists in refusing to name its assessors, the Court of Sessions nominates them; and the magistrates thus appointed are invested with the same authority as elected officers.

which there is no appeal, which can at once reduce him to insignificance, and deprive him of his charge. This system undoubtedly possesses great advantages, but its execution is attended with a practical difficulty, which it is important to point out.

I have already observed, that the administrative tribunal, which is called the Court of Sessions, has no right of inspection over the town officers. It can only interfere when the conduct of a magistrate is specially brought under its notice; and this is the delicate part of the system. The Americans of New England have no public prosecutor for the Court of Sessions,* and it may readily be perceived that it would be difficult to create one. If an accusing magistrate had merely been appointed in the chief town of each county, and he had been unassisted by agents in the townships, he would not have been better acquainted with what was going on in the county than the members of the Court of Sessions. But to appoint his agents in each township would have been to centre in his person the most formidable of powers, that of a judicial administration. Moreover, laws are the children of habit, and nothing of the kind exists in the legislation of England. The Americans have, therefore, divided the offices of inspection and complaint, as well as all the other functions of the administration. Grand-jurors are bound by the law to apprise the court to which they belong of all the misdemeanors which may have been committed in their county.† There are certain great offences which are officially prosecuted by the State;‡ but, more frequently, the task of punishing

* I say the Court of Sessions, because, in common courts, there is an officer [the district attorney] who exercises some of the functions of a public prosecutor.

† The Grand-jurors are, for instance, bound to inform the court of the bad state of the roads.

‡ If, for instance, the treasurer of the county holds back his accounts.

delinquents devolves upon the fiscal officer, whose province it is to receive the fine: thus, the treasurer of the township is charged with the prosecution of such administrative offences as fall under his notice. But a more especial appeal is made by American legislation to the private interest of each citizen;* and this great principle is constantly to be met with in studying the laws of the United States. American legislators are more apt to give men credit for intelligence than for honesty; and they rely not a little on personal interest for the execution of the laws. When an individual is really and sensibly injured by an administrative abuse, his personal interest is a guaranty that he will prosecute. But if a legal formality be required, which, however advantageous to the community, is of small importance to individuals, plaintiffs may be less easily found; and thus, by a tacit agreement, the laws may fall into disuse. Reduced by their system to this extremity, the Americans are obliged to encourage informers by bestowing on them a portion of the penalty in certain cases; † and they thus insure the execution of the laws by the dangerous expedient of degrading the morals of the people.

* Thus, to take one example out of a thousand, if a private individual breaks his carriage, or is wounded, in consequence of the badness of a road, he can sue the township or the county for damages at the sessions.

† In cases of invasion or insurrection, if the town officers neglect to furnish the necessary stores and ammunition for the militia, the township may be condemned to a fine of from 200 to 500 dollars. It may readily be imagined that, in such a case, it might happen that no one would care to prosecute; hence the law adds, that any citizen may enter a complaint for offences of this kind, and that half the fine shall belong to the prosecutor. See Act of 6th March, 1810. The same clause is frequently to be met with in the Laws of Massachusetts. Not only are private individuals thus incited to prosecute the public officers, but the public officers are encouraged in the same manner to bring the disobedience of private individuals to justice. If a citizen refuses to perform the work which has been assigned to him upon a road, the road-surveyor may prosecute him, and, if convicted, he receives half the penalty for himself.

Above the county magistrates, there is, properly speaking, no administrative power, but only a power of government.

GENERAL REMARKS ON THE ADMINISTRATION IN THE UNITED STATES.

Differences of the States of the Union in their Systems of Administration. — Activity and Perfection of the Town Authorities decreases towards the South. — Power of the Magistrates increases; that of the Voter diminishes. — Administration passes from the Township to the County. — States of New York: Ohio: Pennsylvania. — Principles of Administration applicable to the whole Union. — Election of Public Officers, and Inalienability of their Functions. — Absence of Gradation of Ranks. — Introduction of Judicial Procedures into the Administration.

I HAVE already said that, after examining the constitution of the township and the county of New England in detail, I should take a general view of the remainder of the Union. Townships and town arrangements exist in every State; but in no other part of the Union is a township to be met with precisely similar to those of New England. The farther we go towards the South, the less active does the business of the township or parish become; it has fewer magistrates, duties, and rights; the population exercises a less immediate influence on affairs; town-meetings are less frequent, and the subjects of debate less numerous. The power of the elected magistrate is augmented, and that of the voter diminished, whilst the public spirit of the local communities is less excited and less influential.* These differences may be perceived to a certain extent in the State of New York; they are very sensible in Penn-

---

* For details, see the Revised Statutes of the State of New York, Part I. See, in the Digest of the Laws of Pennsylvania, the words ASSESSORS, COLLECTOR, CONSTABLES, OVERSEER OF THE POOR, SUPERVISORS OF HIGHWAYS: and in the Acts of a general nature of the State of Ohio, the Act of the 25th of February, 1834, relating to townships, p. 412.

sylvania; but they become less striking as we advance to
the Northwest. The majority of the emigrants who settle
in the Northwestern States are natives of New England,
and they carry the administrative habits of their mother
country with them into the country which they adopt.
A township in Ohio is not unlike a township in Massachusetts.

We have seen that, in Massachusetts, the mainspring of
public administration lies in the township. It forms the
common centre of the interests and affections of the citizens. But this ceases to be the case as we descend to the
States in which knowledge is less generally diffused, and
where the township consequently offers fewer guaranties
of a wise and active administration. As we leave New
England, therefore, we find that the importance of the
town is gradually transferred to the county, which becomes
the centre of administration, and the intermediate power
between the government and the citizen. In Massachusetts, the business of the county is conducted by the Court
of Sessions, which is composed of a *quorum* appointed by
the Governor and his Council; but the county has no representative assembly, and its expenditure is voted by the
State legislature. In the great State of New York, on the
contrary, and in those of Ohio and Pennsylvania, the inhabitants of each county choose a certain number of representatives, who constitute the assembly of the county.*
The county assembly has the right of taxing the inhabitants to a certain extent; and it is, in this respect, a real

---

* See the Revised Statutes of the State of New York, Part I. chap. xi.
Vol. I. p. 340, *Id.*, chap. xii. p. 366; also, in the Acts of the State of
Ohio, an act relating to county commissioners, 25th February, 1824, p. 263.
See the Digest of the Laws of Pennsylvania, at the words COUNTY-RATES
and LEVIES, p. 170.

In the State of New York, each township elects a representative, who has
a share in the administration of the county as well as in that of the township.

legislative body: at the same time, it exercises an executive power in the county, frequently directs the administration of the townships, and restricts their authority
within much narrower bounds than in Massachusetts.

Such are the principal differences which the systems of
county and town administration present in the Federal
States. Were it my intention to examine the subject in
detail, I should have to point out still further differences
in the executive details of the several communities. But
I have said enough to show the general principles on which
the administration in the United States rests. These principles are differently applied: their consequences are more
or less numerous in various localities; but they are always substantially the same. The laws differ, and their
outward features change; but the same spirit animates
them. If the township and the county are not everywhere
organized in the same manner, it is at least true that, in
the United States, the county and the township are always
based upon the same principle; namely, that every one is
the best judge of what concerns himself alone, and the
most proper person to supply his own wants. The township and the county are therefore bound to take care of
their special interests: the State governs, but does not
execute the laws. Exceptions to this principle may be
met with, but not a contrary principle.

The first consequence of this doctrine has been to cause
all the magistrates to be chosen either by the inhabitants,
or at least from among them. As the officers are everywhere elected or appointed for a certain period, it has been
impossible to establish the rules of a hierarchy of authorities; there are almost as many independent functionaries
as there are functions, and the executive power is disseminated in a multitude of hands. Hence arose the necessity
of introducing the control of the courts of justice over the
administration, and the system of pecuniary penalties, by

which the secondary bodies and their representatives are constrained to obey the laws. This system obtains from one end of the Union to the other. The power of punishing administrative misconduct, or of performing, in urgent cases, administrative acts, has not, however, been bestowed on the same judges in all the States. The Anglo-Americans derived the institution of justices of the peace from a common source; but although it exists in all the States, it is not always turned to the same use. The justices of the peace everywhere participate in the administration of the townships and the counties,* either as public officers, or as the judges of public misdemeanors; but in most of the States, the more important public offences come under the cognizance of the ordinary tribunals.

Thus, the election of public officers, or the inalienability of their functions, the absence of a gradation of powers, and the introduction of judicial action over the secondary branches of the administration, are the principal and universal characteristics of the American system from Maine to the Floridas. In some States (and that of New York has advanced most in this direction) traces of a centralized administration begin to be discernible. In the State of New York, the officers of the central government exercise, in certain cases, a sort of inspection or control over the secondary bodies.† At other times, they constitute a sort

* In some of the Southern States, the county courts are charged with all the detail of the administration. See the Statutes of the State of Tennessee, Art. JUDICIARY, TAXES, &c.

† For instance, the direction of public instruction is centralized in the hands of the government. The legislature names the members of the University, who are denominated Regents; the Governor and Lieutenant-Governor of the State are necessarily of the number. The Regents of the University annually visit the colleges and academies, and make their report to the legislature. Their superintendence is not inefficient, for several reasons: the Colleges, in order to become corporations, stand in need of a char-

of court of appeal for the decision of affairs.* In the State of New York, judicial penalties are less used than in other places as a means of administration; and the right of prosecuting the offences of public officers is vested in fewer hands.† The same tendency is faintly observable in some other States; ‡ but, in general, the prominent feature of the administration in the United States is its excessive decentralization.

ter, which is only granted on the recommendation of the Regents: every year, funds are distributed by the State for the encouragement of learning, and the Regents are the distributors of this money. The school-commissioners are obliged to send an annual report to the general Superintendent of the Schools. A similar report is annually made to the same person on the number and condition of the poor.

* If any one conceives himself to be wronged by the school-commissioners (who are town officers), he can appeal to the Superintendent of the Primary Schools, whose decision is final.

Provisions similar to those above cited are to be met with from time to time in the laws of the State of New York; but, in general, these attempts at centralization are feeble and unproductive. The great authorities of the State have the right of watching and controlling the subordinate agents, without that of rewarding or punishing them. The same individual is never empowered to give an order and to punish disobedience; he has, therefore, the right of commanding, without the means of exacting compliance. In 1830, the Superintendent of Schools, in his annual report to the legislature, complained that several school-commissioners had neglected, notwithstanding his application, to furnish him with the accounts which were due. He added that, if this omission continued, he should be obliged to prosecute them, as the law directs, before the proper tribunals.

† Thus, the district-attorney is directed to recover all fines below the sum of fifty dollars, unless such a right has been specially awarded to another magistrate.

‡ Several traces of centralization may be discovered in Massachusetts; for instance, the committees of the town schools are directed to make an annual report to the Secretary of State.

OF THE STATE.

I HAVE described the townships and the administration; it now remains for me to speak of the State and the government. This is ground I may pass over rapidly, without fear of being misunderstood; for all I have to say is to be found in the various written constitutions, copies of which are easily to be procured. These constitutions rest upon a simple and rational theory; most of their forms have been adopted by all constitutional nations, and are become familiar to us.

Here, then, I have only to give a brief account; I shall endeavor afterwards to pass judgment upon what I now describe.

LEGISLATIVE POWER OF THE STATE.

Division of the Legislative Body into two Houses. — Senate. — House of Representatives. — Different Functions of these two Bodies.

THE legislative power of the State is vested in two assemblies, the first of which generally bears the name of the Senate.

The Senate is commonly a legislative body; but it sometimes becomes an executive and judicial one. It takes part in the government in several ways, according to the constitution of the different States;* but it is in the nomination of public functionaries that it most commonly assumes an executive power. It partakes of judicial power in the trial of certain political offences, and sometimes also in the decision of certain civil cases.† The number of its members is always small.

The other branch of the legislature, which is usually

---

* In Massachusetts, the Senate is not invested with any administrative functions.

† As in the State of New York.

called the House of Representatives, has no share whatever in the administration, and takes a part in the judicial power only as it impeaches public functionaries before the Senate.

The members of the two houses are nearly everywhere subject to the same conditions of eligibility. They are chosen in the same manner, and by the same citizens. The only difference which exists between them is, that the term for which the Senate is chosen is, in general, longer than that of the House of Representatives. The latter seldom remain in office longer than a year; the former usually sit two or three years.

By granting to the senators the privilege of being chosen for several years, and being renewed *seriatim*, the law takes care to preserve in the legislative body a nucleus of men already accustomed to public business, and capable of exercising a salutary influence upon the new-comers.

The Americans plainly did not desire, by this separation of the legislative body into two branches, to make one house hereditary and the other elective, one aristocratic and the other democratic. It was not their object to create in the one a bulwark to power, whilst the other represented the interests and passions of the people. The only advantages which result from the present constitution of the two houses in the United States are, the division of the legislative power, and the consequent check upon political movements; together with the creation of a tribunal of appeal for the revision of the laws.

Time and experience, however, have convinced the Americans that, even if these are its only advantages, the division of the legislative power is still a principle of the greatest necessity. Pennsylvania was the only one of the United States which at first attempted to establish a single House of Assembly; and Franklin himself was so far carried away by the logical consequences of the principle of the sovereignty of the people, as to have concurred in the measure : but the Pennsylvanians were soon obliged to change the law, and to create two houses. Thus the principle of the division of the legislative power was finally established, and its necessity may henceforward be regarded as a demonstrated truth. This theory, nearly unknown to the republics of antiquity, — first introduced into the world almost by accident, like so many other great truths, and misunderstood by several modern nations, — is at length become an axiom in the political science of the present age.

THE EXECUTIVE POWER OF THE STATE.

Office of Governor in an American State. — His Relation to the Legislature. — His Rights and his Duties. — His Dependence on the People.

THE executive power of the State is *represented* by the Governor. It is not by accident that I have used this word ; the Governor *represents* this power, although he enjoys but a portion of its rights. The supreme magistrate, under the title of Governor, is the official moderator and counsellor of the legislature. He is armed with a veto or suspensive power, which allows him to stop, or at least to retard, its movements at pleasure. He lays the wants of the country before the legislative body, and points out the means which he thinks may be usefully employed in providing for them ; he is the natural executor of its decrees in all the undertakings which interest the nation at large.* In the absence of the legislature, the Governor is bound to take all necessary steps to guard the State against violent shocks and unforeseen dangers.

* Practically speaking, it is not always the Governor who executes the plans of the Legislature ; it often happens that the latter, in voting a measure, names special agents to superintend the execution of it.

The whole military power of the State is at the disposal of the Governor. He is the commander of the militia, and head of the armed force. When the authority, which is by general consent awarded to the laws, is disregarded, the Governor puts himself at the head of the armed force of the State, to quell resistance and restore order.

Lastly, the Governor takes no share in the administration of the townships and counties, except it be indirectly in the nomination of Justices of the Peace, which nomination he has not the power to cancel.*

The Governor is an elected magistrate, and is generally chosen for one or two years only; so that he always continues to be strictly dependent upon the majority who returned him.

POLITICAL EFFECTS OF DECENTRALIZED ADMINISTRATION IN THE UNITED STATES.

Necessary Distinction between a Centralized Government and a Centralized Administration. — Administration not Centralized in the United States : great Centralization of the Government. — Some bad Consequences resulting to the United States from the extremely decentralized Administration. — Administrative Advantages of this Order of Things. — The Power which administers is less Regular, less Enlightened, less Learned, but much greater than in Europe. — Political Advantages of this Order of Things. — In the United States, the Country makes itself felt everywhere. — Support given to the Government by the Community. — Provincial Institutions more necessary in Proportion as the social Condition becomes more Democratic. — Reason of this.

CENTRALIZATION is a word in general and daily use, without any precise meaning being attached to it. Nevertheless, there exist two distinct kinds of centralization, which it is necessary to discriminate with accuracy.

---

* In some of the States, justices of the peace are not appointed by the Governor.

Certain interests are common to all parts of a nation, such as the enactment of its general laws, and the maintenance of its foreign relations. Other interests are peculiar to certain parts of the nation; such, for instance, as the business of the several townships. When the power which directs the former or general interests is concentrated in one place or in the same persons, it constitutes a centralized government. To concentrate in like manner into one place the direction of the latter or local interests, constitutes what may be termed a centralized administration.

Upon some points, these two kinds of centralization coincide; but by classifying the objects which fall more particularly within the province of each, they may easily be distinguished.

It is evident that a centralized government acquires immense power when united to centralized administration. Thus combined, it accustoms men to set their own will habitually and completely aside; to submit, not only for once, or upon one point, but in every respect, and at all times. Not only, therefore, does this union of power subdue them compulsorily, but it affects their ordinary habits; it isolates them, and then influences each separately.

These two kinds of centralization mutually assist and attract each other; but they must not be supposed to be inseparable. It is impossible to imagine a more completely centralized government than that which existed in France under Louis XIV.; when the same individual was the author and the interpreter of the laws, and the representative of France at home and abroad, he was justified in asserting that he constituted the state. Nevertheless, the administration was much less centralized under Louis XIV. than it is at the present day.

In England, the centralization of the government is carried to great perfection; the state has the compact vigor of one man, and its will puts immense masses in motion, and turns its whole power where it pleases. But England, which has done so great things for the last fifty years, has never centralized its administration. Indeed, I cannot conceive that a nation can live and prosper without a powerful centralization of government. But I am of opinion that a centralized administration is fit only to enervate the nations in which it exists, by incessantly diminishing their local spirit. Although such an administration can bring together at a given moment, on a given point, all the disposable resources of a people, it injures the renewal of those resources. It may insure a victory in the hour of strife, but it gradually relaxes the sinews of strength. It may help admirably the transient greatness of a man, but not the durable prosperity of a nation.

Observe, that whenever it is said that a state cannot act because it is not centralized, it is the centralization of the government which is spoken of. It is frequently asserted, and we assent to the proposition, that the German empire has never been able to bring all its powers into action. But the reason was, that the state was never able to enforce obedience to its general laws; the several members of that great body always claimed the right, or found the means, of refusing their co-operation to the representatives of the common authority, even in the affairs which concerned the mass of the people; in other words, there was no centralization of government. The same remark is applicable to the Middle Ages; the cause of all the miseries of feudal society was, that the control, not only of administration, but of government, was divided amongst a thousand hands, and broken up in a thousand different ways. The want of a centralized government prevented the nations of Europe from advancing with energy in any straightforward course.

We have shown that, in the United States, there is no

centralized administration, and no hierarchy of public functionaries. Local authority has been carried farther than
any European nation could endure without great inconvenience, and it has even produced some disadvantageous
consequences in America. But in the United States, the
centralization of the government is perfect; and it would
be easy to prove that the national power is more concentrated there than it has ever been in the old nations of
Europe. Not only is there but one legislative body in
each State, — not only does there exist but one source of
political authority, — but numerous assemblies in districts
or counties have not, in general, been multiplied, lest they
should be tempted to leave their administrative duties and
interfere with the government. In America, the legislature of each State is supreme; nothing can impede its
authority, — neither privileges, nor local immunities, nor
personal influence, nor even the empire of reason, since it
represents that majority which claims to be the sole organ
of reason. Its own determination is, therefore, the only
limit to its action. In juxtaposition with it, and under its
immediate control, is the representative of the executive
power, whose duty it is to constrain the refractory to submit by superior force. The only symptom of weakness
lies in certain details of the action of the government.
The American republics have no standing armies to in-
timidate a discontented minority; but as no minority has
as yet been reduced to declare open war, the necessity of
an army has not been felt. The State usually employs the
officers of the township or the county to deal with the citizens. Thus, for instance, in New England, the town
assessor fixes the rate of taxes; the town collector receives
them; the town treasurer transmits the amount to the public treasury; and the disputes which may arise are brought
before the ordinary courts of justice. This method of collecting taxes is slow as well as inconvenient, and it would

prove a perpetual hindrance to a government whose pecuniary demands were large. It is desirable that, in whatever materially affects its existence, the government should be served by officers of its own, appointed by itself, removable at its pleasure, and accustomed to rapid methods of proceeding. But it will always be easy for the central government, organized as it is in America, to introduce more energetic and efficacious modes of action according to its wants.

The want of a centralized government will not, then, as has often been asserted, prove the destruction of the republics of the New World; far from the American governments being not sufficiently centralized, I shall prove hereafter that they are too much so. The legislative bodies daily encroach upon the authority of the government, and their tendency, like that of the French Convention, is to appropriate it entirely to themselves. The social power thus centralized is constantly changing hands, because it is subordinate to the power of the people. It often forgets the maxims of wisdom and foresight in the consciousness of its strength. Hence arises its danger. Its vigor, and not its impotence, will probably be the cause of its ultimate destruction.

The system of decentralized administration produces several different effects in America. The Americans seem to me to have outstepped the limits of sound policy, in isolating the administration of the government: for order, even in secondary affairs, is a matter of national importance.* As the State has no administrative functionaries

---

* The authority which represents the State ought not, I think, to waive the right of inspecting the local administration, even when it does not itself administer. Suppose, for instance, that an agent of the government was stationed at some appointed spot in each county, to prosecute the misdemeanors of the town and county officers, would not a more uniform order be the result, without in any way compromising the independence of the

of its own, stationed on different points of its territory, to whom it can give a common impulse, the consequence is, that it rarely attempts to issue any general police regulations. The want of these regulations is severely felt, and is frequently observed by Europeans. The appearance of disorder which prevails on the surface leads him at first to imagine that society is in a state of anarchy: nor does he perceive his mistake till he has gone deeper into the subject. Certain undertakings are of importance to the whole State; but they cannot be put in execution, because there is no State administration to direct them. Abandoned to the exertions of the towns or counties, under the care of elected and temporary agents, they lead to no result, or at least to no durable benefit.

The partisans of centralization in Europe are wont to maintain that the government can administer the affairs of each locality better than the citizens could do it for themselves: this may be true, when the central power is enlightened, and the local authorities are ignorant; when it is alert, and they are slow; when it is accustomed to act, and they to obey. Indeed, it is evident that this double tendency must augment with the increase of centralization, and that the readiness of the one and the incapacity of the others must become more and more prominent. But I deny that it is so, when the people are as enlightened, as awake to their interests, and as accustomed to reflect on

township? Nothing of the kind, however, exists in America: there is nothing above the county courts, which have, as it were, only an incidental cognizance of the administrative offences they ought to repress.

[Mr. Spencer properly remarks, that "such an agent as the author here suggests would soon come to be considered a public informer, the most odious of all characters in the United States; and he would lose all efficiency and strength." Whereas, as it is, the constant presence of the district attorney, and the meeting of a grand jury three or four times a year in every county, to whom every aggrieved person has free access, are sufficient precautions against the misconduct or neglect of the local officers. — Am. Ed.]

them, as the Americans are. I am persuaded, on the contrary, that, in this case, the collective strength of the citizens will always conduce more efficaciously to the public welfare than the authority of the government. I know it is difficult to point out with certainty the means of arousing a sleeping population, and of giving it passions and knowledge which it does not possess; it is, I am well aware, an arduous task to persuade men to busy themselves about their own affairs. It would frequently be easier to interest them in the punctilios of court etiquette, than in the repairs of their common dwelling. But whenever a central administration affects completely to supersede the persons most interested, I believe that it is either misled, or desirous to mislead. However enlightened and skilful a central power may be, it cannot of itself embrace all the details of the life of a great nation. Such vigilance exceeds the powers of man. And when it attempts unaided to create and set in motion so many complicated springs, it must submit to a very imperfect result, or exhaust itself in bootless efforts.

Centralization easily succeeds, indeed, in subjecting the external actions of men to a certain uniformity, which we come at last to love for its own sake, independently of the objects to which it is applied, like those devotees who worship the statue, and forget the deity it represents. Centralization imparts without difficulty an admirable regularity to the routine of business; provides skilfully for the details of the social police; represses small disorders and petty misdemeanors; maintains society in a *statu quo* alike secure from improvement and decline; and perpetuates a drowsy regularity in the conduct of affairs, which the heads of the administration are wont to call good order and public tranquillity; * in short, it excels in prevention, but not

* China appears to me to present the most perfect instance of that species of well-being which a highly centralized administration may furnish to

in action.* Its force deserts it, when society is to be profoundly moved, or accelerated in its course; and if once the co-operation of private citizens is necessary to the furtherance of its measures, the secret of its impotence is disclosed. Even whilst the centralized power, in its despair, invokes the assistance of the citizens, it says to them: "You shall act just as I please, as much as I please, and in the direction which I please. You are to take charge of the details, without aspiring to guide the system; you are to work in darkness; and afterwards you may judge my work by its results." These are not the conditions on which the alliance of the human will is to be obtained; it must be free in its gait, and responsible for its acts, or (such is the constitution of man) the citizen had rather remain a passive spectator, than a dependent actor, in schemes with which he is unacquainted.

It is undeniable, that the want of those uniform regulations which control the conduct of every inhabitant of France, is not unfrequently felt in the United States. Gross instances of social indifference and neglect are to be met with; and from time to time, disgraceful blemishes are seen, in complete contrast with the surrounding civilization. Useful undertakings, which cannot succeed without perpetual attention and rigorous exactitude, are frequently abandoned; for in America, as well as in other countries, the people proceed by sudden impulses and momentary exertions. The European, accustomed to find a functionary always at hand to interfere with all he un-

---

its subjects. Travellers assure us that the Chinese have tranquillity without happiness, industry without improvement, stability without strength, and public order without public morality. The condition of society there is always tolerable, never excellent. I imagine that, when China is opened to European observation, it will be found to contain the most perfect model of a centralized administration which exists in the universe.

* This is a lively and faithful description of the system which Dickens has taught us to stigmatize by the name of "red-tape." — AM. ED.

dertakes, reconciles himself with difficulty to the complex mechanism of the administration of the townships. In general, it may be affirmed that the lesser details of the police, which render life easy and comfortable, are neglected in America, but that the essential guaranties of man in society are as strong there as elsewhere. In America, the power which conducts the administration is far less regular, less enlightened, and less skilful, but a hundred-fold greater, than in Europe. In no country in the world, do the citizens make such exertions for the common weal. I know of no people who have established schools so numerous and efficacious, places of public worship better suited to the wants of the inhabitants, or roads kept in better repair. Uniformity or permanence of design, the minute arrangement of details,* and the perfection of administrative system, must not be sought for in the United States: what

---

* A writer of talent, who, in a comparison of the finances of France with those of the United States, has proved that ingenuity cannot always supply the place of the knowledge of facts, justly reproaches the Americans for the sort of confusion which exists in the accounts of the expenditure in the townships; and after giving the model of a Departmental Budget in France, he adds: "We are indebted to centralization, that admirable invention of a great man, for the order and method which prevail alike in all the municipal budgets, from the largest city to the humblest *commune.*" Whatever may be my admiration of this result, when I see the *communes* of France, with their excellent system of accounts, plunged into the grossest ignorance of their true interests, and abandoned to so incorrigible an apathy that they seem to vegetate rather than to live; when, on the other hand, I observe the activity, the information, and the spirit of enterprise in those American townships whose budgets are neither methodical nor uniform; I see that society there is always at work. I am struck by the spectacle; for to my mind, the end of a good government is to insure the welfare of a people, and not merely to establish order in the midst of its misery. I am therefore led to suppose, that the prosperity of the American townships and the apparent confusion of their finances, the distress of the French *communes* and the perfection of their budget, may be attributable to the same cause. At any rate, I am suspicious of a good which is united with so many evils, and I am not averse to an evil which is compensated by so many benefits.

we find there is, the presence of a power which, if it is somewhat wild, is at least robust, and an existence checkered with accidents, indeed, but full of animation and effort.

Granting, for an instant, that the villages and counties of the United States would be more usefully governed by a central authority, which they had never seen, than by functionaries taken from among them, — admitting, for the sake of argument, that there would be more security in America, and the resources of society would be better employed there, if the whole administration centred in a single arm, — still the *political* advantages which the Americans derive from their decentralized system would induce me to prefer it to the contrary plan. It profits me but little, after all, that a vigilant authority always protects the tranquillity of my pleasures, and constantly averts all dangers from my path, without my care or concern, if this same authority is the absolute master of my liberty and my life, and if it so monopolizes movement and life, that when it languishes everything languishes around it, that when it sleeps everything must sleep, and that when it dies the state itself must perish.

There are countries in Europe, where the natives consider themselves as a kind of settlers, indifferent to the fate of the spot which they inhabit. The greatest changes are effected there without their concurrence, and (unless chance may have apprised them of the event) without their knowledge; nay, more, the condition of his village, the police of his street, the repairs of the church or the parsonage, do not concern him; for he looks upon all these things as unconnected with himself, and as the property of a powerful stranger whom he calls the government. He has only a life-interest in these possessions, without the spirit of ownership or any ideas of improvement. This want of interest in his own affairs goes so far, that if his own safety or that of his children is at last endangered, instead of trying to avert the peril, he will fold his arms, and wait till the whole nation comes to his aid. This man, who has so completely sacrificed his own free will, does not, more than any other person, love obedience; he cowers, it is true, before the pettiest officer; but he braves the law with the spirit of a conquered foe, as soon as its superior force is withdrawn: he perpetually oscillates between servitude and license.

When a nation has arrived at this state, it must either change its customs and its laws, or perish; for the source of public virtues is dried up; and though it may contain subjects, it has no citizens. Such communities are a natural prey to foreign conquests; and if they do not wholly disappear from the scene, it is only because they are surrounded by other nations similar or inferior to themselves; it is because they still have an indefinable instinct of patriotism; and an involuntary pride in the name of their country, or a vague reminiscence of its bygone fame, suffices to give them an impulse of self-preservation.

Nor can the prodigious exertions made by certain nations to defend a country in which they had lived, so to speak, as strangers, be adduced in favor of such a system; for it will be found that, in these cases, their main incitement was religion. The permanence, the glory, or the prosperity of the nation were become parts of their faith; and in defending their country, they defended also that Holy City of which they were all citizens. The Turkish tribes have never taken an active share in the conduct of their affairs; but they accomplished stupendous enterprises, as long as the victories of the Sultan were triumphs of the Mohammedan faith. In the present age, they are in rapid decay, because their religion is departing, and despotism only remains. Montesquieu, who attributed to absolute power an authority peculiar to itself, did it, as I conceive, an undeserved honor; for despotism, taken by itself, can maintain nothing durable. On close inspection, we shall find that religion, and not fear, has ever been the cause of the long-lived prosperity of an absolute government. Do what you may, there is no true power among men except in the free union of their will; and patriotism or religion are the only two motives in the world which can long urge all the people towards the same end.

Laws cannot rekindle an extinguished faith; but men may be interested by the laws in the fate of their country. It depends upon the laws to awaken and direct the vague impulse of patriotism, which never abandons the human heart; and if it be connected with the thoughts, the passions, and the daily habits of life, it may be consolidated into a durable and rational sentiment. Let it not be said that it is too late to make the experiment; for nations do not grow old as men do, and every fresh generation is a new people ready for the care of the legislator.

It is not the *administrative*, but the *political* effects of decentralization, that I most admire in America. In the United States, the interests of the country are everywhere kept in view; they are an object of solicitude to the people of the whole Union, and every citizen is as warmly attached to them as if they were his own. He takes pride in the glory of his nation; he boasts of its success, to which he conceives himself to have contributed; and he rejoices in the general prosperity by which he profits. The feeling he entertains toward the state is analogous to that which unites him to his family, and it is by a kind of selfishness that he interests himself in the welfare of his country.

To the European, a public officer represents a superior force; to an American, he represents a right. In America, then, it may be said that no one renders obedience to man, but to justice and to law. If the opinion which the citizen entertains of himself is exaggerated, it is at least salutary;

he unhesitatingly confides in his own powers, which appear to him to be all-sufficient. When a private individual meditates an undertaking, however directly connected it may be with the welfare of society, he never thinks of soliciting the co-operation of the government; but he publishes his plan, offers to execute it, courts the assistance of other individuals, and struggles manfully against all obstacles. Undoubtedly he is often less successful than the state might have been in his position; but in the end, the sum of these private undertakings far exceeds all that the government could have done.

As the administrative authority is within the reach of the citizens, whom in some degree it represents, it excites neither their jealousy nor hatred: as its resources are limited, every one feels that he must not rely solely on its aid. Thus, when the administration thinks fit to act within its own limits, it is not abandoned to itself, as in Europe; the duties of private citizens are not supposed to have lapsed because the state has come into action; but every one is ready, on the contrary, to guide and support it. This action of individuals, joined to that of the public authorities, frequently accomplishes what the most energetic centralized administration would be unable to do.*

It would be easy to adduce several facts in proof of what I advance, but I had rather give only one, with which I am best acquainted. In America, the means which the authorities have at their disposal for the discovery of crimes and the arrest of criminals are few. A state police does not exist, and passports are unknown. The criminal police of the United States cannot be compared to that of France; the magistrates and public agents are not numerous; they do not always initiate the measures for arresting the guilty; and the examinations of prisoners are rapid and oral. Yet I believe that in no country does

* See Appendix I.

crime more rarely elude punishment. The reason is, that every one conceives himself to be interested in furnishing evidence of the crime, and in seizing the delinquent. During my stay in the United States, I witnessed the spontaneous formation of committees in a county for the pursuit and prosecution of a man who had committed a great crime. In Europe, a criminal is an unhappy man who is struggling for his life against the agents of power, whilst the people are merely a spectator of the conflict: in America, he is looked upon as an enemy of the human race, and the whole of mankind is against him.

I believe that provincial institutions are useful to all nations, but nowhere do they appear to me to be more necessary than amongst a democratic people. In an aristocracy, order can always be maintained in the midst of liberty; and as the rulers have a great deal to lose, order is to them a matter of great interest. In like manner, an aristocracy protects the people from the excesses of despotism, because it always possesses an organized power ready to resist a despot. But a democracy without provincial institutions has no security against these evils. How can a populace, unaccustomed to freedom in small concerns, learn to use it temperately in great affairs? What resistance can be offered to tyranny in a country where each individual is weak, and where the citizens are not united by any common interest? Those who dread the license of the mob, and those who fear absolute power, ought alike to desire the gradual development of provincial liberties.

I am also convinced, that democratic nations are most likely to fall beneath the yoke of a centralized administration, for several reasons, amongst which is the following.

The constant tendency of these nations is to concentrate all the strength of the government in the hands of the only power which directly represents the people; because, beyond the people, nothing is to be perceived but a mass of equal individuals. But when the same power already has all the attributes of government, it can scarcely refrain from penetrating into the details of the administration, and an opportunity of doing so is sure to present itself in the long run, as was the case in France. In the French Revolution, there were two impulses in opposite directions, which must never be confounded; the one was favorable to liberty, the other to despotism. Under the ancient monarchy, the king was the sole author of the laws; and below the power of the sovereign, certain vestiges of provincial institutions, half destroyed, were still distinguishable. These provincial institutions were incoherent, ill arranged, and frequently absurd; in the hands of the aristocracy, they had sometimes been converted into instruments of oppression. The Revolution declared itself the enemy at once of royalty and of provincial institutions; it confounded in indiscriminate hatred all that had preceded it, — despotic power and the checks to its abuses; and its tendency was at once to republicanize and to centralize. This double character of the French Revolution is a fact which has been adroitly handled by the friends of absolute power. Can they be accused of laboring in the cause of despotism, when they are defending that centralized administration which was one of the great innovations of the Revolution? * In this manner, popularity may be united with hostility to the rights of the people, and the secret slave of tyranny may be the professed lover of freedom.

I have visited the two nations in which the system of provincial liberty has been most perfectly established, and I have listened to the opinions of different parties in those countries. In America, I met with men who secretly aspired to destroy the democratic institutions of the Union;

* See Appendix K.

in England, I found others who openly attacked the aristocracy; but I found no one who did not regard provincial independence as a great good. In both countries, I heard a thousand different causes assigned for the evils of the state; but the local system was never mentioned amongst them. I heard citizens attribute the power and prosperity of their country to a multitude of reasons; but they *all* placed the advantages of local institutions in the foremost rank.

Am I to suppose that when men, who are naturally so divided on religious opinions and on political theories, agree on one point, (and that one which they can best judge, as it is one of which they have daily experience,) they are all in error? The only nations which deny the utility of provincial liberties are those which have fewest of them; in other words, those only censure the institution who do not know it.

CHAPTER VI.

JUDICIAL POWER IN THE UNITED STATES, AND ITS INFLU-
ENCE ON POLITICAL SOCIETY.

The Anglo-Americans have retained the Characteristics of Judicial Power
which are common to other Nations. — They have, however, made it a
powerful political Organ. — How. — In what the Judicial System of the
Anglo-Americans differs from that of all other Nations. — Why the
American Judges have the Right of declaring Laws to be unconstitutional. — How they use this Right. — Precautions taken by the Legislator to prevent its Abuse.

I HAVE thought it right to devote a separate chapter
to the judicial authorities of the United States, lest
their great political importance should be lessened in the
reader's eyes by a merely incidental mention of them.
Confederations have existed in other countries beside
America; I have seen republics elsewhere than upon the
shores of the New World alone: the representative system
of government has been adopted in several states of Europe; but I am not aware that any nation of the globe
has hitherto organized a judicial power in the same manner as the Americans. The judicial organization of the
United States is the institution which a stranger has the
greatest difficulty in understanding. He hears the authority of a judge invoked in the political occurrences of
every day, and he naturally concludes that, in the United
States, the judges are important political functionaries:
nevertheless, when he examines the nature of the tribunals, they offer at the first glance nothing which is contrary to the usual habits and privileges of those bodies;

and the magistrates seem to him to interfere in public affairs only by chance, but by a chance which recurs every day.

When the Parliament of Paris remonstrated, or refused to register an edict, or when it summoned a functionary accused of malversation to its bar, its political influence as a judicial body was clearly visible; but nothing of the kind is to be seen in the United States. The Americans have retained all the ordinary characteristics of judicial authority, and have carefully restricted its action to the ordinary circle of its functions.

The first characteristic of judicial power in all nations is the duty of arbitration. But rights must be contested in order to warrant the interference of a tribunal; and an action must be brought before the decision of a judge can be had. As long, therefore, as a law is uncontested, the judicial authority is not called upon to discuss it, and it may exist without being perceived. When a judge in a given case attacks a law relating to that case, he extends the circle of his customary duties, without, however, stepping beyond it, since he is in some measure obliged to decide upon the law in order to decide the case. But if he pronounces upon a law without proceeding from a case, he clearly steps beyond his sphere, and invades that of the legislative authority.

The second characteristic of judicial power is, that it pronounces on special cases, and not upon general principles. If a judge, in deciding a particular point, destroys a general principle by passing a judgment which tends to reject all the inferences from that principle, and consequently to annul it, he remains within the ordinary limits of his functions. But if he directly attacks a general principle without having a particular case in view, he leaves the circle in which all nations have agreed to confine his authority; he assumes a more important, and perhaps a more useful influence, than that of the magistrate; but he ceases to represent the judicial power.

The third characteristic of the judicial power is, that it can only act when it is called upon, or when, in legal phrase, it has taken cognizance of an affair. This characteristic is less general than the other two; but, notwithstanding the exceptions, I think it may be regarded as essential. The judicial power is, by its nature, devoid of action; it must be put in motion in order to produce a result. When it is called upon to repress a crime, it punishes the criminal; when a wrong is to be redressed, it is ready to redress it; when an act requires interpretation, it is prepared to interpret it; but it does not pursue criminals, hunt out wrongs, or examine evidence of its own accord. A judicial functionary who should take the initiative, and usurp the censureship of the laws, would in some measure do violence to the passive nature of his authority.

The Americans have retained these three distinguishing characteristics of the judicial power: an American judge can only pronounce a decision when litigation has arisen, he is conversant only with special cases, and he cannot act until the cause has been duly brought before the court. His position is, therefore, perfectly similar to that of the magistrates of other nations; and yet he is invested with immense political power. How comes that about? If the sphere of his authority and his means of action are the same as those of other judges, whence does he derive a power which they do not possess? The cause of this difference lies in the simple fact, that the Americans have acknowledged the right of the judges to found their decisions on the *Constitution* rather than on the *laws*. In other words, they have not permitted them to apply such laws as may appear to them to be unconstitutional.

I am aware that a similar right has been sometimes claimed — but claimed in vain — by courts of justice in

other countries; but in America it is recognized by all the
authorities; and not a party, not so much as an individual,
is found to contest it.   This fact can be explained only by
the principles of the American constitutions.   In France,
the constitution is * — or, at least, is supposed to be — immutable; and the received theory is, that no power has the
right of changing any part of it.   In England, the constitution may change continually; † or rather, it does not in
reality exist; the Parliament is at once a legislative and
a constituent assembly.   The political theories of America
are more simple and more rational.   An American constitution is not supposed to be immutable, as in France; nor
is it susceptible of modification by the ordinary powers of
society, as in England.   It constitutes a detached whole,
which, as it represents the will of the whole people, is no
less binding on the legislator than on the private citizen,
but which may be altered by the will of the people in predetermined cases, according to established rules.   In America, the constitution may therefore vary; but as long as it
exists, it is the origin of all authority, and the sole vehicle
of the predominating force.

   It is easy to perceive how these differences must act upon
the position and the rights of the judicial bodies in the three
countries I have cited.   If, in France, the tribunals were
authorized to disobey the laws on the ground of their being
opposed to the constitution, the constituent power would in
fact be placed in their hands, since they alone would have
the right of interpreting a constitution, of which no authority could change the terms.   They would, therefore, take
the place of the nation, and exercise as absolute a sway
over society as the inherent weakness of judicial power
would allow them to do.   Undoubtedly, as the French
judges are incompetent to declare a law to be unconstitutional, the power of changing the constitution is indirectly

* See Appendix L.   † See Appendix M.

given to the legislative body, since no legal barrier would oppose the alterations which it might prescribe. But it is still better to grant the power of changing the constitution of the people to men who represent (however imperfectly) the will of the people, than to men who represent no one but themselves.

It would be still more unreasonable to invest the English judges with the right of resisting the decisions of the legislative body, since the Parliament which makes the laws also makes the constitution; and consequently, a law emanating from the three estates of the realm can in no case be unconstitutional. But neither of these remarks is applicable to America.

In the United States, the constitution governs the legislator as much as the private citizen: as it is the first of laws, it cannot be modified by a law; and it is therefore just that the tribunals should obey the constitution in preference to any law. This condition belongs to the very essence of the judicature; for to select that legal obligation by which he is most strictly bound, is in some sort the natural right of every magistrate.

In France, the constitution is also the first of laws, and the judges have the same right to take it as the ground of their decisions; but were they to exercise this right, they must perforce encroach on rights more sacred than their own, namely, on those of society, in whose name they are acting. In this case, reasons of state clearly prevail over ordinary motives. In America, where the nation can always reduce its magistrates to obedience by changing its constitution, no danger of this kind is to be feared. Upon this point, therefore, the political and the logical reason agree, and the people as well as the judges preserve their privileges.

Whenever a law which the judge holds to be unconstitutional is invoked in a tribunal of the United States, he

may refuse to admit it as a rule; this power is the only one
which is peculiar to the American magistrate, but it gives
rise to immense political influence. In truth, few laws can
escape the searching analysis of the judicial power for any
length of time, for there are few which are not prejudicial
to some private interest or other, and none which may not
be brought before a court of justice by the choice of parties, or by the necessity of the case. But as soon as a
judge has refused to apply any given law in a case, that
law immediately loses a portion of its moral force. Those
to whom it is prejudicial learn that means exist of overcoming its authority; and similar suits are multiplied, until it
becomes powerless. The alternative, then, is, that the
people must alter the constitution, or the legislature must
repeal the law. The political power which the Americans
have intrusted to their courts of justice is therefore immense; but the evils of this power are considerably diminished by the impossibility of attacking the laws except
through the courts of justice. If the judge had been empowered to contest the law on the ground of theoretical
generalities, — if he were able to take the initiative, and to
censure the legislator, — he would play a prominent political part; and as the champion or the antagonist of a party,
he would have brought the hostile passions of the nation
into the conflict. But when a judge contests a law in an
obscure debate on some particular case, the importance of
his attack is concealed from public notice; his decision
bears upon the interest of an individual, and the law is
slighted only incidentally. Moreover, although it is censured, it is not abolished; its moral force may be diminished, but its authority is not taken away; and its final
destruction can be accomplished only by the reiterated
attacks of judicial functionaries. It will be seen, also,
that by leaving it to private interest to censure the law,
and by intimately uniting the trial of the law with the

trial of an individual, legislation is protected from wanton assaults, and from the daily aggressions of party spirit. The errors of the legislator are exposed only to meet a real want; and it is always a positive and appreciable fact which must serve as the basis of a prosecution.

I am inclined to believe this practice of the American courts to be at once most favorable to liberty and to public order. If the judge could only attack the legislator openly and directly, he would sometimes be afraid to oppose him; and at other times, party spirit might encourage him to brave it at every turn. The laws would consequently be attacked when the power from which they emanated was weak, and obeyed when it was strong; — that is to say, when it would be useful to respect them, they would often be contested; and when it would be easy to convert them into an instrument of oppression, they would be respected. But the American judge is brought into the political arena independently of his own will. He only judges the law because he is obliged to judge a case. The political question which he is called upon to resolve is connected with the interests of the parties, and he cannot refuse to decide it without a denial of justice. He performs his functions as a citizen, by fulfilling the precise duties which belong to his profession as a magistrate. It is true that, upon this system, the judicial censorship of the courts of justice over the legislature cannot extend to all laws indiscriminately, inasmuch as some of them can never give rise to that precise species of contest which is termed a lawsuit; and even when such a contest is possible, it may happen that no one cares to bring it before a court of justice. The Americans have often felt this inconvenience; but they have left the remedy incomplete, lest they should give it an efficacy which might in some cases prove dangerous. Within these limits, the power vested in the American courts of justice, of pronouncing a statute to be unconstitutional, forms one of the most powerful barriers which has ever been devised against the tyranny of political assemblies.

OTHER POWERS GRANTED TO AMERICAN JUDGES.

In the United States, all the Citizens have the Right of indicting the Public Functionaries before the ordinary Tribunals. — How they use this Right. — Art. 75 of the French Constitution of the Year VIII. — The Americans and the English cannot understand the Purport of this Article.

IT is hardly necessary to say that, in a free country like America, all the citizens have the right of indicting public functionaries before the ordinary tribunals, and that all the judges have the power of convicting public officers. The right granted to the courts of justice of punishing the agents of the executive government, when they violate the laws, is so natural a one, that it cannot be looked upon as an extraordinary privilege. Nor do the springs of government appear to me to be weakened in the United States, by rendering all public officers responsible to the tribunals. The Americans seem, on the contrary, to have increased by this means that respect which is due to the authorities, and at the same time, to have made these authorities more careful not to offend. I was struck by the small number of political trials which occur in the United States; but I had no difficulty in accounting for this circumstance. A prosecution, of whatever nature it may be, is always a difficult and expensive undertaking. It is easy to attack a public man in the journals, but the motives for bringing him before the tribunals must be serious. A solid ground of complaint must exist, before any one thinks of prosecuting a public officer, and these officers are careful not to furnish such grounds of complaint, when they are afraid of being prosecuted.

This does not depend upon the republican form of American institutions, for the same thing happens in England. These two nations do not regard the impeachment of the principal officers of state as the guaranty of their independence. But they hold that it is rather by minor prosecutions, which the humblest citizen can institute at any time, that liberty is protected, and not by those great judicial procedures, which are rarely employed until it is too late.

In the Middle Ages, when it was very difficult to reach offenders, the judges inflicted frightful punishments on the few who were arrested; but this did not diminish the number of crimes. It has since been discovered that, when justice is more certain and more mild, it is more efficacious. The English and the Americans hold that tyranny and oppression are to be treated like any other crime, by lessening the penalty and facilitating conviction.

In the year VIII. of the French Republic, a constitution was drawn up in which the following clause was introduced: " Art. 75. All the agents of the government below the rank of ministers can be prosecuted for offences relating to their several functions only by virtue of a decree of the Council of State; in which case, the prosecution takes place before the ordinary tribunals." This clause survived the " Constitution of the year VIII.," and is still maintained, in spite of the just complaints of the nation. I have always found a difficulty in explaining its meaning to Englishmen or Americans, and have hardly understood it myself. They at once perceived that, the Council of State in France being a great tribunal established in the centre of the kingdom, it was a sort of tyranny to send all complainants before it as a preliminary step. But when I told them that the Council of State was not a judicial body, in the common sense of the term, but an administrative council composed of men dependent on the Crown, — so that the king, after having ordered one of his servants, called a

Prefect, to commit an injustice, has the power of commanding another of his servants, called a Councillor of State, to prevent the former from being punished, — when I showed them, that the citizen who has been injured by an order of the sovereign is obliged to ask the sovereign's permission to obtain redress, they refused to credit so flagrant an abuse, and were tempted to accuse me of falsehood or ignorance. It frequently happened, before the Revolution, that a Parliament * issued a warrant against a public officer who had committed an offence. Sometimes the royal authority intervened, and quashed the proceedings. Despotism then showed itself openly, and men obeyed it only by submitting to superior force. It is painful to perceive how much lower we are sunk than our forefathers; since we allow things to pass, under the color of justice and the sanction of law, which violence alone imposed upon them.

* A French "Parliament" was a judicial body. — AM. ED.

CHAPTER VII.

POLITICAL JURISDICTION IN THE UNITED STATES.

Definition of Political Jurisdiction. — What is understood by Political Jurisdiction in France, in England, and in the United States. — In America,
the Political Judge has to do only with Public Officers. — He more frequently decrees Removal from Office than an ordinary Penalty. — Political Jurisdiction as it exists in the United States is, notwithstanding its
Mildness, and perhaps in Consequence of that Mildness, a most Powerful Instrument in the Hands of the Majority.

I UNDERSTAND by political jurisdiction, that temporary right of pronouncing a legal decision with
which a political body may be invested.

In absolute governments, it is useless to introduce any
extraordinary forms of procedure; the prince, in whose
name an offender is prosecuted, is as much the sovereign
of the courts of justice as of everything else, and the idea
which is entertained of his power is of itself a sufficient
security. The only thing he has to fear is, that the external formalities of justice should be neglected, and that
his authority should be dishonored, from a wish to
strengthen it. But in most free countries, in which the
majority can never have the same influence over the tribunals as an absolute monarch, the judicial power has
occasionally been vested for a time in the representatives
of the people. It has been thought better to introduce a
temporary confusion between the functions of the different
authorities, than to violate the necessary principle of the
unity of government.

England, France, and the United States have established

this political jurisdiction by law; and it is curious to see the different use which these three great nations have made of it. In England and in France, the House of Lords and the Chamber of Peers constitute the highest criminal court of their respective nations; and although they do not habitually try all political offences, they are competent to try them all. Another political body has the right of bringing the accusation before the Peers: the only difference which exists between the two countries in this respect is, that in England the Commons may impeach whomsoever they please before the Lords, whilst in France, the Deputies can only employ this mode of prosecution against the ministers of the Crown. In both countries, the Upper House may make use of all the existing penal laws of the nation to punish the delinquents.

In the United States, as well as in Europe, one branch of the legislature is authorized to impeach, and the other to judge: the House of Representatives arraigns the offender, and the Senate punishes him. But the Senate can only try such persons as are brought before it by the House of Representatives, and those persons must belong to the class of public functionaries. Thus the jurisdiction of the Senate is less extensive than that of the Peers of France, whilst the right of impeachment by the Representatives is more general than that of the Deputies. But the great difference which exists between Europe and America is, that, in Europe, the political tribunals can apply all the enactments of the penal code, whilst in America, when they have deprived the offender of his official rank, and have declared him incapable of filling any political office for the future, their jurisdiction terminates, and that of the ordinary tribunals begins.

Suppose, for instance, that the President of the United States has committed the crime of high-treason; the House of Representatives impeaches him, and the Senate degrades him from office; he must then be tried by a jury, which alone can deprive him of liberty or life. This accurately illustrates the subject we are treating. The political jurisdiction which is established by the laws of Europe is intended to reach great offenders, whatever may be their birth, their rank, or their power in the State; and to this end, all the privileges of a court of justice are temporarily given to a great political assembly. The legislator is then transformed into a magistrate; he is called upon to prove, to classify, and to punish the offence; and as he exercises all the authority of a judge, the law imposes upon him all the duties of that high office, and requires all the formalities of justice. When a public functionary is impeached before an English or a French political tribunal, and is found guilty, the sentence deprives him *ipso facto* of his functions, and may pronounce him incapable of resuming them or any others for the future. But in this case, the political interdict is a consequence of the sentence, and not the sentence itself. In Europe, then, the sentence of a political tribunal is a judicial verdict, rather than an administrative measure. In the United States, the contrary takes place; and although the decision of the Senate is judicial in its form, since the Senators are obliged to comply with the rules and formalities of a court of justice; although it is judicial, also, in respect to the motives on which it is founded, since the Senate is generally obliged to take an offence at common law as the basis of its sentence; yet the political judgment is rather an administrative than a judicial act. If it had been the intention of the American legislator really to invest a political body with great judicial authority, its action would not have been limited to public functionaries, since the most dangerous enemies of the state may not have any public functions; and this is especially true in republics, where party influence has the most force, and where the strength of many a leader is increased by his exercising no legitimate power.

If the American legislator had wished to give society itself the means of preventing great offences by the fear of punishment, according to the practice of ordinary justice, all the resources of the penal code would have been given to the political tribunals. But he gave them only an imperfect weapon, which can never reach the most dangerous offenders; since men who aim at the entire subversion of the laws are not likely to murmur at a political interdict.

The main object of the political jurisdiction which obtains in the United States is, therefore, to take away the power from him who would make a bad use of it, and prevent him from ever acquiring it again. This is evidently an administrative measure, sanctioned by the formalities of a judicial decision. In this matter, the Americans have created a mixed system; they have surrounded the act which removes a public functionary with all the securities of a political trial, and they have deprived political condemnations of their severest penalties. Every link of the system may easily be traced from this point; we at once perceive why the American constitutions subject all the civil functionaries to the jurisdiction of the Senate, whilst the military, whose crimes are nevertheless more formidable, are exempted from that tribunal. In the civil service, none of the American functionaries can be said to be removable; the places which some of them occupy are inalienable, and the others are chosen for a term which cannot be shortened.* It is, therefore, necessary to try them all in order to deprive them of their authority. But military officers are dependent on the chief magistrate of

---

* This is a great mistake. In no country in the world do civil officers hold their posts by so short and uncertain a tenure as in the United States. This is true both of the Federal and the State governments, rotation in office being now held up (falsely and injuriously, as we believe) to be a republican principle. Every change of administration, every election of a new Governor or a new President, leads to the appointment of a new set of officers,

the State, who is himself a civil functionary; and the decision which condemns him is a blow upon them all.

If we now compare the American and the European systems, we shall meet with differences no less striking in the effects which each of them produces or may produce. In France and England, the jurisdiction of political bodies is looked upon as an extraordinary resource, which is only to be employed in order to rescue society from unwonted dangers. It is not to be denied that these tribunals, as they are constituted in Europe, violate the conservative principle of the division of powers in the state, and threaten incessantly the lives and liberties of the subject. The same political jurisdiction in the United States is only indirectly hostile to the division of powers; it cannot menace the lives of the citizens, and it does not hover, as in Europe, over the heads of the whole community, since it reaches those only who have voluntarily submitted to its authority by accepting office. It is, at the same time, less formidable and less efficacious; indeed, it has not been considered by the legislators of the United States as an extreme remedy for the more violent evils of society, but as an ordinary means of government. In this respect, it probably exercises more real influence on the social body in America than in Europe. We must not be misled by the apparent mildness of American legislation in all that relates to political jurisdiction. It is to be observed, in the first place, that in the United States, the tribunal which passes judgment is composed of the same elements, and subject to the same influences, as the body which impeaches the offender, and that this gives an almost irresistible impulse to the vin-

down even to the lowest clerks in the several departments. The country thus loses all the benefit of experience in the conduct of its affairs, the offices being all held at any one time by a set of raw hands. The only exception is in the case of the Judges of the Supreme Court, who are now the only functionaries that cannot be removed except by impeachment. — AM. ED.

dictive passions of parties. If political judges in the United
States cannot inflict so heavy penalties as those in Europe,
there is the less chance of their acquitting an offender; the
conviction, if it is less formidable, is more certain. The
principal object of the political tribunals of Europe is to
punish the offender; of those in America, to deprive him
of his power. A political sentence in the United States
may, therefore, be looked upon as a preventive measure;
and there is no reason for tying down the judges to the
exact definitions of criminal law. Nothing can be more
alarming than the vagueness with which political offences,
properly so called, are described in the laws of America.
Article II. Section 4 of the Constitution of the United
States runs thus: — " The President, Vice-President, and
all civil officers of the United States, shall be removed from
office on impeachment for, and conviction of, treason, bribery, *or other high crimes and misdemeanors*." Many of the
constitutions of the States are even less explicit. " Public
officers," says the Constitution of Massachusetts, " shall be
impeached for misconduct or maladministration." The
Constitution of Virginia declares that " all the civil officers
who shall have offended against the State by maladministration, corruption, or other high crimes, may be impeached
by the House of Delegates." In some of the States, the
constitutions do not specify any offences, in order to subject the public functionaries to an unlimited responsibility.*
I venture to affirm, that it is precisely their mildness which
renders the American laws so formidable in this respect.
We have shown that, in Europe, the removal of a functionary and his political disqualification are the consequences of
the penalty he is to undergo, and that, in America, they
constitute the penalty itself. The consequence is, that in
Europe, political tribunals are invested with terrible powers
which they are afraid to use, and the fear of punishing too

* See the Constitutions of Illinois, Maine, Connecticut, and Georgia.

much hinders them from punishing at all. But in America, no one hesitates to inflict a penalty from which humanity does not recoil. To condemn a political opponent to death, in order to deprive him of his power, is to commit what all the world would execrate as a horrible assassination; but to declare that opponent unworthy to exercise that authority, and to deprive him of it, leaving him uninjured in life and limb, may seem to be the fair issue of the struggle. But this sentence, which it is so easy to pronounce, is not the less fatally severe to most of those upon whom it is inflicted. Great criminals may undoubtedly brave its vain rigor; but ordinary offenders will dread it as a condemnation which destroys their position in the world, casts a blight upon their honor, and condemns them to a shameful inactivity worse than death. The influence exercised in the United States upon the progress of society by the jurisdiction of political bodies is the more powerful in proportion as it seems less frightful. It does not directly coerce the subject, but it renders the majority more absolute over those in power; it does not give an unbounded authority to the legislature which can only be exerted at some great crisis, but it establishes a temperate and regular influence, which is at all times available. If the power is decreased, it can, on the other hand, be more conveniently employed, and more easily abused. By preventing political tribunals from inflicting judicial punishments, the Americans seem to have eluded the worst consequences of legislative tyranny, rather than tyranny itself; and I am not sure that political jurisdiction, as it is constituted in the United States, is not, all things considered, the most formidable weapon which has ever been placed in the grasp of a majority. When the American republics begin to degenerate, it will be easy to verify the truth of this observation, by remarking whether the number of political impeachments is increased.*

* See Appendix N.

CHAPTER VIII.

THE FEDERAL CONSTITUTION.

I HAVE hitherto considered each State as a separate whole, and have explained the different springs which the people there put in motion, and the different means of action which it employs. But all the States which I have considered as independent are yet forced to submit, in certain cases, to the supreme authority of the Union. The time is now come to examine the portion of sovereignty which has been granted to the Union, and to cast a rapid glance over the Federal Constitution.

HISTORY OF THE FEDERAL CONSTITUTION.

Origin of the first Union. — Its Weakness. — Congress appeals to the Constituent Authority. — Interval of two Years between this Appeal and the Promulgation of the new Constitution.

THE thirteen Colonies, which simultaneously threw off the yoke of England towards the end of the last century, had, as I have already said, the same religion, the same language, the same customs, and almost the same laws; they were struggling against a common enemy; and these reasons were sufficiently strong to unite them one to another, and to consolidate them into one nation. But as each of them had always had a separate existence, and a government within its reach, separate interests and peculiar customs had sprung up, which were opposed to such a compact and intimate union as would have absorbed the individual importance of each in the general importance of all. Hence arose two opposite tendencies, — the one prompting the Anglo-Americans to unite, the other to divide, their strength.

As long as the war with the mother country lasted, the principle of union was kept alive by necessity; and although the laws which constituted it were defective, the common tie subsisted in spite of their imperfections.* But no sooner was peace concluded, than the faults of this legislation became manifest, and the state seemed to be suddenly dissolved. Each Colony became an independent republic, and assumed an absolute sovereignty. The Federal government, condemned to impotence by its Constitution, and no longer sustained by the presence of a common danger, witnessed the outrages offered to its flag by the great nations of Europe, whilst it was scarcely able to maintain its ground against the Indian tribes, and to pay the interest of the debt which had been contracted during the war of independence. It was already on the verge of destruction, when it officially proclaimed its inability to conduct the government, and appealed to the constituent authority.†

If America ever approached (for however brief a time) that lofty pinnacle of glory to which the proud imagination of its inhabitants is wont to point, it was at this solemn moment, when the national power abdicated, as it were, its authority. All ages have furnished the spectacle of a people struggling with energy to win its independence; and the efforts of the Americans in throwing off the English yoke have been considerably exaggerated. Separated from

---

* See the Articles of the first Confederation, formed in 1778. This Constitution was not adopted by all the States until 1781. See also the analysis given of this Constitution in the Federalist, from No. 15 to No. 22 inclusive, and Story's "Commentaries on the Constitution of the United States," pp. 85–115.

† Congress made this declaration on the 21st of February, 1787.

their enemies by three thousand miles of ocean, and backed by a powerful ally, the United States owed their victory much more to their geographical position than to the valor of their armies or the patriotism of their citizens.　It would be ridiculous to compare the American war to the wars of the French Revolution, or the efforts of the Americans to those of the French, when France, attacked by the whole of Europe, without money, without credit, without allies, threw forward a twentieth part of her population to meet her enemies, and with one hand carried the torch of revolution beyond the frontiers, whilst she stifled with the other a flame that was devouring the country within.　But it is new in the history of society, to see a great people turn a calm and scrutinizing eye upon itself, when apprised by the legislature that the wheels of its government are stopped, — to see it carefully examine the extent of the evil, and patiently wait two whole years until a remedy is discovered, to which it voluntarily submitted without its costing a tear or a drop of blood from mankind.

When the inadequacy of the first constitution was discovered, America had the double advantage of that calm which had succeeded the effervescence of the Revolution, and of the aid of those great men whom the Revolution had created.　The assembly which accepted the task of composing the second constitution was small ; * but George Washington was its President, and it contained the finest minds and the noblest characters which had ever appeared in the New World.　This national Convention, after long and mature deliberation, offered to the acceptance of the people the body of general laws which still rules the Union. All the States adopted it successively.†　The new Federal

* It consisted of fifty-five members ; Washington, Madison, Hamilton, and the two Morrises were amongst the number.

† It was not adopted by the legislative bodies, but representatives were elected by the people for this sole purpose ; and the new Constitution was discussed at length in each of these assemblies.

government commenced its functions in 1789, after an interregnum of two years. The Revolution of America terminated precisely when that of France began.

SUMMARY OF THE FEDERAL CONSTITUTION.

Division of Authority between the Federal Government and the States. — The Government of the States is the Rule, the Federal Government the Exception.

THE first question which awaited the Americans was, so to divide the sovereignty that each of the different States which composed the Union should continue to govern itself in all that concerned its internal prosperity, whilst the entire nation, represented by the Union, should continue to form a compact body, and to provide for all general exigencies. The problem was a complex and difficult one. It was as impossible to determine beforehand, with any degree of accuracy, the share of authority which each of the two governments was to enjoy, as to foresee all the incidents in the life of a nation.

The obligations and the claims of the Federal government were simple and easily definable, because the Union had been formed with the express purpose of meeting certain great general wants ; but the claims and obligations of the individual States, on the other hand, were complicated and various, because their government had penetrated into all the details of social life. The attributes of the Federal government were therefore carefully defined, and all that was not included among them was declared to remain to the governments of the several States. Thus the government of the States remained the rule, and that of the Confederation was the exception.*

* It is to be observed, that, whenever the *exclusive* right of regulating certain matters is not reserved to Congress by the Constitution, the States may

But as it was foreseen that, in practice, questions might arise as to the exact limits of this exceptional authority, and it would be dangerous to submit these questions to the decision of the ordinary courts of justice, established in the different States by the States themselves, a high Federal court was created,* one of whose duties was to maintain the balance of power between the two rival governments, as it had been established by the Constitution.†

POWERS OF THE FEDERAL GOVERNMENT.

Power of declaring War, making Peace, and levying General Taxes vested in the Federal Government. — What Part of the Internal Policy of the Country it may direct. — The Government of the Union in some Respects more centralized than the King's Government in the old French Monarchy.

THE people in themselves are only individuals; and the special reason why they need to be united under one government is, that they may appear to advantage before foreigners. The exclusive right of making peace and war, of

legislate concerning them till Congress sees fit to take up the affair. For instance, Congress has the right of making a general law on bankruptcy, which, however, it neglects to do. Each State is then at liberty to make such a law for itself. This point, however, has been established only after discussion in the law courts, and may be said to belong more properly to jurisprudence.

* The action of this court is indirect, as we shall hereafter show.

† It is thus that the Federalist, No. 45, explains this division of sovereignty between the Union and the States: "The powers delegated by the Constitution to the Federal government are few and defined. Those which are to remain in the State governments are numerous and indefinite. The former will be exercised principally on external objects, as war, peace, negotiation, and foreign commerce. The powers reserved to the several States will extend to all the objects which, in the ordinary course of affairs, concern the internal order and prosperity of the State."

I shall often have occasion to quote the Federalist in this work. When concluding treaties of commerce, raising armies, and equipping fleets, was therefore granted to the Union. The necessity of a national government was less imperiously felt in the conduct of the internal affairs of society; but there are certain general interests which can only be attended to with advantage by a general authority. The Union was invested with the power of controlling the monetary system, carrying the mails, and opening the great roads which were to unite the different parts of the country.* The independence of the government of each State in its sphere was recognized; yet the Federal government was authorized to interfere in the internal affairs of the States † in a few predetermined cases, in which an indiscreet use of their independence might compromise the safety of the whole Union. Thus, whilst the power of modifying and changing their legislation at pleasure was preserved to each of the confederate republics, they are forbidden to enact *ex-post-facto* laws, or to grant any titles of nobility. Lastly, as it was necessary that the Federal government should be able to fulfil its engagements, it has an unlimited power of levying taxes.

In examining the division of powers, as established by

the bill, which has since become the Constitution of the United States, was before the people, and the discussions were still pending, three men, who had already acquired a portion of that celebrity which they have since enjoyed, — John Jay, Hamilton, Madison, — undertook together to explain to the nation the advantages of the measure which was proposed. With this view, they published in a journal a series of articles, which now form a complete treatise. They entitled their journal "The Federalist," a name which has been retained in the work. The Federalist is an excellent book, which ought to be familiar to the statesmen of all countries, though it specially concerns America.

* Several other powers of the same kind exist, such as that of legislating on bankruptcy, and granting patents. The necessity of confiding such matters to the Federal government is obvious enough.

† Even in these cases, its interference is indirect. The Union interferes by means of the tribunals, as will be hereafter shown.

the Federal Constitution, remarking on the one hand the portion of sovereignty which has been reserved to the several States, and on the other, the share of power which has been given to the Union, it is evident that the Federal legislators entertained very clear and accurate notions respecting the centralization of government. The United States form not only a republic, but a confederation; yet the national authority is more centralized there than it was in several of the absolute monarchies of Europe. I will cite only two examples.

Thirteen supreme courts of justice existed in France, which, generally speaking, had the right of interpreting the law without appeal; and those provinces which were styled *pays d'État* were authorized to refuse their assent to an impost which had been levied by the sovereign, who represented the nation.

In the Union, there is but one tribunal to interpret, as there is one legislature to make, the laws; and an impost voted by the representatives of the nation is binding upon all the citizens. In these two essential points, therefore, the Union is more centralized than the French monarchy, although the Union is only an assemblage of confederate republics.

In Spain, certain provinces had the right of establishing a system of custom-house duties peculiar to themselves, although that privilege belongs, by its very nature, to the national sovereignty. In America, Congress alone has the right of regulating the commercial relations of the States with each other. The government of the confederation is therefore more centralized in this respect than the kingdom of Spain. It is true, that the power of the crown in France or Spain was always able to obtain by force whatever the constitution of the country denied, and that the ultimate result was consequently the same; but I am here discussing the theory of the constitution.

After having settled the limits within which the Federal government was to act, the next point was to determine how it should be put in action.

LEGISLATIVE POWERS OF THE FEDERAL GOVERNMENT.

Division of the Legislative Body into Two Branches. — Difference in the Manner of forming the Two Houses. — The Principle of the Independence of the States predominates in the Formation of the Senate. That of the Sovereignty of the Nation in the Composition of the House of Representatives. — Singular Effect of the Fact that a Constitution can be Logical only when the Nation is Young.

THE plan which had been laid down beforehand in the constitutions of the several States was followed, in many respects, in the organization of the powers of the Union. The Federal legislature of the Union was composed of a Senate and a House of Representatives. A spirit of compromise caused these two assemblies to be constituted on different principles. I have already shown that two interests were opposed to each other in the establishment of the Federal Constitution. These two interests had given rise to two opinions. It was the wish of one party to convert the Union into a league of independent States, or a sort of congress, at which the representatives of the several nations would meet to discuss certain points of common interest. The other party desired to unite the inhabitants of the American Colonies into one and the same people, and to establish a government, which should act as the sole representative of the nation, although in a limited sphere. The practical consequences of these two theories were very different.

If the object was, that a league should be established instead of a national government, then the majority of the States, instead of the majority of the inhabitants of the Union, would make the laws: for every State, great or small, would then remain in full independence, and enter the Union upon a footing of perfect equality. If, however, the inhabitants of the United States were to be considered as belonging to one and the same nation, it would be natural that the majority of the citizens of the Union should make the law. Of course, the lesser States could not subscribe to the application of this doctrine without, in fact, abdicating their existence in respect to the sovereignty of the Confederation; since they would cease to be a co-equal and co-authoritative power, and become an insignificant fraction of a great people. The former system would have invested them with excessive authority, the latter would have destroyed their influence altogether. Under these circumstances, the result was, that the rules of logic were broken, as is usually the case when interests are opposed to arguments. A middle course was hit upon by the legislators, which brought together by force two systems theoretically irreconcilable.

The principle of the independence of the States triumphed in the formation of the Senate, and that of the sovereignty of the nation in the composition of the House of Representatives. Each State was to send two Senators to Congress, and a number of Representatives proportioned to its population.* It results from this arrangement that

* Every ten years, Congress fixes anew the number of Representatives which each State is to furnish. The total number was 69 in 1789, and 240 in 1833.

The Constitution decided that there should not be more than one Representative for every 30,000 persons; but no minimum was fixed on. Congress has not thought fit to augment the number of Representatives in proportion to the increase of population. The first Act which was passed on the subject (14th of April, 1792) decided that there should be one Representative for every 33,000 inhabitants. The Act which was passed in 1852 fixes the proportion at one for 93,423, and made the House consist of 234 members. The population represented is composed of all the freemen, and of three fifths of the slaves.

the State of New York has at the present day thirty-three Representatives, and only two Senators; the State of Delaware has two Senators, and only one Representative; the State of Delaware is therefore equal to the State of New York in the Senate, whilst the latter has thirty-three times the influence of the former in the House of Representatives. Thus, the minority of the nation in the Senate may paralyze the decisions of the majority represented in the other House, which is contrary to the spirit of constitutional government.

These facts show how rare and difficult it is rationally and logically to combine all the several parts of legislation. The course of time always gives birth to different interests, and sanctions different principles, among the same people; and when a general constitution is to be established, these interests and principles are so many natural obstacles to the rigorous application of any political system with all its consequences. The early stages of national existence are the only periods at which it is possible to make legislation strictly logical; and when we perceive a nation in the enjoyment of this advantage, we should not hastily conclude that it is wise, but only remember that it is young. When the Federal Constitution was formed, the interest of independence for the separate States, and the interest of union for the whole people, were the only two conflicting interests which existed amongst the Anglo-Americans; and a compromise was necessarily made between them.

It is, however, just to acknowledge, that this part of the Constitution has not hitherto produced those evils which might have been feared. All the States are young and contiguous; their customs, their ideas, and their wants are not dissimilar; and the differences which result from their size are not enough to set their interests much at variance. The small States have consequently never leagued themselves together in the Senate to oppose the designs of the

larger ones. Besides, there is so irresistible an authority
in the legal expression of the will of a people, that the
Senate could offer but a feeble opposition to the vote of the
majority expressed by the House of Representatives.

It must not be forgotten, moreover, that it was not in
the power of the American legislators to reduce to a single
nation the people for whom they were making laws. The
object of the Federal Constitution was not to destroy the
independence of the States, but to restrain it. By acknowledging the real power of these secondary communities, (and
it was impossible to deprive them of it,) they disavowed
beforehand the habitual use of constraint in enforcing the
decisions of the majority. This being laid down, the introduction of the influence of the States into the mechanism
of the Federal government was by no means to be wondered at; since it only attested the existence of an acknowledged power, which was to be humored, and not forcibly
checked.

A FURTHER DIFFERENCE BETWEEN THE SENATE AND THE HOUSE OF REPRESENTATIVES.

The Senate named by the State Legislatures; the Representatives by the
People. — Double Election of the former; single Election of the latter.
— Term of the different Offices. — Peculiar Functions of each House.

THE Senate differs from the other House, not only in the
very principle of representation, but also in the mode of its
election, in the term for which it is chosen, and in the
nature of its functions. The House of Representatives
is chosen by the people, the Senate by the legislatures of
each State; the former is directly elected, the latter is
elected by an elected body; the term for which the Representatives are chosen is only two years, that of the Senators is six. The functions of the House of Representatives
are purely legislative, and the only share it takes in the

judicial power is in the impeachment of public officers. The Senate co-operates in the work of legislation, and tries those political offences which the House of Representatives submits to its decision. It also acts as the great executive council of the nation; the treaties which are concluded by the President must be ratified by the Senate; and the appointments he may make, in order to be definitive, must be approved by the same body.

THE EXECUTIVE POWER.

Dependence of the President. — He is Elective and Responsible. — Free in his own Sphere, under the Inspection, but not under the Direction, of the Senate. — His Salary fixed at his Entry into Office. — Suspensive Veto.

THE American legislators undertook a difficult task in attempting to create an executive power dependent on the majority of the people, and nevertheless sufficiently strong to act without restraint in its own sphere. It was indispensable to the maintenance of the republican form of government, that the representative of the executive power should be subject to the will of the nation.

The President is an elective magistrate. His honor, his property, his liberty, and his life are the securities which the people have for the temperate use of his power. But in the exercise of his authority, he is not perfectly independent; the Senate takes cognizance of his relations with foreign powers, and of his distribution of public appointments, so that he can neither corrupt nor be corrupted. The legislators of the Union acknowledge that the executive power could not fulfil its task with dignity and advantage, unless it enjoyed more stability and strength than had been granted it in the separate States.

The President is chosen for four years, and he may be re-elected; so that the chances of a future administration may inspire him with hopeful undertakings for the public good, and give him the means of carrying them into execution. The President was made the sole representative of the executive power of the Union; and care was taken not to render his decisions subordinate to the vote of a council, — a dangerous measure, which tends at the same time to clog the action of the government and to diminish its responsibility. The Senate has the right of annulling certain acts of the President; but it cannot compel him to take any steps, nor does it participate in the exercise of the executive power.

The action of the legislature on the executive power may be direct, and we have just shown that the Americans carefully obviated this influence; but it may, on the other hand, be indirect. Legislative assemblies which have the power of depriving an officer of state of his salary encroach upon his independence; and as they are free to make the laws, it is to be feared lest they should gradually appropriate to themselves a portion of that authority which the Constitution had vested in his hands. This dependence of the executive power is one of the defects inherent in republican constitutions. The Americans have not been able to counteract the tendency which legislative assemblies have to get possession of the government, but they have rendered this propensity less irresistible. The salary of the President is fixed, at the time of his entering upon office, for the whole period of his magistracy. The President is, moreover, armed with a suspensive veto, which allows him to oppose the passing of such laws as might destroy the portion of independence which the Constitution awards him. Yet the struggle between the President and the legislature must always be an unequal one, since the latter is certain of bearing down all resistance by persevering in its plans; but the suspensive veto forces it, at least, to reconsider the matter, and, if the motion be persisted in, it must then be backed by a majority of two thirds of the whole house. The veto is, moreover, a sort of appeal to the people. The executive power, which, without this security, might have been secretly oppressed, adopts this means of pleading its cause and stating its motives. But if the legislature perseveres in its design, can it not always overpower all resistance? I reply that in the constitutions of all nations, of whatever kind they may be, a certain point exists at which the legislator must have recourse to the good sense and the virtue of his fellow-citizens. This point is nearer and more prominent in republics, whilst it is more remote and more carefully concealed in monarchies; but it always exists somewhere. There is no country in which everything can be provided for by the laws, or in which political institutions can prove a substitute for common sense and public morality.

IN WHAT THE POSITION OF A PRESIDENT OF THE UNITED STATES DIFFERS FROM THAT OF A CONSTITUTIONAL KING OF FRANCE.

Executive Power in the United States as limited and exceptional as the Sovereignty which it represents. — Executive Power in France, like the State Sovereignty, extends to everything. — The King a Branch of the Legislature. — The President the mere Executor of the Law. — Other Differences resulting from the Duration of the two Powers. — The President checked in the Exercise of the Executive Authority. — The King Independent in its Exercise. — In spite of these Differences, France is more akin to a Republic than the Union to a Monarchy. — Comparison of the Number of Public Officers depending upon the Executive Power in the two Countries.

THE executive power has so important an influence on the destinies of nations, that I wish to dwell for an instant on this portion of my subject, in order more clearly to explain the part it sustains in America. In order to form a clear and precise idea of the position of the President of the United States, it may be well to compare it with that of one of the constitutional kings of Europe. In this comparison, I shall pay but little attention to the external signs of power, which are more apt to deceive the eye of the observer than to guide his researches. When a monarchy is being gradually transformed into a republic, the executive power retains the titles, the honors, the etiquette, and even the funds of royalty, long after its real authority has disappeared. The English, after having cut off the head of one king, and expelled another from his throne, were still wont to address the successors of those princes only upon their knees. On the other hand, when a republic falls under the sway of a single man, the demeanor of the sovereign remains as simple and unpretending as if his authority was not yet paramount. When the Emperors exercised an unlimited control over the fortunes and the lives of their fellow-citizens, it was customary to call them Cæsar in conversation; and they were in the habit of supping without formality at their friends' houses. It is therefore necessary to look below the surface.

The sovereignty of the United States is shared between the Union and the States, whilst, in France, it is undivided and compact: hence arises the first and most notable difference which exists between the President of the United States and the King of France. In the United States, the executive power is as limited and exceptional as the sovereignty in whose name it acts; in France, it is as universal as the authority of the State. The Americans have a Federal, and the French a national government.

This cause of inferiority results from the nature of things, but it is not the only one; the second in importance is as follows. Sovereignty may be defined to be the right of making laws. In France, the King really exercises a portion of the sovereign power, since the laws have no weight if he refuses to sanction them; he is, moreover, the executor of all they ordain. The President is also the executor of the laws; but he does not really co-operate in making them, since the refusal of his assent does not prevent their passage. He is not, therefore, a part of the sovereign power, but only its agent. But not only does the King of France constitute a portion of the sovereign power; he also contributes to the nomination of the legislature, which is the other portion. He participates in it through appointing the members of one chamber, and dissolving the other at his pleasure; whereas the President of the United States has no share in the formation of the legislative body, and cannot dissolve it. The King has the same right of bringing forward measures as the Chambers, — a right which the President does not possess. The King is represented in each assembly by his ministers, who explain his intentions, support his opinions, and maintain the principles of the government. The President and his ministers are alike excluded from Congress, so that his influence and his opinions can only penetrate indirectly into that great body. The King of France is, therefore, on an equal footing with the legislature, which can no more act without him than he can without it. The President is placed beside the legislature like an inferior and dependent power.

Even in the exercise of the executive power, properly so called, — the point upon which his position seems to be most analogous to that of the King of France, — the President labors under several causes of inferiority. The authority of the King, in France, has, in the first place, the advantage of duration over that of the President; and durability is one of the chief elements of strength; nothing is either loved or feared but what is likely to endure. The President of the United States is a magistrate elected for four years. The King, in France, is an hereditary sovereign.

In the exercise of the executive power, the President of the United States is constantly subject to a jealous supervision. He may prepare, but he cannot conclude, a treaty; he may nominate, but he cannot appoint, a public officer.* The King of France is absolute within the sphere of executive power.

The President of the United States is responsible for his actions; but the person of the King is declared inviolable by French law.

Nevertheless, public opinion as a directing power is no less above the head of the one than of the other. This power is less definite, less evident, and less sanctioned by the laws in France than in America; but it really exists there. In America, it acts by elections and decrees; in France, it proceeds by revolutions. Thus, notwithstanding the different constitutions of these two countries, public opinion is the predominant authority in both of them. The fundamental principle of legislation — a principle essentially republican — is the same in both countries, although its developments may be more or less free, and its consequences different. Whence I am led to conclude,

---

* The Constitution has left it doubtful whether the President is obliged to consult the Senate in the removal as well as in the appointment of Federal officers. The Federalist (No. 77) seemed to establish the affirmative; but in 1789, Congress formally decided, that, as the President was responsible for his actions, he ought not to be forced to employ agents who had forfeited his esteem. See Kent's Commentaries, Vol. I. p. 289. [See also Daniel Webster's speech on the Appointing and Removing Power, Webster's Works, IV. 185; Marshall's Washington, V. 196; Sergeant & Rawle's Reports, V. 451. The decision of Congress upon this subject in 1789 was by a very small majority in the House, and in the Senate it passed only by the casting vote of the Vice-President. And this decision is only by *inference* from the Act thus passed, which provides, that, when the Secretary of the Treasury should be removed by the President, his assistant shall discharge the duties of the office. Mr. Spencer rightly observes, that the power has been "repeatedly denied in and out of Congress, and must be considered as yet an unsettled question." — AM. ED.]

that France with its King is nearer akin to a republic, than the Union with its President is to a monarchy.

In all that precedes, I have touched only upon the main points of distinction; if I could have entered into details, the contrast would have been still more striking.

I have remarked that the authority of the President in the United States is only exercised within the limits of a partial sovereignty, whilst that of the King in France is undivided. I might have gone on to show that the power of the King's government in France exceeds its natural limits, however extensive these may be, and penetrates in a thousand different ways into the administration of private interests. Amongst the examples of this influence may be quoted that which results from the great number of public functionaries, who all derive their appointments from the executive government. This number now exceeds all previous limits; it amounts to 138,000 * nominations, each of which may be considered as an element of power. The President of the United States has not the exclusive right of making any public appointments, and their whole number scarcely exceeds 12,000.†

* The sums annually paid by the state to these officers amount to 200,000,000 francs (eight millions sterling).

† This number is extracted from the "National Calendar" for 1833.

It results from this comparison, that the King of France has eleven times as many places at his disposal as the President, although the population of France is not much more than double that of the Union.

[The vast increase of the population of the United States, since De Tocqueville wrote, from thirteen millions to nearly thirty millions, and the consequent necessary enlargement of the machinery of government, has nearly reversed these proportions. The patronage of the President of the United States is now enormous, and has become a dominant feature in the operation of our national government. Reckoning the subordinate officers in the Post-Office and Customs departments, all of whom derive their appointments either directly or indirectly from the President, and continue in office only during his pleasure, and most of whom, in fact, give place to new incumbents at every change of administration, it is easy to see that the in-

ACCIDENTAL CAUSES WHICH MAY INCREASE THE INFLUENCE
OF THE EXECUTIVE GOVERNMENT.

External Security of the Union. — Army of six thousand Men. — Few
Ships. — The President has great Prerogatives, but no Opportunity of
exercising them. — In the Prerogatives which he does exercise, he is
Weak.

IF the executive government is feebler in America than
in France, the cause is perhaps more attributable to the
circumstances than to the laws of the country.

It is chiefly in its foreign relations that the executive
power of a nation finds occasion to exert its skill and its
strength. If the existence of the Union were perpetually
threatened, if its chief interests were in daily connection
with those of other powerful nations, the executive government would assume an increased importance in proportion to the measures expected of it, and to those which it
would execute. The President of the United States, it is
true, is the commander-in-chief of the army, but the army
is composed of only six thousand men; he commands the
fleet, but the fleet reckons but few sail; he conducts the
foreign relations of the Union, but the United States are
a nation without neighbors. Separated from the rest of
the world by the ocean, and too weak as yet to aim at the
dominion of the seas, they have no enemies, and their interests rarely come into contact with those of any other
nation of the globe. This proves that the practical operation of the government must not be judged by the theory
of its constitution. The President of the United States
possesses almost royal prerogatives, which he has no opportunity of exercising, and the privileges which he can at

fluence of the executive government, through the number of places at its
disposal, has become excessive, and imperils both the moral character and the
stability of our republican institutions. — AM. ED.]

present use are very circumscribed. The laws allow him to be strong, but circumstances keep him weak.

On the other hand, the great strength of the royal prerogative in France arises from circumstances far more than from the laws. There the executive government is constantly struggling against immense obstacles, and has immense resources in order to overcome them; so that it is enlarged by the extent of its achievements, and by the importance of the events it controls, without modifying its constitution. If the laws had made it as feeble and as circumscribed as that of the American Union, its influence would soon become still more preponderant.

WHY THE PRESIDENT OF THE UNITED STATES DOES NOT NEED A MAJORITY IN THE TWO HOUSES IN ORDER TO CARRY ON THE GOVERNMENT.

It is an established axiom in Europe, that a constitutional king cannot govern when opposed by the two branches of the legislature. But several Presidents of the United States have been known to lose the majority in the legislative body, without being obliged to abandon the supreme power, and without inflicting any serious evil upon society. I have heard this fact quoted to prove the independence and the power of the executive government in America: a moment's reflection will convince us, on the contrary, that it is a proof of its weakness.

A king in Europe requires the support of the legislature to enable him to perform the duties imposed upon him by the constitution, because those duties are enormous. A constitutional king in Europe is not merely the executor of the law, but the execution of its provisions devolves so completely upon him, that he has the power of paralyzing its force if it opposes his designs. He requires the assistance of the legislative assemblies to make the law, but those

assemblies need his aid to execute it. These two authorities cannot subsist without each other, and the mechanism of government is stopped as soon as they are at
variance.

In America, the President cannot prevent any law from
being passed, nor can he evade the obligation of enforcing
it. His sincere and zealous co-operation is no doubt useful,
but is not indispensable, in carrying on public affairs. In
all his important acts, he is directly or indirectly subject to
the legislature; and of his own free authority, he can do
but little. It is therefore his weakness, and not his power,
which enables him to remain in opposition to Congress. In
Europe, harmony must reign between the crown and the
legislature, because a collision between them may prove
serious; in America, this harmony is not indispensable,
because such a collision is impossible.

ELECTION OF THE PRESIDENT.

The Dangers of the Elective System increase in Proportion to the Extent
of the Prerogative. — This System possible in America, because no
powerful Executive Authority is required. — How Circumstances favor
the Establishment of the Elective System. — Why the Election of the
President does not change the Principles of the Government. — Influence of the Election of the President on Secondary Functionaries.

THE dangers of the system of election, applied to the
chief of the executive government of a great people, have
been sufficiently exemplified by experience and by history. I wish to speak of them in reference to America
alone.

These dangers may be more or less formidable in proportion to the place which the executive power occupies,
and to the importance it possesses in the state; and they
may vary according to the mode of election, and the cir-

cumstances in which the electors are placed. The most
weighty argument against the election of a chief magistrate
is, that it offers so splendid a lure to private ambition, and
is so apt to inflame men in the pursuit of power, that, when
legitimate means are wanting, force may not unfrequently
seize what right denied. It is clear that, the greater the
prerogatives of executive authority are, the greater is the
temptation; the more the ambition of the candidates is excited, the more warmly are their interests espoused by a
throng of partisans, who hope to share the power when
their patron has won the prize. The dangers of the elective system increase, therefore, in the exact ratio of the
influence exercised by the executive power in the affairs of
the state. The revolutions of Poland are not solely attributable to the elective system in general, but to the fact
that the elected monarch was the sovereign of a powerful
kingdom.

Before we can discuss the absolute advantages of the
elective system, we must make preliminary inquiries as to
whether the geographical position, the laws, the habits, the
manners, and the opinions of the people, amongst whom it
is to be introduced, will admit of the establishment of a
weak and dependent executive government; for to attempt
to render the representative of the state a powerful sovereign, and at the same time elective, is, in my opinion, to
entertain two incompatible designs. To reduce hereditary
royalty to the condition of an elective authority, the only
means that I am acquainted with are to circumscribe its
sphere of action beforehand, gradually to diminish its prerogatives, and to accustom the people by degrees to live
without its protection. But this is what the republicans
of Europe never think of doing: as many of them hate
tyranny only because they are exposed to its severity, it is
oppression, and not the extent of the executive power,
which excites their hostility; and they attack the former,

without perceiving how nearly it is connected with the latter.

Hitherto, no citizen has cared to expose his honor and his life in order to become the President of the United States, because the power of that office is temporary, limited, and subordinate. The prize of fortune must be great to encourage adventurers in so desperate a game. No candidate has as yet been able to arouse the dangerous enthusiasm or the passionate sympathies of the people in his favor, for the simple reason that, when he is at the head of the government, he has but little power, little wealth, and little glory to share amongst his friends; and his influence in the state is too small for the success or the ruin of a faction to depend upon his elevation to power.

The great advantage of hereditary monarchies is, that, as the private interest of a family is always intimately connected with the interests of the state, these state interests are never neglected for a moment; and if the affairs of a monarchy are not better conducted than those of a republic, at least there is always some one to conduct them, well or ill, according to his capacity. In elective states, on the contrary, the wheels of government cease to act, as it were, of their own accord, at the approach of an election, and even for some time previous to that event. The laws may, indeed, accelerate the operation of the election, which may be conducted with such simplicity and rapidity that the seat of power will never be left vacant; but, notwithstanding these precautions, a break necessarily occurs in the minds of the people.

At the approach of an election, the head of the executive government thinks only of the struggle which is coming on; he no longer has anything to look forward to; he can undertake nothing new, and he will only prosecute with indifference those designs which another will perhaps terminate. " I am so near the time of my retirement from

office," said President Jefferson, on the 21st of January,
1809, (six weeks before the election,*) " that I feel no
passion, I take no part, I express no sentiment.   It appears
to me just to leave to my successor the commencement of
those measures which he will have to prosecute, and for
which he will be responsible."   On the other hand, the
eyes of the nation are centred on a single point ; all are
watching the gradual birth of so important an event.

The wider the influence of the executive power extends,
the greater and the more necessary is its constant action,
the more fatal is the term of suspense ; and a nation
which is accustomed to the government, or, still more,
one used to the administration of a powerful executive
authority, would be infallibly convulsed by an election.
In the United States, the action of the government may
be slackened with impunity, because it is always weak and
circumscribed.

One of the principal vices of the elective system is, that
it always introduces a certain degree of instability into the
internal and external policy of the state.   But this disadvantage is less sensibly felt if the share of power vested in
the elected magistrate is small.   In Rome, the principles
of the government underwent no variation, although the
Consuls were changed every year, because the Senate,
which was an hereditary assembly, possessed the directing
authority.   In most of the European monarchies, if the
king were elective, the kingdom would be revolutionized
at every new election.   In America, the President exercises
a certain influence on state affairs, but he does not conduct

---

* De Tocqueville is in error here.   The election was really determined
three months before, in November, 1808 ; and Jefferson, writing six weeks
before his successor, already chosen, *was to come into office,* merely expresses
his intention to leave Mr. Madison to initiate his own policy, instead of embarrassing him by leaving projects or measures begun, but not completed.
— AM. ED.

them; the preponderating power is vested in the representatives of the whole nation. The political maxims of the country depend, therefore, on the mass of the people, not on the President alone; and consequently, in America, the elective system has no very prejudicial influence on the fixity of the government. But the want of fixed principles is an evil so inherent in the elective system, that it is still very perceptible in the narrow sphere to which the authority of the President extends.

The Americans have admitted that the head of the executive power, in order to discharge his duty and bear the whole weight of responsibility, ought to be free to choose his own agents, and to remove them at pleasure: the legislative bodies watch the conduct of the President more than they direct it. The consequence is, that, at every new election, the fate of all the Federal public officers is in suspense. It is sometimes made a subject of complaint, that, in the constitutional monarchies of Europe, the fate of the humbler servants of an administration often depends upon that of the ministers. But in elective governments this evil is far greater; and the reason of it is very obvious. In a constitutional monarchy, successive ministries are rapidly formed; but as the principal representative of the executive power is never changed, the spirit of innovation is kept within bounds; the changes which take place are in the details, rather than in the principles, of the administrative system: but to substitute one system for another, as is done in America every four years by law, is to cause a sort of revolution. As to the misfortunes which may fall upon individuals in consequence of this state of things, it must be allowed that the uncertain tenure of the public offices does not produce the evil consequences in America which might be expected from it elsewhere. It is so easy to acquire an independent position in the United States, that the public officer who loses his place may be deprived of the comforts of life, but not of the means of subsistence.

I remarked at the beginning of this chapter, that the dangers of the elective system, applied to the head of the state, are augmented or decreased by the peculiar circumstances of the people which adopts it. However the functions of the executive power may be restricted, it must always exercise a great influence upon the foreign policy of the country; for a negotiation cannot be opened, or successfully carried on, otherwise than by a single agent. The more precarious and the more perilous the position of a people becomes, the more absolute is the want of a fixed and consistent external policy, and the more dangerous does the system of electing the chief magistrate become. The policy of the Americans in relation to the whole world is exceedingly simple; and it may almost be said that nobody stands in need of them, nor do they stand in need of anybody. Their independence is never threatened. In their present condition, therefore, the functions of the executive power are no less limited by circumstances than by the laws; and the President may frequently change his policy, without involving the state in difficulty or destruction.

Whatever the prerogatives of the executive power may be, the period which immediately precedes an election, and that during which the election is taking place, must always be considered as a national crisis, which is perilous in proportion to the internal embarrassments and the external dangers of the country. Few of the nations of Europe could escape the calamities of anarchy or of conquest every time they might have to elect a new sovereign. In America, society is so constituted that it can stand without assistance, upon its own basis; nothing is to be feared from the pressure of external dangers; and the election of the President is a cause of agitation, but not of ruin.

MODE OF ELECTION.

Skill of the American Legislators shown in the Mode of Election adopted by them. — Creation of a special Electoral Body. — Separate Votes of these Electors. — Case in which the House of Representatives is called upon to choose the President. — Results of the twelve Elections which have taken place since the Constitution has been established.

BESIDES the dangers which are inherent in the system, many others may arise from the mode of election; but these may be obviated by the precautions of the legislator. When a people met in arms, on some public spot, to choose its head, it was exposed to all the chances of civil war resulting from such a mode of proceeding, besides the dangers of the elective system in itself. The Polish laws, which subjected the election of the sovereign to the veto of a single individual, suggested the murder of that individual, or prepared the way for anarchy.

In the examination of the institutions, and the political as well as social condition of the United States, we are struck by the admirable harmony of the gifts of fortune and the efforts of man. That nation possessed two of the main causes of internal peace; it was a new country, but it was inhabited by a people grown old in the exercise of freedom. Besides, America had no hostile neighbors to dread; and the American legislators, profiting by these favorable circumstances, created a weak and subordinate executive power, which could without danger be made elective.

It then only remained for them to choose the least dangerous of the various modes of election; and the rules which they laid down upon this point admirably correspond to the securities which the physical and political constitution of the country already afforded. Their object was to find the mode of election which would best express the choice of the people with the least possible excitement and suspense. It was admitted, in the first place, that the simple majority should decide the point; but the difficulty was, to obtain this majority without an interval of delay, which it was most important to avoid. It rarely happens that an individual can receive at the first trial a majority of the suffrages of a great people; and this difficulty is enhanced in a republic of confederate states, where local influences are far more developed and more powerful. The means by which it was proposed to obviate this second obstacle was, to delegate the electoral powers of the nation to a body which should represent it. This mode of election rendered a majority more probable; for the fewer the electors are, the greater is the chance of their coming to an agreement. It also offered an additional probability of a judicious choice. It then remained to be decided whether this right of election was to be intrusted to the legislature itself, the ordinary representative of the nation, or whether a special electoral college should be formed for the sole purpose of choosing a President. The Americans chose the latter alternative, from a belief that those who were chosen only to make the laws would represent but imperfectly the wishes of the nation in the election of its chief magistrate; and that, as they are chosen for more than a year, the constituency they represented might have changed its opinion in that time. It was thought that, if the legislature was empowered to elect the head of the executive power, its members would, for some time before the election, be exposed to the manœuvres of corruption and the tricks of intrigue; whereas the special electors would, like a jury, remain mixed up with the crowd till the day of action, when they would appear for a moment only to give their votes.

It was therefore determined that every State should name a certain number of Electors,* who in their turn

* As many as it sends members to Congress. The number of Electors at the election of 1833 was 288.

should elect the President; and as it had been observed, that the assemblies to which the choice of a chief magistrate had been intrusted in elective countries inevitably became the centres of passion and cabal; that they sometimes usurped powers which did not belong to them; and that their proceedings, or the uncertainty which resulted from them, were sometimes prolonged so much as to endanger the welfare of the state, — it was determined that the Electors should all vote upon the same day, without being convoked to the same place.* This double election rendered a majority probable, though not certain; for it was possible that the Electors might not, any more than their constituents, come to an agreement. In this case, it would be necessary to have recourse to one of three measures; either to appoint new Electors, or to consult a second time those already appointed, or to give the election to another authority. The first two of these alternatives, independently of the uncertainty of their results, were likely to delay the final decision, and to perpetuate an agitation which must always be accompanied with danger. The third expedient was therefore adopted, and it was agreed that the votes should be transmitted, sealed, to the President of the Senate, and that they should be opened and counted on an appointed day, in the presence of the Senate and the House of Representatives. If none of the candidates has received a majority, the House of Representatives then proceeds immediately to elect the President; but with the condition that it must fix upon one of the three candidates who have the highest number of votes in the Electoral College.†

---

* The Electors of the same State assemble, but they transmit to the central government the list of their individual votes, and not the mere result of the vote of the majority.

† In this case, it is the majority of the States, and not the majority of the members, which decides the question; so that New York has not more influence in the debate than Rhode Island. Thus the citizens of the Union are first consulted as members of one and the same community; and, if they

Thus, it is only in case of an event which cannot often happen, and which can never be foreseen, that the election is intrusted to the ordinary Representatives of the nation; and even then, they are obliged to choose a citizen who has already been designated by a powerful minority of the special Electors. It is by this happy expedient that the respect which is due to the popular voice is combined with the utmost celerity of execution, and with those precautions which the interests of the country demand. But the decision of the question by the House of Representatives does not necessarily offer an immediate solution of the difficulty; for the majority of that assembly may still be doubtful, and in this case the Constitution prescribes no remedy. Nevertheless, by restricting the number of candidates to three, and by referring the matter to the judgment of an enlightened public body, it has smoothed all the obstacles * which are not inherent in the elective system itself.

In the forty-four years which have elapsed since the promulgation of the Federal Constitution, the United States have twelve times chosen a President. Ten of these elections took place at once by the simultaneous votes of the special Electors in the different States. The House of Representatives has only twice exercised its conditional privilege of deciding in cases of uncertainty: the first time was at the election of Mr. Jefferson in 1801; the second was in 1825, when Mr. J. Quincy Adams was named.†

cannot agree, recourse is had to the division of the States, each of which has a separate and independent vote. This is one of the singularities of the Federal Constitution, which can be explained only by the jar of conflicting interests.

* Jefferson, in 1801, was not elected until the thirty-sixth time of balloting.

† Seventy-two years having now elapsed, there have been nineteen Presidential elections, and still the House of Representatives has been required to act in the election only twice. — AM. ED.

CRISIS OF THE ELECTION.

The Election may be considered as a Moment of National Crisis. — Why. — Passions of the People. — Anxiety of the President. — Calm which succeeds the Agitation of the Election.

I HAVE shown what the circumstances are which favored the adoption of the elective system in the United States, and what precautions were taken by the legislators to obviate its dangers. The Americans are accustomed to all kinds of elections; and they knew by experience the utmost degree of excitement which is compatible with security. The vast extent of the country and the dissemination of the inhabitants render a collision between parties less probable and less dangerous there than elsewhere. The political circumstances under which the elections have been carried on have not, as yet, caused any real danger. Still, the epoch of the election of the President of the United States may be considered as a crisis in the affairs of the nation.

The influence which the President exercises on public business is no doubt feeble and indirect; but the choice of the President, though of small importance to each individual citizen, concerns the citizens collectively; and however trifling an interest may be, it assumes a great degree of importance as soon as it becomes general. The President possesses, in comparison with the kings of Europe, but few means of creating partisans; but the places which are at his disposal are sufficiently numerous to interest, directly or indirectly, several thousand electors in his success.* Moreover, political parties in the United States are led to rally round an individual in order to acquire a more tangi-

* Owing to the increase of patronage already referred to as necessarily produced by the vast increase of the population, this influence has now become excessive, and very dangerous. — AM. ED.

ble shape in the eyes of the crowd; and the name of the candidate for the Presidency is put forward as the symbol and personification of their theories. For these reasons, parties are strongly interested in gaining the election, not so much with a view to the triumph of their principles under the auspices of the President elect, as to show, by his election, that the supporters of those principles now form the majority.

For a long while before the appointed time is come, the election becomes the important, and (so to speak) the all-engrossing, topic of discussion. The ardor of faction is redoubled; and all the artificial passions which the imagination can create in a happy and peaceful land are agitated and brought to light. The President, moreover, is absorbed by the cares of self-defence. He no longer governs for the interest of the state, but for that of his re-election; he does homage to the majority, and instead of checking its passions, as his duty commands, he frequently courts its worst caprices. As the election draws near, the activity of intrigue and the agitation of the populace increase; the citizens are divided into hostile camps, each of which assumes the name of its favorite candidate; the whole nation glows with feverish excitement; the election is the daily theme of the public papers, the subject of private conversation, the end of every thought and every action, the sole interest of the present. It is true, that, as soon as the choice is determined, this ardor is dispelled; the calm returns; and the river, which had nearly broken its banks, sinks to its usual level: but who can refrain from astonishment that such a storm should have arisen?

RE-ELECTION OF THE PRESIDENT.

When the Head of the Executive Power is re-eligible, it is the State which
is the Source of Intrigue and Corruption. — The Desire of being re-
elected is the chief Aim of a President of the United States. — Disadvantage of the Re-election peculiar to America. — The Natural Evil of
Democracy is, that it gradually subordinates all Authority to the slightest Desires of the Majority. — The Re-election of the President encourages this Evil.

Were the legislators of the United States right or wrong
in allowing the re-election of the President? It seems, at
first sight, contrary to all reason, to prevent the head of
the executive power from being elected a second time.
The influence which the talents and the character of a
single individual may exercise upon the fate of a whole
people, especially in critical circumstances or arduous
times, is well known. A law preventing the re-election
of the chief magistrate would deprive the citizens of their
best means of insuring the prosperity and the security of
the commonwealth; and, by a singular inconsistency, a
man would be excluded from the government at the very
time when he had proved his ability to govern well.

But if these arguments are strong, perhaps still more
powerful reasons may be advanced against them. Intrigue
and corruption are the natural vices of elective government; but when the head of the state can be re-elected,
these evils rise to a great height, and compromise the very
existence of the country. When a simple candidate seeks
to rise by intrigue, his manœuvres must be limited to a
very narrow sphere; but when the chief magistrate enters
the lists, he borrows the strength of the government for
his own purposes. In the former case, the feeble resources
of an individual are in action; in the latter, the state
itself, with its immense influence, is busied in the work of
corruption and cabal. The private citizen, who employs

culpable practices to acquire power, can act in a manner
only indirectly prejudicial to the public prosperity. But if
the representative of the executive descends into the combat, the cares of government dwindle for him into second-
rate importance, and the success of his election is his first
concern. All public negotiations, as well as all laws, are to
him nothing more than electioneering schemes; places
become the reward of services rendered, not to the nation,
but to its chief; and the influence of the government, if
not injurious to the country, is at least no longer beneficial
to the community for which it was created.

It is impossible to consider the ordinary course of affairs
in the United States without perceiving that the desire of
being re-elected is the chief aim of the President; that the
whole policy of his administration, and even his most indifferent measures, tend to this object; and that, especially
as the crisis approaches, his personal interest takes the
place of his interest in the public good. The principle of
re-eligibility renders the corrupting influence of elective
governments still more extensive and pernicious. It tends
to degrade the political morality of the people, and to substitute management and intrigue for patriotism.

In America, it injures still more directly the very sources
of national existence. Every government seems to be
afflicted by some evil which is inherent in its nature, and
the genius of the legislator consists in having a clear view
of this evil. A state may survive the influence of a host
of bad laws, and the mischief they cause is frequently exaggerated; but a law which encourages the growth of the
canker within must prove fatal in the end, although its
bad consequences may not be immediately perceived.

The principle of destruction in absolute monarchies lies
in the unlimited and unreasonable extension of the royal
power; and a measure tending to remove the constitutional
provisions which counterbalance this influence would be

radically bad, even if its immediate consequences were unattended with evil.   By parity of reasoning, in countries governed by a democracy, where the people is perpetually drawing all authority to itself, the laws which increase or accelerate this action directly attack the very principle of the government.

The greatest merit of the American legislators is, that they clearly discerned this truth, and had the courage to act up to it.   They conceived that a certain authority above the body of the people was necessary, which should enjoy a degree of independence in its sphere, without being entirely beyond the popular control; an authority which would be forced to comply with the *permanent* determinations of the majority, but which would be able to resist its caprices, and refuse its most dangerous demands.   To this end, they centred the whole executive power of the nation in a single arm; they granted extensive prerogatives to the President, and armed him with the veto to resist the encroachments of the legislature.

But by introducing the principle of re-election, they partly destroyed their work; they conferred on the President a great power, but made him little inclined to use it. If ineligible a second time, the President would not be independent of the people, for his responsibility would not cease; but the favor of the people would not be so necessary to him as to induce him to submit in every respect to its desires.   If re-eligible, (and this is especially true at the present day, when political morality is relaxed, and when great men are rare,) the President of the United States becomes an easy tool in the hands of the majority. He adopts its likings and its animosities, he anticipates its wishes, he forestalls its complaints, he yields to its idlest cravings, and instead of guiding it, as the legislature intended that he should do, he merely follows its bidding. Thus, in order not to deprive the state of the talents of an individual, those talents have been rendered almost useless; and to keep an expedient for extraordinary perils, the country has been exposed to continual dangers.

FEDERAL COURTS OF JUSTICE.*

Political Importance of the Judiciary in the United States. — Difficulty of treating this Subject. — Utility of Judicial Power in Confederations. — What Tribunals could be introduced into the Union. — Necessity of establishing Federal Courts of Justice. — Organization of the National Judiciary. — The Supreme Court. — In what it differs from all known Tribunals.

I HAVE examined the legislative and executive power of the Union, and the judicial power now remains to be considered; but here I cannot conceal my fears from the reader. Their judicial institutions exercise a great influence on the condition of the Anglo-Americans, and they occupy a very important place amongst political institutions, properly so called: in this respect, they are peculiarly deserving of our attention. But I am at a loss how to explain the political action of the American tribunals without entering into some technical details respecting their constitution and their forms of proceeding; and I cannot descend to these minutiæ without wearying the reader by the natural dryness of the subject, or falling into obscurity through a desire to be succinct. I can scarcely hope to escape these different evils. Ordinary readers will complain that I am tedious, lawyers that I am too concise. But these are the natural disadvantages of my subject, and especially of the point which I am now to discuss.

The great difficulty was, not to know how to constitute the Federal government, but to find out a method of enforcing its laws. Governments have generally but two

* See Chapter VI., entitled "Judicial Power in the United States." This chapter explains the general principles of the American judiciary.

means of overcoming the opposition of the governed ; namely, the physical force which is at their own disposal, and the moral force which they derive from the decisions of the courts of justice.

A government which should have no other means of exacting obedience than open war, must be very near its ruin, for one of two things would then probably happen to it. If it was weak and temperate, it would resort to violence only at the last extremity, and would connive at many partial acts of insubordination ; then the state would gradually fall into anarchy. If it was enterprising and powerful, it would every day have recourse to physical strength, and thus would soon fall into a military despotism. Thus its activity and its inertness would be equally prejudicial to the community.

The great end of justice is, to substitute the notion of right for that of violence, and to place a legal barrier between the government and the use of physical force. It is a strange thing, the authority which is accorded to the intervention of a court of justice by the general opinion of mankind! It clings even to the mere formalities of justice, and gives a bodily influence to the mere shadow of the law. The moral force which courts of justice possess renders the use of physical force very rare, and is frequently substituted for it ; but if force proves to be indispensable, its power is doubled by the association of the idea of law.

A federal government stands in greater need than any other of the support of judicial institutions, because it is naturally weak, and exposed to formidable opposition.* If

---

* Federal laws are those which most require courts of justice, and those, at the same time, which have most rarely established them. The reason is, that confederations have usually been formed by independent states, which had no real intention of obeying the central government ; and though they readily ceded the right of command to the central government, they carefully reserved the right of non-compliance to themselves.

it were always obliged to resort to violence in the first instance, it could not fulfil its task. The Union, therefore,
stood in special need of a judiciary to make its citizens
obey the laws, and to repel the attacks which might be
directed against them. But what tribunals were to exercise these privileges ? Were they to be intrusted to the
courts of justice which were already organized in every
State ? Or was it necessary to create Federal courts ? It
may easily be proved that the Union could not adapt to its
wants the judicial power of the States. The separation of
the judiciary from the other powers of the state is necessary for the security of each, and the liberty of all. But
it is no less important to the existence of the nation,
that the several powers of the state should have the same
origin, follow the same principles, and act in the same
sphere ; in a word, that they should be correlative and homogeneous. No one, I presume, ever thought of causing
offences committed in France to be tried by a foreign court
of justice, in order to insure the impartiality of the judges.
The Americans form but one people in relation to their
Federal government ; but in the bosom of this people divers political bodies have been allowed to subsist, which
are dependent on the national government in a few points,
and independent in all the rest, — which have all a distinct
origin, maxims peculiar to themselves, and special means
of carrying on their affairs. To intrust the execution of
the laws of the Union to tribunals instituted by these
political bodies, would be to allow foreign judges to preside
over the nation. Nay, more ; not only is each State foreign to the Union at large, but it is a perpetual adversary,
since whatever authority the Union loses turns to the advantage of the States. Thus, to enforce the laws of the
Union by means of the State tribunals would be to allow
not only foreign, but partial, judges to preside over the
nation.

But the number, still more than the mere character, of the State tribunals, made them unfit for the service of the nation. When the Federal Constitution was formed, there were already thirteen courts of justice in the United States, which decided causes without appeal. That number is now increased to twenty-four [thirty-four]. To suppose that a state can subsist, when its fundamental laws are subjected to four-and-twenty different interpretations at the same time, is to advance a proposition alike contrary to reason and to experience.

The American legislators therefore agreed to create a Federal judicial power to apply the laws of the Union, and to determine certain questions affecting general interests, which were carefully defined beforehand. The entire judicial power of the Union was centred in one tribunal, called the Supreme Court of the United States. But, to facilitate the expedition of business, inferior courts were appended to it, which were empowered to decide causes of small importance without appeal, and, with appeal, causes of more magnitude. The members of the Supreme Court are appointed neither by the people nor the legislature, but by the President of the United States, acting with the advice of the Senate. In order to render them independent of the other authorities, their office was made inalienable; and it was determined that their salary, when once fixed, should not be diminished by the legislature.* It was easy to proclaim the principle of a Federal judiciary, but difficulties multiplied when the extent of its jurisdiction was to be determined.

* The Union was divided into districts, in each of which a resident Federal judge was appointed, and the court in which he presided was termed a "District Court." Each of the judges of the Supreme Court annually visits a certain portion of the country, in order to try the most important causes upon the spot: the court presided over by this magistrate is styled a "Circuit Court." Lastly, all the most serious cases of litigation are brought, either primarily or by appeal, before the Supreme Court, which holds a

MEANS OF DETERMINING THE JURISDICTION OF THE FEDERAL COURTS.

Difficulty of determining the Jurisdiction of the different Courts of Justice in Confederations. — The Courts of the Union obtained the Right of fixing their own Jurisdiction. — In what respects this Rule attacks the Portion of Sovereignty reserved to the several States. — The Sovereignty of these States restricted by the Laws and by the Interpretation of the Laws. — Danger thus incurred by the several States more apparent than real.

As the constitution of the United States recognized two distinct sovereignties, in presence of each other, represented in a judicial point of view by two distinct classes of courts of justice, the utmost care taken in defining their separate jurisdictions would have been insufficient to prevent frequent collisions between those tribunals. The question then arose, to whom the right of deciding the competency of each court was to be referred.

In nations which constitute a single body politic, when a question of jurisdiction is debated between two courts, a third tribunal is generally within reach to decide the difference; and this is effected without difficulty, because, in these nations, questions of judicial competency have no connection with questions of national sovereignty. But it was impossible to create an arbiter between a superior court of the Union and the superior court of a separate State, which would not belong to one of these two classes. It was therefore necessary to allow one of these courts to

solemn session once a year, at which all the judges of the Circuit Courts must attend. The jury was introduced into the Federal courts, in the same manner, and for the same cases, as into the courts of the States.

It will be observed that no analogy exists between the Supreme Court of the United States and the French *Cour de Cassation*, since the latter only hears appeals. The Supreme Court judges of the fact, as well as the law, of the case; the *Cour de Cassation* does not pronounce a decision of its own, but refers the cause to another tribunal.

judge its own cause, and to take or to retain cognizance of the point which was contested.   To grant this privilege to the different courts of the States would have been to destroy the sovereignty of the Union *de facto*, after having established it *de jure;* for the interpretation of the Constitution would soon have restored to the States that portion of independence of which the terms of the Constitution deprived them.   The object of creating a Federal tribunal was to prevent the State courts from deciding, each after its own fashion, questions affecting the national interests, and so to form a uniform body of jurisprudence for the interpretation of the laws of the Union.   This end would not have been attained if the courts of the several States, even while they abstained from deciding cases avowedly Federal in their nature, had been able to decide them by pretending that they were not Federal.   The Supreme Court of the United States was therefore invested with the right of determining all questions of jurisdiction.*

This was a severe blow to the sovereignty of the States, which was thus restricted not only by the laws, but by the interpretation of them, — by one limit which was known, and by another which was dubious, — by a rule which was certain, and one which was arbitrary.   It is true, the Constitution had laid down the precise limits of the Federal supremacy; but whenever this supremacy is contested by one of the States, a Federal tribunal decides the question. Nevertheless, the dangers with which the independence of the States is threatened by this mode of proceeding are less serious than they appear to be.   We shall see hereafter,

---

* In order to diminish the number of these suits, however, it was decided that, in a great many Federal causes, the courts of the States should be empowered to decide conjointly with those of the Union, the losing party having then a right of appeal to the Supreme Court of the United States.   The Supreme Court of Virginia contested the right of the Supreme Court of the United States to judge an appeal from its decisions, but unsuccessfully.   See Kent's Commentaries, Vol. I. pp. 300, 370, *et seq.*

that, in America, the real power is vested in the States far more than in the Federal government. The Federal judges are conscious of the relative weakness of the power in whose name they act; and they are more inclined to abandon the right of jurisdiction, in cases where the law gives it to them, than to assert a privilege to which they have no legal claim.

DIFFERENT CASES OF JURISDICTION.

The Matter and the Party are the First Conditions of the Federal Jurisdiction. — Suits in which Ambassadors are engaged. — Or the Union. — Or a separate State. — By whom tried. — Causes resulting from the Laws of the Union. — Why judged by the Federal Tribunals. — Causes relating to the Non-performance of Contracts tried by the Federal Courts. — Consequences of this Arrangement.

AFTER establishing the competency of the Federal courts, the legislators of the Union defined the cases which should come within their jurisdiction. It was determined, on the one hand, that certain parties must always be brought before the Federal courts, without regard to the special nature of the suit; and, on the other, that certain causes must always be brought before the same courts, no matter who were the parties to them. The party and the cause were therefore admitted to be the two bases of Federal jurisdiction.

Ambassadors represent nations in amity with the Union, and whatever concerns these personages concerns in some degree the whole Union. When an ambassador, therefore, is a party in a suit, its issue affects the welfare of the nation, and a Federal tribunal is naturally called upon to decide it.

The Union itself may be involved in legal proceedings, and, in this case, it would be contrary to reason and to the customs of all nations to appeal to a tribunal representing any other sovereignty than its own: the Federal courts alone, therefore, take cognizance of these affairs.

When two parties belonging to two different States are engaged in a suit, the case cannot with propriety be brought before a court of either State. The surest expedient is to select a tribunal which can excite the suspicions of neither party, and this is naturally a Federal court.

When the two parties are not private individuals, but States, an important political motive is added to the same consideration of equity. The quality of the parties, in this case, gives a national importance to all their disputes; and the most trifling litigation between two States may be said to involve the peace of the whole Union.*

The nature of the cause frequently prescribes the rule of competency. Thus, all questions which concern maritime affairs evidently fall under the cognizance of the Federal tribunals.† Almost all these questions depend on the interpretation of the law of nations; and, in this respect, they essentially interest the Union in relation to foreign powers. Moreover, as the sea is not included within the limits of any one State jurisdiction rather than another, only the national courts can hear causes which originate in maritime affairs.

The Constitution comprises under one head almost all the cases which, by their very nature, come before the

---

* The Constitution also says that the Federal courts shall decide "controversies between a State and the citizens of another State." And here a most important question arose, — whether the jurisdiction given by the Constitution, in cases in which a State is a party, extended to suits brought *against* a State as well as *by* it, or was exclusively confined to the latter. The question was most elaborately considered in the case of *Chisholm* v. *Georgin*, and was decided by the majority of the Supreme Court in the affirmative. The decision created general alarm among the States, and an amendment was proposed and ratified, by which the power was entirely taken away so far as it regards suits brought *against* a State.

† As, for instance, all cases of piracy.

Federal courts. The rule which it lays down is simple, but pregnant with an entire system of ideas, and with a multitude of facts. It declares that the judicial power of the Supreme Court shall extend to all cases in law and equity *arising under the laws of the United States.*

Two examples will put the intention of the legislator in the clearest light.

The Constitution prohibits the States from making laws on the value and circulation of money. If, notwithstanding this prohibition, a State passes a law of this kind, with which the interested parties refuse to comply because it is contrary to the Constitution, the case must come before a Federal court, because it arises under the laws of the United States. Again, if difficulties arise in the levying of import duties which have been voted by Congress, the Federal court must decide the case, because it arises under the interpretation of a law of the United States.

This rule is in perfect accordance with the fundamental principles of the Federal Constitution. The Union, as it was established in 1789, possesses, it is true, a limited sovereignty; but it was intended that, within its limits, it should form one and the same people.* Within those limits, the Union is sovereign. When this point is established and admitted, the inference is easy; for if it be acknowledged that the United States, within the bounds prescribed by their Constitution, constitute but one people, it is impossible to refuse them the rights which belong to other nations. But it has been allowed, from the origin of society, that every nation has the right of deciding by its own courts those questions which concern the execution

---

* This principle was, in some measure, restricted by the introduction of the several States as independent powers into the Senate, and by allowing them to vote separately in the House of Representatives when the President is elected by that body. But these are exceptions, and the contrary principle is the rule.

of its own laws. To this it is answered, that the Union is in so singular a position, that, in relation to some matters, it constitutes but one people, and in relation to all the rest, it is a nonentity. But the inference to be drawn is, that, in the laws relating to these matters, the Union possesses all the rights of absolute sovereignty. The difficulty is to know what these matters are; and when once it is resolved, (and we have shown how it was resolved, in speaking of the means of determining the jurisdiction of the Federal courts,) no further doubt can arise; for as soon as it is established that a suit is Federal, that is to say, that it belongs to the share of sovereignty reserved by the Constitution to the Union, the natural consequence is, that it should come within the jurisdiction of a Federal court.

Whenever the laws of the United States are attacked, or whenever they are resorted to in self-defence, the Federal courts must be appealed to. Thus the jurisdiction of the tribunals of the Union extends and narrows its limits exactly in the same ratio as the sovereignty of the Union augments or decreases. We have shown that the principal aim of the legislators of 1789 was to divide the sovereign authority into two parts. In the one, they placed the control of all the general interests of the Union, in the other, the control of the special interests of its component States. Their chief solicitude was, to arm the Federal government with sufficient power to enable it to resist, within its sphere, the encroachments of the several States. As for these communities, the general principle of independence within certain limits of their own was adopted in their behalf; there the central government cannot control, nor even inspect, their conduct. In speaking of the division of authority, I observed that this latter principle had not always been respected, since the States are prevented from passing certain laws, which apparently belong to their own particular sphere of interest. When a State of the Union passes a law of this kind, the citizens who are injured by its execution can appeal to the Federal courts.

Thus the jurisdiction of the Federal courts extends, not only to all the cases which arise under the laws of the Union, but also to those which arise under laws made by the several States in opposition to the Constitution. The States are prohibited from making *ex-post-facto* laws in criminal cases; and any person condemned by virtue of a law of this kind, can appeal to the judicial power of the Union. The States are likewise prohibited from making laws which may impair the obligation of contracts.* If a citizen thinks that an obligation of this kind is impaired by a law passed in his State, he may refuse to obey it, and may appeal to the Federal courts.†

* It is perfectly clear, says Mr. Story, (Commentaries, p. 503, or in the large edition § 1379,) that any law which enlarges, abridges, or in any manner changes the intention of the parties, resulting from the stipulations in the contract, necessarily impairs it. He gives in the same place a very careful definition of what is understood by a contract in Federal jurisprudence. The definition is very broad. A grant made by the State to a private individual, and accepted by him, is a contract, and cannot be revoked by any future law. A charter granted by the State to a company is a contract, and equally binding on the State as on the grantee. The clause of the Constitution here referred to insures, therefore, the existence of a great part of acquired rights, but not of all. Property may legally be held, though it may not have passed into the possessor's hands by means of a contract; and its possession is an acquired right, not guaranteed by the Federal Constitution.

† A remarkable instance of this is given by Mr. Story (p. 508, or in the large edition § 1388). "Dartmouth College in New Hampshire had been founded by a charter granted to certain individuals before the American Revolution, and its trustees formed a corporation under this charter. The legislature of New Hampshire had, without the consent of this corporation, passed an act changing the terms of the original charter of the College, and transferring all the rights, privileges, and franchises derived from the old charter to new trustees appointed under the act. The constitutionality of the act was contested, and the cause was carried up to the Supreme (Federal) Court, where it was held, that the Provincial charter was a contract within the meaning of the Constitution, and that the amendatory act was utterly void, as impairing the obligation of that charter."

This provision appears to me to be the most serious attack upon the independence of the States. The rights accorded to the Federal government for purposes obviously national are definite and easily understood : but those with which this clause invests it are neither clearly appreciable nor accurately defined. For there are many political laws which affect the existence of contracts, which might thus furnish a pretext for the encroachments of the central authority.*

* The apprehensions expressed in this paragraph seem to be unfounded. The object of the clause in the Constitution respecting contracts is not so much to strengthen the Federal government as to protect private individuals against harmful and unjust State legislation. It does not limit the power of the States, except by prohibiting them from committing positive wrong. They can still legislate upon the subject of *future* contracts ; they can prescribe what contracts shall be formed, and how ; but they cannot impair any that are *already made.* Any law which should authorize the breach of a contract already made, or in any way impair its obligation, would be obviously unjust.

Moreover, as Mr. Spencer observes, the author is in error " in supposing the judiciary of the United States, and particularly the Supreme Court, to be a part of the *political* Federal government, and a ready instrument to execute its designs upon the State authorities. Although the judges are in form commissioned by the United States, yet they are in fact appointed by the delegates of the States, in the Senate of the United States, concurrently with and acting upon the nomination of the President. In truth, the judiciary have no political duties to perform ; they are arbiters chosen by the Federal and State governments jointly, and, when appointed, as independent of one as of the other. They cannot be removed without the consent of the States represented in the Senate ; and they can be removed without the consent of the President, and against his wishes. Such is the theory of the Constitution. And it has been felt practically, in the rejection by the Senate of persons nominated as judges by a President of the same political party with a majority of the Senators. Two instances of this kind occurred during the administration of Mr. Jefferson." — Am. Ed.

PROCEDURE OF THE FEDERAL COURTS.

Natural Weakness of the Judicial Power in Confederations. — Legislators ought, as much as possible, to bring Private Individuals, and not States, before the Federal Courts. — How the Americans have succeeded in this. —Direct Prosecution of Private Individuals in the Federal Courts. — Indirect Prosecution of the States which violate the Laws of the Union. — The Decrees of the Supreme Court enervate, but do not destroy, the State Laws.

I HAVE shown what the rights of the Federal courts are, and it is no less important to show how they are exercised. The irresistible authority of justice in countries in which the sovereignty is undivided, is derived from the fact, that the tribunals of those countries represent the entire nation at issue with the individual against whom their decree is directed; and the idea of power is thus introduced to corroborate the idea of right. But it is not always so in countries in which the sovereignty is divided; in them, the judicial power is more frequently opposed to a fraction of the nation, than to an isolated individual, and its moral authority and physical strength are consequently diminished. In Federal states, the power of the judge is naturally decreased, and that of the justiciable parties is augmented. The aim of the legislator in confederate states ought therefore to be, to render the position of the courts of justice analogous to that which they occupy in countries where the sovereignty is undivided; in other words, his efforts ought constantly to tend to maintain the judicial power of the confederation as the representative of the nation, and the justiciable party as the representative of an individual interest.

Every government, whatever may be its constitution, requires the means of constraining its subjects to discharge their obligations, and of protecting its privileges from their assaults. As far as the direct action of the government on the community is concerned, the Constitution of the United States contrived, by a master-stroke of policy, that the Federal courts, acting in the name of the laws, should take cognizance only of parties in an individual capacity. For, as it had been declared that the Union consisted of one and the same people within the limits laid down by the Constitution, the inference was that the government created by this constitution, and acting within these limits, was invested with all the privileges of a national government, one of the principal of which is the right of transmitting its injunctions directly to the private citizen. When, for instance, the Union votes an impost, it does not apply to the States for the levying of it, but to every American citizen, in proportion to his assessment. The Supreme Court, which is empowered to enforce the execution of this law of the Union, exerts its influence not upon a refractory State, but upon the private tax-payer; and, like the judicial power of other nations, it acts only upon the person of an individual. It is to be observed that the Union chose its own antagonist; and as that antagonist is feeble, he is naturally worsted.

But the difficulty increases when the proceedings are not brought forward *by*, but *against*, the Union. The Constitution recognizes the legislative power of the States; and a law enacted by that power may violate the rights of the Union. In this case, a collision is unavoidable between that body and the State which has passed the law: and it only remains to select the least dangerous remedy. The general principles which I have before established show what this remedy is.*

It may be conceived that, in the case under consideration, the Union might have sued the State before a Federal court, which would have annulled the act; this would have been the most natural proceeding. But the judicial power

---

* See Chapter VI., on Judicial Power in America.

would thus have been placed in direct opposition to the State, and it was desirable to avoid this predicament as much as possible. The Americans hold that it is nearly impossible that a new law should not injure some private interests by its provisions. These private interests are assumed by the American legislators as the means of assailing such measures as may be prejudicial to the Union, and it is to these interests that the protection of the Supreme Court is extended.

Suppose a State sells a portion of its public lands to a company, and that, a year afterwards, it passes a law by which the lands are otherwise disposed of, and that clause of the Constitution which prohibits laws impairing the obligation of contracts is thereby violated. When the purchaser under the second act appears to take possession, the possessor under the first act brings his action before the tribunals of the Union, and causes the title of the claimant to be pronounced null and void.* Thus, in point of fact, the judicial power of the Union is contesting the claims of the sovereignty of a State; but it acts only indirectly, and upon an application of detail. It attacks the law in its consequences, not in its principle, and rather weakens than destroys it.

The last case to be provided for was, that each State formed a corporation enjoying a separate existence and distinct civil rights, and that it could therefore sue or be sued before a tribunal. Thus, a State could bring an action against another State. In this instance, the Union was not called upon to contest a State law, but to try a suit in which a State was a party. This suit was perfectly similar to any other cause, except that the quality of the parties was different; and here the danger pointed out at the beginning of this chapter still exists, with less chance of being avoided. It is inherent in the very essence of Fed-

* See Kent's Commentaries, Vol. I. p. 387.

eral constitutions, that they should create parties in the bosom of the nation, which present powerful obstacles to the free course of justice.

HIGH RANK OF THE SUPREME COURT AMONGST THE GREAT POWERS OF STATE.

No Nation ever constituted so great a Judicial Power as the Americans. — Extent of its Prerogatives. — Its Political Influence. — The Tranquillity and the very Existence of the Union depend on the Discretion of the seven Federal Judges.

WHEN we have examined in detail the organization of the Supreme Court, and the entire prerogatives which it exercises, we shall readily admit that a more imposing judicial power was never constituted by any people. The Supreme Court is placed higher than any known tribunal, both by the nature of its rights and the class of justiciable parties which it controls.

In all the civilized countries of Europe, the government has always shown the greatest reluctance to allow the cases in which it was itself interested to be decided by the ordinary course of justice. This repugnance is naturally greater as the government is more absolute; and, on the other hand, the privileges of the courts of justice are extended with the increasing liberties of the people: but no European nation has yet held that all judicial controversies, without regard to their origin, can be left to the judges of common law.

In America, this theory has been actually put in practice; and the Supreme Court of the United States is the sole tribunal of the nation. Its power extends to all cases arising under laws and treaties made by the national authorities, to all cases of admiralty and maritime jurisdiction, and, in general, to all points which affect the law of nations.

It may even be affirmed that, although its constitution is essentially judicial, its prerogatives are almost entirely political. Its sole object is to enforce the execution of the laws of the Union ; and the Union only regulates the relations of the government with the citizens, and of the nation with foreign powers: the relations of citizens amongst themselves are almost all regulated by the sovereignty of the States.

A second and still greater cause of the preponderance of this court may be adduced. In the nations of Europe, the courts of justice are only called upon to try the controversies of private individuals ; but the Supreme Court of the United States summons sovereign powers to its bar. When the clerk of the court advances on the steps of the tribunal, and simply says, " The State of New York *versus* The State of Ohio," it is impossible not to feel that the court which he addresses is no ordinary body ; and when it is recollected that one of these parties represents one million, and the other two millions of men, one is struck by the responsibility of the seven judges, whose decision is about to satisfy or to disappoint so large a number of their fellow-citizens.

The peace, the prosperity, and the very existence of the Union are vested in the hands of the seven Federal judges. Without them, the Constitution would be a dead letter: the Executive appeals to them for assistance against the encroachments of the legislative power ; the Legislature demands their protection against the assaults of the Executive ; they defend the Union from the disobedience of the States, the States from the exaggerated claims of the Union, the public interest against private interests, and the conservative spirit of stability against the fickleness of the democracy. Their power is enormous, but it is the power of public opinion. They are all-powerful as long as the people respect the law ; but they would be impotent against popular neglect or contempt of the law. The force of public opinion is the most intractable of agents, because its exact limits cannot be defined; and it is not less dangerous to exceed, than to remain below, the boundary prescribed.

The Federal judges must not only be good citizens, and men of that information and integrity which are indispensable to all magistrates, but they must be statesmen, wise to discern the signs of the times, not afraid to brave the obstacles which can be subdued, nor slow to turn away from the current when it threatens to sweep them off, and the supremacy of the Union and the obedience due to the laws along with them.

The President, who exercises a limited power, may err without causing great mischief in the state. Congress may decide amiss without destroying the Union, because the electoral body in which the Congress originates may cause it to retract its decision by changing its members. But if the Supreme Court is ever composed of imprudent or bad men, the Union may be plunged into anarchy or civil war.

The original cause of this danger, however, does not lie in the constitution of the tribunal, but in the very nature of federal governments. We have seen that, in confederate states, it is especially necessary to strengthen the judicial power, because in no other nations do those independent persons who are able to contend with the social body exist in greater power, or in a better condition to resist the physical strength of the government. But the more a power requires to be strengthened, the more extensive and independent it must be made; and the dangers which its abuse may create are heightened by its independence and its strength. The source of the evil is not, therefore, in the constitution of the power, but in the constitution of the state which renders the existence of such a power necessary.

IN WHAT RESPECTS THE FEDERAL CONSTITUTION IS SUPERIOR TO THAT OF THE STATES.

How the Constitution of the Union can be compared with that of the States. — Superiority of the Constitution of the Union attributable to the Wisdom of the Federal Legislators. — Legislature of the Union less dependent on the People than that of the States. — Executive Power more independent in its Sphere. — Judicial Power less subjected to the Will of the Majority. — Practical Consequence of these Facts. — The Dangers inherent in a Democratic Government diminished by the Federal Legislators, and increased by the Legislators of the States.

THE Federal Constitution differs essentially from that of the States in the ends which it is intended to accomplish; but in the means by which these ends are attained, a greater analogy exists between them. The objects of the governments are different, but their forms are the same; and in this special point of view, there is some advantage in comparing them with each other.

I am of opinion, for several reasons, that the Federal Constitution is superior to any of the State constitutions.

The present Constitution of the Union was formed at a later period than those of the majority of the States, and it may have profited by this additional experience. But we shall be convinced that this is only a secondary cause of its superiority, when we recollect that eleven [twenty-one] new States have since been added to the Union, and that these new republics have almost always rather exaggerated than remedied the defects which existed in the former constitutions.

The chief cause of the superiority of the Federal Constitution lay in the character of the legislators who composed it. At the time when it was formed, the ruin of the Confederation seemed imminent, and its danger was universally known. In this extremity, the people chose the men who most deserved the esteem, rather than those who had gained the affections, of the country. I have already observed, that, distinguished as almost all the legislators of the Union were for their intelligence, they were still more so for their patriotism. They had all been nurtured at a time when the spirit of liberty was braced by a continual struggle against a powerful and dominant authority. When the contest was terminated, whilst the excited passions of the populace persisted, as usual, in warring against dangers which had ceased to exist, these men stopped short; they cast a calmer and more penetrating look upon their country; they perceived that a definitive revolution had been accomplished, and that the only dangers which America had now to fear were those which might result from the abuse of freedom. They had the courage to say what they believed to be true, because they were animated by a warm and sincere love of liberty; and they ventured to propose restrictions, because they were resolutely opposed to destruction.*

Most of the State constitutions assign one year for the duration of the House of Representatives, and two years for that of the Senate; so that members of the legislative body are constantly and narrowly tied down by the slight-

---

* At this time, Alexander Hamilton, who was one of the principal founders of the Constitution, ventured to express the following sentiments in the Federalist, No. 71 : —

" There are some who would be inclined to regard the servile pliancy of the Executive to a prevailing current, either in the community or in the legislature, as its best recommendation. But such men entertain very crude notions, as well of the purposes for which government was instituted, as of the true means by which the public happiness may be promoted. The republican principle demands, that the deliberative sense of the community should govern the conduct of those to whom they intrust the management of their affairs; but it does not require an unqualified complaisance to every sudden breeze of passion, or to every transient impulse which the people may receive from the arts of men who flatter their prejudices to betray their interests. It is a just observation, that the people commonly *intend the public good.* This often applies to their very errors. But their good sense would

est desires of their constituents. The legislators of the Union were of opinion that this excessive dependence of the legislature altered the nature of the main consequences of the representative system, since it vested not only the source of authority, but the government, in the people. They increased the length of the term, in order to give the representatives freer scope for the exercise of their own judgment.

The Federal Constitution, as well as the State constitutions, divided the legislative body into two branches. But in the States, these two branches were composed of the same elements, and elected in the same manner. The consequence was, that the passions and inclinations of the populace were as rapidly and easily represented in one chamber as in the other, and that laws were made with violence and precipitation. By the Federal Constitution, the two houses originate in like manner in the choice of the people; but the conditions of eligibility and the mode of election were changed, in order that, if, as is the case in certain nations, one branch of the legislature should not represent the same interests as the other, it might at least represent more wisdom. A mature age was necessary to

despise the adulator who should pretend that they always *reason right* about the *means* of promoting it. They know from experience that they sometimes err; and the wonder is, that they so seldom err as they do, beset, as they continually are, by the wiles of parasites and sycophants; by the snares of the ambitious, the avaricious, the desperate; by the artifices of men who possess their confidence more than they deserve it, and of those who seek to possess rather than to deserve it. When occasions present themselves in which the interests of the people are at variance with their inclinations, it is the duty of the persons whom they have appointed to be the guardians of those interests to withstand the temporary delusion, in order to give them time and opportunity for more cool and sedate reflection. Instances might be cited, in which a conduct of this kind has saved the people from very fatal consequences of their own mistakes, and has procured lasting monuments of their gratitude to the men who had courage and magnanimity enough to serve them at the peril of their displeasure."

become a Senator, and the Senate was chosen by an elected assembly of a limited number of members.

To concentrate the whole social force in the hands of the
legislative body is the natural tendency of democracies; for
as this is the power which emanates the most directly from
the people, it has the greater share of the people's overwhelming power, and it is naturally led to monopolize
every species of influence. This concentration of power
is at once very prejudicial to a well-conducted administration, and favorable to the despotism of the majority. The
legislators of the States frequently yielded to these democratic propensities, which were invariably and courageously
resisted by the founders of the Union.

In the States, the executive power is vested in the hands
of a magistrate, who is apparently placed upon a level with
the legislature, but who is in reality only the blind agent
and the passive instrument of its will. He can derive no
power from the duration of his office, which terminates
in one year, or from the exercise of prerogatives, for he
can scarcely be said to have any. The legislature can
condemn him to inaction by intrusting the execution of its
laws to special committees of its own members, and can
annul his temporary dignity by cutting down his salary.*
The Federal Constitution vests all the privileges and all the
responsibility of the executive power in a single individual.
The duration of the Presidency is fixed at four years; the
salary cannot be altered during this term; the President is
protected by a body of official dependents, and armed with
a suspensive veto : in short, every effort was made to confer a strong and independent position upon the executive
authority, within the limits which were prescribed to it.

---

* Not always. In several of the States, the compensation of the Governor
cannot be lessened during his term of office. So, also, the Governor's term
is not always for a single year. In many of the States it is two, in some
it is three, years. — AM. ED.

In the State constitutions, the judicial power is that which is the most independent of the legislative authority; nevertheless, in all the States, the legislature has reserved to itself the right of regulating the emoluments of the judges, a practice which necessarily subjects them to its immediate influence. In some States, the judges are appointed only temporarily, which deprives them of a great portion of their power and their freedom. In others, the legislative and judicial powers are entirely confounded. The Senate of New York, for instance, constitutes in certain cases the superior court of the State. The Federal Constitution, on the other hand, carefully separates the judicial power from all the others; and it provides for the independence of the judges, by declaring that their salary shall not be diminished, and that their functions shall be inalienable.

The practical consequences of these different systems may easily be perceived. An attentive observer will soon remark that the business of the Union is incomparably better conducted than that of any individual State. The conduct of the Federal government is more fair and temperate than that of the States; it has more prudence and discretion, its projects are more durable and more skilfully combined, its measures are executed with more vigor and consistency.

I recapitulate the substance of this chapter in a few words.

The existence of democracies is threatened by two principal dangers, viz. the complete subjection of the legislature to the will of the electoral body, and the concentration of all the other powers of the government in the legislative branch.

The development of these evils has been favored by the legislators of the States; but the legislators of the Union have done all they could to render them less formidable.

CHARACTERISTICS OF THE FEDERAL CONSTITUTION OF THE
UNITED STATES OF AMERICA AS COMPARED WITH ALL
OTHER FEDERAL CONSTITUTIONS.

The American Union appears to resemble all other Confederations. — Yet
its Effects are different. — Reason of this. — In what this Union differs
from all other Confederations. — The American Government not a Federal, but an imperfect National Government.

THE United States of America do not afford the first or
the only instance of a confederation, several of which have
existed in modern Europe, without adverting to those of
antiquity. Switzerland, the Germanic Empire, and the
Republic of the Low Countries, either have been, or still
are, confederations. In studying the constitutions of these
different countries, one is surprised to see that the powers
with which they invested the federal government are
nearly the same with those awarded by the American Constitution to the government of the United States. They
confer upon the central power the same rights of making
peace and war, of raising money and troops, and of providing for the general exigencies and the common interests
of the nation. Nevertheless, the federal government of
these different states has always been as remarkable for its
weakness and inefficiency as that of the American Union
is for its vigor and capacity. Again, the first American
Confederation perished through the excessive weakness of
its government; and yet this weak government had as
large rights and privileges as those of the Federal government of the present day, and in some respects even larger.
But the present Constitution of the United States contains
certain novel principles, which exercise a most important
influence, although they do not at once strike the observer.

This Constitution, which may at first sight be confounded with the federal constitutions which have preceded
it, rests in truth upon a wholly novel theory, which may

be considered as a great discovery in modern political science. In all the confederations which preceded the American Constitution of 1789, the allied states for a common object agreed to obey the injunctions of a federal government; but they reserved to themselves the right of ordaining and enforcing the execution of the laws of the union. The American States which combined in 1789 agreed, that the Federal government should not only dictate the laws, but should execute its own enactments. In both cases, the right is the same, but the exercise of the right is different; and this difference produced the most momentous consequences.

In all the confederations which preceded the American Union, the federal government, in order to provide for its wants, had to apply to the separate governments; and if what it prescribed was disagreeable to any one of them, means were found to evade its claims. If it was powerful, it then had recourse to arms; if it was weak, it connived at the resistance which the law of the union, its sovereign, met with, and did nothing, under the plea of inability. Under these circumstances, one of two results invariably followed: either the strongest of the allied states assumed the privileges of the federal authority, and ruled all the others in its name;* or the federal government was abandoned by its natural supporters, anarchy arose between the confederates, and the union lost all power of action.†

In America, the subjects of the Union are not States,

* This was the case in Greece, when Philip undertook to execute the decrees of the Amphictyons; in the Low Countries, where the province of Holland always gave the law; and, in our own time, in the Germanic Confederation, in which Austria and Prussia make themselves the agents of the Diet, and rule the whole confederation in its name.

† Such has always been the situation of the Swiss Confederation, which would have perished ages ago but for the mutual jealousies of its neighbors.

but private citizens : the national government levies a tax, not upon the State of Massachusetts, but upon each inhabitant of Massachusetts. The old confederate governments presided over communities, but that of the Union presides over individuals. Its force is not borrowed, but self-derived ; and it is served by its own civil and military officers, its own army, and its own courts of justice. It cannot be doubted that the national spirit, the passions of the multitude, and the provincial prejudices of each State, still tend singularly to diminish the extent of the Federal authority thus constituted, and to facilitate resistance to its mandates ; but the comparative weakness of a restricted sovereignty is an evil inherent in the Federal system. In America, each State has fewer opportunities and temptations to resist : nor can such a design be put in execution, (if indeed it be entertained,) without an open violation of the laws of the Union, a direct interruption of the ordinary course of justice, and a bold declaration of revolt ; in a word, without taking the decisive step which men always hesitate to adopt.

In all former confederations, the privileges of the Union furnished more elements of discord than of power, since they multiplied the claims of the nation without augmenting the means of enforcing them : and hence the real weak ness of federal governments has almost always been in the exact ratio of their nominal power. Such is not the case in the American Union, in which, as in ordinary governments, the Federal power has the means of enforcing all it is empowered to demand.

The human understanding more easily invents new things than new words, and we are hence constrained to employ many improper and inadequate expressions. When several nations form a permanent league, and establish a supreme authority, which, although it cannot act upon private individuals, like a national government, still acts upon each of the confederate states in a body, this government, which is so essentially different from all others, is called Federal. Another form of society is afterwards discovered, in which several states are fused into one with regard to certain common interests, although they remain distinct, or only confederate, with regard to all other concerns. In this case, the central power acts directly upon the governed, whom it rules and judges in the same manner as a national government, but in a more limited circle. Evidently this is no longer a federal government, but an incomplete national government, which is neither exactly national nor exactly federal; but the new word which ought to express this novel thing does not yet exist.

Ignorance of this new species of confederation has been the cause which has brought all unions to civil war, to servitude, or to inertness; and the states which formed these leagues have been either too dull to discern, or too pusillanimous to apply, this great remedy. The first American confederation perished by the same defects.

But in America, the confederate States had been long accustomed to form a portion of one empire before they had won their independence; they had not contracted the habit of governing themselves completely; and their national prejudices had not taken deep root in their minds. Superior to the rest of the world in political knowledge, and sharing that knowledge equally amongst themselves, they were little agitated by the passions which generally oppose the extension of federal authority in a nation, and those passions were checked by the wisdom of their greatest men. The Americans applied the remedy with firmness, as soon as they were conscious of the evil; they amended their laws, and saved the country.

ADVANTAGES OF THE FEDERAL SYSTEM IN GENERAL, AND
ITS SPECIAL UTILITY IN AMERICA.

Happiness and Freedom of small Nations. — Power of great Nations. —
Great Empires favorable to the Growth of Civilization. — Strength of-
ten the first Element of National Prosperity. — Aim of the Federal System to unite the twofold Advantages resulting from a small and from a
large Territory. — Advantages derived by the United States from this
System. The Law adapts itself to the Exigencies of the Population;
Population does not conform to the Exigencies of the Law. — Activity,
Progress, the Love and Enjoyment of Freedom, in American Communities — Public Spirit of the Union is only the Aggregate of Provincial
Patriotism. — Principles and Things circulate freely over the Territory
of the United States. — The Union is happy and free as a little Nation,
and respected as a great one.

In small states, the watchfulness of society penetrates
into every part, and the spirit of improvement enters into
the smallest details; the ambition of the people being
necessarily checked by its weakness, all the efforts and
resources of the citizens are turned to the internal well-
being of the community, and are not likely to evaporate in
the fleeting breath of glory. The powers of every individual being generally limited, his desires are proportionally
small. Mediocrity of fortune makes the various conditions
of life nearly equal, and the manners of the inhabitants are
orderly and simple. Thus, all things considered, and al-
lowance being made for the various degrees of morality
and enlightenment, we shall generally find in small nations more persons in easy circumstances, more contentment and tranquillity, than in large ones.

When tyranny is established in the bosom of a small
state, it is more galling than elsewhere, because, acting in
a narrower circle, everything in that circle is affected by
it. It supplies the place of those great designs which it
cannot entertain, by a violent or exasperating interference
in a multitude of minute details; and it leaves the political

world, to which it properly belongs, to meddle with the arrangements of private life. Tastes as well as actions are to be regulated ; and the families of the citizens, as well as the state, are to be governed. This invasion of rights occurs, however, but seldom, freedom being in truth the natural state of small communities. The temptations which the government offers to ambition are too weak, and the resources of private individuals are too slender, for the sovereign power easily to fall into the grasp of a single man ; and should such an event occur, the subjects of the state can easily unite and overthrow the tyrant and the tyranny at once by a common effort.

Small nations have therefore ever been the cradle of political liberty ; and the fact that many of them have lost their liberty by becoming larger, shows that their freedom was more a consequence of their small size than of the character of the people.

The history of the world affords no instance of a great nation retaining the form of republican government for a long series of years ; * and this has led to the conclusion that such a thing is impracticable. For my own part, I think it imprudent to attempt to limit what is possible, and to judge the future, for men who are every day deceived in relation to the actual and the present, and often taken by surprise in the circumstances with which they are most familiar. But it may be said with confidence, that a great republic will always be exposed to more perils than a small one.

All the passions which are most fatal to republican institutions increase with an increasing territory, whilst the virtues which favor them do not augment in the same proportion. The ambition of private citizens increases with the power of the state ; the strength of parties, with

---

* I do not speak of a confederation of small republics, but of a great consolidated republic.

the importance of the ends they have in view; but the
love of country, which ought to check these destructive
agencies, is not stronger in a large than in a small republic.
It might, indeed, be easily proved that it is less powerful
and less developed. Great wealth and extreme poverty,
capital cities of large size, a lax morality, selfishness, and
antagonism of interests, are the dangers which almost invariably arise from the magnitude of states. Several of
these evils scarcely injure a monarchy, and some of them
even contribute to its strength and duration. In monarchical states, the government has its peculiar strength; it
may use, but it does not depend on, the community; and
the more numerous the people, the stronger is the prince.
But the only security which a republican government possesses against these evils lies in the support of the majority.
This support is not, however, proportionably greater in a
large republic than in a small one; and thus, whilst the
means of attack perpetually increase, both in number and
influence, the power of resistance remains the same; or it
may rather be said to diminish, since the inclinations and
interests of the people are more diversified by the increase
of the population, and the difficulty of forming a compact
majority is constantly augmented. It has been observed,
moreover, that the intensity of human passions is heightened not only by the importance of the end which they
propose to attain, but by the multitude of individuals who
are animated by them at the same time. Every one has
had occasion to remark, that his emotions in the midst of
a sympathizing crowd are far greater than those which he
would have felt in solitude. In great republics, political
passions become irresistible, not only because they aim at
gigantic objects, but because they are felt and shared by
millions of men at the same time.

It may, therefore, be asserted as a general proposition,
that nothing is more opposed to the well-being and the

freedom of men than vast empires. Nevertheless, it is important to acknowledge the peculiar advantages of great states. For the very reason that the desire of power is more intense in these communities than amongst ordinary men, the love of glory is also more developed in the hearts of certain citizens, who regard the applause of a great people as a reward worthy of their exertions, and an elevating encouragement to man. If we would learn why great nations contribute more powerfully to the increase of knowledge and the advance of civilization than small states, we shall discover an adequate cause in the more rapid and energetic circulation of ideas, and in those great cities which are the intellectual centres where all the rays of human genius are reflected and combined. To this it may be added, that most important discoveries demand a use of national power which the government of a small state is unable to make: in great nations, the government has more enlarged ideas, and is more completely disengaged from the routine of precedent and the selfishness of local feeling; its designs are conceived with more talent, and executed with more boldness.

In time of peace, the well-being of small nations is undoubtedly more general and complete; but they are apt to suffer more acutely from the calamities of war than those great empires whose distant frontiers may long avert the presence of the danger from the mass of the people, who are therefore more frequently afflicted than ruined by the contest.

But in this matter, as in many others, the decisive argument is the necessity of the case. If none but small nations existed, I do not doubt that mankind would be more happy and more free; but the existence of great nations is unavoidable.

Political strength thus becomes a condition of national prosperity. It profits a state but little to be affluent and free, if it is perpetually exposed to be pillaged or subjugated; its manufactures and commerce are of small advantage, if another nation has the empire of the seas and gives the law in all the markets of the globe. Small nations are often miserable, not because they are small, but because they are weak; and great empires prosper, less because they are great, than because they are strong. Physical strength is therefore one of the first conditions of the happiness, and even of the existence, of nations. Hence it occurs, that, unless very peculiar circumstances intervene, small nations are always united to large empires in the end, either by force or by their own consent. I know not a more deplorable condition than that of a people unable to defend itself or to provide for its own wants.

The Federal system was created with the intention of combining the different advantages which result from the magnitude and the littleness of nations; and a glance at the United States of America discovers the advantages which they have derived from its adoption.

In great centralized nations, the legislator is obliged to give a character of uniformity to the laws, which does not always suit the diversity of customs and of districts; as he takes no cognizance of special cases, he can only proceed upon general principles; and the population are obliged to conform to the exigencies of the legislation, since the legislation cannot adapt itself to the exigencies and the customs of the population; which is a great cause of trouble and misery. This disadvantage does not exist in confederations; Congress regulates the principal measures of the national government; and all the details of the administration are reserved to the provincial legislatures. One can hardly imagine how much this division of sovereignty contributes to the well-being of each of the States which compose the Union. In these small communities, which are never agitated by the desire of aggrandizement or the care of self-defence, all public authority and private energy are turned towards internal improvements. The central government of each State, which is in immediate juxtaposition to the citizens, is daily apprised of the wants which arise in society; and new projects are proposed every year, which are discussed at town-meetings or by the legislature, and which are transmitted by the press to stimulate the zeal and to excite the interest of the citizens. This spirit of improvement is constantly alive in the American republics, without compromising their tranquillity; the ambition of power yields to the less refined and less dangerous desire for well-being. It is generally believed in America, that the existence and the permanence of the republican form of government in the New World depend upon the existence and the duration of the Federal system; and it is not unusual to attribute a large share of the misfortunes which have befallen the new States of South America to the injudicious erection of great republics, instead of a divided and confederate sovereignty.

It is incontestably true, that the tastes and the habits of republican government in the United States were first created in the townships and the provincial assemblies. In a small State, like that of Connecticut, for instance, where cutting a canal or laying down a road is a great political question, where the State has no army to pay and no wars to carry on, and where much wealth or much honor cannot be given to the rulers, no form of government can be more natural or more appropriate than a republic. But it is this same republican spirit, it is these manners and customs of a free people, which have been created and nurtured in the different States, which must be afterwards applied to the country at large. The public spirit of the Union is, so to speak, nothing more than an aggregate or summary of the patriotic zeal of the separate provinces. Every citizen of the United States transports, so to speak, his attachment to his little republic into the common store of American patriotism. In defending the Union, he defends the increasing prosperity of his own State or county, the right of conducting its affairs, and the hope of causing measures of improvement to be adopted in it which may be favorable to his own interests; and these are motives which are wont to stir men more than the general interests of the country and the glory of the nation.

On the other hand, if the temper and the manners of the inhabitants especially fitted them to promote the welfare of a great republic, the federal system renders their task less difficult. The confederation of all the American States presents none of the ordinary inconveniences resulting from great agglomerations of men. The Union is a great republic in extent, but the paucity of objects for which its government acts assimilates it to a small State. Its acts are important, but they are rare. As the sovereignty of the Union is limited and incomplete, its exercise is not dangerous to liberty; for it does not excite those insatiable desires of fame and power which have proved so fatal to great republics. As there is no common centre to the country, great capital cities, colossal wealth, abject poverty, and sudden revolutions are alike unknown; and political passion, instead of spreading over the land like a fire on the prairies, spends its strength against the interests and the individual passions of every State.

Nevertheless, tangible objects and ideas circulate throughout the Union as freely as in a country inhabited by one people. Nothing checks the spirit of enterprise. The government invites the aid of all who have talents or knowledge to serve it. Inside of the frontiers of the Union, profound peace prevails, as within the heart of some great empire; abroad, it ranks with the most powerful nations of the earth: two thousand miles of coast are open to the commerce of the world; and as it holds the keys of a New World, its flag is respected in the most remote seas. The Union is happy and free as a small people, and glorious and strong as a great nation.

WHY THE FEDERAL SYSTEM IS NOT PRACTICABLE FOR ALL NATIONS, AND HOW THE ANGLO-AMERICANS WERE ENABLED TO ADOPT IT.

Every Federal System has inherent Faults which baffle the Efforts of the Legislator. — The Federal System is complex. — It demands a daily Exercise of the Intelligence of the Citizens. — Practical Knowledge of Government common amongst the Americans. — Relative Weakness of the Government of the Union another Defect inherent in the Federal System. — The Americans have diminished without remedying it. — The Sovereignty of the separate States apparently weaker, but really stronger, than that of the Union. — Why. — Natural Causes of Union then must exist between Confederate Nations beside the Laws. — What these Causes are amongst the Anglo-Americans. — Maine and Georgia, separated by a Distance of a thousand Miles, more naturally united than Normandy and Brittany. — War the main Peril of Confederations. — This proved even by the Example of the United States. — The Union has no great Wars to fear. — Why. — Dangers which Europeans would incur if they adopted the Federal System of the Americans.

WHEN a legislator succeeds, after many efforts, in exercising an indirect influence upon the destiny of nations, his genius is lauded by mankind, whilst, in point of fact, the geographical position of the country which he is unable to change, a social condition which arose without his co-operation, manners and opinions which he cannot trace to their source, and an origin with which he is unacquainted, exercise so irresistible an influence over the courses of society, that he is himself borne away by the current after an ineffectual resistance. Like the navigator, he may direct the vessel which bears him, but he can neither change its structure, nor raise the winds, nor lull the waters which swell beneath him.

I have shown the advantages which the Americans derive from their Federal system ; it remains for me to point out the circumstances which enabled them to adopt it, as its benefits cannot be enjoyed by all nations. The accidental defects of the federal system which originate in the laws may be corrected by the skill of the legislator, but there are evils inherent in the system which cannot be remedied by any effort. The people must therefore find in themselves the strength necessary to bear the natural imperfections of their government.

The most prominent evil of all federal systems is the complicated nature of the means they employ. Two sovereignties are necessarily in presence of each other. The legislator may simplify and equalize, as far as possible, the action of these two sovereignties, by limiting each of them to a sphere of authority accurately defined ; but he cannot combine them into one, or prevent them from coming into collision at certain points. The federal system, therefore, rests upon a theory which is complicated, at the best, and which demands the daily exercise of a considerable share of discretion on the part of those it governs.

A proposition must be plain, to be adopted by the understanding of a people. A false notion which is clear and precise will always have more power in the world than a true principle which is obscure or involved. Hence it happens that parties, which are like small communities in the heart of the nation, invariably adopt some principle or name as a symbol, which very inadequately represents the end they have in view and the means which they employ, but without which they could neither act nor subsist. The governments which are founded upon a single principle or a single feeling, which is easily defined, are perhaps not the best, but they are unquestionably the strongest and the most durable in the world.

In examining the Constitution of the United States, which is the most perfect federal constitution that ever existed, one is startled at the variety of information and the amount of discernment which it presupposes in the people whom it is meant to govern. The government of the Union depends almost entirely upon legal fictions; the Union is an ideal nation, which exists, so to speak, only in the mind, and whose limits and extent can only be discerned by the understanding.

After the general theory is comprehended, many difficulties remain to be solved in its application; for the sovereignty of the Union is so involved in that of the States, that it is impossible to distinguish its boundaries at the first glance. The whole structure of the government is artificial and conventional; and it would be ill adapted to a people which has not been long accustomed to conduct its own affairs, or to one in which the science of politics has not descended to the humblest classes of society. I have never been more struck by the good sense and the practical judgment of the Americans, than in the manner in which they elude the numberless difficulties resulting from their Federal Constitution. I scarcely ever met with a plain American citizen who could not distinguish with surprising facility the obligations created by the laws of Congress from those created by the laws of his own State, and who, after having discriminated between the matters which come under the cognizance of the Union and those which the local legislature is competent to regulate, could not point out the exact limit of the separate jurisdictions of the Federal courts and the tribunals of the State.

The Constitution of the United States resembles those fine creations of human industry which insure wealth and renown to their inventors, but which are profitless in other hands. This truth is exemplified by the condition of Mexico at the present time. The Mexicans were desirous of establishing a federal system, and they took the Federal Constitution of their neighbors, the Anglo-Americans, as their model, and copied it almost entirely.* But, although they had borrowed the letter of the law, they could not introduce the spirit and the sense which give it life. They were involved in ceaseless embarrassments by the mechanism of their double government; the sovereignty of the States and that of the Union perpetually exceeded their respective privileges, and came into collision; and to the present day Mexico is alternately the victim of anarchy and the slave of military despotism.

The second and most fatal of all defects, and that which I believe to be inherent in the federal system, is the relative weakness of the government of the union. The principle upon which all confederations rest is that of a divided sovereignty. Legislators may render this partition less perceptible, they may even conceal it for a time from the public eye, but they cannot prevent it from existing; and a divided must always be weaker than an entire sovereignty. The remarks made on the Constitution of the United States have shown with what skill the Americans, while restraining the power of the Union within the narrow limits of a federal government, have given it the semblance, and to a certain extent the force, of a national government. By this means, the legislators of the Union have diminished the natural danger of confederations, but have not entirely obviated it.

The American government, it is said, does not address itself to the States, but transmits its injunctions directly to the citizens, and compels them by isolation to comply with its demands. But if the Federal law were to clash with the interests and the prejudices of a State, it might be feared that all the citizens of that State would conceive themselves to be interested in the cause of a single individual who should refuse to obey. If all the citizens of the State were aggrieved at the same time and in the same

* See the Mexican Constitution of 1824.

manner by the authority of the Union, the Federal government would vainly attempt to subdue them individually; they would instinctively unite in a common defence, and would find an organization already prepared for them in the sovereignty which their State is allowed to enjoy. Fiction would give way to reality, and an organized portion of the nation might then contest the central authority.

The same observation holds good with regard to the Federal jurisdiction. If the courts of the Union violated an important law of a State in a private case, the real, though not the apparent contest, would be between the aggrieved State represented by a citizen, and the Union represented by its courts of justice.*

He would have but a partial knowledge of the world who should imagine that it is possible, by the aid of legal fictions, to prevent men from finding out and employing those means of gratifying their passions which have been left open to them. The American legislators, though they have rendered a collision between the two sovereignties less probable, have not destroyed the causes of such a misfortune. It may even be affirmed, that, in case of such a collision, they have not been able to insure the victory of the Federal element in a case of this kind. The Union is possessed of money and troops, but the States have kept

* For instance, the Union possesses by the Constitution the right of selling unoccupied lands for its own profit. Suppose that the State of Ohio should claim the same right in behalf of certain tracts lying within its own boundaries, upon the plea that the Constitution refers to those lands alone which do not belong to the jurisdiction of any particular State, and consequently should choose to dispose of them itself. The litigation would be carried on, it is true, in the names of the purchasers from the State of Ohio and the purchasers from the Union, and not in the names of Ohio and the Union. But what would become of this legal fiction, if the Federal purchaser was confirmed in his right by the courts of the Union, whilst the other competitor was ordered to retain possession by the tribunals of the State of Ohio?

the affections and the prejudices of the people. The sovereignty of the Union is an abstract being, which is connected with but few external objects; the sovereignty of the States is perceptible by the senses, easily understood, and constantly active. The former is of recent creation, the latter is coeval with the people itself. The sovereignty of the Union is factitious, that of the States is natural and self-existent, without effort, like the authority of a parent. The sovereignty of the nation affects a few of the chief interests of society; it represents an immense but remote country, a vague and ill-defined sentiment. The authority of the States controls every individual citizen at every hour and in all circumstances; it protects his property, his freedom, and his life; it affects at every moment his well-being or his misery. When we recollect the traditions, the customs, the prejudices of local and familiar attachment with which it is connected, we cannot doubt the superiority of a power which rests on the instinct of patriotism so natural to the human heart.

Since legislators cannot prevent such dangerous collisions as occur between the two sovereignties which coexist in the federal system, their first object must be, not only to dissuade the confederate states from warfare, but to encourage such dispositions as lead to peace. Hence it is that the federal compact cannot be lasting unless there exist in the communities which are leagued together a certain number of inducements to union which render their common dependence agreeable, and the task of the government light. The federal system cannot succeed without the presence of favorable circumstances added to the influence of good laws. All the nations which have ever formed a confederation have been held together by some common interests, which served as the intellectual ties of association.

But men have sentiments and principles, as well as material interests. A certain uniformity of civilization is not less necessary to the durability of a confederation, than a uniformity of interests in the states which compose it. In Switzerland, the difference between the civilization of the Canton of Uri and that of the Canton of Vaud is like the difference between the fifteenth and the nineteenth centuries; therefore, properly speaking, Switzerland has never had a federal government. The union between these two Cantons subsists only upon the map; and this would soon be perceived if an attempt were made by a central authority to prescribe the same laws to the whole territory.

The circumstance which makes it easy to maintain a Federal government in America is, that the States not only have similar interests, a common origin, and a common language, but that they are also arrived at the same stage of civilization; which almost always renders a union feasible. I do not know of any European nation, however small, which does not present less uniformity in its different provinces than the American people, which occupies a territory as extensive as one half of Europe. The distance from Maine to Georgia is about one thousand miles; but the difference between the civilization of Maine and that of Georgia is slighter than the difference between the habits of Normandy and those of Brittany. Maine and Georgia, which are placed at the opposite extremities of a great empire, have therefore more real inducements to form a confederation than Normandy and Brittany, which are separated only by a brook.

The geographical position of the country increased the facilities which the American legislators derived from the manners and customs of the inhabitants; and it is to this circumstance that the adoption and the maintenance of the Federal system are mainly attributable.

The most important occurrence in the life of a nation is the breaking out of a war. In war, a people act as one man against foreign nations, in defence of their very existence. The skill of the government, the good sense of the community, and the natural fondness which men almost always entertain for their country, may be enough, as long as the only object is to maintain peace in the interior of the state, and to favor its internal prosperity ; but that the nation may carry on a great war, the people must make more numerous and painful sacrifices; and to suppose that a great number of men will, of their own accord, submit to these exigencies, is to betray an ignorance of human nature. All the nations which have been obliged to sustain a long and serious warfare have consequently been led to augment the power of their government. Those who have not succeeded in this attempt have been subjugated. A long war almost always reduces nations to the wretched alternative of being abandoned to ruin by defeat, or to despotism by success. War therefore renders the weakness of a government most apparent and most alarming; and I have shown that the inherent defect of federal governments is that of being weak.

The federal system not only has no centralized administration, and nothing which resembles one, but the central government itself is imperfectly organized, which is always a great cause of weakness when the nation is opposed to other countries which are themselves governed by a single authority. In the Federal Constitution of the United States, where the central government has more real force than in any other confederation, this evil is still extremely sensible. A single example will illustrate the case.

The Constitution confers upon Congress the right of " calling forth the militia to execute the laws of the Union, suppress insurrections, and repel invasions "; and another article declares that the President of the United States is the commander-in-chief of the militia. In the war of 1812, the President ordered the militia of the Northern

States to march to the frontiers; but Connecticut and Massachusetts, whose interests were impaired by the war, refused to obey the command. They argued that the Constitution authorizes the Federal government to call forth the militia in case of *insurrection* or *invasion;* but in the present instance, there was neither invasion nor insurrection. They added, that the same Constitution which conferred upon the Union the right of calling the militia into active service, reserved to the States that of naming the officers; and consequently (as they understood the clause) no officer of the Union had any right to command the militia, even during war, except the President in person: and in this case, they were ordered to join an army commanded by another individual. These absurd and pernicious doctrines received the sanction not only of the Governors and the legislative bodies, but also of the courts of justice in both States; and the Federal government was constrained to raise elsewhere the troops which it required.*

How happens it, then, that the American Union, with all the relative perfection of its laws, is not dissolved by the occurrence of a great war? It is because it has no great wars to fear. Placed in the centre of an immense continent, which offers a boundless field for human industry, the Union is almost as much insulated from the world as if all its frontiers were girt by the ocean. Canada con-

---

* Kent's Commentaries, Vol. I. p. 244. I have selected an example which relates to a time long after the promulgation of the present Constitution. If I had gone back to the days of the Confederation, I might have given still more striking instances. The whole nation was at that time in a state of enthusiastic excitement; the Revolution was represented by a man who was the idol of the people; but at that very period, Congress had, to say the truth, no resources at all at its disposal. Troops and supplies were perpetually wanting. The best-devised projects failed in the execution, and the Union, constantly on the verge of destruction, was saved by the weakness of its enemies far more than by its own strength.

tains only a million of inhabitants, and its population is divided into two inimical nations. The rigor of the climate limits the extension of its territory, and shuts up its ports during the six months of winter. From Canada to the Gulf of Mexico a few savage tribes are to be met with, which retire, perishing in their retreat, before six thousand soldiers. To the south, the Union has a point of contact with the empire of Mexico; and it is thence that serious hostilities may one day be expected to arise. But for a long while to come, the uncivilized state of the Mexican people, the depravity of their morals, and their extreme poverty, will prevent that country from ranking high amongst nations. As for the powers of Europe, they are too distant to be formidable.*

The great advantage of the United States does not, then, consist in a Federal Constitution which allows them to carry on great wars, but in a geographical position which renders such wars extremely improbable.

No one can be more inclined than I am to appreciate the advantages of the Federal system, which I hold to be one of the combinations most favorable to the prosperity and freedom of man. I envy the lot of those nations which have been able to adopt it; but I cannot believe that any confederate people could maintain a long or an equal contest with a nation of similar strength in which the government is centralized. A people which should divide its sovereignty into fractional parts, in the presence of the great military monarchies of Europe, would, in my opinion, by that very act abdicate its power, and perhaps its existence and its name. But such is the admirable position of the New World, that man has no other enemy than himself; and that, in order to be happy and to be free, he has only to determine that he will be so.

* See Appendix O.

CHAPTER IX.

THUS far, I have examined the institutions of the United States; I have passed their legislation in review, and have described the present forms of political society in that country. But above these institutions, and beyond all these characteristic forms, there is a sovereign power — that of the people — which may destroy or modify them at its pleasure. It remains to be shown in what manner this power, superior to the laws, acts; what are its instincts and its passions, what the secret springs which retard, accelerate, or direct its irresistible course, what the effects of its unbounded authority, and what the destiny which is reserved for it.

HOW IT CAN BE STRICTLY SAID THAT THE PEOPLE GOVERN IN THE UNITED STATES.

In America, the people appoint the legislative and the executive power, and furnish the jurors who punish all infractions of the laws. The institutions are democratic, not only in their principle, but in all their consequences; and the people elect their representatives *directly*, and for the most part *annually*, in order to insure their dependence. The people are, therefore, the real directing power; and although the form of government is representative, it is evident that the opinions, the prejudices, the interests, and even the passions of the people are hindered by no permanent obstacles from exercising a perpetual influence on the daily conduct of affairs. In the United States, the majority governs in the name of the people, as is the case in all countries in which the people are supreme. This majority is principally composed of peaceable citizens, who, either by inclination or by interest, sincerely wish the welfare of their country. But they are surrounded by the incessant agitation of parties, who attempt to gain their co-operation and support.

CHAPTER X.

PARTIES IN THE UNITED STATES.

Great Distinction to be made between Parties. — Parties which are to each other as rival Nations. — Parties properly so called. — Difference between great and small Parties. — Epochs which produce them. — Their Characteristics. — America has had great Parties. — They are extinct. — Federalists. — Republicans. — Defeat of the Federalists. — Difficulty of creating Parties in the United States. — What is done with this Intention. — Aristocratic or Democratic Character to be met with in all Parties. — Struggle of General Jackson against the Bank.

A GREAT distinction must be made between parties. Some countries are so large that the different populations which inhabit them, although united under the same government, have contradictory interests; and they may consequently be in a perpetual state of opposition. In this case, the different fractions of the people may more properly be considered as distinct nations than as mere parties; and if a civil war breaks out, the struggle is carried on by rival states rather than by factions in the same state.

But when the citizens entertain different opinions upon subjects which affect the whole country alike, — such, for instance, as the principles upon which the government is to be conducted, — then distinctions arise which may correctly be styled parties. Parties are a necessary evil in free governments; but they have not at all times the same character and the same propensities.

At certain periods, a nation may be oppressed by such

insupportable evils as to conceive the design of effecting a total change in their political constitution ; at other times, the mischief lies still deeper, and the existence of society itself is endangered. Such are the times of great revolutions and of great parties. But between these epochs of misery and confusion there are periods during which human society seems to rest, and mankind to take breath. This pause is, indeed, only apparent ; for time does not stop its course for nations any more than for men ; they are all advancing every day towards a goal with which they are unacquainted. We imagine them to be stationary only when their progress escapes our observation, as men who are going at a foot-pace seem to be standing still to those who run.

But however this may be, there are certain epochs at which the changes that take place in the social and political constitution of nations are so slow and insensible, that men imagine they have reached a final state ; and the human mind, believing itself to be firmly based upon sure foundations, does not extend its researches beyond a certain horizon. These are the times of small parties and of intrigue.

The political parties which I style great are those which cling to principles rather than to their consequences ; to general, and not to special cases ; to ideas, and not to men. These parties are usually distinguished by nobler features, more generous passions, more genuine convictions, and a more bold and open conduct, than the others. In them, private interest, which always plays the chief part in political passions, is more studiously veiled under the pretext of the public good ; and it may even be sometimes concealed from the eyes of the very persons whom it excites and impels.

Minor parties, on the other hand, are generally deficient in political good faith. As they are not sustained or digni-

fied by lofty purposes, they ostensibly display the selfishness of their character in their actions. They glow with
a factitious zeal; their language is vehement; but their
conduct is timid and irresolute. The means which they
employ are as wretched as the end at which they aim.
Hence it happens, that, when a calm state succeeds a
violent revolution, great men seem suddenly to disappear,
and the powers of the human mind to lie concealed. Society is convulsed by great parties, it is only agitated by
minor ones; it is torn by the former, by the latter it is
degraded; and if the first sometimes save it by a salutary
perturbation, the last invariably disturb it to no good end.

America has had great parties, but has them no longer;
and if her happiness is thereby considerably increased, her
morality has suffered. When the war of independence
was terminated, and the foundations of the new government were to be laid down, the nation was divided between two opinions, — two opinions which are as old as
the world, and which are perpetually to be met with, under
different forms and various names, in all free communities,
— the one tending to limit, the other to extend indefinitely,
the power of the people. The conflict between these two
opinions never assumed that degree of violence in America
which it has frequently displayed elsewhere. Both parties
of the Americans were agreed upon the most essential
points; and neither of them had to destroy an old constitution, or to overthrow the structure of society, in order to
triumph. In neither of them, consequently, were a great
number of private interests affected by success or defeat:
but moral principles of a high order, such as the love of
equality and of independence, were concerned in the
struggle, and these sufficed to kindle violent passions.

The party which desired to limit the power of the
people, endeavored to apply its doctrines more especially
to the Constitution of the Union, whence it derived its

name of *Federal*. The other party, which affected to be exclusively attached to the cause of liberty, took that of *Republican*. America is the land of democracy, and the Federalists, therefore, were always in a minority; but they reckoned on their side almost all the great men whom the war of independence had produced, and their moral power was very considerable. Their cause was, moreover, favored by circumstances. The ruin of the first Confederation had impressed the people with a dread of anarchy, and the Federalists profited by this transient disposition of the multitude. For ten or twelve years, they were at the head of affairs, and they were able to apply some, though not all, of their principles; for the hostile current was becoming from day to day too violent to be checked. In 1801, the Republicans got possession of the government: Thomas Jefferson was elected President; and he increased the influence of their party by the weight of his great name, the brilliancy of his talents, and his immense popularity.

The means by which the Federalists had maintained their position were artificial, and their resources were temporary: it was by the virtues or the talents of their leaders, as well as by fortunate circumstances, that they had risen to power. When the Republicans attained that station in their turn, their opponents were overwhelmed by utter defeat. An immense majority declared itself against the retiring party, and the Federalists found themselves in so small a minority, that they at once despaired of future success. From that moment, the Republican or Democratic party has proceeded from conquest to conquest, until it has acquired absolute supremacy in the country. The Federalists, perceiving that they were vanquished without resource, and isolated in the midst of the nation, fell into two divisions, of which one joined the victorious Republicans, and the other laid down their banners and changed their name. Many years have elapsed since they wholly ceased to exist as a party.

The accession of the Federalists to power was, in my opinion, one of the most fortunate incidents which accompanied the formation of the great American Union: they resisted the inevitable propensities of their country and their age. But whether their theories were good or bad, they had the fault of being inapplicable, as a whole, to the society which they wished to govern, and that which occurred under the auspices of Jefferson must therefore have taken place sooner or later. But their government at least gave the new republic time to acquire a certain stability, and afterwards to support without inconvenience the rapid growth of the very doctrines which they had combated. A considerable number of their principles, moreover, were embodied at last in the political creed of their opponents; and the Federal Constitution, which subsists at the present day, is a lasting monument of their patriotism and their wisdom.

Great political parties, then, are not to be met with in the United States at the present time. Parties, indeed, may be found which threaten the future of the Union; but there are none which seem to contest the present form of government, or the present course of society. The parties by which the Union is menaced do not rest upon principles, but upon material interests. These interests constitute, in the different provinces of so vast an empire, rival nations rather than parties. Thus, upon a recent occasion [1832], the North contended for the system of commercial prohibition, and the South took up arms in favor of free trade, simply because the North is a manufacturing and the South an agricultural community; and the restrictive system which was profitable to the one, was prejudicial to the other.

In the absence of great parties, the United States swarm with lesser controversies; and public opinion is divided into a thousand minute shades of difference upon questions of detail. The pains which are taken to create parties are inconceivable, and at the present day it is no easy task. In the United States, there is no religious animosity, because all religion is respected, and no sect is predominant; there is no jealousy of rank, because the people are everything, and none can contest their authority; lastly, there is no public misery to serve as a means of agitation, because the physical position of the country opens so wide a field to industry, that man only needs to be let alone to be able to accomplish prodigies. Nevertheless, ambitious men will succeed in creating parties, since it is difficult to eject a person from authority upon the mere ground that his place is coveted by others. All the skill of the actors in the political world lies in the art of creating parties. A political aspirant in the United States begins by discerning his own interest, and discovering those other interests which may be collected around, and amalgamated with it. He then contrives to find out some doctrine or principle which may suit the purposes of this new association, and which he adopts in order to bring forward his party and secure its popularity: just as the *imprimatur* of the king was in former days printed upon the title-page of a volume, and was thus incorporated with a book to which it in no wise belonged. This being done, the new party is ushered into the political world.

All the domestic controversies of the Americans at first appear to a stranger to be incomprehensible or puerile, and he is at a loss whether to pity a people who take such arrant trifles in good earnest, or to envy that happiness which enables a community to discuss them. But when he comes to study the secret propensities which govern the factions of America, he easily perceives that the greater part of them are more or less connected with one or the other of those two great divisions which have always existed in free communities. The deeper we penetrate into the inmost thought of these parties, the more do we perceive that the object of the one is to limit, and that of the other to extend, the authority of the people. I do not assert that the ostensible purpose, or even that the secret aim, of American parties is to promote the rule of aristocracy or democracy in the country; but I affirm that aristocratic or democratic passions may easily be detected at the bottom of all parties, and that, although they escape a superficial observation, they are the main point and soul of every faction in the United States.

To quote a recent example: — when President Jackson attacked the Bank, the country was excited, and parties were formed; the well-informed classes rallied round the Bank, the common people round the President. But it must not be imagined that the people had formed a rational opinion upon a question which offers so many difficulties to the most experienced statesmen. By no means. The Bank is a great establishment, which has an independent existence; and the people, accustomed to make and unmake whatsoever they please, are startled to meet with this obstacle to their authority. In the midst of the perpetual fluctuation of society, the community is irritated by so permanent an institution, and is led to attack it, in order to see whether it can be shaken, like everything else.

REMAINS OF THE ARISTOCRATIC PARTY IN THE UNITED STATES.

Secret Opposition of wealthy Individuals to Democracy. — Their Retirement. — Their Taste for exclusive Pleasures and for Luxury at Home. — Their Simplicity abroad. — Their affected Condescension towards the People.

IT sometimes happens, in a people amongst whom various opinions prevail, that the balance of parties is lost, and one of them obtains an irresistible preponderance, overpowers all obstacles, annihilates its opponents, and appropriates all the resources of society to its own use. The vanquished despair of success, hide their heads, and are silent. The nation seems to be governed by a single principle, universal stillness prevails, and the prevailing party assumes the credit of having restored peace and unanimity to the country. But under this apparent unanimity still exist profound differences of opinion, and real opposition.

This is what occurred in America; when the democratic party got the upper hand, it took exclusive possession of the conduct of affairs, and from that time, the laws and the customs of society have been adapted to its caprices. At the present day, the more affluent classes of society have no influence in political affairs; and wealth, far from conferring a right, is rather a cause of unpopularity than a means of attaining power. The rich abandon the lists, through unwillingness to contend, and frequently to contend in vain, against the poorer classes of their fellow-citizens. As they cannot occupy in public a position equivalent to what they hold in private life, they abandon the former, and give themselves up to the latter; and they constitute a private society in the state, which has its own tastes and pleasures. They submit to this state of things as an irremediable evil, but they are careful not to show that they are galled by its continuance; one often hears them laud the advantages of a republican government and democratic institutions when they are in public. Next to hating their enemies, men are most inclined to flatter them.

Mark, for instance, that opulent citizen, who is as anxious as a Jew of the Middle Ages to conceal his wealth. His dress is plain, his demeanor unassuming; but the interior of his dwelling glitters with luxury, and none but a few chosen guests, whom he haughtily styles his equals, are allowed to penetrate into this sanctuary. No European noble is more exclusive in his pleasures, or more jealous of the smallest advantages which a privileged station confers. But the same individual crosses the city to reach a dark counting-house in the centre of traffic, where every one may accost him who pleases. If he meets his cobbler upon the way, they stop and converse; the two citizens discuss the affairs of the state, and shake hands before they part.

But beneath this artificial enthusiasm, and these obsequious attentions to the preponderating power, it is easy to perceive that the rich have a hearty dislike of the democratic institutions of their country. The people form a power which they at once fear and despise. If the maladministration of the democracy ever brings about a revolutionary crisis, and monarchical institutions ever become practicable in the United States, the truth of what I advance will become obvious.

The two chief weapons which parties use in order to obtain success are the *newspapers* and public *associations*.

CHAPTER XI.

LIBERTY OF THE PRESS IN THE UNITED STATES.

Difficulty of restraining the Liberty of the Press. — Particular Reasons which some Nations have for cherishing this Liberty. — The Liberty of the Press a necessary Consequence of the Sovereignty of the People as it is understood in America. — Violent Language of the Periodical Press in the United States. — The Periodical Press has some peculiar Instincts, proved by the Example of the United States. — Opinion of the Americans upon the Judicial Repression of the Abuses of the Press — Why the Press is less powerful in America than in France.

THE influence of the liberty of the press does not affect political opinions alone, but extends to all the opinions of men, and modifies customs as well as laws. In another part of this work, I shall attempt to determine the degree of influence which the liberty of the press has exercised upon civil society in the United States, and to point out the direction which it has given to the ideas, as well as the tone which it has imparted to the character and the feelings, of the Anglo-Americans. At present, I purpose only to examine the effects produced by the liberty of the press in the political world.

I confess that I do not entertain that firm and complete attachment to the liberty of the press which is wont to be excited by things that are supremely good in their very nature. I approve of it from a consideration more of the evils it prevents, than of the advantages it insures.

If any one could point out an intermediate and yet a tenable position between the complete independence and the entire servitude of opinion, I should, perhaps, be inclined to adopt it; but the difficulty is, to discover this intermediate position.   Intending to correct the licentiousness of the press, and to restore the use of orderly language, you first try the offender by a jury; but if the jury acquits him, the opinion which was that of a single individual becomes the opinion of the whole country.   Too much and too little has therefore been done; go farther, then.   You bring the delinquent before permanent magistrates; but even here, the cause must be heard before it can be decided; and the very principles which no book would have ventured to avow are blazoned forth in the pleadings, and what was obscurely hinted at in a single composition is thus repeated in a multitude of other publications.   The language is only the expression, and (if I may so speak) the body, of the thought, but it is not the thought itself. Tribunals may condemn the body, but the sense, the spirit, of the work is too subtile for their authority.   Too much has still been done to recede, too little to attain your end; you must go still farther.   Establish a censorship of the press.   But the tongue of the public speaker will still make itself heard, and your purpose is not yet accomplished; you have only increased the mischief.   Thought is not, like physical strength, dependent upon the number of its agents; nor can authors be counted like the troops which compose an army.   On the contrary, the authority of a principle is often increased by the small number of men by whom it is expressed.   The words of one strong-minded man, addressed to the passions of a listening assembly, have more power than the vociferations of a thousand orators; and if it be allowed to speak freely in any one public place, the consequence is the same as if free speaking was allowed in every village.   The liberty of speech must therefore be destroyed, as well as the liberty of the press.   And now you have succeeded, everybody is reduced to silence.   But your object was to repress the abuses of liberty, and you are brought to the feet of a despot. You have been led from the extreme of independence to the extreme of servitude, without finding a single tenable position on the way at which you could stop.

There are certain nations which have peculiar reasons for cherishing the liberty of the press, independently of the general motives which I have just pointed out. For in certain countries which profess to be free, every individual agent of the government may violate the laws with impunity, since the constitution does not give to those who are injured a right of complaint before the courts of justice. In this case, the liberty of the press is not merely one of the guaranties, but it is the only guaranty, of their liberty and security which the citizens possess. If the rulers of these nations proposed to abolish the independence of the press, the whole people might answer, Give us the right of prosecuting your offences before the ordinary tribunals, and perhaps we may then waive our right of appeal to the tribunal of public opinion.

In countries where the doctrine of the sovereignty of the people ostensibly prevails, the censorship of the press is not only dangerous, but absurd. When the right of every citizen to a share in the government of society is acknowledged, every one must be presumed to be able to choose between the various opinions of his contemporaries, and to appreciate the different facts from which inferences may be drawn. The sovereignty of the people and the liberty of the press may therefore be regarded as correlative; just as the censorship of the press and universal suffrage are two things which are irreconcilably opposed, and which cannot long be retained among the institutions of the same people. Not a single individual of the [thirty] millions who inhabit the United States has, as yet, dared to propose any restrictions on the liberty of the press. The first newspaper over which I cast my eyes, upon my arrival in America, contained the following article : —

"In all this affair, the language of Jackson [the President] has been that of a heartless despot, solely occupied with the preservation of his own authority. Ambition is his crime, and it will be his punishment, too: intrigue is his native element, and intrigue will confound his tricks, and deprive him of his power. He governs by means of corruption, and his immoral practices will redound to his shame and confusion. His conduct in the political arena has been that of a shameless and lawless game-ster. He succeeded at the time; but the hour of retribution ap-proaches, and he will be obliged to disgorge his winnings, to throw aside his false dice, and to end his days in some retirement, where he may curse his madness at his leisure; for repentance is a virtue with which his heart is likely to remain forever unac-quainted."

Many persons in France think, that the violence of the press originates in the instability of the social state, in our political passions, and the general feeling of uneasiness which consequently prevails; and it is therefore supposed that, as soon as society has resumed a certain degree of composure, the press will abandon its present vehemence. For my own part, I would willingly attribute to these causes the extraordinary ascendency which the press has acquired over the nation; but I do not think that they do exercise much influence upon its language. The periodi-cal press appears to me to have passions and instincts of its own, independent of the circumstances in which it is placed; and the present condition of America corroborates this opinion.

America is perhaps, at this moment, the country of the whole world which contains the fewest germs of revolu-tion; but the press is not less destructive in its principles there than in France, and it displays the same violence without the same reasons for indignation. In America, as in France, it constitutes a singular power, so strangely composed of mingled good and evil, that liberty could not live without it, and public order can hardly be maintained against it. Its power is certainly much greater in France than in the United States; though nothing is more rare in the latter country than to hear of a prosecution being instituted against it. The reason of this is perfectly simple: the Americans, having once admitted the doctrine of the sovereignty of the people, apply it with perfect sincerity. It was never their intention out of elements which are changing every day to create institutions which should last forever; and there is consequently nothing criminal in an attack upon the existing laws, provided a violent infraction of them is not intended. They are also of opinion that courts of justice are powerless to check the abuses of the press; and that, as the subtilty of human language perpetually eludes judicial analysis, offences of this nature somehow escape the hand which attempts to seize them. They hold that, to act with efficacy upon the press, it would be necessary to find a tribunal, not only devoted to the existing order of things, but capable of surmounting the influence of public opinion; a tribunal which should conduct its proceedings without publicity, which should pronounce its decrees without assigning its motives, and punish the intentions, even more than the language, of a writer. Whoever should be able to create and maintain a tribunal of this kind, would waste his time in prosecuting the liberty of the press; for he would be the absolute master of the whole community, and would be as free to rid himself of the authors as of their writings. In this question, therefore, there is no medium between servitude and license; in order to enjoy the inestimable benefits which the liberty of the press insures, it is necessary to submit to the inevitable evils which it creates. To expect to acquire the former, and to escape the latter, is to cherish one of those illusions which commonly mislead nations in their times of sickness, when, tired with faction and exhausted by effort, they attempt to make hostile opinions and contrary principles coexist upon the same soil.

The small influence of the American journals is attributable to several reasons, amongst which are the following.

The liberty of writing, like all other liberty, is most formidable when it is a novelty; for a people who have never been accustomed to hear state affairs discussed before them, place implicit confidence in the first tribune who presents himself. The Anglo-Americans have enjoyed this liberty ever since the foundation of the Colonies; moreover, the press cannot create human passions, however skilfully it may kindle them where they exist. In America, political life is active, varied, even agitated, but is rarely affected by those deep passions which are excited only when material interests are impaired: and in the United States, these interests are prosperous. A glance at a French and an American newspaper is sufficient to show the difference which exists in this respect between the two nations. In France, the space allotted to commercial advertisements is very limited, and the news-intelligence is not considerable; but the essential part of the journal is the discussion of the politics of the day. In America, three quarters of the enormous sheet are filled with advertisements, and the remainder is frequently occupied by political intelligence or trivial anecdotes: it is only from time to time, that one finds a corner devoted to passionate discussions, like those which the journalists of France every day give to their readers.

It has been demonstrated by observation, and discovered by the sure instinct even of the pettiest despots, that the influence of a power is increased in proportion as its direction is centralized. In France, the press combines a twofold centralization; almost all its power is centred in the same spot, and, so to speak, in the same hands; for its organs are far from numerous. The influence of a public press thus constituted, upon a sceptical nation, must be almost unbounded. It is an enemy with whom a government may sign an occasional truce, but which it is difficult to resist for any length of time.

Neither of these kinds of centralization exists in America. The United States have no metropolis; the intelligence and the power of the people are disseminated through all the parts of this vast country, and instead of radiating from a common point, they cross each other in every direction; the Americans have nowhere established any central direction of opinion, any more than of the conduct of affairs. This difference arises from local circumstances, and not from human power; but it is owing to the laws of the Union that there are no licenses to be granted to printers, no securities demanded from editors, as in France, and no stamp duty, as in France and England. The consequence is, that nothing is easier than to set up a newspaper, as a small number of subscribers suffices to defray the expenses.

Hence the number of periodical and semi-periodical pub lications in the United States is almost incredibly large. The most enlightened Americans attribute the little in fluence of the press to this excessive dissemination of its power; and it is an axiom of political science in that country, that the only way to neutralize the effect of the public journals is to multiply their number. I cannot see how a truth which is so self-evident should not already have been more generally admitted in Europe. I can see why the persons who hope to bring about revolutions by means of the press, should be desirous of confining it to a few powerful organs; but it is inconceivable that the official partisans of the existing state of things, and the natural supporters of the laws, should attempt to diminish the influence of the press by concentrating its power. The governments of Europe seem to treat the press with the courtesy which the knights of old showed to their opponents; having found from their own experience that centralization is a powerful weapon, they have furnished their enemies with it, in order doubtless to have more glory for overcoming them.

In America, there is scarcely a hamlet which has not its newspaper. It may readily be imagined, that neither discipline nor unity of action can be established among so many combatants; and each one consequently fights under his own standard. All the political journals of the United States are, indeed, arrayed on the side of the administration or against it; but they attack and defend it in a thousand different ways. They cannot form those great currents of opinion which sweep away the strongest dikes. This division of the influence of the press produces other consequences scarcely less remarkable. The facility with which newspapers can be established produces a multitude of them; but as the competition prevents any considerable profit, persons of much capacity are rarely led to engage in these undertakings. Such is the number of the public prints, that, even if they were a source of wealth, writers of ability could not be found to direct them all. The journalists of the United States are generally in a very humble position, with a scanty education and a vulgar turn of mind. The will of the majority is the most general of laws, and it establishes certain habits to which every one must then conform; the aggregate of these common habits is what is called the class-spirit (*esprit de corps*) of each profession; thus there is the class-spirit of the bar, of the court, &c. The class-spirit of the French journalists consists in a violent, but frequently an eloquent and lofty, manner of discussing the great interests of the state; and the exceptions to this mode of writing are only occasional. The characteristics of the American journalist consist in an open and coarse appeal to the passions of his readers;

he abandons principles to assail the characters of individuals, to track them into private life, and disclose all their weaknesses and vices.

Nothing can be more deplorable than this abuse of the powers of thought; I shall have occasion to point out hereafter the influence of the newspapers upon the taste and the morality of the American people; but my present subject exclusively concerns the political world. It cannot be denied, that the political effects of this extreme license of the press tend indirectly to the maintenance of public order. The individuals who already stand high in the esteem of their fellow-citizens are afraid to write in the newspapers, and they are thus deprived of the most powerful instrument which they can use to excite the passions of the multitude to their own advantage.*

The personal opinions of the editors have no weight in the eyes of the public: what they seek in a newspaper is a knowledge of facts, and it is only by altering or distorting those facts, that a journalist can contribute to the support of his own views.

But although the press is limited to these resources, its influence in America is immense. It causes political life to circulate through all the parts of that vast territory. Its eye is constantly open to detect the secret springs of political designs, and to summon the leaders of all parties in turn to the bar of public opinion. It rallies the interests of the community round certain principles, and draws up the creed of every party; for it affords a means of intercourse between those who hear and address each other, without ever coming into immediate contact. When many organs of the press adopt the same line of conduct, their influence in the long run becomes irresistible; and public

* They only write in the papers when they choose to address the people in their own name; as, for instance, when they are called upon to repel calumnious imputations, or to correct a misstatement of facts.

opinion, perpetually assailed from the same side, eventually yields to the attack.   In the United States, each separate journal exercises but little authority; but the power of the periodical press is second only to that of the people.*

The Opinions established in the United States, under the Influence of the Liberty of the Press, are frequently more firmly rooted than those which are formed elsewhere under the Sanction of a Censor.

IN the United States, the democracy perpetually brings new men to the conduct of public affairs; and the administration consequently seldom preserves consistency or order in its measures.   But the general principles of the government are more stable, and the chief opinions which regulate society are more durable, there than in many other countries.   When once the Americans have taken up an idea, whether it be well or ill founded, nothing is more difficult than to eradicate it from their minds.   The same tenacity of opinion has been observed in England, where, for the last century, greater freedom of thought and more invincible prejudices have existed than in any other country of Europe.   I attribute this to a cause which may, at first sight, appear to have an opposite tendency, namely, to the liberty of the press.   The nations amongst whom this liberty exists cling to their opinions as much from pride as from conviction.   They cherish them because they hold them to be just, and because they chose them of their own free will; and they adhere to them, not only because they are true, but because they are their own.   Several other reasons conduce to the same end.

It was remarked by a man of genius, that "ignorance lies at the two ends of knowledge."   Perhaps it would have been more correct to say, that strong convictions are found only at the two ends, and that doubt lies in the middle.

* See Appendix P.

The human intellect, in truth, may be considered in three distinct states, which frequently succeed one another.

A man believes firmly, because he adopts a proposition without inquiry. He doubts as soon as objections present themselves. But he frequently succeeds in satisfying these doubts, and then he begins again to believe. This time, he has not a dim and casual glimpse of the truth, but sees it clearly before him, and advances by the light it gives.*

When the liberty of the press acts upon men who are in the first of these three states, it does not immediately disturb their habit of believing implicitly without investigation, but it changes every day the objects of their unreflecting convictions. The human mind continues to discern but one point at a time upon the whole intellectual horizon, and that point is constantly changing. This is the period of sudden revolutions. Woe to the generations which first abruptly adopt the freedom of the press.

The circle of novel ideas, however, is soon travelled over. Experience comes to undeceive men, and plunges them into doubt and general mistrust. We may rest assured that the majority of mankind will always stop in one of these two states, will either believe they know not wherefore, or will not know what to believe. Few are those who can ever attain to that other state of rational and independent conviction, which true knowledge can produce out of the midst of doubt.

It has been remarked that, in times of great religious fervor, men sometimes change their religious opinions; whereas, in times of general scepticism, every one clings to his old persuasion. The same thing takes place in politics under the liberty of the press. In countries where all the theories of social science have been contested in their turn,

* It may, however, be doubted whether this rational and self-guiding conviction arouses as much fervor or enthusiastic devotedness in men, as their first dogmatical belief.

men who have adopted one of them stick to it, not so much because they are sure of its truth, as because they are not sure that there is any better to be had. In the present age, men are not very ready to die for their opinions, but they are rarely inclined to change them; there are few martyrs, as well as few apostates.

Another still more valid reason may be adduced: when no opinions are looked upon as certain, men cling to the mere instincts and material interests of their position, which are naturally more tangible, definite, and permanent than any opinions in the world.

It is a very difficult question to decide, whether an aristocracy or a democracy governs the best. But it is certain that democracy annoys one part of the community, and that aristocracy oppresses another. It is a truth which is self-established, and one which it is needless to discuss, that " you are rich and I am poor."

CHAPTER XII.

POLITICAL ASSOCIATIONS IN THE UNITED STATES.

Daily Use which the Anglo-Americans make of the Right of Association. — Three Kinds of Political Associations. — How the Americans apply the Representative System to Associations. — Dangers resulting to the State. — Great Convention of 1831 relative to the Tariff. — Legislative Character of this Convention. — Why the unlimited Exercise of the Right of Association is less dangerous in the United States than elsewhere. — Why it may be looked upon as necessary. — Utility of Associations among a democratic People.

IN no country in the world has the principle of association been more successfully used, or applied to a greater multitude of objects, than in America. Besides the permanent associations, which are established by law, under the names of townships, cities, and counties, a vast number of others are formed and maintained by the agency of private individuals.

The citizen of the United States is taught from infancy to rely upon his own exertions, in order to resist the evils and the difficulties of life; he looks upon the social authority with an eye of mistrust and anxiety, and he claims its assistance only when he is unable to do without it. This habit may be traced even in the schools, where the children in their games are wont to submit to rules which they have themselves established, and to punish misdemeanors which they have themselves defined. The same spirit pervades every act of social life. If a stoppage occurs in a thoroughfare, and the circulation of vehicles is hindered, the neighbors immediately form themselves into a deliberative body; and this extemporaneous assembly gives rise to an executive power, which remedies the inconvenience before anybody has thought of recurring to a pre-existing authority superior to that of the persons immediately concerned. If some public pleasure is concerned, an association is formed to give more splendor and regularity to the entertainment. Societies are formed to resist evils which are exclusively of a moral nature, as to diminish the vice of intemperance. In the United States, associations are established to promote the public safety, commerce, industry, morality, and religion. There is no end which the human will despairs of attaining through the combined power of individuals united into a society.

I shall have occasion hereafter to show the effects of association in civil life; I confine myself for the present to the political world. When once the right of association is recognized, the citizens may use it in different ways.

An association consists simply in the public assent which a number of individuals give to certain doctrines; and in the engagement which they contract to promote in a certain manner the spread of those doctrines. The right of associating with such views is very analogous to the liberty of unlicensed printing; but societies thus formed possess more authority than the press. When an opinion is represented by a society, it necessarily assumes a more exact and explicit form. It numbers its partisans, and compromises them in its cause: they, on the other hand, become acquainted with each other, and their zeal is increased by their number. An association unites into one channel the efforts of diverging minds, and urges them vigorously towards the one end which it clearly points out.

The second degree in the exercise of the right of association is the power of meeting. When an association is allowed to establish centres of action at certain important points in the country, its activity is increased, and its influence extended. Men have the opportunity of seeing each other; means of execution are combined; and opinions are maintained with a warmth and energy which written language can never attain.

Lastly, in the exercise of the right of political association, there is a third degree: the partisans of an opinion may unite in electoral bodies, and choose delegates to represent them in a central assembly. This is, properly speaking, the application of the representative system to a party.

Thus, in the first instance, a society is formed between individuals professing the same opinion, and the tie which keeps it together is of a purely intellectual nature. In the second case, small assemblies are formed, which represent only a fraction of the party. Lastly, in the third case, they constitute, as it were, a separate nation in the midst of the nation, a government within the government. Their delegates, like the real delegates of the majority, represent the whole collective force of their party; and, like them, also, have an appearance of nationality and all the moral power which results from it. It is true that they have not the right, like the others, of making the laws; but they have the power of attacking those which are in force, and of drawing up beforehand those which ought to be enacted.

If, among a people who are imperfectly accustomed to the exercise of freedom, or are exposed to violent political passions, by the side of the majority who make the laws be placed a minority who only deliberate and get laws ready for adoption, I cannot but believe that public tranquillity would there incur very great risks. There is doubtless a wide difference between proving that one law is in itself better than another, and proving that the former ought to be substituted for the latter. But the imagination of the multitude is very apt to overlook this difference, which is so apparent to the minds of thinking men.

It sometimes happens that a nation is divided into two nearly equal parties, each of which affects to represent the majority. If, near the directing power, another power be established, which exercises almost as much moral authority as the former, we are not to believe that it will long be content to speak without acting ; or that it will always be restrained by the abstract consideration that associations are meant to direct opinions, but not to enforce them, — to suggest, but not to make, the laws.

The more I consider the independence of the press in its principal consequences, the more am I convinced that, in the modern world, it is the chief, and, so to speak, the constitutive element of liberty. A nation which is determined to remain free is therefore right in demanding, at any price, the exercise of this independence. But the *unlimited* liberty of political association cannot be entirely assimilated to the liberty of the press. The one is at the same time less necessary, and more dangerous, than the other. A nation may confine it within certain limits without forfeiting any part of its self-directing power ; and it may sometimes be obliged to do so, in order to maintain its own authority.

In America, the liberty of association for political purposes is unlimited. An example will show in the clearest light to what an extent this privilege is tolerated.

The question of a tariff or free trade has much agitated the minds of Americans. The tariff was not only a subject of debate as a matter of opinion, but it affected some great material interests of the States. The North attributed a portion of its prosperity, and the South nearly all its sufferings, to this system. For a long time, the tariff was the sole source of the political animosities which agitated the Union.

In 1831, when the dispute was raging with the greatest violence, a private citizen of Massachusetts proposed, by means of the newspapers, to all the enemies of the tariff, to send delegates to Philadelphia, in order to consult together upon the best means of restoring freedom of trade. This proposal circulated in a few days, by the power of the press, from Maine to New Orleans: the opponents of the tariff adopted it with enthusiasm; meetings were held in all quarters, and delegates were appointed. The majority of these delegates were well known, and some of them had earned a considerable degree of celebrity. South Carolina alone, which afterwards took up arms in the same cause, sent sixty-three delegates. On the 1st of October, 1831, this assembly, which, according to the American custom, had taken the name of a Convention, met at Philadelphia; it consisted of more than two hundred members. Its debates were public, and they at once assumed a legislative character; the extent of the powers of Congress, the theories of free trade, and the different provisions of the tariff were discussed. At the end of ten days, the Convention broke up, having drawn up an address to the American people, in which it declared: — 1. That Congress had not the right of making a tariff, and that the existing tariff was unconstitutional. 2. That the prohibition of free trade was prejudicial to the interests of any nation, and to those of the American people especially.

It must be acknowledged that the unrestrained liberty of political association has not hitherto produced, in the United States, the fatal results which might perhaps be expected from it elsewhere. The right of association was imported from England, and it has always existed in America; the exercise of this privilege is now incorporated with the manners and customs of the people. At the present time, the liberty of association has become a necessary guaranty against the tyranny of the majority. In the United States, as soon as a party has become dominant, all public authority passes into its hands: its private supporters occupy all the offices, and have all the force of the administration at their disposal. As the most distinguished members of the opposite party cannot surmount the barrier which excludes them from power, they must establish themselves outside of it, and oppose the whole moral authority of the minority to the physical power which domineers over it. Thus a dangerous expedient is used to obviate a still more formidable danger.

The omnipotence of the majority appears to me to be so full of peril to the American republics, that the dangerous means used to bridle it seem to be more advantageous than prejudicial. And here I will express an opinion which may remind the reader of what I said when speaking of the freedom of townships. There are no countries in which associations are more needed, to prevent the despotism of faction or the arbitrary power of a prince, than those which are democratically constituted. In aristocratic nations, the body of the nobles and the wealthy are in themselves natural associations, which check the abuses of power. In countries where such associations do not exist, if private individuals cannot create an artificial and temporary substitute for them, I can see no permanent protection against the most galling tyranny; and a great people may be oppressed with impunity by a small faction, or by a single individual.

The meeting of a great political convention, (for there are conventions of all kinds,) which may frequently become a necessary measure, is always a serious occurrence, even in America, and one which judicious patriots cannot regard without alarm. This was very perceptible in the Convention of 1831, at which all the most distinguished members strove to moderate its language, and to restrain its objects within certain limits. It is probable that this Convention exercised a great influence on the minds of the malcontents, and prepared them for the open revolt against the commercial laws of the Union which took place in 1832.

It cannot be denied that the unrestrained liberty of association for political purposes is the privilege which a people
is longest in learning how to exercise. If it does not
throw the nation into anarchy, it perpetually augments the
chances of that calamity. On one point, however, this
perilous liberty offers a security against dangers of another
kind; in countries where associations are free, secret societies are unknown. In America, there are factions, but no
conspiracies.

Different Ways in which the Right of Association is understood in Europe and in the United States. — Different Use which is made of it.

THE most natural privilege of man, next to the right of
acting for himself, is that of combining his exertions with
those of his fellow-creatures, and of acting in common
with them. The right of association therefore appears to
me almost as inalienable in its nature as the right of personal liberty. No legislator can attack it without impairing
the foundations of society. Nevertheless, if the liberty
of association is only a source of advantage and prosperity
to some nations, it may be perverted or carried to excess
by others, and from an element of life may be changed
into a cause of destruction. A comparison of the different methods which associations pursue, in those countries
in which liberty is well understood, and in 'those where
liberty degenerates into license, may be useful both to governments and to parties.

Most Europeans look upon association as a weapon
which is to be hastily fashioned, and immediately tried in
the conflict. A society is formed for discussion, but the
idea of impending action prevails in the minds of all those
who constitute it. It is, in fact, an army; and the time
given to speech serves to reckon up the strength and to
animate the courage of the host, after which they march

against the enemy. Resources which lie within the bounds of law may suggest themselves, to the persons who compose it, as means, but never as the only means, of success.

Such, however, is not the manner in which the right of association is understood in the United States. In America, the citizens who form the minority associate, in order, first, to show their numerical strength, and so to diminish the moral power of the majority; and, secondly, to stimulate competition, and thus to discover those arguments which are most fitted to act upon the majority: for they always entertain hopes of drawing over the majority to their own side, and then disposing of the supreme power in its name. Political associations in the United States are therefore peaceable in their intentions, and strictly legal in the means which they employ; and they assert with perfect truth, that they aim at success only by lawful expedients.

The difference which exists in this respect between Americans and Europeans depends on several causes. In Europe, there are parties which differ so much from the majority, that they can never hope to acquire its support, and yet they think they are strong enough in themselves to contend against it. When a party of this kind forms an association, its object is, not to convince, but to fight. In America, the individuals who hold opinions much opposed to those of the majority can do nothing against it; and all other parties hope to win it over to their own principles. The exercise of the right of association becomes dangerous, then, in proportion as great parties find themselves wholly unable to acquire the majority. In a country like the United States, in which the differences of opinion are mere differences of hue, the right of association may remain unrestrained without evil consequences. Our inexperience of liberty leads us to regard the liberty of association only as a right of attacking the government. The first notion which presents itself to a party, as well as to an individual, when it has acquired a consciousness of its own strength, is that of violence: the notion of persuasion arises at a later period, and is derived from experience. The English, who are divided into parties which differ essentially from each other, rarely abuse the right of association, because they have long been accustomed to exercise it. In France, the passion for war is so intense, that there is no undertaking so mad, or so injurious to the welfare of the state, that a man does not consider himself honored in defending it at the risk of his life.

But perhaps the most powerful of the causes which tend to mitigate the violence of political associations in the United States is universal suffrage. In countries in which universal suffrage exists, the majority is never doubtful, because neither party can reasonably pretend to represent that portion of the community which has not voted. The associations know as well as the nation at large, that they do not represent the majority. This results, indeed, from the very fact of their existence; for if they did represent the preponderating power, they would change the law instead of soliciting its reform. The consequence of this is, that the moral influence of the government which they attack is much increased, and their own power is much enfeebled.

In Europe, there are few associations which do not affect to represent the majority, or which do not believe that they represent it. This conviction or this pretension tends to augment their force amazingly, and contributes no less to legalize their measures. Violence may seem to be excusable, in defence of the cause of oppressed right. Thus it is, in the vast complication of human laws, that extreme liberty sometimes corrects the abuses of liberty, and that extreme democracy obviates the dangers of democracy. In Europe, associations consider themselves, in some degree, as the legislative and executive council of the people, which is unable to speak for itself; moved by this belief, they act and they command. In America, where they represent in the eyes of all only a minority of the nation, they argue and petition.

The means which associations in Europe employ, are in accordance with the end which they propose to obtain. As the principal aim of these bodies is to act, and not to debate, to fight rather than to convince, they are naturally led to adopt an organization which is not civic and peaceable, but partakes of the habits and maxims of military life. They centralize, also, the direction of their forces as much as possible, and intrust the power of the whole party to a small number of leaders.

The members of these associations respond to a watchword, like soldiers on duty; they profess the doctrine of passive obedience; say rather, that in uniting together they at once abjure the exercise of their own judgment and free will: and the tyrannical control which these societies exercise, is often far more insupportable than the authority possessed over society by the government which they attack. Their moral force is much diminished by these proceedings, and they lose the sacred character which always attaches to a struggle of the oppressed against their oppressors. He who in given cases consents to obey his fellows with servility, and who submits his will, and even his thoughts, to their control, how can he pretend that he wishes to be free?

The Americans have also established a government in their associations, but it is invariably borrowed from the forms of the civil administration. The independence of each individual is formally recognized; as in society, all the members advance at the same time towards the same end; but they are not all obliged to follow the same track. No one abjures the exercise of his reason and free will; but every one exerts that reason and will to promote a common undertaking.

CHAPTER XIII.

GOVERNMENT OF THE DEMOCRACY IN AMERICA.

I AM well aware of the difficulties which attend this part of my subject; but although every expression which I am about to use may clash, upon some points, with the feelings of the different parties which divide my country, I shall still speak my whole thought.

In Europe, we are at a loss how to judge the true character and the permanent instincts of democracy, because in Europe two conflicting principles exist, and we do not know what to attribute to the principles themselves, and what to the passions which the contest produces. Such, however, is not the case in America; there the people reign without impediment, and they have no perils to dread, and no injuries to avenge. In America, democracy is given up to its own propensities; its course is natural, and its activity is unrestrained; there, consequently, its real character must be judged. And to no people can this inquiry be more vitally interesting than to the French nation, who are blindly driven onwards, by a daily and irresistible impulse, towards a state of things which may prove either despotic or republican, but which will assuredly be democratic.

UNIVERSAL SUFFRAGE.

I HAVE already observed that universal suffrage has been adopted in all the States of the Union: it consequently exists in communities which occupy very different positions in the social scale. I have had opportunities of observing its effects in different localities, and amongst races of men who are nearly strangers to each other in their language, their religion, and their modes of life; in Louisiana as well as in New England, in Georgia as in Canada. I have remarked that universal suffrage is far from producing in America either all the good or all the evil consequences which may be expected from it in Europe, and that its effects generally differ very much from those which are attributed to it.

THE CHOICE OF THE PEOPLE, AND THE INSTINCTIVE PREFERENCES OF THE AMERICAN DEMOCRACY.

In the United States, the ablest Men are rarely placed at the Head of Affairs. — Reason of this Peculiarity. — The Envy which prevails in the lower Orders of France against the higher Classes is not a French, but a purely democratic Feeling. — Why the most distinguished Men in America frequently seclude themselves from public Affairs.

MANY people in Europe are apt to believe without saying it, or to say without believing it, that one of the great advantages of universal suffrage is, that it intrusts the direction of affairs to men who are worthy of the public confidence. They admit that the people are unable to govern of themselves, but they aver that the people always wish the welfare of the state, and instinctively designate those who are animated by the same good wishes, and who are the most fit to wield the supreme authority. I confess that the observations I made in America by no means coincide with these opinions. On my arrival in the United States, I was surprised to find so much distinguished talent among the subjects, and so little among the heads of the government. It is a constant fact, that, at the present day, the ablest men in the United States are rarely placed at the head of affairs; and it must be acknowledged that such has been the result, in proportion as democracy has outstepped all its former limits. The race of American statesmen has evidently dwindled most remarkably in the course of the last fifty years.

Several causes may be assigned for this phenomenon. It is impossible, after the most strenuous exertions, to raise the intelligence of the people above a certain level. Whatever may be the facilities of acquiring information, whatever may be the profusion of easy methods and cheap science, the human mind can never be instructed and developed without devoting considerable time to these objects.

The greater or the less possibility of subsisting without labor is therefore the necessary boundary of intellectual improvement. This boundary is more remote in some countries, and more restricted in others; but it must exist somewhere, as long as the people are constrained to work in order to procure the means of subsistence, that is to say, as long as they continue to be the people. It is therefore quite as difficult to imagine a state in which all the citizens should be very well informed, as a state in which they should all be wealthy; these two difficulties are correlative. I readily admit that the mass of the citizens sincerely wish to promote the welfare of the country; nay, more, I even allow that the lower classes mix fewer considerations of personal interest with their patriotism than the higher orders; but it is always more or less difficult for them to discern the best means of attaining the end which they sincerely desire. Long and patient observation and much acquired knowledge are requisite to form a just estimate of the character of a single individual. Men of the greatest genius often fail to do it, and can it be supposed that the vulgar will always succeed? The people have neither the time nor the means for an investigation of this kind. Their conclusions are hastily formed from a superficial inspection of the more prominent features of a question. Hence it often happens that mountebanks of all sorts are able to please the people, whilst their truest friends frequently fail to gain their confidence.

Moreover, the democracy not only lack that soundness of judgment which is necessary to select men really deserving of their confidence, but often have not the desire or the inclination to find them out. It cannot be denied that democratic institutions strongly tend to promote the feeling of envy in the human heart; not so much because they afford to every one the means of rising to the same level with others, as because those means perpetually disappoint the persons who employ them. Democratic institutions awaken and foster a passion for equality which they can never entirely satisfy. This complete equality eludes the grasp of the people at the very moment when they think they have grasped it, and " flies," as Pascal says, " with an eternal flight "; the people are excited in the pursuit of an advantage, which is more precious because it is not sufficiently remote to be unknown, or sufficiently near to be enjoyed. The lower orders are agitated by the chance of success, they are irritated by its uncertainty; and they pass from the enthusiasm of pursuit to the exhaustion of ill-success, and lastly to the acrimony of disappointment. Whatever transcends their own limits appears to be an obstacle to their desires, and there is no superiority, however legitimate it may be, which is not irksome in their sight.

It has been supposed that the secret instinct, which leads the lower orders to remove their superiors as much as possible from the direction of public affairs, is peculiar to France. This, however, is an error; the instinct to which I allude is not French, it is democratic; it may have been heightened by peculiar political circumstances, but it owes its origin to a higher cause.

In the United States, the people do not hate the higher classes of society, but are not favorably inclined towards them, and carefully exclude them from the exercise of authority. They do not dread distinguished talents, but are rarely fond of them. In general, every one who rises without their aid seldom obtains their favor.

Whilst the natural instincts of democracy induce the people to reject distinguished citizens as their rulers, an instinct not less strong induces able men to retire from the political arena, in which it is so difficult to retain their independence, or to advance without becoming servile. This opinion has been candidly expressed by Chancellor Kent, who says, in speaking with high praise of that part of the Constitution which empowers the executive to nominate the judges: "It is indeed probable that the men who are best fitted to discharge the duties of this high office would have too much reserve in their manners, and too much austerity in their principles, for them to be returned by the majority at an election where universal suffrage is adopted." Such were the opinions which were printed without contradiction in America in the year 1830!

I hold it to be sufficiently demonstrated, that universal suffrage is by no means a guaranty of the wisdom of the popular choice. Whatever its advantages may be, this is not one of them.

CAUSES WHICH MAY PARTLY CORRECT THESE TENDENCIES OF THE DEMOCRACY.

Contrary Effects produced on Nations as on Individuals by great Dangers. — Why so many distinguished Men stood at the Head of Affairs in America fifty Years ago. — Influence which Intelligence and Morality exercise upon the popular Choice. — Example of New England. — States of the Southwest. — How certain Laws influence the Choice of the People. — Election by an elected Body. — Its Effects upon the Composition of the Senate.

WHEN serious dangers threaten the state, the people frequently succeed in selecting the citizens who are the most able to save it. It has been observed that man rarely retains his customary level in very critical circumstances; he rises above, or sinks below, his usual condition, and the same thing is true of nations. Extreme perils sometimes quench the energy of a people, instead of stimulating it; they excite, without directing its passions; and instead of clearing, they confuse its powers of perception. The Jews fought and killed each other amid the smoking ruins of their temple. But it is more common, both with nations and individuals, to find extraordinary virtues developed from the very imminence of the danger. Great characters are then brought into relief, as the edifices which are usually concealed by the gloom of night are illuminated by the glare of a conflagration. At those dangerous times, genius no longer hesitates to come forward; and the people, alarmed by the perils of their situation, bury their envious passions in a short oblivion. Great names may then be drawn from the urn of election.

I have already observed, that the American statesmen of the present day are very inferior to those who stood at the head of affairs fifty years ago. This is as much a consequence of the circumstances, as of the laws, of the country. When America was struggling in the high cause of independence, to throw off the yoke of another country, and when it was about to usher a new nation into the world, the spirits of its inhabitants were roused to the height which their great objects required. In this general excitement, distinguished men were ready to anticipate the call of the community, and the people clung to them for support, and placed them at their head. But such events are rare; and it is from the ordinary course of affairs that our judgment must be formed.

If passing occurrences sometimes check the passions of democracy, the intelligence and the morals of the community exercise an influence on them which is not less powerful, and far more permanent. This is very perceptible in the United States.

In New England, where education and liberty are the daughters of morality and religion, — where society has acquired age and stability enough to enable it to form principles and hold fixed habits, — the common people are accustomed to respect intellectual and moral superiority, and to submit to it without complaint, although they set at naught all those privileges which wealth and birth have introduced among mankind. In New England, consequently, the democracy makes a more judicious choice than it does elsewhere.

But as we descend towards the South, to those States in which the constitution of society is more recent and less strong, where instruction is less general, and the principles of morality, religion, and liberty are less happily combined, we perceive that talents and virtues become more rare among those who are in authority.

Lastly, when we arrive at the new Southwestern States, in which the constitution of society dates but from yesterday, and presents only an agglomeration of adventurers and speculators, we are amazed at the persons who are invested with public authority, and we are led to ask by what force, independent of the legislation and of the men who direct it, the state can be protected and society be made to flourish.

There are certain laws of a democratic nature which contribute, nevertheless, to correct, in some measure, these dangerous tendencies of democracy. On entering the House of Representatives at Washington, one is struck by the vulgar demeanor of that great assembly. Often there is not a distinguished man in the whole number. Its members are almost all obscure individuals, whose names bring no associations to mind. They are mostly village lawyers, men in trade, or even persons belonging to the lower classes of society. In a country in which education is very general, it is said that the representatives of the people do not always know how to write correctly.

At a few yards' distance is the door of the Senate, which contains within a small space a large proportion of the celebrated men of America. Scarcely an individual is to be seen in it who has not had an active and illustrious career: the Senate is composed of eloquent advocates, distinguished generals, wise magistrates, and statesmen of note, whose arguments would do honor to the most remarkable parliamentary debates of Europe.

How comes this strange contrast, and why are the ablest citizens found in one assembly rather than in the other? Why is the former body remarkable for its vulgar elements, whilst the latter seems to enjoy a monopoly of intelligence and talent? Both of these assemblies emanate from the people; both are chosen by universal suffrage; and no voice has hitherto been heard to assert, in America, that the Senate is hostile to the interests of the people. From what cause, then, does so startling a difference arise? The only reason which appears to me adequately to account for it is, that the House of Representatives is elected by the people directly, while the Senate is elected by elected bodies. The whole body of the citizens name the legislature of each State, and the Federal Constitution converts these legislatures into so many electoral bodies, which return the members of the Senate. The Senators are elected by an indirect application of the popular vote: for the legislatures which appoint them are not aristocratic or privileged bodies, which elect in their own right; but they are chosen by the totality of the citizens; they are generally elected every year, and new members may be chosen every year enough to determine the Senatorial appointments. But this transmission of the popular authority through an assembly of chosen men operates an important change in it, by refining its discretion and improving its choice. Men who are chosen in this manner accurately represent the majority of the nation which governs them; but they represent only the elevated thoughts which are current in the community, and the generous propensities which prompt its nobler actions, rather than the petty passions which disturb, or the vices which disgrace it.

The time must come when the American republics will be obliged more frequently to introduce the plan of election by an elected body into their system of representation, or run the risk of perishing miserably amongst the shoals of democracy.

I do not hesitate to avow, that I look upon this peculiar system of election as the only means of bringing the exercise of political power to the level of all classes of the people. Those who hope to convert this institution into the exclusive weapon of a party, and those who fear to use it, seem to me to be equally in error.

INFLUENCE WHICH THE AMERICAN DEMOCRACY HAS EXER-
CISED ON THE LAWS RELATING TO ELECTIONS.

When Elections are rare, they expose the State to a violent Crisis. — When
they are frequent, they keep up a feverish Excitement. — The Americans
have preferred the second of these two Evils. — Mutability of the Laws.
— Opinions of Hamilton, Madison, and Jefferson on this Subject.

WHEN elections recur only at long intervals, the state is
exposed to violent agitation every time they take place.
Parties then exert themselves to the utmost, in order to
gain a prize which is so rarely within their reach; and as
the evil is almost irremediable for the candidates who fail,
everything is to be feared from their disappointed ambition.
If, on the other hand, the legal struggle is soon to be repeated, the defeated parties take patience.

When elections occur frequently, their recurrence keeps
society in a feverish excitement, and gives a continual instability to public affairs. Thus, on the one hand, the state
is exposed to the perils of a revolution, — on the other, to
perpetual mutability; the former system threatens the very
existence of the government, the latter prevents any steady
and consistent policy. The Americans have preferred the
second of these evils to the first; but they were led to this
conclusion by instinct more than by reason, for a taste for
variety is one of the characteristic passions of democracy.
Hence their legislation is strangely mutable.

Many Americans consider the instability of their laws as
a necessary consequence of a system whose general results
are beneficial. But no one in the United States affects to
deny the fact of this instability, or contends that it is not a
great evil.

Hamilton, after having demonstrated the utility of a
power which might prevent, or at least impede, the promulgation of bad laws, adds: " It may perhaps be said, that
the power of preventing bad laws includes that of prevent-

ing good ones, and may be used to the one purpose as well as to the other. But this objection will have little weight with those who can properly estimate the mischiefs of that inconstancy and mutability in the laws which form the greatest blemish in the character and genius of our govern-ments." (Federalist, No. 73.)

And again, in No. 62 of the same work, he observes : " The facility and excess of law-making seem to be the dis-eases to which our governments are most liable."

Jefferson himself, the greatest democrat whom the de-mocracy of America has as yet produced, pointed out the same dangers.

" The instability of our laws," said he, " is really a very serious inconvenience. I think that we ought to have ob-viated it by deciding that a whole year should always be allowed to elapse between the bringing in of a bill and the final passing of it. It should afterwards be discussed and put to the vote without the possibility of making any al-teration in it ; and if the circumstances of the case required a more speedy decision, the question should not be decided by a simple majority, but by a majority of at least two thirds of both houses."

PUBLIC OFFICERS UNDER THE CONTROL OF THE AMERICAN DEMOCRACY.

Simple Exterior of American public Officers. — No official Costume. — All public Officers are remunerated. — Political Consequences of this Sys-tem. — No public Career exists in America. — Results of this Fact.

PUBLIC officers in the United States are confounded with the crowd of citizens ; they have neither palaces, nor guards, nor ceremonial costumes. This simple exterior of persons in authority is connected, not only with the pecu-liarities of the American character, but with the funda-mental principles of society. In the estimation of the democracy, a government is not a benefit, but a necessary evil. A certain degree of power must be granted to public officers, for they would be of no use without it. But the ostensible semblance of authority is by no means indispensable to the conduct of affairs ; and it is needlessly offensive to the susceptibility of the public. The public officers themselves are well aware, that they enjoy the superiority over their fellow-citizens which they derive from their authority, only on condition of putting themselves on a level with the whole community by their manners. A public officer in the United States is uniformly simple in his manners, accessible to all the world, attentive to all requests, and obliging in his replies. I was pleased by these characteristics of a democratic government; I admired the manly independence which respects the office more than the officer, and thinks less of the emblems of authority than of the man who bears them.

I believe that the influence which costumes really exercise, in an age like that in which we live, has been a good deal exaggerated. I never perceived that a public officer in America was the less respected, whilst in the discharge of his duties, because his own merit was set off by no adventitious signs. On the other hand, it is very doubtful whether a peculiar dress induces public men to respect themselves, when they are not otherwise inclined to do so. When a magistrate (and in France such instances are not rare) snubs the parties before him, or indulges his wit at their expense, or shrugs his shoulders at their pleas of defence, or smiles complacently as the charges are enumerated, I should like to deprive him of his robes of office, to see whether, when he is reduced to the garb of a private citizen, he would not recall some portion of the natural dignity of mankind.

No public officer in the United States has an official costume, but every one of them receives a salary. And this, also, still more naturally than what precedes, results from democratic principles. A democracy may allow some magisterial pomp, and clothe its officers in silks and gold, without seriously compromising its principles. Privileges of this kind are transitory; they belong to the place, and not to the man. But if public officers are unpaid, a class of rich and independent public functionaries will be created, who will constitute the basis of an aristocracy; and if the people still retain their right of election, the choice can be made only from a certain class of citizens.

When a democratic republic renders gratuitous offices which had formerly been remunerated, it may safely be inferred that the state is advancing towards monarchy. And when a monarchy begins to remunerate such officers as had hitherto been unpaid, it is a sure sign that it is approaching a despotic or a republican form of government. The substitution of paid for unpaid functionaries is of itself, in my opinion, sufficient to constitute a real revolution.

I look upon the entire absence of unpaid offices in America as one of the most prominent signs of the absolute dominion which democracy exercises in that country. All public services, of whatsoever nature they may be, are paid; so that every one has not merely a right, but also the means, of performing them. Although, in democratic states, all the citizens are qualified to hold offices, all are not tempted to try for them. The number and the capacities of the candidates, more than the conditions of the candidateship, restrict the choice of the electors.

In nations where the principle of election extends to everything, no political career can, properly speaking, be said to exist. Men arrive as if by chance at the post which they hold, and they are by no means sure of retaining it. This is especially true when the elections are held annually. The consequence is, that, in tranquil times, public functions offer but few lures to ambition. In the

United States, those who engage in the perplexities of political life are persons of very moderate pretensions. The pursuit of wealth generally diverts men of great talents and strong passions from the pursuit of power ; and it frequently happens that a man does not undertake to direct the fortunes of the state until he has shown himself incompetent to conduct his own. The vast number of very ordinary men who occupy public stations is quite as attributable to these causes, as to the bad choice of the democracy. In the United States, I am not sure that the people would choose men of superior abilities, even if they wished to be elected ; but it is certain that candidates of this description do not come forward.

ARBITRARY POWER OF MAGISTRATES* UNDER THE RULE OF THE AMERICAN DEMOCRACY.

For what Reason the arbitrary Power of Magistrates is greater in Absolute Monarchies and in Democratic Republics than it is in Limited Monarchies. — Arbitrary Power of the Magistrates in New England.

IN two kinds of government the magistrates exercise considerable arbitrary power, — namely, under the absolute government of an individual, and under that of a democracy. This identical result proceeds from very similar causes.

In despotic states, the fortune of no one is secure ; public officers are not more safe than private persons. The sovereign, who has under his control the lives, the property, and sometimes the honor, of the men whom he employs, thinks he has nothing to fear from them, and allows them great latitude of action, because he is convinced that they will not use it against him. In despotic states, the sover-

---

* I here use the word *magistrates* in its widest sense ; I apply it to all officers to whom the execution of the laws is intrusted.

eign is so much attached to his power, that he dislikes the constraint even of his own regulations, and likes to see his agents acting irregularly, and, as it were, by chance, in order to be sure that their actions will never counteract his desires.

In democracies, as the majority has every year the right of taking away the power of the officers whom it had appointed, it has no reason to fear any abuse of their authority. As the people are always able to signify their will to those who conduct the government, they prefer leaving them to their own free action, instead of prescribing an invariable rule of conduct, which would at once fetter their activity and the popular authority.

It may even be observed, on attentive consideration, that, under the rule of a democracy, the arbitrary action of the magistrate must be still greater than in despotic states. In the latter, the sovereign can immediately punish all the faults with which he becomes acquainted, but he cannot hope to become acquainted with all those which are committed. In democracies, on the contrary, the sovereign power is not only supreme, but universally present. The American functionaries are, in fact, much more free in the sphere of action which the law traces out for them than any public officer in Europe. Very frequently, the object which they are to accomplish is simply pointed out to them, and the choice of the means is left to their own discretion.

In New England, for instance, the selectmen of each township are bound to draw up the list of persons who are to serve on the jury; the only rule which is laid down to guide them in their choice is, that they are to select citizens possessing the elective franchise and enjoying a fair reputation.* In France, the lives and liberties of the subjects would be thought to be in danger, if a public officer of any

---

* It should be added, that the jurors are afterwards drawn from these lists by lot.

kind was intrusted with so formidable a right. In New England, the same magistrates are empowered to post the names of habitual drunkards in public houses, and to prohibit the inhabitants of a town from supplying them with liquor.* Such a censorial power would be revolting to the population of the most absolute monarchies; here, however, it is submitted to without difficulty.

Nowhere has so much been left by the law to the arbitrary determination of the magistrate as in democratic republics, because they have nothing to fear from arbitrary power. It may even be asserted that the freedom of the magistrate increases as the elective franchise is extended, and as the duration of the time of office is shortened. Hence arises the great difficulty of converting a democratic republic into a monarchy. The magistrate ceases to be elective, but he retains the rights and the habits of an elected officer, which lead directly to despotism.

It is only in limited monarchies that the law, which prescribes the sphere in which public officers are to act, superintends all their measures. The cause of this may be easily detected. In limited monarchies, the power is divided between the king and the people, both of whom are interested in the stability of the magistrate. The king does not venture to place the public officers under the control of the people, lest they should be tempted to betray his interests; on the other hand, the people fear lest the magistrates should serve to oppress the liberties of the country if they were entirely dependent upon the crown: they cannot,

* See Act of 28th February, 1787. [But this law is obsolete. And M. de Tocqueville's other instance is not happily chosen. In England, which is a limited monarchy, the jury lists are drawn up by the sheriff, and such a power is more formidable in the hands of one man than of several. In truth, the doctrine of the author here is a very questionable one. Magistrates in America do not have so much trusted to their discretion as in England or France. Their modes of action are prescribed beforehand by law, and defined with jealous care. — Am. Ed.]

therefore, be said to depend on either the one or the other. The same cause which induces the king and the people to render public officers independent, suggests the necessity of such securities as may prevent their independence from encroaching upon the authority of the former, or upon the liberties of the latter. They consequently agree as to the necessity of restricting the functionary to a line of conduct laid down beforehand, and find it for their interest to impose upon him certain regulations which he cannot evade.

INSTABILITY OF THE ADMINISTRATION IN THE UNITED STATES.

In America, the Public Acts of a Community frequently leave fewer Traces than the Occurrences in a Family. — Newspapers the only Historical Remains. — Instability of the Administration prejudicial to the Art of Government.

THE authority which public men possess in America is so brief, and they are so soon commingled with the ever-changing population of the country, that the acts of a community frequently leave fewer traces than the events in a private family. The public administration is, so to speak, oral and traditionary. But little is committed to writing, and that little is soon wafted away forever, like the leaves of the Sibyl, by the smallest breeze.

The only historical remains in the United States are the newspapers; if a number be wanting, the chain of time is broken, and the present is severed from the past. I am convinced that, in fifty years, it will be more difficult to collect authentic documents concerning the social condition of the Americans at the present day, than it is to find remains of the administration of France during the Middle Ages; and if the United States were ever invaded by barbarians, it would be necessary to have recourse to the

history of other nations, in order to learn anything of the
people who now inhabit them.

The instability of the administration has penetrated into
the habits of the people ; it even appears to suit the general
taste, and no one cares for what occurred before his time ;
no methodical system is pursued ; no archives are formed ;
and no documents are brought together when it would be
very easy to do so.* Where they exist, little store is set
upon them. I have amongst my papers several original
public documents, which were given to me in the public
offices, in answer to some of my inquiries. In America,
society seems to live from hand to mouth, like an army
in the field. Nevertheless, the art of administration is
undoubtedly a science, and no sciences can be improved
if the discoveries and observations of successive generations
are not connected together, in the order in which they
occur. One man, in the short space of his life, remarks
a fact, another conceives an idea ; the former invents a
means of execution, the latter reduces a truth to a formula ;
and mankind gather the fruits of individual experience on
their way, and gradually form the sciences. But the persons who conduct the administration in America can seldom afford any instruction to each other ; and when they
assume the direction of society, they simply possess those

---

* One would think that M. de Tocqueville had never seen the volumi-
nous documents which are printed every year, here in America, by the order
of the State legislatures and of Congress. In the aggregate, they already
form a respectable library, so that the future historian will suffer rather from
the embarrassment of riches than from the want of materials. Instead of
complaining that "little is committed to writing," in America, and that
"that little is soon wafted away forever," he ought to censure the inordinate loquacity of Presidents, Governors, legislators, and other public officers, whose interminable messages, reports, and supplementary documents
are preserved by the public printers in many huge volumes, which nobody,
indeed, ever thinks of perusing, but which are even difficult to consult on
account of their number and magnitude. — AM. ED.

attainments which are widely disseminated in the community, and no knowledge peculiar to themselves. Democracy, pushed to its furthest limits, is therefore prejudicial to the art of government; and, for this reason, it is better adapted to a people already versed in the conduct of administration, than to a nation which is uninitiated in public affairs.

This remark, indeed, is not exclusively applicable to the science of administration. Although a democratic government is founded upon a very simple and natural principle, it always presupposes the existence of a high degree of culture and enlightenment in society.* At first, it might be supposed to belong to the earliest ages of the world; but maturer observation will convince us that it could only come last in the succession of human history.

CHARGES LEVIED BY THE STATE UNDER THE RULE OF THE AMERICAN DEMOCRACY.

In all Communities, Citizens are divisible into certain Classes. — Habits of each of these Classes in the Direction of Public Finances. — Why Public Expenditure must tend to increase when the People govern. — What renders the Extravagance of a Democracy less to be feared in America. — Public Expenditure under a Democracy.

BEFORE we can tell whether a democratic government is economical or not, we must establish a standard of comparison. The question would be of easy solution, if we were to draw a parallel between a democratic republic and an absolute monarchy. The public expenditure in the former would be found to be more considerable than under the latter; such is the case with all free states compared with those which are not so. It is certain that despotism

---

* It is needless to observe, that I speak here of the democratic form of government as applied to a people, and not merely to a tribe.

ruins individuals by preventing them from producing wealth, much more than by depriving them of what they have already produced; it dries up the source of riches, whilst it usually respects acquired property. Freedom, on the contrary, produces far more goods than it destroys; and the nations which are favored by free institutions invariably find that their resources increase even more rapidly than their taxes.

My present object is to compare free nations with each other, and to point out the influence of democracy upon the finances of a state.

Communities, as well as organic bodies, are subject in their formation to certain fixed rules, from which they cannot depart. They are composed of certain elements which are common to them at all times and under all circumstances. The people may always be mentally divided into three classes. The first of these classes consists of the wealthy; the second, of those who are in easy circumstances; and the third is composed of those who have little or no property, and who subsist by the work which they perform for the two superior orders. The proportion of the individuals in these several divisions may vary according to the condition of society; but the divisions themselves can never be obliterated.

It is evident that each of these classes will exercise an influence peculiar to its own instincts upon the administration of the finances of the state. If the first of the three exclusively possesses the legislative power, it is probable that it will not be sparing of the public funds, because the taxes which are levied on a large fortune only diminish the sum of superfluities, and are, in fact, but little felt. If the second class has the power of making the laws, it will certainly not be lavish of taxes, because nothing is so onerous as a large impost levied upon a small income. The government of the middle classes appears to me the most economical, I will not say the most enlightened, and certainly not the most generous, of free governments.

Let us now suppose that the legislative authority is vested in the lowest order: there are two striking reasons which show that the tendency of the expenditures will be to increase, not to diminish.

As the great majority of those who create the laws have no taxable property, all the money which is spent for the community appears to be spent to their advantage, at no cost of their own; and those who have some little property readily find means of so regulating the taxes, that they weigh upon the wealthy and profit the poor; although the rich cannot take the same advantage when they are in possession of the government.

In countries in which the poor * should have the exclusive power of making the laws, no great economy of public expenditure ought to be expected: that expenditure will always be considerable; either because the taxes cannot weigh upon those who levy them, or because they are levied in such a manner as not to reach these poorer classes. In other words, the government of the democracy is the only one under which the power which votes the taxes escapes the payment of them.

In vain will it be objected, that the true interest of the people is to spare the fortunes of the rich, since they must suffer in the long run from the general impoverishment which will ensue. Is it not the true interest of kings, also, to render their subjects happy, and of the nobles to admit recruits into their order on suitable grounds? If remote advantages had power to prevail over the passions and the

---

* The word *poor* is used here, and throughout the remainder of this chapter, in a relative, not in an absolute sense. Poor men in America would often appear rich in comparison with the poor of Europe; but they may with propriety be styled poor in comparison with their more affluent countrymen.

exigencies of the moment, no such thing as a tyrannical sovereign or an exclusive aristocracy could ever exist.

Again, it may be objected that the poor never have the sole power of making the laws; but I reply, that, wherever universal suffrage has been established, the majority unquestionably exercises the legislative authority; and if it be proved that the poor always constitute the majority, may it not be added, with perfect truth, that, in the countries in which they possess the elective franchise, they possess the sole power of making the laws? It is certain that, in all the nations of the world, the greater number has always consisted of those persons who hold no property, or of those whose property is insufficient to exempt them from the necessity of working in order to procure a comfortable subsistence. Universal suffrage does, therefore, in point of fact, invest the poor with the government of society.

The disastrous influence which popular authority may sometimes exercise upon the finances of a state was clearly seen in some of the democratic republics of antiquity, in which the public treasure was exhausted in order to relieve indigent citizens, or to supply games and theatrical amusements for the populace. It is true, that the representative system was then almost unknown, and that, at the present time, the influence of popular passions is less felt in the conduct of public affairs; but it may well be believed that, in the end, the delegate will conform to the principles of his constituents, and favor their propensities as much as their interests.

The extravagance of democracy is, however, less to be dreaded in proportion as the people acquire a share of property, because, on the one hand, the contributions of the rich are then less needed, and, on the other, it is more difficult to impose taxes which shall not reach the imposers. On this account, universal suffrage would be less dangerous in France than in England, where nearly all the taxable property is vested in the hands of a few. America, where the great majority of the citizens possess some fortune, is in a still more favorable position than France.

There are further causes which may increase the amount of public expenditure in democratic countries. When an aristocracy governs, those who conduct the affairs of state are exempted, by their very station in society, from any want: content with their lot, power and renown are the only objects for which they strive; placed far above the obscure crowd, they do not always clearly perceive how the well-being of the mass of the people will redound to their own grandeur. They are not, indeed, callous to the sufferings of the poor; but they cannot feel those miseries as acutely as if they were themselves partakers of them. Provided that the people appear to submit to their lot, the rulers are satisfied, and demand nothing further from the government. An aristocracy is more intent upon the means of maintaining than of improving its condition.

When, on the contrary, the people are invested with the supreme authority, they are perpetually seeking for something better, because they feel the hardships of their lot. The thirst for improvement extends to a thousand different objects; it descends to the most trivial details, and especially to those changes which are accompanied with considerable expense, since the object is to improve the condition of the poor, who cannot pay for the improvement. Moreover, all democratic communities are agitated by an ill-defined excitement, and a kind of feverish impatience, that creates a multitude of innovations, almost all of which are expensive.

In monarchies and aristocracies, those who are ambitious flatter the natural taste which the rulers have for power and renown, and thus often incite them to very costly undertakings. In democracies, where the rulers are poor

and in want, they can be courted only by such means as
will improve their well-being, and these improvements cannot take place without money.   When a people begin to
reflect on their situation, they discover a multitude of
wants which they had not before been conscious of, and to
satisfy these exigencies recourse must be had to the coffers
of the state.   Hence it happens that the public charges
increase in proportion to the civilization of the country,
and imposts are augmented as knowledge becomes more
diffused.

The last cause which renders a democratic government
dearer than any other is, that a democracy does not always
lessen its expenditures even when it wishes to do so, because it does not understand the art of being economical.
As it frequently changes its purposes, and still more frequently its agents, its undertakings are often ill conducted
or left unfinished: in the former case, the state spends
sums out of all proportion to the end which it proposes to
accomplish; in the latter, the expense brings no return.

TENDENCIES OF THE AMERICAN DEMOCRACY AS REGARDS THE SALARIES OF PUBLIC OFFICERS.

In Democracies, those who establish high Salaries have no chance of profiting by them. — Tendency of the American Democracy to increase the
Salaries of subordinate Officers, and to lower those of the more important Functionaries. — Reason of this. — Comparative Statement of the
Salaries of Public Officers in the United States and in France.

THERE is a powerful reason which usually induces democracies to economize upon the salaries of public officers.
Those who fix the amount of the salaries, being very numerous, have but little chance of obtaining office so as to
be in receipt of those salaries.   In aristocratic countries,
on the contrary, the individuals who appoint high salaries
have almost always a vague hope of profiting by them.

These appointments may be looked upon as a capital which they create for their own use, or at least as a resource for their children.

It must be allowed, moreover, that a democratic state is most parsimonious towards its principal agents. In America, the secondary officers are much better, and the higher functionaries much worse paid, than elsewhere.

These opposite effects result from the same cause: the people fix the salaries of the public officers in both cases; and the scale of remuneration is determined by the comparison of their own wants. It is held to be fair, that the servants of the public should be placed in the same easy circumstances as the public themselves;* but when the question turns upon the salaries of the great officers of state, this rule fails, and chance alone guides the popular decision. The poor have no adequate conception of the wants which the higher classes of society feel. The sum which is scanty to the rich appears enormous to him whose wants do not extend beyond the necessaries of life; and in his estimation, the Governor of a State, with his twelve hundred or two thousand dollars a year, is a fortunate and enviable being.† If you try to convince him that the representative of a great people ought to appear with some splendor in the eyes of foreign nations, he will at first assent to your assertion; but when he reflects on

---

* The easy circumstances in which secondary functionaries are placed in the United States result, also, from another cause, which is independent of the general tendencies of democracy: every kind of private business is very lucrative, and the state would not be served at all if it did not pay its servants well. The country is in the position of a commercial house, which is obliged to sustain a costly competition, notwithstanding its tastes are economical.

† The State of Ohio, which contains a million of inhabitants, gives its Governor a salary of only 1,200 dollars a year. [Now that its population exceeds two millions, the Governor's salary has been raised to 1,800 dollars — Am. Ed.]

his own humble dwelling, and the small earnings of his hard toil, he remembers all that he could do with a salary which you judge to be insufficient, and he is startled and almost frightened at the view of so much wealth. Besides, the secondary public officer is almost on a level with the people, whilst the others are raised above them. The former may therefore excite his sympathy, but the latter begin to arouse his envy.

This is clearly seen in the United States, where the salaries seem, if I may so speak, to decrease as the authority of those who receive them is augmented.*

Under the rule of an aristocracy, on the contrary, the high officers receive munificent salaries, while the inferior

---

* To render this assertion perfectly evident, it will suffice to examine the scale of salaries of the agents of the Federal government. I have added the salaries of the corresponding officers in France, to complete the comparison.

UNITED STATES.	FRANCE.
Treasury Department.	*Ministère de Finances.*
Messenger, ... $ 700	Huissier, . . . 1,500 fr. ($ 300)
Clerk with lowest salary, . . 1,000	Clerk with lowest sala-
Clerk with highest salary, . 1,600	ry, 1,000 to 1,800 fr. ($ 200 – 360)
Chief Clerk, ... 2,000	Clerk with highest sala-
Secretary of State, . . . 6,000	ry, 3,200 to 3,600 fr. ($ 640 – 720)
The President, ... 25,000	Secrétaire-général, 20,000 fr. ($ 4,000)
	The Minister, 80,000 fr. ($ 16,000)
	The King, 12,000,000 fr. ($ 2,400,000)

[Since M. de Tocqueville wrote, all these salaries of American officers, except that of the President, have been somewhat enlarged ; but the addition made to them is not more than enough to make up for the increased expenses of living. — AM. ED.]

I have perhaps done wrong in selecting France as my standard of comparison. In France, as the democratic tendencies of the nation exercise an ever-increasing influence upon the government, the Chambers show a disposition to raise the low salaries, and to lower the principal ones. Thus, the Minister of Finance, who received 160,000 fr. under the Empire, receives 80,000 fr. in 1835 ; the *Directeurs-Généraux* of Finance, who then received 50,000 fr., now receive only 20,000 fr.

ones often have not more than enough to procure the necessaries of life. The reason of this fact is easily discoverable from causes very analogous to those which I have just pointed out. As a democracy is unable to conceive the pleasures of the rich, or to witness them without envy, so an aristocracy is slow to understand the privations of the poor, or rather is unacquainted with them. The poor man is not, properly speaking, of the same kind as the rich one; but he is a being of another species. An aristocracy therefore cares but little for the condition of its subordinate agents; and their salaries are raised only when they refuse to serve for too scanty a remuneration.

It is the parsimonious conduct of democracy towards its principal officers, which has caused more economical propensities to be attributed to it than it really possesses. It is true that it scarcely allows the means of decent maintenance to those who conduct its affairs; but it lavishes enormous sums to succor the wants or facilitate the enjoyments of the people.* The money raised by taxation may be better employed; but it is not economically used. In general, democracy gives largely to the people, and very sparingly to those who govern them. The reverse is the case in aristocratic countries, where the money of the state profits the persons who are at the head of affairs.

* See the American budgets for the support of paupers, and for gratuitous instruction. In 1831, over $250,000 were spent in the State of New York for the maintenance of the poor; and at least $1,000,000 were devoted to public instruction. [In 1858, the total expenditure for the relief of the poor in the State of New York was $1,491,391; and for common schools, $3,653,995. — AM. ED.] The State of New York contained only 1,900,000 inhabitants in the year 1830, which is not more than double the amount of population in the *Département du Nord* in France. [In 1855, the population of New York was 3,466,212.]

DIFFICULTY OF DISTINGUISHING THE CAUSES WHICH INCLINE THE AMERICAN GOVERNMENT TO ECONOMY.

WE are liable to frequent errors in seeking among facts for the real influence which laws exercise upon the fate of mankind, since nothing is more difficult to appreciate than a fact. One nation is naturally fickle and enthusiastic ; another is sober and calculating ; and these characteristics originate in their physical constitution, or in remote causes with which we are unacquainted.

There are nations which are fond of parade, bustle, and festivity, and which do not regret millions spent upon the gayeties of an hour. Others, on the contrary, are attached to more quiet enjoyments, and seem almost ashamed of appearing to be pleased. In some countries, high value is set upon the beauty of public edifices ; in others, the productions of art are treated with indifference, and everything which is unproductive is regarded with contempt. In some, renown, in others, money, is the ruling passion.

Independently of the laws, all these causes exercise a powerful influence upon the conduct of the finances of the state. If the Americans never spend the money of the people in public festivities, it is not merely because the taxes are under the control of the people, but because the people take no delight in festivities. If they repudiate all ornament from their architecture, and set no store on any but practical and homely advantages, it is not because they live under democratic institutions, but because they are a commercial nation. The habits of private life are continued in public ; and we ought carefully to distinguish that economy which depends upon their institutions from that which is the natural result of their habitudes and manners.

WHETHER THE EXPENDITURE OF THE UNITED STATES CAN
BE COMPARED WITH THAT OF FRANCE.

Two Points to be established in order to estimate the Extent of the Public
Charges, viz. the National Wealth, and the Rate of Taxation. — The
Wealth and the Charges of France not accurately known. — Why the
Wealth and Charges of the Union cannot be accurately known. — Researches of the Author to discover the Amount of Taxation of Pennsylvania. — General Symptoms which may serve to indicate the Amount
of the Public Charges in a given Nation. — Result of this Investigation
for the Union.

MANY attempts have recently been made in France to
compare the public expenditure of that country with the
expenditure of the United States. All these attempts
have, however, been fruitless ; and a few words will suffice
to show that they could not have a satisfactory result.

In order to estimate the amount of the public charges of
a people, two preliminaries are indispensable : it is necessary, in the first place, to know the wealth of that people ;
and, in the second, to learn what portion of that wealth is
devoted to the expenditure of the state. To show the
amount of taxation without showing the resources which
are destined to meet it, would be a futile task ; for it is not
the expenditure, but the relation of the expenditure to the
revenue, which it is desirable to know. The same rate of
taxation which may easily be supported by a wealthy con-
tributor will reduce a poor one to extreme misery.

The wealth of nations is composed of several elements ;
real property is the first of these, and personal property the
second. It is difficult to know precisely the amount of
cultivable land in a country, and its natural or acquired
value ; and it is still more difficult to estimate the whole
personal property which is at the disposal of a nation, and
which eludes the strictest analysis by the diversity and the
number of shapes under which it may occur. And, in-

deed, we find that the nations of Europe which have been the longest civilized, including even those in which the administration is most centralized, have not succeeded, as yet, in determining the exact amount of their wealth.

In America, the attempt has never been made; for how would such an investigation be possible in a new country, where society has not yet settled into fixed and tranquil habits, — where the national government is not assisted by a multitude of agents whose exertions it can command and direct to one end, — and where statistics are not studied, because no one is able to collect the necessary documents, or find time to peruse them? Thus the primary elements of the calculations which have been made in France cannot be obtained in the Union; the relative wealth of the two countries is unknown: the property of the former is not yet accurately determined, and no means exist of computing that of the latter.

I consent therefore, for the moment, to abandon this necessary term of the comparison, and I confine myself to a computation of the actual amount of taxation, without investigating the ratio of the taxation to the revenue. But the reader will perceive that my task has not been facilitated by thus narrowing the circle of my researches.

It cannot be doubted that the central administration of France, assisted by all the public officers who are at its disposal, might determine precisely the amount of the direct and indirect taxes levied upon the citizens. But this investigation, which no private individual can undertake, has not hitherto been completed by the French government, or, at least, its results have not been made public. We are acquainted with the sum total of the charges of the state; we know the amount of the departmental expenditure; but the expenses of the *communes* have not been computed, and the total of the public expenses of France is consequently unknown.

If we now turn to America, we perceive that the diffi
culties are multiplied and enhanced. The Union publishes
an exact return of the amount of its expenditure; the
budgets of the four and twenty States publish similar returns; but the expenses of the counties and the townships
are unknown.*

* The Americans, as we have seen, have four separate budgets, — the
Union, the States, the counties, and the townships having each severally
their own. During my stay in America, I made every endeavor to discover the amount of the public expenditure in the townships and counties
of the principal States of the Union; and I readily obtained the budget
of the larger townships, but found it quite impossible to procure that of the
smaller ones. I possess, however, some documents relating to county expenses which, although incomplete, are still curious. I have to thank Mr.
Richards, former Mayor of Philadelphia, for the budgets of thirteen of the
counties of Pennsylvania, — viz. Lebanon, Centre, Franklin, Fayette, Mont-
gomery, Luzerne, Dauphin, Butler, Alleghany, Columbia, Northampton,
Northumberland, and Philadelphia, — for the year 1830. Their population
at that time consisted of 495,207 inhabitants. On looking at the map of
Pennsylvania, it will be seen that these thirteen counties are scattered in
every direction, and so generally affected by the causes which usually influence the condition of a country, that they may fairly be supposed to furnish
a correct average of the financial state of the counties of Pennsylvania in
general. The expenses of these counties amounted, in the year 1830, to
about $ 342,900, or nearly 69 cents for each inhabitant; and, calculating
that each of them contributed in the same year about $ 2.43 towards the
Union, and about 72 cents to the State of Pennsylvania, it appears that they
each contributed, as their share of all the public expenses (except those of
the townships), the sum of $ 3.84. This calculation is doubly incomplete,
as it applies only to a single year and to one part of the public charges; but
it has at least the merit of not being conjectural.

[This estimate probably errs by excess. In the American Almanac for
1847, a careful computation, founded on numerous returns, makes the aggregate of national expenditure for each inhabitant 97 cents; of State expenditure, 50 cents; of town or city, including county, expenditure, 92 cents;
— making the total cost of government for each person $ 2.39. Mr. Liv-
ingston, in a calculation made in 1832, estimated the cost of government in
the United States at an average of $ 2.15 for each person. In 1838, Mr.
H. C. Carey of Philadelphia estimated it at $ 2.19. Allowing for the dif-
ferences created by the lapse of years, these three estimates, founded on independent data, agree remarkably well. — AM. ED.]

The Federal authority cannot oblige the State governments to throw any light upon this point; and even if these governments were inclined to give their simultaneous aid, it may be doubted whether they are able to furnish a satisfactory answer. Independently of the natural difficulties of the task, the political organization of the country would hinder the success of their efforts. The county and town magistrates are not appointed by the authorities of the State, and are not subjected to their control. It is therefore allowable to suppose, that, even if the State was desirous of obtaining the returns which we require, its design would be counteracted by the neglect of those subordinate officers whom it would be obliged to employ.* It is

---

* Those who have attempted to compare the expenses of France and America have at once perceived, that no such comparison could be drawn between the total expenditures of the two countries; but they have endeavored to contrast detached portions of this expenditure. It may readily be shown, that this second system is not at all less defective than the first.

If I attempt to compare the French budget with the budget of the Union, it must be remembered that the latter embraces much fewer objects than the centralized government of the former country, and that the American expenditure must consequently be much smaller. If I contrast the budgets of the departments with those of the States which constitute the Union, it must be observed, that, as the States have the supervision of more numerous and important interests than the departments, their expenditure is naturally more considerable. As for the budgets of the counties, nothing of the kind occurs in the French system of finances; and it is doubtful whether the corresponding expenses in France should be referred to the budget of the state, or to those of the municipal divisions.

Municipal expenses exist in both countries, but they are not always analogous. In America, the townships discharge a variety of offices which are reserved in France to the departments, or to the state. It may, moreover, be asked what is to be understood by the municipal expenses of America. The organization of the municipal bodies or townships differs in the several States. Are we to be guided by what occurs in New England or in Georgia, in Pennsylvania or in Illinois?

A kind of analogy may very readily be perceived between certain budgets in the two countries; but as the elements of which they are composed always differ more or less, no fair comparison can be instituted between them.

in fact useless to inquire what the Americans might do to
forward this inquiry, since it is certain that they have hitherto done nothing.   There does not exist a single individual at the present day, in America or in Europe, who can
inform us what each citizen of the Union annually contributes to the public charges of the nation.*

Hence we must conclude, that it is no less difficult to
compare the social expenditure, than it is to estimate the
relative wealth, of France and America.   I will even add,
that it would be dangerous to attempt this comparison;
for when statistics are not based upon computations which

---

* Even if we knew the exact pecuniary contributions of every French
and American citizen to the coffers of the state, we should only come at a
portion of the truth.   Governments not only demand supplies of money,
but call for personal services, which may be looked upon as equivalent to a
given sum.   When a state raises an army, besides the pay of the troops
which is furnished by the entire nation, each soldier must give up his time,
the value of which depends on the use he might make of it if he were not
in the service.   The same remark applies to the militia; the citizen who is
in the militia devotes a certain portion of valuable time to the maintenance
of the public security, and in reality surrenders to the state those earnings
which he is prevented from gaining.   Many other instances might be cited.
The governments of France and America both levy taxes of this kind, which
weigh upon the citizens; but who can estimate with accuracy their relative
amount in the two countries?

This, however, is not the last of the difficulties which prevent us from
comparing the expenditure of the Union with that of France.   The French
government contracts certain obligations which are not assumed by the state
in America, and *vice versâ*.   The French government pays the clergy; in
America, the voluntary principle prevails.   In America, there is a legal provision for the poor; in France, they are abandoned to the charity of the
public.   The French public officers are paid by a fixed salary; in America,
they are allowed certain perquisites.   In France, contributions in labor take
place on very few roads, — in America, upon almost all the thoroughfares:
in the former country, the roads are free to all travellers; in the latter, turn-
pikes abound.   All these differences in the manner in which taxes are levied
in the two countries enhance the difficulty of comparing their expenditure;
for there are certain expenses which the citizens would not be subject to, or
which would at any rate be less considerable, if the state did not undertake
to act in their name.

are strictly accurate, they mislead instead of guiding aright. The mind is easily imposed upon by the affectation of exactitude which marks even the misstatements of statistics; and it adopts with confidence the errors which are apparelled in the forms of mathematical truth.

We abandon, therefore, the numerical investigation, with the hope of meeting with data of another kind. In the absence of positive documents, we may form an opinion as to the proportion which the taxation of a people bears to its real wealth, by observing whether its external appearance is flourishing; whether, after having paid the dues of the state, the poor man retains the means of subsistence, and the rich the means of enjoyment; and whether both classes seem contented with their position, seeking, however, to ameliorate it by perpetual exertions, so that industry is never in want of capital, nor capital unemployed by industry. The observer who draws his inferences from these signs will, undoubtedly, be led to the conclusion, that the American of the United States contributes a much smaller portion of his income to the state than the citizen of France. Nor, indeed, can the result be otherwise.

A portion of the French debt is the consequence of two invasions; and the Union has no similar calamity to fear. The position of France obliges it to maintain a large standing army; the isolation of the Union enables it to have only six thousand soldiers. The French have a fleet of three hundred sail; the Americans have [1832] only fifty-two vessels. How, then, can the inhabitant of the Union be taxed as heavily as the inhabitant of France? No parallel can be drawn between the finances of two countries so differently situated.

It is by examining what actually takes place in the Union, and not by comparing the Union with France, that we can judge whether the American government is really economical. On casting my eyes over the different republics which form the confederation, I perceive that their governments often lack perseverance in their undertakings, and that they exercise no steady control over the men whom they employ. I naturally infer that they must often spend the money of the people to no purpose, or consume more of it than is really necessary for their enterprises. Faithful to its popular origin, the government makes great efforts to satisfy the wants of the lower orders, to open to them the road to power, and to diffuse knowledge and comfort among them. The poor are maintained, immense sums are annually devoted to public instruction, all services are remunerated, and the humblest agents are liberally paid. This kind of government appears to be useful and rational, but I am constrained to admit that it is expensive.

Wherever the poor direct public affairs, and dispose of the national resources, it appears certain that, as they profit by the expenditure of the state, they will often augment that expenditure.

I conclude, therefore, without having recourse to inaccurate statistics, and without hazarding a comparison which might prove incorrect, that the democratic government of the Americans is not a cheap government, as is sometimes asserted; and I fear not to predict that, if the United States are ever involved in serious difficulties, taxation will speedily be raised as high there as in most of the aristocracies or the monarchies of Europe.

CORRUPTION AND THE VICES OF THE RULERS IN A DEMOCRACY, AND CONSEQUENT EFFECTS UPON PUBLIC MORALITY.

In Aristocracies, Rulers sometimes endeavor to corrupt the People. — In Democracies, Rulers frequently show themselves to be corrupt. — In the former, their Vices are directly prejudicial to the Morality of the People. — In the latter, their indirect Influence is still more pernicious.

A DISTINCTION must be made, when aristocracies and democracies mutually accuse each other of facilitating corruption. In aristocratic governments, those who are placed at the head of affairs are rich men, who are desirous only of power. In democracies, statesmen are poor, and have their fortunes to make. The consequence is, that, in aristocratic states, the rulers are rarely accessible to corruption, and have little craving for money; whilst the reverse is the case in democratic nations.

But in aristocracies, as those who wish to attain the head of affairs possess considerable wealth, and as the number of persons by whose assistance they may rise is comparatively small, the government is, if I may so speak, put up at auction. In democracies, on the contrary, those who are covetous of power are seldom wealthy, and the number of those who confer power is extremely great. Perhaps, in democracies, the number of men who might be bought is not smaller, but buyers are rarely to be found; and, besides, it would be necessary to buy so many persons at once, that the attempt would be useless.

Many of the men who have governed France during the last forty years have been accused of making their fortunes at the expense of the state or its allies; a reproach which was rarely addressed to the public men of the old monarchy. But in France, the practice of bribing electors is almost unknown, whilst it is notoriously and publicly carried on in England. In the United States, I never heard any one accused of spending his wealth in buying votes; but I have often heard the probity of public officers questioned; still more frequently have I heard their success attributed to low intrigues and immoral practices.

If, then, the men who conduct an aristocracy sometimes endeavor to corrupt the people, the heads of a democracy are themselves corrupt. In the former case, the morality of the people is directly assailed; in the latter, an indirect influence is exercised which is still more to be dreaded.

As the rulers of democratic nations are almost always

suspected of dishonorable conduct, they in some measure lend the authority of the government to the base practices of which they are accused. They thus afford dangerous examples, which discourage the struggles of virtuous independence and cloak with authority the secret designs of wickedness. If it be asserted that evil passions are found in all ranks of society; that they ascend the throne by hereditary right; and that we may find despicable characters at the head of aristocratic nations, as well as in the bosom of a democracy, — the plea has but little weight in my estimation. The corruption of men who have casually risen to power has a coarse and vulgar infection in it, which renders it dangerous to the multitude. On the contrary, there is a kind of aristocratic refinement, and an air of grandeur, in the depravity of the great, which frequently prevent it from spreading abroad.

The people can never penetrate into the dark labyrinth of court intrigue, and will always have difficulty in detecting the turpitude which lurks under elegant manners, refined tastes, and graceful language. But, to pillage the public purse, and to sell the favors of the state, are arts which the meanest villain can understand, and hope to practise in his turn.

Besides, what is to be feared is, not so much the immorality of the great, as the fact that immorality may lead to greatness. In a democracy, private citizens see a man of their own rank in life, who rises from that obscure position in a few years to riches and power; the spectacle excites their surprise and their envy; and they are led to inquire how the person who was yesterday their equal, is to-day their ruler. To attribute his rise to his talents or his virtues is unpleasant; for it is tacitly to acknowledge that they are themselves less virtuous or less talented than he was. They are therefore led, and often rightly, to impute his success mainly to some of his vices; and an odious connection is thus formed between the ideas of turpitude and power, unworthiness and success, utility and dishonor.

EFFORTS OF WHICH A DEMOCRACY IS CAPABLE.

The Union has only had one Struggle hitherto for its Existence. — Enthusiasm at the Commencement of the War. — Indifference towards its Close. — Difficulty of establishing Military Conscription or Impressment of Seamen in America. — Why a Democratic People is less capable than any other of sustained Effort.

I WARN the reader that I here speak of a government which follows the real will of the people, and not of a government which simply commands in their name. Nothing is so irresistible as a tyrannical power commanding in the name of the people, because, whilst wielding the moral power which belongs to the will of the greater number, it acts at the same time with the quickness and persistence of a single man.

It is difficult to say what degree of effort a democratic government may be capable of making on the occurrence of a national crisis. No great democratic republic has hitherto existed in the world. To style the oligarchy which ruled over France in 1793 by that name, would be an insult to the republican form of government. The United States afford the first example of the kind.

The American Union has now subsisted for half a century, and its existence has only once been attacked, namely, during the War of Independence. At the commencement of that long war, extraordinary efforts were made with enthusiasm for the service of the country.*

---

* One of the most singular, in my opinion, was the resolution which the Americans took of temporarily abandoning the use of tea. Those who know that men usually cling more to their habits than to their life, will doubtless admire this great though obscure sacrifice, which was made by a whole people.

But as the contest was prolonged, private selfishness began to reappear. No money was brought into the public treasury; few recruits could be raised for the army; the people still wished to acquire independence, but would not employ the only means by which it could be obtained. "Tax laws," says Hamilton, in the Federalist (No. 12), "have in vain been multiplied; new methods to enforce the collection have in vain been tried; the public expectation has been uniformly disappointed; and the treasuries of the States have remained empty. The popular system of administration inherent in the nature of popular government, coinciding with the real scarcity of money incident to a languid and mutilated state of trade, has hitherto defeated every experiment for extensive collections, and has at length taught the different legislatures the folly of attempting them."

Since that period, the United States have not had a single serious war to carry on. In order, therefore, to know what sacrifices democratic nations may impose upon themselves, we must wait until the American people are obliged to put half their entire income at the disposal of the government, as was done by the English; or to send forth a twentieth part of its population to the field of battle, as was done by France.

In America, the conscription is unknown, and men are induced to enlist by bounties.* The notions and habits of the people of the United States are so opposed to compulsory recruiting, that I do not think it can ever be sanctioned by the laws. What is termed the conscription in France, is assuredly the heaviest tax upon the people; yet how could a great Continental war be carried on without

---

* It is not entirely correct to say that the conscription is unknown in the United States. Troops were drafted from the militia occasionally during the Revolution, and in the course of the war with England in 1812. — AM. ED.

it? The Americans have not adopted the British practice of impressing seamen, and they have nothing which corresponds to the French system of maritime conscription; the navy, as well as the merchant service, is supplied by volunteers. But it is not easy to conceive how a people can sustain a great maritime war, without having recourse to one or the other of these two systems. Indeed, the Union, which has already fought with honor upon the seas, has never had a numerous fleet, and the equipment of its few vessels has always been very expensive.

I have heard American statesmen confess, that the Union will with difficulty maintain its power on the seas, without adopting the system of impressment or maritime conscription; but the difficulty is to induce the people, who exercise the supreme authority, to submit to such measures.

It is incontestable that, in times of danger, a free people display far more energy than any other. But I incline to believe that this is especially true of those free nations in which the aristocratic element preponderates. Democracy appears to me better adapted for the conduct of society in times of peace, or for a sudden effort of remarkable vigor, than for the prolonged endurance of the great storms which beset the political existence of nations. The reason is very evident; enthusiasm prompts men to expose themselves to dangers and privations; but without reflection, they will not support them long. There is more calculation even in the impulses of bravery, than is generally supposed; and although the first efforts are made by passion alone, perseverance is maintained only by a distinct view of what one is fighting for. A portion of what is dear to us is hazarded, in order to save the remainder.

But it is this clear perception of the future, founded upon judgment and experience, which is frequently wanting in democracies. The people are more apt to feel than to reason; and if their present sufferings are great, it is to be feared that the still greater sufferings attendant upon defeat will be forgotten.

Another cause tends to render the efforts of a democratic government less persevering than those of an aristocracy. Not only are the lower less awake than the higher orders to the good or evil chances of the future, but they suffer more acutely from present privations. The noble exposes his life, indeed, but the chance of glory is equal to the chance of harm. If he sacrifices a large portion of his income to the state, he deprives himself for a time of some of the pleasures of affluence; but to the poor man, death has no glory, and the imposts which are merely irksome to the rich often deprive him of the necessaries of life.

This relative weakness of democratic republics in critical times is, perhaps, the greatest obstacle to the foundation of such a republic in Europe. In order that one such state should exist in the European world, it would be necessary that similar institutions should be simultaneously introduced into all the other nations.

I am of opinion that a democratic government tends, in the long run, to increase the real strength of society; but it can never combine, upon a single point and at a given time, so much power as an aristocracy or an absolute monarchy. If a democratic country remained during a whole century subject to a republican government, it would probably, at the end of that period, be richer, more populous, and more prosperous, than the neighboring despotic states. But during that century, it would often have incurred the risk of being conquered by them.

SELF-CONTROL OF THE AMERICAN DEMOCRACY.

The American People acquiesce slowly, and sometimes do not acquiesce, in
what is beneficial to its Interests. — The Faults of the American Democracy are, for the most part, reparable.

THE difficulty which a democracy finds in conquering
the passions and subduing the desires of the moment from
a view to the future, is observable in the United States in
the most trivial things.   The people, surrounded by flat-
terers, find great difficulty in surmounting their inclinations ; whenever they are required to undergo a privation
or any inconvenience, even to attain an end sanctioned by
their own rational conviction, they almost always refuse at
first to comply.   The deference of the Americans to the
laws has been justly applauded ; but it must be added, that,
in America, the legislation is made by the people and for
the people.   Consequently, in the United States, the law
favors those classes which elsewhere are most interested in
evading it.   It may therefore be supposed, that an offensive law, of which the majority should not see the immediate utility, would either not be enacted or not obeyed.

In America, there is no law against fraudulent bank-
ruptcies, not because they are few, but because they are
many.   The dread of being prosecuted as a bankrupt is
greater in the minds of the majority than the fear of being
ruined by the bankruptcy of others ; and a sort of guilty
tolerance is extended by the public conscience to an offence
which every one condemns in his individual capacity.   In
the new States of the Southwest, the citizens generally
take justice into their own hands, and murders are of frequent occurrence.   This arises from the rude manners and
the ignorance of the inhabitants of those deserts, who do
not perceive the utility of strengthening the law, and who
prefer duels to prosecutions.

Some one observed to me one day, in Philadelphia, that almost all crimes in America are caused by the abuse of intoxicating liquors, which the lower classes can procure in great abundance from their cheapness. " How comes it," said I, " that you do not put a duty upon brandy? " " Our legislators," rejoined my informant, " have frequently thought of this expedient; but the task is difficult: a revolt might be apprehended; and the members who should vote for such a law would be sure of losing their seats." " Whence I am to infer," replied I, " that drunkards are the majority in your country, and that temperance is unpopular."

When these things are pointed out to the American statesmen, they answer, " Leave it to time, and experience of the evil will teach the people their true interests." This is frequently true: though a democracy is more liable to error than a monarch or a body of nobles, the chances of its regaining the right path, when once it has acknowledged its mistake, are greater also; because it is rarely embarrassed by interests which conflict with those of the majority, and resist the authority of reason. But a democracy can obtain truth only as the result of experience; and many nations may perish whilst they are awaiting the consequences of their errors. The great privilege of the Americans does not consist in being more enlightened than other nations, but in being able to repair the faults they may commit.

It must be added, that a democracy cannot profit by past experience, unless it has arrived at a certain pitch of knowledge and civilization. There are nations whose first education has been so vicious, and whose character presents so strange a mixture of passion, ignorance, and erroneous notions upon all subjects, that they are unable to discern the causes of their own wretchedness, and they fall a sacrifice to ills of which they are ignorant.

I have crossed vast tracts of country formerly inhabited by powerful Indian nations who are now extinct; I have passed some time among remnants of tribes, which witness the daily decline of their numbers, and of the glory of their independence; and I have heard these Indians themselves anticipate the impending doom of their race. Every European can perceive means which would rescue these unfortunate beings from the destruction otherwise inevitable. They alone are insensible to the remedy; they feel the woes which year after year heaps upon their heads, but they will perish to a man without accepting the cure. Force would have to be employed to compel them to live.

The incessant revolutions which have convulsed the South American states for the last quarter of a century are regarded with astonishment, and we are constantly hoping that, erelong, they will return to what is called their *natural state.* But who can affirm that revolutions are not, at the present time, the most natural state of the South American Spaniards? In that country, society is struggling in the depths of an abyss whence its own efforts are insufficient to rescue it. The inhabitants of that fair portion of the Western hemisphere seem obstinately bent on the work of destroying each other. If they fall into momentary quiet, from exhaustion, that repose soon prepares them for a new frenzy. When I consider their condition, alternating between misery and crime, I am tempted to believe that despotism itself would be a blessing to them, if it were possible that the words despotism and blessing could ever be united in my mind.

CONDUCT OF FOREIGN AFFAIRS BY THE AMERICAN DEMOCRACY.

Direction given to the Foreign Policy of the United States by Washington and Jefferson. — Almost all the Defects inherent in Democratic Institutions are brought to Light in the Conduct of Foreign Affairs; their Advantages are less perceptible.

WE have seen that the Federal Constitution intrusts the permanent direction of the external interests of the nation to the President and the Senate,* which tends in some degree to detach the general foreign policy of the Union from the direct control of the people. It cannot, therefore, be asserted with truth, that the foreign affairs of the state are conducted by the democracy.

The policy of America received a direction from two men, — Washington and Jefferson, — which it observes to the present day. Washington said, in the admirable Farewell Address which he made to his fellow-citizens, and which may be regarded as his political testament: —

" The great rule of conduct for us in regard to foreign nations is, in extending our commercial relations, to have with them as little *political* connection as possible. So far as we have already formed engagements, let them be fulfilled with perfect good faith. Here let us stop.

" Europe has a set of primary interests, which to us have none, or a very remote relation. Hence she must be engaged in frequent controversies, the causes of which are essentially foreign to our concerns. Hence, therefore, it must be unwise in us to implicate ourselves, by artificial ties, in the ordinary vicissitudes of her politics, or the

---

* " The President," says the Constitution, Art. II. sect. 2, § 2, "shall have power, by and with the advice and consent of the Senate, to make treaties, provided two thirds of the Senators present concur." The reader is reminded that the Senators are returned for a term of six years, and that they are chosen by the legislature of each State.

ordinary combinations and collisions of her friendships or enmities.

" Our detached and distant situation invites and enables us to pursue a different course. If we remain one people, under an efficient government, the period is not far off when we may defy material injury from external annoyance ; when we may take such an attitude as will cause the neutrality we may at any time resolve upon to be scrupulously respected ; when belligerent nations, under the impossibility of making acquisitions upon us, will not lightly hazard the giving us provocation ; when we may choose peace or war, as our interest, guided by justice, shall counsel.

" Why forego the advantages of so peculiar a situation ? Why quit our own to stand upon foreign ground ? Why, by interweaving our destiny with that of any part of Europe, entangle our peace and prosperity in the toils of European ambition, rivalship, interest, humor, or caprice ?

" It is our true policy to steer clear of permanent alliances with any portion of the foreign world, — so far, I mean, as we are now at liberty to do it ; for let me not be understood as capable of patronizing infidelity to existing engagements. I hold the maxim no less applicable to public than to private affairs, that honesty is always the best policy. I repeat it, therefore, let those engagements be observed in their genuine sense ; but in my opinion it is unnecessary, and would be unwise, to extend them.

" Taking care always to keep ourselves, by suitable establishments, in a respectable defensive posture, we may safely trust to temporary alliances for extraordinary emergencies."

In a previous part of the same Address, Washington makes this admirable and just remark: "The nation which indulges towards another an habitual hatred, or an habitual fondness, is in some degree a slave. It is a slave to its animosity or to its affection, either of which is sufficient to lead it astray from its duty and its interest."

The political conduct of Washington was always guided by these maxims. He succeeded in maintaining his country in a state of peace whilst all the other nations of the globe were at war; and he laid it down as a fundamental doctrine, that the true interest of the Americans consisted in a perfect neutrality with regard to the internal dissensions of the European powers.

Jefferson went still further, and introduced this other maxim into the policy of the Union, — that "the Americans ought never to solicit any privileges from foreign nations, in order not to be obliged to grant similar privileges themselves."

These two principles, so plain and just as to be easily understood by the people, have greatly simplified the foreign policy of the United States. As the Union takes no part in the affairs of Europe, it has, properly speaking, no foreign interests to discuss, since it has, as yet, no powerful neighbors on the American continent. The country is as much removed from the passions of the Old World by its position as by its wishes, and it is neither called upon to repudiate nor to espouse them; whilst the dissensions of the New World are still concealed within the bosom of the future.

The Union is free from all pre-existing obligations; it can profit by the experience of the old nations of Europe, without being obliged, as they are, to make the best of the past, and to adapt it to their present circumstances. It is not, like them, compelled to accept an immense inheritance bequeathed by their forefathers, — an inheritance of glory mingled with calamities, and of alliances conflicting with national antipathies. The foreign policy of the United States is eminently expectant; it consists more in abstaining than in acting.

It is therefore very difficult to ascertain, at present, what degree of sagacity the American democracy will display in the conduct of the foreign policy of the country; upon this point, its adversaries as well as its friends must suspend their judgment. As for myself, I do not hesitate to say that it is especially in the conduct of their foreign relations that democracies appear to me decidedly inferior to other governments. Experience, instruction, and habit almost always succeed in creating in a democracy a homely species of practical wisdom, and that science of the petty occurrences of life which is called good sense. Good sense may suffice to direct the ordinary course of society; and amongst a people whose education is completed, the advantages of democratic liberty in the internal affairs of the country may more than compensate for the evils inherent in a democratic government. But it is not always so in the relations with foreign nations.

Foreign politics demand scarcely any of those qualities which are peculiar to a democracy; they require, on the contrary, the perfect use of almost all those in which it is deficient. Democracy is favorable to the increase of the internal resources of a state; it diffuses wealth and comfort, promotes public spirit, and fortifies the respect for law in all classes of society: all these are advantages which have only an indirect influence over the relations which one people bears to another. But a democracy can only with great difficulty regulate the details of an important undertaking, persevere in a fixed design, and work out its execution in spite of serious obstacles. It cannot combine its measures with secrecy, or await their consequences with patience. These are qualities which more especially belong to an individual or an aristocracy; and they are precisely the qualities by which a nation, like an individual, attains a dominant position.

If, on the contrary, we observe the natural defects of

aristocracy, we shall find that, comparatively speaking, they do not injure the direction of the external affairs of the state. The capital fault of which aristocracies may be accused is, that they work for themselves, and not for the people. In foreign politics, it is rare for the interest of the aristocracy to be distinct from that of the people.

The propensity which induces democracies to obey impulse rather than prudence, and to abandon a mature design for the gratification of a momentary passion, was clearly seen in America on the breaking out of the French Revolution. It was then as evident to the simplest capacity, as it is at the present time, that the interest of the Americans forbade them to take any part in the contest which was about to deluge Europe with blood, but which could not injure their own country. But the sympathies of the people declared themselves with so much violence in favor of France, that nothing but the inflexible character of Washington, and the immense popularity which he enjoyed, could have prevented the Americans from declaring war against England. And even then, the exertions which the austere reason of that great man made to repress the generous but imprudent passions of his fellow-citizens nearly deprived him of the sole recompense which he ever claimed, — that of his country's love. The majority reprobated his policy, but it was afterwards approved by the whole nation.*

* See the fifth volume of Marshall's "Life of Washington." "In a government constituted like that of the United States," he says, "it is impossible for the chief magistrate, however firm he may be, to oppose for any length of time the torrent of popular opinion; and the prevalent opinion of that day seemed to incline to war. In fact, in the session of Congress held at the time, it was frequently seen that Washington had lost the majority in the House of Representatives." The violence of the language used against him in public was extreme, and, in a political meeting, they did not scruple to compare him indirectly with the traitor Arnold. "By the opposition," says Marshall, "the friends of the administration were declared to be an

If the Constitution and the favor of the public had not intrusted the direction of the foreign affairs of the country to Washington, it is certain that the American nation would at that time have adopted the very measures which it now condemns.

Almost all the nations which have exercised a powerful influence upon the destinies of the world, by conceiving, following out, and executing vast designs, from the Romans to the English, have been governed by aristocratic institutions. Nor will this be a subject of wonder, when we recollect that nothing in the world has so absolute a fixity of purpose as an aristocracy. The mass of the people may be led astray by ignorance or passion; the mind of a king may be biassed, and made to vacillate in his designs, and, besides, a king is not immortal. But an aristocratic body is too numerous to be led astray by intrigue; and yet not numerous enough to yield readily to the intoxication of unreflecting passion. An aristocracy is a firm and enlightened individual that never dies.

aristocratic and corrupt faction, who, from a desire to introduce monarchy, were hostile to France, and under the influence of Britain; that they were a paper nobility, whose extreme sensibility at every measure which threatened the funds induced a tame submission to injuries and insults which the interests and honor of the nation required them to resist."

CHAPTER XIV.

WHAT ARE THE REAL ADVANTAGES WHICH AMERICAN SOCIETY DERIVES FROM A DEMOCRATIC GOVERNMENT.

BEFORE entering upon the present chapter, I must remind the reader of what I have more than once observed in this book. The political constitution of the United States appears to me to be one of the forms of government which a democracy may adopt; but I do not regard the American Constitution as the best, or as the only one, which a democratic people may establish. In showing the advantages which the Americans derive from the government of democracy, I am therefore very far from affirming, or believing, that similar advantages can be obtained only from the same laws.

GENERAL TENDENCY OF THE LAWS UNDER THE AMERICAN DEMOCRACY, AND INSTINCTS OF THOSE WHO APPLY THEM.

Defects of a Democratic Government easy to be discovered. — Its Advantages discerned only by long Observation. — Democracy in America often inexpert, but the general Tendency of the Laws is advantageous. — In the American Democracy, Public Officers have no Permanent Interests distinct from those of the Majority. — Results of this State of Things.

THE defects and weaknesses of a democratic government may readily be discovered; they are demonstrated by flagrant instances, whilst its salutary influence is insensible, and, so to speak, occult. A glance suffices to detect its faults, but its good qualities can be discerned only by long observation. The laws of the American democracy are frequently defective or incomplete; they sometimes attack vested rights, or sanction others which are dangerous to the community; and even if they were good, their frequency would still be a great evil. How comes it, then, that the American republics prosper and continue?

In the consideration of laws, a distinction must be carefully observed between the end at which they aim, and the means by which they pursue that end; between their absolute and their relative excellence. If it be the intention of the legislator to favor the interests of the minority at the expense of the majority, and if the measures he takes are so combined as to accomplish the object he has in view with the least possible expense of time and exertion, the law may be well drawn up, although its purpose is bad; and the more efficacious it is, the more dangerous it will be.

Democratic laws generally tend to promote the welfare of the greatest possible number; for they emanate from the majority of the citizens, who are subject to error, but who cannot have an interest opposed to their own advantage. The laws of an aristocracy tend, on the contrary, to concentrate wealth and power in the hands of the minority; because an aristocracy, by its very nature, constitutes a minority. It may therefore be asserted, as a general proposition, that the purpose of a democracy in its legislation is more useful to humanity than that of an aristocracy. This is, however, the sum total of its advantages.

Aristocracies are infinitely more expert in the science of legislation than democracies ever can be. They are possessed of a self-control which protects them from the errors of temporary excitement; and they form far-reaching designs, which they know how to mature till a favorable opportunity arrives. Aristocratic government proceeds with the dexterity of art; it understands how to make the collective force of all its laws converge at the same time to a given point. Such is not the case with democracies, whose laws are almost always ineffective or inopportune. The means of democracy are therefore more imperfect than those of aristocracy, and the measures which it unwittingly adopts are frequently opposed to its own cause; but the object it has in view is more useful.

Let us now imagine a community so organized by nature, or by its constitution, that it can support the transitory action of bad laws, and that it can await, without destruction, the *general tendency* of its legislation: we shall then conceive how a democratic government, notwithstanding its faults, may be best fitted to produce the prosperity of this community. This is precisely what has occurred in the United States; and I repeat, what I have before remarked, that the great advantage of the Americans consists in their being able to commit faults which they may afterwards repair.

An analogous observation may be made respecting public officers. It is easy to perceive that the American democracy frequently errs in the choice of the individuals to whom it intrusts the power of the administration; but it is more difficult to say why the state prospers under their rule. In the first place, it is to be remarked, that if, in a democratic state, the governors have less honesty and less capacity than elsewhere, the governed are more enlightened and more attentive to their interests. As the people in democracies are more constantly vigilant in their affairs, and more jealous of their rights, they prevent their representatives from abandoning that general line of conduct which their own interest prescribes. In the second place, it must be remembered, that, if the democratic magistrate is more apt to misuse his power, he possesses it for a shorter time. But there is yet another reason which is still more general and conclusive. It is no doubt of importance to the welfare of nations that they should be governed by men of talents and virtue; but it is perhaps still more important for them that the interests of those men should not differ from the interests of the community at large; for if such were the case, their virtues might become almost useless, and their talents might be turned to a bad account. I have said that it is important that the interests of the persons in authority should not differ from or oppose the interests of the community at large; but I do not insist upon their having the same interests as the *whole* population, because I am not aware that such a state of things ever existed in any country.

No political form has hitherto been discovered which is equally favorable to the prosperity and the development of all the classes into which society is divided. These classes continue to form, as it were, so many distinct communities in the same nation; and experience has shown that it is no less dangerous to place the fate of these classes exclusively in the hands of any one of them, than it is to make one people the arbiter of the destiny of another. When the rich alone govern, the interest of the poor is always endangered; and when the poor make the laws, that of the rich incurs very serious risks. The advantage of democracy does not consist, therefore, as has sometimes been asserted, in favoring the prosperity of all, but simply in contributing to the well-being of the greatest number.

The men who are intrusted with the direction of public affairs in the United States are frequently inferior, both in capacity and morality, to those whom an aristocracy would raise to power. But their interest is identified and confounded with that of the majority of their fellow-citizens. They may frequently be faithless, and frequently mistaken; but they will never systematically adopt a line of conduct hostile to the majority; and they cannot give a dangerous or exclusive tendency to the government.

The maladministration of a democratic magistrate, more-over, is an isolated fact, which has influence only during the short period for which he is elected. Corruption and incapacity do not act as common interests, which may connect men permanently with one another. A corrupt or incapable magistrate will not concert his measures with another magistrate, simply because the latter is as corrupt and incapable as himself; and these two men will never unite their endeavors to promote the corruption and inaptitude of their remote posterity. The ambition and the manœuvres of the one will serve, on the contrary, to unmask the other. The vices of a magistrate, in democratic states, are usually wholly personal.

But under aristocratic governments, public men are swayed by the interest of their order, which, if it is sometimes confounded with the interests of the majority, is very frequently distinct from them. This interest is the common and lasting bond which unites them together; it induces them to coalesce and combine their efforts to attain an end which is not always the happiness of the greatest number: and it serves not only to connect the persons in authority with each other, but to unite them with a considerable portion of the community, since a numerous body of citizens belong to the aristocracy, without being invested with official functions. The aristocratic magistrate is therefore constantly supported by a portion of the community, as well as by the government of which he is a member.

The common purpose which, in aristocracies, connects the interest of the magistrates with that of a portion of their contemporaries, identifies it also with that of future generations; they labor for the future as well as for the present. The aristocratic magistrate is urged at the same time, towards the same point, by the passions of the community, by his own, and, I may almost add, by those of his posterity. Is it, then, wonderful that he does not resist such repeated impulses? And, indeed, aristocracies are often carried away by their class-spirit, without being corrupted by it; and they unconsciously fashion society to their own ends, and prepare it for their own descendants.

The English aristocracy is perhaps the most liberal which has ever existed, and no body of men has ever, uninterruptedly, furnished so many honorable and enlightened individuals to the government of a country. It cannot, however, escape observation, that, in the legislation of England, the interests of the poor have been often sacrificed to the advantage of the rich, and the rights of the majority to the privileges of a few. The consequence is, that England, at the present day, combines the extremes of good and evil fortune in the bosom of her society; and the miseries and privations of her poor almost equal her power and renown.

In the United States, where the public officers have no class-interests to promote, the general and constant influence of the government is beneficial, although the individuals who conduct it are frequently unskilful, and sometimes contemptible. There is, indeed, a secret tendency in democratic institutions, which makes the exertions of the citizens subservient to the prosperity of the community, in spite of their vices and mistakes; whilst in aristocratic institutions, there is a secret bias, which, notwithstanding the talents and virtues of those who conduct the government, leads them to contribute to the evils which oppress their fellow-creatures. In aristocratic governments, public men may frequently do harm without intending it; and in democratic states, they bring about good results which they never thought of.

PUBLIC SPIRIT IN THE UNITED STATES.

Instinctive Patriotism. — Patriotism of Reflection. — Their different Characteristics. — Nations ought to strive to acquire the second when the first has disappeared. — Efforts of the Americans to acquire it. — Interest of the Individual intimately connected with that of the Country.

THERE is one sort of patriotic attachment, which principally arises from that instinctive, disinterested, and undefinable feeling which connects the affections of man with his birthplace. This natural fondness is united with a taste for ancient customs, and a reverence for traditions of the past; those who cherish it love their country as they love the mansion of their fathers. They love the tranquillity which it affords them; they cling to the peaceful habits which they have contracted within its bosom; they are attached to the reminiscences which it awakens; and they are even pleased by living there in a state of obedience. This patriotism is sometimes stimulated by religious enthusiasm, and then it is capable of making prodigious efforts. It is in itself a kind of religion : it does not reason, but it acts from the impulse of faith and sentiment. In some nations, the monarch is regarded as a personification of the country; and, the fervor of patriotism being converted into the fervor of loyalty, they take a sympathetic pride in his conquests, and glory in his power. There was a time, under the ancient monarchy, when the French felt a sort of satisfaction in the sense of their dependence upon the arbitrary will of their king; and they were wont to say with pride, " We live under the most powerful king in the world."

But, like all instinctive passions, this kind of patriotism incites great transient exertions, but no continuity of effort. It may save the state in critical circumstances, but often allows it to decline in times of peace. Whilst the manners of a people are simple, and its faith unshaken, — whilst society is steadily based upon traditional institutions, whose legitimacy has never been contested, — this instinctive patriotism is wont to endure.

But there is another species of attachment to country, which is more rational than the one we have been describing. It is, perhaps, less generous and less ardent, but it is more fruitful and more lasting: it springs from knowledge; it is nurtured by the laws; it grows by the exercise of civil rights; and, in the end, it is confounded with the personal interests of the citizen. A man comprehends the influence which the well-being of his country has upon his own; he is aware that the laws permit him to contribute to that prosperity, and he labors to promote it, at first because it benefits him, and secondly because it is in part his own work.

But epochs sometimes occur in the life of a nation, when the old customs of a people are changed, public morality is destroyed, religious belief shaken, and the spell of tradition broken, whilst the diffusion of knowledge is yet imperfect, and the civil rights of the community are ill secured, or confined within narrow limits. The country then assumes a dim and dubious shape in the eyes of the citizens; they no longer behold it in the soil which they inhabit, for that soil is to them an inanimate clod; nor in the usages of their forefathers, which they have learned to regard as a debasing yoke; nor in religion, for of that they doubt; nor in the laws, which do not originate in their own authority; nor in the legislator, whom they fear and despise. The country is lost to their senses; they can neither discover it under its own nor under borrowed features, and they retire into a narrow and unenlightened selfishness. They are emancipated from prejudice, without having acknowledged the empire of reason; they have neither the instinctive patriotism of a monarchy, nor the reflecting patriotism of a republic; but they have stopped between the two in the midst of confusion and distress.

In this predicament, to retreat is impossible; for a people cannot recover the sentiments of their youth, any more than a man can return to the innocent tastes of childhood: such things may be regretted, but they cannot be renewed. They must go forward, and accelerate the union of private with public interests, since the period of disinterested patriotism is gone by forever.

I am certainly far from affirming, that, in order to obtain this result, the exercise of political rights should be immediately granted to all men. But I maintain that the most powerful, and perhaps the only, means which we still possess of interesting men in the welfare of their country, is to make them partakers in the government. At the present time, civic zeal seems to me to be inseparable from the exercise of political rights; and I think that the number of citizens will be found to augment or decrease in Europe in proportion as those rights are extended.

How happens it that in the United States, where the inhabitants arrived but as yesterday upon the soil which they now occupy, and brought neither customs nor traditions with them there; where they met each other for the first time with no previous acquaintance; where, in short, the instinctive love of country can scarcely exist; — how happens it that every one takes as zealous an interest in the affairs of his township, his county, and the whole State, as if they were his own? It is because every one, in his sphere, takes an active part in the government of society.

The lower orders in the United States understand the influence exercised by the general prosperity upon their own welfare; simple as this observation is, it is too rarely made by the people. Besides, they are wont to regard this prosperity as the fruit of their own exertions. The citizen looks upon the fortune of the public as his own, and he labors for the good of the State, not merely from a sense of pride or duty, but from what I venture to term cupidity.

It is unnecessary to study the institutions and the history of the Americans in order to know the truth of this remark, for their manners render it sufficiently evident. As the American participates in all that is done in his country, he thinks himself obliged to defend whatever may be censured in it; for it is not only his country which is then attacked, it is himself. The consequence is, that his national pride resorts to a thousand artifices, and descends to all the petty tricks of personal vanity.

Nothing is more embarrassing, in the ordinary intercourse of life, than this irritable patriotism of the Americans. A stranger may be well inclined to praise many of the institutions of their country, but he begs permission to blame some things in it,—a permission which is inexorably refused. America is therefore a free country, in which, lest anybody should be hurt by your remarks, you are not allowed to speak freely of private individuals, or of the state; of the citizens, or of the authorities; of public or of private undertakings; or, in short, of anything at all, except, perhaps, the climate and the soil; and even then, Americans will be found ready to defend both, as if they had concurred in producing them.

In our times, we must choose between the patriotism of all and the government of a few; for the social force and activity which the first confers are irreconcilable with the pledges of tranquillity which are given by the second.

NOTION OF RIGHTS IN THE UNITED STATES.

No great People without a Notion of Right. — How the Notion of Right can be given to a People. — Respect for Right in the United States.— Whence it arises.

AFTER the general idea of virtue, I know no higher principle than that of right; or rather these two ideas are united in one. The idea of right is simply that of virtue introduced into the political world. It was the idea of right which enabled men to define anarchy and tyranny; and which taught them how to be independent without arrogance, and to obey without servility. The man who submits to violence is debased by his compliance; but when he submits to that right of authority which he acknowledges in a fellow-creature, he rises in some measure above the person who gives the command. There are no great men without virtue; and there are no great nations, — it may almost be added, there would be no society, — without respect for right; for what is a union of rational and intelligent beings who are held together only by the bond of force?

I am persuaded that the only means which we possess, at the present time, of inculcating the idea of right, and of rendering it, as it were, palpable to the senses, is to endow all with the peaceful exercise of certain rights : this is very clearly seen in children, who are men without the strength and the experience of manhood. When a child begins to move in the midst of the objects which surround him, he is instinctively led to appropriate to himself everything which he can lay his hands upon; he has no notion of the property of others; but as he gradually learns the value of things, and begins to perceive that he may in his turn be despoiled, he becomes more circumspect, and he ends by respecting those rights in others which he wishes to have respected in himself. The principle which the child derives from the possession of his toys is taught to the man by the objects which he may call his own. In America, the most democratic of nations, those complaints against property in general, which are so frequent in Europe, are never heard, because in America there are no paupers. As every one has property of his own to defend, every one recognizes the principle upon which he holds it.

The same thing occurs in the political world. In America, the lowest classes have conceived a very high notion of political rights, because they exercise those rights; and they refrain from attacking the rights of others, in order that their own may not be violated. Whilst in Europe, the same classes sometimes resist even the supreme power, the American submits without a murmur to the authority of the pettiest magistrate.

This truth appears even in the trivial details of national life. In France, few pleasures are exclusively reserved for the higher classes; the poor are generally admitted wherever the rich are received; and they consequently behave with propriety, and respect whatever promotes the enjoyments which they themselves share. In England, where wealth has a monopoly of amusement as well as of power, complaints are made, that, whenever the poor happen to enter the places reserved for the pleasures of the rich, they do wanton mischief: can this be wondered at, since care has been taken that they should have nothing to lose?

The government of the democracy brings the notion of political rights to the level of the humblest citizens, just as the dissemination of wealth brings the notion of property within the reach of all men; to my mind, this is one of its greatest advantages. I do not say it is easy to teach men how to exercise political rights; but I maintain that, when it is possible, the effects which result from it are highly important; and I add, that, if there ever was a time at which such an attempt ought to be made, that time is now. Do you not see that religious belief is shaken, and the divine notion of right is declining? — that morality is debased, and the notion of moral right is therefore fading away? Argument is substituted for faith, and calculation for the impulses of sentiment. If, in the midst of this general disruption, you do not succeed in connecting the notion of right with that of private interest, which is the only immutable point in the human heart, what means will you

have of governing the world except by fear ?   When I am
told that the laws are weak and the people are turbulent,
that passions are excited and the authority of virtue is paralyzed, and therefore no measures must be taken to increase
the rights of the democracy, I reply, that, for these very
reasons, some measures of the kind ought to be taken ; and
I believe that governments are still more interested in taking them than society at large, for governments may perish,
but society cannot die.

But I do not wish to exaggerate the example which
America furnishes.   There the people were invested with
political rights at a time when they could not be abused,
for the inhabitants were few in number, and simple in their
manners.   As they have increased, the Americans have
not augmented the power of the democracy ; they have
rather extended its domain.

It cannot be doubted that the moment at which political
rights are granted to a people that had before been without
them is a very critical one, — that the measure, though
often necessary, is always dangerous.   A child may kill
before he is aware of the value of life ; and he may deprive another person of his property, before he is aware
that his own may be taken from him.   The lower orders,
when first they are invested with political rights, stand, in
relation to those rights, in the same position as the child
does to the whole of nature ; and the celebrated adage
may then be applied to them, *Homo puer robustus.*   This
truth may be perceived even in America.   The States in
which the citizens have enjoyed their rights longest, are
those in which they make the best use of them.

It cannot be repeated too often, that nothing is more fertile in prodigies than the art of being free ; but there is
nothing more arduous than the apprenticeship of liberty.
It is not so with despotism : despotism often promises to
make amends for a thousand previous ills ; it supports the

right, it protects the oppressed, and it maintains public order. The nation is lulled by the temporary prosperity which it produces, until it is roused to a sense of its misery. Liberty, on the contrary, is generally established with difficulty in the midst of storms; it is perfected by civil discord; and its benefits cannot be appreciated until it is already old.

RESPECT FOR THE LAW IN THE UNITED STATES.

Respect of the Americans for the Law. — Parental Affection which they entertain for it. — Personal Interest of every one to increase the Power of the Law.

It is not always feasible to consult the whole people, either directly or indirectly, in the formation of the law; but it cannot be denied that, when this is possible, the authority of the law is much augmented. This popular origin, which impairs the excellence and the wisdom of legislation, contributes much to increase its power. There is an amazing strength in the expression of the will of a whole people; and when it declares itself, even the imagination of those who would wish to contest it is overawed. The truth of this fact is well known by parties; and they consequently strive to make out a majority whenever they can. If they have not the greater number of voters on their side, they assert that the true majority abstained from voting; and if they are foiled even there, they have recourse to those persons who had no right to vote.

In the United States, except slaves, servants,* and paupers supported by the townships, there is no class of persons who do not exercise the elective franchise, and who do not indirectly contribute to make the laws. Those

* This is a strange mistake; in the United States, servants have as good a right to vote as their employers, and often vote against them. — Am. Ed.

who wish to attack the laws must consequently either change the opinion of the nation, or trample upon its decision.

A second reason, which is still more direct and weighty, may be adduced : in the United States, every one is personally interested in enforcing the obedience of the whole community to the law ; for as the minority may shortly rally the majority to its principles, it is interested in professing that respect for the decrees of the legislator which it may soon have occasion to claim for its own. However irksome an enactment may be, the citizen of the United States complies with it, not only because it is the work of the majority, but because it is his own, and he regards it as a contract to which he is himself a party.

In the United States, then, that numerous and turbulent multitude does not exist, who, regarding the law as their natural enemy, look upon it with fear and distrust. It is impossible, on the contrary, not to perceive that all classes display the utmost reliance upon the legislation of their country, and are attached to it by a kind of parental affection.

I am wrong, however, in saying all classes ; for as, in America, the European scale of authority is inverted, the wealthy are there placed in a position analogous to that of the poor in the Old World, and it is the opulent classes who frequently look upon the law with suspicion. I have already observed that the advantage of democracy is not, as has been sometimes asserted, that it protects the interests of all, but simply that it protects those of the majority. In the United States, where the poor rule, the rich have always something to fear from the abuse of their power. This natural anxiety of the rich may produce a secret dissatisfaction ; but society is not disturbed by it, for the same reason which withholds the confidence of the rich from the legislative authority, makes them obey its mandates : their wealth, which prevents them from making the law, prevents them from withstanding it. Amongst civilized nations, only those who have nothing to lose ever revolt; and if the laws of a democracy are not always worthy of respect, they are always respected; for those who usually infringe the laws cannot fail to obey those which they have themselves made, and by which they are benefited; whilst the citizens who might be interested in the infraction of them are induced, by their character and station, to submit to the decisions of the legislature, whatever they may be. Besides, the people in America obey the law, not only because it is their work, but because it may be changed if it be harmful; a law is observed because, first, it is a self-imposed evil, and, secondly, it is an evil of transient duration.

ACTIVITY WHICH PERVADES ALL PARTS OF THE BODY POLITIC IN THE UNITED STATES; INFLUENCE WHICH IT EXERCISES UPON SOCIETY.

More difficult to conceive the Political Activity which pervades the United States, than the Freedom and Equality which reign there. — The great Activity which perpetually agitates the Legislative Bodies is only an Episode, a Prolongation of the general Activity. — Difficult for an American to confine himself to his own Business. — Political Agitation extends to all social Intercourse. — Commercial Activity of the Americans partly attributable to this Cause. — Indirect Advantages which Society derives from a Democratic Government.

On passing from a free country into one which is not free, the traveller is struck by the change; in the former, all is bustle and activity; in the latter, everything seems calm and motionless. In the one, amelioration and progress are the topics of inquiry; in the other, it seems as if the community wished only to repose in the enjoyment of advantages already acquired. Nevertheless, the country which exerts itself so strenuously to become happy, is generally more wealthy and prosperous than that which appears so contented with its lot; and when we compare them, we can scarcely conceive how so many new wants are daily felt in the former, whilst so few seem to exist in the latter.

If this remark is applicable to those free countries which have preserved monarchical forms and aristocratic institutions, it is still more so to democratic republics. In these States, it is not a portion only of the people who endeavor to improve the state of society, but the whole community is engaged in the task; and it is not the exigencies and convenience of a single class for which provision is to be made, but the exigencies and convenience of all classes at once.

It is not impossible to conceive the surprising liberty which the Americans enjoy; some idea may likewise be formed of their extreme equality; but the political activity which pervades the United States must be seen in order to be understood. No sooner do you set foot upon American ground, than you are stunned by a kind of tumult; a confused clamor is heard on every side; and a thousand simultaneous voices demand the satisfaction of their social wants. Everything is in motion around you; here, the people of one quarter of a town are met to decide upon the building of a church; there, the election of a representative is going on; a little further, the delegates of a district are posting to the town in order to consult upon some local improvements; in another place, the laborers of a village quit their ploughs to deliberate upon the project of a road or a public school. Meetings are called for the sole purpose of declaring their disapprobation of the conduct of the government; whilst in other assemblies, citizens salute the authorities of the day as the fathers of their country. Societies are formed which regard drunkenness as the principal cause of the evils of the state, and solemnly bind themselves to give an example of temperance.*

The great political agitation of American legislative bodies, which is the only one that attracts the attention of foreigners, is a mere episode, or a sort of continuation, of that universal movement which originates in the lowest classes of the people, and extends successively to all the ranks of society. It is impossible to spend more effort in the pursuit of happiness.

The cares of politics engross a prominent place in the occupations of a citizen in the United States; and almost the only pleasure which an American knows is to take a part in the government, and to discuss its measures. This feeling pervades the most trifling habits of life; even the women frequently attend public meetings, and listen to political harangues as a recreation from their household labors. Debating clubs are, to a certain extent, a substitute for theatrical entertainments: an American cannot converse, but he can discuss; and his talk falls into a dissertation. He speaks to you as if he was addressing a meeting; and if he should chance to become warm in the discussion, he will say " Gentlemen " to the person with whom he is conversing.

In some countries, the inhabitants seem unwilling to avail themselves of the political privileges which the law gives them; it would seem that they set too high a value upon their time to spend it on the interests of the community; and they shut themselves up in a narrow selfishness, marked out by four sunk fences and a quickset hedge. But if an American were condemned to confine his activity to his own affairs, he would be robbed of one half of his

---

* At the time of my stay in the United States, the Temperance Societies already consisted of more than 270,000 members; and their effect had been to diminish the consumption of strong liquors by 500,000 gallons per annum in Pennsylvania alone.

existence; he would feel an immense void in the life which he is accustomed to lead, and his wretchedness would be unbearable.* I am persuaded, that, if ever a despotism should be established in America, it will be more difficult to overcome the habits which freedom has formed, than to conquer the love of freedom itself.

This ceaseless agitation which democratic government has introduced into the political world, influences all social intercourse. I am not sure that, upon the whole, this is not the greatest advantage of democracy; and I am less inclined to applaud it for what it does, than for what it causes to be done.

It is incontestable that the people frequently conduct public business very ill; but it is impossible that the lower orders should take a part in public business without extending the circle of their ideas, and quitting the ordinary routine of their thoughts. The humblest individual who co-operates in the government of society acquires a certain degree of self-respect; and as he possesses authority, he can command the services of minds more enlightened than his own. He is canvassed by a multitude of applicants, and, in seeking to deceive him in a thousand ways, they really enlighten him. He takes a part in political undertakings which he did not originate, but which give him a taste for undertakings of the kind. New improvements are daily pointed out to him in the common property, and this gives him the desire of improving that property which is his own. He is perhaps neither happier nor better than those who came before him, but he is better informed and more active. I have no doubt that the democratic institutions of the United States, joined to the physical constitu-

---

* The same remark was made at Rome under the first Cæsars. Montesquieu somewhere alludes to the excessive despondency of certain Roman citizens, who, after the excitement of political life, were all at once flung back into the stagnation of private life.

tion of the country, are the cause (not the direct, as is so often asserted, but the indirect cause) of the prodigious commercial activity of the inhabitants. It is not created by the laws, but the people learn how to promote it by the experience derived from legislation.

When the opponents of democracy assert that a single man performs what he undertakes better than the government of all, it appears to me that they are right. The government of an individual, supposing an equality of knowledge on either side, is more consistent, more persevering, more uniform, and more accurate in details, than that of a multitude, and it selects with more discrimination the men whom it employs. If any deny this, they have never seen a democratic government, or have judged upon partial evidence. It is true that, even when local circumstances and the dispositions of the people allow democratic institutions to exist, they do not display a regular and methodical system of government. Democratic liberty is far from accomplishing all its projects with the skill of an adroit despotism. It frequently abandons them before they have borne their fruits, or risks them when the consequences may be dangerous; but in the end, it produces more than any absolute government; if it does fewer things well, it does a greater number of things. Under its sway, the grandeur is not in what the public administration does, but in what is done without it or outside of it. Democracy does not give the people the most skilful government, but it produces what the ablest governments are frequently unable to create; namely, an all-pervading and restless activity, a superabundant force, and an energy which is inseparable from it, and which may, however unfavorable circumstances may be, produce wonders. These are the true advantages of democracy.

In the present age, when the destinies of Christendom seem to be in suspense, some hasten to assail democracy as a hostile power, whilst it is yet growing; and others already adore this new deity which is springing forth from chaos. But both parties are imperfectly acquainted with the object of their hatred or their worship; they strike in the dark, and distribute their blows at random.

We must first understand what is wanted of society and its government. Do you wish to give a certain elevation to the human mind, and teach it to regard the things of this world with generous feelings, to inspire men with a scorn of mere temporal advantages, to form and nourish strong convictions, and keep alive the spirit of honorable devotedness? Is it your object to refine the habits, embellish the manners, and cultivate the arts, to promote the love of poetry, beauty, and glory? Would you constitute a people fitted to act powerfully upon all other nations, and prepared for those high enterprises which, whatever be their results, will leave a name forever famous in history? If you believe such to be the principal object of society, avoid the government of the democracy, for it would not lead you with certainty to the goal.

But if you hold it expedient to divert the moral and intellectual activity of man to the production of comfort, and the promotion of general well-being; if a clear understanding be more profitable to man than genius; if your object be not to stimulate the virtues of heroism, but the habits of peace; if you had rather witness vices than crimes, and are content to meet with fewer noble deeds, provided offences be diminished in the same proportion; if, instead of living in the midst of a brilliant society, you are contented to have prosperity around you; if, in short, you are of opinion that the principal object of a government is not to confer the greatest possible power and glory upon the body of the nation, but to insure the greatest enjoyment, and to avoid the most misery, to each of the individuals who compose it, — if such be your desire, then equalize the conditions of men, and establish democratic institutions.

But if the time be past at which such a choice was possible, and if some power superior to that of man already hurries us, without consulting our wishes, towards one or the other of these two governments, let us endeavor to make the best of that which is allotted to us, and, by finding out both its good and its evil tendencies, be able to foster the former and repress the latter to the utmost.

CHAPTER XV.

UNLIMITED POWER OF THE MAJORITY IN THE UNITED STATES, AND ITS CONSEQUENCES.

Natural Strength of the Majority in Democracies. — Most of the American Constitutions have increased this Strength by artificial Means. — How this has been done. — Pledged Delegates. — Moral Power of the Majority. — Opinion as to its Infallibility. — Respect for its Rights, how augmented in the United States.

THE very essence of democratic government consists in the absolute sovereignty of the majority; for there is nothing in democratic states which is capable of resisting it. Most of the American constitutions have sought to increase this natural strength of the majority by artificial means.*

The legislature is, of all political institutions, the one which is most easily swayed by the will of the majority. The Americans determined that the members of the legislature should be elected by the people *directly*, and for a *very brief term*, in order to subject them, not only to the general convictions, but even to the daily passions, of their constituents. The members of both houses are taken from the same classes in society, and nominated in the same manner; so that the movements of the legislative

---

* We have seen, in examining the Federal Constitution, that the efforts of the legislators of the Union were directed against this absolute power. The consequence has been, that the Federal government is more independent in its sphere than that of the States. But the Federal government scarcely ever interferes in any but foreign affairs; and the governments of the States in reality direct society in America.

bodies are almost as rapid, and quite as irresistible, as those of a single assembly.   It is to a legislature thus constituted, that almost all the authority of the government has been intrusted.

At the same time that the law increased the strength of those authorities which of themselves were strong, it enfeebled more and more those which were naturally weak.   It deprived the representatives of the executive power of all stability and independence; and, by subjecting them completely to the caprices of the legislature, it robbed them of the slender influence which the nature of a democratic government might have allowed them to exercise.   In several States, the judicial power was also submitted to the election of the majority; and in all of them, its existence was made to depend on the pleasure of the legislative authority, since the representatives were empowered annually to regulate the stipend of the judges.

Custom has done even more than law.   A proceeding is becoming more and more general in the United States, which will, in the end, do away with the guaranties of representative government: it frequently happens that the voters, in electing a delegate, point out a certain line of conduct to him, and impose upon him certain positive obligations which he is pledged to fulfil.   With the exception of the tumult, this comes to the same thing as if the majority itself held its deliberations in the market-place.

Several other circumstances concur to render the power of the majority in America not only preponderant, but irresistible.   The moral authority of the majority is partly based upon the notion, that there is more intelligence and wisdom in a number of men united than in a single individual, and that the number of the legislators is more important than their quality.   The theory of equality is thus applied to the intellects of men; and human pride is thus assailed in its last retreat by a doctrine which the minority hesitate to admit, and to which they will but slowly assent. Like all other powers, and perhaps more than any other, the authority of the many requires the sanction of time in order to appear legitimate. At first, it enforces obedience by constraint; and its laws are not *respected* until they have been long maintained.

The right of governing society, which the majority supposes itself to derive from its superior intelligence, was introduced into the United States by the first settlers; and this idea, which of itself would be sufficient to create a free nation, has now been amalgamated with the manners of the people and the minor incidents of social life.

The French, under the old monarchy, held it for a maxim that the king could do no wrong; and if he did do wrong, the blame was imputed to his advisers. This notion made obedience very easy; it enabled the subject to complain of the law, without ceasing to love and honor the lawgiver. The Americans entertain the same opinion with respect to the majority.

The moral power of the majority is founded upon yet another principle, which is, that the interests of the many are to be preferred to those of the few. It will readily be perceived that the respect here professed for the rights of the greater number must naturally increase or diminish according to the state of parties. When a nation is divided into several great irreconcilable interests, the privilege of the majority is often overlooked, because it is intolerable to comply with its demands.

If there existed in America a class of citizens whom the legislating majority sought to deprive of exclusive privileges which they had possessed for ages, and to bring down from an elevated station to the level of the multitude, it is probable that the minority would be less ready to submit to its laws. But as the United States were colonized by men holding equal rank, there is as yet no natural or permanent disagreement between the interests of its different inhabitants.

There are communities in which the members of the minority can never hope to draw over the majority to their side, because they must then give up the very point which is at issue between them. Thus, an aristocracy can never become a majority whilst it retains its exclusive privileges, and it cannot cede its privileges without ceasing to be an aristocracy.

In the United States, political questions cannot be taken up in so general and absolute a manner; and all parties are willing to recognize the rights of the majority, because they all hope at some time to be able to exercise them to their own advantage. The majority, therefore, in that country, exercise a prodigious actual authority, and a power of opinion which is nearly as great; no obstacles exist which can impede or even retard its progress, so as to make it heed the complaints of those whom it crushes upon its path. This state of things is harmful in itself, and dangerous for the future.

HOW THE OMNIPOTENCE OF THE MAJORITY INCREASES, IN AMERICA, THE INSTABILITY OF LEGISLATION AND ADMINISTRATION INHERENT IN DEMOCRACY.

The Americans increase the Mutability of Law which is inherent in a Democracy by changing the Legislature every Year, and investing it with almost unbounded Authority. — The same Effect is produced upon the Administration. — In America, the Pressure for social Improvements is vastly greater, but less continuous, than in Europe.

I HAVE already spoken of the natural defects of democratic institutions; each one of them increases in the same ratio as the power of the majority. To begin with the most evident of them all, the mutability of the laws is an

evil inherent in a democratic government, because it is natural to democracies to raise new men to power. But this
evil is more or less sensible in proportion to the authority
and the means of action which the legislature possesses.

In America, the authority exercised by the legislatures is
supreme; nothing prevents them from accomplishing their
wishes with celerity, and with irresistible power, and they
are supplied with new representatives every year. That is
to say, the circumstances which contribute most powerfully to democratic instability, and which admit of the free
application of caprice to the most important objects, are
here in full operation. Hence America is, at the present
day, the country of all others where laws last the shortest
time. Almost all the American constitutions have been
amended within thirty years: there is therefore not one
American State which has not modified the principles of
its legislation in that time. As for the laws themselves,
a single glance at the archives of the different States of
the Union suffices to convince one, that in America the
activity of the legislator never slackens. Not that the
American democracy is naturally less stable than any
other, but it is allowed to follow, in the formation of the
laws, the natural instability of its desires.*

The omnipotence of the majority, and the rapid as well
as absolute manner in which its decisions are executed in
the United States, not only render the law unstable, but
exercise the same influence upon the execution of the law
and the conduct of the administration. As the majority is

* The legislative acts promulgated by the State of Massachusetts alone,
from the year 1780 to the present time, already fill three stout volumes; and
it must not be forgotten that the collection to which I allude was revised in
1823, when many old laws which had fallen into disuse were omitted. The
State of Massachusetts, which is not more populous than a department of
France, may be considered as the most stable, the most consistent, and the
most sagacious in its undertakings, of the whole Union.

the only power which it is important to court, all its projects are taken up with the greatest ardor; but no sooner is its attention distracted, than all this ardor ceases; whilst in the free states of Europe, where the administration is at once independent and secure, the projects of the legislature continue to be executed, even when its attention is directed to other objects.

In America, certain improvements are prosecuted with much more zeal and activity than elsewhere; in Europe, the same ends are promoted by much less social effort more continuously applied.

Some years ago, several pious individuals undertook to ameliorate the condition of the prisons. The public were moved by their statements, and the reform of criminals became a popular undertaking. New prisons were built; and, for the first time, the idea of reforming as well as punishing the delinquent formed a part of prison discipline.

But this happy change, in which the public had taken so hearty an interest, and which the simultaneous exertions of the citizens rendered irresistible, could not be completed in a moment. Whilst the new penitentiaries were being erected, and the will of the majority was hastening the work, the old prisons still existed, and contained a great number of offenders. These jails became more unwholesome and corrupt in proportion as the new establishments were reformed and improved, forming a contrast which may readily be understood. The majority was so eagerly employed in founding the new prisons, that those which already existed were forgotten; and, as the general attention was diverted to a novel object, the care which had hitherto been bestowed upon the others ceased. The salutary regulations of discipline were first relaxed, and afterwards broken; so that, in the immediate neighborhood of a prison which bore witness to the mild and enlightened spirit of our times, dungeons existed which reminded one of the barbarism of the Middle Ages.

TYRANNY OF THE MAJORITY.

How the Principle of the Sovereignty of the People is to be understood. — Impossibility of conceiving a Mixed Government. — The Sovereign Power must exist somewhere. — Precautions to be taken to control its Action. — These Precautions have not been taken in the United States. — Consequences.

I HOLD it to be an impious and detestable maxim, that, politically speaking, the people have a right to do anything; and yet I have asserted that all authority originates in the will of the majority. Am I, then, in contradiction with myself?

A general law, which bears the name of justice, has been made and sanctioned, not only by a majority of this or that people, but by a majority of mankind. The rights of every people are therefore confined within the limits of what is just. A nation may be considered as a jury which is empowered to represent society at large, and to apply justice, which is its law. Ought such a jury, which represents society, to have more power than the society itself, whose laws it executes?

When I refuse to obey an unjust law, I do not contest the right of the majority to command, but I simply appeal from the sovereignty of the people to the sovereignty of mankind. Some have not feared to assert that a people can never outstep the boundaries of justice and reason in those affairs which are peculiarly its own; and that consequently full power may be given to the majority by which they are represented. But this is the language of a slave.

A majority taken collectively is only an individual, whose opinions, and frequently whose interests, are opposed to those of another individual, who is styled a minority. If it be admitted that a man possessing absolute power may misuse that power by wronging his adversaries, why should not a majority be liable to the same reproach? Men do not change their characters by uniting with each other; nor does their patience in the presence of obstacles increase with their strength.* For my own part, I cannot believe it; the power to do everything, which I should refuse to one of my equals, I will never grant to any number of them.

I do not think that, for the sake of preserving liberty, it is possible to combine several principles in the same government, so as really to oppose them to one another. The form of government which is usually termed *mixed* has always appeared to me a mere chimera. Accurately speaking, there is no such thing as a *mixed government*, in the sense usually given to that word, because, in all communities, some one principle of action may be discovered which preponderates over the others. England, in the last century, — which has been especially cited as an example of this sort of government, — was essentially an aristocratic state, although it comprised some great elements of democracy; for the laws and customs of the country were such that the aristocracy could not but preponderate in the long run, and direct public affairs according to its own will. The error arose from seeing the interests of the nobles perpetually contending with those of the people, without considering the issue of the contest, which was really the important point. When a community actually has a mixed government, — that is to say, when it is equally divided between adverse principles, — it must either experience a revolution, or fall into anarchy.

I am therefore of opinion, that social power superior to all others must always be placed somewhere; but I think

---

* No one will assert that a people cannot forcibly wrong another people; but parties may be looked upon as lesser nations within a great one, and they are aliens to each other: if, therefore, it be admitted that a nation can act tyrannically towards another nation, it cannot be denied that a party may do the same towards another party.

that liberty is endangered when this power finds no obstacle which can retard its course, and give it time to moderate its own vehemence.

Unlimited power is in itself a bad and dangerous thing. Human beings are not competent to exercise it with discretion. God alone can be omnipotent, because his wisdom and his justice are always equal to his power. There is no power on earth so worthy of honor in itself, or clothed with rights so sacred, that I would admit its uncontrolled and all-predominant authority. When I see that the right and the means of absolute command are conferred on any power whatever, be it called a people or a king, an aristocracy or a democracy, a monarchy or a republic, I say there is the germ of tyranny, and I seek to live elsewhere, under other laws.

In my opinion, the main evil of the present democratic institutions of the United States does not arise, as is often asserted in Europe, from their weakness, but from their irresistible strength. I am not so much alarmed at the excessive liberty which reigns in that country, as at the inadequate securities which one finds there against tyranny.

When an individual or a party is wronged in the United States, to whom can he apply for redress? If to public opinion, public opinion constitutes the majority; if to the legislature, it represents the majority, and implicitly obeys it; if to the executive power, it is appointed by the majority, and serves as a passive tool in its hands. The public force consists of the majority under arms; the jury is the majority invested with the right of hearing judicial cases; and in certain States, even the judges are elected by the majority. However iniquitous or absurd the measure of which you complain, you must submit to it as well as you can.*

* A striking instance of the excesses which may be occasioned by the despotism of the majority occurred at Baltimore during the war of 1812.

If, on the other hand, a legislative power could be so constituted as to represent the majority without necessarily being the slave of its passions, an executive so as to retain a proper share of authority, and a judiciary so as to remain independent of the other two powers, a government

At that time, the war was very popular in Baltimore. A journal which had taken the other side excited by its opposition the indignation of the inhabitants. The mob assembled, broke the printing-presses, and attacked the house of the editors. The militia was called out, but did not obey the call; and the only means of saving the wretches who were threatened by the frenzy of the mob, was to throw them into prison as common malefactors. But even this precaution was ineffectual; the mob collected again during the night; the magistrates again made a vain attempt to call out the militia; the prison was forced, one of the newspaper editors was killed upon the spot, and the others were left for dead. The guilty parties, when they were brought to trial, were acquitted by the jury.

I said one day to an inhabitant of Pennsylvania, "Be so good as to explain to me how it happens, that in a State founded by Quakers, and celebrated for its toleration, free Blacks are not allowed to exercise civil rights. They pay taxes; is it not fair that they should vote?"

"You insult us," replied my informant, "if you imagine that our legislators could have committed so gross an act of injustice and intolerance."

"Then the Blacks possess the right of voting in this country?"

"Without doubt."

"How comes it, then, that at the polling-booth, this morning, I did not perceive a single Negro in the meeting?"

"This is not the fault of the law: the Negroes have an undisputed right of voting; but they voluntarily abstain from making their appearance."

"A very pretty piece of modesty on their part!" rejoined I.

"Why, the truth is, that they are not disinclined to vote, but they are afraid of being maltreated; in this country, the law is sometimes unable to maintain its authority, without the support of the majority. But in this case, the majority entertains very strong prejudices against the Blacks, and the magistrates are unable to protect them in the exercise of their legal rights."

"Then the majority claims the right not only of making the laws, but of breaking the laws it has made?"

[In Massachusetts, and some other States, free Blacks vote as regularly as any other class of citizens. — AM. ED.]

would be formed which would still be democratic, without incurring hardly any risk of tyranny.

I do not say that there is a frequent use of tyranny in America at the present day; but I maintain that there is no sure barrier against it, and that the causes which mitigate the government there are to be found in the circumstances and the manners of the country, more than in its laws.*

* This whole chapter is a glowing description of the evils which are to be feared in the United States from an abuse of the immense power of the majority. In the main, it is a truthful picture; and yet the author allows himself to be so far heated by his own rhetoric as to forget the checks and limitations of this dominant power which he has himself elsewhere noticed. The very complexity of our frame of government enables us to set off and balance the strength of one majority against another. Thus the Federal and the State governments mutually restrain and limit each other, while each is restricted by many provisions in its own written Constitution, which are of the nature of a Bill of Rights. No law can be passed by the Federal Legislature without the concurrence of a majority of the States represented in the Senate, wherein little Delaware, with only one hundred thousand inhabitants, has as potent a voice as the Empire State of New York, with its three and a half millions. Even the sturdy little New England township, so admirably described elsewhere by M. de Tocqueville, succeeds in causing its rights to be respected in the State Legislature, where it is immensely outnumbered, because the other townships would make common cause with it against any crying injustice, fearing that its case may become their own at some future day. Moreover, the majority in a State, or even in the United States, though a mighty, is also an unwieldy power, acting only at long intervals, once a year, or once in four years, and then through so many agents, and so much machinery, that the force of its blows is greatly impaired before they reach their object. It is only a figure of speech to say that the majority of the people make the laws, because they choose the members of the Legislature. The delegates thus chosen respect their constituents, it is true, and strive in the main to conform to their wishes; and yet they act very differently from what those constituents would do, if allowed to come together whenever they pleased, and directly enact any law that pleased them, upon any subject. The necessary delays in law-making, the compliance with established forms, the suspensive veto of a Governor or a President, the fear which each individual legislator entertains lest the proposed enactment, though it may gratify his present

EFFECTS OF THE OMNIPOTENCE OF THE MAJORITY UPON
THE ARBITRARY AUTHORITY OF AMERICAN PUBLIC OF-
FICERS.

Liberty left by the American Laws to Public Officers within a certain
Sphere. — Their Power.

A DISTINCTION must be drawn between tyranny and
arbitrary power. Tyranny may be exercised by means of
the law itself, and in that case it is not arbitrary ; arbitrary
power may be exercised for the public good, in which case
it is not tyrannical. Tyranny usually employs arbitrary
means, but, if necessary, it can do without them.

In the United States, the omnipotence of the majority,
which is favorable to the legal despotism of the legislature,
likewise favors the arbitrary authority of the magistrate.

passion or the present passions of his constituents, may work harm to him
or them in the long run, — all these are salutary safeguards against the
abuse of a mighty power.

Again, it is only a figure of speech to represent the majority and the
minority as two individuals contending with each other, though very unequally matched. A majority is not one man, but a multitude of men, and
a multitude which cannot, by any degree of political skill and discipline,
be made to think or act as one man. The individuals who compose it are
the majority only on this or that subject; on half a dozen other subjects,
every one of them may be a member of a minority; on some points —
his own private interests, for example — he may stand alone. Thus situated, he is not at all likely to make an unscrupulous use of the vast strength
of the greater number, but will generally favor moderate and conciliatory
counsels. He will also reflect, that the change of a very few votes may
place the majority on the other side in respect to the very subjects on which
it is now with him; and any violent expedient which he may now adopt
will then be a formidable precedent to be used against him.

As to the riots in Baltimore and elsewhere, or the prejudice which so
generally operates in America to the disadvantage of the Negroes, M. de
Tocqueville forgets that such things are not peculiar to democracies. Witness the No-Popery riots of 1780, the Bristol riots on occasion of the
Reform Bill, the frequent *emeutes* at Paris, and a thousand other historical
cases. — AM. ED.

The majority has absolute power both to make the law and to watch over its execution ; and as it has equal authority over those who are in power, and the community at large, it considers public officers as its passive agents, and readily confides to them the task of carrying out its designs. The details of their office, and the privileges which they are to enjoy, are rarely defined beforehand. It treats them as a master does his servants, since they are always at work in his sight, and he can direct or reprimand them at any instant.

In general, the American functionaries are far more independent within the sphere which is prescribed to them than the French civil officers. Sometimes, even, they are allowed by the popular authority to exceed those bounds ; and as they are protected by the opinion, and backed by the power, of the majority, they dare do things which even a European, accustomed as he is to arbitrary power, is astonished at. By this means, habits are formed in the heart of a free country which may some day prove fatal to its liberties.

POWER EXERCISED BY THE MAJORITY IN AMERICA UPON OPINION.

In America, when the Majority has once irrevocably decided a Question, all Discussion ceases. — Reason of this. — Moral Power exercised by the Majority upon Opinion. — Democratic Republics have applied Despotism to the Minds of Men.

IT is in the examination of the exercise of thought in the United States, that we clearly perceive how far the power of the majority surpasses all the powers with which we are acquainted in Europe. Thought is an invisible and subtile power, that mocks all the efforts of tyranny. At the present time, the most absolute monarchs in Europe cannot prevent certain opinions hostile to their authority from circulating in secret through their dominions, and even in their courts. It is not so in America; as long as the majority is still undecided, discussion is carried on; but as soon as its decision is irrevocably pronounced, every one is silent, and the friends as well as the opponents of the measure unite in assenting to its propriety. The reason of this is perfectly clear: no monarch is so absolute as to combine all the powers of society in his own hands, and to conquer all opposition, as a majority is able to do, which has the right both of making and of executing the laws.

The authority of a king is physical, and controls the actions of men without subduing their will. But the majority possesses a power which is physical and moral at the same time, which acts upon the will as much as upon the actions, and represses not only all contest, but all controversy.

I know of no country in which there is so little independence of mind and real freedom of discussion as in America. In any constitutional state in Europe, every sort of religious and political theory may be freely preached and disseminated; for there is no country in Europe so subdued by any single authority, as not to protect the man who raises his voice in the cause of truth from the consequences of his hardihood. If he is unfortunate enough to live under an absolute government, the people are often upon his side; if he inhabits a free country, he can, if necessary, find a shelter behind the throne. The aristocratic part of society supports him in some countries, and the democracy in others. But in a nation where democratic institutions exist, organized like those of the United States, there is but one authority, one element of strength and success, with nothing beyond it.

In America, the majority raises formidable barriers around the liberty of opinion: within these barriers, an author may write what he pleases; but woe to him if he goes beyond them. Not that he is in danger of an *auto-da-fé*, but he is exposed to continued obloquy and persecution. His political career is closed forever, since he has offended the only authority which is able to open it. Every sort of compensation, even that of celebrity, is refused to him. Before publishing his opinions, he imagined that he held them in common with others; but no sooner has he declared them, than he is loudly censured by his opponents, whilst those who think like him, without having the courage to speak out, abandon him in silence. He yields at length, overcome by the daily effort which he has to make, and subsides into silence, as if he felt remorse for having spoken the truth.

Fetters and headsmen were the coarse instruments which tyranny formerly employed; but the civilization of our age has perfected despotism itself, though it seemed to have nothing to learn. Monarchs had, so to speak, materialized oppression: the democratic republics of the present day have rendered it as entirely an affair of the mind, as the will which it is intended to coerce. Under the absolute sway of one man, the body was attacked in order to subdue the soul; but the soul escaped the blows which were directed against it, and rose proudly superior. Such is not the course adopted by tyranny in democratic republics; there the body is left free, and the soul is enslaved. The master no longer says, " You shall think as I do, or you shall die"; but he says, " You are free to think differently from me, and to retain your life, your property, and all that you possess; but you are henceforth a stranger among your people. You may retain your civil rights, but they will be useless to you, for you will never be chosen by your fellow-citizens, if you solicit their votes; and they will affect to scorn you, if you ask for their esteem. You will remain among men, but you will be deprived of the rights of mankind. Your fellow-creatures will shun you like an

impure being; and even those who believe in your innocence will abandon you, lest they should be shunned in
their turn. Go in peace! I have given you your life,
but it is an existence worse than death."

Absolute monarchies had dishonored despotism; let us
beware lest democratic republics should reinstate it, and
render it less odious and degrading in the eyes of the many,
by making it still more onerous to the few.

Works have been published in the proudest nations of
the Old World, expressly intended to censure the vices
and the follies of the times: Labruyère inhabited the palace of Louis XIV., when he composed his chapter upon
the Great, and Molière criticised the courtiers in the pieces
which were acted before the court. But the ruling power
in the United States is not to be made game of. The
smallest reproach irritates its sensibility, and the slightest
joke which has any foundation in truth renders it indig-
nant; from the forms of its language up to the solid virtues of its character, everything must be made the subject
of encomium. No writer, whatever be his eminence, can
escape paying this tribute of adulation to his fellow-citizens.
The majority lives in the perpetual utterance of self-applause; and there are certain truths which the Americans
can only learn from strangers or from experience.

If America has not as yet had any great writers, the
reason is given in these facts; there can be no literary
genius without freedom of opinion, and freedom of opinion
does not exist in America. The Inquisition has never
been able to prevent a vast number of anti-religious books
from circulating in Spain. The empire of the majority
succeeds much better in the United States, since it actually
removes any wish to publish them. Unbelievers are to be
met with in America, but there is no public organ of
infidelity. Attempts have been made by some governments to protect morality by prohibiting licentious books.

In the United States, no one is punished for this sort of books, but no one is induced to write them; not because all the citizens are immaculate in conduct, but because the majority of the community is decent and orderly.

In this case the use of the power is unquestionably good; and I am discussing the nature of the power itself. This irresistible authority is a constant fact, and its judicious exercise is only an accident.*

EFFECTS OF THE TYRANNY OF THE MAJORITY UPON THE NATIONAL CHARACTER OF THE AMERICANS. — THE COURTIER-SPIRIT IN THE UNITED STATES.

Effects of the Tyranny of the Majority more sensibly felt hitherto on the Manners than on the Conduct of Society. — They check the Development of great Characters. — Democratic Republics, organized like the United States, infuse the Courtier-spirit into the Mass of the People. — Proofs of this Spirit in the United States, — Why there is more Patriotism in the People than in those who govern in their Name.

THE tendencies which I have just mentioned are as yet but slightly perceptible in political society; but they already exercise an unfavorable influence upon the national character of the Americans. I attribute the small number of distinguished men in political life to the ever-increasing despotism of the majority in the United States.

When the American Revolution broke out, they arose in great numbers; for public opinion then served, not to tyrannize over, but to direct the exertions of individuals. Those celebrated men, sharing the agitation of mind com-

* De Tocqueville's remarks on this subject are rhetorical, and altogether too highly colored. It is notorious, that, in politics, morality, and religion, the most offensive opinions are preached and printed every week here in America, apparently for no other purpose than that of shocking the sentiments of the great bulk of the community. Instead of complaining of the bondage of thought, the judicious observer will rather grieve at the extreme licentiousness of the rostrum and the press. — AM. ED.

mon at that period, had a grandeur peculiar to themselves, which was reflected back upon the nation, but was by no means borrowed from it.

In absolute governments, the great nobles who are nearest to the throne flatter the passions of the sovereign, and voluntarily truckle to his caprices. But the mass of the nation does not degrade itself by servitude; it often submits from weakness, from habit, or from ignorance, and sometimes from loyalty. Some nations have been known to sacrifice their own desires to those of the sovereign with pleasure and pride, thus exhibiting a sort of independence of mind in the very act of submission. These nations are miserable, but they are not degraded. There is a great difference between doing what one does not approve, and feigning to approve what one does; the one is the weakness of a feeble person, the other befits the temper of a lackey.

In free countries, where every one is more or less called upon to give his opinion on affairs of state, — in democratic republics, where public life is incessantly mingled with domestic affairs, where the sovereign authority is accessible on every side, and where its attention can always be attracted by vociferation, — more persons are to be met with who speculate upon its weaknesses, and live upon ministering to its passions, than in absolute monarchies. Not because men are naturally worse in these states than elsewhere, but the temptation is stronger and of easier access at the same time. The result is a more extensive debasement of character.

Democratic republics extend the practice of currying favor with the many, and introduce it into all classes at once : this is the most serious reproach that can be addressed to them. This is especially true in democratic states organized like the American republics, where the power of the majority is so absolute and irresistible that one must give up his rights as a citizen, and almost abjure his qualities as a man, if he intends to stray from the track which it prescribes.

In that immense crowd which throngs the avenues to power in the United States, I found very few men who displayed that manly candor and masculine independence of opinion which frequently distinguished the Americans in former times, and which constitutes the leading feature in distinguished characters wheresoever they may be found. It seems, at first sight, as if all the minds of the Americans were formed upon one model, so accurately do they follow the same route. A stranger does, indeed, sometimes meet with Americans who dissent from the rigor of these formularies, — with men who deplore the defects of the laws, the mutability and the ignorance of democracy, — who even go so far as to observe the evil tendencies which impair the national character, and to point out such remedies as it might be possible to apply ; but no one is there to hear them except yourself, and you, to whom these secret reflections are confided, are a stranger and a bird of passage. They are very ready to communicate truths which are useless to you, but they hold a different language in public.

If ever these lines are read in America, I am well assured of two things ; — in the first place, that all who peruse them will raise their voices to condemn me ; and, in the second place, that many of them will acquit me at the bottom of their conscience.

I have heard of patriotism in the United States, and I have found true patriotism among the people, but never among the leaders of the people. This may be explained by analogy : despotism debases the oppressed much more than the oppressor : in absolute monarchies, the king often has great virtues, but the courtiers are invariably servile. It is true that American courtiers do not say " Sire," or " Your Majesty," — a distinction without a difference.

They are forever talking of the natural intelligence of the people whom they serve : they do not debate the question which of the virtues of their master is pre-eminently worthy of admiration, for they assure him that he possesses all the virtues without having acquired them, or without caring to acquire them ; they do not give him their daughters and their wives to be raised at his pleasure to the rank of his concubines ; but, by sacrificing their opinions, they prostitute themselves. Moralists and philosophers in America are not obliged to conceal their opinions under the veil of allegory ; but before they venture upon a harsh truth, they say, " We are aware that the people whom we are addressing are too superior to the weaknesses of human nature to lose the command of their temper for an instant. We should not hold this language if we were not speaking to men whom their virtues and their intelligence render more worthy of freedom than all the rest of the world." The sycophants of Louis XIV. could not flatter more dexterously.

For my part, I am persuaded that, in all governments, whatever their nature may be, servility will cower to force, and adulation will follow power. The only means of preventing men from degrading themselves is to invest no one with that unlimited authority which is the sure method of debasing them.

THE GREATEST DANGERS OF THE AMERICAN REPUBLICS PROCEED FROM THE OMNIPOTENCE OF THE MAJORITY.

Democratic Republics liable to perish from a Misuse of their Power, and not from Impotence. — The Governments of the American Republics are more Centralized and more Energetic than those of the Monarchies of Europe. — Dangers resulting from this. — Opinions of Madison and Jefferson upon this Point.

GOVERNMENTS usually perish from impotence or from tyranny. In the former case, their power escapes from

them ; it is wrested from their grasp in the latter. Many
observers who have witnessed the anarchy of democratic
states, have imagined that the government of those states
was naturally weak and impotent. The truth is, that,
when war is once begun between parties, the government
loses its control over society. But I do not think that a
democratic power is naturally without force or resources ;
say, rather, that it is almost always by the abuse of its
force, and the misemployment of its resources, that it becomes a failure. Anarchy is almost always produced by
its tyranny or its mistakes, but not by its want of strength.

It is important not to confound stability with force, or
the greatness of a thing with its duration. In democratic
republics, the power which directs * society is not stable ;
for it often changes hands, and assumes a new direction.
But, whichever way it turns, its force is almost irresistible.
The governments of the American republics appear to me
to be as much centralized as those of the absolute monarchies of Europe, and more energetic than they are. I do not,
therefore, imagine that they will perish from weakness.†

If ever the free institutions of America are destroyed,
that event may be attributed to the omnipotence of the
majority, which may at some future time urge the minor-
ities to desperation, and oblige them to have recourse to
physical force. Anarchy will then be the result, but it
will have been brought about by despotism.

Mr. Madison expresses the same opinion in the Federalist, No. 51. " It is of great importance in a republic, not

---

* This power may be centralized in an assembly, in which case it will be
strong without being stable; or it may be centralized in an individual, in
which case it will be less strong, but more stable.

† I presume that it is scarcely necessary to remind the reader here, as well
as throughout this chapter, that I am speaking, not of the Federal governments, but of the several governments of each State, which the majority
controls at its pleasure.

only to guard the society against the oppression of its rulers, but to guard one part of the society against the injustice of the other part. Justice is the end of government. It is the end of civil society. It ever has been, and ever will be, pursued until it be obtained, or until liberty be lost in the pursuit. In a society, under the forms of which the stronger faction can readily unite and oppress the weaker, anarchy may as truly be said to reign as in a state of nature, where the weaker individual is not secured against the violence of the stronger: and as, in the latter state, even the stronger individuals are prompted by the uncertainty of their condition to submit to a government which may protect the weak as well as themselves, so, in the former state, will the more powerful factions be gradually induced by a like motive to wish for a government which will protect all parties, the weaker as well as the more powerful. It can be little doubted, that, if the State of Rhode Island was separated from the Confederacy and left to itself, the insecurity of right under the popular form of government within such narrow limits would be displayed by such reiterated oppressions of the factious majorities, that some power altogether independent of the people would soon be called for by the voice of the very factions whose misrule had proved the necessity of it."

Jefferson also said: "The executive power in our government is not the only, perhaps not even the principal, object of my solicitude. The tyranny of the legislature is really the danger most to be feared, and will continue to be so for many years to come. The tyranny of the executive power will come in its turn, but at a more distant period."

I am glad to cite the opinion of Jefferson upon this subject rather than that of any other, because I consider him the most powerful advocate democracy has ever had.

CHAPTER XVI.

CAUSES WHICH MITIGATE THE TYRANNY OF THE MAJORITY
IN THE UNITED STATES.

ABSENCE OF CENTRALIZED ADMINISTRATION.

The National Majority does not pretend to do everything. — Is obliged to
employ the Town and County Magistrates to execute its sovereign Will.

I HAVE already pointed out the distinction between
a centralized government and a centralized administration. The former exists in America, but the latter is
nearly unknown there. If the directing power of the
American communities had both these instruments of government at its disposal, and united the habit of executing
its commands to the right of commanding; if, after having
established the general principles of government, it descended to the details of their application; and if, having
regulated the great interests of the country, it could descend to the circle of individual interests, freedom would
soon be banished from the New World.

But in the United States, the majority, which so frequently displays the tastes and the propensities of a despot,
is still destitute of the most perfect instruments of tyranny.

In the American republics, the central government has
never as yet busied itself but with a small number of
objects, sufficiently prominent to attract its attention. The
secondary affairs of society have never been regulated by
its authority; and nothing has hitherto betrayed its desire
of even interfering in them. The majority is become

more and more absolute, but has not increased the prerogatives of the central government; those great prerogatives have been confined to a certain sphere; and, although the despotism of the majority may be galling upon one point, it cannot be said to extend to all. However the predominant party in the nation may be carried away by its passions, however ardent it may be in the pursuit of its projects, it cannot oblige all the citizens to comply with its desires in the same manner, and at the same time, throughout the country. When the central government which represents that majority has issued a decree, it must intrust the execution of its will to agents, over whom it frequently has no control, and whom it cannot perpetually direct. The townships, municipal bodies, and counties form so many concealed breakwaters, which check or part the tide of popular determination. If an oppressive law were passed, liberty would still be protected by the mode of executing that law; the majority cannot descend to the details and what may be called the puerilities of administrative tyranny. It does not even imagine that it can do so, for it has not a full consciousness of its authority. It knows only the extent of its natural powers, but is unacquainted with the art of increasing them.

This point deserves attention; for if a democratic republic, similar to that of the United States, were ever founded in a country where the power of one man had previously established a centralized administration, and had sunk it deep into the habits and the laws of the people, I do not hesitate to assert, that, in such a republic, a more insufferable despotism would prevail than in any of the absolute monarchies of Europe; or, indeed, than any which could be found on this side of Asia.

THE PROFESSION OF THE LAW IN THE UNITED STATES SERVES TO COUNTERPOISE THE DEMOCRACY.

Utility of ascertaining what are the natural Instincts of the Legal Profession. — These Men are to act a prominent Part in future Society. — How the peculiar Pursuits of Lawyers give an aristocratic Turn to their Ideas. — Accidental Causes which may check this Tendency. — Ease with which the Aristocracy coalesces with Legal Men. — Use of Lawyers to a Despot. — The Profession of the Law constitutes the only aristocratic Element with which the natural Elements of Democracy will combine. — Peculiar Causes which tend to give an aristocratic Turn of Mind to English and American Lawyers. — The Aristocracy of America is on the Bench and at the Bar. — Influence of Lawyers upon American Society. — Their peculiar Magisterial Spirit affects the Legislature, the Administration, and even the People.

In visiting the Americans and studying their laws, we perceive that the authority they have intrusted to members of the legal profession, and the influence which these individuals exercise in the government, is the most powerful existing security against the excesses of democracy. This effect seems to me to result from a general cause, which it is useful to investigate, as it may be reproduced elsewhere.

The members of the legal profession have taken a part in all the movements of political society in Europe for the last five hundred years. At one time, they have been the instruments of the political authorities, and at another, they have succeeded in converting the political authorities into their instruments. In the Middle Ages, they afforded a powerful support to the Crown; and since that period, they have exerted themselves effectively to limit the royal prerogative. In England, they have contracted a close alliance with the aristocracy: in France, they have shown themselves its most dangerous enemies. Under all these circumstances, have the members of the legal profession been swayed by sudden and fleeting impulses, or have they been more or less impelled by instincts which are natural to them, and which will always recur in history? I am incited to this investigation, for perhaps this particular class of men will play a prominent part in the political society which is soon to be created.

Men who have made a special study of the laws derive from this occupation certain habits of order, a taste for formalities, and a kind of instinctive regard for the regular connection of ideas, which naturally render them very hostile to the revolutionary spirit and the unreflecting passions of the multitude.

The special information which lawyers derive from their studies insures them a separate rank in society, and they constitute a sort of privileged body in the scale of intellect. This notion of their superiority perpetually recurs to them in the practice of their profession : they are the masters of a science which is necessary, but which is not very generally known : they serve as arbiters between the citizens ; and the habit of directing to their purpose the blind passions of parties in litigation, inspires them with a certain contempt for the judgment of the multitude. Add to this, that they naturally constitute *a body ;* not by any previous understanding, or by an agreement which directs them to a common end ; but the analogy of their studies and the uniformity of their methods connect their minds together, as a common interest might unite their endeavors.

Some of the tastes and the habits of the aristocracy may consequently be discovered in the characters of lawyers. They participate in the same instinctive love of order and formalities ; and they entertain the same repugnance to the notions of the multitude, and the same secret contempt of the government of the people. I do not mean to say that the natural propensities of lawyers are sufficiently strong to sway them irresistibly ; for they, like most other men, are governed by their private interests, and especially by the interests of the moment.

In a state of society in which the members of the legal profession cannot hold that rank in the political world which they enjoy in private life, we may rest assured that they will be the foremost agents of revolution. But it must then be inquired, whether the cause which then induces them to innovate and destroy results from a permanent disposition or from an accident. It is true that lawyers mainly contributed to the overthrow of the French monarchy in 1789; but it remains to be seen whether they acted thus because they had studied the laws, or because they were prohibited from making them.

Five hundred years ago, the English nobles headed the people, and spoke in their name; at the present time, the aristocracy support the throne, and defend the royal prerogative. But aristocracy has, notwithstanding this, its peculiar instincts and propensities. We must be careful not to confound isolated members of a body with the body itself. In all free governments, of whatsoever form they may be, members of the legal profession will be found in the front ranks of all parties. The same remark is also applicable to the aristocracy; almost all the democratic movements which have agitated the world have been directed by nobles. A privileged body can never satisfy the ambition of all its members: it has always more talents and more passions than it can find places to content and employ; so that a considerable number of individuals are usually to be met with, who are inclined to attack those very privileges which they cannot soon enough turn to their own account.

I do not, then, assert that *all* the members of the legal profession are, at *all* times, the friends of order and the opponents of innovation, but merely that most of them are usually so. In a community in which lawyers are allowed to occupy without opposition that high station which naturally belongs to them, their general spirit will be eminently conservative and anti-democratic. When an aristocracy excludes the leaders of that profession from its ranks, it excites enemies who are the more formidable as they are independent of the nobility by their labors, and feel themselves to be their equals in intelligence, though inferior in opulence and power. But whenever an aristocracy consents to impart some of its privileges to these same individuals, the two classes coalesce very readily, and assume, as it were, family interests.

I am, in like manner, inclined to believe that a monarch will always be able to convert legal practitioners into the most serviceable instruments of his authority. There is a far greater affinity between this class of persons and the executive power, than there is between them and the people, though they have often aided to overturn the former; just as there is a greater natural affinity between the nobles and the monarch, than between the nobles and the people, although the higher orders of society have often, in concert with the lower classes, resisted the prerogative of the crown.

Lawyers are attached to public order beyond every other consideration, and the best security of public order is authority. It must not be forgotten, also, that, if they prize freedom much, they generally value legality still more: they are less afraid of tyranny than of arbitrary power; and, provided the legislature undertakes of itself to deprive men of their independence, they are not dissatisfied.

I am therefore convinced that the prince who, in presence of an encroaching democracy, should endeavor to impair the judicial authority in his dominions, and to diminish the political influence of lawyers, would commit a great mistake: he would let slip the substance of authority to grasp the shadow. He would act more wisely in introducing lawyers into the government; and if he intrusted despotism to them under the form of violence, perhaps he would find it again in their hands under the external features of justice and law.

The government of democracy is favorable to the political power of lawyers; for when the wealthy, the noble, and the prince are excluded from the government, the lawyers take possession of it, in their own right, as it were, since they are the only men of information and sagacity, beyond the sphere of the people, who can be the object of the popular choice. If, then, they are led by their tastes towards the aristocracy and the prince, they are brought in contact with the people by their interests. They like the government of democracy, without participating in its propensities and without imitating its weaknesses; whence they derive a twofold authority from it and over it. The people in democratic states do not mistrust the members of the legal profession, because it is known that they are interested to serve the popular cause; and the people listen to them without irritation, because they do not attribute to them any sinister designs. The lawyers do not, indeed, wish to overthrow the institutions of democracy, but they constantly endeavor to turn it away from its real direction by means which are foreign to its nature. Lawyers belong to the people by birth and interest, and to the aristocracy by habit and taste; they may be looked upon as the connecting link of the two great classes of society.

The profession of the law is the only aristocratic element which can be amalgamated without violence with the natural elements of democracy, and be advantageously and permanently combined with them. I am not ignorant of the defects inherent in the character of this body of men; but without this admixture of lawyer-like sobriety with the democratic principle, I question whether democratic institutions could long be maintained; and I cannot believe that a republic could hope to exist at the present time, if the influence of lawyers in public business did not increase in proportion to the power of the people.

. This aristocratic character, which I hold to be common to the legal profession, is much more distinctly marked in the United States and in England than in any other country. This proceeds not only from the legal studies of the English and American lawyers, but from the nature of the law, and the position which these interpreters of it occupy, in the two countries. The English and the Americans have retained the law of precedents; that is to say, they continue to found their legal opinions and the decisions of their courts upon the opinions and decisions of their predecessors. In the mind of an English or American lawyer, a taste and a reverence for what is old is almost always united with a love of regular and lawful proceedings.

This predisposition has another effect upon the character of the legal profession and upon the general course of society. The English and American lawyers investigate what has been done; the French advocate inquires what should have been done: the former produce precedents; the latter, reasons. A French observer is surprised to hear how often an English or an American lawyer quotes the opinions of others, and how little he alludes to his own; whilst the reverse occurs in France. There the most trifling litigation is never conducted without the introduction of an entire system of ideas peculiar to the counsel employed; and the fundamental principles of law are discussed in order to obtain a perch of land by the decision of the court. This abnegation of his own opinion, and this implicit deference to the opinion of his forefathers, which are common to the English and American lawyer, this servitude of thought which he is obliged to profess, necessarily give him more timid habits and more conservative inclinations in England and America than in France.

The French codes are often difficult of comprehension,

but they can be read by every one; nothing, on the other hand, can be more obscure and strange to the uninitiated, than a legislation founded upon precedents. The absolute need of legal aid which is felt in England and the United States, and the high opinion which is entertained of the ability of the legal profession, tend to separate it more and more from the people, and to erect it into a distinct class. The French lawyer is simply a man extensively acquainted with the statutes of his country; but the English or American lawyer resembles the hierophants of Egypt, for, like them, he is the sole interpreter of an occult science.

The position which lawyers occupy in England and America exercises no less influence upon their habits and opinions. The English aristocracy, which has taken care to attract to its sphere whatever is at all analogous to itself, has conferred a high degree of importance and authority upon the members of the legal profession. In English society, lawyers do not occupy the first rank, but they are contented with the station assigned to them: they constitute, as it were, the younger branch of the English aristocracy; and they are attached to their elder brothers, although they do not enjoy all their privileges. The English lawyers consequently mingle the aristocratic tastes and ideas of the circles in which they move, with the aristocratic interests of their profession.

And, indeed, the lawyer-like character which I am endeavoring to depict is most distinctly to be met with in England: there, laws are esteemed not so much because they are good as because they are old; and if it be necessary to modify them in any respect, to adapt them to the changes which time operates in society, recourse is had to the most inconceivable subtilties in order to uphold the traditionary fabric, and to maintain that nothing has been done which does not square with the intentions, and complete the labors, of former generations. The very individuals who conduct these changes disclaim any desire of innovation, and had rather resort to absurd expedients than plead guilty to so great a crime. This spirit appertains more especially to the English lawyers ; they appear indifferent to the real meaning of what they treat, and they direct all their attention to the letter, — seeming inclined to abandon reason and humanity, rather than to swerve one tittle from the law. English legislation may be compared to the stock of an old tree, upon which lawyers have ingrafted the most dissimilar shoots, in the hope that, although their fruits may differ, their foliage at least will be confounded with the venerable trunk which supports them all.*

In America, there are no nobles or literary men, and the people are apt to mistrust the wealthy ; lawyers consequently form the highest political class, and the most cultivated portion of society. They have therefore nothing to gain by innovation, which adds a conservative interest to their natural taste for public order. If I were asked where I place the American aristocracy, I should reply, without hesitation, that it is not among the rich, who are united by no common tie, but that it occupies the judicial bench and the bar.

The more we reflect upon all that occurs in the United States, the more shall we be persuaded that the lawyers, as a body, form the most powerful, if not the only, counterpoise to the democratic element. In that country, we easily perceive how the legal profession is qualified by its attributes, and even by its faults, to neutralize the vices

* All this is the criticism of a lively and intelligent Frenchman, unfamiliar with the principles and modes of procedure peculiar to the English Common Law, and exaggerating these very peculiarities of it, because they are so unlike the legal maxims and methods in which he has himself been nurtured from childhood. — AM. ED.

inherent in popular government. When the American people are intoxicated by passion, or carried away by the impetuosity of their ideas, they are checked and stopped by the almost invisible influence of their legal counsellors. These secretly oppose their aristocratic propensities to the nation's democratic instincts, their superstitious attachment to what is old to its love of novelty, their narrow views to its immense designs, and their habitual procrastination to its ardent impatience.

The courts of justice are the visible organs by which the legal profession is enabled to control the democracy. The judge is a lawyer, who, independently of the taste for regularity and order which he has contracted in the study of law, derives an additional love of stability from the inalienability of his own functions. His legal attainments have already raised him to a distinguished rank amongst his fellows ; his political power completes the distinction of his station, and gives him the instincts of the privileged classes.

Armed with the power of declaring the laws to be unconstitutional,* the American magistrate perpetually interferes in political affairs. He cannot force the people to make laws, but at least he can oblige them not to disobey their own enactments, and not to be inconsistent with themselves. I am aware that a secret tendency to diminish the judicial power exists in the United States ; and by most of the Constitutions of the several States, the government can, upon the demand of the two houses of the legislature, remove the judges from their station. Some other State Constitutions make the members of the judiciary elective, and they are even subjected to frequent re-elections. I venture to predict that these innovations will sooner or later be attended with fatal consequences ; and that it will be found out at some future period, that, by thus lessening the independence of the judiciary, they have

---

* See Chapter VI. p. 125, on the Judicial Power in the United States.

attacked not only the judicial power, but the democratic republic itself.

It must not, moreover, be supposed that the legal spirit is confined, in the United States, to the courts of justice; it extends far beyond them. As the lawyers form the only enlightened class whom the people do not mistrust, they are naturally called upon to occupy most of the public stations. They fill the legislative assemblies, and are at the head of the administration; they consequently exercise a powerful influence upon the formation of the law, and upon its execution. The lawyers are, however, obliged to yield to the current of public opinion, which is too strong for them to resist; but it is easy to find indications of what they would do, if they were free to act. The Americans, who have made so many innovations in their political laws, have introduced very sparing alterations in their civil laws, and that with great difficulty, although many of these laws are repugnant to their social condition. The reason of this is, that, in matters of civil law, the majority are obliged to defer to the authority of the legal profession, and the American lawyers are disinclined to innovate when they are left to their own choice.

It is curious for a Frenchman to hear the complaints which are made in the United States, against the stationary spirit of legal men, and their prejudices in favor of existing institutions.

The influence of legal habits extends beyond the precise limits I have pointed out. Scarcely any political question arises in the United States which is not resolved, sooner or later, into a judicial question. Hence all parties are obliged to borrow, in their daily controversies, the ideas, and even the language, peculiar to judicial proceedings. As most public men are, or have been, legal practitioners, they introduce the customs and technicalities of their profession into the management of public affairs. The jury extends this habitude to all classes. The language of the law thus becomes, in some measure, a vulgar tongue ; the spirit of the law, which is produced in the schools and courts of justice, gradually penetrates beyond their walls into the bosom of society, where it descends to the lowest classes, so that at last the whole people contract the habits and the tastes of the judicial magistrate. The lawyers of the United States form a party which is but little feared and scarcely perceived, which has no badge peculiar to itself, which adapts itself with great flexibility to the exigencies of the time, and accommodates itself without resistance to all the movements of the social body. But this party extends over the whole community, and penetrates into all the classes which compose it ; it acts upon the country imperceptibly, but finally fashions it to suit its own purposes.

TRIAL BY JURY IN THE UNITED STATES CONSIDERED AS A POLITICAL INSTITUTION.

Trial by Jury, which is one of the Forms of the Sovereignty of the People, ought to be compared with the other Laws which establish that Sovereignty. — Composition of the Jury in the United States. — Effect of Trial by Jury upon the National Character. — It educates the People. — How it tends to establish the Influence of the Magistrates, and to extend the Legal Spirit among the People.

Since my subject has led me to speak of the administration of justice in the United States, I will not pass over it without adverting to the institution of the jury. Trial by jury may be considered in two separate points of view ; as a judicial, and as a political institution. If it was my purpose to inquire how far trial by jury, especially in civil cases, insures a good administration of justice, I admit that its utility might be contested. As the jury was first established when society was in its infancy, and when courts of justice merely decided simple questions of fact, it is not an easy task to adapt it to the wants of a highly civilized community, when the mutual relations of men are multiplied to a surprising extent, and have assumed an enlightened and intellectual character.*

My present purpose is to consider the jury as a political institution; any other course would divert me from my subject. Of trial by jury, considered as a judicial institution, I shall here say but little. When the English adopted trial by jury, they were a semi-barbarous people; they have since become one of the most enlightened nations of the earth; and their attachment to this institution seems to have increased with their increasing cultivation. They have emigrated and colonized every part of the habitable globe; some have formed colonies, others independent states; the mother country has maintained its monarchical constitution; many of its offspring have founded powerful republics; but everywhere they have boasted of the privilege of trial by jury.† They have established it, or hastened to re-establish it, in all their settlements. A judicial institution which thus obtains the

* The consideration of trial by jury as a judicial institution, and the appreciation of its effects in the United States, together with an inquiry into the manner in which the Americans have used it, would suffice to form a book, and a book upon a very useful and curious subject. The State of Louisiana would throw the most light upon the subject, as it has a mingled population of French and English. The two systems of law, as well as the two nations, are there found side by side, and are gradually combining with each other. The most useful books to consult would be the *Digeste des Lois de la Louisiane*; and the *Traité sur les Règles des Actions civiles*, printed in French and English at New Orleans, in 1830.

† All the English and American jurists are unanimous upon this head. Mr. Story, Judge of the Supreme Court of the United States, speaks, in his Commentaries on the Constitution, of the advantages of trial by jury in civil cases: "The inestimable privilege of a trial by jury in civil cases," says he, "a privilege scarcely inferior to that in criminal cases, which is counted by all persons to be essential to political and civil liberty."

suffrages of a great people for so long a series of ages, which is zealously reproduced at every stage of civilization, in all the climates of the earth, and under every form of human government, cannot be contrary to the spirit of justice.*

But to leave this part of the subject. It would be a very narrow view to look upon the jury as a mere judicial institution; for, however great its influence may be upon the decisions of the courts, it is still greater on the desti-

---

* If it were our province to point out the utility of the jury as a judicial institution, many arguments might be brought forward, and amongst others the following: —

In proportion as you introduce the jury into the business of the courts, you are enabled to diminish the number of judges; which is a great advantage. When judges are very numerous, death is perpetually thinning the ranks of the judicial functionaries, and leaving places vacant for new-comers. The ambition of the magistrates is therefore continually excited, and they are naturally made dependent upon the majority, or the person who fills up the vacant appointments: the officers of the courts then rise like the officers of an army. This state of things is entirely contrary to the sound administration of justice, and to the intentions of the legislator. The office of a judge is made inalienable in order that he may remain independent; but of what advantage is it that his independence should be protected, if he be tempted to sacrifice it of his own accord? When judges are very numerous, many of them must necessarily be incapable; for a great magistrate is a man of no common powers: I know not if a half-enlightened tribunal is not the worst of all combinations for attaining those objects which it is the purpose of courts of justice to accomplish. For my own part, I had rather submit the decision of a case to ignorant jurors directed by a skilful judge, than to judges a majority of whom are imperfectly acquainted with jurisprudence and with the laws.

[I venture to remind the reader, lest this note should appear somewhat redundant to an English eye, that the jury is an institution which has only been naturalized in France within the present century; that it is even now exclusively applied to those criminal causes which come before the Courts of Assize, or to the prosecutions of the public press; and that the judges and counsellors of the numerous local tribunals of France — forming a body of many thousand judicial functionaries — try all civil causes, appeals from criminal causes, and minor offences, without the jury. — *English Translator's Note.*]

nies of society at large. The jury is, above all, a political institution, and it must be regarded in this light in order to be duly appreciated.

By the jury, I mean a certain number of citizens chosen by lot, and invested with a temporary right of judging. Trial by jury, as applied to the repression of crime, appears to me an eminently republican element in the government, for the following reasons.

The institution of the jury may be aristocratic or democratic, according to the class from which the jurors are taken; but it always preserves its republican character, in that it places the real direction of society in the hands of the governed, or of a portion of the governed, and not in that of the government. Force is never more than a transient element of success, and after force, comes the notion of right. A government which should be able to reach its enemies only upon a field of battle would soon be destroyed. The true sanction of political laws is to be found in penal legislation; and if that sanction be wanting, the law will sooner or later lose its cogency. He who punishes the criminal is therefore the real master of society. Now, the institution of the jury raises the people itself, or at least a class of citizens, to the bench of judges. The institution of the jury consequently invests the people, or that class of citizens, with the direction of society.*

In England, the jury is returned from the aristocratic portion of the nation; † the aristocracy makes the laws,

---

* An important remark must, however, be made. Trial by jury does unquestionably invest the people with a general control over the actions of the citizens, but it does not furnish means of exercising this control in all cases, or with an absolute authority. When an absolute monarch has the right of trying offences by his representatives, the fate of the prisoner is, as it were, decided beforehand. But even if the people were predisposed to convict, the composition and the non-responsibility of the jury would still afford some chances favorable to the protection of innocence.

† In France, the qualification of the jurors is the same as the electoral

applies the laws, and punishes infractions of the laws everything is established upon a consistent footing, and England may with truth be said to constitute an aristocratic republic. In the United States, the same system is applied to the whole people. Every American citizen is qualified to be an elector, a juror, and is eligible to office.* The system of the jury, as it is understood in America, appears to me to be as direct and as extreme a consequence of the sovereignty of the people as universal suffrage. They are two instruments of equal power, which contribute to the supremacy of the majority. All the sovereigns who have chosen to govern by their own authority, and to direct society instead of obeying its directions, have destroyed or enfeebled the institution of the jury. The Tudor monarchs sent to prison jurors who refused to convict, and Napoleon caused them to be selected by his agents.

However clear most of these truths may seem to be, they do not command universal assent; and, in France at least, the trial by jury is still but imperfectly understood. If the question arises as to the proper qualification of jurors, it is confined to a discussion of the intelligence and knowledge of the citizens who may be returned, as if the jury was merely a judicial institution. This appears to me the

qualification, namely, the payment of 200 francs per annum in direct taxes: they are chosen by lot. In England, they are returned by the sheriff; the qualifications of jurors were raised to £10 per annum in England, and £6 in Wales, of freehold lands or copyhold, by the statute W. and M., c. 24; leaseholders for a time determinable upon life or lives, of the clear yearly value of £20 per annum over and above the rent reserved, are qualified to serve on juries; and jurors in the courts of Westminster and City of London must be householders, and possessed of real and personal estate of the value of £100. The qualifications, however, prescribed in different statutes vary according to the object for which the jury is impanelled. See Blackstone's Commentaries, Book III. c. 23. — *English Translator's Note.*

* See Appendix Q.

least important part of the subject. The jury is pre-eminently a political institution ; it should be regarded as one
form of the sovereignty of the people : when that sovereignty is repudiated, it must be rejected, or it must be
adapted to the laws by which that sovereignty is established. The jury is that portion of the nation to which
the execution of the laws is intrusted, as the legislature is
that part of the nation which makes the laws ; and in order that society may be governed in a fixed and uniform
manner, the list of citizens qualified to serve on juries must
increase and diminish with the list of electors. This I hold
to be the point of view most worthy of the attention of the
legislator ; all that remains is merely accessory.

I am so entirely convinced that the jury is pre-eminently
a political institution, that I still consider it in this light
when it is applied in civil causes. Laws are always unstable unless they are founded upon the manners of a nation :
manners are the only durable and resisting power in a people. When the jury is reserved for criminal offences, the
people only witness its occasional action in particular cases :
they become accustomed to do without it in the ordinary
course of life ; and it is considered as an instrument, but
not as the only instrument, of obtaining justice. This is
true *a fortiori*, when the jury is applied only to certain
criminal causes.

When, on the contrary, the jury acts also on civil causes,
its application is constantly visible ; it affects all the interests of the community ; every one co-operates in its work :
it thus penetrates into all the usages of life, it fashions the
human mind to its peculiar forms, and is gradually associated with the idea of justice itself.

The institution of the jury, if confined to criminal
causes, is always in danger ; but when once it is introduced into civil proceedings, it defies the aggressions of
time and man. If it had been as easy to remove the jury

from the manners as from the laws of England, it would have perished under the Tudors ; and the civil jury did in reality, at that period, save the liberties of England. In whatever manner the jury be applied, it cannot fail to exercise a powerful influence upon the national character ; but this influence is prodigiously increased when it is introduced into civil causes. The jury, and more especially the civil jury, serves to communicate the spirit of the judges to the minds of all the citizens ; and this spirit, with the habits which attend it, is the soundest preparation for free institutions. It imbues all classes with a respect for the thing judged, and with the notion of right. If these two elements be removed, the love of independence becomes a mere destructive passion. It teaches men to practise equity ; every man learns to judge his neighbor as he would himself be judged. And this is especially true of the jury in civil causes ; for, whilst the number of persons who have reason to apprehend a criminal prosecution is small, every one is liable to have a lawsuit. The jury teaches every man not to recoil before the responsibility of his own actions, and impresses him with that manly confidence without which no political virtue can exist. It invests each citizen with a kind of magistracy ; it makes them all feel the duties which they are bound to discharge towards society, and the part which they take in its government. By obliging men to turn their attention to other affairs than their own, it rubs off that private selfishness which is the rust of society.

The jury contributes powerfully to form the judgment and to increase the natural intelligence of a people ; and this, in my opinion, is its greatest advantage. It may be regarded as a gratuitous public school, ever open, in which every juror learns his rights, enters into daily communication with the most learned and enlightened members of the upper classes, and becomes practically acquainted with the laws, which are brought within the reach of his capacity by the efforts of the bar, the advice of the judge, and even by the passions of the parties. I think that the practical intelligence and political good sense of the Americans are mainly attributable to the long use which they have made of the jury in civil causes.

I do not know whether the jury is useful to those who have lawsuits; but I am certain it is highly beneficial to those who judge them; and I look upon it as one of the most efficacious means for the education of the people which society can employ.

What I have said applies to all nations; but the remark I am about to make is peculiar to the Americans and to democratic communities. I have already observed that, in democracies, the members of the legal profession, and the judicial magistrates, constitute the only aristocratic body which can moderate the movements of the people. This aristocracy is invested with no physical power; it exercises its conservative influence upon the minds of men: and the most abundant source of its authority is the institution of the civil jury. In criminal causes, when society is contending against a single man, the jury is apt to look upon the judge as the passive instrument of social power, and to mistrust his advice. Moreover, criminal causes turn entirely upon simple facts, which common sense can readily appreciate; upon this ground, the judge and the jury are equal. Such, however, is not the case in civil causes; then the judge appears as a disinterested arbiter between the conflicting passions of the parties. The jurors look up to him with confidence, and listen to him with respect, for in this instance, his intellect entirely governs theirs. It is the judge who sums up the various arguments which have wearied their memory, and who guides them through the devious course of the proceedings; he points their attention to the exact question of fact, which they are called upon to decide, and tells them how to answer the question of law. His influence over them is almost unlimited.

If I am called upon to explain why I am but little moved by the arguments derived from the ignorance of jurors in civil causes, I reply, that in these proceedings, whenever the question to be solved is not a mere question of fact, the jury has only the semblance of a judicial body. The jury only sanctions the decision of the judge ; they sanction this decision by the authority of society which they represent, and he, by that of reason and of law.*

In England and in America, the judges exercise an influence upon criminal trials which the French judges have never possessed. The reason of this difference may easily be discovered ; the English and American magistrates have established their authority in civil causes, and only transfer it afterwards to tribunals of another kind, where it was not first acquired. In some cases, and they are frequently the most important ones, the American judges have the right of deciding causes alone.† Upon these occasions, they are accidentally placed in the position which the French judges habitually occupy : but their moral power is much greater ; they are still surrounded by the recollection of the jury, and their judgment has almost as much authority as the voice of the community represented by that institution. Their influence extends far beyond the limits of the courts ; in the recreations of private life, as well as in the turmoil of public business, in public and in the legislative assemblies, the American judge is constantly surrounded by men who are accustomed to regard his intelligence as superior to their own ; and after having exercised his power in the decision of causes, he continues to influence

* See Appendix R.

† The Federal judges act alone upon almost all the questions most important to the government of the country.

the habits of thought, and even the characters, of those who acted with him in his official capacity.

The jury, then, which seems to restrict the rights of the judiciary, does in reality consolidate its power; and in no country are the judges so powerful as where the people share their privileges. It is especially by means of the jury in civil causes, that the American magistrates imbue even the lower classes of society with the spirit of their profession. Thus the jury, which is the most energetic means of making the people rule, is also the most efficacious means of teaching it how to rule well.

CHAPTER XVII.

PRINCIPAL CAUSES WHICH TEND TO MAINTAIN THE DEMO-CRATIC REPUBLIC IN THE UNITED STATES.

A DEMOCRATIC republic exists in the United States; and the principal object of this book has been to explain the causes of its existence. Several of these causes have been involuntarily passed by, or only hinted at, as I was borne along by my subject. Others I have been unable to discuss at all; and those on which I have dwelt most are, as it were, buried in the details of this work.

I think, therefore, that, before I proceed to speak of the future, I ought to collect within a small compass the reasons which explain the present. In this retrospective chapter I shall be brief; for I shall take care to remind the reader only very summarily of what he already knows, and shall select only the most prominent of those facts which I have not yet pointed out.

All the causes which contribute to the maintenance of the democratic republic in the United States are reducible to three heads: —

I. The peculiar and accidental situation in which Providence has placed the Americans.

II. The laws.

III. The manners and customs of the people.

ACCIDENTAL OR PROVIDENTIAL CAUSES WHICH CONTRIBUTE TO MAINTAIN THE DEMOCRATIC REPUBLIC IN THE UNITED STATES.

The Union has no Neighbors. — No Metropolis. — The Americans have had the Chance of Birth in their Favor. — America an empty Country. — How this Circumstance contributes powerfully to maintain the Democratic Republic in America. — How the American Wilds are peopled. — Avidity of the Anglo-Americans in taking Possession of the Solitudes of the New World. — Influence of Physical Prosperity upon the Political Opinions of the Americans.

A THOUSAND circumstances, independent of the will of man, facilitate the maintenance of a democratic republic in the United States. Some of these are known, the others may easily be pointed out; but I shall confine myself to the principal ones.

The Americans have no neighbors, and consequently they have no great wars, or financial crises, or inroads, or conquest, to dread; they require neither great taxes, nor large armies, nor great generals; and they have nothing to fear from a scourge which is more formidable to republics than all these evils combined, namely, military glory. It is impossible to deny the inconceivable influence which military glory exercises upon the spirit of a nation. General Jackson, whom the Americans have twice elected to be the head of their government, is a man of violent temper and very moderate talents; nothing in his whole career ever proved him qualified to govern a free people; and indeed, the majority of the enlightened classes of the Union has always opposed him. But he was raised to the Presidency, and has been maintained there, solely by the recollection of a victory which he gained, twenty years ago, under the walls of New Orleans; a victory which was, however, a very ordinary achievement, and which could only be remembered in a country where battles are rare.

Now the people who are thus carried away by the illusions of glory are unquestionably the most cold and calculating, the most unmilitary, if I may so speak, and the most prosaic, of all the nations of the earth.

America has no great capital* city, whose direct or indirect influence is felt over the whole extent of the country; this I hold to be one of the first causes of the main tenance of republican institutions in the United States. In cities, men cannot be prevented from concerting together, and awakening a mutual excitement which prompts sudden and passionate resolutions. Cities may be looked upon as large assemblies, of which all the inhabitants are members; their populace exercise a prodigious influence upon the magistrates, and frequently execute their own wishes without the intervention of public officers.

* The United States have no metropolis; but they already contain several very large cities. Philadelphia reckoned 161,000 inhabitants, and New York 202,000, in the year 1830. The lower orders which inhabit these cities constitute a rabble even more formidable than the populace of European towns. They consist of freed blacks, in the first place, who are condemned by the laws and by public opinion to an hereditary state of misery and degradation. They also contain a multitude of Europeans, who have been driven to the shores of the New World by their misfortunes or their misconduct; and these men inoculate the United States with all our vices, without bringing with them any of those interests which counteract their baneful influence. As inhabitants of a country where they have no civil rights, they are ready to turn all the passions which agitate the community to their own advantage; thus, within the last few months, serious riots have broken out in Philadelphia and in New York. Disturbances of this kind are unknown in the rest of the country, which is nowise alarmed by them, because the population of the cities has hitherto exercised neither power nor influence over the rural districts.

Nevertheless, I look upon the size of certain American cities, and especially on the nature of their population, as a real danger which threatens the future security of the democratic republics of the New World; and I venture to predict that they will perish from this circumstance, unless the government succeeds in creating an armed force, which, while it remains under the control of the majority of the nation, will be independent of the town-population, and able to repress its excesses.

To subject the provinces to the metropolis is, therefore, to place the destiny of the empire in the hands, not only of a portion of the community, which is unjust, but in the hands of a populace carrying out its own impulses, which is very dangerous. The preponderance of capital cities is therefore a serious injury to the representative system; and it exposes modern republics to the same defect as the republics of antiquity, whch all perished from not having known this system.

It would be easy for me to enumerate many secondary causes which have contributed to establish, and now concur to maintain, the democratic republic of the United States. But among these favorable circumstances I discern two principal ones, which I hasten to point out. I have already observed that the origin of the Americans, or what I have called their point of departure, may be looked upon as the first and most efficacious cause to which the present prosperity of the United States may be attributed. The Americans had the chances of birth in their favor; and their forefathers imported that equality of condition and of intellect into the country whence the democratic republic has very naturally taken its rise. Nor was this all; for besides this republican condition of society, the early settlers bequeathed to their descendants the customs, manners, and opinions which contribute most to the success of a republic. When I reflect upon the consequences of this primary fact, methinks I see the destiny of America embodied in the first Puritan who landed on those shores, just as the whole human race was represented by the first man.

The chief circumstance which has favored the establishment and the maintenance of a democratic republic in the United States, is the nature of the territory which the Americans inhabit. Their ancestors gave them the love of equality and of freedom; but God himself gave them the means of remaining equal and free, by placing them upon a boundless continent. General prosperity is favorable to the stability of all governments, but more particularly of a democratic one, which depends upon the will of the majority, and especially upon the will of that portion of the community which is most exposed to want. When the people rule, they must be rendered happy, or they will overturn the state : and misery stimulates them to those excesses to which ambition rouses kings. The physical causes, independent of the laws, which promote general prosperity, are more numerous in America than they ever have been in any other country in the world, at any other period of history. In the United States, not only is legislation democratic, but Nature herself favors the cause of the people.

In what part of human history can be found anything similar to what is passing before our eyes in North America ? The celebrated communities of antiquity were all founded in the midst of hostile nations, which they were obliged to subjugate, before they could flourish in their place. Even the moderns have found, in some parts of South America, vast regions inhabited by a people of inferior civilization, but who had already occupied and cultivated the soil. To found their new states, it was necessary to extirpate or subdue a numerous population, and they made civilization blush for its own success. But North America was inhabited only by wandering tribes, who had no thought of profiting by the natural riches of the soil ; that vast country was still, properly speaking, an empty continent, a desert land awaiting its inhabitants.

Everything is extraordinary in America, the social condition of the inhabitants, as well as the laws ; but the soil upon which these institutions are founded is more extraordinary than all the rest. When the earth was given to men by the Creator, the earth was inexhaustible ; but men were weak and ignorant; and when they had learned to take advantage of the treasures which it contained, they already covered its surface, and were soon obliged to earn by the sword an asylum for repose and freedom. Just then North America was discovered, as if it had been kept in reserve by the Deity, and had just risen from beneath the waters of the deluge.

That continent still presents, as it did in the primeval time, rivers which rise from never-failing sources, green and moist solitudes, and limitless fields which the plough-share of the husbandman has never turned. In this state, it is offered to man, not barbarous, ignorant, and isolated, as he was in the early ages, but already in possession of the most important secrets of nature, united to his fellow-men, and instructed by the experience of fifty centuries. At this very time, thirteen [twenty-five] millions of civil-ized Europeans are peaceably spreading over those fertile plains, with whose resources and extent they are not yet themselves accurately acquainted. Three or four thousand soldiers drive before them the wandering races of the abo-rigines; these are followed by the pioneers, who pierce the woods, scare off the beasts of prey, explore the courses of the inland streams, and make ready the triumphal march of civilization across the desert.

Often, in the course of this work, I have alluded to the favorable influence of the material prosperity of America upon the institutions of that country. This reason had already been given by many others before me, and is the only one which, being palpable to the senses, as it were, is familiar to Europeans. I shall not, then, enlarge upon a subject so often handled and so well understood, beyond the addition of a few facts. An erroneous notion is gen-erally entertained, that the deserts of America are peopled by European emigrants, who annually disembark upon the coasts of the New World, whilst the American population increase and multiply upon the soil which their forefathers tilled. The European settler usually arrives in the United States without friends, and often without resources; in order to subsist, he is obliged to work for hire, and he rarely proceeds beyond that belt of industrious population which adjoins the ocean. The desert cannot be explored without capital or credit; and the body must be accustomed to the rigors of a new climate, before it can be exposed in the midst of the forest. It is the Americans themselves who daily quit the spots which gave them birth, to acquire extensive domains in a remote region. Thus the European leaves his cottage for the Transatlantic shores, and the American, who is born on that very coast, plunges in his turn into the wilds of central America. This double emigration is incessant; it begins in the middle of Europe, it crosses the Atlantic Ocean, and it advances over the solitudes of the New World. Millions of men are marching at once towards the same horizon: their language, their religion, their manners differ; their object is the same. Fortune has been promised to them somewhere in the West, and to the West they go to find it.

No event can be compared with this continuous removal of the human race, except perhaps those irruptions which caused the fall of the Roman Empire. Then, as well as now, crowds of men were impelled in the same direction, to meet and struggle on the same spot; but the designs of Providence were not the same. Then, every new-comer brought with him destruction and death; now, each one brings the elements of prosperity and life. The future still conceals from us the remote consequences of this migration of the Americans towards the West; but we can readily apprehend its immediate results. As a portion of the inhabitants annually leave the States in which they were born, the population of these States increases very slowly, although they have long been established. Thus, in Connecticut, which yet contains only fifty-nine inhabitants to the square mile, the population has not been increased by more than one quarter in forty years, whilst that of England has been augmented by one third in the same period. The European emigrant always lands, therefore, in a country which is but half full, and where hands are in request: he becomes a workman in easy circumstances; his son goes to seek his fortune in unpeopled regions, and becomes a rich land-owner. The former amasses the capital which the latter invests; and the stranger as well as the native is unacquainted with want.

The laws of the United States are extremely favorable to the division of property; but a cause more powerful than the laws prevents property from being divided to excess.* This is very perceptible in the States which are at last beginning to be thickly peopled; Massachusetts is the most populous part of the Union; but it contains only eighty inhabitants to the square mile, which is much less than in France, where one hundred and sixty-two are reckoned to the same extent of country. But in Massachusetts, estates are very rarely divided; the eldest son generally takes the land, and the others go to seek their fortune in their desert. The law has abolished the right of primogeniture, but circumstances have concurred to reestablish it under a form of which none can complain, and by which no just rights are impaired.

A single fact will suffice to show the prodigious number of individuals who thus leave New England to settle in the wilds. We were assured in 1830, that thirty-six of the members of Congress were born in the little State of Connecticut. The population of Connecticut, which constitutes only one forty-third part of that of the United States, thus furnished one eighth of the whole body of representa-

* In New England, estates are very small, but they are rarely subjected to further division.

tives. The State of Connecticut of itself, however, sends only five delegates to Congress; and the thirty-one others sit for the new Western States. If these thirty-one individuals had remained in Connecticut, it is probable that, instead of becoming rich land-owners, they would have remained humble laborers, that they would have lived in obscurity without being able to rise into public life, and that, far from becoming useful legislators, they might have been unruly citizens.

These reflections do not escape the observation of the Americans any more than of ourselves. "It cannot be doubted," says Chancellor Kent, in his Treatise on American Law, "that the division of landed estates must produce great evils, when it is carried to such excess as that each parcel of land is insufficient to support a family; but these disadvantages have never been felt in the United States, and many generations must elapse before they can be felt. The extent of our inhabited territory, the abundance of adjacent land, and the continual stream of emigration flowing from the shores of the Atlantic towards the interior of the country, suffice as yet, and will long suffice, to prevent the parcelling out of estates."

It would be difficult to describe the avidity with which the American rushes forward to secure this immense booty which fortune offers. In the pursuit, he fearlessly braves the arrow of the Indian and the diseases of the forest; he is unimpressed by the silence of the woods; the approach of beasts of prey does not disturb him; for he is goaded onwards by a passion stronger than the love of life. Before him lies a boundless continent, and he urges onward as if time pressed, and he was afraid of finding no room for his exertions. I have spoken of the emigration from the older States; but how shall I describe that which takes place from the more recent ones? Fifty years have scarcely elapsed since that of Ohio was founded; the greater part of its inhabitants were not born within its confines; its capital has been built only thirty years, and its territory is still covered by an immense extent of uncultivated fields; yet already the population of Ohio is proceeding westward, and most of the settlers who descend to the fertile prairies of Illinois are citizens of Ohio. These men left their first country to improve their condition; they quit their second, to ameliorate it still more; fortune awaits them everywhere, but not happiness. The desire of prosperity is become an ardent and restless passion in their minds, which grows by what it feeds on. They early broke the ties which bound them to their natal earth, and they have contracted no fresh ones on their way. Emigration was at first necessary to them; and it soon becomes a sort of game of chance, which they pursue for the emotions it excites, as much as for the gain it procures.

Sometimes the progress of man is so rapid that the desert reappears behind him. The woods stoop to give him a passage, and spring up again when he is past. It is not uncommon, in crossing the new States of the West, to meet with deserted dwellings in the midst of the wilds; the traveller frequently discovers the vestiges of a log-house in the most solitary retreat, which bear witness to the power, and no less to the inconstancy, of man. In these abandoned fields, and over these ruins of a day, the primeval forest soon scatters a fresh vegetation; the beasts resume the haunts which were once their own; and Nature comes smiling to cover the traces of man with green branches and flowers, which obliterate his ephemeral track.

I remember, that, in crossing one of the woodland districts which still cover the State of New York, I reached the shores of a lake which was embosomed in forests coeval with the world. A small island, covered with woods whose thick foliage concealed its banks, rose from the centre of the waters. Upon the shores of the lake, no object attested the presence of man, except a column of smoke, which might be seen on the horizon rising from the tops of the trees to the clouds, and seeming to hang from heaven rather than to be mounting to it. An Indian canoe was hauled up on the sand, which tempted me to visit the islet that had first attracted my attention, and in a few minutes I set foot upon its banks. The whole island formed one of those delicious solitudes of the New World, which almost lead civilized man to regret the haunts of the savage. A luxuriant vegetation bore witness to the incomparable fruitfulness of the soil. The deep silence, which is common to the wilds of North America, was only broken by the monotonous cooing of the wood-pigeons, and the tapping of the woodpecker upon the bark of trees. I was far from supposing that this spot had ever been inhabited, so completely did Nature seem to be left to herself; but when I reached the centre of the isle, I thought that I discovered some traces of man. I then proceeded to examine the surrounding objects with care, and I soon perceived that a European had undoubtedly been led to seek a refuge in this place. Yet what changes had taken place in the scene of his labors! The logs which he had hastily hewn to build himself a shed had sprouted afresh; the very props were intertwined with living verdure, and his cabin was transformed into a bower. In the midst of these shrubs, a few stones were to be seen, blackened with fire and sprinkled with thin ashes; here the hearth had no doubt been, and the chimney in falling had covered it with rubbish. I stood for some time in silent admiration of the resources of Nature and the littleness of man; and when I was obliged to leave that enchanting solitude, I exclaimed with sadness, " Are ruins, then, already here?"

In Europe, we are wont to look upon a restless disposition, an unbounded desire of riches, and an excessive love of independence, as propensities very dangerous to society.

Yet these are the very elements which insure a long and peaceful future to the republics of America. Without these unquiet passions, the population would collect in certain spots, and would soon experience wants like those of the Old World, which it is difficult to satisfy; for such is the present good fortune of the New World, that the vices of its inhabitants are scarcely less favorable to society than their virtues. These circumstances exercise a great influence on the estimation in which human actions are held in the two hemispheres. What we should call cupidity, the Americans frequently term a laudable industry; and they blame as faint-heartedness what we consider to be the virtue of moderate desires.

In France, simple tastes, orderly manners, domestic affections, and the attachment which men feel to the place of their birth, are looked upon as great guaranties of the tranquillity and happiness of the state. But in America, nothing seems to be more prejudicial to society than such virtues. The French Canadians, who have faithfully preserved the traditions of their ancient manners, are already embarrassed for room upon their small territory; and this little community, which has so recently begun to exist, will shortly be a prey to the calamities incident to old nations. In Canada, the most enlightened, patriotic, and humane inhabitants make extraordinary efforts to render the people dissatisfied with those simple enjoyments which still content them. There the seductions of wealth are vaunted with as much zeal as the charms of a moderate competency in the Old World; and more exertions are made to excite the passions of the citizens there, than to calm them elsewhere. If we listen to their accounts, we shall hear that nothing is more praiseworthy than to exchange the pure and tranquil pleasures which even the poor man tastes in his own country, for the sterile delights of prosperity under a foreign sky; to leave the patrimonial hearth, and the turf beneath which one's forefathers sleep, — in short, to abandon the living and the dead, in quest of fortune.

At the present time, America presents a field for human effort far more extensive than any sum of labor which can be applied to work it. In America, too much knowledge cannot be diffused ; for all knowledge, whilst it may serve him who possesses it, turns also to the advantage of those who are without it. New wants are not to be feared there, since they can be satisfied without difficulty ; the growth of human passions need not be dreaded, since all passions may find an easy and a legitimate object ; nor can men there be made too free, since they are scarcely ever tempted to misuse their liberties.

The American republics of the present day are like companies of adventurers, formed to explore in common the waste lands of the New World, and busied in a flourishing trade. The passions which agitate the Americans most deeply are not their political, but their commercial, passions ; or, rather, they introduce the habits of business into their political life. They love order, without which affairs do not prosper ; and they set an especial value upon regular conduct, which is the foundation of a solid business. They prefer the good sense which amasses large fortunes to that enterprising genius which frequently dissipates them ; general ideas alarm their minds, which are accustomed to positive calculations ; and they hold practice in more honor than theory.

It is in America that one learns to understand the influence which physical prosperity exercises over political actions, and even over opinions which ought to acknowledge no sway but that of reason ; and it is more especially among strangers that this truth is perceptible. Most of the European emigrants to the New World carry with them that wild love of independence and change which our calamities are so apt to produce. I sometimes met with Europeans in the United States, who had been obliged to leave their country on account of their political opinions. They all astonished me by the language they held, but one of them surprised me more than all the rest. As I was crossing one of the most remote districts of Pennsylvania, I was benighted, and obliged to beg for hospitality at the gate of a wealthy planter, who was a Frenchman by birth. He bade me sit down beside his fire, and we began to talk with that freedom which befits persons who meet in the backwoods, two thousand leagues from their native country. I was aware that my host had been a great leveller and an ardent demagogue forty years ago, and that his name was in history. I was therefore not a little surprised to hear him discuss the rights of property as an economist or a land-owner might have done : he spoke of the necessary gradations which fortune establishes among men, of obedience to established laws, of the influence of good morals in commonwealths, and of the support which religious opinions give to order and to freedom; he even went so far as to quote the authority of our Saviour in support of one of his political opinions.

I listened, and marvelled at the feebleness of human reason. How can we discover whether a proposition is true or false, in the midst of the uncertainties of science and the conflicting lessons of experience? A new fact disperses all my doubts. I was poor, I have become rich ; and I am not to expect that prosperity will act upon my conduct, and leave my judgment free. In truth, my opinions change with my fortune ; and the happy circumstances which I turn to my advantage furnish me with that decisive argument which was before wanting.

The influence of prosperity acts still more freely upon Americans than upon strangers. The American has always seen public order and public prosperity intimately united, and proceeding side by side before his eyes; he cannot even imagine that one can subsist without the other: he has therefore nothing to forget; nor has he, like so many Europeans, to unlearn the lessons of his early education.

INFLUENCE OF THE LAWS UPON THE MAINTENANCE OF THE DEMOCRATIC REPUBLIC IN THE UNITED STATES.

Three principal Causes of the Maintenance of the Democratic Republic. — Federal Union. — Township Institutions. — Judicial Power.

THE principal aim of this book has been to make known the laws of the United States; if this purpose has been accomplished, the reader is already enabled to judge for himself which are the laws that really tend to maintain the democratic republic, and which endanger its existence. If I have not succeeded in explaining this in the whole course of my work, I cannot hope to do so in a single chapter. It is not my intention to retrace the path I have already pursued; and a few lines will suffice to recapitulate what I have said.

Three circumstances seem to me to contribute more than all others to the maintenance of the democratic republic in the United States.

The first is that federal form of government which the Americans have adopted, and which enables the Union to combine the power of a great republic with the security of a small one;

The second consists in those township institutions which limit the despotism of the majority, and at the same time impart to the people a taste for freedom, and the art of being free;

The third is to be found in the constitution of the judicial power. I have shown how the courts of justice serve to repress the excesses of democracy, and how they check and direct the impulses of the majority without stopping its activity.

INFLUENCE OF MANNERS UPON THE MAINTENANCE OF THE DEMOCRATIC REPUBLIC IN THE UNITED STATES.

I HAVE previously remarked that the manners of the people may be considered as one of the great general causes to which the maintenance of a democratic republic in the United States is attributable. I here use the word *manners* with the meaning which the ancients attached to the word *mores;* for I apply it not only to manners properly so called, — that is, to what might be termed *the habits of the heart*, — but to the various notions and opinions current among men, and to the mass of those ideas which constitute their character of mind. I comprise under this term, therefore, the whole moral and intellectual condition of a people. My intention is not to draw a picture of American manners, but simply to point out such features of them as are favorable to the maintenance of their political institutions.

RELIGION CONSIDERED AS A POLITICAL INSTITUTION, WHICH POWERFULLY CONTRIBUTES TO THE MAINTENANCE OF THE DEMOCRATIC REPUBLIC AMONGST THE AMERICANS.

North America peopled by Men who professed a Democratic and Republican Christianity. — Arrival of the Catholics. — Why the Catholics now form the most Democratic and most Republican Class.

BY the side of every religion is to be found a political opinion, which is connected with it by affinity. If the human mind be left to follow its own bent, it will regulate the temporal and spiritual institutions of society in a uniform manner; and man will endeavor, if I may so speak, to *harmonize* earth with heaven.

The greatest part of British America was peopled by men who, after having shaken off the authority of the

Pope, acknowledged no other religious supremacy: they brought with them into the New World a form of Christianity, which I cannot better describe than by styling it a democratic and republican religion. This contributed powerfully to the establishment of a republic and a democracy in public affairs; and from the beginning, politics and religion contracted an alliance which has never been dissolved.

About fifty years ago, Ireland began to pour a Catholic population into the United States; and on their part, the Catholics of America made proselytes, so that, at the present moment, more than a million of Christians, professing the truths of the Church of Rome, are to be found in the Union. These Catholics are faithful to the observances of their religion; they are fervent and zealous in the belief of their doctrines. Yet they constitute the most republican and the most democratic class in the United States. This fact may surprise the observer at first, but the causes of it may easily be discovered upon reflection.

I think that the Catholic religion has erroneously been regarded as the natural enemy of democracy. Amongst the various sects of Christians, Catholicism seems to me, on the contrary, to be one of the most favorable to equality of condition among men. In the Catholic Church, the religious community is composed of only two elements; the priest and the people. The priest alone rises above the rank of his flock, and all below him are equal.

On doctrinal points, the Catholic faith places all human capacities upon the same level; it subjects the wise and ignorant, the man of genius and the vulgar crowd, to the details of the same creed; it imposes the same observances upon the rich and needy, it inflicts the same austerities upon the strong and the weak; it listens to no compromise with mortal man, but, reducing all the human race to the same standard, it confounds all the distinctions of society at the foot of the same altar, even as they are confounded in the sight of God. If Catholicism predisposes the faithful to obedience, it certainly does not prepare them for inequality : but the contrary may be said of Protestantism, which generally tends to make men independent, more than to render them equal. Catholicism is like an absolute monarchy ; if the sovereign be removed, all the other classes of society are more equal than in republics.

It has not unfrequently occurred that the Catholic priest has left the service of the altar to mix with the governing powers of society, and to take his place amongst the civil ranks of men. This religious influence has sometimes been used to secure the duration of that political state of things to which he belonged. Thus we have seen Catholics taking the side of aristocracy from a religious motive. But no sooner is the priesthood entirely separated from the government, as is the case in the United States, than it is found that no class of men are more naturally disposed than the Catholics to transfer the doctrine of the equality of condition into the political world.

If, then, the Catholic citizens of the United States are not forcibly led by the nature of their tenets to adopt democratic and republican principles, at least they are not necessarily opposed to them ; and their social position, as well as their limited number, obliges them to adopt these opinions. Most of the Catholics are poor, and they have no chance of taking a part in the government unless it be open to all the citizens. They constitute a minority, and all rights must be respected in order to insure to them the free exercise of their own privileges. These two causes induce them, even unconsciously, to adopt political doctrines which they would perhaps support with less zeal if they were rich and preponderant.

The Catholic clergy of the United States have never attempted to oppose this political tendency ; but they seek rather to justify it. The Catholic priests in America have divided the intellectual world into two parts: in the one, they place the doctrines of revealed religion, which they assent to without discussion; in the other, they leave those political truths, which they believe the Deity has left open to free inquiry. Thus the Catholics of the United States are at the same time the most submissive believers and the most independent citizens.

It may be asserted, then, that in the United States no religious doctrine displays the slightest hostility to democratic and republican institutions. The clergy of all the different sects there hold the same language; their opinions are in agreement with the laws, and the human mind flows onwards, so to speak, in one undivided current.

I happened to be staying in one of the largest cities in the Union, when I was invited to attend a public meeting in favor of the Poles, and of sending them supplies of arms and money. I found two or three thousand persons collected in a vast hall, which had been prepared to receive them. In a short time, a priest, in his ecclesiastical robes, advanced to the front of the platform: the spectators rose, and stood uncovered in silence, whilst he spoke in the following terms:—

"Almighty God! the God of armies! Thou who didst strengthen the hearts and guide the arms of our fathers when they were fighting for the sacred rights of their national independence! Thou who didst make them triumph over a hateful oppression, and hast granted to our people the benefits of liberty and peace! turn, O Lord, a favorable eye upon the other hemisphere; pitifully look down upon an heroic nation which is even now struggling as we did in the former time, and for the same rights. Thou, who didst create man in the same image, let not tyranny mar thy work, and establish inequality upon the earth. Almighty God! do thou watch over the destiny

of the Poles, and make them worthy to be free.   May thy
wisdom direct their councils, may thy strength sustain
their arms!   Shed forth thy terror over their enemies;
scatter the powers which take counsel against them; and
permit not the injustice which the world has witnessed for
fifty years to be consummated in our time.   O Lord, who
holdest alike the hearts of nations and of men in thy powerful hand, raise up allies to the sacred cause of right;
arouse the French nation from the apathy in which its
rulers retain it, that it may go forth again to fight for the
liberties of the world.

"Lord, turn not thou thy face from us, and grant that
we may always be the most religious, as well as the freest,
people of the earth.   Almighty God, hear our supplica-
tions this day.   Save the Poles, we beseech thee, in the
name of thy well-beloved Son, our Lord Jesus Christ, who
died upon the cross for the salvation of all men.   Amen."

The whole meeting responded, "Amen!" with devotion.

INDIRECT INFLUENCE OF RELIGIOUS OPINIONS UPON POLIT-
ICAL SOCIETY IN THE UNITED STATES.

Christian Morality common to all Sects. — Influence of Religion upon the
    Manners of the Americans. — Respect for the Marriage Tie. — How
    Religion confines the Imagination of the Americans within certain Lim-
    its, and checks the Passion for Innovation. — Opinion of the Americans
    on the political Utility of Religion. — Their Exertions to extend and
    secure its Authority.

I HAVE just shown what the direct influence of religion
upon politics is in the United States; but its indirect influence appears to me to be still more considerable, and it
never instructs the Americans more fully in the art of
being free than when it says nothing of freedom.

The sects which exist in the United States are innu-

merable.   They all differ in respect to the worship which
is due to the Creator; but they all agree in respect to the
duties which are due from man to man.   Each sect adores
the Deity in its own peculiar manner; but all sects preach
the same moral law in the name of God.   If it be of the
highest importance to man, as an individual, that his religion should be true, it is not so to society.   Society has no
future life to hope for or to fear; and provided the citizens
profess a religion, the peculiar tenets of that religion are
of little importance to its interests.   Moreover, all the
sects of the United States are comprised within the great
unity of Christianity, and Christian morality is everywhere
the same.

It may fairly be believed, that a certain number of
Americans pursue a peculiar form of worship from habit
more than from conviction.   In the United States, the
sovereign authority is religious, and consequently hypocrisy
must be common; but there is no country in the world
where the Christian religion retains a greater influence
over the souls of men than in America; and there can be
no greater proof of its utility, and of its conformity to
human nature, than that its influence is powerfully felt
over the most enlightened and free nation of the earth.

I have remarked that the American clergy in general,
without even excepting those who do not admit religious
liberty, are all in favor of civil freedom; but they do not
support any particular political system.   They keep aloof
from parties, and from public affairs.   In the United
States, religion exercises but little influence upon the laws,
and upon the details of public opinion; but it directs the
manners of the community, and, by regulating domestic
life, it regulates the state.

I do not question that the great austerity of manners
which is observable in the United States arises, in the first
instance, from religious faith.   Religion is often unable to

restrain man from the numberless temptations which chance offers ; nor can it check that passion for gain which everything contributes to arouse : but its influence over the mind of woman is supreme, and women are the protectors of morals. There is certainly no country in the world where the tie of marriage is more respected than in America, or where conjugal happiness is more highly or worthily appreciated. In Europe, almost all the disturbances of society arise from the irregularities of domestic life. To despise the natural bonds and legitimate pleasures of home, is to contract a taste for excesses, a restlessness of heart, and fluctuating desires. Agitated by the tumultuous passions which frequently disturb his dwelling, the European is galled by the obedience which the legislative powers of the state exact. But when the American retires from the turmoil of public life to the bosom of his family, he finds in it the image of order and of peace. There his pleasures are simple and natural, his joys are innocent and calm ; and as he finds that an orderly life is the surest path to happiness, he accustoms himself easily to moderate his opinions as well as his tastes. Whilst the European endeavors to forget his domestic troubles by agitating society, the American derives from his own home that love of order which he afterwards carries with him into public affairs.

In the United States, the influence of religion is not confined to the manners, but it extends to the intelligence, of the people. Amongst the Anglo-Americans, some profess the doctrines of Christianity from a sincere belief in them, and others do the same because they fear to be suspected of unbelief. Christianity, therefore, reigns without obstacle, by universal consent ; the consequence is, as I have before observed, that every principle of the moral world is fixed and determinate, although the political world is abandoned to the debates and the experiments of men.

Thus the human mind is never left to wander over a boundless field; and, whatever may be its pretensions, it is checked from time to time by barriers which it cannot surmount. Before it can innovate, certain primary principles are laid down, and the boldest conceptions are subjected to certain forms which retard and stop their completion.

The imagination of the Americans, even in its greatest flights, is circumspect and undecided; its impulses are checked, and its works unfinished. These habits of restraint recur in political society, and are singularly favorable both to the tranquillity of the people and the durability of the institutions they have established. Nature and circumstances have made the inhabitants of the United States bold, as is sufficiently attested by the enterprising spirit with which they seek for fortune. If the mind of the Americans were free from all trammels, they would shortly become the most daring innovators and the most persistent disputants in the world. But the revolutionists of America are obliged to profess an ostensible respect for Christian morality and equity, which does not permit them to violate wantonly the laws that oppose their designs; nor would they find it easy to surmount the scruples of their partisans, even if they were able to get over their own. Hitherto, no one in the United States has dared to advance the maxim that everything is permissible for the interests of society, — an impious adage, which seems to have been invented in an age of freedom to shelter all future tyrants. Thus, whilst the law permits the Americans to do what they please, religion prevents them from conceiving, and forbids them to commit, what is rash or unjust.

Religion in America takes no direct part in the government of society, but it must be regarded as the first of their political institutions; for if it does not impart a taste for freedom, it facilitates the use of it. Indeed, it is in this same point of view that the inhabitants of the United States themselves look upon religious belief. I do not know whether all the Americans have a sincere faith in their religion, — for who can search the human heart? — but I am certain that they hold it to be indispensable to the maintenance of republican institutions. This opinion is not peculiar to a class of citizens, or to a party, but it belongs to the whole nation, and to every rank of society.

In the United States, if a politician attacks a sect, this may not prevent the partisans of that very sect from supporting him; but if he attacks all the sects together, every one abandons him, and he remains alone.

Whilst I was in America, a witness, who happened to be called at the Sessions of the county of Chester (State of New York), declared that he did not believe in the existence of God, or in the immortality of the soul. The judge refused to admit his evidence, on the ground that the witness had destroyed beforehand all the confidence of the court in what he was about to say.* The newspapers related the fact without any further comment.

---

* The New York Spectator of August 23, 1831, relates the fact in the following terms: " The Court of Common Pleas of Chester County (New York) a few days since rejected a witness who declared his disbelief in the existence of God. The presiding judge remarked, that he had not before been aware that there was a man living who did not believe in the existence of God ; that this belief constituted the sanction of all testimony in a court of justice ; and that he knew of no cause in a Christian country where a witness had been permitted to testify without such belief."

[The exclusion of the testimony of atheists is not a peculiarity of American jurisprudence, but is a principle of the English Common Law, which is still enforced in England as well as in this country. It is not upheld as a mark of respect for the Christian religion, or because an atheist is unworthy of belief, but because no man is allowed to testify in a court of justice except he is under oath, and an oath has no meaning, because it has no sanction, in the mouth of one who does not believe in a just God and a future retribution. The atheist is excluded, therefore, not because he does not believe what others believe, but because he cannot be sworn.—Am. Ed.]

The Americans combine the notions of Christianity and of liberty so intimately in their minds, that it is impossible to make them conceive the one without the other; and with them, this conviction does not spring from that barren, traditionary faith which seems to vegetate rather than to live in the soul.

I have known of societies formed by the Americans to send out ministers of the Gospel into the new Western States, to found schools and churches there, lest religion should be suffered to die away in those remote settlements, and the rising States be less fitted to enjoy free institutions than the people from whom they came. I met with wealthy New-Englanders who abandoned the country in which they were born, in order to lay the foundations of Christianity and of freedom on the banks of the Missouri, or in the prairies of Illinois. Thus religious zeal is perpetually warmed in the United States by the fires of patriotism. These men do not act exclusively from a consideration of a future life; eternity is only one motive of their devotion to the cause. If you converse with these missionaries of Christian civilization, you will be surprised to hear them speak so often of the goods of this world, and to meet a politician where you expected to find a priest. They will tell you, that " all the American republics are collectively involved with each other; if the republics of the West were to fall into anarchy, or to be mastered by a despot, the republican institutions which now flourish upon the shores of the Atlantic Ocean would be in great peril. It is therefore our interest that the new States should be religious, in order that they may permit us to remain free."

Such are the opinions of the Americans: and if any hold that the religious spirit which I admire is the very thing most amiss in America, and that the only element wanting to the freedom and happiness of the human race on the other side of the ocean is to believe with Spinoza in the eternity of the world, or with Cabanis that thought is secreted by the brain, I can only reply, that those who hold this language have never been in America, and that they have never seen a religious or a free nation. When they return from a visit to that country, we shall hear what they have to say.

There are persons in France who look upon republican institutions only as a means of obtaining grandeur ; they measure the immense space which separates their vices and misery from power and riches, and they aim to fill up this gulf with ruins, that they may pass over it. These men are the *condottieri* of liberty, and fight for their own advantage, whatever be the colors they wear. The republic will stand long enough, they think, to draw them up out of their present degradation. It is not to these that I address myself. But there are others who look forward to a republican form of government as a tranquil and lasting state, towards which modern society is daily impelled by the ideas and manners of the time, and who sincerely desire to prepare men to be free. When these men attack religious opinions, they obey the dictates of their passions, and not of their interests. Despotism may govern without faith, but liberty cannot. Religion is much more necessary in the republic which they set forth in glowing colors, than in the monarchy which they attack ; it is more needed in democratic republics than in any others. How is it possible that society should escape destruction, if the moral tie be not strengthened in proportion as the political tie is relaxed ? and what can be done with a people who are their own masters, if they be not submissive to the Deity ?

PRINCIPAL CAUSES WHICH RENDER RELIGION POWERFUL IN AMERICA.

Care taken by the Americans to separate the Church from the State. — The Laws, Public Opinion, and even the Exertions of the Clergy, concur to promote this End. — Influence of Religion upon the Mind in the United States attributable to this Cause. — Reason of this. — What is the Natural State of Men with regard to Religion at the Present Time. — What are the Peculiar and Incidental Causes which prevent Men, in certain Countries, from arriving at this State.

THE philosophers of the eighteenth century explained in a very simple manner the gradual decay of religious faith. Religious zeal, said they, must necessarily fail the more generally liberty is established and knowledge diffused. Unfortunately, the facts by no means accord with their theory. There are certain populations in Europe whose unbelief is only equalled by their ignorance and debasement; whilst in America, one of the freest and most enlightened nations in the world fulfil with fervor all the outward duties of religion.

On my arrival in the United States, the religious aspect of the country was the first thing that struck my attention; and the longer I stayed there, the more I perceived the great political consequences resulting from this new state of things. In France, I had almost always seen the spirit of religion and the spirit of freedom marching in opposite directions. But in America, I found they were intimately united, and that they reigned in common over the same country. My desire to discover the causes of this phe nomenon increased from day to day. In order to satisfy it, I questioned the members of all the different sects; I sought especially the society of the clergy, who are the depositaries of the different creeds, and are especially interested in their duration. As a member of the Roman Catholic Church, I was more particularly brought into contact with several of its priests, with whom I became intimately acquainted.   To each of these men I expressed my astonishment and explained my doubts : I found that they differed upon matters of detail alone, and that they all attributed the peaceful dominion of religion in their country mainly to the separation of church and state.   I do not hesitate to affirm, that, during my stay in America, I did not meet a single individual, of the clergy or the laity, who was not of the same opinion upon this point.

This led me to examine more attentively than I had hitherto done the station which the American clergy occupy in political society.   I learned with surprise that they filled no public appointments ; * I did not see one of them in the administration, and they are not even represented in the legislative assemblies.†   In several States,‡ the law excludes them from political life, public opinion in all. And when I came to inquire into the prevailing spirit of the clergy, I found that most of its members seemed to retire of their own accord from the exercise of power, and that they made it the pride of their profession to abstain from politics.

* Unless this term be applied to the functions which many of them fill in the schools.   Almost all education is intrusted to the clergy.   [This is too sweeping.   Clergymen often serve upon school committees, or fill professorships in colleges, as they frequently do in Europe.   But they are not so numerous as the laity in either of these offices. — Am. Ed.]

† They are not represented *as such*.   But they are often elected to represent their townships, or even their States in Congress. — Am. Ed.

‡ See the " Constitution of New York," Art. VII. § 4 : —

" And whereas the ministers of the Gospel are, by their profession, dedicated to the service of God and the care of souls, and ought not to be diverted from the great duties of their functions ; therefore no minister of the Gospel, or priest of any denomination whatsoever, shall at any time hereafter, under any pretence or description whatever, be eligible to, or capable of holding, any civil or military office or place within this State."

See also the Constitutions of North Carolina, Art. XXXI. ; Virginia ; South Carolina, Art. I. § 23 ; Kentucky, Art. II. § 26 ; Tennessee, Art. VIII. § 1 ; Louisiana, Art. II. § 22.

I heard them inveigh against ambition and deceit, under whatever political opinions these vices might chance to lurk ; but I learned from their discourses that men are not guilty in the eye of God for any opinions concerning political government which they may profess with sincerity, any more than they are for their mistakes in building a house, or in driving a furrow. I perceived that these ministers of the Gospel eschewed all parties, with the anxiety attendant upon personal interest. These facts convinced me that what I had been told was true ; and it then became my object to investigate their causes, and to inquire how it happened that the real authority of religion was increased by a state of things which diminished its apparent force : these causes did not long escape my researches.

The short space of threescore years can never content the imagination of man ; nor can the imperfect joys of this world satisfy his heart. · Man alone, of all created beings, displays a natural contempt of existence, and yet a boundless desire to exist ; he scorns life, but he dreads annihilation. These different feelings incessantly urge his soul to the contemplation of a future state, and religion directs his musings thither. Religion, then, is simply another form of hope ; and it is no less natural to the human heart than hope itself. Men cannot abandon their religious faith without a kind of aberration of intellect, and a sort of violent distortion of their true nature ; they are invincibly brought back to more pious sentiments. Unbelief is an accident, and faith is the only permanent state of mankind. If we consider religious institutions merely in a human point of view, they may be said to derive an inexhaustible element of strength from man himself, since they belong to one of the constituent principles of human nature.

I am aware that, at certain times, religion may strengthen this influence, which originates in itself, by the artificial power of the laws, and by the support of those temporal institutions which direct society.   Religions intimately united with the governments of the earth have been known to exercise sovereign power founded on terror and faith; but when a religion contracts an alliance of this nature, I do not hesitate to affirm that it commits the same error as a man who should sacrifice his future to his present welfare; and in obtaining a power to which it has no claim, it risks that authority which is rightfully its own. When a religion founds its empire only upon the desire of immortality which lives in every human heart, it may aspire to universal dominion; but when it connects itself with a government, it must adopt maxims which are applicable only to certain nations.   Thus, in forming an alliance with a political power, religion augments its authority over a few, and forfeits the hope of reigning over all.

As long as a religion rests only upon those sentiments which are the consolation of all affliction, it may attract the affections of all mankind.   But if it be mixed up with the bitter passions of the world, it may be constrained to defend allies whom its interests, and not the principle of love, have given to it; or to repel as antagonists men who are still attached to it, however opposed they may be to the powers with which it is allied.   The church cannot share the temporal power of the state, without being the object of a portion of that animosity which the latter excites.

The political powers which seem to be most firmly established have frequently no better guaranty for their duration than the opinions of a generation, the interests of the time, or the life of an individual.   A law may modify the social condition which seems to be most fixed and determinate; and with the social condition, everything else must change. The powers of society are more or less fugitive, like the years which we spend upon earth; they succeed each other with rapidity, like the fleeting cares of life; and no government has ever yet been founded upon an invariable disposition of the human heart, or upon an imperishable interest.

As long as a religion is sustained by those feelings, propensities, and passions which are found to occur under the same forms at all periods of history, it may defy the efforts of time ; or, at least, it, can be destroyed only by another religion. But when religion clings to the interests of the world, it becomes almost as fragile a thing as the powers of earth. It is the only one of them all which can hope for immortality ; but if it be connected with their ephemeral power, it shares their fortunes, and may fall with those transient passions which alone supported them. The alliance which religion contracts with political powers must needs be onerous to itself, since it does not require their assistance to live, and by giving them its assistance it may be exposed to decay.

The danger which I have just pointed out always exists, but it is not always equally visible. In some ages, governments seem to be imperishable ; in others, the existence of society appears to be more precarious than the life of man. Some constitutions plunge the citizens into a lethargic somnolence, and others rouse them to feverish excitement. When governments seem so strong, and laws so stable, men do not perceive the dangers which may accrue from a union of church and state. When governments appear weak, and laws inconstant, the danger is self-evident, but it is no longer possible to avoid it. We must therefore learn how to perceive it from afar.

In proportion as a nation assumes a democratic condition of society, and as communities display democratic propensities, it becomes more and more dangerous to connect religion with political institutions ; for the time is coming when authority will be bandied from hand to hand, when political theories will succeed each other, and when men, laws, and constitutions will disappear or be modified from

day to day, and this not for a season only, but unceasingly.
Agitation and mutability are inherent in the nature of
democratic republics, just as stagnation and sleepiness are
the law of absolute monarchies.

If the Americans, who change the head of the government once in four years, who elect new legislators every
two years, and renew the State officers every twelve-
month, — if the Americans, who have given up the political
world to the attempts of innovators, had not placed religion beyond their reach, where could it take firm hold in
the ebb and flow of human opinions? where would be that
respect which belongs to it, amidst the struggles of faction? and what would become of its immortality, in the
midst of universal decay? The American clergy were the
first to perceive this truth, and to act in conformity with it.
They saw that they must renounce their religious influence,
if they were to strive for political power; and they chose
to give up the support of the state, rather than to share its
vicissitudes.

In America, religion is perhaps less powerful than it has
been at certain periods and among certain nations; but its
influence is more lasting. It restricts itself to its own
resources, but of these none can deprive it: its circle is
limited, but it pervades it and holds it under undisputed
control.

On every side in Europe, we hear voices complaining of
the absence of religious faith, and inquiring the means of
restoring to religion some remnant of its former authority.
It seems to me that we must first attentively consider what
ought to be *the natural state* of men, with regard to religion, at the present time; and when we know what we
have to hope and to fear, we may discern the end to which
our efforts ought to be directed.

The two great dangers which threaten the existence of
religion are schism and indifference. In ages of fervent

devotion, men sometimes abandon their religion, but they only shake one off in order to adopt another. Their faith changes its objects, but suffers no decline. The old religion then excites enthusiastic attachment or bitter enmity in either party; some leave it with anger, others cling to it with increased devotedness, and although persuasions differ, irreligion is unknown. Such, however, is not the case when a religious belief is secretly undermined by doctrines which may be termed negative, since they deny the truth of one religion without affirming that of any other. Prodigious revolutions then take place in the human mind, without the apparent co-operation of the passions of man, and almost without his knowledge. Men lose the objects of their fondest hopes, as if through forgetfulness. They are carried away by an imperceptible current, which they have not the courage to stem, but which they follow with regret, since it bears them away from a faith they love, to a scepticism that plunges them into despair.

In ages which answer to this description, men desert their religious opinions from lukewarmness rather than from dislike; they are not rejected, but they fall away. But if the unbeliever does not admit religion to be true, he still considers it useful. Regarding religious institutions in a human point of view, he acknowledges their influence upon manners and legislation. He admits that they may serve to make men live in peace, and prepare them gently for the hour of death. He regrets the faith which he has lost; and as he is deprived of a treasure of which he knows the value, he fears to take it away from those who still possess it.

On the other hand, those who continue to believe are not afraid openly to avow their faith. They look upon those who do not share their persuasion as more worthy of pity than of opposition; and they are aware, that, to acquire the esteem of the unbelieving, they are not obliged to follow their example. They are not hostile, then, to any one in the world; and as they do not consider the society in which they live as an arena in which religion is bound to face its thousand deadly foes, they love their contemporaries, whilst they condemn their weaknesses and lament their errors.

As those who do not believe conceal their incredulity, and as those who believe display their faith, public opinion pronounces itself in favor of religion: love, support, and honor are bestowed upon it, and it is only by searching the human soul that we can detect the wounds which it has received. The mass of mankind, who are never without the feeling of religion, do not perceive anything at variance with the established faith. The instinctive desire of a future life brings the crowd about the altar, and opens the hearts of men to the precepts and consolations of religion.

But this picture is not applicable to us; for there are men amongst us who have ceased to believe in Christianity, without adopting any other religion; others are in the perplexities of doubt, and already affect not to believe; and others, again, are afraid to avow that Christian faith which they still cherish in secret.

Amidst these lukewarm partisans and ardent antagonists, a small number of believers exists, who are ready to brave all obstacles, and to scorn all dangers, in defence of their faith. They have done violence to human weakness, in order to rise superior to public opinion. Excited by the effort they have made, they scarcely know where to stop; and as they know that the first use which the French made of independence was to attack religion, they look upon their contemporaries with dread, and recoil in alarm from the liberty which their fellow-citizens are seeking to obtain. As unbelief appears to them to be a novelty, they comprise all that is new in one indiscriminate animosity. They are at war with their age and country, and they look upon every opinion which is put forth there as the necessary enemy of faith.

Such is not the natural state of men with regard to religion at the present day; and some extraordinary or incidental cause must be at work in France, to prevent the human mind from following its natural inclination, and drive it beyond the limits at which it ought naturally to stop.

I am fully convinced that this extraordinary and incidental cause is the close connection of politics and religion. The unbelievers of Europe attack the Christians as their political opponents, rather than as their religious adversaries; they hate the Christian religion as the opinion of a party, much more than as an error of belief; and they reject the clergy less because they are the representatives of the Deity, than because they are the allies of government.

In Europe, Christianity has been intimately united to the powers of the earth. Those powers are now in decay, and it is, as it were, buried under their ruins. The living body of religion has been bound down to the dead corpse of superannuated polity; cut but the bonds which restrain it, and it will rise once more. I know not what could restore the Christian Church of Europe to the energy of its earlier days; that power belongs to God alone; but it may be for human policy to leave to faith the full exercise of the strength which it still retains.

HOW THE EDUCATION, THE HABITS, AND THE PRACTICAL
EXPERIENCE OF THE AMERICANS PROMOTE THE SUCCESS
OF THEIR DEMOCRATIC INSTITUTIONS.

What is to be understood by the Education of the American People. — The
Human Mind more superficially instructed in the United States than in
Europe. — No one completely uninstructed. — Reason of this. — Rapidity with which Opinions are diffused even in the half cultivated States
of the West. — Practical Experience more serviceable to the Americans
than Book-Learning.

I HAVE but little to add to what I have already said, concerning the influence which the instruction and the habits
of the Americans exercise upon the maintenance of their
political institutions.

America has hitherto produced very few writers of distinction; it possesses no great historians, and not a single
eminent poet.*   The inhabitants of that country look upon
literature properly so called with a kind of disapprobation;
and there are towns of second-rate importance in Europe,
in which more literary works are annually published than
in the twenty-four States of the Union put together.†
The spirit of the Americans is averse to general ideas; it

* This statement was rather too sweeping even in 1833, when M. de
Tocqueville wrote.   But now, when the list of our historians contains the
names of Prescott, Sparks, Bancroft, Motley, Palfrey, and Hildreth, and
that of our poets includes those of Longfellow, Bryant, Dana, Sprague,
Lowell, and a crowd of others, our author's remark is only curious as
evincing the suddenness and rapidity with which literary talent has been
developed in the United States. — AM. ED.

† It is not too much to say, that as many books are now annually printed
and sold in the United States as in England.   Certainly, what is now called
" the reading public " is larger in America, in proportion to the population,
than in any other country in the world.   This is a consequence partly of
the wide diffusion of education, which enables so many to read books, and
partly of the general prosperity of the people, which enables still more to
buy them.   Literary pursuits are also held in high honor in society; a successful author is second to no one in estimation with the upper classes, or in
favor with the common people. — AM. ED.

does not seek theoretical discoveries. Neither politics nor manufactures direct them to such speculations; and although new laws are perpetually enacted in the United States, no great writers there have hitherto inquired into the general principles of legislation. The Americans have lawyers and commentators, but no jurists; and they furnish examples rather than lessons to the world. The same observation applies to the mechanical arts. In America, the inventions of Europe are adopted with sagacity; they are perfected, and adapted with admirable skill to the wants of the country. Manufactures exist, but the science of manufacture is not cultivated; and they have good workmen, but very few inventors.* Fulton was obliged to proffer his services to foreign nations for a long time, before he was able to devote them to his own country.

The observer who is desirous of forming an opinion on the state of instruction amongst the Anglo-Americans must consider the same object from two different points of view. If he singles out only the learned, he will be astonished to find how few they are; but if he counts the ignorant, the American people will appear to be the most enlightened in the world. The whole population, as I observed in another place, is situated between these two extremes.

In New England, every citizen receives the elementary notions of human knowledge; he is taught, moreover, the doctrines and the evidences of his religion, the history of his country, and the leading features of its Constitution. In the States of Connecticut and Massachusetts, it is extremely rare to find a man imperfectly acquainted with all these things, and a person wholly ignorant of them is a sort of phenomenon.

---

* This assertion is the very reverse of the truth. In no country in the world, during the last fifty years, has inventive industry been so far developed or so successful as in America. Europe copies and adopts American inventions, but furnishes very few comparatively in return. — Am. Ed.

When I compare the Greek and Roman republics with these American States; the manuscript libraries of the former, and their rude population, with the innumerable journals and the enlightened people of the latter; when I remember all the attempts which are made to judge the modern republics by the aid of those of antiquity, and to infer what will happen in our time from what took place two thousand years ago, — I am tempted to burn my books, in order to apply none but novel ideas to so novel a condition of society.

What I have said of New England must not, however, be applied indistinctly to the whole Union : as we advance towards the West or the South, the instruction of the people diminishes.   In the States which border on the Gulf of Mexico, a certain number of individuals may be found, as in France, who are devoid even of the rudiments of instruction.   But there is not a single district in the United States sunk in complete ignorance, and for a very simple reason.   The nations of Europe started from the darkness of a barbarous condition, to advance towards the light of civilization : their progress has been unequal ; some of them have improved apace, whilst others have loitered in their course, and some have stopped, and are still sleeping upon the way.

Such has not been the case in the United States.   The Anglo-Americans, already civilized, settled upon that territory which their descendants occupy ; they had not to begin to learn, and it was sufficient for them not to forget.   Now the children of these same Americans are the persons who, year by year, transport their dwellings into the wilds, and, with their dwellings, their acquired information and their esteem for knowledge.   Education has taught them the utility of instruction, and has enabled them to transmit that instruction to their posterity.   In the United States, society has no infancy, but it is born in man's estate.

The Americans never use the word " peasant," because they have no idea of the class which that term denotes ; the ignorance of more remote ages, the simplicity of rural life, and the rusticity of the villager, have not been preserved amongst them ; and they are alike unacquainted with the virtues, the vices, the coarse habits, and the simple graces of an early stage of civilization.   At the extreme borders of the Confederate States, upon the confines of society and the wilderness, a population of bold adventurers have taken up their abode, who pierce the solitudes of the American woods, and seek a country there, in order to escape the poverty which awaited them in their native home.   As soon as the pioneer reaches the place which is to serve him for a retreat, he fells a few trees and builds a log-house.   Nothing can offer a more miserable aspect than these isolated dwellings.   The traveller who approaches one of them towards nightfall sees the flicker of the hearth-flame through the chinks in the walls ; and at night, if the wind rises, he hears the roof of boughs shake to and fro in the midst of the great forest-trees.   Who would not suppose that this poor hut is the asylum of rudeness and ignorance ?   Yet no sort of comparison can be drawn between the pioneer and the dwelling which shelters him.   Everything about him is primitive and wild, but he is himself the result of the labor and experience of eighteen centuries. He wears the dress and speaks the language of cities ; he is acquainted with the past, curious about the future, and ready for argument upon the present ; he is, in short, a highly civilized being, who consents for a time to inhabit the backwoods, and who penetrates into the wilds of the New World with the Bible, an axe, and some newspapers. It is difficult to imagine the incredible rapidity with which thought circulates in the midst of these deserts.*   I do not

---

* I travelled along a portion of the frontier of the United States in a sort of cart, which was termed the mail. We passed, day and night, with

think that so much intellectual activity exists in the most enlightened and populous districts of France.*

It cannot be doubted that, in the United States, the instruction of the people powerfully contributes to the support of the democratic republic; and such must always be the case, I believe, where the instruction which enlightens the understanding is not separated from the moral education which amends the heart. But I would not exaggerate this advantage, and I am still further from thinking, as so many people do think in Europe, that men can be instantaneously made citizens by teaching them to read and write. True information is mainly derived from experience; and if the Americans had not been gradually accustomed to govern themselves, their book-learning would not help them much at the present day.

I have lived much with the people in the United States, and I cannot express how much I admire their experience and their good sense. An American should never be led to speak of Europe; for he will then probably display

great rapidity, along the roads, which were scarcely marked out through immense forests. When the gloom of the woods became impenetrable, the driver lighted branches of pine, and we journeyed along by the light they cast. From time to time, we came to a hut in the midst of the forest; this was a post-office. The mail dropped an enormous bundle of letters at the door of this isolated dwelling, and we pursued our way at full gallop, leaving the inhabitants of the neighboring log-houses to send for their share of the treasure.

* In 1832, each inhabitant of Michigan paid 23 cents to the post-office revenue; and each inhabitant of the Floridas paid 20 cents. (See National Calendar, 1833, p. 244.) In the same year, each inhabitant of the *Département du Nord* paid not quite 20 cents to the revenue of the French post-office. (See the *Compte rendu de l'Administration des Finances*, 1833, p. 623.) Now the State of Michigan only contained at that time 7 inhabitants per square league, and Florida only 5. The instruction and the commercial activity of these districts are inferior to those of most of the States in the Union; whilst the *Département du Nord*, which contains 3,400 inhabitants per square league, is one of the most enlightened and manufacturing parts of France.

much presumption and very foolish pride. He will take up with those crude and vague notions which are so useful to the ignorant all over the world. But if you question him respecting his own country, the cloud which dimmed his intelligence will immediately disperse; his language will become as clear and precise as his thoughts. He will inform you what his rights are, and by what means he exercises them; he will be able to point out the customs which obtain in the political world. You will find that he is well acquainted with the rules of the administration, and that he is familiar with the mechanism of the laws. The citizen of the United States does not acquire his practical science and his positive notions from books; the instruction he has acquired may have prepared him for receiving those ideas, but it did not furnish them. The American learns to know the laws by participating in the act of legislation; and he takes a lesson in the forms of government from governing. The great work of society is ever going on before his eyes, and, as it were, under his hands.

In the United States, politics are the end and aim of education; in Europe, its principal object is to fit men for private life. The interference of the citizens in public affairs is too rare an occurrence to be provided for beforehand. Upon casting a glance over society in the two hemispheres, these differences are indicated even by their external aspect.

In Europe, we frequently introduce the ideas and habits of private life into public affairs; and as we pass at once from the domestic circle to the government of the state, we may frequently be heard to discuss the great interests of society in the same manner in which we converse with our friends. The Americans, on the other hand, transport the habits of public life into their manners in private; in their country, the jury is introduced into the games of schoolboys, and parliamentary forms are observed in the order of a feast.

THE LAWS CONTRIBUTE MORE TO THE MAINTENANCE OF
THE DEMOCRATIC REPUBLIC IN THE UNITED STATES
THAN THE PHYSICAL CIRCUMSTANCES OF THE COUNTRY,
AND THE MANNERS MORE THAN THE LAWS.

All the Nations of America have a Democratic State of Society. — Yet
Democratic Institutions are supported only among the Anglo-Americans. — The Spaniards of South America, as much favored by Physical
Causes as the Anglo-Americans, unable to maintain a Democratic Republic. — Mexico, which has adopted the Constitution of the United
States, in the same Predicament. — The Anglo-Americans of the West
less able to maintain it than those of the East. — Reason of these Differences.

I HAVE remarked that the maintenance of democratic
institutions in the United States is attributable to the circumstances, the laws, and the manners of that country.*
Most Europeans are acquainted with only the first of these
three causes, and they are apt to give it a preponderant
importance which it does not really possess.

It is true that the Anglo-Americans settled in the New
World in a state of social equality; the low-born and the
noble were not to be found amongst them; and professional prejudices were always as unknown as the prejudices of birth. Thus, as the condition of society was
democratic, the rule of democracy was established without
difficulty. But this circumstance is not peculiar to the
United States; almost all the American colonies were
founded by men equal amongst themselves, or who became
so by inhabiting them. In no one part of the New World
have Europeans been able to create an aristocracy. Nevertheless, democratic institutions prosper nowhere but in the
United States.

* I remind the reader of the general signification which I give to the
word *manners*, — namely, the moral and intellectual characteristics of men
in society.

The American Union has no enemies to contend with; it stands in the wilds like an island in the ocean. But the Spaniards of South America were no less isolated by nature; yet their position has not relieved them from the charge of standing armies. They make war upon each other when they have no foreign enemies to oppose; and the Anglo-American democracy is the only one which has hitherto been able to maintain itself in peace.

The territory of the Union presents a boundless field to human activity, and inexhaustible materials for labor. The passion for wealth takes the place of ambition, and the heat of faction is mitigated by a consciousness of prosperity. But in what portion of the globe shall we find more fertile plains, mightier rivers, or more unexplored and inexhaustible riches, than in South America? Yet South America has been unable to maintain democratic institutions. If the welfare of nations depended on their being placed in a remote position, with an unbounded space of habitable territory before them, the Spaniards of South America would have no reason to complain of their fate. And although they might enjoy less prosperity than the inhabitants of the United States, their lot might still be such as to excite the envy of some nations in Europe. There are, however, no nations upon the face of the earth more miserable than those of South America.

Thus, not only are physical causes inadequate to produce results analogous to those which occur in North America, but they cannot raise the population of South America above the level of European states, where they act in a contrary direction. Physical causes do not therefore affect the destiny of nations so much as has been supposed.

I have met with men in New England who were on the point of leaving a country where they might have remained in easy circumstances, to seek their fortune in the wilds. Not far from that region, I found a French population in Canada, closely crowded on a narrow territory, although the same wilds were at hand; and whilst the emigrant from the United States purchased an extensive estate with the earnings of a short term of labor, the Canadian paid as much for land as he would have done in France.   Thus Nature offers the solitudes of the New World to Europeans also; but they do not always know how to make use of her gifts.   Other inhabitants of America have the same physical conditions of prosperity as the Anglo-Americans, but without their laws and their manners; and these people are miserable.   The laws and manners of the Anglo-Americans are therefore that special and predominant cause of their greatness which is the object of my inquiry.

I am far from supposing that the American laws are preeminently good in themselves: I do not hold them to be applicable to all democratic nations; and several of them seem to me to be dangerous, even in the United States. But it cannot be denied that American legislation, taken as a whole, is extremely well adapted to the genius of the people and the nature of the country which it is intended to govern.   The American laws are therefore good, and to them must be attributed a large portion of the success which attends the government of democracy in America: but I do not believe them to be the principal cause of that success; and if they seem to me to have more influence than the nature of the country upon the social happiness of the Americans, there is still reason to believe that their effect is inferior to that produced by the manners of the people.

The Federal laws undoubtedly constitute the most important part of the legislation of the United States.   Mexico, which is not less fortunately situated than the Anglo-American Union, has adopted these same laws, but is unable to accustom itself to the government of democracy.

Some other cause is therefore at work, independently of physical circumstances and peculiar laws, which enables the democracy to rule in the United States.

Another still more striking proof may be adduced. Almost all the inhabitants of the territory of the Union are the descendants of a common stock; they speak the same language, they worship God in the same manner, they are affected by the same physical causes, and they obey the same laws. Whence, then, do their characteristic differences arise? Why, in the Eastern States of the Union, does the republican government display vigor and regularity, and proceed with mature deliberation? Whence does it derive the wisdom and the durability which mark its acts, whilst in the Western States, on the contrary, society seems to be ruled by chance? There, public business is conducted with an irregularity, and a passionate, almost feverish excitement, which do not announce a long or sure duration.

I am no longer comparing the Anglo-Americans with foreign nations; but I am contrasting them with each other, and endeavoring to discover why they are so unlike. The arguments which are derived from the nature of the country and the difference of legislation are here all set aside. Recourse must be had to some other cause; and what other cause can there be, except the manners of the people?

It is in the Eastern States that the Anglo-Americans have been longest accustomed to the government of democracy, and have adopted the habits and conceived the opinions most favorable to its maintenance. Democracy has gradually penetrated into their customs, their opinions, and their forms of social intercourse; it is to be found in all the details of daily life, as well as in the laws. In the Eastern States, the book instruction and practical education of the people have been most perfected, and religion has been most thoroughly amalgamated with liberty. Now, these habits, opinions, customs, and convictions are precisely what I have denominated *manners.*

In the Western States, on the contrary, a portion of the same advantages are still wanting. Many of the Americans of the West were born in the woods, and they mix the ideas and customs of savage life with the civilization of their fathers. Their passions are more intense, their religious morality less authoritative, and their convictions less firm. The inhabitants exercise no sort of control over their fellows, for they are scarcely acquainted with each other. The nations of the West display, to a certain extent, the inexperience and the rude habits of a people in their infancy; for, although they are composed of old elements, their assemblage is of recent date.

The manners of the Americans of the United States are, then, the peculiar cause which renders that people the only one of the American nations that is able to support a democratic government; and it is the influence of manners which produces the different degrees of order and prosperity that may be distinguished in the several Anglo-American democracies. Thus the effect which the geographical position of a country may have upon the duration of democratic institutions is exaggerated in Europe. Too much importance is attributed to legislation, too little to manners. These three great causes serve, no doubt, to regulate and direct the American democracy; but if they were to be classed in their proper order, I should say that physical circumstances are less efficient than the laws, and the laws infinitely less so than the manners of the people. I am convinced that the most advantageous situation and the best possible laws cannot maintain a constitution in spite of the manners of a country; whilst the latter may turn to some advantage the most unfavorable positions and the worst laws. The importance of manners is a common truth to which study and experience incessantly direct our attention. It may be regarded as a central point in the range of observation, and the common termination of all my inquiries. So seriously do I insist upon this head, that, if I have hitherto failed in making the reader feel the important influence of the practical experience, the habits, the opinions, in short, of the manners of the Americans, upon the maintenance of their institutions, I have failed in the principal object of my work.

WHETHER LAWS AND MANNERS ARE SUFFICIENT TO MAINTAIN DEMOCRATIC INSTITUTIONS IN OTHER COUNTRIES BESIDES AMERICA.

The Anglo-Americans, if transported into Europe, would be obliged to modify their Laws. — Distinction to be made between Democratic Institutions and American Institutions. — Democratic Laws may be conceived better than, or at least different from, those which the American Democracy has adopted. — The Example of America only proves that it is possible, by the Aid of Manners and Legislation, to regulate Democracy.

I HAVE asserted that the success of democratic institutions in the United States is more attributable to the laws themselves, and the manners of the people, than to the nature of the country. But does it follow that the same causes would of themselves produce the same results, if they were put in operation elsewhere; and if the country is no adequate substitute for laws and manners, can laws and manners in their turn take the place of a country? It will readily be understood that the elements of a reply to this question are wanting: other inhabitants are to be found in the New World besides the Anglo-Americans, and, as these are affected by the same physical circumstances as the latter, they may fairly be compared with them.

But there are no nations out of America which have adopted the same laws and manners, though destitute of the physical advantages peculiar to the Anglo-Americans. No standard of comparison therefore exists, and we can only hazard an opinion.

It appears to me, in the first place, that a careful distinction must be made between the institutions of the United States and democratic institutions in general. When I reflect upon the state of Europe, its mighty nations, its populous cities, its formidable armies, and the complex nature of its politics, I cannot suppose that even the Anglo-Americans, if they were transported to our hemisphere, with their ideas, their religion, and their manners, could exist without considerably altering their laws. But a democratic nation may be imagined, organized differently from the American people. Is it then impossible to conceive a government really established upon the will of the majority, but in which the majority, repressing its natural instinct of equality, should consent, with a view to the order and the stability of the state, to invest a family or an individual with all the attributes of executive power ? Might not a democratic society be imagined, in which the forces of the nation would be more centralized than they are in the United States ; where the people would exercise a less direct and less irresistible influence upon public affairs, and yet every citizen, invested with certain rights, would participate, within his sphere, in the conduct of the government? What I have seen amongst the Anglo-Americans induces me to believe that democratic institutions of this kind, prudently introduced into society, so as gradually to mix with the habits, and to be interfused with the opinions of the people, might exist in other countries besides America. If the laws of the United States were the only imaginable democratic laws, or the most perfect which it is possible to conceive, I should admit that their success in America affords no proof of the success of democratic institutions in general, in a country less favored by nature. But as the laws of America appear to me to be defective in several respects, and as I can readily imagine others, the peculiar advantages of that country do not prove to me that democratic institutions cannot succeed in a nation less favored by circumstances, if ruled by better laws.

If human nature were different in America from what it is elsewhere, or if the social condition of the Americans created habits and opinions amongst them different from those which originate in the same social condition in the Old World, the American democracies would afford no means of predicting what may occur in other democracies. If the Americans displayed the same propensities as all other democratic nations, and if their legislators had relied upon the nature of the country and the favor of circumstances to restrain those propensities within due limits, the prosperity of the United States, being attributable to purely physical causes, would afford no encouragement to a people inclined to imitate their example, without sharing their natural advantages. But neither of these suppositions is borne out by facts.

In America, the same passions are to be met with as in Europe, — some originating in human nature, others in the democratic condition of society. Thus, in the United States, I found that restlessness of heart which is natural to men when all ranks are nearly equal, and the chances of elevation are the same to all. I found there the democratic feeling of envy expressed under a thousand different forms. I remarked that the people there frequently displayed, in the conduct of affairs, a mixture of ignorance and presumption ; and I inferred that, in America, men are liable to the same failings and exposed to the same evils as amongst ourselves. But, upon examining the state of society more attentively, I speedily discovered that the Americans had made great and successful efforts to counteract these imperfections of human nature, and to correct the natural defects of democracy. Their divers municipal laws appeared to me so many means of restraining the restless ambition of the citizens within a narrow sphere, and of turning those same passions which might have worked havoc in the state, to the good of the township or the parish. The American legislators seem to have succeeded to some extent in opposing the idea of right to the feelings of envy; the permanence of religious morality to the continual shifting of politics; the experience of the people to their theoretical ignorance; and their practical knowledge of business to the impatience of their desires.

The Americans, then, have not relied upon the nature of their country to counterpoise those dangers which originate in their Constitution and their political laws. To evils which are common to all democratic nations, they have applied remedies which none but themselves had ever thought of; and, although they were the first to make the experiment, they have succeeded in it. The manners and laws of the Americans are not the only ones which may suit a democratic people; but the Americans have shown that it would be wrong to despair of regulating democracy by the aid of manners and laws. If other nations should borrow this general and pregnant idea from the Americans, without, however, intending to imitate them in the peculiar application which they have made of it; if they should attempt to fit themselves for that social condition which it seems to be the will of Providence to impose upon the generations of this age, and so to escape from the despotism or the anarchy which threatens them, — what reason is there to suppose that their efforts would not be crowned with success? The organization and the establishment of democracy in Christendom is the great

political problem of our times. The Americans, unquestionably, have not resolved this problem, but they furnish
useful data to those who undertake to resolve it.

IMPORTANCE OF WHAT PRECEDES WITH RESPECT TO THE STATE OF EUROPE.

IT may readily be discovered with what intention I
undertook the foregoing inquiries. The question here discussed is interesting not only to the United States, but to
the whole world; it concerns, not a nation only, but all
mankind. If those nations whose social condition is democratic could remain free only while they inhabit uncultivated
regions, we must despair of the future destiny of the human
race; for democracy is rapidly acquiring a more extended
sway, and the wilds are gradually peopled with men. If
it were true that laws and manners are insufficient to maintain democratic institutions, what refuge would remain open
to the nations, except the despotism of one man? I am
aware that there are many worthy persons at the present
time who are not alarmed at this alternative, and who are
so tired of liberty as to be glad of repose far from its
storms. But these persons are ill acquainted with the
haven towards which they are bound. Preoccupied by
their remembrances, they judge of absolute power by what
it has been, and not by what it might become in our times.

If absolute power were re-established amongst the democratic nations of Europe, I am persuaded that it would assume a new form, and appear under features unknown to
our fathers. There was a time in Europe when the laws
and the consent of the people had invested princes with
almost unlimited authority, but they scarcely ever availed
themselves of it. I do not speak of the prerogatives of
the nobility, of the authority of high courts of justice, of

corporations and their chartered rights, or of provincial privileges, which served to break the blows of sovereign authority, and to keep up a spirit of resistance in the nation. Independently of these political institutions,—which, however opposed they might be to personal liberty, served to keep alive the love of freedom in the mind, and which may be esteemed useful in this respect, — the manners and opinions of the nation confined the royal authority within barriers which were not less powerful because less conspicuous. Religion, the affections of the people, the benevolence of the prince, the sense of honor, family pride, provincial prejudices, custom, and public opinion limited the power of kings, and restrained their authority within an invisible circle. The constitution of nations was despotic at that time, but their manners were free. Princes had the right, but they had neither the means nor the desire, of doing whatever they pleased.

But what now remains of those barriers which formerly arrested tyranny? Since religion has lost its empire over the souls of men, the most prominent boundary which divided good from evil is overthrown; everything seems doubtful and indeterminate in the moral world; kings and nations are guided by chance, and none can say where are the natural limits of despotism and the bounds of license. Long revolutions have forever destroyed the respect which surrounded the rulers of the state; and, since they have been relieved from the burden of public esteem, princes may henceforward surrender themselves without fear to the intoxication of arbitrary power.

When kings find that the hearts of their subjects are turned towards them, they are clement, because they are conscious of their strength; and they are chary of the affection of their people, because the affection of their people is the bulwark of the throne. A mutual interchange of good-will then takes place between the prince

and the people, which resembles the gracious intercourse
of domestic life. The subjects may murmur at the sovereign's decree, but they are grieved to displease him; and
the sovereign chastises his subjects with the light hand of
parental affection.

But when once the spell of royalty is broken in the
tumult of revolution, — when successive monarchs have
crossed the throne, so as alternately to display to the people the weakness of their right, and the harshness of their
power, — the sovereign is no longer regarded by any as the
father of the state, and he is feared by all as its master. If
he is weak, he is despised; if he is strong, he is detested.
He is himself full of animosity and alarm; he finds that
he is a stranger in his own country, and he treats his subjects like conquered enemies.

When the provinces and the towns formed so many different nations in the midst of their common country, each
of them had a will of its own, which was opposed to the
general spirit of subjection; but, now that all the parts of
the same empire, after having lost their immunities, their
customs, their prejudices, their traditions, and even their
names, have become accustomed to obey the same laws, it
is not more difficult to oppress them all together than it
was formerly to oppress one of them separately.

Whilst the nobles enjoyed their power, and indeed long
after that power was lost, the honor of aristocracy conferred an extraordinary degree of force upon their personal
opposition. Men could then be found who, notwithstanding their weakness, still entertained a high opinion of their
personal value, and dared to cope single-handed with the
public authority. But at the present day, when all ranks
are more and more confounded, — when the individual disappears in the throng, and is easily lost in the midst of
a common obscurity, when the honor of monarchy has
almost lost its power, without being succeeded by virtue,

and when nothing can enable man to rise above himself, — who shall say at what point the exigencies of power and the servility of weakness will stop ?

As long as family feeling was kept alive, the antagonist of oppression was never alone ; he looked about him, and found his clients, his hereditary friends, and his kinsfolk. If this support was wanting, he felt himself sustained by his ancestors, and animated by his posterity. But when patrimonial estates are divided, and when a few years suffice to confound the distinctions of race, where can family feeling be found ?   What force can there be in the customs of a country which has changed, and is still perpetually changing, its aspect, — in which every act of tyranny already has a precedent, and every crime an example, — in which there is nothing so old that its antiquity can save it from destruction, and nothing so unparalleled that its novelty can prevent it from being done?   What resistance can be offered by manners of so pliant a make that they have already often yielded ?   What strength can even public opinion have retained, when no twenty persons are connected by a common tie, — when not a man, nor a family, nor chartered corporation, nor class, nor free institution, has the power of representing or exerting that opinion, and when every citizen, being equally weak, equally poor, and equally isolated, has only his personal impotence to oppose to the organized force of the government?

The annals of France furnish nothing analogous to the condition in which that country might then be thrown. But it may more aptly be assimilated to the times of old, and to those hideous eras of Roman oppression, when the manners of the people were corrupted, their traditions obliterated, their habits destroyed, their opinions shaken, and freedom, expelled from the laws, could find no refuge in the land ; when nothing protected the citizens, and the citizens no longer protected themselves ; when human nature was the sport of man, and princes wearied out the clemency of Heaven before they exhausted the patience of their subjects. Those who hope to revive the monarchy of Henry IV. or of Louis XIV. appear to me to be afflicted with mental blindness; and when I consider the present condition of several European nations,—a condition to which all the others tend,—I am led to believe that they will soon be left with no other alternative than democratic liberty or the tyranny of the Cæsars.

Is not this deserving of consideration? If men must really come to this point, that they are to be entirely emancipated or entirely enslaved,—all their rights to be made equal, or all to be taken away from them; if the rulers of society were compelled either gradually to raise the crowd to their own level, or to allow all the citizens to fall below that of humanity,—would not the doubts of many be resolved, the consciences of many be confirmed, and the community prepared to make great sacrifices with little difficulty? In that case, the gradual growth of democratic manners and institutions should be regarded, not as the best, but as the only means of preserving freedom; and, without liking the government of democracy, it might be adopted as the most applicable, and the fairest remedy for the present ills of society.

It is difficult to make the people participate in the government; but it is still more difficult to supply them with experience, and to inspire them with the feelings which they need in order to govern well. I grant that the wishes of the democracy are capricious, its instruments rude, its laws imperfect. But, if it were true that soon no just medium would exist between the rule of democracy and the dominion of a single man, should we not rather incline towards the former, than submit voluntarily to the latter? And if complete equality be our fate, is it not better to be levelled by free institutions than by a despot?

Those who, after having read this book, should imagine that my intention in writing it was to propose the laws and manners of the Anglo-Americans for the imitation of all democratic communities, would make a great mistake; they must have paid more attention to the form than to the substance of my thought. My aim has been to show, by the example of America, that laws, and especially manners, may allow a democratic people to remain free. But I am very far from thinking that we ought to follow the example of the American democracy, and copy the means which it has employed to attain this end; for I am well aware of the influence which the nature of a country and its political antecedents exercise upon its political constitution; and I should regard it as a great misfortune for mankind if liberty were to exist all over the world under the same features.

But I am of opinion that, if we do not succeed in gradually introducing democratic institutions into France; if we despair of imparting to all the citizens those ideas and sentiments which first prepare them for freedom, and afterwards allow them to enjoy it, — there will be no independence at all, either for the middling classes or the nobility, for the poor or for the rich, but an equal tyranny over all; and I foresee that, if the peaceable dominion of the majority be not founded amongst us in time, we shall sooner or later fall under the unlimited authority of a single man.

CHAPTER XVIII.

THE PRESENT AND PROBABLE FUTURE CONDITION OF THE
THREE RACES WHICH INHABIT THE TERRITORY OF THE
UNITED STATES.

THE principal task which I had imposed upon myself
is now performed: I have shown, as far as I was able,
the laws and the manners of the American democracy.
Here I might stop; but the reader would perhaps feel that
I had not satisfied his expectations.

An absolute and immense democracy is not all that we
find in America; the inhabitants of the New World may
be considered from more than one point of view. In the
course of this work, my subject has often led me to speak
of the Indians and the Negroes; but I have never had time
to stop in order to show what place these two races occupy
in the midst of the democratic people whom I was engaged
in describing. I have shown in what spirit and according
to what laws the Anglo-American Union was formed; but
I could give only a hurried and imperfect glance at the
dangers which menace that confederation, and could not
furnish a detailed account of its chances of duration independently of its laws and manners. When speaking
of the united republics, I hazarded no conjectures upon
the permanence of republican forms in the New World;
and when making frequent allusion to the commercial
activity which reigns in the Union, I was unable to inquire into the future of the Americans as a commercial
people.

These topics are collaterally connected with my subject without forming a part of it; they are American, without being democratic; and to portray democracy has been my principal aim. It was therefore necessary to postpone these questions, which I now take up as the proper termination of my work.

The territory now occupied or claimed by the American Union spreads from the shores of the Atlantic to those of the Pacific Ocean. On the east and west, its limits are those of the continent itself. On the south, it advances nearly to the Tropics, and it extends upward to the icy regions of the North.

The human beings who are scattered over this space do not form, as in Europe, so many branches of the same stock. Three races, naturally distinct, and, I might almost say, hostile to each other, are discoverable amongst them at the first glance. Almost insurmountable barriers had been raised between them by education and law, as well as by their origin and outward characteristics; but fortune has brought them together on the same soil, where, although they are mixed, they do not amalgamate, and each race fulfils its destiny apart.

Amongst these widely differing families of men, the first which attracts attention — the superior in intelligence, in power, and in enjoyment — is the White, or European, the MAN pre-eminently so called; below him appear the Negro and the Indian. These two unhappy races have nothing in common, neither birth, nor features, nor language, nor habits. Their only resemblance lies in their misfortunes. Both of them occupy an equally inferior position in the country they inhabit; both suffer from tyranny; and if their wrongs are not the same, they originate from the same authors.

If we reasoned from what passes in the world, we should

almost say that the European is to the other races of mankind what man himself is to the lower animals : he makes
them subservient to his use, and when he cannot subdue,
he destroys them.   Oppression has, at one stroke, deprived
the descendants of the Africans of almost all the privileges
of humanity.   The Negro of the United States has lost
even the remembrance of his country ; the language which
his forefathers spoke is never heard around him ; he ab-
jured their religion and forgot their customs when he
ceased to belong to Africa, without acquiring any claim
to European privileges.   But he remains half-way between
the two communities, isolated between two races ; sold by
the one, repulsed by the other ; finding not a spot in the
universe to call by the name of country, except the faint
image of a home which the shelter of his master's roof
affords.

The Negro has no family : woman is merely the temporary companion of his pleasures, and his children are on
an equality with himself from the moment of their birth.
Am I to call it a proof of God's mercy, or a visitation of
his wrath, that man, in certain states, appears to be insensible to his extreme wretchedness, and almost obtains a
depraved taste for the cause of his misfortunes ?   The
Negro, plunged in this abyss of evils, scarcely feels his
own calamitous situation.   Violence made him a slave,
and the habit of servitude gives him the thoughts and
desires of a slave ; he admires his tyrants more than he
hates them, and finds his joy and his pride in the servile
imitation of those who oppress him.   His understanding
is degraded to the level of his soul.

The Negro enters upon slavery as soon as he is born ;
nay, he may have been purchased in the womb, and have
begun his slavery before he began his existence.   Equally
devoid of wants and of enjoyment, and useless to himself,
he learns, with his first notions of existence, that he is the

property of another, who has an interest in preserving his life, and that the care of it does not devolve upon himself; even the power of thought appears to him a useless gift of Providence, and he quietly enjoys all the privileges of his debasement.

If he becomes free, independence is often felt by him to be a heavier burden than slavery; for, having learned, in the course of his life, to submit to everything except reason, he is too unacquainted with her dictates to obey them. A thousand new desires beset him, and he has not the knowledge and energy necessary to resist them: these are masters which it is necessary to contend with, and he has learnt only to submit and obey. In short, he is sunk to such a depth of wretchedness, that, while servitude brutalizes, liberty destroys him.

Oppression has been no less fatal to the Indian than to the Negro race, but its effects are different. Before the arrival of white men in the New World, the inhabitants of North America lived quietly in their woods, enduring the vicissitudes and practising the virtues and vices common to savage nations. The Europeans, having dispersed the Indian tribes and driven them into the deserts, condemned them to a wandering life, full of inexpressible sufferings.

Savage nations are only controlled by opinion and custom. When the North American Indians had lost the sentiment of attachment to their country; when their families were dispersed, their traditions obscured, and the chain of their recollections broken; when all their habits were changed, and their wants increased beyond measure, — European tyranny rendered them more disorderly and less civilized than they were before. The moral and physical condition of these tribes continually grew worse, and they became more barbarous as they became more wretched. Nevertheless, the Europeans have not been able to change the character of the Indians; and, though they have had power to destroy, they have never been able to subdue and civilize them.

The lot of the Negro is placed on the extreme limit of servitude, while that of the Indian lies on the uttermost verge of liberty; and slavery does not produce more fatal effects upon the first, than independence upon the second. The Negro has lost all property in his own person, and he cannot dispose of his existence without committing a sort of fraud. But the savage is his own master as soon as he is able to act; parental authority is scarcely known to him; he has never bent his will to that of any of his kind, nor learned the difference between voluntary obedience and a shameful subjection; and the very name of law is unknown to him. To be free, with him, signifies to escape from all the shackles of society. As he delights in this barbarous independence, and would rather perish than sacrifice the least part of it, civilization has little hold over him.

The Negro makes a thousand fruitless efforts to insinuate himself amongst men who repulse him; he conforms to the tastes of his oppressors, adopts their opinions, and hopes by imitating them to form a part of their community. Having been told from infancy that his race is naturally inferior to that of the whites, he assents to the proposition, and is ashamed of his own nature. In each of his features he discovers a trace of slavery, and, if it were in his power, he would willingly rid himself of everything that makes him what he is.

The Indian, on the contrary, has his imagination inflated with the pretended nobility of his origin, and lives and dies in the midst of these dreams of pride. Far from desiring to conform his habits to ours, he loves his savage life as the distinguishing mark of his race, and repels every advance to civilization, less, perhaps, from hatred of it, than from a dread of resembling the Europeans.* While he has nothing to oppose to our perfection in the arts but the resources of the desert, to our tactics nothing but undisciplined courage,   whilst our well-digested plans are met only by the spontaneous instincts of savage life, — who can wonder if he fails in this unequal contest?

The Negro, who earnestly desires to mingle his race with that of the European, cannot do so; while the Indian, who might succeed to a certain extent, disdains to make the attempt. The servility of the one dooms him to slavery, the pride of the other to death.

I remember that, while I was travelling through the forests which still cover the State of Alabama, I arrived

---

* The native of North America retains his opinions and the most insignificant of his habits with a degree of tenacity which has no parallel in history. For more than two hundred years, the wandering tribes of North America have had daily intercourse with the whites, and they have never derived from them a custom or an idea. Yet the Europeans have exercised a powerful influence over the savages: they have made them more licentious, but not more European. In the summer of 1831, I happened to be beyond Lake Michigan, at a place called Green-Bay, which serves as the extreme frontier between the United States and the Indians of the Northwest. Here I became acquainted with an American officer, Major H., who, after talking to me at length about the inflexibility of the Indian character, related the following fact: "I formerly knew a young Indian," said he, "who had been educated at a college in New England, where he had greatly distinguished himself, and had acquired the external appearance of a civilized man. When the war broke out between ourselves and the English in 1812, I saw this young man again; he was serving in our army, at the head of the warriors of his tribe; for the Indians were admitted amongst the ranks of the Americans, on condition only that they would abstain from their horrible custom of scalping their victims. On the evening of the battle of * * *, C. came, and sat himself down by the fire of our bivouac. I asked him what had been his fortune that day: he related his exploits; and growing warm and animated by the recollection of them, he concluded by suddenly opening the breast of his coat, saying, 'You must not betray me: — see here!' And I actually beheld," said the Major, "between his body and his shirt, the skin and hair of an English head, still dripping with blood."

one day at the log-house of a pioneer. I did not wish to
penetrate into the dwelling of the American, but retired
to rest myself for a while on the margin of a spring, which
was not far off, in the woods. While I was in this place,
(which was in the neighborhood of the Creek territory,)
an Indian woman appeared, followed by a Negress, and
holding by the hand a little white girl of five or six years
old, whom I took to be the daughter of the pioneer. A
sort of barbarous luxury set off the costume of the Indian;
rings of metal were hanging from her nostrils and ears;
her hair, which was adorned with glass beads, fell loosely
upon her shoulders; and I saw that she was not married,
for she still wore that necklace of shells which the bride
always deposits on the nuptial couch. The Negress was
clad in squalid European garments. All three came and
seated themselves upon the banks of the fountain; and the
young Indian, taking the child in her arms, lavished upon
her such fond caresses as mothers give; while the Negress
endeavored, by various little artifices, to attract the attention of the young Creole. The child displayed in her
slightest gestures a consciousness of superiority which
formed a strange contrast with her infantine weakness;
as if she received the attentions of her companions with
a sort of condescension. The Negress was seated on the
ground before her mistress, watching her smallest desires,
and apparently divided between an almost maternal affection for the child and servile fear; whilst the savage displayed, in the midst of her tenderness, an air of freedom
and pride which was almost ferocious. I had approached
the group, and was contemplating them in silence; but
my curiosity was probably displeasing to the Indian woman, for she suddenly rose, pushed the child roughly
from her, and, giving me an angry look, plunged into the
thicket.

I had often chanced to see individuals together in the

same place, who belonged to the three races which people North America. I had perceived from many different traits the preponderance of the whites. But in the picture which I have just been describing, there was something peculiarly touching; a bond of affection here united the oppressors with the oppressed, and the effort of Nature to bring them together rendered still more striking the immense distance placed between them by prejudice and the laws.

THE PRESENT AND PROBABLE FUTURE CONDITION OF THE INDIAN TRIBES WHICH INHABIT THE TERRITORY POSSESSED BY THE UNION.

Gradual Disappearance of the Native Tribes. — Manner in which it takes place. — Miseries accompanying the forced Migrations of the Indians. — The Savages of North America had only two Ways of escaping Destruction, War or Civilization. — They are no longer able to make War. — Reasons why they refused to become Civilized when it was in their Power, and why they cannot become so now that they desire it. — Instance of the Creeks and Cherokees. — Policy of the particular States towards these Indians. — Policy of the Federal Government.

NONE of the Indian tribes which formerly inhabited the territory of New England — the Narragansetts, the Mohicans, the Pequods — have any existence but in the recollection of man. The Lenapes, who received William Penn, a hundred and fifty years ago, upon the banks of the Delaware, have disappeared; and I myself met with the last of the Iroquois, who were begging alms. The nations I have mentioned formerly covered the country to the sea-coast; but a traveller at the present day must penetrate more than a hundred leagues into the interior of the continent to find an Indian. Not only have these wild tribes receded, but they are destroyed;* and as they

* In the thirteen original States, there are only 6,273 Indians remaining.

give way or perish, an immense and increasing people fill
their place.   There is no instance upon record of so prodigious a growth or so rapid a destruction : the manner
in which the latter change takes place is not difficult to
describe.

When the Indians were the sole inhabitants of the wilds
whence they have since been expelled, their wants were
few.   Their arms were of their own manufacture, their
only drink was the water of the brook, and their clothes
consisted of the skins of animals, whose flesh furnished
them with food.

The Europeans introduced amongst the savages of North
America fire-arms, ardent spirits, and iron : they taught
them to exchange for manufactured stuffs the rough garments which had previously satisfied their untutored simplicity.   Having acquired new tastes, without the arts
by which they could be gratified, the Indians were obliged
to have recourse to the workmanship of the whites ; but
in return for their productions, the savage had nothing to
offer except the rich furs which still abounded in his woods.
Hence the chase became necessary, not merely to provide
for his subsistence, but to satisfy the frivolous desires of
Europeans.   He no longer hunted merely to obtain food,
but to procure the only objects of barter which he could
offer.*   Whilst the wants of the natives were thus increasing, their resources continued to diminish.

* Messrs. Clarke and Cass, in their report to Congress, the 4th of February, 1829, p. 23, remarked : "The time when the Indians generally could
supply themselves with food and clothing, without any of the articles of civilized life, has long since passed away.   The more remote tribes, beyond the
Mississippi, who live where immense herds of buffalo are yet to be found,
and who follow those animals in their periodical migrations, could more
easily than any others recur to the habits of their ancestors, and live without the white man or any of his manufactures.   But the buffalo is constantly
receding.   The smaller animals — the bear, the deer, the beaver, the otter,
the musk-rat, etc. — principally minister to the comfort and support of the

From the moment when a European settlement is formed in the neighborhood of the territory occupied by the Indians, the beasts of chase take the alarm.* Thousands of savages, wandering in the forests, and destitute of any fixed dwelling, did not disturb them; but as soon as the continuous sounds of European labor are heard in their neighborhood, they begin to flee away, and retire to the West, where their instinct teaches them that they will still find deserts of immeasurable extent. "The buffalo is constantly receding," say Messrs. Clarke and Cass in their Report of the year 1829; "a few years since they approached the base of the Alleghany; and a few years hence they may even be rare upon the immense plains which extend to the base of the Rocky Mountains." I have been assured that this effect of the approach of the whites is often felt at two hundred leagues' distance from their frontier. Their influence is thus exerted over tribes whose name is unknown to them; and who suffer the evils

Indians; and these cannot be taken without guns, ammunition, and traps. Among the Northwestern Indians, particularly, the labor of supplying a family with food is excessive. Day after day is spent by the hunter without success, and during this interval his family must subsist upon bark or roots, or perish. Want and misery are around them and among them. Many die every winter from actual starvation."

The Indians will not live as Europeans live; and yet they can neither subsist without them, nor exactly after the fashion of their fathers. This is demonstrated by a fact which I likewise give upon official authority. Some Indians of a tribe on the banks of Lake Superior had killed a European; the American government interdicted all traffic with the tribe to which the guilty parties belonged, until they were delivered up to justice. This measure had the desired effect.

* "Five years ago," says Volney in his *Tableau des États-Unis*, p. 370, "in going from Vincennes to Kaskaskia, a territory which now forms part of the State of Illinois, but which at the time I mention was completely wild (1797), you could not cross a prairie without seeing herds of from four to five hundred buffaloes. There are now none remaining; they swam across the Mississippi, to escape from the hunters, and more particularly from the bells of the American cows."

of usurpation long before they are acquainted with the authors of their distress.*

Bold adventurers soon penetrate into the country the Indians have deserted, and when they have advanced about fifteen or twenty leagues from the extreme frontiers of the whites, they begin to build habitations for civilized beings in the midst of the wilderness. This is done without difficulty, as the territory of a hunting nation is ill defined; it is the common property of the tribe, and belongs to no one in particular, so that individual interests are not concerned in protecting any part of it.

A few European families, occupying points very remote from each other, soon drive away the wild animals which remain between their places of abode. The Indians, who had previously lived in a sort of abundance, then find it difficult to subsist, and still more difficult to procure the articles of barter which they stand in need of. To drive away their game has the same effect as to render sterile the fields of our agriculturists; deprived of the means of subsistence, they are reduced, like famished wolves, to prowl through the forsaken woods in quest of prey. Their instinctive love of country attaches them to the soil which gave them birth,† even after it has ceased to yield anything

---

* The truth of what I here advance may be easily proved by consulting the tabular statement of Indian tribes inhabiting the United States and their territories. (Legislative Documents, 20th Congress, No. 117, pp. 90–105.) It is there shown that the tribes in the centre of America are rapidly decreasing, although the Europeans are still at a considerable distance from them.

† "The Indians," say Messrs. Clarke and Cass, in their Report to Congress, p. 15, "are attached to their country by the same feelings which bind us to ours; and, besides, there are certain superstitious notions connected with the alienation of what the Great Spirit gave to their ancestors, which operate strongly upon the tribes who have made few or no cessions, but which are gradually weakened as our intercourse with them is extended. 'We will not sell the spot which contains the bones of our fathers,' is almost always the first answer to a proposition for a sale."

but misery and death. At length, they are compelled to acquiesce and depart: they follow the traces of the elk, the buffalo, and the beaver, and are guided by these wild animals in the choice of their future country. Properly speaking, therefore, it is not the Europeans who drive away the natives of America; it is famine;—a happy distinction, which had escaped the casuists of former times, and for which we are indebted to modern discovery!

It is impossible to conceive the frightful sufferings which attend these forced migrations. They are undertaken by a people already exhausted and reduced; and the countries to which the new-comers betake themselves are inhabited by other tribes, which receive them with jealous hostility. Hunger is in the rear, war awaits them, and misery besets them on all sides. To escape from so many enemies, they separate, and each individual endeavors to procure secretly the means of supporting his existence by isolating himself, living in the immensity of the desert like an outcast in civilized society. The social tie, which distress had long since weakened, is then dissolved; they have no longer a country, and soon they will not be a people; their very families are obliterated; their common name is forgotten; their language perishes; and all traces of their origin disappear. Their nation has ceased to exist, except in the recollection of the antiquaries of America, and a few of the learned of Europe.

I should be sorry to have my reader suppose that I am coloring the picture too highly: I saw with my own eyes many of the miseries which I have just described, and was the witness of sufferings which I have not the power to portray.

At the end of the year 1831, whilst I was on the left bank of the Mississippi, at a place named by Europeans Memphis, there arrived a numerous band of Choctaws (or Chactas, as they are called by the French in Louisiana).

These savages had left their country, and were endeavoring to gain the right bank of the Mississippi, where they hoped to find an asylum which had been promised them by the American government. It was then the middle of winter, and the cold was unusually severe; the snow had frozen hard upon the ground, and the river was drifting huge masses of ice. The Indians had their families with them; and they brought in their train the wounded and the sick, with children newly born, and old men upon the verge of death. They possessed neither tents nor wagons, but only their arms and some provisions. I saw them embark to pass the mighty river, and never will that solemn spectacle fade from my remembrance. No cry, no sob, was heard amongst the assembled crowd; all were silent. Their calamities were of ancient date, and they knew them to be irremediable. The Indians had all stepped into the bark which was to carry them across, but their dogs remained upon the bank. As soon as these animals perceived that their masters were finally leaving the shore, they set up a dismal howl, and, plunging all together into the icy waters of the Mississippi, swam after the boat.

The ejectment of the Indians often takes place at the present day in a regular, and, as it were, a legal manner. When the European population begins to approach the limit of the desert inhabited by a savage tribe, the government of the United States usually sends forward envoys, who assemble the Indians in a large plain, and, having first eaten and drunk with them, address them thus: "What have you to do in the land of your fathers? Before long, you must dig up their bones in order to live. In what respect is the country you inhabit better than another? Are there no woods, marshes, or prairies, except where you dwell? And can you live nowhere but under your own sun? Beyond those mountains which you see at the horizon, beyond the lake which

bounds your territory on the west, there lie vast countries where beasts of chase are yet found in great abundance; sell us your lands, then, and go to live happily
in those solitudes." After holding this language, they
spread before the eyes of the Indians fire-arms, woollen
garments, kegs of brandy, glass necklaces, bracelets of
tinsel, ear-rings, and looking-glasses.* If, when they have
beheld all these riches, they still hesitate, it is insinuated
that they cannot refuse the required consent, and that
the government itself will not long have the power of
protecting them in their rights. What are they to do?
Half convinced and half compelled, they go to inhabit
new deserts, where the importunate whites will not let
them remain ten years in peace. In this manner do the
Americans obtain, at a very low price, whole provinces,
which the richest sovereigns of Europe could not purchase.†

* See, in the Legislative Documents of Congress (Doc. 117), the narrative of what takes place on these occasions. This curious passage is from
the formerly mentioned Report, made to Congress by Messrs. Clarke and
Cass, in February, 1829.

"The Indians," says the Report, "reach the treaty-ground poor, and almost naked. Large quantities of goods are taken there by the traders, and
are seen and examined by the Indians. The women and children become
importunate to have their wants supplied, and their influence is soon exerted
to induce a sale. Their improvidence is habitual and unconquerable. The
gratification of his immediate wants and desires is the ruling passion of an
Indian. The expectation of future advantages seldom produces much effect.
The experience of the past is lost, and the prospects of the future disregarded. It would be utterly hopeless to demand a cession of land, unless the
means were at hand of gratifying their immediate wants; and when their
condition and circumstances are fairly considered, it ought not to surprise us
that they are so anxious to relieve themselves."

† On the 19th of May, 1830, Mr. Edward Everett affirmed before the
House of Representatives, that the Americans had already acquired by *treaty*,
to the east and west of the Mississippi, 230,000,000 of acres. In 1808, the
Osages gave up 48,000,000 acres for an annual payment of 1,000 dollars.
In 1818, the Quapaws yielded up 20,000,000 acres for 4,000 dollars. They

These are great evils; and it must be added that they appear to me to be irremediable. I believe that the Indian nations of North America are doomed to perish; and that whenever the Europeans shall be established on the shores of the Pacific Ocean, that race of men will have ceased to exist.* The Indians had only the alternative of war or civilization; in other words, they must either destroy the Europeans or become their equals.

At the first settlement of the colonies, they might have found it possible, by uniting their forces, to deliver themselves from the small bodies of strangers who landed on their continent.† They several times attempted to do it,

reserved for themselves a territory of 1,000,000 acres for a hunting-ground. A solemn oath was taken that it should be respected: but before long it was invaded like the rest.

Mr. Bell, in his "Report of the Committee on Indian Affairs," February 24, 1830, has these words: "To pay an Indian tribe what their ancient hunting-grounds are worth to them after the game is fled or destroyed, as a mode of appropriating wild lands claimed by Indians, has been found more convenient, and certainly it is more agreeable to the forms of justice, as well as more merciful, than to assert the possession of them by the sword. Thus the practice of buying Indian titles is but the substitute which humanity and expediency have imposed, in place of the sword, in arriving at the actual enjoyment of property claimed by the right of discovery, and sanctioned by the natural superiority allowed to the claims of civilized communities over those of savage tribes. Up to the present time, so invariable has been the operation of certain causes, first in diminishing the value of forest lands to the Indians, and secondly, in disposing them to sell readily, that the plan of buying their right of occupancy has never threatened to retard, in any perceptible degree, the prosperity of any of the States." (Legislative Documents, 21st Congress, No. 227, p. 6).

* This seems, indeed, to be the opinion of almost all American statesmen. "Judging of the future by the past," says Mr. Cass, "we cannot err in anticipating a progressive diminution of their numbers, and their eventual extinction, unless our border should become stationary, and they be removed beyond it, or unless some radical change should take place in the principles of our intercourse with them, which it is easier to hope for than to expect."

† Amongst other warlike enterprises, there was one of the Wampanoags,

and were on the point of succeeding; but the disproportion of their resources at the present day, when compared with those of the whites, is too great to allow such an enterprise to be thought of. But from time to time among the Indians, men of sagacity and energy foresee the final destiny which awaits the native population, and exert themselves to unite all the tribes in common hostility to the Europeans; but their efforts are unavailing. The tribes which are in the neighborhood of the whites are too much weakened to offer an effectual resistance; whilst the others, giving way to that childish carelessness of the morrow which characterizes savage life, wait for the near approach of danger before they prepare to meet it: some are unable, others are unwilling, to act.

It is easy to foresee that the Indians will never civilize themselves, or that it will be too late when they may be inclined to make the experiment.

Civilization is the result of a long social process, which takes place in the same spot, and is handed down from one generation to another, each one profiting by the experience of the last. Of all nations, those submit to civilization with the most difficulty who habitually live by the chase. Pastoral tribes, indeed, often change their place of abode; but they follow a regular order in their migrations, and often return to their old stations, whilst the dwelling of the hunter varies with that of the animals he pursues.

Several attempts have been made to diffuse knowledge amongst the Indians, leaving unchecked their wandering propensities, by the Jesuits in Canada, and by the Puritans in New England;* but none of these endeavors have been

and other confederate tribes, under Metacom, in 1675, against the colonists of New England; the English were also engaged in war with them in Virginia in 1622.

* See the historians of New England, the *Histoire de la Nouvelle France*, by Charlevoix, and the work entitled *Lettres édifiantes*.

crowned by any lasting success. Civilization began in the cabin, but soon retired to expire in the woods. The great error of these legislators of the Indians was their not understanding that, in order to succeed in civilizing a people, it is first necessary to fix them, which cannot be done without inducing them to cultivate the soil; the Indians ought in the first place to have been accustomed to agriculture. But not only are they destitute of this indispensable preliminary to civilization, — they would even have great difficulty in acquiring it. Men who have once abandoned themselves to the restless and adventurous life of the hunter feel an insurmountable disgust for the constant and regular labor which tillage requires. We see this proved even in our own societies; but it is far more visible among races whose partiality for the chase is a part of their national character.

Independently of this general difficulty, there is another, which applies peculiarly to the Indians. They consider labor not merely as an evil, but as a disgrace; so that their pride contends against civilization as obstinately as their indolence.*

There is no Indian so wretched as not to retain under his hut of bark a lofty idea of his personal worth; he considers the cares of industry as degrading occupations; he compares the husbandman to the ox which traces the furrow; and in each of our handicrafts, he can see only the labor of slaves. Not that he is devoid of admiration for the power and intellectual greatness of the whites; but, although the result of our efforts surprises him, he con-

---

* "In all the tribes," says Volney, in his *Tableau des États-Unis*, (p. 423,) "there still exists a generation of old warriors, who cannot forbear, when they see their countrymen using the hoe, from exclaiming against the degradation of ancient manners, and asserting that the savages owe their decline to these innovations; adding, that they have only to return to their primitive habits, in order to recover their power and glory."

temns the means by which we obtain it; and while he acknowledges our ascendency, he still believes in his own superiority. War and hunting are the only pursuits which appear to him worthy of a man.* The Indian, in the dreary solitudes of his woods, cherishes the same ideas, the same opinions, as the noble of the Middle Ages in his castle; and he only needs to become a conqueror to complete the resemblance. Thus, however strange it may seem, it is in the forests of the New World, and not amongst the Europeans who people its coasts, that the ancient prejudices of Europe still exist.

More than once, in the course of this work, I have endeavored to explain the prodigious influence which the social condition appears to exercise upon the laws and the manners of men; and I beg to add a few words on the same subject.

When I perceive the resemblance which exists between the political institutions of our ancestors, the Germans, and the wandering tribes of North America, — between the customs described by Tacitus, and those of which I have sometimes been a witness, — I cannot help thinking that the same cause has brought about the same results in both hemispheres; and that, in the midst of the apparent

* The following description occurs in an official document: "Until a young man has been engaged with an enemy, and has performed some acts of valor, he gains no consideration, but is regarded nearly as a woman. In their great war-dances, all the warriors in succession strike the post, as it is called, and recount their exploits. On these occasions, their auditory consists of the kinsmen, friends, and comrades of the narrator. The profound impression which his discourse produces on them is manifested by the silent attention it receives, and by the loud shouts which hail its termination. The young man who finds himself at such a meeting without anything to recount is very unhappy; and instances have sometimes occurred of young warriors, whose passions had been thus inflamed, quitting the war-dance suddenly, and going off alone to seek for trophies which they might exhibit and adventures which they might be allowed to relate."

diversity of human affairs, certain primary facts may be discovered, from which all the others are derived. In what we usually call the German institutions, then, I am inclined to perceive only barbarian habits, and the opinions of savages in what we style feudal principles.

However strongly the vices and prejudices of the North American Indians may be opposed to their becoming agricultural and civilized, necessity sometimes drives them to it. Several of the Southern tribes, considerably numerous, and amongst others the Cherokees and the Creeks,* found themselves, as it were, surrounded by Europeans, who had landed on the shores of the Atlantic, and, either descending the Ohio, or proceeding up the Mississippi, arrived simultaneously upon their borders. These tribes had not been driven from place to place, like their Northern brethren; but they had been gradually shut up within narrow limits, like game driven into an enclosure before the huntsmen plunge among them. The Indians, who were thus placed between civilization and death, found themselves obliged to live ignominiously by labor, like the whites. They took to agriculture, and, without entirely forsaking their old habits or manners, sacrificed only as much as was necessary to their existence.

The Cherokees went further; they created a written

---

* These nations are now swallowed up in the States of Georgia, Tennessee, Alabama, and Mississippi. There were formerly in the South four great nations (remnants of which still exist), the Choctaws, the Chickasaws, the Creeks, and the Cherokees. The remnants of these four nations amounted in 1830 to about 75,000 individuals. It is computed that there are now remaining in the territory occupied or claimed by the Anglo-American Union about 300,000 Indians. (See "Proceedings of the Indian Board in the City of New York.") The official documents supplied to Congress make the number amount to 313,130. The reader who is curious to know the names and numerical strength of all the tribes which inhabit the Anglo-American territory should consult the documents I have just referred to. (Legislative Documents, 20th Congress, No. 117, pp. 90–105.)

language, established a permanent form of government, and, as everything proceeds rapidly in the New World, before they all of them had clothes, they set up a newspaper.*

The development of European habits has been much accelerated among these Indians by the mixed race which has sprung up.† Deriving intelligence from the father's side, without entirely losing the savage customs of the mother, the half-blood forms the natural link between civilization and barbarism. Wherever this race has multiplied, the savage state has become modified, and a great change has taken place in the manners of the people.‡

* I brought back with me to France one or two copies of this singular publication.

† See, in the Report of the Committee on Indian Affairs, 21st Congress, No. 227, p. 23, the reasons for the multiplication of Indians of mixed blood among the Cherokees. The principal cause dates from the War of Independence. Many Anglo-Americans of Georgia, having taken the side of England, were obliged to retreat among the Indians, where they married.

‡ Unhappily, the mixed race has been less numerous and less influential in North America than in any other country. The American continent was peopled by two great nations of Europe, the French and the English. The former were not slow in connecting themselves with the daughters of the natives; but there was an unfortunate affinity between the Indian character and their own: instead of giving the tastes and habits of civilized life to the savages, the French too often grew passionately fond of Indian life. They became the most dangerous inhabitants of the desert, and won the friendship of the Indian by exaggerating his vices and his virtues. M. de Senonville, the Governor of Canada, wrote thus to Louis XIV. in 1685: "It has long been believed that, in order to civilize the savages, we ought to draw them nearer to us. But there is every reason to suppose we have been mistaken. Those which have been brought into contact with us have not become French, and the French who have lived among them are changed into savages, affecting to dress and live like them." ("History of New France," by Charlevoix, Vol. II. p. 345.) The Englishman, on the contrary, continuing obstinately attached to the customs and the most insignificant habits of his forefathers, has remained in the midst of the American solitudes just what he was in the bosom of European cities; he would not allow of any communication with savages whom he despised, and avoided with care the

The success of the Cherokees proves that the Indians are capable of civilization, but it does not prove that they will succeed in it. This difficulty which the Indians find in submitting to civilization proceeds from a general cause, the influence of which it is almost impossible for them to escape. An attentive survey of history demonstrates that, in general, barbarous nations have raised themselves to civilization by degrees, and by their own efforts. Whenever they derived knowledge from a foreign people, they stood towards them in the relation of conquerors, and not of a conquered nation. When the conquered nation is enlightened, and the conquerors are half savage, as in the invasion of the Roman empire by the Northern nations, or that of China by the Mongols, the power which victory bestows upon the barbarian is sufficient to keep up his importance among civilized men, and permit him to rank as their equal until he becomes their rival. The one has might on his side, the other has intelligence ; the former admires the knowledge and the arts of the conquered, the latter envies the power of the conquerors. The barbarians at length admit civilized man into their palaces, and he in turn opens his schools to the barbarians. But when the side on which the physical force lies also possesses an intellectual superiority, the conquered party seldom become civilized ; it retreats, or is destroyed. It may therefore be said, in a general way, that savages go forth in arms to seek knowledge, but do not receive it when it comes to them.

If the Indian tribes which now inhabit the heart of the continent could summon up energy enough to attempt to civilize themselves, they might possibly succeed. Superior already to the barbarous nations which surround them,

union of his race with theirs. Thus, while the French exercised no salutary influence over the Indians, the English have always remained alien from them.

they would gradually gain strength and experience, and when the Europeans should appear upon their borders, they would be in a state, if not to maintain their independence, at least to assert their right to the soil, and to incorporate themselves with the conquerors. But it is the misfortune of Indians to be brought into contact with a civilized people, who are also (it must be owned) the most grasping nation on the globe, whilst they are still semi-barbarian ; to find their masters in their instructors, and to receive knowledge and oppression at once. Living in the freedom of the woods, the North American Indian was destitute, but he had no feeling of inferiority towards any one ; as soon, however, as he desires to penetrate into the social scale of the whites, he can only take the lowest rank in society, for he enters, ignorant and poor, within the pale of science and wealth. After having led a life of agitation, beset with evils and dangers, but at the same time filled with proud emotions,* he is obliged to submit

* There is in the adventurous life of the hunter a certain irresistible charm, which seizes the heart of man, and carries him away in spite of reason and experience. This is plainly shown by the " Memoirs of Tanner." Tanner was a European who was carried away at the age of six by the Indians, and remained thirty years with them in the woods. Nothing can be conceived more appalling than the miseries which he describes. He tells us of tribes without a chief, families without a nation to call their own, men in a state of isolation, wrecks of powerful tribes wandering at random amid the ice and snow and desolate solitudes of Canada. Hunger and cold pursue them ; every day their life is in jeopardy. Amongst these men, manners have lost their empire, traditions are without power. They become more and more savage. Tanner shared in all these miseries ; he was aware of his European origin ; he was not kept away from the whites by force ; on the contrary, he came every year to trade with them, entered their dwellings, and witnessed their enjoyments ; he knew that whenever he chose to return to civilized life, he was perfectly able to do so, — and he remained thirty years in the deserts. When he came into civilized society, he declared that the rude existence, the miseries of which he described, had a secret charm for him which he could not define : he returned to it again and again ; at length he abandoned it with poignant regret ; and when he was at length fixed

to a wearisome, obscure, and degraded state.   To gain the bread which nourishes him by hard and ignoble labor, — this is in his eyes the only result of which civilization can boast ; and even this he is not always sure to obtain.

When the Indians undertake to imitate their European neighbors, and to till the earth like them, they are immediately exposed to a formidable competition.   The white man is skilled in the craft of agriculture ; the Indian is a rough beginner in an art with which he is unacquainted. The former reaps abundant crops without difficulty, the latter meets with a thousand obstacles in raising the fruits of the earth.

The European is placed amongst a population whose wants he knows and partakes.   The savage is isolated in the midst of a hostile people, with whose manners, language, and laws he is imperfectly acquainted, but without whose assistance he cannot live.   He can only procure the materials of comfort by bartering his commodities for the goods of the European, for the assistance of his countrymen is wholly insufficient to supply his wants.   Thus, when the Indian wishes to sell the produce of his labor, he cannot always find a purchaser, whilst the European readily obtains a market ; the former can only produce at considerable cost what the latter sells at a low rate.   Thus the Indian has no sooner escaped those evils to which barbarous nations are exposed, than he is subjected to the still greater miseries of civilized communities ; and he finds it scarcely less difficult to live in the midst of our abundance, than in the depth of his own forest.

among the whites, several of his children refused to share his tranquil and easy situation.   I saw Tanner myself at the lower end of Lake Superior : he seemed to me more like a savage than a civilized being.   His book is written without either taste or order ; but he gives, even unconsciously, a lively picture of the prejudices, the passions, the vices, and, above all, the destitution, in the midst of which he lived.

He has not yet lost the habits of his erratic life; the traditions of his fathers and his passion for the chase are still alive within him. The wild enjoyments which formerly animated him in the woods painfully excite his troubled imagination; the privations which he endured there appear less keen, his former perils less appalling. He contrasts the independence which he possessed amongst his equals with the servile position which he occupies in civilized society. On the other hand, the solitudes which were so long his free home are still at hand; a few hours' march will bring him back to them once more. The whites offer him a sum, which seems to him considerable, for the half-cleared ground whence he obtains sustenance with difficulty. This money of the Europeans may possibly enable him to live a happy and tranquil life far away from them; and he quits the plough, resumes his native arms, and returns to the wilderness forever.* The condition of

* This destructive influence of highly civilized nations upon others which are less so, has been observed among the Europeans themselves. About a century ago, the French founded the town of Vincennes upon the Wabash, in the middle of the desert; and they lived there in great plenty, until the arrival of the American settlers, who first ruined the previous inhabitants by their competition, and afterwards purchased their lands at a very low rate. At the time when M. de Volney, from whom I borrow these details, passed through Vincennes, the number of the French was reduced to a hundred individuals, most of whom were about to migrate to Louisiana or to Canada. These French settlers were worthy people, but idle and uninstructed: they had contracted many of the habits of savages. The Americans, who were perhaps their inferiors in a moral point of view, were immeasurably superior to them in intelligence: they were industrious, well informed, rich, and accustomed to govern their own community.

I myself saw in Canada, where the intellectual difference between the two races is less striking, that the English are the masters of commerce and manufacture in the Canadian country, that they spread on all sides, and confine the French within limits which scarcely suffice to contain them. In like manner, in Louisiana, almost all activity in commerce and manufacture centres in the hands of the Anglo-Americans.

But the case of Texas is still more striking: the State of Texas is a part

the Creeks and Cherokees, to which I have already alluded, sufficiently corroborates the truth of this sad picture.

The Indians, in the little which they have done, have unquestionably displayed as much natural genius as the peoples of Europe in their greatest undertakings; but nations as well as men require time to learn, whatever may be their intelligence and their zeal. Whilst the savages were endeavoring to civilize themselves, the Europeans continued to surround them on every side, and to confine them within narrower limits; the two races gradually met, and they are now in immediate contact with each other. The Indian is already superior to his barbarous parent, but he is still far below his white neighbor. With their resources and acquired knowledge, the Europeans soon appropriated to themselves most of the advantages which the natives might have derived from the possession of the soil: they have settled among them, have purchased land at a low rate, or have occupied it by force, and the Indians have been ruined by a competition which they had not the means of sustaining. They were isolated in their own country, and their race only constituted a little colony of troublesome strangers in the midst of a numerous and dominant people.*

of Mexico, and is upon the frontier between that country and the United States. In the course of the last few years, the Anglo-Americans have penetrated into this province, which is still thinly peopled; they purchase land, they produce the commodities of the country, and supplant the original population. It may easily be foreseen, that, if Mexico takes no steps to check this change, the province of Texas will very shortly cease to belong to that government.

If the different degrees — comparatively slight — which exist in European civilization produce results of such magnitude, it is easy to understand what must happen when the most perfect European civilization comes in contact with Indian barbarism.

* See in the Legislative Documents (21st Congress, No. 89) instances of excesses of every kind committed by the whites upon the territory of the Indians, either in taking possession of a part of their lands, until compelled

Washington said, in one of his messages to Congress, "We are more enlightened and more powerful than the Indian nations; we are therefore bound in honor to treat them with kindness, and even with generosity." But this virtuous and high-minded policy has not been followed. The rapacity of the settlers is usually backed by the tyranny of the government. Although the Cherokees and the Creeks are established upon territory which they inhabited before the arrival of the Europeans, and although the Americans have frequently treated with them as with foreign nations, the surrounding States have not been willing to acknowledge them as an independent people, and have undertaken to subject these children of the woods to Anglo-American magistrates, laws, and customs.* Destitution had driven these unfortunate Indians to civilization, and oppression now drives them back to barbarism: many

to retire by the troops of Congress, or carrying off their cattle, burning their houses, cutting down their corn, and doing violence to their persons.

The Union has a representative agent continually employed to reside among the Indians; and the report of the Cherokee agent, which is among the documents I have referred to, is almost always favorable to the Indians. "The intrusion of whites," he says, "upon the lands of the Cherokees will cause ruin to the poor, helpless, and inoffensive inhabitants." And he further remarks upon the attempt of the State of Georgia to establish a boundary line for the country of the Cherokees, that the line, having been made by the whites alone, and entirely upon *ex parte* evidence of their several rights, was of no validity whatever.

* In 1829, the State of Alabama divided the Creek territory into counties, and subjected the Indian population to European magistrates.

In 1830, the State of Mississippi assimilated the Choctaws and Chickasaws to the white population, and declared that any of them who should take the title of chief should be punished by a fine of 1,000 dollars and a year's imprisonment. When these laws were announced to the Choctaws, who inhabited that district, the tribe assembled, their chief communicated to them the intentions of the whites, and read to them some of the laws to which it was intended that they should submit; and they unanimously declared that it was better at once to retreat again into the wilds.

of them abandon the soil which they had begun to clear, and return to the habits of savage life.

If we consider the tyrannical measures which have been adopted by the legislatures of the Southern States, the conduct of their Governors, and the decrees of their courts of justice, we shall be convinced that the entire expulsion of the Indians is the final result to which all the efforts of their policy are directed. The Americans of that part of the Union look with jealousy upon the lands which the natives still possess;* they are aware that these tribes have not yet lost the traditions of savage life, and before civilization has permanently fixed them to the soil, it is intended to force them to depart by reducing them to despair. The Creeks and Cherokees, oppressed by the several States, have appealed to the central government, which is by no means insensible to their misfortunes, and is sincerely desirous of saving the remnant of the natives, and of maintaining them in the free possession of that territory which the Union has guaranteed to them.† But the several States oppose so formidable a resistance to the execution of this design, that the government is obliged to consent to the extirpation of a few barbarous tribes, already half destroyed, in order not to endanger the safety of the American Union.

But the Federal government, which is not able to protect the Indians, would fain mitigate the hardships of their lot; and, with this intention, it has undertaken to transport them into remote regions at the public cost.

---

* The Georgians, who are so much troubled by the proximity of the Indians, inhabit a territory which does not at present contain more than seven inhabitants to the square mile. In France, there are one hundred and sixty-two inhabitants to the same extent of country.

† In 1818, Congress appointed commissioners to visit the Arkansas territory, accompanied by a deputation of Creeks, Choctaws, and Chickasaws. This expedition was commanded by Messrs. Kennerly, M'Coy, Wash Hood, and John Bell. See the different Reports of the Commissioners, and their journal, in the Documents of Congress, No. 87, House of Representatives.

Between the 33d and 37th degrees of north latitude, a vast tract of country lies, which has taken the name of Arkansas, from the principal river that waters it. It is bounded on the one side by the confines of Mexico, on the other by the Mississippi. Numberless streams cross it in every direction; the climate is mild, and the soil productive, and it is inhabited only by a few wandering hordes of savages. The government of the Union wishes to transport the broken remnants of the indigenous population of the South to the portion of this country which is nearest to Mexico, and at a great distance from the American settlements.

We were assured, towards the end of the year 1831, that 10,000 Indians had already gone to the shores of the Arkansas, and fresh detachments were constantly following them. But Congress has been unable to create a unanimous determination in those whom it is disposed to protect. Some, indeed, joyfully consent to quit the seat of oppression; but the most enlightened members of the community refuse to abandon their recent dwellings and their springing crops; they are of opinion that the work of civilization, once interrupted, will never be resumed; they fear that those domestic habits which have been so recently contracted may be irrevocably lost in the midst of a country which is still barbarous, and where nothing is prepared for the subsistence of an agricultural people; they know that their entrance into those wilds will be opposed by hostile hordes, and that they have lost the energy of barbarians, without having yet acquired the resources of civilization to resist their attacks. Moreover, the Indians readily discover that the settlement which is proposed to them is merely temporary. Who can assure them that they will at length be allowed to dwell in peace in their new retreat? The United States pledge themselves to maintain them there; but the territory which they now occupy was formerly secured to them by the most solemn oaths.* The American government does not indeed now rob them of their lands, but it allows perpetual encroachments on them. In a few years, the same white population which now flocks around them will doubtless track them anew to the solitudes of the Arkansas; they will then be exposed to the same evils, without the same remedies; and as the limits of the earth will at last fail them, their only refuge is the grave.

The Union treats the Indians with less cupidity and violence than the several States, but the two governments are alike deficient in good faith. The States extend what they call the benefits of their laws to the Indians, believing that the tribes will recede rather than submit to them; and the central government, which promises a permanent refuge to these unhappy beings in the West, is well aware of its inability to secure it to them.† Thus the tyranny

* The fifth article of the treaty made with the Creeks in August, 1790, is in the following words: "The United States solemnly guarantee to the Creek nation all their land within the limits of the United States."

The seventh article of the treaty concluded in 1791 with the Cherokees says: "The United States solemnly guarantee to the Cherokee nation all their lands not hereby ceded." The following article declared that, if any citizen of the United States, or other settler not of the Indian race, should establish himself upon the territory of the Cherokees, the United States would withdraw their protection from that individual, and give him up to be punished as the Cherokee nation should think fit.

† This does not prevent them from promising in the most solemn manner to do so. See the letter of the President addressed to the Creek Indians, 23d March, 1829. "Beyond the great river Mississippi, where a part of your nation has gone, your father has provided a country large enough for all of you, and he advises you to remove to it. There your white brothers will not trouble you; they will have no claim to the land, and you can live upon it, you and all your children, as long as the grass grows, or the water runs, in peace and plenty. *It will be yours forever.*"

The Secretary of War, in a letter written to the Cherokees, April 18th, 1829, declares to them that they cannot expect to retain possession of the

of the States obliges the savages to retire; the Union, by its promises and resources, facilitates their retreat; and these measures tend to precisely the same end.*

"By the will of our Father in Heaven, the Governor of the whole world," said the Cherokees, in their petition to Congress,† "the red man of America has become small, and the white man great and renowned. When the ancestors of the people of these United States first came to the shores of America, they found the red man strong: though he was ignorant and savage, yet he received them kindly, and gave them dry land to rest their weary feet. They met in peace, and shook hands in token of friendship. Whatever the white man wanted and asked of the Indian, the latter willingly gave. At that time, the Indian was the lord, and the white man the suppliant. But now the scene has changed. The strength of the red man has become weakness. As his neighbors increased in numbers, his power became less and less; and now, of the many and powerful tribes who once covered these United States, only a few are to be seen, — a few whom a sweeping pestilence has left. The Northern tribes, who were once so numerous and powerful, are now nearly extinct. Thus it has happened to

lands at that time occupied by them, but gives them the most positive assurance of uninterrupted peace if they would remove beyond the Mississippi: as if the power which could not grant them protection then, would be able to afford it them hereafter!

* To obtain a correct idea of the policy pursued by the several States and the Union with respect to the Indians, it is necessary to consult, — 1st. "The Laws of the Colonial and State Governments relating to the Indian Inhabitants." (See the Legislative Documents, 21st Congress, No. 319.) 2d. "The Laws of the Union on the same subject, and especially that of March 30th, 1802." (See Story's "Laws of the United States.") 3d. "The Report of Mr. Cass, Secretary of War, relative to Indian Affairs, November 29th, 1823."

† December 18th, 1829.

the red man of America. Shall we, who are remnants, share the same fate?

"The land on which we stand we have received as an inheritance from our fathers, who possessed it from time immemorial, as a gift from our common Father in Heaven. They bequeathed it to us as their children, and we have sacredly kept it, as containing the remains of our beloved men. This right of inheritance we have never ceded, nor ever forfeited. Permit us to ask, what better right can the people have to a country than the right of inheritance and immemorial peaceable possession? We know it is said of late by the State of Georgia and by the Executive of the United States, that we have forfeited this right; but we think this is said gratuitously. At what time have we made the forfeit? What great crime have we committed, whereby we must forever be divested of our country and rights? Was it when we were hostile to the United States, and took part with the king of Great Britain, during the struggle for independence? If so, why was not this forfeiture declared in the first treaty of peace between the United States and our beloved men? Why was not such an article as the following inserted in the treaty: 'The United States give peace to the Cherokees, but, for the part they took in the late war, declare them to be but tenants at will, to be removed when the convenience of the States within whose chartered limits they live shall require it'? That was the proper time to assume such a possession. But it was not thought of; nor would our forefathers have agreed to any treaty whose tendency was to deprive them of their rights and their country."

Such is the language of the Indians: what they say is true; what they foresee seems inevitable. From whichever side we consider the destinies of the aborigines of North America, their calamities appear irremediable: if they continue barbarous, they are forced to retire; if they attempt to civilize themselves, the contact of a more civilized community subjects them to oppression and destitution. They perish if they continue to wander from waste to waste, and if they attempt to settle, they still must perish. The assistance of Europeans is necessary to instruct them, but the approach of Europeans corrupts and repels them into savage life. They refuse to change their habits as long as their solitudes are their own, and it is too late to change them when at last they are constrained to submit.

The Spaniards pursued the Indians with blood-hounds, like wild beasts ; they sacked the New World like a city taken by storm, with no discernment or compassion ; but destruction must cease at last, and frenzy has a limit: the remnant of the Indian population which had escaped the massacre mixed with its conquerors, and adopted in the end their religion and their manners.* The conduct of the Americans of the United States towards the aborigines is characterized, on the other hand, by a singular attachment to the formalities of law. Provided that the Indians retain their barbarous condition, the Americans take no part in their affairs ; they treat them as independent nations, and do not possess themselves of their hunting-grounds without a treaty of purchase ; and if an Indian nation happen to be so encroached upon as to be unable to subsist upon their territory, they kindly take them by the hand and transport them to a grave far from the land of their fathers.

The Spaniards were unable to exterminate the Indian race by those unparalleled atrocities which brand them with indelible shame, nor did they even succeed in wholly

---

* The honor of this result is, however, by no means due to the Spaniards. If the Indian tribes had not been tillers of the ground at the time of the arrival of the Europeans, they would unquestionably have been destroyed in South as well as in North America.

depriving it of its rights; but the Americans of the United States have accomplished this twofold purpose with singular felicity, tranquilly, legally, philanthropically, without shedding blood, and without violating a single great principle of morality in the eyes of the world.* It is impossible to destroy men with more respect for the laws of humanity.

SITUATION OF THE BLACK POPULATION IN THE UNITED STATES, AND DANGERS WITH WHICH ITS PRESENCE THREATENS THE WHITES.

Why it is more difficult to abolish Slavery, and to efface all Vestiges of it amongst the Moderns, than it was amongst the Ancients. — In the United States, the Prejudices of the Whites against the Blacks seem to increase in Proportion as Slavery is abolished. — Situation of the Negroes in the Northern and Southern States. — Why the Americans abolish Slavery. — Servitude, which debases the Slave, impoverishes the Master. — Contrast between the left and the right Bank of the Ohio. — To what attributable. — The Black Race, as well as Slavery, recedes towards the South. — Explanation of this Fact. — Difficulties attendant upon the Abolition of Slavery in the South. — Dangers to come. — General Anxiety. — Foundation of a Black Colony in Africa. — Why the Americans of the South increase the Hardships of Slavery, whilst they are distressed at its Continuance.

THE Indians will perish in the same isolated condition in which they have lived; but the destiny of the Negroes is in some measure interwoven with that of the Europeans.

* See, amongst other documents, the Report made by Mr. Bell in the name of the Committee on Indian Affairs, February 24th, 1830, in which it is most logically established, and most learnedly proved, that "the fundamental principle, that the Indians had no right, by virtue of their ancient possession, either of soil or sovereignty, has never been abandoned either expressly or by implication."

In perusing this Report, which is evidently drawn up by a skilful hand,

These two races are fastened to each other without intermingling; and they are alike unable to separate entirely or to combine. The most formidable of all the ills which threaten the future of the Union arises from the presence of a black population upon its territory; and in contemplating the cause of the present embarrassments, or the future dangers of the United States, the observer is invariably led to this as a primary fact.

Generally speaking, men must make great and unceasing efforts before permanent evils are created; but there is one calamity which penetrated furtively into the world, and which was at first scarcely distinguishable amidst the ordinary abuses of power: it originated with an individual whose name history has not preserved; it was wafted like some accursed germ upon a portion of the soil; but it afterwards nurtured itself, grew without effort, and spread naturally with the society to which it belonged. This calamity is slavery. Christianity suppressed slavery, but the Christians of the sixteenth century re-established it, — as an exception, indeed, to their social system, and restricted to one of the races of mankind; but the wound thus inflicted upon humanity, though less extensive, was far more difficult of cure.

It is important to make an accurate distinction between slavery itself and its consequences. The immediate evils produced by slavery were very nearly the same in antiquity as they are amongst the moderns; but the consequences of these evils were different. The slave, amongst the ancients, belonged to the same race as his master, and

one is astonished at the facility with which the author gets rid of all arguments founded upon reason and natural right, which he designates as abstract and theoretical principles. The more I contemplate the difference between civilized and uncivilized man with regard to the principles of justice, the more I observe that the former contests the foundation of those rights, which the latter simply violates.

was often the superior of the two in education * and intelligence.   Freedom was the only distinction between them; and when freedom was conferred, they were easily confounded together.   The ancients, then, had a very simple means of ridding themselves of slavery and its consequences, — that of enfranchisement; and they succeeded as soon as they adopted this measure generally.   Not but that, in ancient states, the vestiges of servitude subsisted for some time after servitude itself was abolished.   There is a natural prejudice which prompts men to despise whomsoever has been their inferior long after he is become their equal; and the real inequality which is produced by fortune or by law is always succeeded by an imaginary inequality which is implanted in the manners of the people.   But, among the ancients, this secondary consequence of slavery had a natural limit; for the freedman bore so entire a resemblance to those born free, that it soon became impossible to distinguish him from them.

The greatest difficulty in antiquity was that of altering the law; amongst the moderns, it is that of altering the manners; and, as far as we are concerned, the real obstacles begin where those of the ancients left off.   This arises from the circumstance that, amongst the moderns, the abstract and transient fact of slavery is fatally united with the physical and permanent fact of color.   The tradition of slavery dishonors the race, and the peculiarity of the race perpetuates the tradition of slavery.   No African has ever voluntarily emigrated to the shores of the New World, whence it follows that all the blacks who are now found there are either slaves or freedmen.   Thus the Negro transmits the eternal mark of his ignominy to all his de-

---

* It is well known that several of the most distinguished authors of antiquity, and amongst them Æsop and Terence, were, or had been, slaves. Slaves were not always taken from barbarous nations; the chances of war reduced highly civilized men to servitude.

scendants; and although the law may abolish slavery, God alone can obliterate the traces of its existence.

The modern slave differs from his master not only in his condition, but in his origin. You may set the Negro free, but you cannot make him otherwise than an alien to the European. Nor is this all; we scarcely acknowledge the common features of humanity in this stranger whom slavery has brought amongst us. His physiognomy is to our eyes hideous, his understanding weak, his tastes low; and we are almost inclined to look upon him as a being intermediate between man and the brutes.* The moderns, then, after they have abolished slavery, have three prejudices to contend against, which are less easy to attack, and far less easy to conquer, than the mere fact of servitude, — the prejudice of the master, the prejudice of the race, and the prejudice of color.

It is difficult for us, who have had the good fortune to be born amongst men like ourselves by nature, and our equals by law, to conceive the irreconcilable differences which separate the Negro from the European in America. But we may derive some faint notion of them from analogy. France was formerly a country in which numerous inequalities existed, that had been created by law. Nothing can be more fictitious than a purely legal inferiority, — nothing more contrary to the instinct of mankind than these permanent divisions established between beings evidently similar. Yet these divisions subsisted for ages; they still subsist in many places; and everywhere they have left imaginary vestiges, which time alone can efface. If it be so difficult to root out an inequality which originates solely in the law, how are those distinctions to be destroyed which seem to be based upon the immutable

---

* To induce the whites to abandon the opinion they have conceived of the moral and intellectual inferiority of their former slaves, the Negroes must change; but as long as this opinion subsists, they cannot change.

laws of Nature herself? When I remember the extreme difficulty with which aristocratic bodies, of whatever nature they may be, are commingled with the mass of the people, and the exceeding care which they take to preserve for ages the ideal boundaries of their caste inviolate, I despair of seeing an aristocracy disappear which is founded upon visible and indelible signs. Those who hope that the Europeans will ever be amalgamated with the Negroes appear to me to delude themselves: I am not led to any such conclusion by my reason, or by the evidence of facts. Hitherto, wherever the whites have been the most powerful, they have held the blacks in degradation or in slavery; wherever the Negroes have been strongest, they have destroyed the whites: this has been the only balance which has ever taken place between the two races.

I see that, in a certain portion of the territory of the United States, at the present day, the legal barrier which separated the two races is falling away, but not that which exists in the manners of the country; slavery recedes, but the prejudice to which it has given birth is immovable. Whoever has inhabited the United States must have perceived, that, in those parts of the Union in which the Negroes are no longer slaves, they have in no wise drawn nearer to the whites. On the contrary, the prejudice of race appears to be stronger in the States which have abolished slavery, than in those where it still exists; and nowhere is it so intolerant as in those States where servitude has never been known.

It is true, that in the North of the Union marriages may be legally contracted between Negroes and whites; but public opinion would stigmatize as infamous a man who should connect himself with a Negress, and it would be difficult to cite a single instance of such a union. The electoral franchise has been conferred upon the Negroes in almost all the States in which slavery has been abolished;

but if they come forward to vote, their lives are in danger.
If oppressed, they may bring an action at law, but they
will find none but whites amongst their judges; and although they may legally serve as jurors, prejudice repels
them from that office. The same schools do not receive
the children of the black and of the European.* In the
theatres, gold cannot procure a seat for the servile race
beside their former masters; in the hospitals, they lie
apart; and although they are allowed to invoke the same
God as the whites, it must be at a different altar, and in
their own churches, with their own clergy. The gates of
Heaven are not closed against them; but their inferiority is continued to the very confines of the other world.
When the Negro dies, his bones are cast aside, and the
distinction of condition prevails even in the equality of
death.† Thus the Negro is free, but he can share neither
the rights, nor the pleasures, nor the labor, nor the afflictions, nor the tomb of him whose equal he has been declared to be; and he cannot meet him upon fair terms in
life or in death.

In the South, where slavery still exists, the Negroes are
less carefully kept apart; they sometimes share the labors
and the recreations of the whites; the whites consent to
intermix with them to a certain extent, and although legislation treats them more harshly, the habits of the people
are more tolerant and compassionate. In the South, the
master is not afraid to raise his slave to his own standing,
because he knows that he can in a moment reduce him to
the dust, at pleasure. In the North, the white no longer

---

* This is a mistake. In most of the public schools in the Northern
States, black and white children may be found side by side in the same class-
room. Blacks may also be found in many of the churches, though in separate seats. — Am. Ed.

† This is eloquent, but it is not true. Negroes are buried in the same
graveyards, and often in the same tombs, with whites. — Am. Ed.

distinctly perceives the barrier which separates him from the degraded race, and he shuns the Negro with the more pertinacity, since he fears lest they should some day be confounded together.

Amongst the Americans of the South, Nature sometimes reasserts her rights, and restores a transient equality between the blacks and the whites; but in the North, pride restrains the most imperious of human passions. The American of the Northern States would, perhaps, allow the Negress to share his licentious pleasures, if the laws of his country did not declare that she may aspire to be the legitimate partner of his bed; but he recoils with horror from her who might become his wife.

Thus it is, in the United States, that the prejudice which repels the Negroes seems to increase in proportion as they are emancipated, and inequality is sanctioned by the manners whilst it is effaced from the laws of the country. But if the relative position of the two races which inhabit the United States is such as I have described, why have the Americans abolished slavery in the North of the Union, why do they maintain it in the South, and why do they aggravate its hardships? The answer is easily given. It is not for the good of the Negroes, but for that of the whites, that measures are taken to abolish slavery in the United States.

The first Negroes were imported into Virginia about the year 1621.* In America, therefore, as well as in the rest of the globe, slavery originated in the South. Thence it spread from one settlement to another; but the number of slaves diminished towards the Northern States, and the Negro population was always very limited in New England.†

* See Beverley's History of Virginia. See also in Jefferson's Memoirs some curious details concerning the introduction of Negroes into Virginia, and the first Act which prohibited the importation of them, in 1778.

† The number of slaves was less considerable in the North, but the ad-

A century had scarcely elapsed since the foundation of the Colonies, when the attention of the planters was struck by the extraordinary fact, that the provinces which were comparatively destitute of slaves increased in population, in wealth, and in prosperity more rapidly than those which contained many of them. In the former, however, the inhabitants were obliged to cultivate the soil themselves, or by hired laborers ; in the latter, they were furnished with hands for which they paid no wages. Yet, though labor and expense were on the one side, and ease with economy on the other, the former had the more advantageous system. This result seemed the more difficult to explain, since the settlers, who all belonged to the same European race, had the same habits, the same civilization, the same laws, and their shades of difference were extremely slight.

Time, however, continued to advance ; and the Anglo-Americans, spreading beyond the coasts of the Atlantic Ocean, penetrated farther and farther into the solitudes of the West ; they met there with a new soil and an unwonted climate ; they had to overcome obstacles of the most various character ; their races intermingled, the inhabitants of the South going up towards the North, those of the North descending to the South. But in the midst of all these causes, the same result occurred at every step ;

vantages resulting from slavery were not more contested there than in the South. In 1740, the Legislature of the State of New York declared that the direct importation of slaves ought to be encouraged as much as possible, and smuggling severely punished, in order not to discourage the fair trader. (Kent's Commentaries, Vol. II. p. 206.) Curious researches, by Belknap, upon slavery in New England, are to be found in the Historical Collections of Massachusetts, Vol. IV. p. 193. It appears that Negroes were introduced there in 1630, but that the legislation and manners of the people were opposed to slavery from the first ; see also, in the same work, the manner in which public opinion, and afterwards the laws, finally put an end to slavery.

in general, the colonies in which there were no slaves became more populous and more prosperous than those in which slavery flourished. The farther they went, the more was it shown that slavery, which is so cruel to the slave, is prejudicial to the master.

But this truth was most satisfactorily demonstrated when civilization reached the banks of the Ohio. The stream which the Indians had distinguished by the name of Ohio, or the Beautiful River, waters one of the most magnificent valleys which has ever been made the abode of man. Undulating lands extend upon both shores of the Ohio, whose soil affords inexhaustible treasures to the laborer; on either bank, the air is equally wholesome and the climate mild; and each of them forms the extreme frontier of a vast State: that which follows the numerous windings of the Ohio upon the left is called Kentucky; that upon the right bears the name of the river. These two States differ only in a single respect; Kentucky has admitted slavery, but the State of Ohio has prohibited the existence of slaves within its borders.* Thus the traveller who floats down the current of the Ohio, to the spot where that river falls into the Mississippi, may be said to sail between liberty and servitude; and a transient inspection of surrounding objects will convince him which of the two is more favorable to humanity.

Upon the left bank of the stream, the population is sparse, — from time to time, one descries a troop of slaves loitering in the half-desert fields; the primeval forest reappears at every turn; society seems to be asleep, man to be idle, and nature alone offers a scene of activity and life.

From the right bank, on the contrary, a confused hum is heard, which proclaims afar the presence of industry;

* Not only is slavery prohibited in Ohio, but no free Negroes are [were] allowed to enter the territory of that State, or to hold property in it.

the fields are covered with abundant harvests; the elegance of the dwellings announces the taste and activity of the laborers; and man appears to be in the enjoyment of that wealth and contentment which is the reward of labor.*

The State of Kentucky was founded in 1775, the State of Ohio only twelve years later; but twelve years are more in America than half a century in Europe; and, at the present day, the population of Ohio exceeds that of Kentucky by two hundred and fifty thousand souls.† These different effects of slavery and freedom may readily be understood; and they suffice to explain many of the differences which we remark between the civilization of antiquity and that of our own time.

Upon the left bank of the Ohio, labor is confounded with the idea of slavery, while upon the right bank, it is identified with that of prosperity and improvement; on the one side, it is degraded, on the other, it is honored; on the former territory, no white laborers can be found, for they would be afraid of assimilating themselves to the Negroes, — all the work is done by slaves; on the latter, no one is idle, for the white population extend their activity and intelligence to every kind of employment. Thus, the men whose task it is to cultivate the rich soil of Kentucky are ignorant and apathetic; whilst those who are active and enlightened either do nothing, or pass over into Ohio, where they may work without shame.

* The activity of Ohio is not confined to individuals, but the undertakings of the State are surprisingly great: a canal has been established between Lake Erie and the Ohio, by means of which the valley of the Mississippi communicates with the river of the North, and the European commodities which arrive at New York may be forwarded by water to New Orleans across five hundred leagues of continent.

† The exact numbers given by the census of 1830 were: Kentucky, 688,844; Ohio, 937,679. [The disproportion has become vastly greater. In 1850, the population of Kentucky was 982,405; of Ohio, 1,980,329; their areas are respectively 37,680 and 39,964 square miles. — Am. Ed.]

It is true that, in Kentucky, the planters are not obliged to pay the slaves whom they employ; but they derive small profits from their labor, whilst the wages paid to free workmen would be returned with interest in the value of their services. The free workman is paid, but he does his work quicker than the slave; and rapidity of execution is one of the great elements of economy. The white sells his services, but they are only purchased when they may be useful; the black can claim no remuneration for his toil, but the expense of his maintenance is perpetual; he must be supported in his old age as well as in manhood, in his profitless infancy as well as in the productive years of youth, in sickness as well as in health. Payment must equally be made in order to obtain the services of either class of men: the free workman receives his wages in money; the slave in education, in food, in care, and in clothing. The money which a master spends in the maintenance of his slaves goes gradually and in detail, so that it is scarcely perceived; the salary of the free workman is paid in a round sum, and appears to enrich only him who receives it; but in the end, the slave has cost more than the free servant, and his labor is less productive.*

* Independently of these causes, which, wherever free workmen abound, render their labor more productive and more economical than that of slaves, another cause may be pointed out which is peculiar to the United States: the sugar-cane has hitherto been cultivated with success only upon the banks of the Mississippi, near the mouth of that river in the Gulf of Mexico. In Louisiana, the cultivation of the sugar-cane is exceedingly lucrative; nowhere does a laborer earn so much by his work; and, as there is always a certain relation between the cost of production and the value of the produce, the price of slaves is very high in Louisiana. But Louisiana is one of the confederate States, and slaves may be carried thither from all parts of the Union; the price given for slaves in New Orleans consequently raises the value of slaves in all the other markets. The consequence of this is, that, in the countries where the land is less productive, the cost of slave-labor is still very considerable, which gives an additional advantage to the competition of free labor.

The influence of slavery extends still fur
the character of the master, and imports
dency to his ideas and tastes. ' Upon bot
Ohio, the character of the inhabitants is enterprising and
energetic; but this vigor is very differently exercised in
the two States. The white inhabitant of Ohio, obliged
to subsist by his own exertions, regards temporal prosperity as the chief aim of his existence; and as the country
which he occupies presents inexhaustible resources to his
industry, and ever-varying lures to his activity, his acquis-
itive ardor surpasses the ordinary limits of human cupidity: he is tormented by the desire of wealth, and he boldly
enters upon every path which fortune opens to him; he
becomes a sailor, a pioneer, an artisan, or a cultivator, with
the same indifference, and supports with equal constancy
the fatigues and the dangers incidental to these various
professions; the resources of his intelligence are astonishing, and his avidity in the pursuit of gain amounts to a
species of heroism.

But the Kentuckian scorns not only labor, but all the
undertakings which labor promotes; as he lives in an idle
independence, his tastes are those of an idle man; money
has lost a portion of its value in his eyes; he covets wealth
much less than pleasure and excitement; and the energy
which his neighbor devotes to gain, turns with him to a
passionate love of field sports and military exercises; he
delights in violent bodily exertion, he is familiar with the
use of arms, and is accustomed from a very early age to
expose his life in single combat. Thus slavery not only
prevents the whites from becoming opulent, but even from
desiring to become so.

As the same causes have been continually producing
opposite effects for the last two centuries in the British
colonies of North America, they have at last established
a striking difference between the commercial capacity of

the inhabitants of the South and those of the North. At the present day, it is only the Northern States which are in possession of shipping, manufactures, railroads, and canals. This difference is perceptible, not only in comparing the North with the South, but in comparing the several Southern States. Almost all those who carry on commercial operations, or endeavor to turn slave labor to account, in the most southern districts of the Union, have emigrated from the North. The natives of the Northern States are constantly spreading over that portion of the American territory, where they have less to fear from competition; they discover resources there which escaped the notice of the inhabitants; and, as they comply with a system which they do not approve, they succeed in turning it to better advantage than those who first founded, and who still maintain it.

Were I inclined to continue this parallel, I could easily prove that almost all the differences which may be remarked between the characters of the Americans in the Southern and in the Northern States have originated in slavery; but this would divert me from my subject, and my present intention is not to point out all the consequences of servitude, but those effects which it has produced upon the material prosperity of the countries which have admitted it.

The influence of slavery upon the production of wealth must have been very imperfectly known in antiquity, as slavery then obtained throughout the civilized world; and the nations which were unacquainted with it were barbarians. And, indeed, Christianity only abolished slavery by advocating the claims of the slave; at the present time, it may be attacked in the name of the master; and, upon this point, interest is reconciled with morality.

As these truths became apparent in the United States, slavery receded before the progress of experience. Servitude had begun in the South, and had thence spread toward the North; but it now retires again. Freedom, which started from the North, now descends uninterruptedly toward the South. Amongst the great States, Pennsylvania now constitutes the extreme limit of slavery to the North; but, even within those limits, the slave system is shaken: Maryland, which is immediately below Pennsylvania, is preparing for its abolition; and Virginia, which comes next to Maryland, is already discussing its utility and its dangers.*

No great change takes place in human institutions, without involving amongst its causes the law of inheritance. When the law of primogeniture obtained in the South, each family was represented by a wealthy individual, who was neither compelled nor induced to labor; and he was surrounded, as by parasitic plants, by the other members of his family, who were then excluded by law from sharing the common inheritance, and who led the same kind of life as himself. The same thing then occurred in all the families of the South which still happens in the noble families of some countries in Europe, namely, that the younger sons remain in the same state of idleness as their elder brother, without being as rich as he is. This

---

* A peculiar reason contributes to detach the two last-mentioned States from the cause of slavery. The former wealth of this part of the Union was principally derived from the cultivation of tobacco. This cultivation is specially carried on by slaves; but within the last few years, the market-price of tobacco has diminished, whilst the value of the slaves remains the same. Thus the ratio between the cost of production and the value of the produce is changed. The inhabitants of Maryland and Virginia are therefore more disposed than they were thirty years ago to give up slave-labor in the cultivation of tobacco, or to give up slavery and tobacco at the same time.

[It is hardly necessary to remind the American reader that the text here was written nearly thirty years ago, and was a tolerably accurate description of the state of affairs then, though circumstances have greatly changed since. — AM. ED.]

identical result seems to be produced in Europe and in America by wholly analogous causes. In the South of the United States, the whole race of whites formed an aristocratic body, headed by a certain number of privileged individuals, whose wealth was permanent, and whose leisure was hereditary. These leaders of the American nobility kept alive the traditional prejudices of the white race in the body of which they were the representatives, and maintained idleness in honor. This aristocracy contained many who were poor, but none who would work; its members preferred want to labor; consequently, Negro laborers and slaves met with no competition; and, whatever opinion might be entertained as to the utility of their industry, it was necessary to employ them, since there was no one else to work.

No sooner was the law of primogeniture abolished, than fortunes began to diminish, and all the families of the country were simultaneously reduced to a state in which labor became necessary to existence, — several of them have since entirely disappeared, — and all of them learned to look forward to the time when it would be necessary for every one to provide for his own wants. Wealthy individuals are still to be met with, but they no longer constitute a compact and hereditary body, nor have they been able to adopt a line of conduct in which they could persevere, and which they could infuse into all ranks of society. The prejudice which stigmatized labor was, in the first place, abandoned by common consent, the number of needy men was increased, and the needy were allowed to gain a subsistence by labor without blushing for their toil. Thus, one of the most immediate consequences of the equal division of estates has been, to create a class of free laborers. As soon as competition began between the free laborer and the slave, the inferiority of the latter became manifest, and slavery was attacked in its fundamental principle, which is, the interest of the master.

As slavery recedes, the black population follows its retrograde course, and returns with it towards those tropical regions whence it originally came. However singular this fact may at first appear to be, it may readily be explained. Although the Americans abolish the principle of slavery, they do not set their slaves free. To illustrate this remark, I will quote the example of the State of New York. In 1788, this State prohibited the sale of slaves within its limits, which was an indirect method of prohibiting the importation of them. Thenceforward the number of Negroes could only increase according to the ratio of the natural increase of population. But eight years later, a more decisive measure was taken, and it was enacted that all children born of slave parents after the 4th of July, 1799, should be free. No increase could then take place, and, although slaves still existed, slavery might be said to be abolished.

As soon as a Northern State thus prohibited the importation, no slaves were brought from the South to be sold in its markets. On the other hand, as the sale of slaves was forbidden in that State, an owner could no longer get rid of his slave (who thus became a burdensome possession) otherwise than by transporting him to the South. But when a Northern State declared that the son of the slave should be born free, the slave lost a large portion of his market-value, since his posterity was no longer included in the bargain, and the owner had then a strong interest in transporting him to the South. Thus the same law prevents the slaves of the South from coming North, and drives those of the North to the South.

But there is another cause more powerful than any that I have described. The want of free hands is felt in a State in proportion as the number of slaves decreases. But in proportion as labor is performed by free hands, slave-labor becomes less productive ; and the slave is then a useless or onerous possession, whom it is important to export to the South, where the same competition is not to be feared. Thus the abolition of slavery does not set the slave free, but merely transfers him to another master, and from the North to the South.

The emancipated Negroes, and those born after the abolition of slavery, do not, indeed, migrate from the North to the South; but their situation with regard to the Europeans is not unlike that of the Indians ; they remain half civilized, and deprived of their rights in the midst of a population which is far superior to them in wealth and knowledge, where they are exposed to the tyranny of the laws * and the intolerance of the people. On some accounts they are still more to be pitied than the Indians, since they are haunted by the reminiscence of slavery, and they cannot claim possession of any part of the soil : many of them perish miserably,† and the rest congregate in the great towns, where they perform the meanest offices, and lead a wretched and precarious existence.

But even if the number of Negroes continued to increase as rapidly as when they were still in slavery, as the number of whites augments with twofold rapidity after the abolition of slavery, the blacks would soon be, as it were, lost in the midst of a strange population.

* The States in which slavery is abolished usually do what they can to render their territory disagreeable to the Negroes as a place of residence; and as a kind of emulation exists between the different States in this respect, the unhappy blacks can only choose the least of the evils which beset them.

† There is a great difference between the mortality of the blacks and of the whites in the States in which slavery is abolished; from 1820 to 1831, only one out of forty-two individuals of the white population died in Philadelphia; but one out of twenty-one of the black population died in the same time. The mortality is by no means so great amongst the Negroes who are still slaves. (See Emerson's Medical Statistics, p. 28.)

A district which is cultivated by slaves is in general less populous than a district cultivated by free labor: moreover, America is still a new country, and a State is therefore not half peopled when it abolishes slavery. No sooner is an end put to slavery, than the want of free labor is felt, and a crowd of enterprising adventurers immediately arrive from all parts of the country, who hasten to profit by the fresh resources which are then opened to industry. The soil is soon divided amongst them, and a family of white settlers takes possession of each portion. Besides, European emigration is exclusively directed to the free States; for what would a poor emigrant do who crosses the Atlantic in search of ease and happiness, if he were to land in a country where labor is stigmatized as degrading?

Thus the white population grows by its natural increase, and, at the same time, by the immense influx of emigrants; whilst the black population receives no emigrants, and is upon its decline. The proportion which existed between the two races is soon inverted. The Negroes constitute a scanty remnant, a poor tribe of vagrants, lost in the midst of an immense people who own the land; and the presence of the blacks is only marked by the injustice and the hardships of which they are the victims.

In several of the Western States, the Negro race never made its appearance; and in all the Northern States, it is rapidly declining. Thus the great question of its future condition is confined within a narrow circle, where it becomes less formidable, though not more easy of solution. The more we descend towards the South, the more difficult does it become to abolish slavery with advantage; and this arises from several physical causes which it is important to point out.

The first of these causes is the climate: it is well known that, in proportion as Europeans approach the tropics, labor becomes more difficult to them. Many of the Americans even assert that, within a certain latitude, it is fatal to them, while the Negroes can work there without danger ; * but I do not think that this opinion, which is so favorable to the indolence of the inhabitants of the South, is confirmed by experience. The southern parts of the Union are not hotter than the south of Italy and of Spain ; † and it may be asked why the European cannot work as well there as in the latter two countries. If slavery has been abolished in Italy and in Spain, without causing the destruction of the masters, why should not the same thing take place in the Union ? I cannot believe that Nature has prohibited the Europeans in Georgia and the Floridas, under pain of death, from raising the means of subsistence from the soil; but their labor would unquestionably be more irksome and less productive ‡ to them than to the inhabitants of New England. As the free workman thus loses a portion of his superiority over the slave in the Southern States, there are fewer inducements to abolish slavery.

All the plants of Europe grow in the northern parts of the Union ; the South has special productions of its own. It has been observed that slave labor is a very expensive

* This is true of the spots in which rice is cultivated ; rice-grounds, which are unwholesome in all countries, are particularly dangerous in those regions which are exposed to the beams of a tropical sun. Europeans would not find it easy to cultivate the soil in that part of the New World, if it must necessarily be made to produce rice ; but may they not subsist without rice-grounds ?

† These States are nearer to the equator than Italy and Spain, but the temperature of the continent of America is much lower than that of Europe.

‡ The Spanish government formerly caused a certain number of peasants from the Azores to be transported into a district of Louisiana called Attakapas, by way of experiment. These settlers still cultivate the soil without the assistance of slaves, but their industry is so languid as scarcely to supply their most necessary wants.

method of cultivating cereal grain. The farmer of corn-land, in a country where slavery is unknown, habitually retains only a small number of laborers in his service, and at seed-time and harvest he hires additional hands, who only live at his cost for a short period. But the agriculturist in a slave state is obliged to keep a large number of slaves the whole year round, in order to sow his fields and to gather in his crops, although their services are required only for a few weeks; for slaves are unable to wait till they are hired, and to subsist by their own labor in the mean time, like free laborers; in order to have their services, they must be bought. Slavery, independently of its general disadvantages, is therefore still more inapplicable to countries in which corn is cultivated, than to those which produce crops of a different kind. The cultivation of tobacco, of cotton, and especially of the sugar-cane, demands, on the other hand, unremitting attention: and women and children are employed in it, whose services are of little use in the cultivation of wheat. Thus slavery is naturally more fitted to the countries from which these productions are derived.

Tobacco, cotton, and the sugar-cane are exclusively grown in the South, and they form the principal sources of the wealth of those States. If slavery were abolished, the inhabitants of the South would be driven to this alternative: they must either change their system of cultivation, — and then they would come into competition with the more active and more experienced inhabitants of the North; or, if they continued to cultivate the same produce without slave labor, they would have to support the competition of the other States of the South, which might still retain their slaves. Thus, peculiar reasons for maintaining slavery exist in the South which do not operate in the North.

But there is yet another motive, which is more cogent

than all the others : the South might, indeed, rigorously speaking, abolish slavery ; but how should it rid its territory of the black population ? Slaves and slavery are driven from the North by the same law ; but this twofold result cannot be hoped for in the South.

In proving that slavery is more natural and more advantageous in the South than in the North, I have shown that the number of slaves must be far greater in the former. It was to the southern settlements that the first Africans were brought, and it is there that the greatest number of them have always been imported. As we advance towards the South, the prejudice which sanctions idleness increases in power. In the States nearest to the tropics, there is not a single white laborer ; the Negroes are consequently much more numerous in the South than in the North. And, as I have already observed, this disproportion increases daily, since the Negroes are transferred to one part of the Union as soon as slavery is abolished in the other. Thus, the black population augments in the South, not only by its natural fecundity, but by the compulsory emigration of the Negroes from the North ; and the African race has causes of increase in the South very analogous to those which accelerate the growth of the European race in the North.

In the State of Maine there is one Negro in three hundred inhabitants ; in Massachusetts, one in one hundred ; in New York, two in one hundred ; in Pennsylvania, three in the same number ; in Maryland, thirty-four ; in Virginia, forty-two ; and lastly, in South Carolina,* fifty-five

* We find it asserted in an Amerian work, entitled "Letters on the Colonization Society," by Mr. Carey, 1833, "That for the last forty years, the black race has increased more rapidly than the white race in the State of South Carolina ; and that, if we take the average population of the five States of the South into which slaves were first introduced, viz. Maryland, Virginia, South Carolina, North Carolina, and Georgia, we shall find that from

per cent of the inhabitants are black. Such was the proportion of the black population to the whites in the year 1830. But this proportion is perpetually changing, as it constantly decreases in the North, and augments in the South.

It is evident that the most southern States of the Union cannot abolish slavery without incurring great dangers, which the North had no reason to apprehend when it emancipated its black population. We have already shown how the Northern States made the transition from slavery to freedom, by keeping the present generation in chains, and setting their descendants free; by this means, the Negroes are only gradually introduced into the society; and whilst the men who might abuse their freedom are kept in servitude, those who are emancipated may learn the art of being free before they become their own masters. But it would be difficult to apply this method in the South. To declare that all the Negroes born after a certain period shall be free, is to introduce the principle and the notion of liberty into the heart of slavery; the blacks whom the law thus maintains in a state of slavery from which their children are delivered, are astonished at so unequal a fate, and their astonishment is only the prelude to their impatience and irritation. Thenceforward slavery loses, in their eyes, that kind of moral power which it derived from time and habit; it is reduced to a mere palpable abuse of force. The Northern States had nothing to fear from the contrast, because in them the blacks were few in number, and the white population was very considerable. But if

1700 to 1830 the whites have augmented in the proportion of 80 to 100, and the blacks in that of 100 to 112.

In the United States, in 1830, the population of the two races stood as follows : —

States where slavery is abolished, 6,565,434 whites; 120,520 blacks. Slave States 3,960,814 whites; 2,208,102 blacks.

this faint dawn of freedom were to show two millions of men their true position, the oppressors would have reason to tremble. After having enfranchised the children of their slaves, the Europeans of the Southern States would very shortly be obliged to extend the same benefit to the whole black population.

In the North, as I have already remarked, a twofold migration ensues upon the abolition of slavery, or even precedes that event when circumstances have rendered it probable; the slaves quit the country to be transported southwards; and the whites of the Northern States, as well as the emigrants from Europe, hasten to fill their place. But these two causes cannot operate in the same manner in the Southern States. On the one hand, the mass of slaves is too great to allow any expectation of their being removed from the country; and on the other hand, the Europeans and Anglo-Americans of the North are afraid to come to inhabit a country in which labor has not yet been reinstated in its rightful honors. Besides, they very justly look upon the States in which the number of the Negroes equals or exceeds that of the whites, as exposed to very great dangers; and they refrain from turning their activity in that direction.

Thus the inhabitants of the South would not be able, while abolishing slavery, like their Northern countrymen, to initiate the slaves gradually into a state of freedom; they have no means of perceptibly diminishing the black population, and they would remain unsupported to repress its excesses. Thus, in the course of a few years, a great people of free Negroes would exist in the heart of a white nation of equal size.

The same abuses of power which now maintain slavery would then become the source of the most alarming perils to the white population of the South. At the present time, the descendants of the Europeans are the sole owners of the land, and the absolute masters of all labor; they alone possess wealth, knowledge, and arms. The black is destitute of all these advantages, but can subsist without them because he is a slave. If he were free, and obliged to provide for his own subsistence, would it be possible for him to remain without these things and to support life? Or would not the very instruments of the present superiority of the white, whilst slavery exists, expose him to a thousand dangers if it were abolished?

As long as the Negro remains a slave, he may be kept in a condition not far removed from that of the brutes; but, with his liberty, he cannot but acquire a degree of instruction which will enable him to appreciate his misfortunes, and to discern a remedy for them. Moreover, there exists a singular principle of relative justice, which is firmly implanted in the human heart. Men are much more forcibly struck by those inequalities which exist within the same class, than with those which may be remarked between different classes. One can understand slavery; but how allow several millions of citizens to exist under a load of eternal infamy and hereditary wretchedness? In the North, the population of freed Negroes feels these hardships and indignities, but its numbers and its powers are small, whilst in the South it would be numerous and strong.

As soon as it is admitted that the whites and the emancipated blacks are placed upon the same territory in the situation of two foreign communities, it will readily be understood that there are but two chances for the future; the Negroes and the whites must either wholly part, or wholly mingle. I have already expressed my conviction as to the latter event.* I do not believe that the white

* This opinion is sanctioned by authorities infinitely weightier than anything that I can say: thus, for instance, it is stated in the Memoirs of Jefferson, "Nothing is more clearly written in the book of destiny than the

and black races will ever live in any country upon an equal footing. But I believe the difficulty to be still greater in the United States than elsewhere. An isolated individual may surmount the prejudices of religion, of his country, or of his race; and if this individual is a king, he may effect surprising changes in society; but a whole people cannot rise, as it were, above itself. A despot who should subject the Americans and their former slaves to the same yoke, might perhaps succeed in commingling their races; but as long as the American democracy remains at the head of affairs, no one will undertake so difficult a task; and it may be foreseen that, the freer the white population of the United States becomes, the more isolated will it remain.*

I have previously observed that the mixed race is the true bond of union between the Europeans and the Indians; just so, the Mulattoes are the true means of transition between the white and the Negro; so that, wherever Mulattoes abound, the intermixture of the two races is not impossible. In some parts of America, the European and the Negro races are so crossed by one another, that it is rare to meet with a man who is entirely black, or entirely white: when they are arrived at this point, the two races may really be said to be combined, or, rather, to have been absorbed in a third race, which is connected with both without being identical with either.

Of all Europeans, the English are those who have mixed least with the Negroes. More Mulattoes are to be

emancipation of the blacks; and it is equally certain, that the two races will never live in a state of equal freedom under the same government, so insurmountable are the barriers which nature, habit, and opinion have established between them."

* If the British West India planters had governed themselves, they would assuredly not have passed the Slave Emancipation Bill which the mother country has recently imposed upon them.

seen in the South of the Union than in the North, but
infinitely fewer than in any other European colony: Mulattoes are by no means numerous in the United States;
they have no force peculiar to themselves, and when quarrels originating in differences of color take place, they generally side with the whites, — just as the lackeys of the
great in Europe assume the contemptuous airs of nobility
toward the lower orders.

The pride of origin, which is natural to the English,
is singularly augmented by the personal pride which democratic liberty fosters amongst the Americans: the white
citizen of the United States is proud of his race, and proud
of himself. But if the whites and the Negroes do not
intermingle in the North of the Union, how should they
mix in the South? Can it be supposed for an instant, that
an American of the Southern States, placed, as he must
forever be, between the white man, with all his physical
and moral superiority, and the Negro, will ever think of
being confounded with the latter? The Americans of the
Southern States have two powerful passions, which will
always keep them aloof; — the first is the fear of being
assimilated to the Negroes, their former slaves; and the
second, the dread of sinking below the whites, their
neighbors.

If I were called upon to predict the future, I should say
that the abolition of slavery in the South will, in the common course of things, increase the repugnance of the white
population for the blacks. I found this opinion upon the
analogous observation I have already made at the North.
I have remarked that the white inhabitants of the North
avoid the Negroes with increasing care, in proportion as
the legal barriers of separation are removed by the legislature; and why should not the same result take place in
the South? In the North, the whites are deterred from
intermingling with the blacks by an imaginary danger; in

the South, where the danger would be real, I cannot believe that the fear would be less.

If, on the one hand, it be admitted (and the fact is unquestionable) that the colored population perpetually accumulate in the extreme South, and increase more rapidly than the whites; and if, on the other hand, it be allowed that it is impossible to foresee a time at which the whites and the blacks will be so intermingled as to derive the same benefits from society, — must it not be inferred that the blacks and the whites will, sooner or later, come to open strife in the Southern States? But if it be asked what the issue of the struggle is likely to be, it will readily be understood that we are here left to vague conjectures. The human mind may succeed in tracing a wide circle, as it were, which includes the future; but, within that circle, chance rules, and eludes all our foresight. In every picture of the future there is a dim spot which the eye of the understanding cannot penetrate. It appears, however, extremely probable that, in the West India Islands, the white race is destined to be subdued, and, upon the continent, the blacks.

In the West India Islands, the white planters are isolated amidst an immense black population; on the continent, the blacks are placed between the ocean and an innumerable people, who already extend above them, in a compact mass, from the icy confines of Canada to the frontiers of Virginia, and from the banks of the Missouri to the shores of the Atlantic. If the white citizens of North America remain united, it is difficult to believe that the Negroes will escape the destruction which menaces them; they must be subdued by want or by the sword. But the black population accumulated along the coast of the Gulf of Mexico have a chance of success, if the American Union should be dissolved when the struggle between the two races begins. The Federal tie once broken, the people of the South could not rely upon any lasting succor from their Northern countrymen. The latter are well aware that the danger can never reach them; and unless they are constrained to march to the assistance of the South by a positive obligation, it may be foreseen that the sympathy of race will be powerless.

Yet, at whatever period the strife may break out, the whites of the South, even if they are abandoned to their own resources, will enter the lists with an immense superiority of knowledge and the means of warfare: but the blacks will have numerical strength and the energy of despair upon their side; and these are powerful resources to men who have taken up arms. The fate of the white population of the Southern States will, perhaps, be similar to that of the Moors in Spain. After having occupied the land for centuries, it will, perhaps, retire by degrees to the country whence its ancestors came, and abandon to the Negroes the possession of a territory which Providence seems to have destined for them, since they can subsist and labor in it more easily than the whites.

The danger of a conflict between the white and the black inhabitants of the Southern States of the Union — a danger which, however remote it may be, is inevitable — perpetually haunts the imagination of the Americans, like a painful dream. The inhabitants of the North make it a common topic of conversation, although directly they have nothing to fear from it; but they vainly endeavor to devise some means of obviating the misfortunes which they foresee. In the Southern States, the subject is not discussed: the planter does not allude to the future in conversing with strangers; he does not communicate his apprehensions to his friends, — he seeks to conceal them from himself. But there is something more alarming in the tacit forebodings of the South, than in the clamorous fears of the North.

This all-pervading disquietude has given birth to an undertaking as yet but little known, but which may change the fate of a portion of the human race. From apprehension of the dangers which I have just described, some American citizens have formed a society for the purpose of exporting to the coast of Guinea, at their own expense, such free Negroes as may be willing to escape from the oppression to which they are subject.*

In 1820, the society to which I allude formed a settlement in Africa, upon the seventh degree of north latitude, which bears the name of Liberia. The most recent intelligence informs us that two thousand five hundred Negroes are collected there. They have introduced the democratic institutions of America into the country of their forefathers. Liberia has a representative system of government, Negro jurymen, Negro magistrates, and Negro priests; churches have been built, newspapers established, and, by a singular turn in the vicissitudes of the world, white men are prohibited from establishing themselves within the settlement.†

This is indeed a strange caprice of fortune. Two hundred years have now elapsed since the inhabitants of Europe undertook to tear the Negro from his family and his home, in order to transport him to the shores of North America. Now the European settlers are engaged in sending back the descendants of those very Negroes to

---

* This society assumed the name of " The Society for the Colonization of the Blacks." See its Annual Reports; and more particularly the fifteenth. See also the pamphlet, to which allusion has already been made, entitled, " Letters on the Colonization Society, and on its probable Results," by Mr. Carey, Philadelphia, April, 1833.

† This last regulation was laid down by the founders of the settlement; they apprehended that a state of things might arise in Africa, similar to that which exists on the frontiers of the United States, and that if the Negroes, like the Indians, were brought into collision with a people more enlightened than themselves, they would be destroyed before they could be civilized.

the continent whence they were originally taken : the barbarous Africans have learned civilization in the midst of bondage, and have become acquainted with free political institutions in slavery. Up to the present time, Africa has been closed against the arts and sciences of the whites ; but the inventions of Europe will perhaps penetrate into those regions, now that they are introduced by Africans themselves. The settlement of Liberia is founded upon a lofty and fruitful idea ; but, whatever may be its results with regard to Africa, it can afford no remedy to the New World.

In twelve years, the Colonization Society has transported two thousand five hundred Negroes to Africa ; in the same space of time, about seven hundred thousand blacks were born in the United States. If the colony of Liberia were able to receive thousands of new inhabitants every year, and if the Negroes were in a state to be sent thither with advantage ; if the Union were to supply the society with annual subsidies,* and to transport the Negroes to Africa in the vessels of the state, — it would still be unable to counterpoise the natural increase of population amongst the blacks ; and, as it could not remove as many men in a year as are born upon its territory within that time, it could not prevent the growth of the evil which is daily increasing in the States.† The Negro race will

---

* Nor would these be the only difficulties attendant upon the undertaking ; if the Union undertook to buy up the Negroes now in America, in order to transport them to Africa, the price of slaves, increasing with their scarcity, would soon become enormous ; and the States of the North would never consent to expend such great sums for a purpose which would profit them but little. If the Union took possession of the slaves in the Southern States by force, or at a rate determined by law, an insurmountable resistance would rise in that part of the country. Both courses are equally impossible.

† In 1830 there were in the United States 2,010,327 slaves and 319,439 free blacks, in all 2,329,766 Negroes : which formed about one fifth of the total

never leave those shores of the American continent to which it was brought by the passions and the vices of Europeans ; and it will not disappear from the New World as long as it continues to exist. The inhabitants of the United States may retard the calamities which they apprehend, but they cannot now destroy their efficient cause.

I am obliged to confess that I do not regard the abolition of slavery as a means of warding off the struggle of the two races in the Southern States. The Negroes may long remain slaves without complaining ; but if they are once raised to the level of freemen, they will soon revolt at being deprived of almost all their civil rights ; and, as they cannot become the equals of the whites, they will speedily show themselves as enemies. In the North, everything facilitated the emancipation of the slaves ; and slavery was abolished without rendering the free Negroes formidable, since their number was too small for them ever to claim their rights. But such is not the case in the South. The question of slavery was a commercial and manufacturing question for the slave-owners in the North ; for those of the South, it is a question of life and death. God forbid that I should seek to justify the principle of Negro slavery, as has been done by some American writers ! I say only, that all the countries which formerly adopted that execrable principle are not equally able to abandon it at the present time.

When I contemplate the condition of the South, I can only discover two modes of action for the white inhabitants of those States ; viz. either to emancipate the Negroes, and to intermingle with them, or, remaining isolated from them, to keep them in slavery as long as possible. All intermediate measures seem to me likely to terminate, and that shortly, in the most horrible of civil wars, and

population of the United States at that time. [In 1850, the numbers were 3,204,313 slaves and 434,495 free colored ; in all, 3,638,808. — AM. ED.]

perhaps in the extirpation of one or the other of the two races. Such is the view which the Americans of the South take of the question, and they act consistently with it. As they are determined not to mingle with the Negroes, they refuse to emancipate them.

Not that the inhabitants of the South regard slavery as necessary to the wealth of the planter; on this point, many of them agree with their Northern countrymen, in freely admitting that slavery is prejudicial to their interests; but they are convinced that the removal of this evil would peril their own existence. The instruction which is now diffused in the South has convinced the inhabitants that slavery is injurious to the slave-owner, but it has also shown them, more clearly than before, that it is almost an impossibility to get rid of it. Hence arises a singular contrast; the more the utility of slavery is contested, the more firmly is it established in the laws; and whilst its principle is gradually abolished in the North, that self-same principle gives rise to more and more rigorous consequences in the South.

The legislation of the Southern States with regard to slaves presents at the present day such unparalleled atrocities as suffice to show that the laws of humanity have been totally perverted, and to betray the desperate position of the community in which that legislation has been promulgated. The Americans of this portion of the Union have not, indeed, augmented the hardships of slavery; they have, on the contrary, bettered the physical condition of the slaves. The only means by which the ancients maintained slavery were fetters and death; the Americans of the South of the Union have discovered more intellectual securities for the duration of their power. They have employed their despotism and their violence against the human mind. In antiquity, precautions were taken to prevent the slave from breaking his chains; at the present day, measures are adopted to deprive him even of the desire of freedom. The ancients kept the bodies of their slaves in bondage, but placed no restraint upon the mind and no check upon education ; and they acted consistently with their established principle, since a natural termination of slavery then existed, and one day or other the slave might be set free, and become the equal of his master. But the Americans of the South, who do not admit that the Negroes can ever be commingled with themselves, have forbidden them, under severe penalties, to be taught to read or write ; and, as they will not raise them to their own level, they sink them as nearly as possible to that of the brutes.

The hope of liberty had always been allowed to the slave, to cheer the hardships of his condition. But the Americans of the South are well aware that emancipation cannot but be dangerous, when the freed man can never be assimilated to his former master. To give a man his freedom, and to leave him in wretchedness and ignominy, is nothing less than to prepare a future chief for a revolt of the slaves. Moreover, it has long been remarked, that the presence of a free Negro vaguely agitates the minds of his less fortunate brethren, and conveys to them a dim notion of their rights. The Americans of the South have consequently taken away from slave-owners the right of emancipating their slaves in most cases, — not indeed by positive prohibition, but by subjecting that step to various formalities which it is difficult to comply with.

I happened to meet with an old man, in the South of the Union, who had lived in illicit intercourse with one of his Negresses, and had had several children by her, who were born the slaves of their father. He had, indeed, frequently thought of bequeathing to them at least their liberty ; but years had elapsed before he could surmount the legal obstacles to their emancipation, and in the mean while his old age was come, and he was about to die. He pictured to himself his sons dragged from market to market, and passing from the authority of a parent to the rod of the stranger, until these horrid anticipations worked his expiring imagination into frenzy. When I saw him, he was a prey to all the anguish of despair; and I then understood how awful is the retribution of Nature upon those who have broken her laws.

These evils are unquestionably great, but they are the necessary and foreseen consequences of the very principle of modern slavery. When the Europeans chose their slaves from a race differing from their own, — which many of them considered as inferior to the other races of mankind, and any notion of intimate union with which they all repelled with horror, — they must have believed that slavery would last forever, since there is no intermediate state which can be durable between the excessive inequality produced by servitude and the complete equality which originates in independence. The Europeans did imperfectly feel this truth, but without acknowledging it even to themselves. Whenever they have had to do with Negroes, their conduct has either been dictated by their interest and their pride, or by their compassion. They first violated every right of humanity by their treatment of the Negro, and they afterwards informed him that those rights were precious and inviolable. They affected to open their ranks to the slaves, but the Negroes who attempted to penetrate into the community were driven back with scorn; and they have incautiously and involuntarily been led to admit freedom instead of slavery, without having the courage to be wholly iniquitous, or wholly just.

If it be impossible to anticipate a period at which the Americans of the South will mingle their blood with that of the Negroes, can they allow their slaves to become free without compromising their own security? And if they are obliged to keep that race in bondage in order to save their own families, may they not be excused for availing themselves of the means best adapted to that end? The events which are taking place in the Southern States appear to me to be at once the most horrible and the most natural results of slavery. When I see the order of nature overthrown, and when I hear the cry of humanity in its vain struggle against the laws, my indignation does not light upon the men of our own time who are the instruments of these outrages; but I reserve my execration for those who, after a thousand years of freedom, brought back slavery into the world once more.

Whatever may be the efforts of the Americans of the South to maintain slavery, they will not always succeed. Slavery, now confined to a single tract of the civilized earth, attacked by Christianity as unjust, and by political economy as prejudicial, and now contrasted with democratic liberty and the intelligence of our age, cannot survive. By the act of the master, or by the will of the slave, it will cease; and, in either case, great calamities may be expected to ensue. If liberty be refused to the Negroes of the South, they will, in the end, forcibly seize it for themselves; if it be given, they will, erelong, abuse it.

WHAT ARE THE CHANCES OF DURATION OF THE AMERICAN UNION, AND WHAT DANGERS THREATEN IT.

What makes the preponderant Force lie in the States rather than in the Union. — The Union will last only as long as all the States choose to belong to it. — Causes which tend to keep them united. — Utility of the Union to resist foreign Enemies, and to exclude Foreigners from America. — No natural Barriers between the several States. — No conflicting Interests to divide them. — Reciprocal Interests of the Northern, Southern, and Western States. — Intellectual Ties of Union. — Uniformity of Opinions. — Dangers of the Union resulting from the different Characters and the Passions of its Citizens. — Character of the Citizens in the South and in the North. — The rapid Growth of the Union one of its greatest Dangers. Progress of the Population to the Northwest. — Power gravitates in the same Direction. — Passions originating from sudden Turns of Fortune. — Whether the existing Government of the Union tends to gain Strength, or to lose it. — Various Signs of its Decrease. — Internal Improvements. — Waste Lands. — Indians. — The Bank. — The Tariff. — General Jackson.

THE maintenance of the existing institutions of the several States depends in part upon the maintenance of the Union itself. We must therefore first inquire into the probable fate of the Union. One point may be assumed at once: if the present confederation were dissolved, it appears to me to be incontestable that the States of which it is now composed would not return to their original isolated condition, but that several Unions would then be formed in the place of one. It is not my intention to inquire into the principles upon which these new Unions would probably be established, but merely to show what the causes are which may effect the dismemberment of the existing confederation.

With this object, I shall be obliged to retrace some of the steps which I have already taken, and to revert to topics which I have before discussed. I am aware that the reader may accuse me of repetition, but the importance of the matter which still remains to be treated is my excuse : I had rather say too much, than not be thoroughly understood ; and I prefer injuring the author to slighting the subject.

The legislators who formed the Constitution of 1789 endeavored to confer a separate existence and superior strength upon the federal power. But they were confined by the conditions of the task which they had undertaken to perform. They were not appointed to constitute the government of a single people, but to regulate the association of several States; and, whatever their inclinations might be, they could not but divide the exercise of sovereignty.

In order to understand the consequences of this division, it is necessary to make a short distinction between the functions of government. There are some objects which are national by their very nature, — that is to say, which affect the nation as a whole, and can only be intrusted to the man or the assembly of men who most completely represent the entire nation. Amongst these may be reckoned war and diplomacy. There are other objects which are provincial by their very nature, — that is to say, which only affect certain localities, and which can only be properly treated in that locality. Such, for instance, is the budget of a municipality. Lastly, there are objects of a mixed nature, which are national inasmuch as they affect all the citizens who compose the nation, and which are provincial inasmuch as it is not necessary that the nation itself should provide for them all. Such are the rights which regulate the civil and political condition of the citizens. No society can exist without civil and political rights. These rights, therefore, interest all the citizens alike; but it is not always necessary to the existence and the prosperity of the nation that these rights should be uniform, nor, consequently, that they should be regulated by the central authority.

There are, then, two distinct categories of objects which are submitted to the sovereign power; and these are found in all well-constituted communities, whatever may be the basis of the political constitution. Between these two extremes, the objects which I have termed mixed may be considered to lie. As these are neither exclusively national nor entirely provincial, the care of them may be given to a national or a provincial government, according to the agreement of the contracting parties, without in any way impairing the object of association.

The sovereign power is usually formed by the union of individuals, who compose a people; and individual powers or collective forces, each representing a small fraction of the sovereign, are the only elements which are found under the general government. In this case, the general government is more naturally called upon to regulate, not only those affairs which are essentially national, but most of those which I have called mixed; and the local governments are reduced to that small share of sovereign authority which is indispensable to their well-being.

But sometimes the sovereign authority is composed of pre-organized political bodies, by virtue of circumstances anterior to their union; and, in this case, the provincial governments assume the control, not only of those affairs which more peculiarly belong to them, but of all or a part of the mixed objects in question. For the confederate nations, which were independent sovereignties before their union, and which still represent a considerable share of the sovereign power, have consented to cede to the general government the exercise only of those rights which are indispensable to the Union.

When the national government, independently of the prerogatives inherent in its nature, is invested with the right of regulating the mixed objects of sovereignty, it possesses a preponderant influence. Not only are its own rights extensive, but all the rights which it does not possess exist by its sufferance; and it is to be feared that the provincial governments may be deprived by it of their natural and necessary prerogatives.

When, on the other hand, the provincial governments are invested with the power of regulating those same affairs of mixed interest, an opposite tendency prevails in society. The preponderant force resides in the province, not in the nation; and it may be apprehended that the national government may, in the end, be stripped of the privileges which are necessary to its existence.

Single nations have therefore a natural tendency to centralization, and confederations to dismemberment.

It now remains to apply these general principles to the American Union. The several States necessarily retained the right of regulating all purely provincial affairs. Moreover, these same States kept the rights of determining the civil and political competency of the citizens, of regulating the reciprocal relations of the members of the community, and of dispensing justice, — rights which are general in their nature, but do not necessarily appertain to the national government. We have seen that the government of the Union is invested with the power of acting in the name of the whole nation, in those cases in which the nation has to appear as a single and undivided power; as, for instance, in foreign relations, and in offering a common resistance to a common enemy; in short, in conducting those affairs which I have styled exclusively national.

In this division of the rights of sovereignty, the share of the Union seems at first sight more considerable than that of the States, but a more attentive investigation shows it to be less so. The undertakings of the government of the Union are more vast, but it has less frequent occasion to act at all. Those of the provincial governments are

comparatively small, but they are incessant, and they keep
alive the authority which they represent. The government of the Union watches over the general interests of
the country ; but the general interests of a people have but
a questionable influence upon individual happiness, whilst
provincial interests produce an immediate effect upon the
welfare of the inhabitants. The Union secures the independence and the greatness of the nation, which do not
immediately affect private citizens; but the several States
maintain the liberty, regulate the rights, protect the fortune, and secure the life and the whole future prosperity,
of every citizen.

The Federal government is far removed from its subjects, whilst the provincial governments are within the
reach of them all, and are ready to attend to the smallest
appeal. The central government has upon its side the
passions of a few superior men who aspire to conduct it ;
but upon the side of the provincial governments are the
interests of all those second-rate individuals who can only
hope to obtain power within their own State, and who
nevertheless exercise more authority over the people because they are nearer to them.

The Americans have, therefore, much more to hope and
to fear from the States than from the Union ; and, according to the natural tendency of the human mind, they are
more likely to attach themselves strongly to the former
than to the latter. In this respect, their habits and feelings harmonize with their interests.

When a compact nation divides its sovereignty, and
adopts a confederate form of government, the traditions,
the customs, and the manners of the people for a long time
struggle against the laws, and give an influence to the central government which the laws forbid. But when a number of confederate states unite to form a single nation, the
same causes operate in an opposite direction. I have no

doubt that, if France were to become a confederate republic like that of the United States, the government would
at first be more energetic than that of the Union; and if
the Union were to alter its constitution to a monarchy like
that of France, I think that the American government
would long remain weaker than the French. When the
national existence of the Anglo-Americans began, their
provincial existence was already of long standing : necessary relations were established between the townships and
the individual citizens of the same States ; and they were
accustomed to consider some objects as common to them
all, and to conduct other affairs as exclusively relating to
their own special interests.

The Union is a vast body, which presents no definite
object to patriotic feeling. The forms and limits of the
state are distinct and circumscribed, since it represents
a certain number of objects which are familiar to the citizens, and dear to them all. It is identified with the soil ;
with the right of property and the domestic affections ;
with the recollections of the past, the labors of the present, and the hopes of the future. Patriotism, then, which
is frequently a mere extension of individual selfishness, is
still directed to the State, and has not passed over to the
Union. Thus, the tendency of the interests, the habits,
and the feelings of the people is to centre political activity
in the States in preference to the Union.

It is easy to estimate the different strength of the two
governments, by remarking the manner in which they exercise their respective powers. Whenever the government
of a State addresses an individual or an assembly of individuals, its language is clear and imperative, — and such is
also the tone of the Federal government when it speaks
to individuals ; but, no sooner has it anything to do with
a State, than it begins to parley, to explain its motives and
justify its conduct, to argue, to advise, and, in short, any-

thing but to command. If doubts are raised as to the limits of the constitutional powers of either government, the provincial government prefers its claim with boldness, and takes prompt and energetic steps to support it. Meanwhile the government of the Union reasons; it appeals to the interests, the good sense, the glory of the nation; it temporizes, it negotiates, and does not consent to act until it is reduced to the last extremity. At first sight, it might readily be imagined that it is the provincial government which is armed with the authority of the nation, and that Congress represents a single State.

The Federal government is, therefore, notwithstanding the precautions of those who founded it, naturally so weak, that, more than any other, it requires the free consent of the governed to enable it to subsist. It is easy to perceive that its object is to enable the States to realize with facility their determination of remaining united; and, as long as this preliminary condition exists, it is wise, strong, and active. The Constitution fits the government to control individuals, and easily to surmount such obstacles as they may be inclined to offer, but it was by no means established with a view to the possible voluntary separation of one or more of the States from the Union.

If the sovereignty of the Union were to engage in a struggle with that of the States, at the present day, its defeat may be confidently predicted; and it is not probable that such a struggle would be seriously undertaken.* As

* The great struggle which is now going on (1862), and a greater one is nowhere recorded in history, proves that M. de Tocqueville overlooked one great obstacle to the dismemberment of the Union. This is found in the strong attachment of the remaining members of the federation, who resist to the death the attempt of their sister States to withdraw, first, because the original compact between them made no provision for such withdrawal except by the voluntary consent of the greater number; and secondly and chiefly, because the remaining States, who are the large majority, are not willing to allow the interests, the power, and the glory of all to be sacrificed by the act

often as a steady resistance is offered to the Federal government, it will be found to yield. Experience has hitherto shown that, whenever a State has demanded anything with perseverance and resolution, it has invariably succeeded; and that, if it has distinctly refused to act, it was left to do as it thought fit.*

But even if the government of the Union had any strength inherent in itself, the physical situation of the country would render the exercise of that strength very difficult.† The United States cover an immense territory, they are separated from each other by great distances, and the population is disseminated over the surface of a country which is still half a wilderness. If the Union were to undertake to enforce by arms the allegiance of the confederate States, it would be in a position very analogous to that of England at the time of the war of independence.

However strong a government may be, it cannot easily escape from the consequences of a principle which it has once admitted as the foundation of its constitution. The Union was formed by the voluntary agreement of the States; and these, in uniting together, have not forfeited their nationality, nor have they been reduced to the con-

of a few. They thus act in strict accordance with their own republican principle, that the will of the majority, duly ascertained and expressed in the manner and under the limitations prescribed by the Constitution, shall be the ultimate and supreme law, from which there can be no appeal. And this determination they are now manifesting with a unanimity and energy such as no nation has ever before shown in defence of its government. — Am. Ed.

* See the conduct of the Northern States in the war of 1812. "During that war," says Jefferson in a letter to General Lafayette, "four of the Eastern States were only attached to the Union like so many inanimate bodies to living men."

† The profound peace of the Union affords no pretext for a standing army; and without a standing army, a government is not prepared to profit by a favorable opportunity to conquer resistance, and take the sovereign power by surprise.

dition of one and the same people. If one of the States chose to withdraw its name from the contract, it would be difficult to disprove its right of doing so,* and the Federal government would have no means of maintaining its claims directly, either by force or by right. In order to enable the Federal government easily to conquer the resistance which may be offered to it by any of its subjects, it would be necessary that one or more of them should be specially interested in the existence of the Union, as has frequently been the case in the history of confederations.

If it be supposed that amongst the States which are united by the Federal tie there are some which exclusively enjoy the principal advantages of union, or whose prosperity entirely depends on the duration of that union, it is unquestionable that they will always be ready to support the central government in enforcing the obedience of the others. But the government would then be exerting a force not derived from itself, but from a principle contrary to its nature. States form confederations in order to derive equal advantages from their union; and in the case just alluded to, the Federal government would derive its power from the unequal distribution of those benefits amongst the States.

If one of the confederate States have acquired a preponderance sufficiently great to enable it to take exclusive possession of the central authority, it will consider the other States as subject provinces, and will cause its own supremacy to be respected under the borrowed name of the sovereignty of the Union. Great things may then be done in the name of the Federal government, but, in reality,

---

* It is enough here to say in reply, that the opinion of our greatest lawyers and statesmen, fortified by repeated judgments of the Supreme Court, is, that a State has no right under the Constitution voluntarily to secede from the Union. — AM. ED.

that government will have ceased to exist.* In both these cases, the power which acts in the name of the confederation becomes stronger the more it abandons the natural state and the acknowledged principles of confederations.

In America, the existing Union is advantageous to all the States, but it is not indispensable to any one of them. Several of them might break the Federal tie without compromising the welfare of the others, although the sum of their joint prosperity would be less. As the existence and the happiness of none of the States are wholly dependent on the present Constitution, they would none of them be disposed to make great personal sacrifices to maintain it. On the other hand, there is no State which seems hitherto to have its ambition much interested in the maintenance of the existing Union. They certainly do not all exercise the same influence in the Federal councils; but no one can hope to domineer over the rest, or to treat them as its inferiors or as its subjects.

It appears to me unquestionable, that, if any portion of the Union seriously desired to separate itself from the other States, they would not be able, nor indeed would they attempt, to prevent it; and that the present Union will only last as long as the States which compose it choose to continue members of the confederation. If this point be admitted, the question becomes less difficult; and our object is, not to inquire whether the States of the existing Union are capable of separating, but whether they will choose to remain united.

Amongst the various reasons which tend to render the existing Union useful to the Americans, two principal ones are especially evident to the observer. Although the

---

* Thus the province of Holland, in the republic of the Low Countries, and the Emperor in the Germanic Confederation, have sometimes put themselves in the place of the Union, and have employed the federal authority to their own advantage.

Americans are, as it were, alone upon their continent, commerce gives them for neighbors all the nations with which they trade. Notwithstanding their apparent isolation, then, the Americans need to be strong, and they can be strong only by remaining united. If the States were to split, they would not only diminish the strength which they now have against foreigners, but they would soon create foreign powers upon their own territory. A system of inland custom-houses would then be established; the valleys would be divided by imaginary boundary lines; the courses of the rivers would be impeded, and a multitude of hindrances would prevent the Americans from using that vast continent which Providence has given them for a dominion. At present, they have no invasion to fear, and consequently no standing armies to maintain, no taxes to levy. If the Union were dissolved, all these burdensome things would erelong be required. The Americans are, then, most deeply interested in the maintenance of their Union. On the other hand, it is almost impossible to discover any private interest which might now tempt a portion of the Union to separate from the other States.

When we cast our eyes upon the map of the United States, we perceive the chain of the Alleghany Mountains, running from the northeast to the southwest, and crossing nearly one thousand miles of country; and we are led to imagine that the design of Providence was to raise, between the valley of the Mississippi and the coasts of the Atlantic Ocean, one of those natural barriers which break the mutual intercourse of men, and form the necessary limits of different States. But the average height of the Alleghanies does not exceed 2,500 feet. Their rounded summits, and the spacious valleys which they enclose within their passes, are of easy access in several directions. Besides, the principal rivers which fall into the Atlantic Ocean, the Hudson, the Susquehanna, and the Potomac, take their rise beyond the Alleghanies, in an open elevated plain, which borders upon the valley of the Mississippi. These streams quit this tract of country, make their way through the barrier which would seem to turn them westward, and, as they wind through the mountains, open an easy and natural passage to man.

No natural barrier divides the regions which are now inhabited by the Anglo-Americans; the Alleghanies are so far from separating nations, that they do not even divide different States. New York, Pennsylvania, and Virginia comprise them within their borders, and extend as much to the west as to the east of the line.

The territory now occupied by the twenty-four States of the Union, and the three great districts which have not yet acquired the rank of States, although they already contain inhabitants, covers a surface of 1,002,600 square miles,* which is about equal to five times the extent of France. Within these limits the quality of the soil, the temperature, and the produce of the country, are extremely various. The vast extent of territory occupied by the Anglo-American republics has given rise to doubts as to the maintenance of their Union. Here a distinction must be made; contrary interests sometimes arise in the different provinces of a vast empire, which often terminate in open dissensions; and the extent of the country is then most prejudicial to the duration of the state. But if the inhabitants of these vast regions are not divided by contrary interests, the extent of the territory is favorable to

* See Darby's View of the United States, p. 435. [In 1860 the number of States has increased to 34; the population to 31,000,000, and the area of the States, 3,189,000 square miles. — *English Translator's Note.*] [And now that the United States comprise a vast region bordering on the Pacific Ocean, the Rocky Mountains, and the barren and mountainous country adjacent to them, form a great natural barrier between the eastern and western portions of the Union. — AM. ED.]

their prosperity; for the unity of the government promotes the interchange of the different productions of the soil, and increases their value by faciliating their consumption.

It is indeed easy to discover different interests in the different parts of the Union, but I am unacquainted with any which are hostile to each other. The Southern States are almost exclusively agricultural. The Northern States are more peculiarly commercial and manufacturing. The States of the West are, at the same time, agricultural and manufacturing. In the South, the crops consist of tobacco, rice, cotton, and sugar; in the North and the West, of wheat and maize: these are different sources of wealth; but union is the means by which these sources are opened and rendered equally advantageous to all.

The North, which ships the produce of the Anglo-Americans to all parts of the world, and brings back the produce of the globe to the Union, is evidently interested in maintaining the confederation in its present condition, in order that the number of American producers and consumers may remain as large as possible. The North is the most natural agent of communication between the South and the West of the Union on the one hand, and the rest of the world upon the other; the North is therefore interested in the union and prosperity of the South and the West, in order that they may continue to furnish raw materials for its manufactures, and cargoes for its shipping.

The South and the West, on their side, are still more directly interested in the preservation of the Union and the prosperity of the North. The produce of the South is, for the most part, exported beyond seas; the South and the West consequently stand in need of the commercial resources of the North. They are likewise interested in the maintenance of a powerful fleet by the Union, to protect them efficaciously. The South and the West have no vessels, but willingly contribute to the expense of a navy; for if the fleets of Europe were to blockade the ports of the South and the delta of the Mississippi, what would become of the rice of the Carolinas, the tobacco of Virginia, and the sugar and cotton which grow in the valley of the Mississippi? Every portion of the Federal budget does, therefore, contribute to the maintenance of material interests which are common to all the confederate States.

Independently of this commercial utility, the South and the West derive great political advantages from their union with each other and with the North. The South contains an enormous slave population, — a population which is already alarming, and still more formidable for the future. The States of the West occupy a single valley; the rivers which intersect their territory rise in the Rocky Mountains or in the Alleghanies, and fall into the Mississippi, which bears them onwards to the Gulf of Mexico. The Western States are consequently entirely cut off, by their position, from the traditions of Europe and the civilization of the Old World. The inhabitants of the South, then, are induced to support the Union in order to avail themselves of its protection against the blacks; and the inhabitants of the West, in order not to be excluded from a free communication with the rest of the globe, and shut up in the wilds of central America. The North cannot but desire the maintenance of the Union, in order to remain, as it now is, the connecting link between that vast body and the other parts of the world.

The material interests of all the parts of the Union are, then, intimately connected; and the same assertion holds true respecting those opinions and sentiments which may be termed the immaterial interests of men.

The inhabitants of the United States talk much of their attachment to their country; but I confess that I do not rely upon that calculating patriotism which is founded upon interest, and which a change in the interests may destroy. Nor do I attach much importance to the language of the Americans, when they manifest, in their daily conversation, the intention of maintaining the Federal system adopted by their forefathers. A government retains its sway over a great number of citizens far less by the voluntary and rational consent of the multitude, than by that instinctive, and to a certain extent involuntary, agreement which results from similarity of feelings and resemblances of opinion. I will never admit that men constitute a social body simply because they obey the same head and the same laws. Society can only exist when a great number of men consider a great number of things under the same aspect, when they hold the same opinions upon many subjects, and when the same occurrences suggest the same thoughts and impressions to their minds.

The observer who examines what is passing in the United States upon this principle, will readily discover that their inhabitants, though divided into twenty-four distinct sovereignties, still constitute a single people; and he may perhaps be led to think that the Anglo-American Union is more truly a united society than some nations of Europe which live under the same legislation and the same prince.

Although the Anglo-Americans have several religious sects, they all regard religion in the same manner. They are not always agreed upon the measures which are most conducive to good government, and they vary upon some of the forms of government which it is expedient to adopt; but they are unanimous upon the general principles which ought to rule human society. From Maine to the Floridas, and from the Missouri to the Atlantic Ocean, the people are held to be the source of all legitimate power. The same notions are entertained respecting liberty and equality, the liberty of the press, the right of association, the jury, and the responsibility of the agents of government.

If we turn from their political and religious opinions to the moral and philosophical principles which regulate the daily actions of life, and govern their conduct, we still find the same uniformity. The Anglo-Americans * acknowledge the moral authority of the reason of the community, as they acknowledge the political authority of the mass of citizens; and they hold that public opinion is the surest arbiter of what is lawful or forbidden, true or false. The majority of them believe that a man, by following his own interest rightly understood, will be led to do what is just and good. They hold that every man is born in possession of the right of self-government, and that no one has the right of constraining his fellow-creatures to be happy. They have all a lively faith in the perfectibility of man; they judge that the diffusion of knowledge must necessarily be advantageous, and the consequences of ignorance fatal; they all consider society as a body in a state of improvement, humanity as a changing scene, in which nothing is, or ought to be, permanent; and they admit that what appears to them to-day to be good, may be superseded by something better to-morrow. I do not give all these opinions as true, but as American opinions.

The Anglo-Americans are not only united by these common opinions, but they are separated from all other nations by a feeling of pride. For the last fifty years, no pains have been spared to convince the inhabitants of the United States that they are the only religious, enlightened, and free people. They perceive that, for the present, their own democratic institutions prosper, whilst those of other countries fail; hence they conceive a high opinion of their

* It is scarcely necessary for me to observe that, by the expression *Anglo-Americans,* I mean to designate only the great majority of the nation; for some isolated individuals, of course, hold very different opinions.

superiority, and are not very remote from believing themselves to be a distinct species of mankind.

Thus, the dangers which threaten the American Union do not originate in diversity of interests or of opinions; but in the various characters and passions of the Americans. The men who inhabit the vast territory of the United States are almost all the issue of a common stock; but climate, and more especially slavery, have gradually introduced marked differences between the British settler of the Southern States and the British settler of the North. In Europe, it is generally believed that slavery has rendered the interests of one part of the Union contrary to those of the other; but I have not found this to be the case. Slavery has not created interests in the South contrary to those of the North, but it has modified the character and changed the habits of the natives of the South.

I have already explained the influence of slavery upon the commercial ability of the Americans in the South; and this same influence equally extends to their manners. The slave is a servant who never remonstrates, and who submits to everything without complaint. He may sometimes assassinate, but he never withstands, his master. In the South, there are no families so poor as not to have slaves.* The citizen of the Southern States becomes a sort of domestic dictator from infancy; the first notion he acquires in life is, that he is born to command, and the first habit which he contracts is that of ruling without resistance. His education tends, then, to give him the character of a haughty and hasty man, — irascible, violent, ardent in his desires, impatient of obstacles, but easily discouraged if he cannot succeed upon his first attempt.

---

* This is not strictly true. There are many "poor whites," as they are termed, in the Southern States, who own no slaves, and earn a scanty subsistence by the labor of their hands, though they labor very unwillingly. — AM. ED.

The American of the North sees no slaves around him in his childhood; he is even unattended by free servants, for he is usually obliged to provide for his own wants. As soon as he enters the world, the idea of necessity assails him on every side : he soon learns to know exactly the natural limits of his power; he never expects to subdue by force those who withstand him ; and he knows that the surest means of obtaining the support of his fellow-creatures is to win their favor. He therefore becomes patient, reflecting, tolerant, slow to act, and persevering in his designs.

In the Southern States, the more pressing wants of life are always supplied; the inhabitants, therefore, are not occupied with the material cares of life, from which they are relieved by others ; and their imagination is diverted to more captivating and less definite objects. The American of the South is fond of grandeur, luxury, and renown, of gayety, pleasure, and, above all, of idleness; nothing obliges him to exert himself in order to subsist; and as he has no necessary occupations, he gives way to indolence, and does not even attempt what would be useful.

But the equality of fortunes and the absence of slavery in the North plunge the inhabitants in those material cares which are disdained by the white population of the South. They are taught from infancy to combat want, and to place wealth above all the pleasures of the intellect or the heart. The imagination is extinguished by the trivial details of life ; and the ideas become less numerous and less general, but far more practical, clearer, and more precise. As prosperity is the sole aim of exertion, it is excellently well attained ; nature and men are turned to the best pecuniary advantage ; and society is dexterously made to contribute to the welfare of each of its members, whilst individual selfishness is the source of general happiness.

The American of the North has not only experience, but knowledge ; yet he values science not as an enjoyment, but as a means, and is only anxious to seize its useful applications. The American of the South is more given to act upon impulse; he is more clever, more frank, more generous, more intellectual, and more brilliant. The former, with a greater degree of activity, common sense, information, and general aptitude, has the characteristic good and evil qualities of the middle classes. The latter has the tastes, the prejudices, the weaknesses, and the magnanimity of all aristocracies.

If two men are united in society, who have the same interests, and, to a certain extent, the same opinions, but different characters, different acquirements, and a different style of civilization, it is most probable that these men will not agree. The same remark is applicable to a society of nations.

Slavery, then, does not attack the American Union directly in its interests, but indirectly in its manners.

The States which gave their assent to the Federal contract in 1790 were thirteen in number; the Union now consists of twenty-four [thirty-four] members. The population, which amounted to nearly four millions in 1790, had more than tripled in the space of forty years; in 1830, it amounted to nearly thirteen millions.* Changes of such magnitude cannot take place without danger.

A society of nations, as well as a society of individuals, has three principal chances of duration, — namely, the wisdom of its members, their individual weakness, and their limited number. The Americans who quit the coasts of the Atlantic Ocean to plunge into the Western wilderness are adventurers, impatient of restraint, greedy of wealth, and frequently men expelled from the States in which they were born. When they arrive in the deserts, they are

* Census of 1790   .   .   .   3,929,328.
    "   1830 .   .   .   . 12,856,165.
    "   1860 .   .   .   31,134,666.

unknown to each other ; they have neither traditions, family feeling, nor the force of example to check their excesses. The authority of the laws is feeble amongst them, — that of morality is still weaker. The settlers who are constantly peopling the valley of the Mississippi are, then, in every respect, inferior to the Americans who inhabit the older parts of the Union. But they already exercise a great influence in its councils ; and they arrive at the government of the commonwealth before they have learnt to govern themselves.*

The greater the individual weakness of the contracting parties, the greater are the chances of the duration of the contract ; for their safety is then dependent upon their union. When, in 1790, the most populous of the American republics did not contain 500,000 inhabitants,† each of them felt its own insignificance as an independent people, and this feeling rendered compliance with the Federal authority more easy. But, when one of the confederate States reckons, like the State of New York, two millions [three and a half millions] of inhabitants, and covers an extent of territory equal to a quarter of France, ‡ it feels its own strength ; and, although it may still support the Union as useful to its prosperity, it no longer regards it as necessary to its existence ; and, while consenting to continue in it, it aims at preponderance in the Federal councils. The mere increase in number of the States weakens the tie that holds them together. All men who are placed at the same point of view do not look at the same objects in the same manner. Still less do they do so when the point of view is different. In proportion,

---

* This indeed is only a temporary danger. I have no doubt that in time society will assume as much stability and regularity in the West as it has already done upon the coast of the Atlantic Ocean.

† Pennsylvania contained 431,373 inhabitants in 1790.

‡ The area of the State of New York is about 46,000 square miles.

then, as the American republics become, more numerous, there is less chance of their unanimity in matters of legislation. At present, the interests of the different parts of the Union are not at variance; but who can foresee the various changes of the future in a country in which new towns are founded every day, and new States almost every year?

Since the first settlement of the British Colonies, the number of inhabitants has about doubled every twenty-two years. I perceive no causes which are likely to check this ratio of increase of the Anglo-American population for the next hundred years; and, before that time has elapsed, I believe that the territories and dependencies of the United States will be covered by more than a hundred millions of inhabitants, and divided into forty States.† I admit that these hundred millions of men have no different interests. I suppose, on the contrary, that they are all equally interested in the maintenance of the Union; but I still say that, for the very reason that they are a hundred millions, forming forty distinct nations unequally strong, the continuance of the Federal government can only be a fortunate accident.

Whatever faith I may have in the perfectibility of man,

---

* If the population continues to double every twenty-two years, as it has done for the last two hundred years, the number of inhabitants in the United States in 1852 will be twenty-four millions; in 1874, forty-eight millions; and in 1896, ninety-six millions. This may still be the case, even if the lands on the eastern slope of the Rocky Mountains should be found unfit for cultivation. The territory which is already occupied can easily contain this number of inhabitants. One hundred millions of men spread over the surface of the twenty-four States, and the three dependencies, which now constitute the Union, would only give 762 inhabitants to the square league; this would be far below the mean population of France, which is 1,006 to the square league; or of England, which 1,457; and it would even be below the population of Switzerland, for that country, notwithstanding its lakes and mountains, contains 783 inhabitants to the square league.

until human nature is altered, and men wholly transformed, I shall refuse to believe in the duration of a government which is called upon to hold together forty different nations, spread over a territory equal to one half of Europe, to avoid all rivalry, ambition, and struggles between them, and to direct their independent activity to the accomplishment of the same designs.

But the greatest peril to which the Union is exposed by its increase arises from the continual displacement of its internal forces. The distance from Lake Superior to the Gulf of Mexico is more than twelve hundred miles, as the crow flies. The frontier of the United States winds along the whole of this immense line; sometimes falling within its limits, but more frequently extending far beyond it, into the waste. It has been calculated that the whites advance every year a mean distance of seventeen miles along the whole of this vast boundary. Obstacles, such as an unproductive district, a lake, or an Indian nation, are sometimes encountered. The advancing column then halts for a while; its two extremities curve round upon themselves, and, as soon as they are reunited, they proceed onwards. This gradual and continuous progress of the European race towards the Rocky Mountains has the solemnity of a providential event; it is like a deluge of men rising unabatedly, and daily driven onwards by the hand of God.

Within this front line of conquering settlers, towns are built, and vast States founded. In 1790, there were only a few thousand pioneers sprinkled along the valleys of the Mississippi; at the present day, these valleys contain as many inhabitants as were to be found in the whole Union in 1790. Their population amounts to nearly four millions. The city of Washington was founded in 1800, in the very centre of the Union; but such are the changes which have taken place, that it now stands at one of the extremities; and the delegates of the most remote Western States, in

order to take their seats in Congress, are already obliged
to perform a journey as long as that from Vienna to Paris.*

All the States are borne onwards at the same time in the
path of fortune, but they do not all increase and prosper
in the same proportion. In the North of the Union, the
detached branches of the Alleghany chain, extending as
far as the Atlantic Ocean, form spacious roads and ports,
constantly accessible to the largest vessels. But from the
Potomac, following the shore, to the mouth of the Mississippi, the coast is sandy and flat. In this part of the
Union, the mouths of almost all the rivers are obstructed ;
and the few harbors which exist amongst these lagunes
afford shallower water to vessels, and much fewer commercial advantages, than those of the North.

This first and natural cause of inferiority is united to
another cause proceeding from the laws. We have seen
that slavery, which is abolished in the North, still exists in
the South ; and I have pointed out its fatal consequences
upon the prosperity of the planter himself.

The North is therefore superior to the South both in
commerce † and manufacture ; the natural consequence of

* The distance from Jefferson, the capital of the State of Missouri, to
Washington, is 1,019 miles.

† The following statements will show the difference between the commercial activity of the South and of the North.

In 1829 the tonnage of all the merchant-vessels belonging to Virginia, the
two Carolinas, and Georgia (the four great Southern States), amounted to
only 5,243 tons. In the same year, the tonnage of the vessels of the State
of Massachusetts alone amounted to 17,322 tons. (See Legislative Documents, 21st Congress, 2d Session, No. 140, p. 214.) Thus Massachusetts
had three times as much shipping as the four above-mentioned States. Nevertheless, the area of the State of Massachusetts is only 7,335 square miles,
and its population amounts to 610,014 inhabitants ; whilst the area of the
four other States I have quoted is 210,000 square miles, and their population
3,047,767. Thus the area of the State of Massachusetts forms only one
thirtieth part of the area of the four States ; and its population is but one
fifth of theirs. [In 1858, the tonnage of the these four Southern States was

which is the more rapid increase of population and wealth within its borders. The States on the shores of the Atlantic Ocean are already half peopled. Most of the land is held by an owner ; and they cannot therefore receive so many emigrants as the Western States, where a boundless field is still open to industry. The valley of the Mississippi is far more fertile than the coast of the Atlantic Ocean. This reason, added to all the others, contributes to drive the Europeans westward, — a fact which may be rigorously demonstrated by figures. It is found that the sum total of the population of all the United States has about tripled in the course of forty years. But in the new States adjacent to the Mississippi, the population has increased thirty-one fold within the same time.

The centre of the Federal power is continually displaced. Forty years ago, the majority of the citizens of the Union was established upon the coast of the Atlantic, in the environs of the spot where Washington now stands ; but the great body of the people are now advancing inland and to the North, so that, in twenty years, the majority will unquestionably be on the western side ot the Alleghanies. If the Union continues, the basin of the Mississippi is evidently marked out, by its fertility and its extent, to be the permanent centre of the Federal government. In thirty or forty years, that tract of country will have assumed its natural rank. It is easy to calculate that its population,

but 4,765, while that of Massachusetts was 32,599.] Slavery is prejudicial to the commercial prosperity of the South in several different ways; by diminishing the spirit of enterprise amongst the whites, and by preventing them from obtaining the sailors whom they require. Sailors are usually taken only from the lowest ranks of the population. But in the Southern States, these lowest ranks are composed of slaves, and it is very difficult to employ them at sea. They are unable to serve as well as a white crew, and apprehensions would always be entertained of their mutinying in the middle of the ocean, or of their escaping in the foreign countries at which they might touch.

compared with that of the coast of the Atlantic, will then be, in round numbers, as 40 to 11. In a few years, the States which founded the Union will lose the direction of its policy, and the population of the valley of the Mississippi will preponderate in the Federal assemblies.

This constant gravitation of the Federal power and influence towards the Northwest is shown every ten years, when a general census of the population is made, and the number of delegates which each State sends to Congress is settled anew.* In 1790, Virginia had nineteen representatives in Congress. This number continued to increase until 1813, when it reached twenty-three; from that time it began to decrease, and, in 1833, Virginia elected only twenty-one.† During the same period, the State of

* It may be seen that, in the course of the last ten years (1820 - 1830), the population of one district, as, for instance, the State of Delaware, has increased in the proportion of five per cent; whilst that of another, as the Territory of Michigan, has increased 250 per cent. Thus the population of Virginia had augmented 13 per cent, and that of the border State of Ohio 61 per cent, in the same time. The general table of these changes, which is given in the National Calendar, is a striking picture of the unequal fortunes of the different States.

† It has just been said, that, in the course of the last term, the population of Virginia has increased 13 per cent; and it is necessary to explain how the number of representatives for a State may decrease, when the population of that State, far from diminishing, is actually upon the increase. I take the State of Virginia, to which I have already alluded, as my term of comparison. The number of representatives of Virginia in 1823 was proportionate to the total number of the representatives of the Union, and to the relation which its population bore to that of the whole Union; in 1833, the number of representatives of Virginia was likewise proportionate to the total number of the representatives of the Union, and to the relation which its population, augmented in the course of ten years, bore to the augmented population of the Union in the same space of time. The new number of Virginian representatives will then be to the old number, on the one hand, as the new number of all the representatives is to the old number; and, on the other hand, as the augmentation of the population of Virginia is to that of the whole population of the country. Thus, if the increase of the popu-

New York followed the contrary direction : in 1790, it had ten representatives in Congress ; in 1813, twenty-seven ; in 1823, thirty-four ; and in 1833, forty. The State of Ohio had only one representative in 1803 ; and in 1833, it had already nineteen. [Virginia now has thirteen, New York thirty-three, and Ohio twenty-one representatives.]

It is difficult to imagine a durable union of a nation which is rich and strong with one which is poor and weak, even if it were proved that the strength and wealth of the one are not the causes of the weakness and poverty of the other. But union is still more difficult to maintain at a time when one party is losing strength, and the other is gaining it. This rapid and disproportionate increase of certain States threatens the independence of the others. New York might perhaps succeed, with its two millions of inhabitants and its forty representatives, in dictating to the other States in Congress. But, even if the more powerful States make no attempt to oppress the smaller ones, the danger still exists ; for there is almost as much in the possibility of the act as in the act itself. The weak generally mistrust the justice and the reason of the strong. The States which increase less rapidly than the others look upon those which are more favored by fortune with envy and suspicion. Hence arise the deep-seated uneasiness and ill-defined agitation which are observable in the South, and which form so striking a contrast to the confidence and prosperity which are common to other parts of the Union. I am inclined to think that the hostile attitude taken

lation of the lesser country be to that of the greater in an exact inverse ratio of the proportion between the new and the old numbers of all the representatives, the number of the representatives of Virginia will remain stationary ; and if the increase of the Virginian population be to that of the whole Union in a feebler ratio than the new number of the representatives of the Union to the old number, the number of the representatives of Virginia must decrease.

by the South recently, is attributable to no other cause. The inhabitants of the Southern States are, of all the Americans, those who are most interested in the main- tenance of the Union ; they would assuredly suffer most from being left to themselves ; and yet they are the only ones who threaten to break the tie of confederation.   It is easy to perceive that the South, which has given four Presidents — Washington, Jefferson, Madison, and Mon- roe — to the Union, which perceives that it is losing its Federal influence, and that the number of its representa- tives in Congress is diminishing from year to year, whilst those of the Northern and Western States are increasing, — the South, which is peopled with ardent and irascible men, is becoming more and more irritated and alarmed. Its inhabitants reflect upon their present position, and re- member their past influence, with the melancholy uneasi- ness of men who suspect oppression.   If they discover a law of the Union which is not unequivocally favorable to their interests, they protest against it as an abuse of force ; and if their ardent remonstrances are not listened to, they threaten to quit an association which loads them with burdens whilst it deprives them of the profits.   " The Tariff," said the inhabitants of Carolina in 1832, " enriches the North and ruins the South ; for, if this were not the case, to what can we attribute the continually increasing power and wealth of the North, with its inclement skies and arid soil ; whilst the South, which may be styled the garden of America, is rapidly declining." *

If the changes which I have described were gradual, so that each generation at least might have time to disappear with the order of things under which it had lived, the danger would be less ; but the progress of society in Amer- ica is precipitate, and almost revolutionary.   The same

* See the report of its committee to the convention which proclaimed the nullification of the Tariff in South Carolina.

citizen may have lived to see his State take the lead in the Union, and afterwards become powerless in the Federal assemblies; and an Anglo-American republic has been known to grow as rapidly as a man, passing from birth and infancy to maturity in the course of thirty years. It must not be imagined, however, that the States which lose their preponderance also lose their population or their riches: no stop is put to their prosperity, and they even go on to increase more rapidly than any kingdom in Europe.* But they believe themselves to be impoverished because their wealth does not augment as rapidly as that of their neighbors; and they think that their power is lost because they suddenly come in contact with a power greater than their own :† thus they are more hurt in their feelings and their passions than in their interests. But this is amply sufficient to endanger the maintenance of the Union. If kings and peoples had only had their true interests in view, ever since the beginning of the world, war would scarcely be known among mankind.

Thus the prosperity of the United .States is the source of their most serious dangers, since it tends to create in some of the confederate States that intoxication which accompanies a rapid increase of fortune; and to awaken in others those feelings of envy, mistrust, and regret which

---

* The population of a country assuredly constitutes the first element of its wealth. In the ten years (1820 – 1830) during which Virginia lost two of its representatives in Congress, its population increased in the proportion of 13.7 per cent; that of Carolina, in the proportion of 15 per cent; and that of Georgia, 15.5 per cent. But the population of Russia, which increases more rapidly than that of any other European country, only augments in ten years at the rate of 9.5 per cent; of France, at the rate of 7 per cent; and of Europe altogether, at the rate of 4.7 per cent.

† It must be admitted, however, that the depreciation which has taken place in the value of tobacco, during the last fifty years, has notably diminished the opulence of the Southern planters : but this circumstance is as independent of the will of their Northern brethren as it is of their own.

usually attend the loss of it. The Americans contemplate this extraordinary progress with exultation; but they would be wiser to consider it with sorrow and alarm. The Americans of the United States must inevitably become one of the greatest nations in the world; their offspring will cover almost the whole of North America; the continent which they inhabit is their dominion, and it cannot escape them. What urges them to take possession of it so soon? Riches, power, and renown cannot fail to be theirs at some future time; but they rush upon this immense fortune as if but a moment remained for them to make it their own.

I think that I have demonstrated, that the existence of the present confederation depends entirely on the continued assent of all the confederates; and, starting from this principle, I have inquired into the causes which may induce some of the States to separate from the others. The Union may, however, perish in two different ways: one of the confederate States may choose to retire from the compact, and so forcibly to sever the Federal tie; and it is to this supposition that most of the remarks that I have made apply: or the authority of the Federal government may be gradually lost by the simultaneous tendency of the united republics to resume their independence. The central power, successively stripped of all its prerogatives, and reduced to impotence by tacit consent, would become incompetent to fulfil its purpose; and the second union would perish, like the first, by a sort of senile imbecility. The gradual weakening of the Federal tie, which may finally lead to the dissolution of the Union, is a distinct circumstance, that may produce a variety of minor consequences before it operates so violent a change. The confederation might still subsist, although its government were reduced to such a degree of inanition as to paralyze the nation, to cause internal anarchy, and to check the general prosperity of the country.

After having investigated the causes which may induce the Anglo-Americans to disunite, it is important to inquire whether, if the Union continues to subsist, their government will extend or contract its sphere of action, and whether it will become more energetic or more weak.

The Americans are evidently disposed to look upon their condition with alarm. They perceive that, in most of the nations of the world, the exercise of the rights of sovereignty tends to fall into a few hands, and they are dismayed by the idea that it may be so in their own country. Even the statesmen feel, or affect to feel, these fears; for in America centralization is by no means popular, and there is no surer means of courting the majority than by inveighing against the encroachments of the central power. The Americans do not perceive that the countries in which this alarming tendency to centralization exists are inhabited by a single people; whilst the Union is composed of different communities, — a fact which is sufficient to baffle all the inferences which might be drawn from analogy. I confess that I am inclined to consider these fears of a great number of Americans as purely imaginary. Far from participating in their dread of the consolidation of power in the hands of the Union, I think that the Federal government is visibly losing strength. To prove this assertion, I shall not have recourse to any remote occurrences, but to circumstances which I have myself witnessed, and which belong to our own time.

An attentive examination of what is going on in the United States will easily convince us that two opposite tendencies exist there, like two currents flowing in contrary directions in the same channel. The Union has now existed for forty-five years, and time has done away with many provincial prejudices which were at first hostile to its power. The patriotic feeling which attached each of the Americans to his own State is become less exclusive;

and the different parts of the Union have become more amicable as they have become better acquainted with each other. The post, that great instrument of intercourse, now reaches into the backwoods; and steamboats have established daily means of communication between the different points of the coast. An inland navigation of unexampled rapidity conveys commodities up and down the rivers of the country. And to these facilities of nature and art may be added those restless cravings, that busy-mindedness, and love of pelf, which are constantly urging the American into active life, and bringing him into contact with his fellow-citizens. He crosses the country in every direction; he visits all the various populations of the land. There is not a province in France in which the natives are so well known to each other as the thirteen millions of men who cover the territory of the United States.

Whilst the Americans intermingle, they assimilate; the differences resulting from their climate, their origin, and their institutions diminish; and they all draw nearer and nearer to the common type. Every year thousands of men leave the North to settle in different parts of the Union: they bring with them their faith, their opinions, and their manners; and as they are more enlightened than the men amongst whom they are about to dwell, they soon rise to the head of affairs, and adapt society to their own advantage. This continual emigration of the North to the South is peculiarly favorable to the fusion of all the different provincial characters into one national character. The civilization of the North appears to be the common standard, to which the whole nation will one day be assimilated.

The commercial ties which unite the confederate States are strengthened by the increasing manufactures of the Americans; and the union which began in their opinions gradually forms a part of their habits: the course of time has swept away the bugbear thoughts which haunted the imaginations of the citizens in 1789. The Federal power is not become oppressive; it has not destroyed the independence of the States; it has not subjected the confederates to monarchical institutions; and the Union has not rendered the lesser States dependent upon the larger ones. The confederation has continued to increase in population, in wealth, and in power. I am therefore convinced that the natural obstacles to the continuance of the American Union are not so powerful now as they were in 1789, and that the enemies of the Union are not so numerous.

And yet a careful examination of the history of the United States for the last forty-five years will readily convince us that the Federal power is declining; nor is it difficult to explain the causes of this phenomenon. When the Constitution of 1789 was promulgated, the nation was a prey to anarchy; the Union, which succeeded this confusion, excited much dread and hatred, but it was warmly supported because it satisfied an imperious want. Although it was then more attacked than it is now, the Federal power soon reached the maximum of its authority, as is usually the case with a government which triumphs after having braced its strength by the struggle. At that time, the interpretation of the Constitution seemed to extend, rather than to repress, the Federal sovereignty; and the Union offered, in several respects, the appearance of a single and undivided people, directed in its foreign and internal policy by a single government. But to attain this point the people had risen, to some extent, above itself.

The Constitution had not destroyed the individuality of the States; and all communities, of whatever nature they may be, are impelled by a secret instinct towards independence. This propensity is still more decided in a country like America, in which every village forms a sort of republic, accustomed to govern itself. It therefore cost the States an effort to submit to the Federal supremacy ; and all efforts, however successful they may be, necessarily subside with the causes in which they originated.

As the Federal government consolidated its authority, America resumed its rank amongst the nations, peace returned to its frontiers, and public credit was restored ; confusion was succeeded by a fixed state of things, which permitted the full and free exercise of industrious enterprise. It was this very prosperity which made the Americans forget the cause which had produced it ; and when once the danger was passed, the energy and the patriotism which had enabled them to brave it disappeared from amongst them. Delivered from the cares which oppressed them, they easily returned to their ordinary habits, and gave themselves up without resistance to their natural inclinations. When a powerful government no longer appeared to be necessary, they once more began to think it irksome. Everything prospered under the Union, and the States were not inclined to abandon the Union ; but they desired to render the action of the power which represented it as light as possible. The general principle of union was adopted, but in every minor detail there was a tendency to independence. The principle of confederation was every day more easily admitted, and more rarely applied ; so that the Federal government, by creating order and peace, brought about its own decline.

As soon as this tendency of public opinion began to be manifested externally, the leaders of parties, who live by the passions of the people, began to work it to their own advantage. The position of the Federal government then became exceedingly critical. Its enemies were in possession of the popular favor ; and they obtained the right of conducting its policy by pledging themselves to lessen its influence. From that time forwards, the government of the

Union, as often as it has entered the lists with the governments of the States, has almost invariably been obliged to
recede. And whenever an interpretation of the terms of
the Federal Constitution has been pronounced, that interpretation has generally been opposed to the Union, and
favorable to the States.*

The Constitution gave to the Federal government the
right of providing for the national interests; and it had
been held that no other authority was so fit to superintend
the " internal improvements " which affected the prosperity of the whole Union; such, for instance, as the cutting
of canals. But the States were alarmed at a power which
could thus dispose of a portion of their territory; they
were afraid that the central government would by this
means acquire a formidable patronage within their own
limits, and exercise influence which they wished to reserve
exclusively to their own agents. The Democratic party,
which has constantly opposed the increase of the Federal
authority, accused Congress of usurpation, and the Chief
Magistrate of ambition. The central government was in-
timidated by these clamors; and it finally acknowledged
its error, promising to confine its influence for the future
within the circle which was prescribed to it.

The Constitution confers upon the Union the right of
treating with foreign nations. The Indian tribes, which
border upon the frontiers of the United States, had usually
been regarded in this light. As long as these savages con-

---

* This assertion may be doubted. The only authorized *interpreter* of the
Constitution is the Supreme Court of the United States; and in most of the
suits before this tribunal, which have involved a question as to the limits of the
Federal and the State authority, the decision has been in favor of the former.
See the Dartmouth College case, that of Chisholm *v.* Georgia, Gibbons *v.* Ogden, Ogden *v.* Saunders, the Cherokee Land case, and many others. Several of the cases which our author goes on to cite are instances of *legislative*,
not *judicial*, interpretation; that is, legally they are no interpretation at all,
being all liable to be overruled by the Supreme Court. — AM. ED.

sented to retire before the civilized settlers, the Federal right was not contested; but as soon as an Indian tribe attempted to fix its residence upon a given spot, the adjacent States claimed possession of the lands, and a right of sovereignty over the natives. The central government soon recognized both these claims; and after it had concluded treaties with the Indians as independent nations, it gave them up as subjects to the legislative tyranny of the States.*

Some of the States which had been founded upon the coast of the Atlantic extended indefinitely to the West, into wild regions where no European had yet penetrated. The States whose confines were irrevocably fixed looked with a jealous eye upon the unbounded regions which were thus opened to their neighbors. The latter then agreed, with a view to conciliate the others, and to facilitate the act of Union, to lay down their own boundaries, and to abandon all the territory which lay beyond them to the confederation at large. † Thenceforward the Federal government became the owner of all the uncultivated lands which lie beyond the borders of the thirteen States first confederated. It had the right of parcelling and selling them, and the sums derived from this source were paid into the public treasury to furnish the means of purchasing tracts of land from the Indians, opening roads to the re-

---

* See, in the Legislative Documents already quoted in speaking of the Indians, the letter of the President of the United States to the Cherokees, his correspondence on this subject with his agents, and his messages to Congress. [In the case here referred to, Georgia did not claim a right of sovereignty over the Indians as her own subjects, but only demanded that they should leave a tract of country, the Indian title to which the Federal government had pledged itself to extinguish. — AM. ED.]

† The first act of cession was made by the State of New York in 1780; Virginia, Massachusetts, Connecticut, South and North Carolina, followed this example at different times, and, lastly, the act of cession of Georgia was made as recently as 1802

mote settlements, and accelerating the advance of civilization. New States have been formed in the course of time,
in the midst of those wilds which were formerly ceded by
the Atlantic States. Congress has gone on to sell, for the
profit of the nation at large, the uncultivated lands which
those new States contained. But the latter at length asserted that, as they were now fully constituted, they ought
to have the right of converting the produce of these sales
exclusively to their own use. As their remonstrances became more and more threatening, Congress thought fit
to deprive the Union of a portion of the privileges which
it had hitherto enjoyed; and, at the end of 1832, it passed
a law by which the greatest part of the revenue derived
from the sale of lands was made over to the new Western
republics, although the lands themselves were not ceded
to them.*

The slightest observation in the United States enables
one to appreciate the advantages which the country derives from the Bank. These advantages are of several
kinds, but one of them is peculiarly striking to the stranger. The notes of the Bank of the United States are
taken upon the borders of the desert for the same value as
at Philadelphia, where the Bank conducts its operations.†

But the Bank of the United States is the object of great
animosity. Its directors proclaimed their hostility to the

---

* It is true that the President refused his assent to this law; but he completely adopted it in principle. See Message of 8th December, 1833. [This
is overstated again. The Western States never claimed the lands, but only
that they should be sold at a low price, so as to encourage their settlement,
and that a fair portion of the purchase-money should be devoted to opening
roads and other internal improvements. — AM. ED.]

† The Bank of the United States was established in 1816, with a capital of
35,000,000 dollars; its charter expired in 1836. In 1832, Congress passed
a law to renew it, but the President put his veto upon the bill. The struggle
continued with great violence on either side, and the speedy fall of the Bank
might have been foreseen.

President; and they were accused, not without probability, of having abused their influence to thwart his election. The President therefore attacked the establishment with all the warmth of personal enmity; and he was encouraged in the pursuit of his revenge by the conviction that he was supported by the secret inclinations of the majority. The Bank may be regarded as the great monetary tie of the Union, just as Congress is the great legislative tie; and the same passions which tend to render the States independent of the central power contributed to the overthrow of the Bank.

The Bank of the United States always held a great number of the notes issued by the provincial banks, which it can at any time oblige them to convert into cash. It has itself nothing to fear from a similar demand, as the extent of its resources enables it to meet all claims. But the existence of the provincial banks is thus threatened, and their operations are restricted, since they are able to issue only a quantity of notes duly proportioned to their capital. They submitted with impatience to this salutary control. The newspapers which they bought over, and the President, whose interest rendered him their instrument, attacked the Bank with the greatest vehemence. They roused the local passions and the blind democratic instinct of the country to aid their cause; and they asserted that the Bank directors formed a permanent aristocratic body, whose influence would ultimately be felt in the government, and affect those principles of equality upon which society rests in America.

The contest between the Bank and its opponents was only an incident in the great struggle which is going on in America between the provinces and the central power, — between the spirit of democratic independence, and that of a proper distribution and subordination of power. I do not mean that the enemies of the Bank were identically the same individuals who, on other points, attacked the Federal government; but I assert that the attacks directed against the Bank of the United States originated in the same propensities which militate against the Federal government, and that the very numerous opponents of the former afford a deplorable symptom of the decreasing strength of the latter.

But the Union has never shown so much weakness as on the celebrated question of the Tariff.* The wars of the French Revolution and of 1812 had created manufacturing establishments in the North of the Union, by cutting off free communication between America and Europe. When peace was concluded, and the channel of intercourse reopened, by which the produce of Europe was transmitted to the New World, the Americans thought fit to establish a system of import duties, for the twofold purpose of protecting their incipient manufactures and of paying off the amount of the debt contracted during the war. The Southern States, which have no manufactures to encourage, and which are exclusively agricultural, soon complained of this measure. I do not pretend to examine here whether their complaints were well or ill founded, but only to recite the facts.

As early as 1820, South Carolina declared, in a petition to Congress, that the Tariff was "unconstitutional, oppressive, and unjust." And the States of Georgia, Virginia, North Carolina, Alabama, and Mississippi subsequently remonstrated against it with more or less vigor. But Congress, far from lending an ear to these complaints, raised the scale of Tariff duties in the years 1824 and 1828, and recognized anew the principle on which it was founded. A doctrine was then proclaimed, or rather revived, in the South, which took the name of Nullification.

* See principally, for the details of this affair, the Legislative Documents, 22d Congress, 2d Session, No. 30.

I have shown in the proper place that the object of the Federal Constitution was not to form a league, but to create a national government. The Americans of the United States form one and the same people, in all the cases which are specified by that Constitution; and upon these points, the will of the nation is expressed, as it is in all constitutional nations, by the voice of the majority. When the majority has once spoken, it is the duty of the minority to submit. Such is the sound legal doctrine, and the only one which agrees with the text of the Constitution, and the known intention of those who framed it.

The partisans of Nullification in the South maintain, on the contrary, that the intention of the Americans in uniting was not to combine themselves into one and the same people, but that they meant only to form a league of independent States; and that each State, consequently, retains its entire sovereignty, if not *de facto*, at least *de jure*, and has the right of putting its own construction upon the laws of Congress, and of suspending their execution within the limits of its own territory, if they seem unconstitutional and unjust.

The entire doctrine of Nullification is comprised in a sentence uttered by Vice-President Calhoun, the head of that party in the South, before the Senate of the United States, in 1833 : " The Constitution is a compact to which the States were parties in their sovereign capacity : now, whenever a compact is entered into by parties which acknowledge no common arbiter to decide in the last resort, each of them has a right to judge for itself in relation to the nature, extent, and obligations of the instrument." It is evident that such a doctrine destroys the very basis of the Federal Constitution, and brings back the anarchy from which the Americans were delivered by the act of 1789.

When South Carolina perceived that Congress turned

a deaf ear to its remonstrances, it threatened to apply the doctrine of Nullification to the Federal Tariff law. Congress persisted in its system, and at length the storm broke out. In the course of 1832, the people of South Carolina* named a national convention, to consult upon the extraordinary measures which remained to be taken; and on the 24th of November of the same year, this convention promulgated a law, under the form of a decree, which annulled the Federal law of the Tariff, forbade the levy of the imposts which that law commands, and refused to recognize the appeal which might be made to the Federal courts of law.† This decree was only to be put in execution in the ensuing month of February; and it was intimated that, if Congress modified the Tariff before that period, South Carolina might be induced to proceed no further with her menaces; and a vague desire was afterwards expressed of submitting the question to an extraordinary assembly of all the confederate States. In the

---

* That is to say, the majority of the people; for the opposite party, called the *Union party*, always formed a very strong and active minority. Carolina may contain about 47,000 voters; 30,000 were in favor of nullification, and 17,000 opposed to it.

† This decree was preceded by a Report of the Committee by which it was framed, containing the explanation of the motives and object of the law. The following passage occurs in it (p. 34): "When the rights reserved by the Constitution to the different States are deliberately violated, it is the duty and the right of those States to interfere, in order to check the progress of the evil; to resist usurpation, and to maintain, within their respective limits, those powers and privileges which belong to them as *independent, sovereign States.* If they were destitute of this right, they would not be sovereign. South Carolina declares that she acknowledges no tribunal upon earth above her authority. She has indeed entered into a solemn compact of union with the other States; but she demands, and will exercise, the right of putting her own construction upon it; and when this compact is violated by her sister States, and by the government which they have created, she is determined to avail herself of the unquestionable right of judging what is the extent of the infraction, and what are the measures best fitted to obtain justice."

mean time, South Carolina armed her militia, and prepared for war.

But Congress, which had slighted its suppliant subjects, listened to their complaints as soon as they appeared with arms in their hands.* A law was passed, by which the tariff duties were to be gradually reduced for ten years, until they were brought so low as not to exceed the supplies necessary to the government. Thus Congress completely abandoned the principle of the Tariff, and substituted a mere fiscal impost for a system of protective duties.† The government of the Union, to conceal its defeat, had recourse to an expedient which is much in vogue with feeble governments. It yielded the point *de facto*, but remained inflexible upon the principles ; and whilst it was altering the Tariff law, it passed another bill, by which the President was invested with extraordinary powers, enabling him to overcome by force a resistance which was then no longer to be feared.

But South Carolina did not consent to leave the Union in the enjoyment of these scanty appearances of success : the same national convention which had annulled the Tariff bill, met again, and accepted the proffered concession ; but, at the same time, it declared its unabated perseverance in the doctrine of nullification ; and, to prove what it said, it annulled the law investing the President with extraordinary powers, although it was very certain that the law would never be carried into effect.

Almost all the controversies of which I have been speaking have taken place under the Presidency of General

* Congress was finally decided to take this step by the conduct of the powerful State of Virginia, whose Legislature offered to serve as a mediator between the Union and South Carolina. Hitherto the latter State had appeared to be entirely abandoned, even by the States which had joined in her remonstrances.

† This bill was brought in by Mr. Clay, and it passed in four days through both houses of Congress, by an immense majority.

Jackson; and it cannot be denied that, in the question of the Tariff, he has supported the rights of the Union with energy and skill. I think, however, that the conduct of this President of the Federal government may be reckoned as one of the dangers which threaten its continuance.

Some persons in Europe have formed an opinion of the influence of General Jackson upon the affairs of his country which appears highly extravagant to those who have seen the subject nearer at hand. We have been told that General Jackson has won battles; that he is an energetic man, prone by nature and habit to the use of force, covetous of power, and a despot by inclination. All this may be true; but the inferences which have been drawn from these truths are very erroneous. It has been imagined that General Jackson is bent on establishing a dictatorship in America, introducing a military spirit, and giving a degree of influence to the central authority which cannot but be dangerous to provincial liberties. But in America the time for similar undertakings, and the age for men of this kind, is not yet come: if General Jackson had thought of exercising his authority in this manner, he would infallibly have forfeited his political station, and compromised his life, — he has not been so imprudent as to attempt anything of the kind.

Far from wishing to extend the Federal power, the President belongs to the party which is desirous of limiting that power to the clear and precise letter of the Constitution, and which never puts a construction upon that act favorable to the government of the Union; far from standing forth as the champion of centralization, General Jackson is the agent of the State jealousies; and he was placed in his lofty station by the passions which are most opposed to the central government. It is by perpetually flattering these passions that he maintains his sta-

tion and his popularity. General Jackson is the slave
of the majority : he yields to its wishes, its propensities,
and its demands, — say, rather, anticipates and forestalls
them.

Whenever the governments of the States come into collision with that of the Union, the President is generally
the first to question his own rights, — he almost always
outstrips the legislature ; and when the extent of the Federal power is controverted, he takes part, as it were,
against himself, — he conceals his official interests, and
labors to diminish his own dignity. Not, indeed, that he
is naturally weak or hostile to the Union ; for when the
majority decided against the claims of nullification, he put
himself at their head, asserted the doctrines which the nation held distinctly and energetically, and was the first to
recommend force ; but General Jackson appears to me, if
I may use the American expression, to be a Federalist by
taste and a Republican by calculation.

General Jackson stoops to gain the favor of the majority ; but when he feels that his popularity is secure, he
overthrows all obstacles in the pursuit of the objects which
the community approves, or of those which it does not
regard with jealousy. Supported by a power which his
predecessors never had, he tramples on his personal enemies, whenever they cross his path, with a facility without
example ; he takes upon himself the responsibility of measures which no one before him would have ventured to
attempt : he even treats the national representatives with
a disdain approaching to insult ; he puts his veto upon the
laws of Congress, and frequently neglects even to reply
to that powerful body. He is a favorite who sometimes
treats his master roughly. The power of General Jackson
perpetually increases, but that of the President declines ;
in his hands, the Federal government is strong, but it will
pass enfeebled into the hands of his successor.

I am strangely mistaken if the Federal government of the United States be not constantly losing strength, retiring gradually from public affairs, and narrowing its circle of action. It is naturally feeble, but it now abandons even the appearance of strength. On the other hand, I thought that I remarked a more lively sense of independence, and a more decided attachment to their separate governments, in the States. The Union is desired, but only as a shadow; they wish it to be strong in certain cases, and weak in all others; in time of warfare, it is to be able to concentrate all the forces of the nation, and all the resources of the country, in its hands; and in time of peace, its existence is to be scarcely perceptible; as if this alternate debility and vigor were natural or possible.

I do not see anything for the present which can check this general tendency of opinion: the causes in which it originated do not cease to operate in the same direction. The change will therefore go on, and it may be predicted that, unless some extraordinary event occurs, the government of the Union will grow weaker and weaker every day.

I think, however, that the period is still remote, at which the Federal power will be entirely extinguished by its inability to protect itself, and to maintain peace in the country. The Union is sanctioned by the manners and desires of the people; its results are palpable, its benefits visible. When it is perceived that the weakness of the Federal government compromises the existence of the Union, I do not doubt that a reaction will take place with a view to increase its strength.

The government of the United States is, of all the Federal governments which have hitherto been established, the one which is most naturally destined to act. As long as it is only indirectly assailed by the interpretation of its laws, and as long as its substance is not seriously impaired, a change of opinion, an internal crisis, or a war, may restore all the vigor which it requires. What I have been most anxious to establish is simply this: Many people in France imagine that a change of opinion is going on in the United States, which is favorable to a centralization of power in the hands of the President and the Congress. I hold that a contrary tendency may distinctly be observed. So far is the Federal government, as it grows old, from acquiring strength, and from threatening the sovereignty of the States, that I maintain it to be growing weaker, and that the sovereignty of the Union alone is in danger. Such are the facts which the present time discloses. The future conceals the final result of this tendency, and the events which may check, retard, or accelerate the changes I have described; I do not affect to be able to remove the veil which hides them.

OF THE REPUBLICAN INSTITUTIONS OF THE UNITED STATES, AND WHAT THEIR CHANCES OF DURATION ARE.

The Union is only an Accident. — Republican Institutions have more Permanence. — A Republic for the Present is the natural State of the Anglo-Americans. — Reason of this. — In order to destroy it, all the Laws must be changed at the same Time, and a great Alteration take place in Manners. — Difficulties which the Americans would experience in creating an Aristocracy.

THE dismemberment of the Union, by introducing war into the heart of those States which are now confederate, with standing armies, a dictatorship, and a heavy taxation, might eventually compromise the fate of republican institutions. But we ought not to confound the future prospects of the republic with those of the Union. The Union is an accident, which will only last as long as circumstances favor it; but a republican form of government seems to me the natural state of the Americans, which nothing but the continued action of hostile causes, always acting in the same direction, could change into a monarchy. The Union exists principally in the law which formed it; one revolution, one change in public opinion, might destroy it forever; but the republic has a deeper foundation to rest upon.

What is understood by a republican government in the United States, is the slow and quiet action of society upon itself. It is a regular state of things really founded upon the enlightened will of the people. It is a conciliatory government, under which resolutions are allowed time to ripen; and in which they are deliberately discussed, and are executed only when mature. The republicans in the United States set a high value upon morality, respect religious belief, and acknowledge the existence of rights. They profess to think that a people ought to be moral, religious, and temperate, in proportion as it is free. What is called the republic in the United States is the tranquil rule of the majority, which, after having had time to examine itself, and to give proof of its existence, is the common source of all the powers of the State. But the power of the majority itself is not unlimited. Above it, in the moral world, are humanity, justice, and reason; and in the political world, vested rights. The majority recognizes these two barriers; and if it now and then overstep them, it is because, like individuals, it has passions, and, like them, it is prone to do what is wrong, whilst it discerns what is right.

But the demagogues of Europe have made strange discoveries. A republic is not, according to them, the rule of the majority, as has hitherto been thought, but the rule of those who are strenuous partisans of the majority. It is not the people who preponderate in this kind of government, but those who know what is good for the people; —

a happy distinction, which allows men to act in the name of nations without consulting them, and to claim their gratitude whilst their rights are trampled under foot. A republican government, moreover, they hold, is the only one which has the right of doing whatever it chooses, and despising what men have hitherto respected, from the highest moral laws to the vulgar rules of common sense. It had been supposed, until our time, that despotism was odious, under whatever form it appeared. But it is a discovery of modern days that there are such things as legitimate tyranny and holy injustice, provided they are exercised in the name of the people.

The ideas which the Americans have adopted respecting the republic, render it easy for them to live under it, and insure its duration. With them, if the republic be often practically bad, at least it is theoretically good; and, in the end, the people always act in conformity to it.

It was impossible, at the foundation of the States, and it would still be difficult, to establish a central administration in America. The inhabitants are dispersed over too great a space, and separated by too many natural obstacles, for one man to undertake to direct the details of their existence. America is therefore pre-eminently the country of provincial and municipal government. To this cause, which was plainly felt by all the Europeans of the New World, the Anglo-Americans added several others peculiar to themselves.

At the time of the settlement of the North American Colonies, municipal liberty had already penetrated into the laws as well as the manners of the English, and the emigrants adopted it, not only as a necessary thing, but as a benefit which they knew how to appreciate. We have already seen how the Colonies were founded: every province, and almost every district, was peopled separately by men who were strangers to each other, or were associated

with very different purposes. The English settlers in the
United States, therefore, early perceived that they were
divided into a great number of small and distinct communities, which belonged to no common centre; and that
each of these little communities must take care of its own
affairs, since there was not any central authority which
was naturally bound and easily enabled to provide for
them. Thus, the nature of the country, the manner in
which the British Colonies were founded, the habits of the
first emigrants, in short, everything, united to promote,
in an extraordinary degree, municipal and provincial liberties.

In the United States, therefore, the mass of the institutions of the country is essentially republican; and, in order
permanently to destroy the laws which form the basis of
the republic, it would be necessary to abolish all the laws
at once. At the present day, it would be even more difficult for a party to found a monarchy in the United States,
than for a set of men to convert France into a republic.
Royalty would not find a system of legislation prepared
for it beforehand; and a monarchy would then really exist,
surrounded by republican institutions. The monarchical
principle would likewise have great difficulty in penetrating into the manners of the Americans.

In the United States, the sovereignty of the people is
not an isolated doctrine, bearing no relation to the prevailing habits and ideas of the people; it may, on the contrary, be regarded as the last link of a chain of opinions
which binds the whole Anglo-American world. That
Providence has given to every human being the degree
of reason necessary to direct himself in the affairs which
interest him exclusively, is the grand maxim upon which
civil and political society rests in the United States. The
father of a family applies it to his children, the master to
his servants, the township to its officers, the province to

its townships, the State to the provinces, the Union to the States; and, when extended to the nation, it becomes the doctrine of the sovereignty of the people.

Thus, in the United States, the fundamental principle of the republic is the same which governs the greater part of human actions; republican notions insinuate themselves into all the ideas, opinions, and habits of the Americans, and are formally recognized by the laws; and, before the laws could be altered, the whole community must be revolutionized. In the United States, even the religion of most of the citizens is republican, since it submits the truths of the other world to private judgment: as in politics, the care of their temporal interests is abandoned to the good sense of the people. Thus, every man is allowed freely to take that road which he thinks will lead him to heaven, —just as the law permits every citizen to have the right of choosing his own government.

It is evident that nothing but a long series of events, all having the same tendency, could substitute for this combination of laws, opinions, and manners, a mass of opposite opinions, manners, and laws.

If republican principles are to perish in America, they can yield only after a laborious social process, often interrupted, and as often resumed; they will have many apparent revivals, and will not become totally extinct until an entirely new people shall have succeeded to those who now exist. There is no symptom or presage of the approach of such a revolution. There is nothing more striking to a person newly arrived in the United States, than the kind of tumultuous agitation in which he finds political society. The laws are incessantly changing, and at first sight it seems impossible that a people so fickle in its desires should avoid adopting, within a short space of time, a completely new form of government. But such apprehensions are premature; the instability which affects political institutions

is of two kinds, which ought not to be confounded.
The first, which modifies secondary laws, is not incompatible with a very settled state of society. The other
shakes the very foundations of the Constitution, and attacks the fundamental principles of legislation ; this species
of instability is always followed by troubles and revolutions, and the nation which suffers under it is in a violent
and transitory state.

Experience shows that these two kinds of legislative instability have no necessary connection ; for they have been
found united or separate, according to times and circumstances. The first is common in the United States, but
not the second : the Americans often change their laws,
but the foundations of the Constitution are respected.

In our days, the republican principle rules in America,
as the monarchical principle did in France under Louis
XIV. The French of that period were not only friends
of the monarchy, but thought it impossible to put anything
in its place ; they received it as we receive the rays of the
sun and the return of the seasons. Amongst them the
royal power had neither advocates nor opponents. In like
manner does the republican government exist in America,
without contention or opposition, without proofs or arguments, by a tacit agreement, a sort of *consensus universalis*.

It is, however, my opinion, that, by changing their administrative forms as often as they do, the inhabitants of
the United States compromise the stability of their government. It may be apprehended that men, perpetually
thwarted in their designs by the mutability of legislation,
will learn to look upon the republic as an inconvenient
form of society ; the evil resulting from the instability of
the secondary enactments might then raise a doubt as to
the nature of the fundamental principles of the Constitution, and indirectly bring about a revolution ; but this
epoch is still very remote.

It may be foreseen even now, that, when the Americans lose their republican institutions, they will speedily arrive at a despotic government, without a long interval of limited monarchy. Montesquieu remarked, that nothing is more absolute than the authority of a prince who immediately succeeds a republic, since the indefinite powers which had fearlessly been intrusted to an elected magistrate are then transferred to an hereditary sovereign. This is true in general, but it is more peculiarly applicable to a democratic republic. In the United States, the magistrates are not elected by a particular class of citizens, but by the majority of the nation; as they are the immediate representatives of the passions of the multitude, and are wholly dependent upon its pleasure, they excite neither hatred nor fear: hence, as I have already shown, very little care has been taken to limit their authority, and they are left in possession of a vast deal of arbitrary power. This state of things has created habits which would outlive itself; the American magistrate would retain his indefinite power, but would cease to be responsible for it; and it is impossible to say what bounds could then be set to tyranny.

Some of our European politicians expect to see an aristocracy arise in America, and already predict the exact period at which it will assume the reins of government. I have previously observed, and I repeat it, that the present tendency of American society appears to me to become more and more democratic. Nevertheless, I do not assert that the Americans will not, at some future time, restrict the circle of political rights, or confiscate those rights to the advantage of a single man; but I cannot believe that they will ever give the exclusive use of them to a privileged class of citizens, or, in other words, that they will ever found an aristocracy.

An aristocratic body is composed of a certain number of citizens, who, without being very far removed from the mass of the people, are, nevertheless, permanently stationed above them;—a body which it is easy to touch, and difficult to strike, — with which the people are in daily contact, but with which they can never combine. Nothing can be imagined more contrary to nature and to the secret instincts of the human heart, than a subjection of this kind; and men who are left to follow their own bent will always prefer the arbitrary power of a king to the regular administration of an aristocracy. Aristocratic institutions cannot subsist without laying down the inequality of men as a fundamental principle, legalizing it beforehand, and introducing it into the family as well as into society; but these are things so repugnant to natural equity, that they can only be extorted from men by constraint.

I do not think a single people can be quoted, since human society began to exist, which has, by its own free will and its own exertions, created an aristocracy within its own bosom. All the aristocracies of the Middle Ages were founded by military conquest; the conqueror was the noble, the vanquished became the serf. Inequality was then imposed by force; and after it had been once introduced into the manners of the country, it maintained itself, and passed naturally into the laws. Communities have existed which were aristocratic from their earliest origin, owing to circumstances anterior to that event, and which became more democratic in each succeeding age. Such was the lot of the Romans, and of the barbarians after them. But a people, having taken its rise in civilization and democracy, which should gradually establish inequality of condition, until it arrived at inviolable privileges and exclusive castes, would be a novelty in the world; and nothing indicates that America is likely to be the first to furnish such an example.

SOME CONSIDERATIONS ON THE CAUSES OF THE COMMERCIAL PROSPERITY OF THE UNITED STATES.

The Americans destined by Nature to be a great Maritime People. — Extent of their Coasts. — Depth of their Ports. — Size of their Rivers. — The Commercial Superiority of the Anglo-Americans less attributable, however, to Physical Circumstances, than to Moral and Intellectual Causes. — Reason of this Opinion. — Future of the Anglo-Americans as a Commercial Nation. — The Dissolution of the Union would not check the Maritime Vigor of the States. — Reason of this. — Anglo-Americans will naturally supply the Wants of the Inhabitants of South America. — They will become, like the English, the Factors of a great Portion of the World.

THE coast of the United States, from the Bay of Fundy to the Sabine River in the Gulf of Mexico, is more than two thousand miles in extent.* These shores form an unbroken line, and are all subject to the same government. No nation in the world possesses vaster, deeper, or more secure ports for commerce than the Americans.

The inhabitants of the United States constitute a great civilized people, which fortune has placed in the midst of an uncultivated country, at a distance of three thousand miles from the central point of civilization. America consequently stands in daily need of Europe. The Americans will, no doubt, ultimately succeed in producing or manufacturing at home most of the articles which they require; but the two continents can never be independent of each other, so numerous are the natural ties between their wants, their ideas, their habits, and their manners.

The Union has peculiar commodities which have now become necessary to us, as they cannot be cultivated, or can be raised only at an enormous expense, upon the soil

* It is hardly necessary to remind the American reader that the annexation of Texas, and the accession of Oregon and California on the Pacific, since M. de Tocqueville wrote, have made this coast-line half as long again. — AM. ED.

of Europe.   The Americans consume only a small portion
of this produce, and they are willing to sell us the rest.
Europe is therefore the market of America, as America is
the market of Europe; and maritime commerce is no less
necessary to enable the inhabitants of the United States to
transport their raw materials to the ports of Europe, than
it is to enable us to supply them with our manufactured
produce.   The United States must therefore either furnish much business to other maritime nations, even if they
should themselves renounce commerce, as the Spaniards of
Mexico have hitherto done, or they must become one of
the first maritime powers of the globe.

The Anglo-Americans have always displayed a decided
taste for the sea.   The Declaration of Independence, by
breaking the commercial bonds which united them to England, gave a fresh and powerful stimulus to their maritime
genius.   Ever since that time, the shipping of the Union
has increased almost as rapidly as the number of its inhabitants.   The Americans themselves now transport to their
own shores nine tenths of the European produce which
they consume.   And they also bring three quarters of the
exports of the New World to the European consumer.
The ships of the United States fill the docks of Havre
and of Liverpool, whilst the number of English and
French vessels at New York is comparatively small.

Thus, not only does the American merchant brave competition on his own ground, but even successfully supports
that of foreign nations in their own ports.   This is readily
explained by the fact, that the vessels of the United States
cross the seas at a cheaper rate.   As long as the mercantile
shipping of the United States preserves this superiority,
it will not only retain what it has acquired, but will constantly increase in prosperity.

It is difficult to say for what reason the Americans can
navigate at a lower rate than other nations; one is at first

led to attribute this superiority to the physical advantages which nature gives them; but it is not so. The American vessels cost almost as much to build as our own; * they are not better built, and they generally last a shorter time. The pay of the American sailor is more considerable than the pay on board European ships, which is proved by the great number of Europeans who are to be found in the merchant-vessels of the United States. How happens it, then, that the Americans sail their vessels at a cheaper rate than we can ours? I am of opinion, that the true cause of their superiority must not be sought for in physical advantages, but that it is wholly attributable to moral and intellectual qualities.

The following comparison will illustrate my meaning. During the campaigns of the Revolution, the French introduced a new system of tactics into the art of war, which perplexed the oldest generals, and very nearly destroyed the most ancient monarchies of Europe. They first undertook to make shift without a number of things which had always been held to be indispensable in warfare; they required novel exertions of their troops, which no civilized nations had ever thought of; they achieved great actions in an incredibly short time, and risked human life without hesitation to obtain the object in view. The French had less money and fewer men than their enemies; their resources were infinitely inferior; nevertheless, they were constantly victorious, until their adversaries chose to imitate their example.

The Americans have introduced a similar system into commerce, — they do for cheapness what the French did for conquest. The European sailor navigates with prudence; he sets sail only when the weather is favorable; if an unforeseen accident befalls him, he puts into port; at

* Materials are, generally speaking, less expensive in America than in Europe, but the price of labor is much higher.

night, he furls a portion of his canvas; and when the whitening billows intimate the vicinity of land, he checks his course, and takes an observation of the sun. The American neglects these precautions, and braves these dangers. He weighs anchor before the tempest is over; by night and by day he spreads his sheets to the wind; he repairs as he goes along such damage as his vessel may have sustained from the storm; and when he at last approaches the term of his voyage, he darts onward to the shore as if he already descried a port. The Americans are often shipwrecked, but no trader crosses the seas so rapidly. And, as they perform the same distance in a shorter time, they can perform it at a cheaper rate.

The European navigator touches at different ports in the course of a long voyage; he loses precious time in making the harbor, or in waiting for a favorable wind to leave it; and he pays daily dues to be allowed to remain there. The American starts from Boston to purchase tea in China: he arrives at Canton, stays there a few days, and then returns. In less than two years, he has sailed as far as the entire circumference of the globe, and has seen land but once. It is true that, during a voyage of eight or ten months, he has drunk brackish water, and lived upon salt meat; that he has been in a continual contest with the sea, with disease, and with weariness; but, upon his return, he can sell a pound of his tea for a half-penny less than the English merchant, and his purpose is accomplished.

I cannot better explain my meaning, than by saying that the Americans show a sort of heroism in their manner of trading. The European merchant will always find it difficult to imitate his American competitor, who, in adopting the system which I have just described, does not follow calculation, but an impulse of his nature.

The inhabitants of the United States experience all the wants and all the desires which result from an advanced civilization; and as they are not surrounded, as in Europe, by a community skilfully organized to satisfy them, they are often obliged to procure for themselves the various articles which education and habit have rendered necessaries. In America, it sometimes happens that the same person tills his field, builds his dwelling, contrives his tools, makes his shoes, and weaves the coarse stuff of which his dress is composed. This is prejudicial to the excellence of the work, but it powerfully contributes to awaken the intelligence of the workman. Nothing tends to materialize man, and to deprive his work of the faintest trace of mind, more than the extreme division of labor. In a country like America, where men devoted to special occupations are rare, a long apprenticeship cannot be required from any one who embraces a profession. The Americans therefore change their means of gaining a livelihood very readily, and they suit their occupations to the exigencies of the moment. Men are to be met with who have successively been lawyers, farmers, merchants, ministers of the Gospel, and physicians. If the American be less perfect in each craft than the European, at least there is scarcely any trade with which he is utterly unacquainted. His capacity is more general, and the circle of his intelligence is greater.

The inhabitants of the United States are never fettered by the axioms of their profession; they escape from all the prejudices of their present station; they are not more attached to one line of operation than to another; they are not more prone to employ an old method than a new one; they have no rooted habits, and they easily shake off the influence which the habits of other nations might exercise upon them, from a conviction that their country is unlike any other, and that its situation is without a precedent in the world. America is a land of wonders, in which everything is in constant motion, and every change seems an improvement. The idea of novelty is there indissolubly connected with the idea of amelioration. No natural boundary seems to be set to the efforts of man ; and, in his eyes, what is not yet done is only what he has not yet attempted to do.

This perpetual change which goes on in the United States, these frequent vicissitudes of fortune, these unforeseen fluctuations in private and public wealth, serve to keep the minds of the people in a perpetual feverish agitation, which admirably invigorates their exertions, and keeps them, so to speak, above the ordinary level of humanity. The whole life of an American is passed like a game of chance, a revolutionary crisis, or a battle. As the same causes are continually in operation throughout the country, they ultimately impart an irresistible impulse to the national character. The American, taken as a chance specimen of his countrymen, must then be a man of singular warmth in his desires, enterprising, fond of adventure, and, above all, of novelty. The same bent is manifest in all that he does : he introduces it into his political laws, his religious doctrines, his theories of social economy, and his domestic occupations ; he bears it with him in the depth of the backwoods, as well as in the business of the city. It is this same passion, applied to maritime commerce, which makes him the cheapest and the quickest trader in the world.

As long as the sailors of the United States retain these mental advantages, and the practical superiority which they derive from them, they will not only continue to supply the wants of the producers and consumers of their own country, but they will tend more and more to become, like the English, the factors of other nations.* This prediction has

---

* It must not be supposed that English vessels are exclusively employed in transporting foreign produce into England, or British produce to foreign countries : at the present day, the merchant shipping of England may be regarded in the light of a vast system of public conveyances, ready to serve

already begun to be realized ; we perceive that the American traders are introducing themselves as intermediate agents in the commerce of several European nations ;* and America will offer a still wider field to their enterprise.

The great colonies which were founded in South America by the Spaniards and the Portuguese have since become empires. Civil war and oppression now lay waste those extensive regions. Population does not increase, and the thinly scattered inhabitants are too much absorbed in the cares of self-defence even to attempt any amelioration of their condition. But it will not always be so. Europe has succeeded by her own efforts in piercing the gloom of the Middle Ages. South America has the same Christian laws and usages as we have ; she contains all the germs of civilization which have grown amidst the nations of Europe or their offsets, added to the advantages to be derived from our example : why, then, should she always remain uncivilized ? It is clear that the question is simply one of time ; at some future period, which may be more or less remote, the inhabitants of South America will form flourishing and enlightened nations.

But when the Spaniards and Portuguese of South America begin to feel the wants common to all civilized nations, they will still be unable to satisfy those wants for themselves ; as the youngest children of civilization, they must perforce admit the superiority of their elder brethren. They will be agriculturists long before they succeed in manufactures or commerce ; and they will require the mediation of strangers to exchange their produce beyond seas for those articles for which a demand will begin to be felt.

It is unquestionable that the Americans of the North

all the producers of the world, and to open communications between all nations. The maritime genius of the Americans prompts them to enter into competition with the English.

* Part of the commerce of the Mediterranean is already carried on by American vessels.

will one day be called upon to supply the wants of the
Americans of the South. Nature has placed them in con-
tiguity, and has furnished the former with every means of
knowing and appreciating those demands, of establishing
permanent relations with those States, and gradually filling
their markets. The merchant of the United States could
only forfeit these natural advantages if he were very inferior to the merchant of Europe; but he is superior to him
in several respects. The Americans of the United States
already exercise a great moral influence upon all the nations of the New World. They are the source of intelligence; and all those who inhabit the same continent are
already accustomed to consider them as the most enlightened, the most powerful, and the most wealthy members
of the great American family. All eyes are therefore
turned towards the United States: these are the models
which the other communities try to imitate to the best of
their power; it is from the Union that they borrow their
political principles and their laws.

The Americans of the United States stand in precisely
the same position with regard to the South Americans as
their fathers, the English, occupy with regard to the Ital-
ians, the Spaniards, the Portuguese, and all those nations
of Europe which receive their articles of daily consumption from England, because they are less advanced in civilization and trade. England is at this time the natural
emporium of almost all the nations which are within its
reach; the American Union will perform the same part
in the other hemisphere; and every community which is
founded or which prospers in the New World, is founded
and prospers to the advantage of the Anglo-Americans.

If the Union were to be dissolved, the commerce of
the States which now compose it would undoubtedly be
checked for a time; but less than one would think. It is
evident that, whatever may happen, the commercial States

will remain united.   They are contiguous, they have the
same opinions, interests, and manners; and they alone
form a great maritime power.   Even if the South of the
Union were to become independent of the North, it would
still require the services of those States.   I have already
observed that the South is not a commercial country, and
nothing indicates that it will become so.   The Americans
of the South of the United States will therefore long be
obliged to have recourse to strangers to export their produce, and supply them with the commodities which satisfy
their wants.   But the Northern States are undoubtedly
able to act as their intermediate agents cheaper than any
other merchants.   They will therefore retain that employment, for cheapness is the sovereign law of commerce.
Sovereign will and national prejudices cannot long resist
the influence of cheapness.   Nothing can be more virulent
than the hatred which exists between the Americans of the
United States and the English.   But in spite of these
hostile feelings, the Americans derive most of their manufactured commodities from England, because England supplies them at a cheaper rate than any other nation.   Thus
the increasing prosperity of America turns, notwithstanding the grudge of the Americans, to the advantage of
British manufactures.

Reason and experience prove that no commercial prosperity can be durable if it cannot be united, in case of
need, to naval force.   This truth is as well understood in
the United States as anywhere else: the Americans are
already able to make their flag respected; in a few years
they will make it feared.   I am convinced that the dismemberment of the Union would not have the effect of
diminishing the naval power of the Americans, but would
powerfully contribute to increase it.*   At present, the

* This prophecy has already been fulfilled in a remarkable manner by
the great struggle which is now going on between the North and the South.
— Am. Ed.

commercial States are connected with others which are not commercial, and which unwillingly behold the increase of a maritime power by which they are only indirectly benefited. If, on the contrary, the commercial States of the Union formed one and the same nation, commerce would become the foremost of their national interests; they would consequently be willing to make great sacrifices to protect their shipping, and nothing would prevent them from pursuing their desires upon this point.

Nations, as well as men, almost always betray the prominent features of their future destiny in their earliest years. When I contemplate the ardor with which the Anglo-Americans prosecute commerce, the advantages which aid them, and the success of their undertakings, I cannot help believing that they will one day become the first maritime power of the globe. They are born to rule the seas, as the Romans were to conquer the world.

CONCLUSION.

I AM approaching the close of my inquiry: hitherto, in speaking of the future destiny of the United States, I have endeavored to divide my subject into distinct portions, in order to study each of them with more attention. My present object is to embrace the whole from one point of view; the remarks I shall make will be less detailed, but they will be more sure. I shall perceive each object less distinctly, but I shall descry the principal facts with more certainty. A traveller, who has just left a vast city, climbs the neighboring hill; as he goes farther off, he loses sight of the men whom he has just quitted; their dwellings are confused in a dense mass; he can no longer distinguish the public squares, and can scarcely trace out the great thoroughfares; but his eye has less difficulty in following the boundaries of the city, and for the first time he sees the shape of the whole. Such is the future destiny of the British race in North America to my eye; the details of the immense picture are lost in the shade, but I conceive a clear idea of the entire subject.

The territory now occupied or possessed by the United States of America forms about one twentieth part of the habitable earth. But extensive as these bounds are, it must not be supposed that the Anglo-American race will always remain within them; indeed, it has already gone far beyond them.

There was a time when we also might have created a great French nation in the American wilds, to counterbalance the influence of the English upon the destinies of the New World. France formerly possessed a territory in North America scarcely less extensive than the whole of Europe. The three greatest rivers of that continent then flowed within her dominions. The Indian tribes which dwelt between the mouth of the St. Lawrence and the delta of the Mississippi were unaccustomed to any other tongue than ours; and all the European settlements scattered over that immense region recalled the traditions of our country. Louisburg, Montmorency, Duquesne, Saint-Louis, Vincennes, New Orleans, (for such were the names they bore,) are words dear to France and familiar to our ears.

But a course of circumstances, which it would be tedious to enumerate,* have deprived us of this magnificent inheritance. Wherever the French settlers were numerically weak and partially established, they have disappeared:

* The foremost of these circumstances is, that nations which are accustomed to township institutions and municipal government are better able than any others to found prosperous colonies. The habit of thinking and governing for one's self is indispensable in a new country, where success necessarily depends in a great measure upon the individual exertions of the settlers.

those who remain are collected on a small extent of country, and are now subject to other laws. The 400,000 French inhabitants of Lower Canada constitute at the present time the remnant of an old nation lost in the midst of a new people. A foreign population is increasing around them unceasingly and on all sides, who already penetrate amongst the former masters of the country, predominate in their cities, and corrupt their language. This population is identical with that of the United States; it is therefore with truth that I asserted that the British race is not confined within the frontiers of the Union, since it already extends to the northeast.

To the northwest, nothing is to be met with but a few insignificant Russian settlements; but to the southwest, Mexico presents a barrier to the Anglo-Americans. Thus, the Spaniards and the Anglo-Americans are, properly speaking, the two races which divide the possession of the New World. The limits of separation between them have been settled by treaty; but although the conditions of that treaty are favorable to the Anglo-Americans, I do not doubt that they will shortly infringe it. Vast provinces, extending beyond the frontiers of the Union towards Mexico, are still destitute of inhabitants. The natives of the United States will people these solitary regions before their rightful occupants. They will take possession of the soil, and establish social institutions, so that, when the legal owner at length arrives, he will find the wilderness under cultivation, and strangers quietly settled in the midst of his inheritance.

The lands of the New World belong to the first occupant; they are the natural reward of the swiftest pioneer. Even the countries which are already peopled will have some difficulty in securing themselves from this invasion. I have already alluded to what is taking place in the province of Texas. The inhabitants of the United States are perpetually migrating to Texas, where they purchase land; and although they conform to the laws of the country, they are gradually founding the empire of their own language and their own manners.* The province of Texas is still part of the Mexican dominions, but it will soon contain no Mexicans; the same thing has occurred wherever the Anglo-Americans have come in contact with a people of a different origin.

It cannot be denied that the British race has acquired an amazing preponderance over all other European races in the New World; and it is very superior to them in civilization, industry, and power. As long as it is surrounded only by desert or thinly-peopled countries, as long as it encounters no dense population upon its route, through which it cannot work its way, it will assuredly continue to spread. The lines marked out by treaties will not stop it; but it will everywhere overleap these imaginary barriers.

The geographical position of the British race in the New World is peculiarly favorable to its rapid increase. Above its northern frontiers the icy regions of the Pole extend; and a few degrees below its southern confines lies the burning climate of the Equator. The Anglo-Americans are therefore placed in the most temperate and habitable zone of the continent.

It is generally supposed that the prodigious increase of population in the United States is posterior to their Declaration of Independence. But this is an error: the population increased as rapidly under the colonial system as at the present day; that is to say, it doubled in about twenty-two years. But this proportion, which is now applied to millions, was then applied to thousands, of inhabitants; and the same fact, which was scarcely noticeable a century ago, is now evident to every observer.

---

* In less than ten years after De Tocqueville wrote, the annexation of Texas fulfilled this prophecy. — Am. Ed.

The English in Canada, who are dependent on a king, augment and spread almost as rapidly as the British settlers of the United States, who live under a republican government. During the war of Independence, which lasted eight years, the population continued to increase without intermission in the same ratio. Although powerful Indian nations allied with the English existed, at that time, upon the western frontiers, the emigration westward was never checked. Whilst the enemy laid waste the shores of the Atlantic, Kentucky, the western parts of Pennsylvania, and the States of Vermont and of Maine, were filling with inhabitants. Nor did the unsettled state of things which succeeded the war prevent the increase of the population, or stop its progress across the wilds. Thus, the difference of laws, the various conditions of peace and war, of order or anarchy, have exercised no perceptible influence upon the continued development of the Anglo-Americans. This may be readily understood, for no causes are sufficiently general to exercise a simultaneous influence over the whole of so extensive a territory. One portion of the country always offers a sure retreat from the calamities which afflict another part; and however great may be the evil, the remedy which is at hand is greater still.

It must not, then, be imagined that the impulse of the British race in the New World can be arrested. The dismemberment of the Union, and the hostilities which might ensue, the abolition of republican institutions, and the tyrannical government which might succeed, may retard this impulse, but they cannot prevent the people from ultimately fulfilling their destinies. No power upon earth can shut out the emigrants from that fertile wilderness which offers resources to all industry, and a refuge from all want. Future events, whatever they may be, will not deprive the Americans of their climate or their inland seas, their great rivers or their exuberant soil. Nor will bad laws, revolutions, and anarchy be able to obliterate that love of prosperity and spirit of enterprise which seem to be the distinctive characteristics of their race, or extinguish altogether the knowledge which guides them on their way.

Thus, in the midst of the uncertain future, one event at least is sure. At a period which may be said to be near, — for we are speaking of the life of a nation, — the Anglo-Americans alone will cover the immense space contained between the polar regions and the tropics, extending from the coasts of the Atlantic to those of the Pacific Ocean. The territory which will probably be occupied by the Anglo-Americans may perhaps equal three quarters of Europe in extent. The climate of the Union is, upon the whole, preferable to that of Europe, and its natural advantages are as great; it is therefore evident that its population will at some future time be proportionate to our own. Europe, divided as it is between so many nations, and torn as it has been by incessant wars growing out of the barbarous manners of the Middle Ages, has yet attained a population of 410 inhabitants to the square league. What cause can prevent the United States from having as numerous a population in time?

Many ages must elapse before the different offsets of the British race in America will cease to present the same physiognomy; and the time cannot be foreseen at which a permanent inequality of condition can be established in the New World. Whatever differences may arise, from peace or war, freedom or oppression, prosperity or want, between the destinies of the different descendants of the great Anglo-American family, they will all preserve at least a similar social condition, and will hold in common the customs and opinions to which that social condition has given birth.

In the Middle Ages, the tie of religion was sufficiently powerful to unite all the different populations of Europe in the same civilization. The British of the New World have a thousand other reciprocal ties; and they live at a time when the tendency to equality is general amongst mankind. The Middle Ages were a period when everything was broken up, — when each people, each province, each city, and each family tended strongly to maintain its distinct individuality. At the present time, an opposite tendency seems to prevail, and the nations seem to be advancing to unity. Our means of intellectual intercourse unite the remotest parts of the earth; and men cannot remain strangers to each other, or be ignorant of what is taking place in any corner of the globe. The consequence is, that there is less difference at the present day between the Europeans and their descendants in the New World, in spite of the ocean which divides them, than there was between certain towns in the thirteenth century, which were separated only by a river. If this tendency to assimilation brings foreign nations closer to each other, it must *a fortiori* prevent the descendants of the same people from becoming aliens to each other.

The time will therefore come, when one hundred and fifty millions of men will be living in North America,* equal in condition, all belonging to one family, owing their origin to the same cause, and preserving the same civilization, the same language, the same religion, the same habits, the same manners, and imbued with the same opinions, propagated under the same forms. The rest is uncertain, but this is certain; and it is a fact new to the world, — a fact which the imagination strives in vain to grasp.

There are at the present time two great nations in the world, which started from different points, but seem to tend towards the same end. I allude to the Russians and the Americans. Both of them have grown up unnoticed;

---

* This would be a population proportionate to that of Europe, taken at a mean rate of 410 inhabitants to the square league.

and whilst the attention of mankind was directed elsewhere, they have suddenly placed themselves in the front
rank among the nations, and the world learned their existence and their greatness at almost the same time.

All other nations seem to have nearly reached their natural limits, and they have only to maintain their power;
but these are still in the act of growth.* All the others
have stopped, or continue to advance with extreme difficulty; these alone are proceeding with ease and celerity
along a path to which no limit can be perceived. The
American struggles against the obstacles which nature opposes to him; the adversaries of the Russian are men.
The former combats the wilderness and savage life; the
latter, civilization with all its arms. The conquests of the
American are therefore gained by the ploughshare; those
of the Russian by the sword. The Anglo-American re-
lies upon personal interest to accomplish his ends, and gives
free scope to the unguided strength and common sense of
the people; the Russian centres all the authority of society
in a single arm. The principal instrument of the former
is freedom; of the latter, servitude. Their starting-point
is different, and their courses are not the same; yet each
of them seems marked out by the will of Heaven to sway
the destinies of half the globe.

* The population of Russia increases more rapidly than that of any other
country in the Old World.

END OF VOLUME I.

DEMOCRACY IN AMERICA

VOLUME II

ADVERTISEMENT

TO THE SECOND PART.

THE Americans have a democratic state of society, which has naturally suggested to them certain laws and certain political manners. It has also created in their minds many feelings and opinions which were unknown in the old aristocratic societies of Europe. It has destroyed or modified the old relations of men to each other, and has established new ones. The aspect of civil society has been as much altered as the face of the political world.

I have treated of the former subject in the work which I published, five years ago, upon American Democracy; the latter is the object of the present book. These two Parts complete each other, and form but a single work.

But I must warn the reader immediately against an error which would be very prejudicial to me. Because I attribute so many different effects to the principle of equality, it might be inferred that I consider this principle as the only cause of everything that takes place in our day. This would be attributing to me a very narrow view of things.

A multitude of the' opinions, sentiments, and instincts which belong to our times owe their origin to circumstances which have nothing to do with the principle of equality, or are even hostile to it. Thus, taking the United States for example, I could easily prove that the nature of the country, the origin of its inhabitants, the religion of the early settlers, their acquired knowledge, their previous habits, have exercised, and still do exercise, independently of democracy, an immense influence upon their modes of thought and feeling. Other causes, equally independent of the principle of equality, would be found in Europe, and would explain much of what is passing there.

I recognize the existence and the efficiency of all these various causes; but my subject does not lead me to speak of them. I have not undertaken to point out the origin and nature of all our inclinations and all our ideas; I have only endeavored to show how far both of them are affected by the equality of men's conditions.

As I am firmly convinced that the democratic revolution which we are now beholding is an irresistible fact, against which it would be neither desirable nor prudent to contend, some persons perhaps may be surprised that, in the course of this book, I have often applied language of strong censure to the democratic communities which this revolution has created. The simple reason is, that precisely because I was not an opponent of democracy, I wished to speak of it with all sincerity. Men will not receive the truth from their enemies, and it is very seldom offered to them by their friends; on this very account, I have frankly uttered it. I believed that many persons would take it upon themselves to inform men of the benefits which they might hope to receive from the establishment of equality, whilst very few would venture to point out from afar the dangers with which it would be attended. It is principally towards these dangers, therefore, that I directed my gaze; and, believing that I had clearly discerned what they are, it would have been cowardice to say nothing about them.

I hope the same impartiality will be found in this second work which people seemed to observe in its predecessor. Placed between the conflicting opinions which divide my countrymen, I have endeavored for the time to stifle in my own bosom the sympathy or the aversion that I felt for either. If the readers of my book find in it a single phrase intended to flatter either of the great parties which have agitated our country, or any one of the petty factions which in our day harass and weaken it, let them raise their voices and accuse me.

The subject which I wished to cover by my investigations is immense; for it includes most of the feelings and opinions produced by the new

condition of the world's affairs.   Such a subject
certainly exceeds my strength, and in the treatment of it I have not been able to satisfy myself.
But though I could not reach the object at which
I aimed, my readers will at least do me the justice
to believe, that I conceived and followed out the
undertaking in a spirit which rendered me worthy of success.

CONTENTS OF VOL. II.

—•—

FIRST BOOK.

INFLUENCE OF DEMOCRACY UPON THE ACTION OF INTELLECT IN THE UNITED STATES.

CHAPTER XX.

CHAPTER XXI.

SECOND BOOK.

INFLUENCE OF DEMOCRACY ON THE FEELINGS OF THE AMERICANS.

CHAPTER I.

CHAPTER II.

CHAPTER III.

CHAPTER IV.

CHAPTER V.

CHAPTER VI.

CHAPTER VII.

CHAPTER VIII.

CHAPTER IX.

CHAPTER X.

CHAPTER XI.

CHAPTER XII.

CHAPTER XIII.

CHAPTER XIV.

CHAPTER XV.

CHAPTER XVI.

CHAPTER XVII.

CHAPTER XVIII.

THIRD BOOK.

INFLUENCE OF DEMOCRACY ON MANNERS PROPERLY SO CALLED.

CHAPTER IX.

CHAPTER X.

CHAPTER XI.

CHAPTER XII.

CHAPTER XIII.

CHAPTER XIV.

CHAPTER XV.

CHAPTER XVI.

CHAPTER XVII.

CHAPTER XVIII.

CHAPTER XIX.

CHAPTER XX.

CHAPTER XXI.

CHAPTER XXII.

CHAPTER XXIII.

CHAPTER XXIV.

CHAPTER XXV.

CHAPTER XXVI.

FOURTH BOOK.

INFLUENCE OF DEMOCRATIC IDEAS AND FEELINGS ON POLITICAL SOCIETY.

CHAPTER I.

CHAPTER II.

DEMOCRACY IN AMERICA.

SECOND PART.

FIRST BOOK.

INFLUENCE OF DEMOCRACY UPON THE ACTION OF INTELLECT IN THE UNITED STATES.

CHAPTER I.

PHILOSOPHICAL METHOD OF THE AMERICANS.

I THINK that in no country in the civilized world is less attention paid to philosophy than in the United States. The Americans have no philosophical school of their own; and they care but little for all the schools into which Europe is divided, the very names of which are scarcely known to them.

Yet it is easy to perceive that almost all the inhabitants of the United States conduct their understanding in the same manner, and govern it by the same rules; that is to say, without ever having taken the trouble to define the rules, they have a philosophical method common to the whole people.

To evade the bondage of system and habit, of family-maxims, class-opinions, and, in some degree, of national prejudices; to accept tradition only as a means of information, and existing facts only as a lesson to be used in doing otherwise and doing better; to seek the reason of things for one's self, and in one's self alone; to tend to results without being bound to means, and to aim at the substance through the form; — such are the principal characteristics of what I shall call the philosophical method of the Americans.

But if I go further, and seek amongst these characteristics the principal one which includes almost all the rest, I discover that, in most of the operations of mind, each American appeals only to the individual effort of his own understanding.

America is therefore one of the countries where the precepts of Descartes are least studied, and are best applied. Nor is this surprising. The Americans do not read the works of Descartes, because their social condition deters them from speculative studies; but they follow his maxims, because this same social condition naturally disposes their minds to adopt them.

In the midst of the continual movement which agitates a democratic community, the tie which unites one generation to another is relaxed or broken; every man there readily loses all trace of the ideas of his forefathers, or takes no care about them.

Men living in this state of society cannot derive their belief from the opinions of the class to which they belong; for, so to speak, there are no longer any classes, or those which still exist are composed of such mobile elements, that the body can never exercise any real control over its members.

As to the influence which the intellect of one man may have on that of another, it must necessarily be very limited in a country where the citizens, placed on an equal footing, are all closely seen by each other; and where, as no signs of incontestable greatness or superiority are perceived in any one of them, they are constantly brought back to their own reason as the most obvious and proximate source of truth. It is not only confidence in this or that man which is destroyed, but the disposition for trusting the authority of any man whatsoever. Every one shuts himself up in his own breast, and affects from that point to judge the world.

The practice which obtains amongst the Americans, of fixing the standard of their judgment in themselves alone, leads them to other habits of mind. As they perceive that they succeed in resolving without assistance all the little difficulties which their practical life presents, they readily conclude that everything in the world may be explained, and that nothing in it transcends the limits of the understanding. Thus they fall to denying what they cannot comprehend; which leaves them but little faith for whatever is extraordinary, and an almost insurmountable distaste for whatever is supernatural. As it is on their own testimony that they are accustomed to rely, they like to discern the object which engages their attention with extreme clearness; they therefore strip off as much as possible all that covers it, they rid themselves of whatever separates them from it, they remove whatever conceals it from sight, in order to view it more closely and in the broad light of day. This disposition of mind soon leads them to contemn forms, which they regard as useless and inconvenient veils placed between them and the truth.

The Americans, then, have not required to extract their philosophical method from books; they have found it in themselves. The same thing may be remarked in what has taken place in Europe. This same method has only been established and made popular in Europe in proportion as the condition of society has become more equal, and men have grown more like each other. Let us consider for a moment the connection of the periods in which this change may be traced.

In the sixteenth century, the Reformers subjected some of the dogmas of the ancient faith to the scrutiny of private judgment; but they still withheld from it the discussion of all the rest. In the seventeenth century, Bacon in the natural sciences, and Descartes in philosophy properly so called, abolished received formulas, destroyed the empire of tradition, and overthrew the authority of the schools. The philosophers of the eighteenth century, generalizing at length the same principle, undertook to submit to the private judgment of each man all the objects of his belief.

Who does not perceive that Luther, Descartes, and Voltaire employed the same method, and that they differed only in the greater or less use which they professed should be made of it? Why did the Reformers confine themselves so closely within the circle of religious ideas? Why did Descartes, choosing only to apply his method to certain matters, though he had made it fit to be applied to all, declare that men might judge for themselves in matters philosophical, but not in matters political? How happened it that, in the eighteenth century, those general applications were all at once drawn from this same method, which Descartes and his predecessors had either not perceived or had rejected? To what, lastly, is the fact to be attributed, that at this period the method we are speaking of suddenly emerged from the schools, to penetrate into society and become the common standard of intelligence; and that, after it had become popular among the French, it has been ostensibly adopted or secretly followed by all the nations of Europe?

The philosophical method here designated may have been born in the sixteenth century, — it may have been more accurately defined and more extensively applied in the seventeenth; but neither in the one nor in the other could it be commonly adopted. Political laws, the condition of society, and the habits of mind which are derived from these causes, were as yet opposed to it.

It was discovered at a time when men were beginning to equalize and assimilate their conditions. It could only be generally followed in ages when those conditions had at length become nearly equal, and men nearly alike.

The philosophical method of the eighteenth century is, then, not only French, but it is democratic; and this explains why it was so readily admitted throughout Europe, where it has contributed so powerfully to change the face of society. It is not because the French have changed their former opinions, and altered their former manners, that they have convulsed the world; but because they were the first to generalize and bring to light a philosophical method, by the aid of which it became easy to attack all that was old, and to open a path to all that was new.

If it be asked why, at the present day, this same method is more rigorously followed and more frequently applied by the French than by the Americans, although the principle of equality is no less complete and of more ancient date amongst the latter people, the fact may be attributed to two circumstances, which it is first essential to have clearly understood.

It must never be forgotten that religion gave birth to Anglo-American society. In the United States, religion is therefore mingled with all the habits of the nation and all the feelings of patriotism, whence it derives a peculiar force. To this reason another of no less power may be added: in America, religion has, as it were, laid down its own limits. Religious institutions have remained wholly distinct from political institutions, so that former laws have been easily changed whilst former belief has remained unshaken. Christianity has therefore retained a strong hold on the public mind in America; and I would more particularly remark, that its sway is not only that of a philosophical doctrine which has been adopted upon inquiry, but of a religion which is believed without discussion. In the United States, Christian sects are infinitely diversified and perpetually modified; but Christianity itself is an established and irresistible fact, which no one undertakes either to attack or to defend. The Americans, having admitted the principal doctrines of the Christian religion without inquiry, are obliged to accept in like manner a great number of moral truths originating in it and connected with it. Hence the activity of individual analysis is restrained within narrow limits, and many of the most important of human opinions are removed from its influence.

The second circumstance to which I have alluded is, that the social condition and the constitution of the Americans are democratic, but they have not had a democratic revolution. They arrived upon the soil they occupy in nearly the condition in which we see them at the present day ; and this is of considerable importance.

There are no revolutions which do not shake existing belief, enervate authority, and throw doubts over commonly received ideas. The effect of all revolutions is, therefore, more or less, to surrender men to their own guidance, and to open to the mind of every man a void and almost unlimited range of speculation. When equality of conditions succeeds a protracted conflict between the different classes of which the elder society was composed, envy, hatred, and uncharitableness, pride and exaggerated self-confidence, seize upon the human heart, and plant their sway in it for a time. This, independently of equality itself, tends powerfully to divide men, — to lead them to mistrust the judgment of each other, and to seek the light of truth nowhere but in themselves. Every one then attempts to be his own sufficient guide, and makes it his boast to form his own opinions on all subjects. Men are no longer bound together by ideas, but by interests ; and it would seem as if human opinions were reduced to a sort of intellectual dust, scattered on every side, unable to collect, unable to cohere.

Thus, that independence of mind which equality supposes to exist is never so great, never appears so excessive, as at the time when equality is beginning to establish itself, and in the course of that painful labor by which it is established. That sort of intellectual freedom which equality may give ought, therefore, to be very carefully distinguished from the anarchy which revolution brings. Each of these two things must be separately considered, in order not to conceive exaggerated hopes or fears of the future.

I believe that the men who will live under the new forms of society will make frequent use of their private judgment, but I am far from thinking that they will often abuse it. This is attributable to a cause of more general application to all democratic countries, and which, in the long run, must needs restrain in them the independence of individual speculation within fixed, and sometimes narrow, limits.

I shall proceed to point out this cause in the next chapter.

CHAPTER II.

OF THE PRINCIPAL SOURCE OF BELIEF AMONG DEMOCRATIC NATIONS.

AT different periods, dogmatical belief is more or less common. It arises in different ways, and it may change its object and its form ; but under no circumstances will dogmatical belief cease to exist, or, in other words, men will never cease to entertain some opinions on trust, and without discussion. If every one undertook to form all his own opinions, and to seek for truth by isolated paths struck out by himself alone, it would follow that no considerable number of men would ever unite in any common belief.

But obviously without such common belief no society can prosper, — say, rather, no society can exist ; for without ideas held in common, there is no common action, and without common action there may still be men, but there is no social body. In order that society should exist, and, *a fortiori*, that a society should prosper, it is required that all the minds of the citizens should be rallied and held together by certain predominant ideas ; and this cannot be the case unless each of them sometimes draws his opinions from the common source, and consents to accept certain matters of belief already formed.

If I now consider man in his isolated capacity, I find that dogmatical belief is not less indispensable to him in order to live alone, than it is to enable him to co-operate with his fellows. If man were forced to demonstrate for himself all the truths of which he makes daily use, his task would never end. He would exhaust his strength in preparatory demonstrations, without ever advancing beyond them. As, from the shortness of his life, he has not the time, nor, from the limits of his intelligence, the capacity, to accomplish this, he is reduced to take upon trust a number of facts and opinions which he has not had either the time or the power to verify for himself, but which men of greater ability have sought out, or which the world adopts. On this groundwork he raises for himself the structure of his own thoughts; he is not led to proceed in this manner by choice, but is constrained by the inflexible law of his condition. There is no philosopher of so great parts in the world, but that he believes a million of things on the faith of other people, and supposes a great many more truths than he demonstrates.

This is not only necessary, but desirable. A man who should undertake to inquire into everything for himself, could devote to each thing but little time and attention. His task would keep his mind in perpetual unrest, which would prevent him from penetrating to the depth of any truth, or of grappling his mind firmly to any conviction. His intellect would be at once independent and powerless. He must therefore make his choice from amongst the various objects of human belief, and adopt many opinions without discussion, in order to search the better into that smaller number which he sets apart for investigation. It is true, that whoever receives an opinion on the word of another, does so far enslave his mind; but it is a salutary servitude which allows him to make a good use of freedom.

A principle of authority must then always occur, under all circumstances, in some part or other of the moral and intellectual world. Its place is variable, but a place it necessarily has. The independence of individual minds may be greater, or it may be less: unbounded it cannot be. Thus the question is, not to know whether any intellectual authority exists in the ages of democracy, but simply where it resides and by what standard it is to be measured.

I have shown in the preceding chapter how the equality of conditions leads men to entertain a sort of instinctive incredulity of the supernatural, and a very lofty and often exaggerated opinion of the human understanding. The men who live at a period of social equality are not there-fore easily led to place that intellectual authority to which they bow either beyond or above humanity. They com-monly seek for the sources of truth in themselves, or in those who are like themselves. This would be enough to prove that, at such periods, no new religion could be estab-lished, and that all schemes for such a purpose would be not only impious, but absurd and irrational. It may be foreseen that a democratic people will not easily give cre-dence to divine missions ; that they will laugh at modern prophets ; and that they will seek to discover the chief arbiter of their belief within, and not beyond, the limits of their kind.

When the ranks of society are unequal, and men unlike each other in condition, there are some individuals wielding the power of superior intelligence, learning, and enlighten-ment, whilst the multitude are sunk in ignorance and preju-dice. Men living at these aristocratic periods are therefore naturally induced to shape their opinions by the standard of a superior person, or superior class of persons, whilst they are averse to recognize the infallibility of the mass of the people.

The contrary takes place in ages of equality. The nearer the people are drawn to the common level of an equal and similar condition, the less prone does each man become to place implicit faith in a certain man or a certain class of men. But his readiness to believe the multitude increases, and opinion is more than ever mistress of the world. Not only is common opinion the only guide which private judgment retains amongst a democratic people, but amongst such a people it possesses a power infinitely beyond what it has elsewhere. At periods of equality, men have no faith in one another, by reason of their common resemblance; but this very resemblance gives them almost unbounded confidence in the judgment of the public; for it would not seem probable, as they are all endowed with equal means of judging, but that the greater truth should go with the greater number.

When the inhabitant of a democratic country compares himself individually with all those about him, he feels with pride that he is the equal of any one of them; but when he comes to survey the totality of his fellows, and to place himself in contrast with so huge a body, he is instantly overwhelmed by the sense of his own insignificance and weakness. The same equality which renders him independent of each of his fellow-citizens, taken severally, exposes him alone and unprotected to the influence of the greater number. The public has therefore, among a democratic people, a singular power, which aristocratic nations cannot conceive of; for it does not persuade to certain opinions, but it enforces them, and infuses them into the intellect by a sort of enormous pressure of the minds of all upon the reason of each.

In the United States, the majority undertakes to supply a multitude of ready-made opinions for the use of individuals, who are thus relieved from the necessity of forming opinions of their own. Everybody there adopts great numbers of theories, on philosophy, morals, and politics, without inquiry, upon public trust; and if we look to it very narrowly, it will be perceived that religion herself holds sway there much less as a doctrine of revelation than as a commonly received opinion.

The fact that the political laws of the Americans are such that the majority rules the community with sovereign sway, materially increases the power which that majority naturally exercises over the mind. For nothing is more customary in man than to recognize superior wisdom in the person of his oppressor. This political omnipotence of the majority in the United States doubtless augments the influence which public opinion would obtain without it over the minds of each member of the community; but the foundations of that influence do not rest upon it. They must be sought for in the principle of equality itself, not in the more or less popular institutions which men living under that condition may give themselves. The intellectual dominion of the greater number would probably be less absolute amongst a democratic people governed by a king, than in the sphere of a pure democracy, but it will always be extremely absolute; and by whatever political laws men are governed in the ages of equality, it may be foreseen that faith in public opinion will become a species of religion there, and the majority its ministering prophet.

Thus intellectual authority will be different, but it will not be diminished; and far from thinking that it will disappear, I augur that it may readily acquire too much preponderance, and confine the action of private judgment within narrower limits than are suited either to the greatness or the happiness of the human race. In the principle of equality I very clearly discern two tendencies; the one leading the mind of every man to untried thoughts, the other which would prohibit him from thinking at all. And I perceive how, under the dominion of certain laws, democracy would extinguish that liberty of the mind to which a democratic social condition is favorable; so that, after having broken all the bondage once imposed on it by ranks or by men, the human mind would be closely fettered to the general will of the greatest number.

If the absolute power of a majority were to be substituted, by democratic nations, for all the different powers

which checked or retarded overmuch the energy of individual minds, the evil would only have changed character.
Men would not have found the means of independent life;
they would simply have discovered (no easy task) a new
physiognomy of servitude.   There is, — and I cannot repeat it too often, — there is here matter for profound reflection to those who look on freedom of thought as a holy
thing, and who hate not only the despot, but despotism.
For myself, when I feel the hand of power lie heavy on
my brow, I care but little to know who oppresses me ; and
I am not the more disposed to pass beneath the yoke because it is held out to me by the arms of a million of men.

CHAPTER III.

WHY THE AMERICANS SHOW MORE APTITUDE AND TASTE FOR GENERAL IDEAS THAN THEIR FOREFATHERS, THE ENGLISH.

THE Deity does not regard the human race collectively. He surveys at one glance and severally all the beings of whom mankind is composed; and he discerns in each man the resemblances which assimilate him to all his fellows, and the differences which distinguish him from them. God, therefore, stands in no need of general ideas; that is to say, he never feels the necessity of collecting a considerable number of analogous objects under the same form for greater convenience in thinking.

Such is, however, not the case with man. If the human mind were to attempt to examine and pass a judgment on all the individual cases before it, the immensity of detail would soon lead it astray, and it would no longer see anything: in this strait, man has recourse to an imperfect but necessary expedient, which at once assists and demonstrates his weakness.

Having superficially considered a certain number of objects, and remarked their resemblance, he assigns to them a common name, sets them apart, and proceeds onwards.

General ideas are no proof of the strength, but rather of the insufficiency, of the human intellect; for there are in nature no beings exactly alike, no things precisely identical, nor any rules indiscriminately and alike applicable to several objects at once. The chief merit of general ideas is, that they enable the human mind to pass a rapid judgment on a great many objects at once; but, on the other

hand, the notions they convey are never otherwise than incomplete, and they always cause the mind to lose as much
in accuracy as it gains in comprehensiveness.

As social bodies advance in civilization, they acquire the
knowledge of new facts, and they daily lay hold almost unconsciously of some particular truths.   The more truths
of this kind a man apprehends, the more general ideas is
he naturally led to conceive.   A multitude of particular
facts cannot be seen separately without at last discovering
the common tie which connects them.   Several individuals
lead to the notion of the species, several species to that of
the genus.   Hence the habit and the taste for general ideas
will always be greatest amongst a people of ancient cultivation and extensive knowledge.

But there are other reasons which impel men to generalize their ideas, or which restrain them from it.

The Americans are much more addicted to the use of
general ideas than the English, and entertain a much
greater relish for them : this appears very singular at first,
when it is remembered that the two nations have the same
origin, that they lived for centuries under the same laws,
and that they still incessantly interchange their opinions
and their manners.   This contrast becomes much more
striking still, if we fix our eyes on our own part of the
world, and compare together the two most enlightened
nations which inhabit it.   It would seem as if the mind of
the English could only tear itself reluctantly and painfully
away from the observation of particular facts, to rise from
them to their causes, and that it only generalizes in spite
of itself.   Amongst the French, on the contrary, the taste
for general ideas would seem to have grown to so ardent a
passion that it must be satisfied on every occasion.   I am
informed every morning when I wake, that some general
and eternal law has just been discovered which I never
heard mentioned before.   There is not a mediocre scribbler

who does not try his hand at discovering truths applicable to a great kingdom, and who is not very ill pleased with himself if he does not succeed in compressing the human race into the compass of an article.

So great a dissimilarity between two very enlightened nations surprises me. If I again turn my attention to England, and observe the events which have occurred there in the last half-century, I think I may affirm that a taste for general ideas increases in that country in proportion as its ancient constitution is weakened.

The state of civilization is therefore insufficient by itself to explain what suggests to the human mind the love of general ideas, or diverts it from them.

When the conditions of men are very unequal, and the inequalities are permanent, individual men gradually become so dissimilar, that each class assumes the aspect of a distinct race: only one of these classes is ever in view at the same instant; and, losing sight of that general tie which binds them all within the vast bosom of mankind, the observation invariably rests, not on man, but on certain men. Those who live in this aristocratic state of society never, therefore, conceive very general ideas respecting themselves; and that is enough to imbue them with an habitual distrust of such ideas, and an instinctive aversion for them.

He, on the contrary, who inhabits a democratic country sees around him, on every hand, men differing but little from each other; he cannot turn his mind to any one portion of mankind, without expanding and dilating his thought till it embrace the whole. All the truths which are applicable to himself appear to him equally and similarly applicable to each of his fellow-citizens and fellow-men. Having contracted the habit of generalizing his ideas in the study which engages him most and interests him most, he transfers the same habit to all his pursuits;

and thus it is that the craving to discover general laws in everything, to include a great number of objects under the same formula, and to explain a mass of facts by a single cause, becomes an ardent, and sometimes an undiscerning, passion in the human mind.

Nothing shows the truth of this proposition more clearly than the opinions of the ancients respecting their slaves. The most profound and capacious minds of Rome and Greece were never able to reach the idea, at once so general and so simple, of the common likeness of men, and of the common birthright of each to freedom: they strove to prove that slavery was in the order of nature, and that it would always exist. Nay, more, everything shows that those of the ancients who had been slaves before they became free, many of whom have left us excellent writings, did themselves regard servitude in no other light.

All the great writers of antiquity belonged to the aristocracy of masters, or, at least, they saw that aristocracy established and uncontested before their eyes. Their mind, after it had expanded itself in several directions, was barred from further progress in this one; and the advent of Jesus Christ upon earth was required to teach that all the members of the human race are by nature equal and alike.

In the ages of equality, all men are independent of each other, isolated, and weak. The movements of the multitude are not permanently guided by the will of any individuals: at such times, humanity seems always to advance of itself. In order, therefore, to explain what is passing in the world, man is driven to seek for some great causes, which, acting in the same manner on all our fellow-creatures, thus induce them all voluntarily to pursue the same track. This again naturally leads the human mind to conceive general ideas, and superinduces a taste for them.

I have already shown in what way the equality of conditions leads every man to investigate truth for himself. It may readily be perceived that a method of this kind must insensibly beget a tendency to general ideas in the human mind. When I repudiate the traditions of rank, professions, and birth, when I escape from the authority of example, to seek out, by the single effort of my reason, the path to be followed, I am inclined to derive the motives of my opinions from human nature itself, which leads me necessarily, and almost unconsciously, to adopt a great number of very general notions.

All that I have here said explains why the English display much less aptitude and taste for the generalization of ideas than their American progeny, and still less again than their neighbors the French; and likewise why the English of the present day display more than their forefathers did.

The English have long been a very enlightened and a very aristocratic nation; their enlightened condition urged them constantly to generalize, and their aristocratic habits confined them to the particular. Hence arose that philosophy, at once bold and timid, broad and narrow, which has hitherto prevailed in England, and which still obstructs and stagnates so many minds in that country.

Independently of the causes I have pointed out in what goes before, others may be discerned less apparent, but no less efficacious, which produce amongst almost every democratic people a taste, and frequently a passion, for general ideas. A distinction must be taken between ideas of this kind. Some of them are the result of slow, minute, and conscientious labor of the mind, and these extend the sphere of human knowledge; others spring up at once from the first rapid exercise of the wits, and beget none but very superficial and uncertain notions.

Men who live in ages of equality have a great deal of curiosity and little leisure; their life is so practical, so confused, so excited, so active, that but little time remains to them for thought. Such men are prone to general ideas, because they spare them the trouble of studying particulars; they contain, if I may so speak, a great deal in a little compass, and give, in a little time, a great return. If, then, upon a brief and inattentive investigation, they think they discern a common relation between certain objects, inquiry is not pushed any further; and without examining in detail how far these several objects agree or differ, they are hastily arranged under one formulary, in order to pass to another subject.

One of the distinguishing characteristics of a democratic period is the taste which all men then have for easy success and present enjoyment. This occurs in the pursuits of the intellect as well as in all others. Most of those who live at a time of equality are full of an ambition at once aspiring and relaxed: they would fain succeed brilliantly and at once, but they would be dispensed from great efforts to obtain success. These conflicting tendencies lead straight to the research of general ideas, by aid of which they flatter themselves that they can delineate vast objects with little pains, and draw the attention of the public without much trouble.

And I know not that they are wrong in thinking thus. For their readers are as much averse to investigating anything to the bottom as they are; and what is generally sought in the productions of mind is easy pleasure and information without labor.

If aristocratic nations do not make sufficient use of general ideas, and frequently treat them with inconsiderate disdain, it is true, on the other hand, that a democratic people is ever ready to carry ideas of this kind to excess, and to espouse them with injudicious warmth.

CHAPTER IV.

WHY THE AMERICANS HAVE NEVER BEEN SO EAGER AS THE
FRENCH FOR GENERAL IDEAS IN POLITICAL AFFAIRS.

I HAVE observed that the Americans show a less decided taste for general ideas than the French. This is
more especially true in politics.

Although the Americans infuse into their legislation far
more general ideas than the English, and although they
strive more than the latter to adjust the practice of affairs
to theory, no political bodies in the United States have
ever shown so much love for general ideas as the Constituent Assembly and the Convention in France. At no time
has the American people laid hold on ideas of this kind
with the passionate energy of the French people in the
eighteenth century, or displayed the same blind confidence
in the value and absolute truth of any theory.

This difference between the Americans and the French
originates in several causes, but principally in the following
one. The Americans form a democratic people, who have
always directed public affairs themselves. The French are
a democratic people, who, for a long time, could only speculate on the best manner of conducting them. The social
condition of the French led them to conceive very general
ideas on the subject of government, whilst their political
constitution prevented them from correcting those ideas
by experiment, and from gradually detecting their insufficiency; whereas, in America, the two things constantly
balance and correct each other.

It may seem, at first sight, that this is very much opposed to what I have said before, that democratic nations derive their love of theory from the very excitement of their active life. A more attentive examination will show that there is nothing contradictory in the proposition.

Men living in democratic countries eagerly lay hold of general ideas, because they have but little leisure, and because these ideas spare them the trouble of studying particulars. This is true; but it is only to be understood of those matters which are not the necessary and habitual subjects of their thoughts. Mercantile men will take up very eagerly, and without any close scrutiny, all the general ideas on philosophy, politics, science, or the arts, which may be presented to them; but for such as relate to commerce, they will not receive them without inquiry, or adopt them without reserve. The same thing applies to statesmen with regard to general ideas in politics.

If, then, there be a subject upon which a democratic people is peculiarly liable to abandon itself, blindly and extravagantly, to general ideas, the best corrective that can be used will be to make that subject a part of their daily practical occupation. They will then be compelled to enter upon details, and the details will teach them the weak points of the theory. This remedy may frequently be a painful one, but its effect is certain.

Thus it happens, that the democratic institutions which compel every citizen to take a practical part in the government moderate that excessive taste for general theories in politics which the principle of equality suggests.

CHAPTER V.

HOW RELIGION IN THE UNITED STATES AVAILS ITSELF OF DEMOCRATIC TENDENCIES.

I HAVE shown, in a preceding chapter, that men cannot do without dogmatical belief; and even that it is much to be desired that such belief should exist amongst them. I now add, that, of all the kinds of dogmatical belief, the most desirable appears to me to be dogmatical belief in matters of religion; and this is a clear inference, even from no higher consideration than the interests of this world.

There is hardly any human action, however particular it may be, which does not originate in some very general idea men have conceived of the Deity, of his relation to mankind, of the nature of their own souls, and of their duties to their fellow-creatures. Nor can anything prevent these ideas from being the common spring whence all the rest emanates.

Men are therefore immeasurably interested in acquiring fixed ideas of God, of the soul, and of their general duties to their Creator and their fellow-men; for doubt on these first principles would abandon all their actions to chance, and would condemn them in some way to disorder and impotence.

This is, then, the subject on which it is most important for each of us to have fixed ideas; and unhappily it is also the subject on which it is most difficult for each of us, left to himself, to settle his opinions by the sole force of his reason. None but minds singularly free from the ordinary cares of life — minds at once penetrating, subtile, and trained by thinking — can, even with much time and care, sound the depths of these so necessary truths. And, indeed, we see that philosophers are themselves almost always surrounded with uncertainties; that at every step the natural light which illuminates their path grows dimmer and less secure; and that, in spite of all their efforts, they have as yet only discovered a few conflicting notions, on which the mind of man has been tossed about for thousands of years, without ever firmly grasping the truth, or finding novelty even in its errors. Studies of this nature are far above the average capacity of men; and, even if the majority of mankind were capable of such pursuits, it is evident that leisure to cultivate them would still be wanting.

Fixed ideas about God and human nature are indispensable to the daily practice of men's lives; but the practice of their lives prevents them from acquiring such ideas.

The difficulty appears to be without a parallel. Amongst the sciences, there are some which are useful to the mass of mankind, and are within its reach; others can be approached only by the few, and are not cultivated by the many, who require nothing beyond their more remote applications: but the daily practice of the science I speak of is indispensable to all, although the study of it is inaccessible to the greater number.

General ideas respecting God and human nature are therefore the ideas above all others which it is most suitable to withdraw from the habitual action of private judgment, and in which there is most to gain and least to lose by recognizing a principle of authority.

The first object, and one of the principal advantages, of religion is to furnish to each of these fundamental questions a solution which is at once clear, precise, intelligible to the mass of mankind, and lasting. There are religions which are false and very absurd; but it may be affirmed that any religion which remains within the circle I have just traced, without pretending to go beyond it, (as many religions have attempted to do, for the purpose of restraining on every side the free movement of the human mind,) imposes a salutary restraint on the intellect ; and it must be admitted that, if it do not save men in another world, it is at least very conducive to their happiness and their greatness in this.

This is more especially true of men living in free countries. When the religion of a people is destroyed, doubt gets hold of the higher powers of the intellect, and half paralyzes all the others. Every man accustoms himself to have only confused and changing notions on the subjects most interesting to his fellow-creatures and himself. His opinions are ill-defended and easily abandoned ; and, in despair of ever resolving by himself the hard problems respecting the destiny of man, he ignobly submits to think no more about them.

Such a condition cannot but enervate the soul, relax the springs of the will, and prepare a people for servitude. Not only does it happen, in such a case, that they allow their freedom to be taken from them ; they frequently themselves surrender it. When there is no longer any principle of authority in religion, any more than in politics, men are speedily frightened at the aspect of this unbounded independence. The constant agitation of all surrounding things alarms and exhausts them. As everything is at sea in the sphere of the mind, they determine at least that the mechanism of society shall be firm and fixed ; and, as they cannot resume their ancient belief, they assume a master.

For my own part, I doubt whether man can ever support at the same time complete religious independence and entire political freedom. And I am inclined to think that, if faith be wanting in him, he must be subject ; and if he be free, he must believe.

Perhaps, however, this great utility of religions is still

more obvious amongst nations where equality of conditions prevails, than amongst others. It must be acknowledged that equality, which brings great benefits into the world, nevertheless suggests to men (as will be shown hereafter) some very dangerous propensities. It tends to isolate them from each other, to concentrate every man's attention upon himself; and it lays open the soul to an inordinate love of material gratification.

The greatest advantage of religion is to inspire diametrically contrary principles. There is no religion which does not place the object of man's desires above and beyond the treasures of earth, and which does not naturally raise his soul to regions far above those of the senses. Nor is there any which does not impose on man some duties toward his kind, and thus draw him at times from the contemplation of himself. This occurs in religions the most false and dangerous.

Religious nations are therefore naturally strong on the very point on which democratic nations are weak, which shows of what importance it is for men to preserve their religion as their conditions become more equal.

I have neither the right nor the intention of examining the supernatural means which God employs to infuse religious belief into the heart of man. I am at this moment considering religions in a purely human point of view; my object is to inquire by what means they may most easily retain their sway in the democratic ages upon which we are entering.

It has been shown that, at times of general cultivation and equality, the human mind consents only with reluctance to adopt dogmatical opinions, and feels their necessity acutely only in spiritual matters. This proves, in the first place, that, at such times, religions ought, more cautiously than at any other, to confine themselves within their own precincts; for in seeking to extend their power beyond religious matters, they incur a risk of not being believed at all. The circle within which they seek to restrict the human intellect ought therefore to be carefully traced, and, beyond its verge, the mind should be left entirely free to its own guidance.

Mohammed professed to derive from Heaven, and has inserted in the Koran, not only religious doctrines, but political maxims, civil and criminal laws, and theories of science. The Gospel, on the contrary, only speaks of the general relations of men to God and to each other, beyond which it inculcates and imposes no point of faith. This alone, besides a thousand other reasons, would suffice to prove that the former of these religions will never long predominate in a cultivated and democratic age, whilst the latter is destined to retain its sway at these as at all other periods.

In continuation of this same inquiry, I find that, for religions to maintain their authority, humanly speaking, in democratic ages, not only must they confine themselves strictly within the circle of spiritual matters, but their power also will depend very much on the nature of the belief they inculcate, on the external forms they assume, and on the obligations they impose.

The preceding observation, that equality leads men to very general and very vast ideas, is principally to be understood in respect to religion. Men who are similar and equal in the world readily conceive the idea of the one God, governing every man by the same laws, and granting to every man future happiness on the same conditions. The idea of the unity of mankind constantly leads them back to the idea of the unity of the Creator; whilst, on the contrary, in a state of society where men are broken up into very unequal ranks, they are apt to devise as many deities as there are nations, castes, classes, or families, and to trace a thousand private roads to Heaven.

It cannot be denied that Christianity itself has felt, to

some extent, the influence which social and political conditions exercise on religious opinions.

When the Christian religion first appeared upon earth, Providence, by whom the world was doubtless prepared for its coming, had gathered a large portion of the human race, like an immense flock, under the sceptre of the Cæsars. The men of whom this multitude was composed were distinguished by numerous differences; but they had thus much in common, that they all obeyed the same laws, and that every subject was so weak and insignificant in respect to the Emperor, that all appeared equal when their condition was contrasted with his. This novel and peculiar state of mankind necessarily predisposed men to listen to the general truths which Christianity teaches, and may serve to explain the facility and rapidity with which they then penetrated into the human mind.

The counterpart of this state of things was exhibited after the destruction of the Empire. The Roman World, being then, as it were, shattered into a thousand fragments, each nation resumed its former individuality. A scale of ranks soon grew up in the bosom of these nations; the different races were more sharply defined, and each nation was divided by castes into several peoples. In the midst of this common effort, which seemed to be dividing human society into as many fragments as possible, Christianity did not lose sight of the leading general ideas which it had brought into the world. But it appeared, nevertheless, to lend itself as much as possible to the new tendencies created by this distribution of mankind into fractions. Men continue to worship one God, the Creator and Preserver of all things; but every people, every city, and, so to speak, every man, thought to obtain some distinct privilege, and win the favor of an especial protector near the throne of Grace. Unable to subdivide the Deity, they multiplied and unduly enhanced the importance of his agents. The homage due to saints and angels became an almost idolatrous worship for most Christians; and it might be feared for a moment that the religion of Christ would retrograde towards the superstitions which it had overcome.

It seems evident, that, the more the barriers are removed which separate one nation from another and one citizen from another, the stronger is the bent of the human mind, as if by its own impulse, towards the idea of a single and all-powerful Being, dispensing equal laws in the same manner to every man. In democratic ages, then, it is more particularly important not to allow the homage paid to secondary agents to be confounded with the worship due to the Creator alone.

Another truth is no less clear, — that religions ought to have fewer external observances in democratic periods than at any others.

In speaking of philosophical method among the Americans, I have shown that nothing is more repugnant to the human mind, in an age of equality, than the idea of subjection to forms. Men living at such times are impatient of figures; to their eyes, symbols appear to be puerile artifices used to conceal or to set off truths which should more naturally be bared to the light of day: they are unmoved by ceremonial observances, and are disposed to attach only a secondary importance to the details of public worship.

Those who have to regulate the external forms of religion in a democratic age should pay a close attention to these natural propensities of the human mind, in order not to run counter to them unnecessarily.

I firmly believe in the necessity of forms, which fix the human mind in the contemplation of abstract truths, and aid it in embracing them warmly and holding them with firmness. Nor do I suppose that it is possible to maintain a religion without external observances; but, on the other hand, I am persuaded that, in the ages upon which we are entering, it would be peculiarly dangerous to multiply them beyond measure; and that they ought rather to be limited to as much as is absolutely necessary to perpetuate the doctrine itself, which is the substance of religion, of which the ritual is only the form.* A religion which should become more minute, more peremptory, and more charged with small observances, at a time when men are becoming more equal, would soon find itself reduced to a band of fanatical zealots in the midst of an infidel people.

I anticipate the objection that, as all religions have general and eternal truths for their object, they cannot thus shape themselves to the shifting inclinations of every age, without forfeiting their claim to certainty in the eyes of mankind. To this I reply again, that the principal opinions which constitute a creed, and which theologians call articles of faith, must be very carefully distinguished from the accessories connected with them. Religions are obliged to hold fast to the former, whatever be the peculiar spirit of the age; but they should take good care not to bind themselves in the same manner to the latter, at a time when everything is in transition, and when the mind, accustomed to the moving pageant of human affairs, reluctantly allows itself to be fixed on any point. The fixity of eternal and secondary things can afford a chance of duration only when civil society is itself fixed; under any other circumstances, I hold it to be perilous.

We shall see that, of all the passions which originate in or are fostered by equality, there is one which it renders peculiarly intense, and which it also infuses into the heart

---

* In all religions, there are some ceremonies which are inherent in the substance of the faith itself, and in these nothing should on any account be changed. This is especially the case with Roman Catholicism, in which the doctrine and the form are frequently so closely united as to form but one point of belief.

of every man, — I mean the love of well-being. The taste for well-being is the prominent and indelible feature of democratic times.

It may be believed that a religion which should undertake to destroy so deep-seated a passion, would in the end be destroyed by it; and if it attempted to wean men entirely from the contemplation of the good things of this world, in order to devote their faculties exclusively to the thought of another, it may be foreseen that the minds of men would at length escape its grasp, to plunge into the exclusive enjoyment of present and material pleasures.

The chief concern of religion is to purify, to regulate, and to restrain the excessive and exclusive taste for well-being which men feel at periods of equality; but it would be an error to attempt to overcome it completely, or to eradicate it. Men cannot be cured of the love of riches; but they may be persuaded to enrich themselves by none but honest means.

This brings me to a final consideration, which comprises, as it were, all the others. The more the conditions of men are equalized and assimilated to each other, the more important is it for religion; whilst it carefully abstains from the daily turmoil of secular affairs, not needlessly to run counter to the ideas which generally prevail, or to the permanent interests which exist in the mass of the people. For, as public opinion grows to be more and more the first and most irresistible of existing powers, the religious principle has no external support strong enough to enable it long to resist its attacks. This is not less true of a democratic people ruled by a despot, than of a republic. In ages of equality kings may often command obedience, but the majority always commands belief: to the majority, therefore, deference is to be paid in whatsoever is not contrary to the faith.

I showed in my former volume how the American clergy

stand aloof from secular affairs. This is the most obvious, but not the only, example of their self-restraint. In America, religion is a distinct sphere, in which the priest is sovereign, but out of which he takes care never to go. Within its limits, he is master of the mind; beyond them, he leaves men to themselves, and surrenders them to the independence and instability which belong to their nature and their age. I have seen no country in which Christianity is clothed with fewer forms, figures, and observances than in the United States; or where it presents more distinct, simple, and general notions to the mind. Although the Christians of America are divided into a multitude of sects, they all look upon their religion in the same light. This applies to Roman Catholicism as well as to the other forms of belief. There are no Romish priests who show less taste for the minute individual observances, for extraordinary or peculiar means of salvation, or who cling more to the spirit, and less to the letter, of the law, than the Roman Catholic priests of the United States. Nowhere is that doctrine of the Church which prohibits the worship reserved to God alone from being offered to the saints, more clearly inculcated or more generally followed. Yet the Roman Catholics of America are very submissive and very sincere.

Another remark is applicable to the clergy of every communion. The American ministers of the Gospel do not attempt to draw or to fix all the thoughts of man upon the life to come; they are willing to surrender a portion of his heart to the cares of the present; seeming to consider the goods of this world as important, though secondary, objects. If they take no part themselves in productive labor, they are at least interested in its progress, and they applaud its results; and whilst they never cease to point to the other world as the great object of the hopes and fears of the believer, they do not forbid him honestly to

court prosperity in this. Far from attempting to show
that these things are distinct and contrary to one another,
they study rather to find out on what point they are most
nearly and closely connected.

All the American clergy know and respect the intellectual supremacy exercised by the majority: they never
sustain any but necessary conflicts with it. They take no
share in the altercations of parties, but they readily adopt
the general opinions of their country and their age: and
they allow themselves to be borne away without opposition
in the current of feeling and opinion by which everything
around them is carried along. They endeavor to amend
their contemporaries, but they do not quit fellowship with
them. Public opinion is therefore never hostile to them:
it rather supports and protects them; and their belief owes
its authority at the same ·time to the strength which is its
own, and to that which it borrows from the opinions of
the majority.

Thus it is, that, by respecting all democratic tendencies
not absolutely contrary to herself, and by making use of
several of them for her own purposes, Religion sustains a
successful struggle with that spirit of individual independence which is her most dangerous opponent.

CHAPTER VI.

THE PROGRESS OF ROMAN CATHOLICISM IN THE UNITED STATES.

AMERICA is the most democratic country in the world, and it is at the same time (according to reports worthy of belief) the country in which the Roman Catholic religion makes most progress.   At first sight, this is surprising.

Two things must here be accurately distinguished: equality inclines men to wish to form their own opinions; but, on the other hand, it imbues them with the taste and the idea of unity, simplicity, and impartiality in the power which governs society.   Men living in democratic times are therefore very prone to shake off all religious authority; but if they consent to subject themselves to any authority of this kind, they choose at least that it should be single and uniform.   Religious powers not radiating from a common centre are naturally repugnant to their minds; and they almost as readily conceive that there should be no religion, as that there should be several.

At the present time, more than in any preceding age, Roman Catholics are seen to lapse into infidelity, and Protestants to be converted to Roman Catholicism.   If the Roman Catholic faith be considered within the pale of the Church, it would seem to be losing ground; without that pale, to be gaining it.   Nor is this difficult of explanation. The men of our days are naturally little disposed to believe; but, as soon as they have any religion, they immediately find in themselves a latent instinct which urges

them unconsciously towards Catholicism. Many of the
doctrines and practices of the Romish Church astonish
them; but they feel a secret admiration for its discipline,
and its great unity attracts them. If Catholicism could
at length withdraw itself from the political animosities to
which it has given rise, I have hardly any doubt but that
the same spirit of the age which appears to be so opposed
to it would become so favorable as to admit of its great
and sudden advancement.

One of the most ordinary weaknesses of the human intellect is to seek to reconcile contrary principles, and to
purchase peace at the expense of logic. Thus there have
ever been, and will ever be, men who, after having submitted some portion of their religious belief to the principle of authority, will seek to exempt several other parts of
their faith from it, and to keep their minds floating at random between liberty and obedience. But I am inclined to
believe that the number of these thinkers will be less in
democratic than in other ages; and that our posterity will
tend more and more to a division into only two parts, —
some relinquishing Christianity entirely, and others returning to the Church of Rome.

CHAPTER VII.

WHAT CAUSES DEMOCRATIC NATIONS TO INCLINE TOWARDS PANTHEISM.

I SHALL show hereafter how the preponderating taste of a democratic people for very general ideas manifests itself in politics; but I wish to point out, at present, its principal effect on philosophy.

It cannot be denied that pantheism has made great progress in our age. The writings of a part of Europe bear visible marks of it: the Germans introduce it into philosophy, and the French into literature. Most of the works of imagination published in France contain some opinions or some tinge caught from pantheistical doctrines, or they disclose some tendency to such doctrines in their authors. This appears to me not to proceed only from an accidental, but from a permanent cause.

When the conditions of society are becoming more equal, and each individual man becomes more like all the rest, more weak and insignificant, a habit grows up of ceasing to notice the citizens, and considering only the people, — of overlooking individuals, to think only of their kind. At such times, the human mind seeks to embrace a multitude of different objects at once; and it constantly strives to connect a variety of consequences with a single cause. The idea of unity so possesses man, and is sought by him so generally, that, if he thinks he has found it, he readily yields himself to repose in that belief. Not content with the discovery that there is nothing in the world but a creation and a Creator, he is still embarrassed by this primary division of things, and seeks to expand and simplify his conception by including God and the Universe in one great Whole.

If there be a philosophical system which teaches that all things material and immaterial, visible and invisible, which the world contains, are to be considered only as the several parts of an immense Being, who alone remains eternal amidst the continual change and ceaseless transformation of all that constitutes him, we may readily infer that such a system, although it destroy the individuality of man, — nay, rather because it destroys that individuality, — will have secret charms for men living in democracies. All their habits of thought prepare them to conceive it, and predispose them to adopt it. It naturally attracts and fixes their imagination ; it fosters the pride, whilst it soothes the indolence, of their minds.

Amongst the different systems by whose aid Philosophy endeavors to explain the Universe, I believe pantheism to be one of those most fitted to seduce the human mind in democratic times. Against it, all who abide in their attachment to the true greatness of man should combine and struggle.

CHAPTER VIII.

HOW EQUALITY SUGGESTS TO THE AMERICANS THE IDEA OF THE INDEFINITE PERFECTIBILITY OF MAN.

EQUALITY suggests to the human mind several ideas which would not have originated from any other source, and it modifies almost all those previously entertained. I take as an example the idea of human perfectibility, because it is one of the principal notions that the intellect can conceive, and because it constitutes of itself a great philosophical theory, which is everywhere to be traced by its consequences in the conduct of human affairs.

Although man has many points of resemblance with the brutes, one trait is peculiar to himself, — he improves: they are incapable of improvement. Mankind could not fail to discover this difference from the beginning. The idea of perfectibility is therefore as old as the world; equality did not give birth to it, but has imparted to it a new character.

When the citizens of a community are classed according to rank, profession, or birth, and when all men are constrained to follow the career which chance has opened before them, every one thinks that the utmost limits of human power are to be discerned in proximity to himself, and no one seeks any longer to resist the inevitable law of his destiny. Not, indeed, that an aristocratic people absolutely deny man's faculty of self-improvement, but they do not hold it to be indefinite; they can conceive amelioration, but not change: they imagine that the future condition of society may be better, but not essentially different; and, whilst they admit that humanity has made progress, and

may still have some to make, they assign to it beforehand
certain impassable limits.

Thus, they do not presume that they have arrived at the
supreme good or at absolute truth, (what people or what
man was ever wild enough to imagine it?) but they cherish a persuasion that they have pretty nearly reached that
degree of greatness and knowledge which our imperfect
nature admits of; and, as nothing moves about them, they
are willing to fancy that everything is in its fit place.
Then it is that the legislator affects to lay down eternal
laws; that kings and nations will raise none but imperishable monuments; and that the present generation undertakes to spare generations to come the care of regulating
their destinies.

In proportion as castes disappear and the classes of society approximate, — as manners, customs, and laws vary,
from the tumultuous intercourse of men, — as new facts
arise, — as new truths are brought to light, — as ancient
opinions are dissipated, and others take their place, — the
image of an ideal but always fugitive perfection presents
itself to the human mind. Continual changes are then every instant occurring under the observation of every man:
the position of some is rendered worse; and he learns but
too well that no people and no individual, how enlightened
soever they may be, can lay claim to infallibility: the condition of others is improved; whence he infers that man is
endowed with an indefinite faculty of improvement. His
reverses teach him that none have discovered absolute
good, — his success stimulates him to the never-ending
pursuit of it. Thus, forever seeking, forever falling to
rise again, — often disappointed, but not discouraged, —
he tends unceasingly towards that unmeasured greatness
so indistinctly visible at the end of the long track which
humanity has yet to tread.

It can hardly be believed how many facts naturally flow

from the philosophical theory of the indefinite perfectibility of man, or how strong an influence it exercises even on those who, living entirely for the purposes of action and not of thought, seem to conform their actions to it, without knowing anything about it.

I accost an American sailor, and inquire why the ships of his country are built so as to last but for a short time; he answers without hesitation, that the art of navigation is every day making such rapid progress, that the finest vessel would become almost useless if it lasted beyond a few years. In these words, which fell accidentally, and on a particular subject, from an uninstructed man, I recognize the general and systematic idea upon which a great people direct all their concerns.

Aristocratic nations are naturally too apt to narrow the scope of human perfectibility; democratic nations, to expand it beyond reason.

CHAPTER IX.

THE EXAMPLE OF THE AMERICANS DOES NOT PROVE THAT A DEMOCRATIC PEOPLE CAN HAVE NO APTITUDE AND NO TASTE FOR SCIENCE, LITERATURE, OR ART.

IT must be acknowledged that in few of the civilized nations of our time have the higher sciences made less progress than in the United States; and in few have great artists, distinguished poets, or celebrated writers, been more rare.* Many Europeans, struck by this fact, have looked upon it as a natural and inevitable result of equality; and they have thought that, if a democratic state of society and democratic institutions were ever to prevail over the whole earth, the human mind would gradually find its beacon-lights grow dim, and men would relapse into a period of darkness.

To reason thus is, I think, to confound several ideas which it is important to divide and examine separately: it is to mingle, unintentionally, what is democratic with what is only American.

The religion professed by the first emigrants, and bequeathed by them to their descendants, — simple in its forms, austere and almost harsh in its principles, and hostile to external symbols and to ceremonial pomp, — is naturally unfavorable to the fine arts, and only yields reluctantly to the pleasures of literature. The Americans are a very old and a very enlightened people, who have fallen upon a new and unbounded country, where they may extend themselves at pleasure, and which they may fertilize without difficulty.

* See notes to Vol. I. pp. 403, 404. — AM. ED.

This state of things is without a parallel in the history of the world. In America, every one finds facilities unknown elsewhere for making or increasing his fortune. The spirit of gain is always on the stretch, and the human mind, constantly diverted from the pleasures of imagination and the labors of the intellect, is there swayed by no impulse but the pursuit of wealth. Not only are manufacturing and commercial classes to be found in the United States, as they are in all other countries; but, what never occurred elsewhere, the whole community are simultaneously engaged in productive industry and commerce.

But I am convinced that, if the Americans had been alone in the world, with the freedom and the knowledge acquired by their forefathers, and the passions which are their own, they would not have been slow to discover that progress cannot long be made in the application of the sciences without cultivating the theory of them; that all the arts are perfected by one another: and, however absorbed they might have been by the pursuit of the principal object of their desires, they would speedily have admitted that it is necessary to turn aside from it occasionally, in order the better to attain it in the end.

The taste for the pleasures of mind is moreover so natural to the heart of civilized man, that amongst the polite nations, which are least disposed to give themselves up to these pursuits, a certain number of persons are always to be found who take part in them. This intellectual craving, once felt, would very soon have been satisfied.

But at the very time when the Americans were naturally inclined to require nothing of science but its special applications to the useful arts and the means of rendering life comfortable, learned and literary Europe was engaged in exploring the common sources of truth, and in improving at the same time all that can minister to the pleasures or satisfy the wants of man.

At the head of the enlightened nations of the Old World the inhabitants of the United States more particularly distinguished one, to which they were closely united by a common origin and by kindred habits. Amongst this people they found distinguished men of science, able artists, writers of eminence, and they were enabled to enjoy the treasures of the intellect without laboring to amass them. In spite of the ocean which intervenes, I cannot consent to separate America from Europe. I consider the people of the United States as that portion of the English people who are commissioned to explore the forests of the New World; whilst the rest of the nation, enjoying more leisure and less harassed by the drudgery of life, may devote their energies to thought, and enlarge in all directions the empire of mind.

The position of the Americans is therefore quite exceptional, and it may be believed that no democratic people will ever be placed in a similar one. Their strictly Puritanical origin, — their exclusively commercial habits, — even the country they inhabit, which seems to divert their minds from the pursuit of science, literature, and the arts, — the proximity of Europe, which allows them to neglect these pursuits without relapsing into barbarism, — a thousand special causes, of which I have only been able to point out the most important, — have singularly concurred to fix the mind of the American upon purely practical objects. His passions, his wants, his education, and everything about him, seem to unite in drawing the native of the United States earthward: his religion alone bids him turn, from time to time, a transient and distracted glance to heaven. Let us cease, then, to view all democratic nations under the example of the American people, and attempt to survey them at length with their own features.

It is possible to conceive a people not subdivided into any castes or scale of ranks; among whom the law, recognizing no privileges, should divide inherited property into equal shares ; but which, at the same time, should be without knowledge and without freedom. Nor is this an empty hypothesis : a despot may find that it is his interest to render his subjects equal and to leave them ignorant, in order more easily to keep them slaves. Not only would a democratic people of this kind show neither aptitude nor taste for science, literature, or art, but it would probably never arrive at the possession of them. The law of descent would of itself provide for the destruction of large fortunes at each succeeding generation ; and no new fortunes would be acquired. The poor man, without either knowledge or freedom, would not so much as conceive the idea of raising himself to wealth ; and the rich man would allow himself to be degraded to poverty, without a notion of self-defence. Between these two members of the community complete and invincible equality would soon be established. No one would then have time or taste to devote himself to the pursuits or pleasures of the intellect ; but all men would remain paralyzed in a state of common ignorance and equal servitude.

When I conceive a democratic society of this kind, I fancy myself in one of those low, close, and gloomy abodes, where the light which breaks in from without soon faints and fades away. A sudden heaviness overpowers me, and I grope through the surrounding darkness, to find an opening which will restore me to the air and the light of day. But all this is not applicable to men already enlightened who retain their freedom, after having abolished those peculiar and hereditary rights which perpetuated the tenure of property in the hands of certain individuals or certain classes.

When men living in a democratic state of society are enlightened, they readily discover that they are not confined and fixed by any limits which constrain them to take up with their present fortune. They all, therefore, conceive the idea of increasing it, — if they are free, they all attempt it ; but all do not succeed in the same manner. The legislature, it is true, no longer grants privileges, but nature grants them. As natural inequality is very great, fortunes become unequal as soon as every man exerts all his faculties to get rich.

The law of descent prevents the establishment of wealthy families, but it does not prevent the existence of wealthy individuals. It constantly brings back the members of the community to a common level, from which they as constantly escape ; and the inequality of fortunes augments in proportion as their knowledge is diffused and their liberty increased.

A sect which arose in our time, and was celebrated for its talents and its extravagance, proposed to concentrate all property in the hands of a central power, whose function it should afterwards be to parcel it out to individuals, according to their merits. This would have been a method of escaping from that complete and eternal equality which seems to threaten democratic society. But it would be a simpler and less dangerous remedy to grant no privilege to any, giving to all equal cultivation and equal independence, and leaving every one to determine his own position. Natural inequality will soon make way for itself, and wealth will spontaneously pass into the hands of the most capable.

Free and democratic communities, then, will always contain a multitude of people enjoying opulence or a competency. The wealthy will not be so closely linked to each other as the members of the former aristocratic class of society ; their inclinations will be different, and they will scarcely ever enjoy leisure as secure or complete ; but they will be far more numerous than those who belonged to that class of society could ever be. These persons will not be strictly confined to the cares of practical life ; and they will still be able, though in different degrees, to indulge in the pursuits and pleasures of the intellect. In those pleasures they will indulge; for, if it be true that the human mind leans on one side to the limited, the material, and the useful, it naturally rises on the other to the infinite, the spiritual, and the beautiful. Physical wants confine it to the earth; but, as soon as the tie is loosened, it will rise of itself.

Not only will the number of those who can take an interest in the productions of mind be greater, but the taste for intellectual enjoyment will descend, step by step, even to those who, in aristocratic societies, seem to have neither time nor ability to indulge in them. When hereditary wealth, the privileges of rank, and the prerogatives of birth have ceased to be, and when every man derives his strength from himself alone, it becomes evident that the chief cause of disparity between the fortunes of men is the mind. Whatever tends to invigorate, to extend, or to adorn the mind, instantly rises to a high value. The utility of knowledge becomes singularly conspicuous even to the eyes of the multitude: those who have no taste for its charms set store upon its results, and make some efforts to acquire it.

In free and enlightened democratic times there is nothing to separate men from each other, or to retain them in their place: they rise or sink with extreme rapidity. All classes live in continual intercourse, from their great proximity to each other. They communicate and intermingle every day; they imitate and emulate one another: this suggests to the people many ideas, notions, and desires which they would never have entertained if the distinctions of rank had been fixed, and society at rest. In such nations, the servant never considers himself as an entire stranger to the pleasures and toils of his master, nor the poor man to those of the rich; the rural population assimilates itself to that of the towns, and the provinces to the capital. No one easily allows himself to be reduced to the mere material cares of life; and the humblest artisan casts at times an eager and a furtive glance into the higher regions of the intellect. People do not read with the same notions or in the same manner as they do in aristocratic communities; but the circle of readers is unceasingly expanded, till it includes all the people.

As soon as the multitude begin to take an interest in the labors of the mind, it finds out that to excel in some of them is a powerful means of acquiring fame, power, or wealth. The restless ambition which equality begets instantly takes this direction, as it does all others. The number of those who cultivate science, letters, and the arts, becomes immense. The intellectual world starts into prodigious activity: every one endeavors to open for himself a path there, and to draw the eyes of the public after him. Something analogous occurs to what happens in society in the United States politically considered. What is done is often imperfect, but the attempts are innumerable; and, although the results of individual effort are commonly very small, the total amount is always very large.

It is therefore not true to assert, that men living in democratic times are naturally indifferent to science, literature, and the arts: only it must be acknowledged that they cultivate them after their own fashion, and bring to the task their own peculiar qualifications and deficiencies.

CHAPTER X.

WHY THE AMERICANS ARE MORE ADDICTED TO PRACTICAL THAN TO THEORETICAL SCIENCE.

IF a democratic state of society and democratic institutions do not retard the onward course of the human mind, they incontestably guide it in one direction in preference to another. Their efforts, thus circumscribed, are still exceedingly great; and I may be pardoned if I pause for a moment to contemplate them.

We had occasion, in speaking of the philosophical method of the American people, to make several remarks, which must here be turned to account.

Equality begets in man the desire of judging of every · thing for himself: it gives him, in all things, a taste for the tangible and the real, a contempt for tradition and for forms. These general tendencies are principally discernible in the peculiar subject of this chapter.

Those who cultivate the sciences amongst a democratic people are always afraid of losing their way in visionary speculation. They mistrust systems; they adhere closely to facts, and study facts with their own senses. As they do not easily defer to the mere name of any fellow-man, they are never inclined to rest upon any man's authority; but, on the contrary, they are unremitting in their efforts to find out the weaker points of their neighbors' doctrine. Scientific precedents have little weight with them; they are never long detained by the subtilty of the schools, nor ready to accept big words for sterling coin; they penetrate, as far as they can, into the principal parts of the subject which occupies them, and they like to expound them in the vulgar tongue. Scientific pursuits then follow a freer and safer course, but a less lofty one.

The mind may, as it appears to me, divide science into three parts.

The first comprises the most theoretical principles, and those more abstract notions, whose application is either unknown or very remote.

The second is composed of those general truths which still belong to pure theory, but lead nevertheless by a straight and short road to practical results.

Methods of application and means of execution make up the third.

Each of these different portions of science may be separately cultivated, although reason and experience prove that neither of them can prosper long, if it be absolutely cut off from the two others.

In America, the purely practical part of science is admirably understood, and careful attention is paid to the theoretical portion, which is immediately requisite to application. On this head, the Americans always display a clear, free, original, and inventive power of mind. But hardly any one in the United States devotes himself to the essentially theoretical and abstract portion of human knowledge. In this respect, the Americans carry to excess a tendency which is, I think, discernible, though in a less degree, amongst all democratic nations.

Nothing is more necessary to the culture of the higher sciences, or of the more elevated departments of science, than meditation; and nothing is less suited to meditation than the structure of democratic society. We do not find there, as amongst an aristocratic people, one class which keeps in repose because it is well off; and another, which does not venture to stir because it despairs of improving its condition. Every one is in motion: some in quest of

power, others of gain. In the midst of this universal
tumult, — this incessant conflict of jarring interests, — this
continual striving of men after fortune, — where is that
calm to be found which is necessary for the deeper combinations of the intellect? How can the mind dwell upon
any single point, when everything whirls around it, and
man himself is swept and beaten onwards by the heady
current which rolls all things in its course?

But the permanent agitation which subsists in the bosom
of a peaceable and established democracy must be distinguished from the tumultuous and revolutionary movements
which almost always attend the birth and growth of democratic society. When a violent revolution occurs amongst
a highly-civilized people, it cannot fail to give a sudden impulse to their feelings and ideas. This is more particularly
true of democratic revolutions, which stir up at once all
the classes of which a people is composed, and beget at the
same time inordinate ambition in the breast of every member of the community. The French made surprising advances in the exact sciences at the very time at which they
were finishing the destruction of the remains of their former feudal society; yet this sudden fecundity is not to be
attributed to democracy, but to the unexampled revolution
which attended its growth. What happened at that period
was a special incident, and it would be unwise to regard
it as the test of a general principle.

Great revolutions are not more common amongst democratic than amongst other nations: I am even inclined to
believe that they are less so. But there prevails amongst
those populations a small, distressing motion, a sort of incessant jostling of men, which annoys and disturbs the
mind without exciting or elevating it.

Men who live in democratic communities not only seldom indulge in meditation, but they naturally entertain
very little esteem for it. A democratic state of society and

democratic institutions keep the greater part of men in
constant activity; and the habits of mind which are suited
to an active life are not always suited to a contemplative
one.   The man of action is frequently obliged to content
himself with the best he can get, because he would never
accomplish his purpose if he chose to carry every detail to
perfection.   He has perpetually occasion to rely on ideas
which he has not had leisure to search to the bottom; for
he is much more frequently aided by the seasonableness of
an idea than by its strict accuracy; and, in the long run,
he risks less in making use of some false principles, than
in spending his time in establishing all his principles, on the
basis of truth.   The world is not led by long or learned
demonstrations: a rapid glance at particular incidents,
the daily study of the fleeting passions of the multitude,
the accidents of the moment and the art of turning them
to account, decide all its affairs.

In the ages in which active life is the condition of almost
every one, men are therefore generally led to attach an excessive value to the rapid bursts and superficial conceptions
of the intellect; and, on the other hand, to depreciate
unduly its slower and deeper labors.   This opinion of the
public influences the judgment of the men who cultivate
the sciences; they are persuaded that they may succeed in
those pursuits without meditation, or are deterred from
such pursuits as demand it.

There are several methods of studying the sciences.
Amongst a multitude of men you will find a selfish, mercantile, and trading taste for the discoveries of the mind,
which must not be confounded with that disinterested passion which is kindled in the heart of a few.   A desire to
utilize knowledge is one thing; the pure desire to know
is another.   I do not doubt that in a few minds, and
at long intervals, an ardent, inexhaustible love of truth
springs up, self-supported, and living in ceaseless fruition,

without ever attaining full satisfaction. This ardent love it is — this proud, disinterested love of what is true — which raises men to the abstract sources of truth, to draw their mother knowledge thence.

If Pascal had had nothing in view but some large gain, or even if he had been stimulated by the love of fame alone, I cannot conceive that he would ever have been able to rally all the powers of his mind, as he did, for the better discovery of the most hidden things of the Creator. When I see him, as it were, tear his soul from all the cares of life to devote it wholly to these researches, and, prematurely snapping the links which bind the frame to life, die of old age before forty, I stand amazed, and perceive that no ordinary cause is at work to produce efforts so extraordinary.

The future will prove whether these passions, at once so rare and so productive, come into being and into growth as easily in the midst of democratic as in aristocratic communities. For myself, I confess that I am slow to believe it.

In aristocratic societies, the class which gives the tone to opinion, and has the guidance of affairs, being permanently and hereditarily placed above the multitude, naturally conceives a lofty idea of itself and of man. It loves to invent for him noble pleasures, to carve out splendid objects for his ambition. Aristocracies often commit very tyrannical and inhuman actions, but they rarely entertain grovelling thoughts; and they show a kind of haughty contempt of little pleasures, even whilst they indulge in them. The effect is greatly to raise the general pitch of society. In aristocratic ages, vast ideas are commonly entertained of the dignity, the power, and the greatness of man. These opinions exert their influence on those who cultivate the sciences, as well as on the rest of the community. They facilitate the natural impulse of the mind to the highest regions of thought; and they naturally prepare it to conceive a sublime, almost a divine, love of truth.

Men of science at such periods are consequently carried away towards theory; and it even happens that they frequently conceive an inconsiderate contempt for practice. "Archimedes," says Plutarch, "was of so lofty a spirit, that he never condescended to write any treatise on the manner of constructing all these engines of war. And as he held this science of inventing and putting together engines, and all arts generally speaking which tended to any useful end in practice, to be vile, low, and mercenary, he spent his talents and his studious hours in writing of those things only whose beauty and subtilty had in them no admixture of necessity." Such is the aristocratic aim of science: it cannot be the same in democratic nations.

The greater part of the men who constitute these nations are extremely eager in the pursuit of actual and physical gratification. As they are always dissatisfied with the position which they occupy, and are always free to leave it, they think of nothing but the means of changing their fortune, or increasing it. To minds thus predisposed, every new method which leads by a shorter road to wealth, every machine which spares labor, every instrument which diminishes the cost of production, every discovery which facilitates pleasures or augments them, seems to be the grandest effort of the human intellect. It is chiefly from these motives that a democratic people addicts itself to scientific pursuits, — that it understands and respects them. In aristocratic ages, science is more particularly called upon to furnish gratification to the mind; in democracies, to the body.

You may be sure that the more a nation is democratic, enlightened, and free, the greater will be the number of these interested promoters of scientific genius, and. the more will discoveries immediately applicable to productive industry confer gain, fame, and even power, on their authors. For in democracies, the working class take a part in public affairs; and public honors, as well as pecuniary remuneration, may be awarded to those who deserve them.

In a community thus organized, it may easily be conceived that the human mind may be led insensibly to the neglect of theory; and that it is urged, on the contrary, with unparalleled energy, to the applications of science, or at least to that portion of theoretical science which is necessary to those who make such applications. In vain will some instinctive inclination raise the mind towards the loftier spheres of the intellect; interest draws it down to the middle zone. There it may develop all its energy and restless activity, and bring forth wonders. These very Americans, who have not discovered one of the general laws of mechanics, have introduced into navigation an engine which changes the aspect of the world.

Assuredly I do not contend that the democratic nations of our time are destined to witness the extinction of the great luminaries of man's intelligence, or even that they will never bring new lights into existence. At the age at which the world has now arrived, and amongst so many cultivated nations perpetually excited by the fever of productive industry, the bonds which connect the different parts of science cannot fail to strike the observer; and the taste for practical science itself, if it be enlightened, ought to lead men not to neglect theory. In the midst of so many attempted applications of so many experiments, repeated every day, it is almost impossible that general laws should not frequently be brought to light; so that great discoveries would be frequent, though great inventors may be few.

I believe, moreover, in high scientific vocations. If the democratic principle does not, on the one hand, induce men to cultivate science for its own sake, on the other, it enormously increases the number of those who do cultivate it. Nor is it credible that, amid so great a multitude, a speculative genius should not from time to time arise inflamed by the love of truth alone. Such an one, we may be sure, would dive into the deepest mysteries of nature, whatever be the spirit of his country and his age. He requires no assistance in his course, — it is enough that he is not checked in it. All that I mean to say is this: permanent inequality of conditions leads men to confine themselves to the arrogant and sterile research of abstract truths, whilst the social condition and the institutions of democracy prepare them to seek the immediate and useful practical results of the sciences. This tendency is natural and inevitable: it is curious to be acquainted with it, and it may be necessary to point it out.

If those who are called upon to guide the nations of our time clearly discerned from afar off these new tendencies, which will soon be irresistible, they would understand that, possessing education and freedom, men living in democratic ages cannot fail to improve the industrial part of science; and that henceforward all the efforts of the constituted authorities ought to be directed to support the highest branches of learning, and to foster the nobler passion for science itself. In the present age, the human mind must be coerced into theoretical studies; it runs of its own accord to practical applications; and, instead of perpetually referring it to the minute examination of secondary effects, it is well to divert it from them sometimes, in order to raise it up to the contemplation of primary causes.

Because the civilization of ancient Rome perished in consequence of the invasion of the Barbarians, we are perhaps too apt to think that civilization cannot perish in any other manner. If the light by which we are guided is ever extinguished, it will dwindle by degrees, and expire of itself. By dint of close adherence to mere applications, principles would be lost sight of; and when the principles were wholly forgotten, the methods derived from them would be ill pursued. New methods could no longer be invented, and men would continue to apply, without intelligence and without art, scientific processes no longer understood.

When Europeans first arrived in China, three hundred years ago, they found that almost all the arts had reached a certain degree of perfection there; and they were surprised that a people which had attained this point should not have gone beyond it. At a later period, they discovered traces of some higher branches of science which had been lost. The nation was absorbed in productive industry; the greater part of its scientific processes had been preserved, but science itself no longer existed there. This served to explain the strange immobility in which they found the minds of this people. The Chinese, in following the track of their forefathers, had forgotten the reasons by which the latter had been guided. They still used the formula, without asking for its meaning; they retained the instrument, but they no longer possessed the art of altering or renewing it. The Chinese, then, had lost the power of change; for them, improvement was impossible. They were compelled, at all times and in all points, to imitate their predecessors, lest they should stray into utter darkness by deviating for an instant from the path already laid down for them. The source of human knowledge was all but dry; and though the stream still ran on, it could neither swell its waters, nor alter its course.

Notwithstanding this, China had subsisted peaceably for centuries. The invaders who had conquered the country assumed the manners of the inhabitants, and order prevailed there. A sort of physical prosperity was everywhere discernible : revolutions were rare, and war was, so to speak, unknown.

It is then a fallacy to flatter ourselves with the reflection that the Barbarians are still far from us; for if there be some nations which allow civilization to be torn from their grasp, there are others who trample it themselves under their feet.

CHAPTER XI.

IN WHAT SPIRIT THE AMERICANS CULTIVATE THE ARTS.

IT would be to waste the time of my readers and my own, if I strove to demonstrate how the general mediocrity of fortunes, the absence of superfluous wealth, the universal desire of comfort, and the constant efforts by which every one attempts to procure it, make the taste for the useful predominate over the love of the beautiful in the heart of man. Democratic nations, amongst whom all these things exist, will therefore cultivate the arts which serve to render life easy, in preference to those whose object is to adorn it. They will habitually prefer the useful to the beautiful, and they will require that the beautiful should be useful.

But I propose to go further; and, after having pointed out this first feature, to sketch several others.

It commonly happens that, in the ages of privilege, the practice of almost all the arts becomes a privilege; and that every profession is a separate walk, upon which it is not allowable for every one to enter. Even when productive industry is free, the fixed character which belongs to aristocratic nations gradually segregates all the persons who practise the same art, till they form a distinct class, always composed of the same families, whose members are all known to each other, and amongst whom a public opinion of their own, and a species of corporate pride, soon spring up. In a class or guild of this kind, each artisan has not only his fortune to make, but his reputation to preserve. He is not exclusively swayed by his own interest, or even by that of his customer, but by that of the body to which he belongs; and the interest of that body is, that each artisan should produce the best possible workmanship. In aristocratic ages, the object of the arts is therefore to manufacture as well as possible, — not with the greatest despatch, or at the lowest rate.

When, on the contrary, every profession is open to all, — when a multitude of persons are constantly embracing and abandoning it, — and when its several members are strangers, indifferent to, and from their numbers hardly seen by, each other, — the social tie is destroyed, and each workman, standing alone, endeavors simply to gain the most money at the least cost. The will of the customer is then his only limit. But at the same time, a corresponding change takes place in the customer also. In countries in which riches, as well as power, are concentrated and retained in the hands of a few, the use of the greater part of this world's goods belongs to a small number of individuals, who are always the same. Necessity, public opinion, or moderate desires, exclude all others from the enjoyment of them. As this aristocratic class remains fixed at the pinnacle of greatness on which it stands, without diminution or increase, it is always acted upon by the same wants, and affected by them in the same manner. The men of whom it is composed naturally derive from their superior and hereditary position a taste for what is extremely well made and lasting. This affects the general way of thinking of the nation in relation to the arts. It often occurs, among such a people, that even the peasant will rather go without the objects he covets, than procure them in a state of imperfection. In aristocracies, then, the handicraftsmen work for only a limited number of fastidious customers: the profit they hope to make depends principally on the perfection of their workmanship.

Such is no longer the case when, all privileges being

abolished, ranks are intermingled, and men are forever
rising or sinking upon the social scale.   Amongst a democratic people, a number of citizens always exist whose pat-
rimony is divided and decreasing.   They have contracted,
under more prosperous circumstances, certain wants, which
remain after the means of satisfying such wants are gone;
and they are anxiously looking out for some surreptitious
method of providing for them.   On the other hand, there
are always in democracies a large number of men whose
fortune is upon the increase, but whose desires grow much
faster than their fortunes: and who gloat upon the gifts of
wealth in anticipation, long before they have means to command them.   Such men are eager to find some short cut
to these gratifications, already almost within their reach.
From the combination of these two causes the result is,
that in democracies there is always a multitude of persons
whose wants are above their means, and who are very willing to take up with imperfect satisfaction, rather than
abandon the object of their desires altogether.

The artisan readily understands these passions, for he
himself partakes in them : in an aristocracy, he would seek
to sell his workmanship at a high price to the few; he now
conceives that the more expeditious way of getting rich is
to sell them at a low price to all.   But there are only two
ways of lowering the price of commodities.   The first is
to discover some better, shorter, and more ingenious
method of producing them: the second is to manufacture
a larger quantity of goods, nearly similar, but of less value.
Amongst a democratic population, all the intellectual faculties of the workman are directed to these two objects : he
strives to invent methods which may enable him not only
to work better, but quicker and cheaper; or, if he cannot
succeed in that, to diminish the intrinsic quality of the
thing he makes, without rendering it wholly unfit for the
use for which it is intended.   When none but the wealthy

had watches, they were almost all very good ones : few are now made which are worth much, but everybody has one in his pocket. Thus the democratic principle not only tends to direct the human mind to the useful arts, but it induces the artisan to produce with great rapidity many imperfect commodities, and the consumer to content himself with these commodities.

Not that, in democracies, the arts are incapable, in case of need, of producing wonders. This may occasionally be the case, if customers appear who are ready to pay for time and trouble. In this rivalry of every kind of industry, in the midst of this immense competition and these countless experiments, some excellent workmen are formed, who reach the utmost limits of their craft. But they have rarely an opportunity of showing what they can do ; they are scrupulously sparing of their powers ; they remain in a state of accomplished mediocrity, which judges itself, and, though well able to shoot beyond the mark before it, aims only at what it hits. In aristocracies, on the contrary, workmen always do all they can ; and when they stop, it is because they have reached the limit of their art.

When I arrive in a country where I find some of the finest productions of the arts, I learn from this fact nothing of the social condition or of the political constitution of the country. But if I perceive that the productions of the arts are generally of an inferior quality, very abundant and very cheap, I am convinced that, amongst the people where this occurs, privilege is on the decline, and that ranks are beginning to intermingle, and will soon be confounded together.

The handicraftsmen of democratic ages endeavor not only to bring their useful productions within the reach of the whole community, but they strive to give to all their commodities attractive qualities which they do not in reality possess. In the confusion of all ranks, every one hopes to appear what he is not, and makes great exertions to succeed in this object. This sentiment, indeed, which is but too natural to the heart of man, does not originate in the democratic principle; but that principle applies it to material objects. The hypocrisy of virtue is of every age, but the hypocrisy of luxury belongs more particularly to the ages of democracy.

To satisfy these new cravings of human vanity, the arts have recourse to every species of imposture; and these devices sometimes go so far as to defeat their own purpose. Imitation diamonds are now made which may be easily mistaken for real ones; as soon as the art of fabricating false diamonds shall become so perfect that they cannot be distinguished from real ones, it is probable that both will be abandoned, and become mere pebbles again.

This leads me to speak of those arts which are called, by way of distinction, the fine arts. I do not believe that it is a necessary effect of a democratic social condition and of democratic institutions to diminish the number of those who cultivate the fine arts; but these causes exert a powerful influence on the manner in which these arts are cultivated. Many of those who had already contracted a taste for the fine arts are impoverished: on the other hand, many of those who are not yet rich begin to conceive that taste, at least by imitation; the number of consumers increases, but opulent and fastidious consumers become more scarce. Something analogous to what I have already pointed out in the useful arts then takes place in the fine arts; the productions of artists are more numerous, but the merit of each production is diminished. No longer able to soar to what is great, they cultivate what is pretty and elegant; and appearance is more attended to than reality.

In aristocracies, a few great pictures are produced; in democratic countries, a vast number of insignificant ones.

In the former, statues are raised of bronze; in the latter, they are modelled in plaster.

When I arrived for the first time at New York, by that part of the Atlantic Ocean which is called the East River, I was surprised to perceive along the shore, at some distance from the city, a number of little palaces of white marble, several of which were of ancient architecture. When I went the next day to inspect more closely one which had particularly attracted my notice, I found that its walls were of whitewashed brick, and its columns of painted wood. All the edifices which I had admired the night before were of the same kind.

The social condition and the institutions of democracy impart, moreover, certain peculiar tendencies to all the imitative arts, which it is easy to point out. They frequently withdraw them from the delineation of the soul, to fix them exclusively on that of the body; and they substitute the representation of motion and sensation for that of sentiment and thought: in a word, they put the Real in the place of the Ideal.

I doubt whether Raphael studied the minute intricacies of the mechanism of the human body as thoroughly as the draughtsmen of our own time. He did not attach the same importance as they do to rigorous accuracy on this point, because he aspired to surpass nature. He sought to make of man something which should be superior to man, and to embellish beauty itself. David and his scholars were, on the contrary, as good anatomists as they were painters. They wonderfully depicted the models which they had before their eyes, but they rarely imagined anything beyond them: they followed nature with fidelity, whilst Raphael sought for something better than nature. They have left us an exact portraiture of man; but he discloses in his works a glimpse of the Divinity.

This remark as to the manner of treating a subject is no

less applicable to the choice of it. The painters of the Renaissance generally sought far above themselves, and away from their own time, for mighty subjects, which left to their imagination an unbounded range. Our painters often employ their talents in the exact imitation of the details of private life, which they have always before their eyes; and they are forever copying trivial objects, the originals of which are only too abundant in nature.

CHAPTER XII.

WHY THE AMERICANS RAISE SOME INSIGNIFICANT MONUMENTS, AND OTHERS THAT ARE VERY GRAND.

I HAVE just observed, that, in democratic ages, monuments of the arts tend to become more numerous and less important. I now hasten to point out the exception to this rule.

In a democratic community, individuals are very weak; but the state, which represents them all, and contains them all in its grasp, is very powerful. Nowhere do citizens appear so insignificant as in a democratic nation; nowhere does the nation itself appear greater, or does the mind more easily take in a wide survey of it. In democratic communities, the imagination is compressed when men consider themselves; it expands indefinitely when they think of the state. Hence it is that the same men who live on a small scale in narrow dwellings, frequently aspire to gigantic splendor in the erection of their public monuments.

The Americans have traced out the circuit of an immense city on the site which they intended to make their capital, but which, up to the present time, is hardly more densely peopled than Pontoise, though, according to them, it will one day contain a million of inhabitants. They have already rooted up trees for ten miles round, lest they should interfere with the future citizens of this imaginary metropolis. They have erected a magnificent palace for Congress in the centre of the city, and have given it the pompous name of the Capitol.

The several States of the Union are every day planning

and erecting for themselves prodigious undertakings, which would astonish the engineers of the great European nations.

Thus democracy not only leads men to a vast number of inconsiderable productions; it also leads them to raise some monuments on the largest scale: but between these two extremes there is a blank. A few scattered specimens of enormous buildings can therefore teach us nothing of the social condition and the institutions of the people by whom they were raised. I may add, though the remark is out of my subject, that they do not make us better acquainted with its greatness, its civilization, and its real prosperity. Whenever a power of any kind shall be able to make a whole people co-operate in a single undertaking, that power, with a little knowledge and a great deal of time, will succeed in obtaining something enormous from efforts so multiplied. But this does not lead to the conclusion that the people are very happy, very enlightened, or even very strong.

The Spaniards found the city of Mexico full of magnificent temples and vast palaces; but that did not prevent Cortes from conquering the Mexican empire with six hundred foot-soldiers and sixteen horses.

If the Romans had been better acquainted with the laws of hydraulics, they would not have constructed all the aqueducts which surround the ruins of their cities, — they would have made a better use of their power and their wealth. If they had invented the steam-engine, perhaps they would not have extended to the extremities of their empire those long artificial ways which are called Roman Roads. These things are the splendid memorials at once of their ignorance and of their greatness.

A people which should leave no other vestige of its track than a few leaden pipes in the earth, and a few iron rods upon its surface, might have been more the master of Nature than the Romans.

CHAPTER XIII.

LITERARY CHARACTERISTICS OF DEMOCRATIC TIMES.

WHEN a traveller goes into a bookseller's shop in the United States, and examines the American books upon the shelves, the number of works appears very great; whilst that of known authors seems, on the contrary, extremely small. He will first find a multitude of elementary treatises, destined to teach the rudiments of human knowledge. Most of these books are written in Europe;* the Americans reprint them, adapting them to their own use. Next comes an enormous quantity of religious works, Bibles, sermons, edifying anecdotes, controversial divinity, and reports of charitable societies; lastly appears the long catalogue of political pamphlets. In America, parties do not write books to combat each other's opinions, but pamphlets, which are circulated for a day with incredible rapidity, and then expire.†

In the midst of all these obscure productions of the human brain appear the more remarkable works of a small number of authors, whose names are, or ought to be, known to Europeans.

Although America is perhaps in our days the civilized

---

* On the contrary, many elementary text-books written in America are republished in England; the reverse is true only in comparatively few cases. It is notorious that better school-books, dictionaries, &c. are written in the United States than in England. — AM. ED.

† This may have been true when M. de Tocqueville wrote; but now-a-days political pamphlets are comparatively obsolete, having been superseded by the newspapers, which reach a vastly larger audience than can be obtained by the ablest pamphlet. — AM. ED.

country in which literature is least attended to, still a large number of persons there take an interest in the productions of mind, and make them, if not the study of their lives, at least the charm of their leisure hours. But England supplies these readers with most of the books which they require. Almost all important English books are republished in the United States. The literary genius of Great Britain still darts its rays into the recesses of the forests of the New World. There is hardly a pioneer's hut which does not contain a few odd volumes of Shakespeare. I remember that I read the feudal drama of Henry V. for the first time in a log-house.

Not only do the Americans constantly draw upon the treasures of English literature, but it may be said with truth that they find the literature of England growing on their own soil. The larger part of that small number of men in the United States who are engaged in the composition of literary works are English in substance, and still more so in form. Thus they transport into the midst of democracy the ideas and literary fashions which are current amongst the aristocratic nation they have taken for their model. They paint with colors borrowed from foreign manners ; and as they hardly ever represent the country they were born in as it really is, they are seldom popular there.

The citizens of the United States are themselves so convinced that it is not for them that books are published, that, before they can make up their minds upon the merit of one of their authors, they generally wait till his fame has been ratified in England ; just as, in pictures, the author of an original is held entitled to judge of the merit of a copy.

The inhabitants of the United States have then, at present, properly speaking, no literature. The only authors whom I acknowledge as American are the journalists. They indeed are not great writers, but they speak the language of their country, and make themselves heard. Other authors are aliens; they are to the Americans what the imitators of the Greeks and Romans were to us at the revival of learning, — an object of curiosity, not of general sympathy. They amuse the mind, but they do not act upon the manners of the people.*

I have already said that this state of things is far from originating in democracy alone, and that the causes of it must be sought for in several peculiar circumstances independent of the democratic principle. If the Americans, retaining the same laws and social condition, had had a different origin, and had been transported into another country, I do not question that they would have had a literature. Even as they are, I am convinced that they will ultimately have one; but its character will be different from that which marks the American literary productions of our time, and that character will be peculiarly its own. Nor is it impossible to trace this character beforehand.

I suppose an aristocratic people amongst whom letters are cultivated; the labors of the mind, as well as the affairs of state, are conducted there by a ruling class in society. The literary as well as the political career is almost entirely confined to this class, or to those nearest to it in rank. These premises suffice for a key to all the rest.

When a small number of the same men are engaged at the same time upon the same objects, they easily concert with one another, and agree upon certain leading rules which are to govern them each and all. If the object which attracts the attention of these men is literature, the productions of the mind will soon be subjected by them to precise canons, from which it will no longer be allowable to depart. If these men occupy an hereditary position in the country, they will be naturally inclined, not only to

* All this is curiously untrue at the present day; but I need only to refer again to the notes on pp. 403, 404, of Vol. I. — AM. ED.

adopt a certain number of fixed rules for themselves, but to follow those which their forefathers laid down for their own guidance ; their code will be at once strict and traditional. As they are not necessarily engrossed by the cares of daily life, — as they have never been so, any more than their fathers were before them, — they have learned to take an interest, for several generations back, in the labors of mind. They have learned to understand literature as an art, to love it in the end for its own sake, and to feel a scholar-like satisfaction in seeing men conform to its rules. Nor is this all : the men of whom I speak began and will end their lives in easy or affluent circumstances ; hence they have naturally conceived a taste for choice gratifications, and a love of refined and delicate pleasures. Nay, more : a kind of softness of mind and heart, which they frequently contract in the midst of this long and peaceful enjoyment of so much welfare, leads them to put aside, even from their pleasures, whatever might be too startling or too acute. They had rather be amused than intensely excited ; they wish to be interested, but not to be carried away.

Now let us fancy a great number of literary performances executed by the men, or for the men, whom I have just described, and we shall readily conceive a style of literature in which everything will be regular and pre-arranged. The slightest work will be carefully touched in its least details ; art and labor will be conspicuous in everything ; each kind of writing will have rules of its own, from which it will not be allowed to swerve, and which distinguish it from all others. Style will be thought of almost as much importance as thought, and the form will be no less considered than the matter ; the diction will be polished, measured, and uniform. The tone of the mind will be always dignified, seldom very animated ; and writers will care more to perfect what they produce, than to multiply their productions. It will sometimes happen that the members of the literary class, always living amongst themselves, and writing for themselves alone, will entirely lose sight of the rest of the world, which will infect them with a false and labored style; they will lay down minute literary rules for their exclusive use, which will insensibly lead them to deviate from common sense, and finally to transgress the bounds of nature. By dint of striving after a mode of parlance different from the vulgar, they will arrive at a sort of aristocratic jargon, which is hardly less remote from pure language than is the coarse dialect of the people. Such are the natural perils of literature amongst aristocracies. Every aristocracy which keeps itself entirely aloof from the people becomes impotent, — a fact which is as true in literature as it is in politics.*

Let us now turn the picture, and consider the other side of it: let us transport ourselves into the midst of a democracy not unprepared by ancient traditions and present culture to partake in the pleasures of mind. Ranks are there intermingled and confounded; knowledge and power are both infinitely subdivided, and, if I may use the expression, scattered on every side. Here, then, is a motley multitude whose intellectual wants are to be supplied. These new votaries of the pleasures of mind have not all received the same education; they do not resemble their fathers, — nay, they perpetually differ from themselves, for they live in a state of incessant change of place, feelings, and fortunes. The mind of each is therefore unattached to that of his

---

* All this is especially true of the aristocratic countries which have been long and peacefully subject to a monarchical government. When liberty prevails in an aristocracy, the higher ranks are constantly obliged to make use of the lower classes; and when they use, they approach them. This frequently introduces something of a democratic spirit into an aristocratic community. There springs up, moreover, in a governing privileged body, an energy and habitually bold policy, a taste for stir and excitement, which must infallibly affect all literary performances.

fellows by tradition or common habits; and they have never had the power, the inclination, or the time to concert together. It is, however, from the bosom of this heterogeneous and agitated mass that authors spring; and from the same source their profits and their fame are distributed.

I can without difficulty understand that, under these circumstances, I must expect to meet in the literature of such a people with but few of those strict conventional rules which are admitted by readers and writers in aristocratic times. If it should happen that the men of some one period were agreed upon any such rules, that would prove nothing for the following period; for, amongst democratic nations, each new generation is a new people. Amongst such nations, then, literature will not easily be subjected to strict rules, and it is impossible that any such rules should ever be permanent.

In democracies, it is by no means the case that all who cultivate literature have received a literary education; and most of those who have some tinge of belles-lettres are either engaged in politics or in a profession which only allows them to taste occasionally and by stealth the pleasures of mind. These pleasures, therefore, do not constitute the principal charm of their lives; but they are considered as a transient and necessary recreation amidst the serious labors of life. Such men can never acquire a sufficiently intimate knowledge of the art of literature to appreciate its more delicate beauties; and the minor shades of expression must escape them. As the time they can devote to letters is very short, they seek to make the best use of the whole of it. They prefer books which may be easily procured, quickly read, and which require no learned researches to be understood. They ask for beauties self-proffered, and easily enjoyed; above all, they must have what is unexpected and new. Accustomed to the struggle, the crosses, and the monotony of practical life, they require strong and rapid emotions, startling passages, — truths or errors brilliant enough to rouse them up, and to plunge them at once, as if by violence, into the midst of the subject.

Why should I say more? or who does not understand what is about to follow, before I have expressed it? Taken as a whole, literature in democratic ages can never present, as it does in the periods of aristocracy, an aspect of order, regularity, science, and art; its form will, on the contrary, ordinarily be slighted, sometimes despised. Style will frequently be fantastic, incorrect, overburdened, and loose, — almost always vehement and bold. Authors will aim at rapidity of execution, more than at perfection of detail. Small productions will be more common than bulky books: there will be more wit than erudition, more imagination than profundity; and literary performances will bear marks of an untutored and rude vigor of thought, — frequently of great variety and singular fecundity. The object of authors will be to astonish rather than to please, and to stir the passions more than to charm the taste.

Here and there, indeed, writers will doubtless occur who will choose a different track, and who will, if they are gifted with superior abilities, succeed in finding readers, in spite of their defects or their better qualities; but these exceptions will be rare; and even the authors who shall so depart from the received practice in the main subject of their works, will always relapse into it in some lesser details.

I have just depicted two extreme conditions: the transition by which a nation passes from the former to the latter is not sudden, but gradual, and marked with shades of very various intensity. In the passage which conducts a lettered people from the one to the other, there is almost always a moment at which the literary genius of democratic nations has its confluence with that of aristocracies, and both seek to establish their joint sway over the human mind. Such epochs are transient, but very brilliant : they are fertile without exuberance, and animated without confusion. The French literature of the eighteenth century may serve as an example.

I should say more than I mean, if I were to assert that the literature of a nation is always subordinate to its social state and its political constitution. I am aware that, independently of these causes, there are several others which confer certain characteristics on literary productions ; but these appear to me to be the chief. The relations which exist between the social and political condition of a people and the genius of its authors are always numerous : whoever knows the one, is never completely ignorant of the other.

CHAPTER XIV.

THE TRADE OF LITERATURE.

DEMOCRACY not only infuses a taste for letters among the trading classes, but introduces a trading spirit into literature.

In aristocracies, readers are fastidious and few in number; in democracies, they are far more numerous and far less difficult to please. The consequence is, that among aristocratic nations no one can hope to succeed without great exertion, and this exertion may earn great fame, but can never procure much money; whilst among democratic nations a writer may flatter himself that he will obtain at a cheap rate a moderate reputation and a large fortune. For this purpose he need not be admired, it is enough that he is liked.

The ever-increasing crowd of readers, and their continual craving for something new, insures the sale of books which nobody much esteems.

In democratic times, the public frequently treat authors as kings do their courtiers; they enrich and despise them. What more is needed by the venal souls who are born in courts, or are worthy to live there?

Democratic literature is always infested with a tribe of writers who look upon letters as a mere trade; and for some few great authors who adorn it, you may reckon thousands of idea-mongers.

CHAPTER XV.

THE STUDY OF GREEK AND LATIN LITERATURE IS PECULIARLY USEFUL IN DEMOCRATIC COMMUNITIES.

WHAT was called the People in the most democratic republics of antiquity was very unlike what we designate by that term. In Athens, all the citizens took part in public affairs; but there were only twenty thousand citizens to more than three hundred and fifty thousand inhabitants. All the rest were slaves, and discharged the greater part of those duties which belong at the present day to the lower, or even to the middle classes. Athens then, with her universal suffrage, was, after all, merely an aristocratic republic, in which all the nobles had an equal right to the government.

The struggle between the patricians and plebeians of Rome must be considered in the same light: it was simply an intestine feud between the elder and younger branches of the same family. All the citizens belonged, in fact, to the aristocracy, and partook of its character.

It is to be remarked, moreover, that, amongst the ancients, books were always scarce and dear; and that very great difficulties impeded their publication and circulation. These circumstances concentrated literary tastes and habits amongst a small number of men, who formed a small literary aristocracy out of the choicer spirits of the great political aristocracy. Accordingly, nothing goes to prove that literature was ever treated as a trade amongst the Greeks and Romans.

These communities, which were not only aristocracies,

but very polished and free nations, of course imparted to their literary productions the special defects and merits which characterize the literature of aristocratic times. And indeed a very superficial survey of the works of ancient authors will suffice to convince us, that, if those writers were sometimes deficient in variety and fertility in their subjects, or in boldness, vivacity, and power of generalization in their thoughts, they always displayed exquisite care and skill in their details. Nothing in their works seems to be done hastily, or at random : every line is written for the eye of the connoisseur, and is shaped after some conception of ideal beauty. No literature places those fine qualities in which the writers of democracies are naturally deficient in bolder relief than that of the ancients : no literature, therefore, ought to be more studied in democratic times. This study is better suited than any other to combat the literary defects inherent in those times : as for their natural literary qualities, these will spring up of their own accord, without its being necessary to learn to acquire them.

It is important that this point should be clearly understood. A particular study may be useful to the literature of a people, without being appropriate to its social and political wants. If men were to persist in teaching nothing but the literature of the dead languages in a community where every one is habitually led to make vehement exertions to augment or to maintain his fortune, the result would be a very polished, but a very dangerous, set of citizens. For as their social and political condition would give them every day a sense of wants, which their education would never teach them to supply, they would perturb the state, in the name of the Greeks and Romans, instead of enriching it by their productive industry.

It is evident, that, in democratic communities, the interest of individuals, as well as the security of the commonwealth, demands that the education of the greater number should be scientific, commercial, and industrial, rather than literary. Greek and Latin should not be taught in all the schools; but it is important that those who, by their natural disposition or their fortune, are destined to cultivate letters or prepared to relish them, should find schools where a complete knowledge of ancient literature may be acquired, and where the true scholar may be formed. A few excellent universities would do more towards the attainment of this object than a multitude of bad grammar-schools, where superfluous matters, badly learned, stand in the way of sound instruction in necessary studies.

All who aspire to literary excellence in democratic nations ought frequently to refresh themselves at the springs of ancient literature: there is no more wholesome medicine for the mind. Not that I hold the literary productions of the ancients to be irreproachable; but I think that they have some special merits, admirably calculated to counterbalance our peculiar defects. They are a prop on the side on which we are in most danger of falling.

CHAPTER XVI.

HOW THE AMERICAN DEMOCRACY HAS MODIFIED THE ENGLISH LANGUAGE.

IF the reader has rightly understood what I have already said on the subject of literature in general, he will have no difficulty in understanding that species of influence which a democratic social condition and democratic institutions may exercise over language itself, which is the chief instrument of thought.

American authors may truly be said to live rather in England than in their own country; since they constantly study the English writers, and take them every day for their models. But it is not so with the bulk of the population, which is more immediately subjected to the peculiar causes acting upon the United States. It is not then to the written, but to the spoken language, that attention must be paid, if we would detect the changes which the idiom of an aristocratic people may undergo when it becomes the language of a democracy.

Englishmen of education, and more competent judges than I can be of the nicer shades of expression, have frequently assured me that the language of the educated classes in the United States is notably different from that of the educated classes in Great Britain. They complain, not only that the Americans have brought into use a number of new words, — the difference and the distance between the two countries might suffice to explain that much, — but that these new words are more especially taken from the jargon of parties, the mechanical arts, or the language of trade.* They assert, in addition to this, that old English words are often used by the Americans in new acceptations; and lastly, that the inhabitants of the United States frequently intermingle phraseology in the strangest manner, and sometimes place words together which are always kept apart in the language of the mother country. These remarks, which were made to me at various times by persons who appeared to be worthy of credit, led me to reflect upon the subject; and my reflections brought me, by theoretical reasoning, to the same point at which my informants had arrived by practical observation.

In aristocracies, language must naturally partake of that state of repose in which everything remains. Few new words are coined, because few new things are made; and, even if new things were made, they would be designated by known words, whose meaning had been determined by tradition. If it happens that the human mind bestirs itself at length, or is roused by light breaking in from without, the novel expressions which are introduced have a learned, intellectual, and philosophical character, which shows that they do not originate in a democracy. After the fall of Constantinople had turned the tide of science and letters towards the west, the French language was almost immedi-

---

* More new words and phrases, by which I mean words and phrases unknown to the standard English authors of the last century, can be found in ten pages of a popular English writer of the present day, than in a hundred of one of his American contemporaries. And the reason is obvious. The Americans, like the Scotch, having the dread of provincialism before their eyes, write with a timid regard to purity, which amounts almost to affectation; whilst the English often abuse their mother tongue on the ground of their original and exclusive right to it, — that is, on the principle that a man may do what he likes with his own. Hume, Robertson, and Dugald Stewart, three Scotchmen, wrote purer English than Gibbon, Johnson, or Jeremy Bentham; and for a similar reason, in our own times, such writers as Carlyle and Grote corrupt and debase our noble mother tongue, while such as Irving and Prescott contribute to refine and purify it. — AM. ED.

ately invaded by a multitude of new words, which all had Greek or Latin roots. An erudite neologism then sprang up in France, which was confined to the educated classes, and which produced no sensible effect, or at least a very gradual one, upon the people.

All the nations of Europe successively exhibited the same change. Milton alone introduced more than six hundred words into the English language, almost all derived from the Latin, the Greek, or the Hebrew. The constant agitation which prevails in a democratic community tends unceasingly, on the contrary, to change the character of the language, as it does the aspect of affairs. In the midst of this general stir and competition of minds, a great number of new ideas are formed, old ideas are lost, or reappear, or are subdivided into an infinite variety of minor shades. The consequence is, that many words must fall into desuetude, and others must be brought into use.

Besides, democratic nations love change for its own sake; and this is seen in their language as much as in their politics. Even when they have no need to change words, they sometimes have the desire.

The genius of a democratic people is not only shown by the great number of words they bring into use, but also by the nature of the ideas these new words represent. Amongst such a people, the majority lays down the law in language, as well as in everything else; its prevailing spirit is as manifest in this as in other respects. But the majority is more engaged in business than in study; in political and commercial interests, than in philosophical speculation or literary pursuits. Most of the words coined or adopted for its use will bear the mark of these habits; they will mainly serve to express the wants of business, the passions of party, or the details of the public administration. In these departments, the language will constantly grow, whilst it will gradually lose ground in metaphysics and theology.

As to the source whence democratic nations are wont to derive their new expressions, and the manner in which they coin them, both may easily be described. Men living in democratic countries know but little of the language which was spoken at Athens or at Rome, and they do not care to dive into the lore of antiquity to find the expression which they want. If they have sometimes recourse to learned etymologies, vanity will induce them to search for roots from the dead languages; but erudition does not naturally furnish them its resources. The most ignorant, it sometimes happens, will use them most. The eminently democratic desire to get above their own sphere will often lead them to seek to dignify a vulgar profession by a Greek or Latin name. The lower the calling is, and the more remote from learning, the more pompous and erudite is its appellation. Thus, the French rope-dancers have transformed themselves into " Acrobates " and " Funambules."

Having little knowledge of the dead languages, democratic nations are apt to borrow words from living tongues; for they have constant mutual intercourse, and the inhabitants of different countries imitate each other the more readily as they grow more like each other every day.

But it is principally upon their own languages that democratic nations attempt to make innovations. From time to time they resume and restore to use forgotten expressions in their vocabulary, or they borrow from some particular class of the community a term peculiar to it, which they introduce with a figurative meaning into the language of daily life. Many expressions which originally belonged to the technical language of a profession or a party, are thus drawn into general circulation.

The most common expedient employed by democratic nations to make an innovation in language consists in giving an unwonted meaning to an expression already in use. This method is very simple, prompt, and convenient; no learning is required to use it aright, and ignorance itself rather facilitates the practice; but that practice is most dangerous to the language. When a democratic people double the meaning of a word in this way, they sometimes render the signification which it retains as ambiguous as that which it acquires. An author begins by a slight deflection of a known expression from its primitive meaning, and, thus modified, he adapts it as well as he can to his subject. A second writer twists the sense of the expression in another way; a third takes possession of it for another purpose; and as there is no common appeal to the sentence of a permanent tribunal which may definitively settle the signification of the word, it remains in an ambulatory condition. The consequence is, that writers hardly ever appear to dwell upon a single thought, but they always seem to aim at a group of ideas, leaving the reader to judge which of them has been hit.

This is a deplorable consequence of democracy. I had rather that the language should be made hideous with words imported from the Chinese, the Tartars, or the Hurons, than that the meaning of a word in our own language should become indeterminate. Harmony and uniformity are only secondary beauties in composition: many of these things are conventional, and, strictly speaking, it is possible to do without them; but without clear phraseology there is no good language.

The principle of equality necessarily introduces several other changes into language.

In aristocratic ages, when each nation tends to stand aloof from all others, and likes to have a physiognomy of its own, it often happens that several communities which have a common origin become nevertheless strangers to each other; so that, without ceasing to understand the same language, they no longer all speak it in the same manner. In these ages, each nation is divided into a cer-

tain number of classes, which see but little of each other,
and do not intermingle. Each of these classes contracts,
and invariably retains, habits of mind peculiar to itself, and
adopts by choice certain words and certain terms, which
afterwards pass from generation to generation, like their
estates. The same idiom then comprises a language of the
poor and a language of the rich, — a language of the commoner and a language of the nobility, — a learned language
and a vulgar one. The deeper the divisions, and the more
impassable the barriers of society become, the more must
this be the case. I would lay a wager that amongst the
castes of India there are amazing variations of language,
and that there is almost as much difference between the
language of a Pariah and that of a Brahmin, as there is in
their dress.

When, on the contrary, men, being no longer restrained
by ranks, meet on terms of constant intercourse, — when
castes are destroyed, and the classes of society are recruited
from and intermixed with each other, all the words of a
language are mingled. Those which are unsuitable to the
greater number perish: the remainder form a common
store, whence every one chooses pretty nearly at random.
Almost all the different dialects which divided the idioms
of European nations are manifestly declining: there is no
patois in the New World, and it is disappearing every day
from the old countries.

The influence of this revolution in social condition is as
much felt in style as it is in language. Not only does
every one use the same words, but a habit springs up of
using them without discrimination. The rules which style
had set up are almost abolished: the line ceases to be drawn
between expressions which seem by their very nature vulgar, and others which appear to be refined. Persons
springing from different ranks of society carry the terms
and expressions they are accustomed to use with them, into

whatever circumstances they may pass ; thus the origin of words is lost like the origin of individuals, and there is as much confusion in language as there is in society.

I am aware that, in the classification of words, there are rules which do not belong to one form of society any more than to another, but which are derived from the nature of things. Some expressions and phrases are vulgar, because the ideas they are meant to express are low in themselves ; others are of a higher character, because the objects they are intended to designate are naturally lofty. No intermixture of ranks will ever efface these differences. But the principle of equality cannot fail to root out whatever is merely conventional and arbitrary in the forms of thought. Perhaps the necessary classification which I have just pointed out will always be less respected by a democratic people than by any other, because, amongst such a people, there are no men who are permanently disposed, by education, culture, and leisure, to study the natural laws of language, and who cause those laws to be respected by their own observance of them.

I shall not quit this topic without touching on a feature of democratic languages, which is, perhaps, more characteristic of them than any other. It has already been shown that democratic nations have a taste, and sometimes a passion, for general ideas, and that this arises from their peculiar merits and defects. This liking for general ideas is displayed in democratic languages by the continual use of generic terms or abstract expressions, and by the manner in which they are employed. This is the great merit and the great imperfection of these languages.

Democratic nations are passionately addicted to generic terms and abstract expressions, because these modes of speech enlarge thought, and assist the operations of the mind by enabling it to include many objects in a small compass. A democratic writer will be apt to speak of *capacities* in the abstract for *men of capacity,* and without specifying the objects to which their capacity is applied: he will talk about *actualities* to designate in one word the things passing before his eyes at the moment; and, in French, he will comprehend under the term *éventualités* whatever may happen in the universe, dating from the moment at which he speaks. Democratic writers are perpetually coining abstract words of this kind, in which they sublimate into further abstraction the abstract terms of the language. Nay, more, to render their mode of speech more succinct, they personify the object of these abstract terms, and make it act like a real person. Thus they would say in French, *La force des choses* veut *que les capacités gouvernent.*

I cannot better illustrate what I mean than by my own example. I have frequently used the word EQUALITY in an absolute sense, — nay, I have personified equality in several places; thus I have said, that equality does such and such things, or refrains from doing others. It may be affirmed that the writers of the age of Louis XIV. would not have spoken in this manner: they would never have thought of using the word *equality* without applying it to some particular thing; and they would rather have renounced the term altogether, than have consented to make it a living personage.

These abstract terms which abound in democratic languages, and which are used on every occasion without attaching them to any particular fact, enlarge and obscure the thoughts they are intended to convey; they render the mode of speech more succinct, and the idea contained in it less clear. But with regard to language, democratic nations prefer obscurity to labor.

I know not, indeed, whether this loose style has not some secret charm for those who speak and write amongst these nations. As the men who live there are frequently left to the efforts of their individual powers of mind, they are almost always a prey to doubt: and as their situation in life is forever changing, they are never held fast to any of their opinions by the immobility of their fortunes. Men living in democratic countries are, then, apt to entertain unsettled ideas, and they require loose expressions to convey them. As they never know whether the idea they express to-day will be appropriate to the new position they may occupy to-morrow, they naturally acquire a liking for abstract terms. An abstract term is like a box with a false bottom; you may put in it what ideas you please, and take them out again without being observed.

Amongst all nations, generic and abstract terms form the basis of language. I do not, therefore, pretend that these terms are found only in democratic languages; I say only, that men have an especial tendency, in the ages of democracy, to multiply words of this kind, — to take them always by themselves in their most abstract acceptation, and to use them on all occasions, even when the nature of the discourse does not require them.

CHAPTER XVII.

OF SOME SOURCES OF POETRY AMONGST DEMOCRATIC NATIONS.

MANY different significations have been given to the word Poetry. It would weary my readers if I were to lead them to discuss which of these definitions ought to be selected: I prefer telling them at once that which I have chosen. In my opinion, Poetry is the search after, and the delineation of, the Ideal.

The Poet is he who, by suppressing a part of what exists, by adding some imaginary touches to the picture, and by combining certain real circumstances which do not in fact happen together, completes and extends the work of nature. Thus, the object of poetry is not to represent what is true, but to adorn it, and to present to the mind some loftier image. Verse, regarded as the ideal beauty of language, may be eminently poetical; but verse does not of itself constitute poetry.

I now proceed to inquire whether, amongst the actions, the sentiments, and the opinions of democratic nations, there are any which lead to a conception of the ideal, and which may for this reason be considered as natural sources of poetry.

It must, in the first place, be acknowledged that the taste for ideal beauty, and the pleasure derived from the expression of it, are never so intense or so diffused amongst a democratic as amongst an aristocratic people. In aristocratic nations, it sometimes happens that the body acts as it were spontaneously, whilst the higher faculties are bound and burdened by repose. Amongst these nations, the people will often display poetic tastes, and their fancy sometimes ranges beyond and above what surrounds them.

But in democracies, the love of physical gratification, the notion of bettering one's condition, the excitement of competition, the charm of anticipated success, are so many spurs to urge men onward in the active professions they have embraced, without allowing them to deviate for an instant from the track. The main stress of the faculties is to this point. The imagination is not extinct; but its chief function is to devise what may be useful, and to represent what is real. The principle of equality not only diverts men from the description of ideal beauty; it also diminishes the number of objects to be described.

Aristocracy, by maintaining society in a fixed position, is favorable to the solidity and duration of positive religions, as well as to the stability of political institutions. It not only keeps the human mind within a certain sphere of belief, but it predisposes the mind to adopt one faith rather than another. An aristocratic people will always be prone to place intermediate powers between God and man. In this respect, it may be said that the aristocratic element is favorable to poetry. When the universe is peopled with supernatural beings, not palpable to sense, but discovered by the mind, the imagination ranges freely; and poets, finding a thousand subjects to delineate, also find a countless audience to take an interest in their productions.

In democratic ages, it sometimes happens, on the contrary, that men are as much afloat in matters of faith as they are in their laws. Scepticism then draws the imagination of poets back to earth, and confines them to the real and visible world. Even when the principle of equality does not disturb religious conviction, it tends to simplify it, and to divert attention from secondary agents, to fix it principally on the Supreme Power.

Aristocracy naturally leads the human mind to the contemplation of the past, and fixes it there. Democracy, on the contrary, gives men a sort of instinctive distaste for what is ancient. In this respect, aristocracy is far more favorable to poetry; for things commonly grow larger and more obscure as they are more remote; and, for this twofold reason, they are better suited to the delineation of the ideal.

After having deprived poetry of the past, the principle of equality robs it in part of the present. Amongst aristocratic nations, there are a certain number of privileged personages, whose situation is, as it were, without and above the condition of man: to these, power, wealth, fame, wit, refinement, and distinction in all things appear peculiarly to belong. The crowd never sees them very closely, or does not watch them in minute details; and little is needed to make the description of such men poetical. On the other hand, amongst the same people, you will meet with classes so ignorant, low, and enslaved, that they are no less fit objects for poetry, from the excess of their rudeness and wretchedness, than the former are from their greatness and refinement. Besides, as the different classes of which an aristocratic community is composed are widely separated, and imperfectly acquainted with each other, the imagination may always represent them with some addition to, or some subtraction from, what they really are.

In democratic communities, where men are all insignificant and very much alike, each man instantly sees all his fellows when he surveys himself. The poets of democratic ages can never, therefore, take any man in particular as the subject of a piece; for an object of slender importance, which is distinctly seen on all sides, will never lend itself to an ideal conception.

Thus the principle of equality, in proportion as it has

established itself in the world, has dried up most of the old springs of poetry. Let us now attempt to show what new ones it may disclose.

When scepticism had depopulated heaven, and the progress of equality had reduced each individual to smaller and better-known proportions, the poets, not yet aware of what they could substitute for the great themes which were departing together with the aristocracy, turned their eyes to inanimate nature. As they lost sight of gods and heroes, they set themselves to describe streams and mountains. Thence originated, in the last century, that kind of poetry which has been called, by way of distinction, *descriptive*. Some have thought that this embellished delineation of all the physical and inanimate objects which cover the earth was the kind of poetry peculiar to democratic ages; but I believe this to be an error, and that it belongs only to a period of transition.

I am persuaded that, in the end, democracy diverts the imagination from all that is external to man, and fixes it on man alone. Democratic nations may amuse themselves for a while with considering the productions of nature; but they are excited in reality only by a survey of themselves. Here, and here alone, the true sources of poetry amongst such nations are to be found; and it may be believed that the poets who shall neglect to draw their inspirations hence, will lose all sway over the minds which they would enchant, and will be left in the end with none but unimpassioned spectators of their transports.

I have shown how the ideas of progression and of the indefinite perfectibility of the human race belong to democratic ages. Democratic nations care but little for what has been, but they are haunted by visions of what will be; in this direction, their unbounded imagination grows and dilates beyond all measure. Here, then, is the widest range open to the genius of poets, which allows them to remove their performances to a sufficient distance from the eye. Democracy, which shuts the past against the poet, opens the future before him.

As all the citizens who compose a democratic community are nearly equal and alike, the poet cannot dwell upon any one of them; but the nation itself invites the exercise of his powers. The general similitude of individuals, which renders any one of them taken separately an improper subject of poetry, allows poets to include them all in the same imagery, and to take a general survey of the people itself. Democratic nations have a clearer perception than any others of their own aspect; and an aspect so imposing is admirably fitted to the delineation of the ideal.

I readily admit that the Americans have no poets; I cannot allow that they have no poetic ideas. In Europe, people talk a great deal of the wilds of America, but the Americans themselves never think about them: they are insensible to the wonders of inanimate nature, and they may be said not to perceive the mighty forests which surround them till they fall beneath the hatchet. Their eyes are fixed upon another sight: the American people views its own march across these wilds, — drying swamps, turning the course of rivers, peopling solitudes, and subduing nature. This magnificent image of themselves does not meet the gaze of the Americans at intervals only; it may be said to haunt every one of them in his least as well as in his most important actions, and to be always flitting before his mind.

Nothing conceivable is so petty, so insipid, so crowded with paltry interests, in one word, so anti-poetic, as the life of a man in the United States. But amongst the thoughts which it suggests, there is always one which is full of poetry, and this is the hidden nerve which gives vigor to the whole frame.

In aristocratic ages, each people, as well as each individual, is prone to stand separate and aloof from all others. In democratic ages, the extreme fluctuations of men, and the impatience of their desires, keep them perpetually on the move ; so that the inhabitants of different countries intermingle, see, listen to, and borrow from each other. It is not only, then, the members of the same community who grow more alike ; communities themselves are assimilated to one another, and the whole assemblage presents to the eye of the spectator one vast democracy, each citizen of which is a nation. This displays the aspect of mankind for the first time in the broadest light. All that belongs to the existence of the human race taken as a whole, to its vicissitudes and its future, becomes an abundant mine of poetry.

The poets who lived in aristocratic ages have been eminently successful in their delineations of certain incidents in the life of a people or a man ; but none of them ever ventured to include within his performances the destinies of mankind, — a task which poets writing in democratic ages may attempt.

At that same time at which every man, raising his eyes above his country, begins at length to discern mankind at large, the Deity is more and more manifest to the human mind in full and entire majesty. If, in democratic ages, faith in positive religion be often shaken, and the belief in intermediate agents, by whatever name they are called, be overcast ; on the other hand, men are disposed to conceive a far broader idea of Providence itself, and its interference in human affairs assumes a new and more imposing appearance to their eyes. Looking at the human race as one great whole, they easily conceive that its destinies are regulated by the same design ; and in the actions of every individual they are led to acknowledge a trace of that universal and eternal plan on which God rules our race. This consideration may be taken as another prolific source of poetry which is opened in democratic times.

Democratic poets will always appear trivial and frigid if they seek to invest gods, demons, or angels with corporeal forms, and if they attempt to draw them down from heaven to dispute the supremacy of earth. But if they strive to connect the great events they commemorate with the general providential designs which govern the universe, and, without showing the finger of the Supreme Governor, reveal the thoughts of the Supreme Mind, their works will be admired and understood, for the imagination of their contemporaries takes this direction of its own accord.

It may be foreseen in like manner, that poets living in democratic times will prefer the delineation of passions and ideas to that of persons and achievements. The language, the dress, and the daily actions of men in democracies are repugnant to conceptions of the ideal. These things are not poetical in themselves; and if it were otherwise, they would cease to be so, because they are too familiar to all those to whom the poet would speak of them. This forces the poet constantly to search below the external surface which is palpable to the senses, in order to read the inner soul: and nothing lends itself more to the delineation of the ideal, than the scrutiny of the hidden depths in the immaterial nature of man. I need not traverse earth and sky to discover a wondrous object woven of contrasts, of infinite greatness and littleness, of intense gloom and amazing brightness, — capable at once of exciting pity, admiration, terror, contempt. I have only to look at myself. Man springs out of nothing, crosses time, and disappears forever in the bosom of God; he is seen but for a moment, wandering on the verge of the two abysses, and there he is lost.

If man were wholly ignorant of himself, he would have no poetry in him; for it is impossible to describe what the mind does not conceive. If man clearly discerned his own nature, his imagination would remain idle, and would have nothing to add to the picture. But the nature of man is sufficiently disclosed for him to apprehend something of himself, and sufficiently obscure for all the rest to be plunged in thick darkness, in which he gropes forever, — and forever in vain, — to lay hold on some completer notion of his being.

Amongst a democratic people, poetry will not be fed with legends or the memorials of old traditions. The poet will not attempt to people the universe with supernatural beings, in whom his readers and his own fancy have ceased to believe; nor will he coldly personify virtues and vices, which are better received under their own features. All these resources fail him; but Man remains, and the poet needs no more. The destinies of mankind — man himself, taken aloof from his country and his age, and standing in the presence of Nature and of God, with his passions, his doubts, his rare prosperities and inconceivable wretchedness — will become the chief, if not the sole, theme of poetry amongst these nations.

Experience may confirm this assertion, if we consider the productions of the greatest poets who have appeared since the world has been turned to democracy. The authors of our age who have so admirably delineated the features of Faust, Childe Harold, Réné, and Jocelyn, did not seek to record the actions of an individual, but to enlarge and to throw light on some of the obscurer recesses of the human heart.

Such are the poems of democracy. The principle of equality does not then destroy all the subjects of poetry: it renders them less numerous, but more vast.

CHAPTER XVIII.

WHY AMERICAN WRITERS AND ORATORS OFTEN USE AN INFLATED STYLE.

I HAVE frequently remarked that the Americans, who generally treat of business in clear, plain language, devoid of all ornament, and so extremely simple as to be often coarse, are apt to become inflated as soon as they attempt a more poetical diction. They then vent their pomposity from one end of a harangue to the other; and to hear them lavish imagery on every occasion, one might fancy that they never spoke of anything with simplicity.

The English less frequently commit a similar fault. The cause of this may be pointed out without much difficulty. In democratic communities, each citizen is habitually engaged in the contemplation of a very puny object, namely, himself. If he ever raises his looks higher, he perceives only the immense form of society at large, or the still more imposing aspect of mankind. His ideas are all either extremely minute and clear, or extremely general and vague: what lies between is a void. When he has been drawn out of his own sphere, therefore, he always expects that some amazing object will be offered to his attention; and it is on these terms alone that he consents to tear himself for a moment from the petty, complicated cares which form the charm and the excitement of his life.

This appears to me sufficiently to explain why men in democracies, whose concerns are in general so paltry, call upon their poets for conceptions so vast and descriptions so unlimited.

The authors, on their part, do not fail to obey a propensity of which they themselves partake; they perpetually inflate their imaginations, and, expanding them beyond all bounds, they not unfrequently abandon the great in order to reach the gigantic. By these means, they hope to attract the observation of the multitude, and to fix it easily upon themselves: nor are their hopes disappointed; for, as the multitude seeks for nothing in poetry but objects of vast dimensions, it has neither the time to measure with accuracy the proportions of all the objects set before it, nor a taste sufficiently correct to perceive at once in what respect they are out of proportion. The author and the public at once vitiate one another.

We have also seen, that, amongst democratic nations, the sources of poetry are grand, but not abundant. They are soon exhausted: and poets, not finding the elements of the ideal in what is real and true, abandon them entirely and create monsters. I do not fear that the poetry of democratic nations will prove insipid, or that it will fly too near the ground; I rather apprehend that it will be forever losing itself in the clouds, and that it will range at last to purely imaginary regions. I fear that the productions of democratic poets may often be surcharged with immense and incoherent imagery, with exaggerated descriptions and strange creations; and that the fantastic beings of their brain may sometimes make us regret the world of reality.

CHAPTER XIX.

SOME OBSERVATIONS ON THE DRAMA AMONGST DEMOCRATIC NATIONS.

WHEN the revolution which has changed the social and political state of an aristocratic people begins to penetrate into literature, it generally first manifests itself in the drama, and it always remains conspicuous there.

The spectator of a dramatic piece is, to a certain extent, taken by surprise by the impression it conveys. He has no time to refer to his memory, or to consult those more able to judge than himself. It does not occur to him to resist the new literary tendencies which begin to be felt by him; he yields to them before he knows what they are.

Authors are very prompt in discovering which way the taste of the public is thus secretly inclined. They shape their productions accordingly; and the literature of the stage, after having served to indicate the approaching literary revolution, speedily completes it altogether. If you would judge beforehand of the literature of a people which is lapsing into democracy, study its dramatic productions.

The literature of the stage, moreover, even amongst aristocratic nations, constitutes the most democratic part of their literature. No kind of literary gratification is so much within the reach of the multitude as that which is derived from theatrical representations. Neither preparation nor study is required to enjoy them: they lay hold on you in the midst of your prejudices and your ignorance. When the yet untutored love of the pleasures of mind begins to affect a class of the community, it immediately draws them to the stage. The theatres of aristocratic nations have always been filled with spectators not belonging to the aristocracy. At the theatre alone, the higher ranks mix with the middle and the lower classes; there alone do the former consent to listen to the opinion of the latter, or at least to allow them to give an opinion at all. At the theatre, men of cultivation and of literary attainments have always had more difficulty than elsewhere in making their taste prevail over that of the people, and in preventing themselves from being carried away by the latter. The pit has frequently made laws for the boxes.

If it be difficult for an aristocracy to prevent the people from getting the upper hand in the theatre, it will readily be understood that the people will be supreme there when democratic principles have crept into the laws and manners, — when ranks are intermixed, — when minds as well as fortunes are brought more nearly together, — and when the upper class has lost, with its hereditary wealth, its power, its traditions, and its leisure. The tastes and propensities natural to democratic nations, in respect to literature, will therefore first be discernible in the drama, and it may be foreseen that they will break out there with vehemence. In written productions, the literary canons of aristocracy will be gently, gradually, and, so to speak, legally modified; at the theatre, they will be riotously overthrown.

The drama brings out most of the good qualities, and almost all the defects, inherent in democratic literature. Democratic communities hold erudition very cheap, and care but little for what occurred at Rome and Athens; they want to hear something which concerns themselves, and the delineation of the present age is what they demand. When the heroes and the manners of antiquity are frequently brought upon the stage, and dramatic authors faithfully observe the rules of antiquated precedent, that is enough to warrant a conclusion that the democratic classes have not yet got the upper hand in the theatres.

Racine makes a very humble apology in the preface to the Britannicus for having disposed of Junia amongst the Vestals, who, according to Aulus Gellius, he says, " admitted no one below six years of age, nor above ten." We may be sure that he would neither have accused nor defended himself for such an offence, if he had written for our contemporaries.

A fact of this kind not only illustrates the state of literature at the time when it occurred, but also that of society itself. A democratic stage does not prove that the nation is in a state of democracy, for, as we have just seen, it may happen even in aristocracies that democratic tastes affect the drama: but when the spirit of aristocracy reigns exclusively on the stage, the fact irrefragably demonstrates that the whole of society is aristocratic; and it may be boldly inferred that the same lettered and learned class which sways the dramatic writers commands the people and governs the country.

The refined tastes and the arrogant bearing of an aristocracy will rarely fail to lead it, when it manages the stage, to make a kind of selection in human nature. Some of the conditions of society claim its chief interest; and the scenes which delineate their manners are preferred upon the stage. Certain virtues, and even certain vices, are thought more particularly to deserve to figure there; and they are applauded whilst all others are excluded. Upon the stage, as well as elsewhere, an aristocratic audience wishes to meet only persons of quality, and to be moved only by the misfortunes of kings. The same remark applies to style: an aristocracy is apt to impose upon dramatic authors certain modes of expression which give the key in which everything is to be delivered. By these means, the stage frequently comes to delineate only one side of man, or sometimes even to represent what is not to be met with in human nature at all, — to rise above nature, and to go beyond it.

In democratic communities, the spectators have no such preferences, and they rarely display any such antipathies : they like to see upon the stage that medley of conditions, feelings, and opinions which occurs before their eyes. The drama becomes more striking, more vulgar, and more true. Sometimes, however, those who write for the stage in democracies also transgress the bounds of human nature ; but it is on a different side from their predecessors. By seeking to represent in minute detail the little singularities of the present moment, and the peculiar characteristics of certain personages, they forget to portray the general features of the race.

When the democratic classes rule the stage, they introduce as much license in the manner of treating subjects as in the choice of them. As the love of the drama is, of all literary tastes, that which is most natural to democratic nations, the number of authors and of spectators, as well as of theatrical representations, is constantly increasing amongst these communities. Such a multitude, composed of elements so different and scattered in so many different places, cannot acknowledge the same rules, or submit to the same laws. No agreement is possible amongst judges so numerous, who know not when they may meet again, and therefore each pronounces his own separate opinion on the piece. If the effect of democracy is generally to question the authority of all literary rules and conventions, on the stage it abolishes them altogether, and puts in their place nothing but the caprice of each author and each public.

The drama also displays in an especial manner the truth of what I have before said in speaking more generally of style and art in democratic literature. In reading the criticisms which were occasioned by the dramatic productions of the age of Louis XIV., one is surprised to remark the great stress which the public laid on the probability of the plot, and the importance which was attached to the perfect consistency of the characters, and to their doing nothing which could not be easily explained and understood. The value which was set upon the forms of language at that period, and the paltry strife about words with which dramatic authors were assailed, are no less surprising. It would seem that the men of the age of Louis XIV. attached very exaggerated importance to those details which may be perceived in the study, but which escape attention on the stage; for, after all, the principal object of a dramatic piece is to be performed, and its chief merit is to affect the audience. But the audience and the readers in that age were the same: on quitting the theatre, they called up the author for judgment to their own firesides.

In democracies, dramatic pieces are listened to, but not read. Most of those who frequent the amusements of the stage do not go there to seek the pleasures of mind, but the keen emotions of the heart. They do not expect to hear a fine literary work, but to see a play; and provided the author writes the language of his country correctly enough to be understood, and that his characters excite curiosity and awaken sympathy, the audience are satisfied. They ask no more of fiction, and immediately return to real life. Accuracy of style is therefore less required, because the attentive observance of its rules is less perceptible on the stage.

As for the probability of the plot, it is incompatible with perpetual novelty, surprise, and rapidity of invention. It is therefore neglected, and the public excuses the neglect. You may be sure that, if you succeed in bringing your audience into the presence of something that affects them, they will not care by what road you brought them there:

and they will never reproach you for having excited their emotions in spite of dramatic rules.

The Americans, when they go to the theatres, very broadly display all the different propensities which I have here described; but it must be acknowledged that, as yet, very few of them go to theatres at all. Although play-goers and plays have prodigiously increased in the United States in the last forty years, the population indulge in this kind of amusement only with the greatest reserve. This is attributable to peculiar causes, which the reader is already acquainted with, and of which a few words will suffice to remind him.

The Puritans who founded the American republics were not only enemies to amusements, but they professed an especial abhorrence for the stage. They considered it as an abominable pastime; and as long as their principles prevailed with undivided sway, scenic performances were wholly unknown amongst them. These opinions of the first fathers of the colony have left very deep traces on the minds of their descendants.

The extreme regularity of habits and the great strictness of morals which are observable in the United States, have as yet been little favorable to the growth of dramatic art. There are no dramatic subjects in a country which has witnessed no great political catastrophes, and in which love invariably leads by a straight and easy road to matrimony. People who spend every day in the week in making money, and the Sunday in going to church, have nothing to invite the Muse of Comedy.

A single fact suffices to show that the stage is not very popular in the United States. The Americans, whose laws allow of the utmost freedom, and even license of language in all other respects, have nevertheless subjected their dramatic authors to a sort of censorship. Theatrical perform-ances can only take place by permission of the municipal authorities.* This may serve to show how much communities are like individuals; they surrender themselves unscrupulously to their ruling passions, and afterwards take the greatest care not to yield too much to the vehemence of tastes which they do not possess.

No portion of literature is connected by closer or more numerous ties with the present condition of society than the drama. The drama of one period can never be suited to the following age, if in the interval an important revolution has affected the manners and laws of the nation.

The great authors of a preceding age may be read; but pieces written for a different public will not attract an audience. The dramatic authors of the past live only in books. The traditional taste of certain individuals, vanity, fashion, or the genius of an actor, may sustain or resuscitate for a time the aristocratic drama amongst a democracy; but it will speedily fall away of itself, — not overthrown, but abandoned.

---

* This is only a regulation of police, and not a censorship of the plays; its object is to forbid improper popular amusements, such as bull-baiting or gambling. But when a theatre is once licensed, the actors can represent any plays that they choose. — AM. ED.

CHAPTER XX.

SOME CHARACTERISTICS OF HISTORIANS IN DEMOCRATIC TIMES.

HISTORIANS who write in aristocratic ages are wont to refer all occurrences to the particular will and character of certain individuals; and they are apt to attribute the most important revolutions to slight accidents. They trace out the smallest causes with sagacity, and frequently leave the greatest unperceived.

Historians who live in democratic ages exhibit precisely opposite characteristics. Most of them attribute hardly any influence to the individual over the destiny of the race, or to citizens over the fate of a people; but, on the other hand, they assign great general causes to all petty incidents. These contrary tendencies explain each other.

When the historian of aristocratic ages surveys the theatre of the world, he at once perceives a very small number of prominent actors, who manage the whole piece. These great personages, who occupy the front of the stage, arrest attention, and fix it on themselves; and whilst the historian is bent on penetrating the secret motives which make these persons speak and act, the others escape his memory. The importance of the things which some men are seen to do, gives him an exaggerated estimate of the influence which one man may possess; and naturally leads him to think, that, in order to explain the impulses of the multitude, it is necessary to refer them to the particular influence of some one individual.

When, on the contrary, all the citizens are independent

of one another, and each of them is individually weak, no one is seen to exert a great, or still less a lasting, power over the community. At first sight, individuals appear to be absolutely devoid of any influence over it; and society would seem to advance alone by the free and voluntary action of all the men who compose it. This naturally prompts the mind to search for that general reason which operates upon so many men's faculties at once, and turns them simultaneously in the same direction.

I am very well convinced that, even amongst democratic nations, the genius, the vices, or the virtues of certain individuals retard or accelerate the natural current of a people's history; but causes of this secondary and fortuitous nature are infinitely more various, more concealed, more complex, less powerful, and consequently less easy to trace, in periods of equality than in ages of aristocracy, when the task of the historian is simply to detach from the mass of general events the particular influence of one man or of a few men. In the former case, the historian is soon wearied by the toil; his mind loses itself in this labyrinth; and, in his inability clearly to discern or conspicuously to point out the influence of individuals, he denies that they have any. He prefers talking about the characteristics of race, the physical conformation of the country, or the genius of civilization, — which abridges his own labors, and satisfies his reader better at less cost.

M. de Lafayette says somewhere in his Memoirs, that the exaggerated system of general causes affords surprising consolations to second-rate statesmen. I will add, that its effects are not less consolatory to second-rate historians; it can always furnish a few mighty reasons to extricate them from the most difficult part of their work, and it indulges the indolence or incapacity of their minds, whilst it confers upon them the honors of deep thinking.

For myself, I am of opinion that, at all times, one great

portion of the events of this world are attributable to very general facts, and another to special influences. These two kinds of cause are always in operation; their proportion only varies. General facts serve to explain more things in democratic than in aristocratic ages, and fewer things are then assignable to individual influences. During periods of aristocracy, the reverse takes place: special influences are stronger, general causes weaker; unless, indeed, we consider as a general cause the fact itself of the inequality of condition, which allows some individuals to baffle the natural tendencies of all the rest.

The historians who seek to describe what occurs in democratic societies are right, therefore, in assigning much to general causes, and in devoting their chief attention to discover them; but they are wrong in wholly denying the special influence of individuals, because they cannot easily trace or follow it.

The historians who live in democratic ages are not only prone to assign a great cause to every incident, but they are also given to connect incidents together so as to deduce a system from them. In aristocratic ages, as the attention of historians is constantly drawn to individuals, the connection of events escapes them; or, rather, they do not believe in any such connection. To them, the clew of history seems every instant crossed and broken by the step of man. In democratic ages, on the contrary, as the historian sees much more of actions than of actors, he may easily establish some kind of sequence and methodical order amongst the former.

Ancient literature, which is so rich in fine historical compositions, does not contain a single great historical system, whilst the poorest of modern literatures abound with them. It would appear that the ancient historians did not make sufficient use of those general theories which our historical writers are ever ready to carry to excess.

Those who write in democratic ages have another more dangerous tendency. When the traces of individual action upon nations are lost, it often happens that the world goes on to move, though the moving agent is no longer discoverable. As it becomes extremely difficult to discern and analyze the reasons which, acting separately on the will of each member of the community, concur in the end to produce movement in the whole mass, men are led to believe that this movement is involuntary, and that societies unconsciously obey some superior force ruling over them. But even when the general fact which governs the private volition of all individuals is supposed to be discovered upon the earth, the principle of human free-will is not secured. A cause sufficiently extensive to affect millions of men at once, and sufficiently strong to bend them all together in the same direction, may well seem irresistible : having seen that mankind do yield to it, the mind is close upon the inference that mankind cannot resist it.

Historians who live in democratic ages, then, not only deny that the few have any power of acting upon the destiny of a people, but they deprive the people themselves of the power of modifying their own condition, and they subject them either to an inflexible Providence or to some blind necessity. According to them, each nation is indissolubly bound by its position, its origin, its antecedents, and its character, to a certain lot which no efforts can ever change. They involve generation in generation, and thus, going back from age to age, and from necessity to necessity, up to the origin of the world, they forge a close and enormous chain, which girds and binds the human race. To their minds it is not enough to show what events have occurred : they would fain show that events could not have occurred otherwise. They take a nation arrived at a certain stage of its history, and they affirm that it could not but follow the track which brought it thither. It is easier to make such an assertion than to show how the nation might have adopted a better course.

In reading the historians of aristocratic ages, and especially those of antiquity, it would seem that, to be master of his lot and to govern his fellow-creatures, man requires only to be master of himself. In perusing the historical volumes which our age has produced, it would seem that man is utterly powerless over himself and over all around him. The historians of antiquity taught how to command: those of our time teach only how to obey; in their writings the author often appears great, but humanity is always diminutive.

If this doctrine of necessity, which is so attractive to those who write history in democratic ages, passes from authors to their readers, till it infects the whole mass of the community and gets possession of the public mind, it will soon paralyze the activity of modern society, and reduce Christians to the level of the Turks.

I would moreover observe, that such doctrines are peculiarly dangerous at the period at which we are arrived. Our contemporaries are but too prone to doubt of human free-will, because each of them feels himself confined on every side by his own weakness; but they are still willing to acknowledge the strength and independence of men united in society. Let not this principle be lost sight of; for the great object in our time is to raise the faculties of men, not to complete their prostration.

CHAPTER XXI.

OF PARLIAMENTARY ELOQUENCE IN THE UNITED STATES.

AMONGST aristocratic nations, all the members of the community are connected with, and dependent upon, each other; the graduated scale of different ranks acts as a tie, which keeps every one in his proper place, and the whole body in subordination. Something of the same kind always occurs in the political assemblies of these nations. Parties naturally range themselves under certain leaders, whom they obey by a sort of instinct, which is only the result of habits contracted elsewhere. They carry the manners of general society into the lesser assemblage.

In democratic countries, it often happens that a great number of citizens are tending to the same point; but each one only moves thither, or at least flatters himself that he moves, of his own accord. Accustomed to regulate his doings by personal impulse alone, he does not willingly submit to dictation from without. This taste and habit of independence accompany him into the councils of the nation. If he consents to connect himself with other men in the prosecution of the same purpose, at least he chooses to remain free to contribute to the common success after his own fashion. Hence it is that, in democratic countries, parties are so impatient of control, and are never manageable except in moments of great public danger. Even then, the authority of leaders, which under such circumstances may be able to make men act or speak, hardly ever reaches the extent of making them keep silence.

Amongst aristocratic nations, the members of political

assemblies are at the same time members of the aristocracy.
Each of them enjoys high established rank in his own
right, and the position which he occupies in the assembly
is often less important in his eyes than that which he fills
in the country. This consoles him for playing no part in
the discussion of public affairs, and restrains him from too
eagerly attempting to play an insignificant one.

In America, it generally happens that a representative
only becomes somebody from his position in the assembly.
He is therefore perpetually haunted by a craving to acquire
importance there, and he feels a petulant desire to be constantly obtruding his opinions upon his fellow-members.
His own vanity is not the only stimulant which urges him
on in this course, but that of his constituents, and the continual necessity of propitiating them. Amongst aristocratic
nations, a member of the legislature is rarely in strict dependence upon his constituents : he is frequently to them
a sort of unavoidable representative ; sometimes they are
themselves strictly dependent upon him ; and if, at length,
they reject him, he may easily get elected elsewhere, or,
retiring from public life, he may still enjoy the pleasures
of splendid idleness. In a democratic country, like the
United States, a representative has hardly ever a lasting
hold on the minds of his constituents. However small an
electoral body may be, the fluctuations of democracy are
constantly changing its aspect : it must therefore be courted
unceasingly. One is never sure of his supporters, and, if
they forsake him, he is left without a resource ; for his
natural position is not sufficiently elevated for him to be
easily known to those not close to him ; and, with the complete state of independence prevailing among the people,
he cannot hope that his friends or the government will
send him down to be returned by an electoral body unacquainted with him. The seeds of his fortune are, therefore, sown in his own neighborhood : from that nook of

earth he must start, to raise himself to command the people and to influence the destinies of the world. Thus it is natural that, in democratic countries, the members of political assemblies should think more of their constituents than of their party, whilst, in aristocracies, they think more of their party than of their constituents.

But what ought to be said to gratify constituents is not always what ought to be said in order to serve the party to which representatives profess to belong. The general interest of a party frequently demands that members belonging to it should not speak on great questions which they understand imperfectly; that they should speak but little on those minor questions which impede the great ones; lastly, and for the most part, that they should not speak at all. To keep silence is the most useful service that an indifferent spokesman can render to the commonwealth.

Constituents, however, do not think so. The population of a district send a representative to take a part in the government of a country, because they entertain a very high notion of his merits. As men appear greater in proportion to the littleness of the objects by which they are surrounded, it may be assumed that the opinion entertained of the delegate will be so much the higher, as talents are more rare among his constituents. It will therefore frequently happen, that, the less constituents ought to expect from their representative, the more they will anticipate from him; and, however incompetent he may be, they will not fail to call upon him for signal exertions, corresponding to the rank they have conferred upon him.

Independently of his position as a legislator of the State, electors also regard their representative as the natural patron of the constituency in the legislature; they almost consider him as the proxy of each of his supporters, and they flatter themselves that he will not be less zealous in defence of their private interests than of those of the country. Thus electors are well assured beforehand that the representative of their choice will be an orator ; that he will speak often if he can, and that, in case he is forced to refrain, he will strive at any rate to compress into his less frequent orations an inquiry into all the great questions of state, combined with a statement of all the petty grievances they have themselves to complain of; so that, though he be not able to come forward frequently, he should on each occasion prove what he is capable of doing ; and that, instead of perpetually lavishing his powers, he should occasionally condense them in a small compass, so as to furnish a sort of complete and brilliant epitome of his constituents and of himself.   On these terms, they will vote for him at the next election.

These conditions drive worthy men of humble abilities to despair ; who, knowing their own powers, would never voluntarily have come forward.   But thus urged on, the representative begins to speak, to the great alarm of his friends ; and, rushing imprudently into the midst of the most celebrated orators, he perplexes the debate and wearies the House.

All laws which tend to make the representative more dependent on the elector, not only affect the conduct of the legislators, as I have remarked elsewhere, but also their language.   They exercise a simultaneous influence on affairs themselves, and on the manner in which affairs are discussed.

There is hardly a member of Congress who can make up his mind to go home without having despatched at least one speech to his constituents ; nor who will endure any interruption until he has introduced into his harangue whatever useful suggestions may be made touching the four and twenty States of which the Union is composed, and especially the district which he represents.   He there-

fore presents to the mind of his auditors a succession of
great general truths (which he himself only comprehends,
and expresses, confusedly), and of petty minutiæ, which he
is but too able to discover and to point out. The consequence is, that the debates of that great assembly are frequently vague and perplexed, and that they seem rather to
drag their slow length along, than to advance towards a
distinct object. Some such state of things will, I believe,
always arise in the public assemblies of democracies.

Propitious circumstances and good laws might succeed
in drawing to the legislature of a democratic people men
very superior to those who are returned by the Americans
to Congress; but nothing will ever prevent the men of slender abilities who sit there from obtruding themselves with
complacency, and in all ways, upon the public. The evil
does not appear to me to be susceptible of entire cure, because it not only originates in the tactics of that assembly,
but in its constitution and in that of the country. The inhabitants of the United States seem themselves to consider
the matter in this light; and they show their long experience of parliamentary life, not by abstaining from making
bad speeches, but by courageously submitting to hear them
made. They are resigned to it, as to an evil which they
know to be inevitable.

We have shown the petty side of political debates in
democratic assemblies, — let us now exhibit the imposing
one. The proceedings within the Parliament of England
for the last one hundred and fifty years have never occasioned any great sensation out of that country; the opinions
and feelings expressed by the speakers have never awakened much sympathy, even amongst the nations placed
nearest to the great arena of British liberty; whereas Europe was excited by the very first debates which took place
in the small colonial assemblies of America, at the time of
the Revolution.

This was attributable not only to particular and fortuitous circumstances, but to general and lasting causes. I can conceive nothing more admirable or more powerful than a great orator debating great questions of state in a democratic assembly. As no particular class is ever represented there by men commissioned to defend its own interests, it is always to the whole nation, and in the name of the whole nation, that the orator speaks. This expands his thoughts, and heightens his power of language. As precedents have there but little weight, — as there are no longer any privileges attached to certain property, nor any rights inherent in certain individuals, — the mind must have recourse to general truths derived from human nature to resolve the particular question under discussion. Hence the political debates of a democratic people, however small it may be, have a degree of breadth which frequently renders them attractive to mankind. All men are interested by them, because they treat of *man*, who is everywhere the same.

Amongst the greatest aristocratic nations, on the contrary, the most general questions are almost always argued on some special grounds derived from the practice of a particular time or the rights of a particular class, which interest that class alone, or at most the people amongst whom that class happens to exist.

It is owing to this, as much as to the greatness of the French people and the favorable disposition of the nations who listen to them, that the great effect which the French political debates sometimes produce in the world must be attributed. The orators of France frequently speak to mankind, even when they are addressing their countrymen only.

SECOND BOOK.

INFLUENCE OF DEMOCRACY ON THE FEELINGS OF THE AMERICANS.

CHAPTER I.

WHY DEMOCRATIC NATIONS SHOW A MORE ARDENT AND ENDURING LOVE OF EQUALITY THAN OF LIBERTY.

THE first and most intense passion which is produced by equality of condition is, I need hardly say, the love of that equality. My readers will therefore not be surprised that I speak of this feeling before all others.

Everybody has remarked that, in our time, and especially in France, this passion for equality is every day gaining ground in the human heart. It has been said a hundred times, that our contemporaries are far more ardently and tenaciously attached to equality than to freedom; but, as I do not find that the causes of the fact have been sufficiently analyzed, I shall endeavor to point them out.

It is possible to imagine an extreme point at which freedom and equality would meet and be confounded together. Let us suppose that all the people take a part in the government, and that each one of them has an equal right to take a part in it. As no one is different from his fellows, none can exercise a tyrannical power; men will be perfectly free, because they are all entirely equal; and they will all be perfectly equal, because they are entirely free. To this ideal state democratic nations tend. This is the only complete form that equality can assume upon earth; but there are a thousand others which, without being equally perfect, are not less cherished by those nations.

The principle of equality may be established in civil society, without prevailing in the political world. Equal rights may exist of indulging in the same pleasures, of entering the same professions, of frequenting the same places; in a word, of living in the same manner and seeking wealth by the same means, — although all men do not take an equal share in the government. A kind of equality may even be established in the political world, though there should be no political freedom there. A man may be the equal of all his countrymen save one, who is the master of all without distinction, and who selects equally from among them all the agents of his power. Several other combinations might be easily imagined, by which very great equality would be united to institutions more or less free, or even to institutions wholly without freedom.

Although men cannot become absolutely equal unless they are entirely free; and consequently equality, pushed to its furthest extent, may be confounded with freedom, yet there is good reason for distinguishing the one from the other. The taste which men have for liberty, and that which they feel for equality, are, in fact, two different things; and I am not afraid to add, that, amongst democratic nations, they are two unequal things.

Upon close inspection, it will be seen that there is in every age some peculiar and preponderating fact with which all others are connected; this fact almost always gives birth to some pregnant idea or some ruling passion, which attracts to itself and bears away in its course all the feelings and opinions of the time: it is like a great stream, towards which each of the neighboring rivulets seems to flow.

Freedom has appeared in the world at different times

and under various forms; it has not been exclusively bound to any social condition, and it is not confined to democracies. Freedom cannot, therefore, form the distinguishing characteristic of democratic ages. The peculiar and preponderating fact which marks those ages as its own is the equality of condition; the ruling passion of men in those periods is the love of this equality. Ask not what singular charm the men of democratic ages find in being equal, or what special reasons they may have for clinging so tenaciously to equality rather than to the other advantages which society holds out to them: equality is the distinguishing characteristic of the age they live in; that, of itself, is enough to explain that they prefer it to all the rest.

But independently of this reason, there are several others, which will at all times habitually lead men to prefer equality to freedom.

If a people could ever succeed in destroying, or even in diminishing, the equality which prevails in its own body, they could do so only by long and laborious efforts. Their social condition must be modified, their laws abolished, their opinions superseded, their habits changed, their manners corrupted. But political liberty is more easily lost; to neglect to hold it fast, is to allow it to escape. Men therefore cling to equality not only because it is dear to them; they also adhere to it because they think it will last forever.

That political freedom may compromise in its excesses the tranquillity, the property, the lives of individuals, is obvious even to narrow and unthinking minds. On the contrary, none but attentive and clear-sighted men perceive the perils with which equality threatens us, and they commonly avoid pointing them out. They know that the calamities they apprehend are remote, and flatter themselves that they will only fall upon future generations, for which the present generation takes but little thought. The evils which freedom sometimes brings with it are immediate; they are apparent to all, and all are more or less affected by them. The evils which extreme equality may produce are slowly disclosed; they creep gradually into the social frame; they are seen only at intervals; and at the moment at which they become most violent, habit already causes them to be no longer felt.

The advantages which freedom brings are only shown by the lapse of time; and it is always easy to mistake the cause in which they originate. The advantages of equality are immediate, and they may always be traced from their source.

Political liberty bestows exalted pleasures, from time to time, upon a certain number of citizens. Equality every day confers a number of small enjoyments on every man. The charms of equality are every instant felt, and are within the reach of all; the noblest hearts are not insensible to them, and the most vulgar souls exult in them. The passion which equality creates must therefore be at once strong and general. Men cannot enjoy political liberty unpurchased by some sacrifices, and they never obtain it without great exertions. But the pleasures of equality are self-proffered: each of the petty incidents of life seems to occasion them; and in order to taste them, nothing is required but to live.

Democratic nations are at all times fond of equality, but there are certain epochs at which the passion they entertain for it swells to the height of fury. This occurs at the moment when the old social system, long menaced, is overthrown after a severe intestine struggle, and the barriers of rank are at length thrown down. At such times, men pounce upon equality as their booty, and they cling to it as to some precious treasure which they fear to lose. The passion for equality penetrates on every side into men's hearts, expands there, and fills them entirely. Tell them not that, by this blind surrender of themselves to an exclusive passion, they risk their dearest interests: they are deaf.

Show them not freedom escaping from their grasp, whilst they are looking another way : they are blind, or, rather, they can discern but one object to be desired in the universe.

What I have said is applicable to all democratic nations ; what I am about to say concerns the French alone. Amongst most modern nations, and especially amongst all those of the continent of Europe, the taste and the idea of freedom only began to exist and to be developed at the time when social conditions were tending to equality, and as a consequence of that very equality. Absolute kings were the most efficient levellers of ranks amongst their subjects. Amongst these nations, equality preceded freedom : equality was therefore a fact of some standing when freedom was still a novelty ; the one had already created customs, opinions, and laws belonging to it, when the other, alone and for the first time, came into actual existence. Thus the latter was still only an affair of opinion and of taste, whilst the former had already crept into the habits of the people, possessed itself of their manners, and given a particular turn to the smallest actions in their lives. Can it be wondered at that the men of our own time prefer the one to the other ?

I think that democratic communities have a natural taste for freedom : left to themselves, they will seek it, cherish it, and view any privation of it with regret. But for equality, their passion is ardent, insatiable, incessant, invincible : they call for equality in freedom ; and if they cannot obtain that, they still call for equality in slavery. They will endure poverty, servitude, barbarism ; but they will not endure aristocracy.

This is true at all times, and especially in our own day. All men and all powers seeking to cope with this irresistible passion will be overthrown and destroyed by it. In our age, freedom cannot be established without it, and despotism itself cannot reign without its support.

CHAPTER II.

OF INDIVIDUALISM * IN DEMOCRATIC COUNTRIES.

I HAVE shown how it is that, in ages of equality, every man seeks for his opinions within himself: I am now to show how it is that, in the same ages, all his feelings are turned towards himself alone. *Individualism* is a novel expression, to which a novel idea has given birth. Our fathers were only acquainted with *égoïsme* (selfishness). Selfishness is a passionate and exaggerated love of self, which leads a man to connect everything with himself, and to prefer himself to everything in the world. Individualism is a mature and calm feeling, which disposes each member of the community to sever himself from the mass of his fellows, and to draw apart with his family and his friends ; so that, after he has thus formed a little circle of his own, he willingly leaves society at large to itself. Selfishness originates in blind instinct : individualism proceeds from erroneous judgment more than from depraved feelings ; it originates as much in deficiencies of mind as in perversity of heart.

Selfishness blights the germ of all virtue : individualism, at first, only saps the virtues of public life ; but, in the long run, it attacks and destroys all others, and is at length

---

* I adopt the expression of the original, however strange it may seem to the English ear, partly because it illustrates the remark on the introduction of general terms into democratic language which was made in a preceding chapter, and partly because I know of no English word exactly equivalent to the expression. The chapter itself defines the meaning attached to it by the author. — *English Translator's Note.*

absorbed in downright selfishness. Selfishness is a vice as old as the world, which does not belong to one form of society more than to another: individualism is of democratic origin, and it threatens to spread in the same ratio as the equality of condition.

Amongst aristocratic nations, as families remain for centuries in the same condition, often on the same spot, all generations become, as it were, contemporaneous. A man almost always knows his forefathers, and respects them: he thinks he already sees his remote descendants, and he loves them. He willingly imposes duties on himself towards the former and the latter; and he will frequently sacrifice his personal gratifications to those who went before and to those who will come after him. Aristocratic institutions have, moreover, the effect of closely binding every man to several of his fellow-citizens. As the classes of an aristocratic people are strongly marked and permanent, each of them is regarded by its own members as a sort of lesser country, more tangible and more cherished than the country at large. As, in aristocratic communities, all the citizens occupy fixed positions, one above the other, the result is, that each of them always sees a man above himself whose patronage is necessary to him, and, below himself, another man whose co-operation he may claim. Men living in aristocratic ages are therefore almost always closely attached to something placed out of their own sphere, and they are often disposed to forget themselves. It is true that, in these ages, the notion of human fellowship is faint, and that men seldom think of sacrificing themselves for mankind; but they often sacrifice themselves for other men. In democratic times, on the contrary, when the duties of each individual to the race are much more clear, devoted service to any one man becomes more rare; the bond of human affection is extended, but it is relaxed.

Amongst democratic nations, new families are constantly

springing up, others are constantly falling away, and all that remain change their condition; the woof of time is every instant broken, and the track of generations effaced. Those who went before are soon forgotten; of those who will come after, no one has any idea: the interest of man is confined to those in close propinquity to himself. As each class approximates to other classes, and intermingles with them, its members become indifferent, and as strangers to one another. Aristocracy had made a chain of all the members of the community, from the peasant to the king: democracy breaks that chain, and severs every link of it.

As social conditions become more equal, the number of persons increases who, although they are neither rich nor powerful enough to exercise any great influence over their fellows, have nevertheless acquired or retained sufficient education and fortune to satisfy their own wants. They owe nothing to any man, they expect nothing from any man; they acquire the habit of always considering themselves as standing alone, and they are apt to imagine that their whole destiny is in their own hands.

Thus, not only does democracy make every man forget his ancestors, but it hides his descendants and separates his contemporaries from him; it throws him back forever upon himself alone, and threatens in the end to confine him entirely within the solitude of his own heart.

CHAPTER III.

INDIVIDUALISM STRONGER AT THE CLOSE OF A DEMOCRATIC REVOLUTION THAN AT OTHER PERIODS.

THE period when the construction of democratic society upon the ruins of an aristocracy has just been completed is especially that at which this isolation of men from one another, and the selfishness resulting from it, most forcibly strike the observation. Democratic communities not only contain a large number of independent citizens, but they are constantly filled with men who, having entered but yesterday upon their independent condition, are intoxicated with their new power. They entertain a presumptuous confidence in their own strength, and, as they do not suppose that they can henceforward ever have occasion to claim the assistance of their fellow-creatures, they do not scruple to show that they care for nobody but themselves.

An aristocracy seldom yields without a protracted struggle, in the course of which implacable animosities are kindled between the different classes of society. These passions survive the victory, and traces of them may be observed in the midst of the democratic confusion which ensues. Those members of the community who were at the top of the late gradations of rank cannot immediately forget their former greatness; they will long regard themselves as aliens in the midst of the newly-composed society. They look upon all those whom this state of society has made their equals as oppressors, whose destiny can excite no sympathy; they have lost sight of their former equals, and feel no longer bound by a common interest to their fate: each of them, standing aloof, thinks that he is reduced to care for himself alone. Those, on the contrary, who were formerly at the foot of the social scale, and who have been brought up to the common level by a sudden revolution, cannot enjoy their newly-acquired independence without secret uneasiness; and if they meet with some of their former superiors on the same footing as themselves, they stand aloof from them with an expression of triumph and fear.

It is, then, commonly at the outset of democratic society that citizens are most disposed to live apart. Democracy leads men not to draw near to their fellow-creatures; but democratic revolutions lead them to shun each other, and perpetuate in a state of equality the animosities which the state of inequality created.

The great advantage of the Americans is, that they have arrived at a state of democracy without having to endure a democratic revolution; and that they are born equal, instead of becoming so.

CHAPTER IV.

THAT THE AMERICANS COMBAT THE EFFECTS OF INDIVIDUALISM BY FREE INSTITUTIONS.

DESPOTISM, which is of a very timorous nature, is never more secure of continuance than when it can keep men asunder; and all its influence is commonly exerted for that purpose. No vice of the human heart is so acceptable to it as selfishness: a despot easily forgives his subjects for not loving him, provided they do not love each other. He does not ask them to assist him in governing the state; it is enough that they do not aspire to govern it themselves. He stigmatizes as turbulent and unruly spirits those who would combine their exertions to promote the prosperity of the community; and, perverting the natural meaning of words, he applauds as good citizens those who have no sympathy for any but themselves.

Thus the vices which despotism produces are precisely those which equality fosters. These two things mutually and perniciously complete and assist each other. Equality places men side by side, unconnected by any common tie; despotism raises barriers to keep them asunder: the former predisposes them not to consider their fellow-creatures, the latter makes general indifference a sort of public virtue.

Despotism, then, which is at all times dangerous, is more particularly to be feared in democratic ages. It is easy to see that in those same ages men stand most in need of freedom. When the members of a community are forced to attend to public affairs, they are necessarily drawn from the circle of their own interests, and snatched at times from self-observation. As soon as a man begins to treat of public affairs in public, he begins to perceive that he is not so independent of his fellow-men as he had at first imagined, and that, in order to obtain their support, he must often lend them his co-operation.

When the public govern, there is no man who does not feel the value of public good-will, or who does not endeavor to court it by drawing to himself the esteem and affection of those amongst whom he is to live. Many of the passions which congeal and keep asunder human hearts, are then obliged to retire and hide below the surface. Pride must be dissembled; disdain dares not break out; selfishness fears its own self. Under a free government, as most public offices are elective, the men whose elevated minds or aspiring hopes are too closely circumscribed in private life constantly feel that they cannot do without the people who surround them. Men learn at such times to think of their fellow-men from ambitious motives; and they frequently find it, in a manner, their interest to forget themselves.

I may here be met by an objection derived from electioneering intrigues, the meanness of candidates, and the calumnies of their opponents. These are occasions of enmity which occur the oftener, the more frequent elections become. Such evils are doubtless great, but they are transient; whereas the benefits which attend them remain. The desire of being elected may lead some men for a time to violent hostility; but this same desire leads all men in the long run mutually to support each other; and, if it happens that an election accidentally severs two friends, the electoral system brings a multitude of citizens permanently together, who would otherwise always have remained unknown to each other. Freedom produces private animosities, but despotism gives birth to general indifference.

The Americans have combated by free institutions the

tendency of equality to keep men asunder, and they have subdued it. The legislators of America did not suppose that a general representation of the whole nation would suffice to ward off a disorder at once so natural to the frame of democratic society, and so fatal: they also thought that it would be well to infuse political life into each portion of the territory, in order to multiply to an infinite extent opportunities of acting in concert for all the members of the community, and to make them constantly feel their mutual dependence on each other. The plan was a wise one. The general affairs of a country only engage the attention of leading politicians, who assemble from time to time in the same places; and, as they often lose sight of each other afterwards, no lasting ties are established between them. But if the object be to have the local affairs of a district conducted by the men who reside there, the same persons are always in contact, and they are, in a manner, forced to be acquainted, and to adapt themselves to one another.

It is difficult to draw a man out of his own circle to interest him in the destiny of the state, because he does not clearly understand what influence the destiny of the state can have upon his own lot. But if it be proposed to make a road cross the end of his estate, he will see at a glance that there is a connection between this small public affair and his greatest private affairs; and he will discover, without its being shown to him, the close tie which unites private to general interest. Thus, far more may be done by intrusting to the citizens the administration of minor affairs than by surrendering to them the control of important ones, towards interesting them in the public welfare, and convincing them that they constantly stand in need one of another in order to provide for it. A brilliant achievement may win for you the favor of a people at one stroke; but to earn the love and respect of the population which sur-

rounds you, a long succession of little services rendered
and of obscure good deeds, — a constant habit of kindness,
and an established reputation for disinterestedness, — will
be required. Local freedom, then, which leads a great
number of citizens to value the affection of their neighbors
and of their kindred, perpetually brings men together, and
forces them to help one another, in spite of the propensities which sever them.

In the United States, the more opulent citizens take
great care not to stand aloof from the people; on the contrary, they constantly keep on easy terms with the lower
classes : they listen to them, they speak to them every day.
They know that the rich in democracies always stand in
need of the poor; and that, in democratic times, you attach
a poor man to you more by your manner than by benefits conferred. The magnitude of such benefits, which sets
off the difference of condition, causes a secret irritation to
those who reap advantage from them; but the charm of
simplicity of manners is almost irresistible : affability carries
men away, and even want of polish is not always displeasing. This truth does not take root at once in the minds of
the rich. They generally resist it as long as the democratic revolution lasts, and they do not acknowledge it
immediately after that revolution is accomplished. They
are very ready to do good to the people, but they still
choose to keep them at arm's length; they think that is
sufficient, but they are mistaken. They might spend fortunes thus without warming the hearts of the population
around them ; — that population does not ask them for
the sacrifice of their money, but of their pride.

It would seem as if every imagination in the United
States were upon the stretch to invent means of increasing
the wealth and satisfying the wants of the public. The
best-informed inhabitants of each district constantly use
their information to discover new truths which may augment the general prosperity ; and, if they have made any

such discoveries, they eagerly surrender them to the mass of the people.

When the vices and weaknesses frequently exhibited by those who govern in America are closely examined, the prosperity of the people occasions, but improperly occasions, surprise. Elected magistrates do not make the American democracy flourish; it flourishes because the magistrates are elective.

It would be unjust to suppose that the patriotism and the zeal which every American displays for the welfare of his fellow-citizens are wholly insincere. Although private interest directs the greater part of human actions in the United States, as well as elsewhere, it does not regulate them all. I must say that I have often seen Americans make great and real sacrifices to the public welfare; and I have remarked a hundred instances in which they hardly ever failed to lend faithful support to each other. The free institutions which the inhabitants of the United States possess, and the political rights of which they make so much use, remind every citizen, and in a thousand ways, that he lives in society. They every instant impress upon his mind the notion that it is the duty, as well as the interest, of men to make themselves useful to their fellow-creatures; and as he sees no particular ground of animosity to them, since he is never either their master or their slave, his heart readily leans to the side of kindness. Men attend to the interests of the public, first by necessity, afterwards by choice: what was intentional becomes an instinct; and by dint of working for the good of one's fellow-citizens, the habit and the taste for serving them is at length acquired.

Many people in France consider equality of condition as one evil, and political freedom as a second. When they are obliged to yield to the former, they strive at least to escape from the latter. But I contend that, in order to combat the evils which equality may produce, there is only one effectual remedy, — namely, political freedom.

CHAPTER V.

OF THE USE WHICH THE AMERICANS MAKE OF PUBLIC ASSO-CIATIONS IN CIVIL LIFE.

I DO not propose to speak of those political associations by the aid of which men endeavor to defend themselves against the despotic action of a majority, or against the aggressions of regal power. That subject I have already treated. If each citizen did not learn, in proportion as he individually becomes more feeble, and consequently more incapable of preserving his freedom single-handed, to combine with his fellow-citizens for the purpose of defending it, it is clear that tyranny would unavoidably increase together with equality.

Those associations only which are formed in civil life, without reference to political objects, are here adverted to. The political associations which exist in the United States are only a single feature in the midst of the immense assemblage of associations in that country. Americans of all ages, all conditions, and all dispositions, constantly form associations. They have not only commercial and manufacturing companies, in which all take part, but associations of a thousand other kinds, — religious, moral, serious, futile, general or restricted, enormous or diminutive. The Americans make associations to give entertainments, to found seminaries, to build inns, to construct churches, to diffuse books, to send missionaries to the antipodes; they found in this manner hospitals, prisons, and schools. If it be proposed to inculcate some truth, or to foster some feeling, by the encouragement of a great example, they form a society.   Wherever, at the head of some new undertaking, you see the government in France, or a man of rank in England, in the United States you will be sure to find an association.

I met with several kinds of associations in America of which I confess I had no previous notion ; and I have often admired the extreme skill with which the inhabitants of the United States succeed in proposing a common object to the exertions of a great many men, and in inducing them voluntarily to pursue it.

I have since travelled over England, whence the Americans have taken some of their laws and many of their customs ; and it seemed to me that the principle of association was by no means so constantly or adroitly used in that country.   The English often perform great things singly, whereas the Americans form associations for the smallest undertakings.   It is evident that the former people consider association as a powerful means of action, but the latter seem to regard it as the only means they have of acting.

Thus, the most democratic country on the face of the earth is that in which men have, in our time, carried to the highest perfection the art of pursuing in common the object of their common desires, and have applied this new science to the greatest number of purposes.   Is this the result of accident ? or is there in reality any necessary connection between the principle of association and that of equality ?

Aristocratic communities always contain, amongst a multitude of persons who by themselves are powerless, a small number of powerful and wealthy citizens, each of whom can achieve great undertakings single-handed.   In aristocratic societies, men do not need to combine in order to act, because they are strongly held together.   Every wealthy and powerful citizen constitutes the head of a permanent and compulsory association, composed of all those who are dependent upon him, or whom he makes subservient to the execution of his designs.

Amongst democratic nations, on the contrary, all the citizens are independent and feeble; they can do hardly anything by themselves, and none of them can oblige his fellow-men to lend him their assistance. They all, therefore, become powerless, if they do not learn voluntarily to help each other. If men living in democratic countries had no right and no inclination to associate for political purposes, their independence would be in great jeopardy; but they might long preserve their wealth and their cultivation: whereas, if they never acquired the habit of forming associations in ordinary life, civilization itself would be endangered. A people amongst whom individuals should lose the power of achieving great things single-handed, without acquiring the means of producing them by united exertions, would soon relapse into barbarism.

Unhappily, the same social condition which renders associations so necessary to democratic nations, renders their formation more difficult amongst those nations than amongst all other. When several members of an aristocracy agree to combine, they easily succeed in doing so: as each of them brings great strength to the partnership, the number of its members may be very limited; and when the members of an association are limited in number, they may easily become mutually acquainted, understand each other, and establish fixed regulations. The same opportunities do not occur amongst democratic nations, where the associated members must always be very numerous for their association to have any power.

I am aware that many of my countrymen are not in the least embarrassed by this difficulty. They contend, that, the more enfeebled and incompetent the citizens become, the more able and active the government ought to be rendered, in order that society at large may execute what individuals can no longer accomplish. They believe this answers the whole difficulty, but I think they are mistaken.

A government might perform the part of some of the largest American companies; and several States, members of the Union, have already attempted it; but what political power could ever carry on the vast multitude of lesser undertakings which the American citizens perform every day, with the assistance of the principle of association? It is easy to foresee that the time is drawing near when man will be less and less able to produce, of himself alone, the commonest necessaries of life. The task of the governing power will therefore perpetually increase, and its very efforts will extend it every day. The more it stands in the place of associations, the more will individuals, losing the notion of combining together, require its assistance: these are causes and effects which unceasingly create each other. Will the administration of the country ultimately assume the management of all the manufactures which no single citizen is able to carry on? And if a time at length arrives when, in consequence of the extreme subdivision of landed property, the soil is split into an infinite number of parcels, so that it can only be cultivated by companies of husbandmen, will it be necessary that the head of the government should leave the helm of state to follow the plough? The morals and the intelligence of a democratic people would be as much endangered as its business and manufactures, if the government ever wholly usurped the place of private companies.

Feelings and opinions are recruited, the heart is enlarged, and the human mind is developed, only by the reciprocal influence of men upon each other. I have shown that these influences are almost null in democratic countries; they must therefore be artificially created, and this can only be accomplished by associations.

When the members of an aristocratic community adopt

a new opinion, or conceive a new sentiment, they give it a
station, as it were, beside themselves, upon the lofty platform where they stand ; and opinions or sentiments so conspicuous to the eyes of the multitude are easily introduced
into the minds or hearts of all around.   In democratic
countries, the governing power alone is naturally in a condition to act in this manner; but it is easy to see that its
action is always inadequate, and often dangerous.   A government can no more be competent to keep alive and to
renew the circulation of opinions and feelings amongst a
great people, than to manage all the speculations of productive industry.   No sooner does a government attempt
to go beyond its political sphere, and to enter upon this
new track, than it exercises, even unintentionally, an insupportable tyranny ; for a government can only dictate strict
rules, the opinions which it favors are rigidly enforced, and
it is never easy to discriminate between its advice and its
commands.   Worse still will be the case, if the government
really believes itself interested in preventing all circulation
of ideas ; it will then stand motionless and oppressed by
the heaviness of voluntary torpor.   Governments, therefore, should not be the only active powers : associations
ought, in democratic nations, to stand in lieu of those
powerful private individuals whom the equality of conditions has swept away.

As soon as several of the inhabitants of the United
States have taken up an opinion or a feeling which they
wish to promote in the world, they look out for mutual
assistance ; and as soon as they have found each other out,
they combine.   From that moment they are no longer isolated men, but a power seen from afar, whose actions serve
for an example, and whose language is listened to.   The
first time I heard in the United States that a hundred
thousand men had bound themselves publicly to abstain
from spirituous liquors, it appeared to me more like a joke

than a serious engagement; and I did not at once perceive why these temperate citizens could not content themselves with drinking water by their own firesides. I at last understood that these hundred thousand Americans, alarmed by the progress of drunkenness around them, had made up their minds to patronize temperance. They acted just in the same way as a man of high rank who should dress very plainly, in order to inspire the humbler orders with a contempt of luxury. It is probable that, if these hundred thousand men had lived in France, each of them would singly have memorialized the government to watch the public houses all over the kingdom.

Nothing, in my opinion, is more deserving of our attention than the intellectual and moral associations of America. The political and industrial associations of that country strike us forcibly; but the others elude our observation, or, if we discover them, we understand them imperfectly, because we have hardly ever seen anything of the kind. It must, however, be acknowledged, that they are as necessary to the American people as the former, and perhaps more so. In democratic countries, the science of association is the mother of science; the progress of all the rest depends upon the progress it has made.

Amongst the laws which rule human societies, there is one which seems to be more precise and clear than all others. If men are to remain civilized, or to become so, the art of associating together must grow and improve in the same ratio in which the equality of conditions is increased.

CHAPTER VI.

OF THE RELATION BETWEEN PUBLIC ASSOCIATIONS AND THE NEWSPAPERS.

WHEN men are no longer united amongst themselves by firm and lasting ties, it is impossible to obtain the co-operation of any great number of them, unless you can persuade every man whose help you require that his private interest obliges him voluntarily to unite his exertions to the exertions of all the others. This can be habitually and conveniently effected only by means of a newspaper: nothing but a newspaper can drop the same thought into a thousand minds at the same moment. A newspaper is an adviser who does not require to be sought, but who comes of his own accord, and talks to you briefly every day of the common weal, without distracting you from your private affairs.

Newspapers therefore become more necessary in proportion as men become more equal, and individualism more to be feared. To suppose that they only serve to protect freedom would be to diminish their importance: they maintain civilization. I shall not deny that, in democratic countries, newspapers frequently lead the citizens to launch together into very ill-digested schemes; but if there were no newspapers, there would be no common activity. The evil which they produce is therefore much less than that which they cure.

The effect of a newspaper is not only to suggest the same purpose to a great number of persons, but to furnish means for executing in common the designs which they may have singly conceived. The principal citizens who inhabit an aristocratic country discern each other from afar; and if they wish to unite their forces, they move towards each other, drawing a multitude of men after them. It frequently happens, on the contrary, in democratic countries, that a great number of men who wish or who want to combine cannot accomplish it, because, as they are very insignificant and lost amidst the crowd, they cannot see, and know not where to find, one another. A newspaper then takes up the notion or the feeling which had occurred simultaneously, but singly, to each of them. All are then immediately guided towards this beacon; and these wandering minds, which had long sought each other in darkness, at length meet and unite. The newspaper brought them together, and the newspaper is still necessary to keep them united.

In order that an association amongst a democratic people should have any power, it must be a numerous body. The persons of whom it is composed are therefore scattered over a wide extent, and each of them is detained in the place of his domicile by the narrowness of his income, or by the small unremitting exertions by which he earns it. Means must then be found to converse every day without seeing each other, and to take steps in common without having met. Thus, hardly any democratic association can do without newspapers.

There is, consequently, a necessary connection between public associations and newspapers: newspapers make associations, and associations make newspapers; and if it has been correctly advanced, that associations will increase in number as the conditions of men become more equal, it is not less certain that the number of newspapers increases in proportion to that of associations. Thus it is, in America, that we find at the same time the greatest number of associations and of newspapers.

This connection between the number of newspapers and that of associations leads us to the discovery of a further connection between the state of the periodical press and the form of the administration in a country, and shows that the number of newspapers must diminish or increase amongst a democratic people, in proportion as its administration is more or less centralized. For, amongst democratic nations, the exercise of local powers cannot be intrusted to the principal members of the community, as in aristocracies. Those powers must either be abolished, or placed in the hands of very large numbers of men, who then in fact constitute an association permanently established by law, for the purpose of administering the affairs of a certain extent of territory; and they require a journal, to bring to them every day, in the midst of their own minor concerns, some intelligence of the state of their public weal. The more numerous local powers are, the greater is the number of men in whom they are vested by law; and as this want is hourly felt, the more profusely do newspapers abound.

The extraordinary subdivision of administrative power has much more to do with the enormous number of American newspapers, than the great political freedom of the country and the absolute liberty of the press. If all the inhabitants of the Union had the suffrage, — but a suffrage which should extend only to the choice of their legislators in Congress, — they would require but few newspapers, because they would have to act together only on very important, but very rare, occasions. But within the great national association, lesser associations have been established by law in every county, every city, and indeed in every village, for the purposes of local administration. The laws of the country thus compel every American to co-operate every day of his life with some of his fellow-citizens for a common purpose, and each one of them requires a newspaper to inform him what all the others are doing.

I am of opinion that a democratic people,* without any national representative assemblies, but with a great number of small local powers, would have in the end more newspapers than another people governed by a centralized administration and an elective legislature. What best explains to me the enormous circulation of the daily press in the United States is, that, amongst the Americans, I find the utmost national freedom combined with local freedom of every kind.

There is a prevailing opinion in France and England, that the circulation of newspapers would be indefinitely increased by removing the taxes which have been laid upon the press. This is a very exaggerated estimate of the effects of such a reform. Newspapers increase in numbers, not according to their cheapness, but according to the more or less frequent want which a great number of men may feel for intercommunication and combination.

In like manner, I should attribute the increasing influence of the daily press to causes more general than those by which it is commonly explained. A newspaper can only subsist on the condition of publishing sentiments or principles common to a large number of men. A newspaper, therefore, always represents an association which is composed of its habitual readers. This association may be more or less defined, more or less restricted, more or less numerous; but the fact that the newspaper keeps alive, is a proof that at least the germ of such an association exists in the minds of its readers.

* I say a *democratic people:* the administration of an aristocratic people may be the reverse of centralized, and yet the want of newspapers be little felt, because local powers are then vested in the hands of a very small number of men, who either act apart, or who know each other, and can easily meet and come to an understanding.

This leads me to a last reflection, with which I shall conclude this chapter. The more equal the conditions of men become, and the less strong men individually are, the more easily do they give way to the current of the multitude, and the more difficult is it for them to adhere by themselves to an opinion which the multitude discard. A newspaper represents an association; it may be said to address each of its readers in the name of all the others, and to exert its influence over them in proportion to their individual weakness. The power of the newspaper press must therefore increase as the social conditions of men become more equal.

CHAPTER VII.

RELATION OF CIVIL TO POLITICAL ASSOCIATIONS.

THERE is only one country on the face of the earth where the citizens enjoy unlimited freedom of association for political purposes. This same country is the only one in the world where the continual exercise of the right of association has been introduced into civil life, and where all the advantages which civilization can confer are procured by means of it.

In all the countries where political associations are prohibited, civil associations are rare. It is hardly probable that this is the result of accident; but the inference should rather be, that there is a natural, and perhaps a necessary, connection between these two kinds of associations.

Certain men happen to have a common interest in some concern; either a commercial undertaking is to be managed, or some speculation in manufactures to be tried: they meet, they combine, and thus, by degrees, they become familiar with the principle of association. The greater the multiplicity of small affairs, the more do men, even without knowing it, acquire facility in prosecuting great undertakings in common.

Civil associations, therefore, facilitate political association; but, on the other hand, political association singularly strengthens and improves associations for civil purposes. In civil life, every man may, strictly speaking, fancy that he can provide for his own wants; in politics, he can fancy no such thing. When a people, then, have any knowledge of public life, the notion of association, and the wish to coalesce, present themselves every day to the minds of the whole community : whatever natural repugnance may restrain men from acting in concert, they will always be ready to combine for the sake of a party. Thus political life makes the love and practice of association more general ; it imparts a desire of union, and teaches the means of combination to numbers of men who otherwise would have always lived apart.

Politics not only give birth to numerous associations, but to associations of great extent. In civil life, it seldom happens that any one interest draws a very large number of men to act in concert ; much skill is required to bring such an interest into existence : but in politics, opportunities present themselves every day. Now it is solely in great associations that the general value of the principle of association is displayed. Citizens who are individually powerless do not very clearly anticipate the strength which they may acquire by uniting together ; it must be shown to them in order to be understood. Hence it is often easier to collect a multitude for a public purpose than a few persons ; a thousand citizens do not see what interest they have in combining together ; ten thousand will be perfectly aware of it. In politics, men combine for great undertakings ; and the use they make of the principle of association in important affairs practically teaches them that it is their interest to help each other in those of less moment. A political association draws a number of individuals at the same time out of their own circle ; however they may be naturally kept asunder by age, mind, and fortune, it places them nearer together, and brings them into contact. Once met, they can always meet again.

Men can embark in few civil partnerships without risking a portion of their possessions ; this is the case with all manufacturing and trading companies. When men are as yet but little versed in the art of association, and are unacquainted with its principal rules, they are afraid, when first they combine in this manner, of buying their experience dear. They therefore prefer depriving themselves of a powerful instrument of success, to running the risks which attend the use of it. They are, however, less reluctant to join political associations, which appear to them to be without danger, because they adventure no money in them. But they cannot belong to these associations for any length of time, without finding out how order is maintained amongst a large number of men, and by what contrivance they are made to advance, harmoniously and methodically, to the same object. Thus they learn to surrender their own will to that of all the rest, and to make their own exertions subordinate to the common impulse, — things which it is not less necessary to know in civil than in political associations. Political associations may therefore be considered as large free schools, where all the members of the community go to learn the general theory of association.

But even if political association did not directly contribute to the progress of civil association, to destroy the former would be to impair the latter. When citizens can only meet in public for certain purposes, they regard such meetings as a strange proceeding of rare occurrence, and they rarely think at all about it. When they are allowed to meet freely for all purposes, they ultimately look upon public association as the universal, or in a manner the sole, means which men can employ to accomplish the different purposes they may have in view. Every new want instantly revives the notion. The art of association then becomes, as I have said before, the mother of action, studied and applied by all.

When some kinds of associations are prohibited and others allowed, it is difficult to distinguish the former from the latter beforehand. In this state of doubt, men abstain from them altogether, and a sort of public opinion passes current, which tends to cause any association whatsoever to be regarded as a bold, and almost an illicit enterprise.*

It is therefore chimerical to suppose that the spirit of association, when it is repressed on some one point, will nevertheless display the same vigor on all others; and that, if men be allowed to prosecute certain undertakings in common, that is quite enough for them eagerly to set about them. When the members of a community are allowed and accustomed to combine for all purposes, they will combine as readily for the lesser as for the more important ones; but if they are only allowed to combine for small affairs, they will be neither inclined nor able to effect it. It is in vain that you will leave them entirely free to prosecute their business on joint-stock account: they will hardly care to avail themselves of the rights you have granted to them; and, after having exhausted your strength in vain efforts to put down prohibited associations, you will be surprised that you cannot persuade men to form the associations you encourage.

* This is more especially true when the executive government has a discretionary power of allowing or prohibiting associations. When certain associations are simply prohibited by law, and the courts of justice have to punish infringements of that law, the evil is far less considerable. Then, every citizen knows beforehand pretty nearly what he has to expect. He judges himself before he is judged by the law, and, abstaining from prohibited associations, he embarks in those which are legally sanctioned. It is by these restrictions that all free nations have always admitted that the right of association might be limited. But if the legislature should invest a man with a power of ascertaining beforehand which associations are dangerous and which are useful, and should authorize him to destroy all associations in the bud, or to allow them to be formed, as nobody would be able to foresee in what cases associations might be established, and in what cases they would be put down, the spirit of association would be entirely paralyzed. The former of these laws would only assail certain associations; the latter would apply to society itself, and inflict an injury upon it. I can conceive that a regular government may have recourse to the former, but I do not concede that any government has the right of enacting the latter.

I do not say that there can be no civil associations in a country where political association is prohibited ; for men can never live in society without embarking in some common undertakings : but I maintain that, in such a country, civil associations will always be few in number, feebly planned, unskilfully managed, that they will never form any vast designs, or that they will fail in the execution of them.

This naturally leads me to think that freedom of association in political matters is not so dangerous to public tranquillity as is supposed ; and that possibly, after having agitated society for some time, it may strengthen the state in the end. In democratic countries, political associations are, so to speak, the only powerful persons who aspire to rule the state. Accordingly, the governments of our time look upon associations of this kind just as sovereigns in the Middle Ages regarded the great vassals of the crown : they entertain a sort of instinctive abhorrence of them, and combat them on all occasions. They bear, on the contrary, a natural good-will to civil associations, because they readily discover that, instead of directing the minds of the community to public affairs, these institutions serve to divert them from such reflections ; and that, by engaging them more and more in the pursuit of objects which cannot be attained without public tranquillity, they deter them from revolutions. But these governments do not attend to the fact, that political associations tend amazingly to multiply and facilitate those of a civil character, and that, in avoiding a dangerous evil, they deprive themselves of an efficacious remedy.

When you see the Americans freely and constantly forming associations for the purpose of promoting some political principle, of raising one man to the head of affairs, or of wresting power from another, you have some difficulty in understanding how men so independent do not constantly fall into the abuse of freedom.   If, on the other hand, you survey the infinite number of trading companies which are in operation in the United States, and perceive that the Americans are on every side unceasingly engaged in the execution of important and difficult plans, which the slightest revolution would throw into confusion, you will readily comprehend why people so well employed are by no means tempted to perturb the state, nor to destroy that public tranquillity by which they all profit.

Is it enough to observe these things separately, or should we not discover the hidden tie which connects them ?   In their political associations, the Americans, of all conditions, minds, and ages, daily acquire a general taste for association, and grow accustomed to the use of it.   There they meet together in large numbers, — they converse, they listen to each other, and they are mutually stimulated to all sorts of undertakings.   They afterwards transfer to civil life the notions they have thus acquired, and make them subservient to a thousand purposes.   Thus it is by the enjoyment of a dangerous freedom that the Americans learn the art of rendering the dangers of freedom less formidable.

If a certain moment in the existence of a nation be selected, it is easy to prove that political associations perturb the state and paralyze productive industry ; but take the whole life of a people, and it may perhaps be easy to demonstrate, that freedom of association in political matters is favorable to the prosperity, and even to the tranquillity, of the community.

I said in the former part of this work : " The unrestrained liberty of political association cannot be entirely assimilated to the liberty of the press.   The one is at the same time less necessary and more dangerous than the other.   A nation may confine it within certain limits, without ceasing to be mistress of itself ; and it may sometimes be obliged to do so, in order to maintain its own authority."   And,

further on, I added : " It cannot be denied that the unrestrained liberty of association for political purposes is the
last degree of liberty which a people is fit for. If it does
not throw them into anarchy, it perpetually brings them,
as it were, to the verge of it." Thus, I do not think that
a nation is always at liberty to invest its citizens with an
absolute right of association for political purposes ; and I
doubt whether, in any country or in any age, it be wise to
set no limits to freedom of association.

A certain nation, it is said, could not maintain tranquillity in the community, cause the laws to be respected, or
establish a lasting government, if the right of association
were not confined within narrow limits. These blessings
are doubtless invaluable ; and I can imagine that, to acquire or to preserve them, a nation may impose upon itself
severe temporary restrictions : but still it is well that the
nation should know at what price these blessings are purchased. I can understand that it may be advisable to cut
off a man's arm in order to save his life ; but it would be
ridiculous to assert that he will be as dexterous as he was
before he lost it.

CHAPTER VIII.

HOW THE AMERICANS COMBAT INDIVIDUALISM BY THE PRIN-
CIPLE OF INTEREST RIGHTLY UNDERSTOOD.

WHEN the world was managed by a few rich and powerful individuals, these persons loved to entertain a lofty idea of the duties of man.   They were fond of professing that it is praiseworthy to forget one's self, and that good should be done without hope of reward, as it is by the Deity himself.   Such were the standard opinions of that time in morals.

I doubt whether men were more virtuous in aristocratic ages than in others; but they were incessantly talking of the beauties of virtue, and its utility was only studied in secret.   But since the imagination takes less lofty flights, and every man's thoughts are centred in himself, moralists are alarmed by this idea of self-sacrifice, and they no longer venture to present it to the human mind.   They therefore content themselves with inquiring, whether the personal advantage of each member of the community does not consist in working for the good of all; and when they have hit upon some point on which private interest and public interest meet and amalgamate, they are eager to bring it into notice.   Observations of this kind are gradually multiplied: what was only a single remark becomes a general principle; and it is held as a truth, that man serves himself in serving his fellow-creatures, and that his private interest is to do good.

I have already shown, in several parts of this work, by what means the inhabitants of the United States almost always manage to combine their own advantage with that of their fellow-citizens: my present purpose is to point out the general rule which enables them to do so. In the United States, hardly anybody talks of the beauty of virtue; but they maintain that virtue is useful, and prove it every day. The American moralists do not profess that men ought to sacrifice themselves for their fellow-creatures *because* it is noble to make such sacrifices; but they boldly aver that such sacrifices are as necessary to him who imposes them upon himself, as to him for whose sake they are made.

They have found out that, in their country and their age, man is brought home to himself by an irresistible force; and, losing all hope of stopping that force, they turn all their thoughts to the direction of it. They therefore do not deny that every man may follow his own interest; but they endeavor to prove that it is the interest of every man to be virtuous. I shall not here enter into the reasons they allege, which would divert me from my subject: suffice it to say, that they have convinced their fellow-countrymen.

Montaigne said long ago, "Were I not to follow the straight road for its straightness, I should follow it for having found by experience that, in the end, it is commonly the happiest and most useful track." The doctrine of interest rightly understood is not then new, but amongst the Americans of our time it finds universal acceptance: it has become popular there; you may trace it at the bottom of all their actions, you will remark it in all they say. It is as often asserted by the poor man as by the rich. In Europe, the principle of interest is much grosser than it is in America, but it is also less common, and especially it is less avowed; amongst us, men still constantly feign great abnegation which they no longer feel.

The Americans, on the contrary, are fond of explaining almost all the actions of their lives by the principle of interest rightly understood; they show with complacency how an enlightened regard for themselves constantly prompts them to assist each other, and inclines them willingly to sacrifice a portion of their time and property to the welfare of the state. In this respect, I think they frequently fail to do themselves justice; for, in the United States, as well as elsewhere, people are sometimes seen to give way to those disinterested and spontaneous impulses which are natural to man: but the Americans seldom allow that they yield to emotions of this kind; they are more anxious to do honor to their philosophy than to themselves.

I might here pause, without attempting to pass a judgment on what I have described. The extreme difficulty of the subject would be my excuse, but I shall not avail myself of it; and I had rather that my readers, clearly perceiving my object, should refuse to follow me, than that I should leave them in suspense.

The principle of interest rightly understood is not a lofty one, but it is clear and sure. It does not aim at mighty objects, but it attains without excessive exertion all those at which it aims. As it lies within the reach of all capacities, every one can without difficulty apprehend and retain it. By its admirable conformity to human weaknesses, it easily obtains great dominion; nor is that dominion precarious, since the principle checks one personal interest by another, and uses, to direct the passions, the very same instrument which excites them.

The principle of interest rightly understood produces no great acts of self-sacrifice, but it suggests daily small acts of self-denial. By itself, it cannot suffice to make a man virtuous; but it disciplines a number of persons in habits of regularity, temperance, moderation, foresight, self-command; and, if it does not lead men straight to virtue by the will, it gradually draws them in that direction by their habits. If the principle of interest rightly understood were to sway the whole moral world, extraordinary virtues would doubtless be more rare; but I think that gross depravity would then also be less common. The principle of interest rightly understood perhaps prevents men from rising far above the level of mankind; but a great number of other men, who were falling far below it, are caught and restrained by it. Observe some few individuals, they are lowered by it; survey mankind, they are raised.

I am not afraid to say, that the principle of interest rightly understood appears to me the best suited of all philosophical theories to the wants of the men of our time, and that I regard it as their chief remaining security against themselves. Towards it, therefore, the minds of the moralists of our age should turn; even should they judge it to be incomplete, it must nevertheless be adopted as necessary.

I do not think, upon the whole, that there is more selfishness amongst us than in America; the only difference is, that there it is enlightened, here it is not. Every American will sacrifice a portion of his private interests to preserve the rest; we would fain preserve the whole, and oftentimes the whole is lost. Everybody I see about me seems bent on teaching his contemporaries, by precept and example, that what is useful is never wrong. Will nobody undertake to make them understand how what is right may be useful?

No power upon earth can prevent the increasing equality of conditions from inclining the human mind to seek out what is useful, or from leading every member of the community to be wrapped up in himself. It must therefore be expected that personal interest will become more than ever the principal, if not the sole, spring of men's actions; but it remains to be seen how each man will understand his personal interest. If the members of a community, as they become more equal, become more ignorant and coarse, it is difficult to foresee to what pitch of stupid excesses their selfishness may lead them; and no one can foretell into what disgrace and wretchedness they would plunge themselves, lest they should have to sacrifice something of their own well-being to the prosperity of their fellow-creatures.

I do not think that the system of interest, as it is professed in America, is, in all its parts, self-evident; but it contains a great number of truths so evident, that men, if they are but educated, cannot fail to see them. Educate, then, at any rate; for the age of implicit self-sacrifice and instinctive virtues is already flitting far away from us, and the time is fast approaching when freedom, public peace, and social order itself will not be able to exist without education.

CHAPTER IX.

THAT THE AMERICANS APPLY THE PRINCIPLE OF INTEREST
RIGHTLY UNDERSTOOD TO RELIGIOUS MATTERS.

IF the principle of interest rightly understood had nothing but the present world in view, it would be very
insufficient, for there are many sacrifices which can only
find their recompense in another; and whatever ingenuity
may be put forth to demonstrate the utility of virtue, it will
never be an easy task to make that man live aright who has
no thought of dying.

It is therefore necessary to ascertain whether the principle of interest rightly understood can be easily reconciled
with religious belief. The philosophers who inculcate this
system of morals tell men that, to be happy in this life,
they must watch their own passions, and steadily control
their excess; that lasting happiness can be secured only by
renouncing a thousand transient gratifications; and that a
man must perpetually triumph over himself in order to
secure his own advantage. The founders of almost all
religions have held the same language. The track they
point out to man is the same, only the goal is more remote;
instead of placing in this world the reward of the sacrifices
they impose, they transport it to another.

Nevertheless, I cannot believe that all those who practise
virtue from religious motives are actuated only by the hope
of a recompense. I have known zealous Christians who
constantly forgot themselves, to work with greater ardor
for the happiness of their fellow-men; and I have heard
them declare that all they did was only to earn the bless-

ings of a future state. I cannot but think that they deceive themselves : I respect them too much to believe them.

Christianity, indeed, teaches that a man must prefer his neighbor to himself, in order to gain eternal life; but Christianity also teaches that men ought to benefit their fellow-creatures for the love of God. A sublime expression ! Man searches by his intellect into the Divine conception, and sees that order is the purpose of God ; he freely gives his own efforts to aid in prosecuting this great design, and, whilst he sacrifices his personal interests to this consummate order of all created things, expects no other recompense than the pleasure of contemplating it.

I do not believe that interest is the sole motive of religious men : but I believe that interest is the principal means which religions themselves employ to govern men, and I do not question that in this way they strike the multitude and become popular. I do not see clearly why the principle of interest rightly understood should undermine the religious opinions of men ; it seems to me more easy to show why it should strengthen them. Let it be supposed that, in order to attain happiness in this world, a man combats his instincts on all occasions, and deliberately calculates every action of his life ; that, instead of yielding blindly to the impetuosity of first desires, he has learned the art of resisting them, and that he has accustomed himself to sacrifice without an effort the pleasure of a moment to the lasting interest of his whole life. If such a man believes in the religion which he professes, it will cost him but little to submit to the restrictions it may impose. Reason herself counsels him to obey, and habit has prepared him to endure these limitations. If he should have conceived any doubts as to the object of his hopes, still he will not easily allow himself to be stopped by them; and he will decide that it is wise to risk some of the advantages of this world, in order to preserve his rights to the great inheritance promised him in another. "To be mistaken in believing that the Christian religion is true," says Pascal, " is no great loss to any one ; but how dreadful to be mistaken in believing it to be false ! "

The Americans do not affect a brutal indifference to a future state ; they affect no puerile pride in despising perils which they hope to escape from. They therefore profess their religion without shame and without weakness ; but there generally is, even in their zeal, something so indescribably tranquil, methodical, and deliberate, that it would seem as if the head, far more than the heart, brought them to the foot of the altar.

The Americans not only follow their religion from interest, but they often place in this world the interest which makes them follow it. In the Middle Ages, the clergy spoke of nothing but a future state ; they hardly cared to prove that a sincere Christian may be a happy man here below. But the American preachers are constantly referring to the earth ; and it is only with great difficulty that they can divert their attention from it. To touch their congregations, they always show them how favorable religious opinions are to freedom and public tranquillity ; and it is often difficult to ascertain from their discourses whether the principal object of religion is to procure eternal felicity in the other world, or prosperity in this.

CHAPTER X.

OF THE TASTE FOR PHYSICAL WELL-BEING IN AMERICA.

IN America, the passion for physical well-being is not always exclusive, but it is general; and if all do not feel it in the same manner, yet it is felt by all. Carefully to satisfy even the least wants of the body, and to provide the little conveniences of life, is uppermost in every mind. Something of an analogous character is more and more apparent in Europe. Amongst the causes which produce these similar consequences in both hemispheres, several are so connected with my subject as to deserve notice.

When riches are hereditarily fixed in families, a great number of men enjoy the comforts of life without feeling an exclusive taste for those comforts. The heart of man is not so much caught by the undisturbed possession of anything valuable, as by the desire, as yet imperfectly satisfied, of possessing it, and by the incessant dread of losing it. In aristocratic communities, the wealthy, never having experienced a condition different from their own, entertain no fear of changing it; the existence of such conditions hardly occurs to them. The comforts of life are not to them the end of life, but simply a way of living; they regard them as existence itself, — enjoyed, but scarcely thought of. As the natural and instinctive taste which all men feel for being well off is thus satisfied without trouble and without apprehension, their faculties are turned elsewhere, and applied to more arduous and lofty undertakings, which excite and engross their minds.

Hence it is that, in the very midst of physical gratifications, the members of an aristocracy often display a haughty contempt of these very enjoyments, and exhibit singular powers of endurance under the privation of them. All the revolutions which have ever shaken or destroyed aristocracies have shown how easily men accustomed to superfluous luxuries can do without the necessaries of life; whereas men who have toiled to acquire a competency can hardly live after they have lost it.

If I turn my observation from the upper to the lower classes, I find analogous effects produced by opposite causes. Amongst a nation where aristocracy predominates in society, and keeps it stationary, the people in the end get as much accustomed to poverty as the rich to their opulence. The latter bestow no anxiety on their physical comforts, because they enjoy them without an effort; the former do not think of things which they despair of obtaining, and which they hardly know enough of to desire them. In communities of this kind, the imagination of the poor is driven to seek another world; the miseries of real life enclose it around, but it escapes from their control, and flies to seek its pleasures far beyond.

When, on the contrary, the distinctions of ranks are confounded together and privileges are destroyed, — when hereditary property is subdivided, and education and freedom widely diffused, the desire of acquiring the comforts of the world haunts the imagination of the poor, and the dread of losing them that of the rich. Many scanty fortunes spring up; those who possess them have a sufficient share of physical gratifications to conceive a taste for these pleasures, — not enough to satisfy it. They never procure them without exertion, and they never indulge in them without apprehension. They are therefore always straining to pursue or to retain gratifications so delightful, so imperfect, so fugitive.

If I were to inquire what passion is most natural to men

who are stimulated and circumscribed by the obscurity of their birth or the mediocrity of their fortune, I could discover none more peculiarly appropriate to their condition than this love of physical prosperity. The passion for physical comforts is essentially a passion of the middle classes: with those classes it grows and spreads, with them it preponderates. From them it mounts into the higher orders of society, and descends into the mass of the people.

I never met in America with any citizen so poor as not to cast a glance of hope and envy on the enjoyments of the rich, or whose imagination did not possess itself by anticipation of those good things which fate still obstinately withheld from him.

On the other hand, I never perceived amongst the wealthier inhabitants of the United States that proud contempt of physical gratifications which is sometimes to be met with even in the most opulent and dissolute aristocracies. Most of these wealthy persons were once poor: they have felt the sting of want; they were long a prey to adverse fortunes; and now that the victory is won, the passions which accompanied the contest have survived it: their minds are, as it were, intoxicated by the small enjoyments which they have pursued for forty years.

Not but that in the United States, as elsewhere, there are a certain number of wealthy persons, who, having come into their property by inheritance, possess without exertion an opulence they have not earned. But even these men are not less devotedly attached to the pleasures of material life. The love of well-being is now become the predominant taste of the nation; the great current of human passions runs in that channel, and sweeps everything along in its course.

CHAPTER XI.

IT may be supposed, from what has just been said, that
the love of physical gratifications must constantly urge
the Americans to irregularities in morals, disturb the peace
of families, and threaten the security of society at large.
But it is not so: the passion for physical gratifications produces in democracies effects very different from those which
it occasions in aristocratic nations.

It sometimes happens that, wearied with public affairs
and sated with opulence, amidst the ruin of religious belief and the decline of the state, the heart of an aristocracy
may by degrees be seduced to the pursuit of sensual enjoyments alone. At other times, the power of the monarch
or the weakness of the people, without stripping the nobility of their fortune, compels them to stand aloof from the
administration of affairs, and, whilst the road to mighty enterprise is closed, abandons them to the inquietude of their
own desires; they then fall back heavily upon themselves,
and seek in the pleasures of the body oblivion of their
former greatness.

When the members of an aristocratic body are thus exclusively devoted to the pursuit of physical gratifications,
they commonly turn in that direction all the energy which
they derive from their long experience of power. Such
men are not satisfied with the pursuit of comfort; they
require sumptuous depravity and splendid corruption. The
worship they pay the senses is a gorgeous one; and they

seem to vie with each other in the art of degrading their own natures. The stronger, the more famous, and the more free an aristocracy has been, the more depraved will it then become; and, however brilliant may have been the lustre of its virtues, I dare predict that they will always be surpassed by the splendor of its vices.

The taste for physical gratifications leads a democratic people into no such excesses. The love of well-being is there displayed as a tenacious, exclusive, universal passion; but its range is confined. To build enormous palaces, to conquer or to mimic nature, to ransack the world in order to gratify the passions of a man, is not thought of: but to add a few roods of land to your field, to plant an orchard, to enlarge a dwelling, to be always making life more comfortable and convenient, to avoid trouble, and to satisfy the smallest wants without effort and almost without cost. These are small objects, but the soul clings to them; it dwells upon them closely and day by day, till they at last shut out the rest of the world, and sometimes intervene between itself and Heaven.

This, it may be said, can only be applicable to those members of the community who are in humble circumstances; wealthier individuals will display tastes akin to those which belonged to them in aristocratic ages. I contest the proposition: in point of physical gratifications, the most opulent members of a democracy will not display tastes very different from those of the people; whether it be that, springing from the people, they really share those tastes, or that they esteem it a duty to submit to them. In democratic society, the sensuality of the public has taken a moderate and tranquil course, to which all are bound to conform: it is as difficult to depart from the common rule by one's vices as by one's virtues. Rich men who live amidst democratic nations are therefore more intent on providing for their smallest wants, than for their extraordinary enjoyments ; they gratify a number of petty desires, without indulging in any great irregularities of passion : thus, they are more apt to become enervated than debauched.

The special taste which the men of democratic times entertain for physical enjoyments is not naturally opposed to the principles of public order ; nay, it often stands in need of order, that it may be gratified. Nor is it adverse to regularity of morals, for good morals contribute to public tranquillity and are favorable to industry. It may even be frequently combined with a species of religious morality : men wish to be as well off as they can in this world, without foregoing their chance of another. Some physical gratifications cannot be indulged in without crime ; from such they strictly abstain. The enjoyment of others is sanctioned by religion and morality ; to these the heart, the imagination, and life itself, are unreservedly given up ; till, in snatching at these lesser gifts, men lose sight of those more precious possessions which constitute the glory and the greatness of mankind.

The reproach I address to the principle of equality is not that it leads men away in the pursuit of forbidden enjoyments, but that it absorbs them wholly in quest of those which are allowed. By these means, a kind of virtuous materialism may ultimately be established in the world, which would not corrupt, but enervate, the soul, and noiselessly unbend its springs of action.

CHAPTER XII.

WHY SOME AMERICANS MANIFEST A SORT OF FANATICAL SPIRITUALISM.

ALTHOUGH the desire of acquiring the good things of this world is the prevailing passion of the American people, certain momentary outbreaks occur, when their souls seem suddenly to burst the bonds of matter by which they are restrained, and to soar impetuously towards Heaven. In all the States of the Union, but especially in the half-peopled country of the Far West, itinerant preachers may be met with, who hawk about the word of God from place to place. Whole families, old men, women, and children, cross rough passes and untrodden wilds, coming from a great distance, to join a camp-meeting, where they totally forget, for several days and nights, in listening to these discourses, the cares of business and even the most urgent wants of the body.

Here and there, in the midst of American society, you meet with men full of a fanatical and almost wild spiritualism, which hardly exists in Europe. From time to time, strange sects arise, which endeavor to strike out extraordinary paths to eternal happiness. Religious insanity is very common in the United States.

Nor ought these facts to surprise us. It was not man who implanted in himself the taste for what is infinite, and the love of what is immortal : these lofty instincts are not the offspring of his capricious will ; their steadfast foundation is fixed in human nature, and they exist in spite of his efforts. He may cross and distort them ; destroy them he cannot.

The soul has wants which must be satisfied; and whatever pains be taken to divert it from itself, it soon grows weary, restless, and disquieted amidst the enjoyments of sense. If ever the faculties of the great majority of mankind were exclusively bent upon the pursuit of material objects, it might be anticipated that an amazing reaction would take place in the souls of some men. They would drift at large in the world of spirits, for fear of remaining shackled by the close bondage of the body.

It is not, then, wonderful, if, in the midst of a community whose thoughts tend earthward, a small number of individuals are to be found who turn their looks to Heaven. I should be surprised if mysticism did not soon make some advance amongst a people solely engaged in promoting their own worldly welfare.

It is said that the deserts of the Thebaid were peopled by the persecutions of the Emperors and the massacres of the Circus; I should rather say, that it was by the luxuries of Rome and the Epicurean philosophy of Greece.

If their social condition, their present circumstances, and their laws did not confine the minds of the Americans so closely to the pursuit of worldly welfare, it is probable that they would display more reserve and more experience whenever their attention is turned to things immaterial, and that they would check themselves without difficulty. But they feel imprisoned within bounds, which they will apparently never be allowed to pass. As soon as they have passed these bounds, their minds know not where to fix themselves, and they often rush unrestrained beyond the range of common sense.

CHAPTER XIII.

WHY THE AMERICANS ARE SO RESTLESS IN THE MIDST OF THEIR PROSPERITY.

IN certain remote corners of the Old World, you may still sometimes stumble upon a small district which seems to have been forgotten amidst the general tumult, and to have remained stationary whilst everything around it was in motion.   The inhabitants are, for the most part, extremely ignorant and poor ; they take no part in the business of the country, and are frequently oppressed by the government ; yet their countenances are generally placid, and their spirits light.

In America, I saw the freest and most enlightened men placed in the happiest circumstances which the world affords : it seemed to me as if a cloud habitually hung upon their brow, and I thought them serious, and almost sad, even in their pleasures.

The chief reason of this contrast is, that the former do not think of the ills they endure, while the latter are forever brooding over advantages they do not possess.   It is strange to see with what feverish ardor the Americans pursue their own welfare ; and to watch the vague dread that constantly torments them, lest they should not have chosen the shortest path which may lead to it.

A native of the United States clings to this world's goods as if he were certain never to die ; and he is so hasty in grasping at all within his reach, that one would suppose he was constantly afraid of not living long enough to enjoy them.   He clutches everything, he holds nothing fast, but soon loosens his grasp to pursue fresh gratifications.

In the United States, a man builds a house in which to spend his old age, and he sells it before the roof is on ; he plants a garden, and lets it just as the trees are coming into bearing ; he brings a field into tillage, and leaves other men to gather the crops ; he embraces a profession, and gives it up ; he settles in a place, which he soon afterwards leaves, to carry his changeable longings elsewhere. If his private affairs leave him any leisure, he instantly plunges into the vortex of politics ; and if, at the end of a year of unremitting labor, he finds he has a few days' vacation, his eager curiosity whirls him over the vast extent of the United States, and he will travel fifteen hundred miles in a few days, to shake off his happiness. Death at length overtakes him, but it is before he is weary of his bootless chase of that complete felicity which forever escapes him.

At first sight, there is something surprising in this strange unrest of so many happy men, restless in the midst of abundance. The spectacle itself is, however, as old as the world ; the novelty is, to see a whole people furnish an exemplification of it.

Their taste for physical gratifications must be regarded as the original source of that secret inquietude which the actions of the Americans betray, and of that inconstancy of which they daily afford fresh examples. He who has set his heart exclusively upon the pursuit of worldly welfare is always in a hurry, for he has but a limited time at his disposal to reach, to grasp, and to enjoy it. The recollection of the shortness of life is a constant spur to him. Besides the good things which he possesses, he every instant fancies a thousand others, which death will prevent him from trying if he does not try them soon. This thought fills him with anxiety, fear, and regret, and keeps his mind in ceaseless trepidation, which leads him perpetually to change his plans and his abode.

If, in addition to the taste for physical well-being, a social condition be superadded, in which neither laws nor customs retain any person in his place, there is a great additional stimulant to this restlessness of temper. Men will then be seen continually to change their track, for fear of missing the shortest cut to happiness.

It may readily be conceived, that, if men, passionately bent upon physical gratifications, desire eagerly, they are also easily discouraged : as their ultimate object is to enjoy, the means to reach that object must be prompt and easy, or the trouble of acquiring the gratification would be greater than the gratification itself. Their prevailing frame of mind, then, is at once ardent and relaxed, violent and enervated. Death is often less dreaded by them than perseverance in continuous efforts to one end.

The equality of conditions leads by a still straighter road to several of the effects which I have here described. When all the privileges of birth and fortune are abolished, when all professions are accessible to all, and a man's own energies may place him at the top of any one of them, an easy and unbounded career seems open to his ambition, and he will readily persuade himself that he is born to no vulgar destinies. But this is an erroneous notion, which is corrected by daily experience. The same equality which allows every citizen to conceive these lofty hopes, renders all the citizens less able to realize them : it circumscribes their powers on every side, whilst it gives freer scope to their desires. Not only are they themselves powerless, but they are met at every step by immense obstacles, which they did not at first perceive. They have swept away the privileges of some of their fellow-creatures which stood in their way, but they have opened the door to universal competition ; the barrier has changed its shape rather than its position. When men are nearly alike, and all follow the same track, it is very difficult for any one individual to

walk quick and cleave a way through the dense throng
which surrounds and presses him.   This constant strife
between the inclinations springing from the equality of
condition and the means it supplies to satisfy them, har-
asses and wearies the mind.

It is possible to conceive men arrived at a degree of freedom which should completely content them ; they would
then enjoy their independence without anxiety and without impatience.   But men will never establish any equality
with which they can be contented.   Whatever efforts a
people may make, they will never succeed in reducing all
the conditions of society to a perfect level ; and even if
they unhappily attained that absolute and complete equality
of position, the inequality of minds would still remain,
which, coming directly from the hand of God, will forever
escape the laws of man.   However democratic, then, the
social state and the political constitution of a people may
be, it is certain that every member of the community will
always find out several points about him which overlook
his own position ; and we may foresee that his looks will
be doggedly fixed in that direction.   When inequality of
conditions is the common law of society, the most marked
inequalities do not strike the eye : when everything is
nearly on the same level, the slightest are marked enough
to hurt it.   Hence, the desire of equality always becomes
more insatiable in proportion as equality is more complete.

Amongst democratic nations, men easily attain a certain
equality of condition ; but they can never attain as much as
they desire.   It perpetually retires from before them, yet
without hiding itself from their sight, and in retiring draws
them on.   At every moment they think they are about
to grasp it ; it escapes at every moment from their hold.
They are near enough to see its charms, but too far off to
enjoy them ; and before they have fully tasted its delights,
they die.

To these causes must be attributed that strange melancholy which oftentimes haunts the inhabitants of democratic countries in the midst of their abundance, and that disgust at life which sometimes seizes upon them in the midst of calm and easy circumstances. Complaints are made in France that the number of suicides increases; in America suicide is rare, but insanity is said to be more common there than anywhere else. These are all different symptoms of the same disease. The Americans do not put an end to their lives, however disquieted they may be, because their religion forbids it; and amongst them materialism may be said hardly to exist, notwithstanding the general passion for physical gratification. The will resists, but reason frequently gives way.

In democratic times, enjoyments are more intense than in the ages of aristocracy, and the number of those who partake in them is vastly larger: but, on the other hand, it must be admitted that man's hopes and desires are oftener blasted, the soul is more stricken and perturbed, and care itself more keen.

CHAPTER XIV.

HOW THE TASTE FOR PHYSICAL GRATIFICATIONS IS UNITED
IN AMERICA TO LOVE OF FREEDOM AND ATTENTION TO
PUBLIC AFFAIRS.

WHEN a democratic state turns to absolute monarchy, the activity which was before directed to
public and to private affairs is all at once centred upon the
latter: the immediate consequence is, for some time, great
physical prosperity; but this impulse soon slackens, and the
amount of productive industry is checked. I know not if
a single trading or manufacturing people can be cited, from
the Tyrians down to the Florentines and the English, who
were not a free people also. There is therefore a close
bond and necessary relation between these two elements, —
freedom and productive industry.

This proposition is generally true of all nations, but especially of democratic nations. I have already shown that
men who live in ages of equality continually require to form
associations in order to procure the things they covet; and,
on the other hand, I have shown how great political freedom improves and diffuses the art of association. Freedom in these ages is therefore especially favorable to the
production of wealth; nor is it difficult to perceive, that
despotism is especially adverse to the same result.

The nature of despotic power in democratic ages is not
to be fierce or cruel, but minute and meddling. Despotism
of this kind, though it does not trample on humanity, is
directly opposed to the genius of commerce and the pursuits of industry.

Thus, the men of democratic times require to be free in order more readily to procure those physical enjoyments for which they are always longing. It sometimes happens, however, that the excessive taste they conceive for these same enjoyments makes them surrender to the first master who appears. The passion for worldly welfare then defeats itself, and, without their perceiving it, throws the object of their desires to a greater distance.

There is, indeed, a most dangerous passage in the history of a democratic people. When the taste for physical gratifications amongst them has grown more rapidly than their education and their experience of free institutions, the time will come when men are carried away, and lose all self-restraint, at the sight of the new possessions they are about to obtain. In their intense and exclusive anxiety to make a fortune, they lose sight of the close connection which exists between the private fortune of each and the prosperity of all. It is not necessary to do violence to such a people in order to strip them of the rights they enjoy; they themselves willingly loosen their hold. The discharge of political duties appears to them to be a troublesome impediment, which diverts them from their occupations and business. If they be required to elect representatives, to support the government by personal service, to meet on public business, they think they have no time, — they cannot waste their precious hours in useless engagements: such idle amusements are unsuited to serious men, who are engaged with the more important interests of life. These people think they are following the principle of self-interest, but the idea they entertain of that principle is a very rude one; and the better to look after what they call their own business, they neglect their chief business, which is to remain their own masters.

As the citizens who labor do not care to attend to public affairs, and as the class which might devote its leisure to these duties has ceased to exist, the place of the government is, as it were, unfilled. If, at that critical moment, some able and ambitious man grasps the supreme power, he will find the road to every kind of usurpation open before him. If he does but attend for some time to the material prosperity of the country, no more will be demanded of him. Above all, he must insure public tranquillity: men who are possessed by the passion for physical gratification generally find out that the turmoil of freedom disturbs their welfare, before they discover how freedom itself serves to promote it. If the slightest rumor of public commotion intrudes into the petty pleasures of private life, they are aroused and alarmed by it. The fear of anarchy perpetually haunts them, and they are always ready to fling away their freedom at the first disturbance.

I readily admit that public tranquillity is a great good; but at the same time, I cannot forget that all nations have been enslaved by being kept in good order. Certainly, it is not to be inferred that nations ought to despise public tranquillity; but that state ought not to content them. A nation which asks nothing of its government but the maintenance of order is already a slave at heart, — the slave of its own well-being, awaiting but the hand that will bind it.

By such a nation, the despotism of faction is not less to be dreaded than the despotism of an individual. When the bulk of the community are engrossed by private concerns, the smallest parties need not despair of getting the upper hand in public affairs. At such times, it is not rare to see upon the great stage of the world, as we see at our theatres, a multitude represented by a few players, who alone speak in the name of an absent or inattentive crowd: they alone are in action, whilst all others are stationary; they regulate everything by their own caprice; they change the laws, and tyrannize at will over the manners of the country; and then men wonder to see into how small a number of weak and worthless hands a great people may fall.

Hitherto, the Americans have fortunately escaped all the perils which I have just pointed out; and in this respect they are really deserving of admiration. Perhaps there is no country in the world where fewer ·idle men are to be met with than in America, or where all who work are more eager to promote their own welfare. But if the passion of the Americans for physical gratifications is vehement, at least it is not indiscriminate; and reason, though unable to restrain it, still directs its course.

An American attends to his private concerns as if he were alone in the world, and the next minute he gives himself up to the common weal as if he had forgotten them. At one time, he seems animated by the most selfish cupidity; at another, by the most lively patriotism. The human heart cannot be thus divided. The inhabitants of the United States alternately display so strong and so similar a passion for their own welfare and for their freedom, that it may be supposed that these passions are united and mingled in some part of their character. And indeed, the Americans believe their freedom to be the best instrument and surest safeguard of their welfare: they are attached to the one by the other. They by no means think that they are not called upon to take a part in public affairs; they believe, on the contrary, that their chief business is to secure for themselves a government which will allow them to acquire the things they covet, and which will not debar them from the peaceful enjoyment of those possessions which they have already acquired.

CHAPTER XV.

HOW RELIGIOUS BELIEF SOMETIMES TURNS THE THOUGHTS OF THE AMERICANS TO IMMATERIAL PLEASURES.

IN the United States, on the seventh day of every week, the trading and working life of the nation seems suspended; all noises cease; a deep tranquillity, say rather the solemn calm of meditation, succeeds the turmoil of the week, and the soul resumes possession and contemplation of itself. Upon this day, the marts of traffic are deserted; every member of the community, accompanied by his children, goes to church, where he listens to strange language, which would seem unsuited to his ear. He is told of the countless evils caused by pride and covetousness; he is reminded of the necessity of checking his desires, of the finer pleasures which belong to virtue alone, and of the true happiness which attends it. On his return home, he does not turn to the ledgers of his business, but he opens the book of Holy Scripture; there he meets with sublime and affecting descriptions of the greatness and goodness of the Creator, of the infinite magnificence of the handiwork of God, and of the lofty destinies of man, his duties, and his immortal privileges.

Thus it is, that the American at times steals an hour from himself; and, laying aside for a while the petty passions which agitate his life, and the ephemeral interests which engross it, he strays at once into an ideal world, where all is great, eternal, and pure.

I have endeavored to point out, in another part of this work, the causes to which the maintenance of the political institutions of the Americans is attributable, and religion appeared to be one of the most prominent amongst them. I am now treating of the Americans in an individual capacity, and I again observe, that religion is not less useful to each citizen than to the whole state. The Americans show, by their practice, that they feel the high necessity of imparting morality to democratic communities by means of religion. What they think of themselves in this respect is a truth of which every democratic nation ought to be thoroughly persuaded.

I do not doubt that the social and political constitution of a people predisposes them to adopt certain doctrines and tastes, which afterwards flourish without difficulty amongst them; whilst the same causes may divert them from certain other opinions and propensities, without any voluntary effort, and, as it were, without any distinct consciousness, on their part. The whole art of the legislator is correctly to discern beforehand these natural inclinations of communities of men, in order to know whether they should be fostered, or whether it may not be necessary to check them. For the duties incumbent on the legislator differ at different times; only the goal towards which the human race ought ever to be tending is stationary: the means of reaching it are perpetually varied.

If I had been born in an aristocratic age, in the midst of a nation where the hereditary wealth of some, and the irremediable penury of others, equally diverted men from the idea of bettering their condition, and held the soul, as it were, in a state of torpor, fixed on the contemplation of another world, I should then wish that it were possible for me to rouse that people to a sense of their wants; I should seek to discover more rapid and easy means for satisfying the fresh desires which I might have awakened; and, directing the most strenuous efforts of the citizens to physical pursuits, I should endeavor to stimulate them to promote their own well-being. If it happened that some men were thus immoderately incited to the pursuit of riches, and caused to display an excessive liking for physical gratifications, I should not be alarmed; these peculiar cases would soon disappear in the general aspect of the whole community.

The attention of the legislators of democracies is called to other cares. Give democratic nations education and freedom, and leave them alone. They will soon learn to draw from this world all the benefits which it can afford; they will improve each of the useful arts, and will day by day render life more comfortable, more convenient, and more easy. Their social condition naturally urges them in this direction; I do not fear that they will slacken their course.

But whilst man takes delight in this honest and lawful pursuit of his own well-being, it is to be apprehended that he may, in the end, lose the use of his sublimest faculties; and that, whilst he is busied in improving all around him, he may at length degrade himself. Here, and here only, does the peril lie. It should therefore be the unceasing object of the legislators of democracies, and of all the virtuous and enlightened men who live there, to raise the souls of their fellow-citizens, and keep them lifted up towards Heaven. It is necessary that all who feel an interest in the future destinies of democratic society should unite, and that all should make joint and continual efforts to diffuse the love of the infinite, lofty aspirations, and a love of pleasures not of earth. If, amongst the opinions of a democratic people, any of those pernicious theories exist which tend to inculcate that all perishes with the body, let men by whom such theories are professed be marked as the natural foes of the whole people.

The materialists are offensive to me in many respects; their doctrines I hold to be pernicious, and I am disgusted at their arrogance. If their system could be of any utility to man, it would seem to be by giving him a modest opinion of himself : but these reasoners show that it is not so ; and when they think they have said enough to prove that they are brutes, they appear as proud as if they had demonstrated that they are gods.

Materialism is, amongst all nations, a dangerous disease of the human mind ; but it is more especially to be dreaded amongst a democratic people, because it readily amalgamates with that vice which is most familiar to the heart under such circumstances. Democracy encourages a taste for physical gratification : this taste, if it become excessive, soon disposes men to believe that all is matter only ; and materialism, in its turn, hurries them on with mad impatience to these same delights : such is the fatal circle within which democratic nations are driven round. It were well that they should see the danger, and hold back.

Most religions are only general, simple, and practical means of teaching men the doctrine of the immortality of the soul. That is the greatest benefit which a democratic people derives from its belief, and hence belief is more necessary to such a people than to all others. When, therefore, any religion has struck its roots deep into a democracy, beware that you do not disturb it ; but rather watch it carefully, as the most precious bequest of aristocratic ages. Seek not to supersede the old religious opinions of men by new ones, lest in the passage from one faith to another, the soul being left for a while stripped of all belief the love of physical gratifications should grow upon it, and fill it wholly.

The doctrine of metempsychosis is assuredly not more rational than that of materialism ; nevertheless, if it were absolutely necessary that a democracy should choose one of the two, I should not hesitate to decide that the community would run less risk of being brutalized by believing that the soul of man will pass into the carcass of a hog, than by believing that the soul of man is nothing at all.

The belief in a supersensual and immortal principle, united for a time to matter, is so indispensable to man's greatness, that its effects are striking, even when it is not united to the doctrine of future reward and punishment, or even when it teaches no more than that, after death, the divine principle contained in man is absorbed in the Deity, or transferred to animate the frame of some other creature. Men holding so imperfect a belief will still consider the body as the secondary and inferior portion of their nature, and will despise it even whilst they yield to its influence; whereas they have a natural esteem and secret admiration for the immaterial part of man, even though they sometimes refuse to submit to its authority. That is enough to give a lofty cast to their opinions and their tastes, and to bid them tend, with no interested motive, and as it were by impulse, to pure feelings and elevated thoughts.

It is not certain that Socrates and his followers had any fixed opinions as to what would befall man hereafter; but the sole point of belief which they did firmly maintain — that the soul has nothing in common with the body, and survives it — was enough to give the Platonic philosophy that sublime aspiration by which it is distinguished.

It is clear, from the works of Plato, that many philosophical writers, his predecessors or contemporaries, professed materialism. These writers have not reached us, or have reached us in mere fragments. The same thing has happened in almost all ages; the greater part of the most famous minds in literature adhere to the doctrines of a spiritual philosophy. The instinct and the taste of the human race maintain those doctrines; they save them oftentimes in spite of men themselves, and raise the names of their defenders above the tide of time. It must not, then, be supposed that, at any period, or under any political condition, the passion for physical gratifications, and the opinions which are superinduced by that passion, can ever content a whole people. The heart of man is of a larger

mould ; it can at once comprise a taste for the possessions
of earth, and the love of those of Heaven : at times, it may
seem to cling devotedly to the one, but it will never be long
without thinking of the other.

If it be easy to see that it is more particularly important
in democratic ages that spiritual opinions should prevail, it
is not easy to say by what means those who govern democratic nations may make them predominate. I am no believer in the prosperity, any more than in the durability,
of official philosophies ; and as to state religions, I have
always held that, if they be sometimes of momentary service to the interests of political power, they always, sooner
or later, become fatal to the Church. Nor do I agree with
those who think that, to raise religion in the eyes of the
people, and to make them do honor to her spiritual doctrines, it is desirable indirectly to give her ministers a political influence which the laws deny them. I am so much
alive to the almost inevitable dangers which beset religious
belief whenever the clergy take part in public affairs, and
I am so convinced that Christianity must be maintained at
any cost in the bosom of modern democracies, that I had
rather shut up the priesthood within the sanctuary, than
allow them to step beyond it.

What means then remain in the hands of constituted authorities to bring men back to spiritual opinions, or to hold
them fast to the religion by which those opinions are suggested ?

My answer will do me harm in the eyes of politicians.
I believe that the sole effectual means which governments
can employ, in order to have the doctrine of the immortality of the soul duly respected, is ever to act as if they
believed in it themselves ; and I think that it is only by
scrupulous conformity to religious morality in great affairs,
that they can hope to teach the community at large to
know, to love, and to observe it in the lesser concerns of life.

CHAPTER XVI.

HOW EXCESSIVE CARE FOR WORLDLY WELFARE MAY IMPAIR THAT WELFARE.

THERE is a closer tie than is commonly supposed between the improvement of the soul and the amelioration of what belongs to the body. Man may leave these two things apart, and consider each of them alternately; but he cannot sever them entirely without at last losing sight of both.

The beasts have the same senses as ourselves, and very nearly the same appetites. We have no sensual passions which are not common to our race and theirs, and which are not to be found, at least in the germ, in a dog as well as in a man. Whence is it, then, that the animals can only provide for their first and lowest wants, whereas we can infinitely vary and endlessly increase our enjoyments?

We are superior to the beasts in this, that we use our souls to find out those material benefits to which they are only led by instinct. In man, the angel teaches the brute the art of satisfying its desires. It is because man is capable of rising above the things of the body, and of contemning life itself, of which the beasts have not the least notion, that he can multiply these same goods of the body to a degree which the inferior races cannot conceive of.

Whatever elevates, enlarges, and expands the soul, renders it more capable of succeeding in those very undertakings which concern it not. Whatever, on the other hand, enervates or lowers it, weakens it for all purposes, the chief as well as the least, and threatens to render it almost equally impotent for both. Hence the soul must remain great and strong, though it were only to devote its strength and greatness from time to time to the service of the body. If men were ever to content themselves with material objects, it is probable that they would lose by degrees the art of producing them; and they would enjoy them in the end, like the brutes, without discernment and without improvement.

CHAPTER XVII.

HOW, WHEN CONDITIONS ARE EQUAL AND SCEPTICISM IS RIFE,
IT IS IMPORTANT TO DIRECT HUMAN ACTIONS TO DISTANT
OBJECTS.

IN ages of faith, the final aim of life is placed beyond life.
The men of those ages, therefore, naturally and almost
involuntarily, accustom themselves to fix their gaze for
many years on some immovable object, towards which
they are constantly tending; and they learn by insensible
degrees to repress a multitude of petty passing desires, in
order to be the better able to content that great and lasting
desire which possesses them. When these same men engage in the affairs of this world, the same habits may be
traced in their conduct. They are apt to set up some
general and certain aim and end to their actions here below, towards which all their efforts are directed: they do
not turn from day to day to chase some novel object of
desire, but they have settled designs which they are never
weary of pursuing.

This explains why religious nations have so often achieved
such lasting results: for whilst they were thinking only of
the other world, they had found out the great secret of success in this. Religions give men a general habit of conducting themselves with a view to futurity: in this respect,
they are not less useful to happiness in this life than to
felicity hereafter; and this is one of their chief political
characteristics.

But in proportion as the light of faith grows dim, the
range of man's sight is circumscribed, as if the end and

aim of human actions appeared every day to be more within his reach. When men have once allowed themselves
to think no more of what is to befall them after life, they
readily lapse into that complete and brutal indifference to
futurity which is but too conformable to some propensities
of mankind. As soon as they have lost the habit of placing
their chief hopes upon remote events, they naturally seek
to gratify without delay their smallest desires; and no
sooner do they despair of living forever, than they are disposed to act as if they were to exist but for a single day.
In sceptical ages, it is always therefore to be feared, that
men may perpetually give way to their daily casual desires; and that, wholly renouncing whatever cannot be
acquired without protracted effort, they may establish nothing great, permanent, and calm.

If the social condition of a people, under these circumstances, becomes democratic, the danger which I here point
out is thereby increased. When every one is constantly
striving to change his position; when an immense field for
competition is thrown open to all; when wealth is amassed
or dissipated in the shortest possible space of time amidst
the turmoil of democracy,— visions of sudden and easy
fortunes, of great possessions easily won and lost, of chance
under all its forms, haunt the mind. The instability of
society itself fosters the natural instability of man's desires.
In the midst of these perpetual fluctuations of his lot, the
present grows upon his mind, until it conceals futurity from
his sight, and his looks go no further than the morrow.

In those countries in which, unhappily, irreligion and democracy coexist, philosophers and those in power ought to
be always striving to place the objects of human actions far
beyond man's immediate range. Adapting himself to the
spirit of his country and his age, the moralist must learn
to vindicate his principles in that position. He must constantly endeavor to show his contemporaries, that, even in

the midst of the perpetual commotion around them, it is easier than they think to conceive and to execute protracted undertakings. He must teach them that, although the aspect of mankind may have changed, the methods by which men may provide for their prosperity in this world are still the same; and that, amongst democratic nations, as well as elsewhere, it is only by resisting a thousand petty selfish passions of the hour, that the general and unquenchable passion for happiness can be satisfied.

The task of those in power is not less clearly marked out. At all times it is important that those who govern nations should act with a view to the future: but this is even more necessary in democratic and sceptical ages than in any others. By acting thus, the leading men of democracies not only make public affairs prosperous, but they also teach private individuals, by their example, the art of managing their private concerns.

Above all, they must strive as much as possible to banish chance from the sphere of politics. The sudden and undeserved promotion of a courtier produces only a transient impression in an aristocratic country, because the aggregate institutions and opinions of the nation habitually compel men to advance slowly in tracks which they cannot get out of. But nothing is more pernicious than similar instances of favor exhibited to a democratic people: they give the last impulse to the public mind in a direction where everything hurries it onwards. At times of scepticism and equality more especially, the favor of the people or of the prince, which chance may confer or chance withhold, ought never to stand in lieu of attainments or services. It is desirable that every advancement should there appear to be the result of some effort; so that no greatness should be of too easy acquirement, and that ambition should be obliged to fix its gaze long upon an object before it is gratified.

Governments must apply themselves to restore to men

that love of the future with which religion and the state of society no longer inspire them ; and, without saying so, they must practically teach the community day by day that wealth, fame, and power are the rewards of labor ; that great success stands at the utmost range of long desires, and that there is nothing lasting but what is obtained by toil.

When men have accustomed themselves to foresee from afar what is likely to befall them in the world, and to feed upon hopes, they can hardly confine their minds within the precise limits of life, and they are ready to break the boundary, and cast their looks beyond. I do not doubt that, by training the members of a community to think of their future condition in this world, they would be gradually and unconsciously brought nearer to religious convictions. Thus, the means which allow men, up to a certain point, to go without religion, are perhaps, after all, the only means we still possess for bringing mankind back, by a long and roundabout path, to a state of faith.

CHAPTER XVIII.

WHY AMONGST THE AMERICANS ALL HONEST CALLINGS ARE CONSIDERED HONORABLE.

AMONGST a democratic people, where there is no hereditary wealth, every man works to earn a living, or has worked, or is born of parents who have worked. The notion of labor is therefore presented to the mind, on every side, as the necessary, natural, and honest condition of human existence. Not only is labor not dishonorable amongst such a people, but it is held in honor : the prejudice is not against it, but in its favor. In the United States, a wealthy man thinks that he owes it to public opinion to devote his leisure to some kind of industrial or commercial pursuit, or to public business. He would think himself in bad repute if he employed his life solely in living. It is for the purpose of escaping this obligation to work, that so many rich Americans come to Europe, where they find some scattered remains of aristocratic society, amongst whom idleness is still held in honor.

Equality of conditions not only ennobles the notion of labor, but it raises the notion of labor as a source of profit.

In aristocracies, it is not exactly labor that is despised, but labor with a view to profit. Labor is honorable in itself, when it is undertaken at the bidding of ambition or virtue. Yet, in aristocratic society, it constantly happens that he who works for honor is not insensible to the attractions of profit. But these two desires only intermingle in the depths of his soul : he carefully hides from every eye the point at which they join; he would fain conceal it from himself. In aristocratic countries there are few public officers who do not affect to serve their country without interested motives. Their salary is an incident of which they think but little, and of which they always affect not to think at all. Thus the notion of profit is kept distinct from that of labor; however they may be united in point of fact, they are not thought of together.

In democratic communities these two notions are, on the contrary, always palpably united. As the desire of well-being is universal, as fortunes are slender or fluctuating, as every one wants either to increase his own resources or to provide fresh ones for his progeny, men clearly see that it is profit which, if not wholly, at least partially, leads them to work. Even those who are principally actuated by the love of fame are necessarily made familiar with the thought that they are not exclusively actuated by that motive; and they discover that the desire of getting a living is mingled in their minds with the desire of making life illustrious.

As soon as, on the one hand, labor is held by the whole community to be an honorable necessity of man's condition, — and, on the other, as soon as labor is always ostensibly performed, wholly or in part, for the purpose of earning remuneration, — the immense interval which separated different callings in aristocratic societies disappears. If all are not alike, all at least have one feature in common. No profession exists in which men do not work for money; and the remuneration which is common to them all gives them all an air of resemblance.

This serves to explain the opinions which the Americans entertain with respect to different callings. In America, no one is degraded because he works, for every one about him works also; nor is any one humiliated by the notion of receiving pay, for the President of the United States also works for pay. He is paid for commanding, other men for obeying orders. In the United States, professions are more or less laborious, more or less profitable; but they are never either high or low: every honest calling is honorable.

CHAPTER XIX.

WHAT CAUSES ALMOST ALL AMERICANS TO FOLLOW INDUS-
TRIAL CALLINGS.

AGRICULTURE is, perhaps, of all the useful arts, that which improves most slowly amongst democratic nations. Frequently, indeed, it would seem to be stationary, because other arts are making rapid strides towards perfection. On the other hand, almost all the tastes and habits which the equality of condition produces naturally lead men to commercial and industrial occupations.

Suppose an active, enlightened, and free man, enjoying a competency, but full of desires : he is too poor to live in idleness ; he is rich enough to feel himself protected from the immediate fear of want, and he thinks how he can better his condition. This man has conceived a taste for physical gratifications, which thousands of his fellow-men indulge in around him ; he has himself begun to enjoy these pleasures, and he is eager to increase his means of satisfying these tastes more completely. But life is slipping away, time is urgent ; — to what is he to turn ? The cultivation of the ground promises an almost certain result to his exertions, but a slow one ; men are not enriched by it without patience and toil. Agriculture is therefore only suited to those who have already large superfluous wealth, or to those whose penury bids them only seek a bare subsistence. The choice of such a man as we have supposed is soon made ; he sells his plot of ground, leaves his dwelling, and embarks in some hazardous but lucrative calling.

Democratic communities abound in men of this kind ;

and, in proportion as the equality of conditions becomes greater, their multitude increases. Thus, democracy not only swells the number of working-men, but it leads men to prefer one kind of labor to another; and, whilst it diverts them from agriculture, it encourages their taste for commerce and manufactures.*

This spirit may be observed even amongst the richest members of the community. In democratic countries, however opulent a man is supposed to be, he is almost always discontented with his fortune, because he finds that he is less rich than his father was, and he fears that his sons will be less rich than himself. Most rich men in democracies are therefore constantly haunted by the desire of obtaining wealth, and they naturally turn their attention to trade and manufactures, which appear to offer the readiest and most efficient means of success. In this respect, they share the instincts of the poor without feeling the same necessities; say, rather, they feel the most imperious of all necessities, that of not sinking in the world.

In aristocracies, the rich are at the same time the governing power. The attention which they unceasingly devote to important public affairs diverts them from the lesser cares

---

* It has often been remarked, that manufacturers and mercantile men are inordinately addicted to physical gratifications, and this has been attributed to commerce and manufactures; but that is, I apprehend, to take the effect for the cause. The taste for physical gratifications is not imparted to men by commerce or manufactures, but it is rather this taste which leads men to embark in commerce and manufactures, as a means by which they hope to satisfy themselves more promptly and more completely. If commerce and manufactures increase the desire of well-being, it is because every passion gathers strength in proportion as it is cultivated, and is increased by all the efforts made to satiate it. All the causes which make the love of worldly welfare predominate in the heart of man, are favorable to the growth of commerce and manufactures. Equality of conditions is one of those causes; it encourages trade, not directly, by giving men a taste for business, but indirectly, by strengthening and expanding in their minds a taste for prosperity.

which trade and manufactures demand.   But if an individual happens to turn his attention to business, the will of the body to which he belongs will immediately prevent him from pursuing it; for, however men may declaim against the rule of numbers, they cannot wholly escape it; and even amongst those aristocratic bodies which most obstinately refuse to acknowledge the rights of the national majority, a private majority is formed which governs the rest.*

In democratic countries, where money does not lead those who possess it to political power, but often removes

---

* Some aristocracies, however, have devoted themselves eagerly to commerce, and have cultivated manufactures with success.   The history of the world furnishes several conspicuous examples.   But, generally speaking, the aristocratic principle is not favorable to the growth of trade and manufactures.   Moneyed aristocracies are the only exception to the rule.   Amongst such aristocracies, there are hardly any desires which do not require wealth to satisfy them; the love of riches becomes, so to speak, the high road of human passions, which is crossed by or connected with all lesser tracks. The love of money and the thirst for that distinction which attaches to power, are then so closely intermixed in the same souls, that it becomes difficult to discover whether men grow covetous from ambition, or whether they are ambitious from covetousness.   This is the case in England, where men seek to get rich in order to arrive at distinction, and seek distinctions as a manifestation of their wealth.   The mind is then seized by both ends, and hurried into trade and manufactures, which are the shortest roads that lead to opulence.

This, however, strikes me as an exceptional and transitory circumstance. When wealth is become the only symbol of aristocracy, it is very difficult for the wealthy to maintain sole possession of political power, to the exclusion of all other men.   The aristocracy of birth and pure democracy are the two extremes of the social and political state of nations: between them moneyed aristocracy finds its place.   The latter approximates to the aristocracy of birth by conferring great privileges on a small number of persons; it so far belongs to the democratic element, that these privileges may be successively acquired by all.   It frequently forms a natural transition between these two conditions of society, and it is difficult to say whether it closes the reign of aristocratic institutions, or whether it already opens the new era of democracy.

them from it, the rich do not know how to spend their leisure. They are driven into active life by the inquietude and the greatness of their desires, by the extent of their resources, and by the taste for what is extraordinary, which is almost always felt by those who rise, by whatsoever means, above the crowd. Trade is the only road open to them. In democracies, nothing is more great or more brilliant than commerce: it attracts the attention of the public, and fills the imagination of the multitude; all energetic passions are directed towards it. Neither their own prejudices nor those of anybody else can prevent the rich from devoting themselves to it. The wealthy members of democracies never form a body which has manners and regulations of its own; the opinions peculiar to their class do not restrain them, and the common opinions of their country urge them on. Moreover, as all the large fortunes which are found in a democratic community are of commercial growth, many generations must succeed each other before their possessors can have entirely laid aside their habits of business.

Circumscribed within the narrow space which politics leave them, rich men in democracies eagerly embark in commercial enterprise: there they can extend and employ their natural advantages; and indeed, it is even by the boldness and the magnitude of their industrial speculations that we may measure the slight esteem in which productive industry would have been held by them, if they had been born amidst an aristocracy.

A similar observation is likewise applicable to all men living in democracies, whether they be poor or rich. Those who live in the midst of democratic fluctuations have always before their eyes the image of chance; and they end by liking all undertakings in which chance plays a part. They are therefore all led to engage in commerce not only for the sake of the profit it holds out to them, but for the love of the constant excitement occasioned by that pursuit.

The United States of America have only been emancipated for half a century from the state of colonial dependence in which they stood to Great Britain: the number of large fortunes there is small, and capital is still scarce. Yet no people in the world have made such rapid progress in trade and manufactures as the Americans: they constitute at the present day the second maritime nation in the world; and although their manufactures have to struggle with almost insurmountable natural impediments, they are not prevented from making great and daily advances.

In the United States, the greatest undertakings and speculations are executed without difficulty, because the whole population are engaged in productive industry, and because the poorest as well as the most opulent members of the commonwealth are ready to combine their efforts for these purposes. The consequence is, that a stranger is constantly amazed by the immense public works executed by a nation which contains, so to speak, no rich men. The Americans arrived but as yesterday on the territory which they inhabit, and they have already changed the whole order of nature for their own advantage. They have joined the Hudson to the Mississippi, and made the Atlantic Ocean communicate with the Gulf of Mexico, across a continent of more than five hundred leagues in extent which separates the two seas. The longest railroads which have been constructed, up to the present time, are in America.

But what most astonishes me in the United States is not so much the marvellous grandeur of some undertakings, as the innumerable multitude of small ones. Almost all the farmers of the United States combine some trade with agriculture; most of them make agriculture itself a trade. It seldom happens that an American farmer settles for good upon the land which he occupies : especially in the districts of the Far West, he brings land into tillage in order to sell it again, and not to farm it : he builds a farm-house on the speculation, that, as the state of the country will soon be changed by the increase of population, a good price may be obtained for it.

Every year, a swarm of people from the North arrive in the Southern States, and settle in the parts where the cotton-plant and the sugar-cane grow. These men cultivate the soil in order to make it produce in a few years enough to enrich them ; and they already look forward to the time when they may return home to enjoy the competency thus acquired. Thus the Americans carry their business-like qualities into agriculture ; and their trading passions are displayed in that, as in their other pursuits.

The Americans make immense progress in productive industry, because they all devote themselves to it at once ; and for this same reason, they are exposed to unexpected and formidable embarrassments. As they are all engaged in commerce, their commercial affairs are affected by such various and complex causes, that it is impossible to foresee what difficulties may arise. As they are all more or less engaged in productive industry, at the least shock given to business, all private fortunes are put in jeopardy at the same time, and the state is shaken. I believe that the return of these commercial panics is an endemic disease of the democratic nations of our age. It may be rendered less dangerous, but it cannot be cured ; because it does not originate in accidental circumstances, but in the temperament of these nations.

CHAPTER XX.

HOW AN ARISTOCRACY MAY BE CREATED BY MANUFACTURES.

I HAVE shown how democracy favors the growth of manufactures, and increases without limit the numbers of the manufacturing classes: we shall now see by what side-road manufacturers may possibly, in their turn, bring men back to aristocracy.

It is acknowledged, that, when a workman is engaged every day upon the same details, the whole commodity is produced with greater ease, promptitude, and economy. It is likewise acknowledged, that the cost of production of manufactured goods is diminished by the extent of the establishment in which they are made, and by the amount of capital employed or of credit. These truths had long been imperfectly discerned, but in our time they have been demonstrated. They have been already applied to many very important kinds of manufactures, and the humblest will gradually be governed by them. I know of nothing in politics which deserves to fix the attention of the legislator more closely than these two new axioms of the science of manufactures.

When a workman is unceasingly and exclusively engaged in the fabrication of one thing, he ultimately does his work with singular dexterity; but, at the same time, he loses the general faculty of applying his mind to the direction of the work. He every day becomes more adroit and less industrious; so that it may be said of him, that, in proportion as the workman improves, the man is degraded. What can be expected of a man who has spent twenty years of his life in making heads for pins? and to what can that mighty human intelligence, which has so often stirred the world, be applied in him, except it be to investigate the best method of making pins' heads? When a workman has spent a considerable portion of his existence in this manner, his thoughts are forever set upon the object of his daily toil; his body has contracted certain fixed habits, which it can never shake off: in a word, he no longer belongs to himself, but to the calling which he has chosen. It is in vain that laws and manners have been at pains to level all the barriers round such a man, and to open to him on every side a thousand different paths to fortune; a theory of manufactures more powerful than manners and laws binds him to a craft, and frequently to a spot, which he cannot leave: it assigns to him a certain place in society, beyond which he cannot go: in the midst of universal movement, it has rendered him stationary.

In proportion as the principle of the division of labor is more extensively applied, the workman becomes more weak, more narrow-minded, and more dependent. The art advances, the artisan recedes. On the other hand, in proportion as it becomes more manifest that the productions of manufactures are by so much the cheaper and better as the manufacture is larger, and the amount of capital employed more considerable, wealthy and educated men come forward to embark in manufactures, which were heretofore abandoned to poor or ignorant handicraftsmen. The magnitude of the efforts required, and the importance of the results to be obtained, attract them. Thus, at the very time at which the science of manufactures lowers the class of workmen, it raises the class of masters.

While the workman concentrates his faculties more and more upon the study of a single detail, the master surveys an extensive whole, and the mind of the latter is enlarged in proportion as that of the former is narrowed. In a short time, the one will require nothing but physical strength without intelligence; the other stands in need of science, and almost of genius, to insure success. This man resembles more and more the administrator of a vast empire, — that man, a brute.

The master and the workman have then here no similarity, and their differences increase every day. They are only connected as the two rings at the extremities of a long chain. Each of them fills the station which is made for him, and which he does not leave : the one is continually, closely, and necessarily dependent upon the other, and seems as much born to obey, as that other is to command. What is this but aristocracy ?

As the conditions of men constituting the nation become more and more equal, the demand for manufactured commodities becomes more general and extensive ; and the cheapness which places these objects within the reach of slender fortunes becomes a great element of success. Hence, there are every day more men of great opulence and education who devote their wealth and knowledge to manufactures; and who seek, by opening large establishments, and by a strict division of labor, to meet the fresh demands which are made on all sides. Thus, in proportion as the mass of the nation turns to democracy, that particular class which is engaged in manufactures becomes more aristocratic. Men grow more alike in the one, more different in the other; and inequality increases in the less numerous class, in the same ratio in which it decreases in the community. Hence it would appear, on searching to the bottom, that aristocracy should naturally spring out of the bosom of democracy.

But this kind of aristocracy by no means resembles those kinds which preceded it. It will be observed at once, that, as it applies exclusively to manufactures and to some manufacturing callings, it is a monstrous exception in the general aspect of society. The small aristocratic societies, which are formed by some manufacturers in the midst of the immense democracy of our age, contain, like the great aristocratic societies of former ages, some men who are very opulent, and a multitude who are wretchedly poor. The poor have few means of escaping from their condition and becoming rich; but the rich are constantly becoming poor, or they give up business when they have realized a fortune. Thus the elements of which the class of the poor is composed are fixed; but the elements of which the class of the rich is composed are not so. To say the truth, though there are rich men, the class of rich men does not exist; for these rich individuals have no feelings or purposes in common, no mutual traditions or mutual hopes; there are individuals, therefore, but no definite class.

Not only are the rich not compactly united amongst themselves, but there is no real bond between them and the poor. Their relative position is not a permanent one; they are constantly drawn together or separated by their interests. The workman is generally dependent on the master, but not on any particular master: these two men meet in the factory, but know not each other elsewhere; and whilst they come into contact on one point, they stand very wide apart on all others. The manufacturer asks nothing of the workman but his labor; the workman expects nothing from him but his wages. The one contracts no obligation to protect, nor the other to defend; and they are not permanently connected either by habit or duty. The aristocracy created by business rarely settles in the midst of the manufacturing population which it directs: the object is not to govern that population, but to use it. An aristocracy thus constituted can have no great hold upon those whom it employs; and, even if it succeed in retaining them at one moment, they escape the next: it knows not how to will, and it cannot act.

The territorial aristocracy of former ages was either bound by law, or thought itself bound by usage, to come to the relief of its serving-men, and to succor their distresses.   But the manufacturing aristocracy of our age first impoverishes and debases the men who serve it, and then abandons them to be supported by the charity of the public.   This is a natural consequence of what has been said before.   Between the workman and the master there are frequent relations, but no real association.

I am of opinion, upon the whole, that the manufacturing aristocracy which is growing up under our eyes is one of the harshest which ever existed in the world; but, at the same time, it is one of the most confined and least dangerous.   Nevertheless, the friends of democracy should keep their eyes anxiously fixed in this direction; for if ever a permanent inequality of conditions and aristocracy again penetrate into the world, it may be predicted that this is the gate by which they will enter.

THIRD BOOK.

INFLUENCE OF DEMOCRACY ON MANNERS PROPERLY
SO CALLED.

CHAPTER I.

HOW MANNERS ARE SOFTENED AS SOCIAL CONDITIONS BECOME MORE EQUAL.

WE perceive that, for several centuries, social conditions have tended to equality, and we discover that
at the same time the manners of society have been softened.
Are these two things merely contemporaneous, or does any
secret link exist between them, so that the one cannot advance without the other ? Several causes may concur to
render the manners of a people less rude ; but, of all these
causes, the most powerful appears to me to be the equality
of conditions. Equality of conditions and greater mildness
in manners are then, in my eyes, not only contemporaneous
occurrences, but correlative facts.

When the fabulists seek to interest us in the actions of
beasts, they invest them with human notions and passions ;
the poets who sing of spirits and angels do the same : there
is no wretchedness so deep, nor any happiness so pure, as
to fill the human mind and touch the heart, unless we are
ourselves held up to our own eyes under other features.

This is strictly applicable to our present subject. When
all men are irrevocably marshalled in an aristocratic community, according to their professions, their property, and
their birth, the members of each class, considering them-

selves as children of the same family, cherish a constant
and lively sympathy towards each other, which can never
be felt in an equal degree by the citizens of a democracy.
But the same feeling does not exist between the several
classes towards each other.

Amongst an aristocratic people, each caste has its own
opinions, feelings, rights, manners, and modes of living.
Thus, the men who compose it do not resemble the mass
of their fellow-citizens; they do not think or feel in the
same manner, and they scarcely believe that they belong to
the same race. They cannot therefore thoroughly understand what others feel, nor judge of others by themselves.
Yet they are sometimes eager to lend each other aid; but
this is not contrary to my previous observation.

These aristocratic institutions, which made the beings of
one and the same race so different, nevertheless bound them
to each other by close political ties. Although the serf
had no natural interest in the fate of the nobles, he did not
the less think himself obliged to devote his person to the
service of that noble who happened to be his lord: and
although the noble held himself to be of a different nature
from that of his serfs, he nevertheless held that his duty
and his honor constrained him to defend, at the risk of his
own life, those who dwelt upon his domains.

It is evident that these mutual obligations did not originate in the law of nature, but in the law of society; and
that the claim of social duty was more stringent than that
of mere humanity. These services were not supposed to
be due from man to man, but to the vassal or to the lord.
Feudal institutions awakened a lively sympathy for the
sufferings of certain men, but none at all for the miseries
of mankind. They infused generosity rather than mildness
into the manners of the time; and although they prompted
men to great acts of self-devotion, they created no real
sympathies, for real sympathies can only exist between

those who are alike; and, in aristocratic ages, men acknowledge none but the members of their own caste to
be like themselves.

When the chroniclers of the Middle Ages, who all belonged to the aristocracy by birth or education, relate the
tragical end of a noble, their grief flows apace; whereas
they tell you at a breath, and without wincing, of massacres and tortures inflicted on the common sort of people.
Not that these writers felt habitual hatred or systematic
disdain for the people; war between the several classes of
the community was not yet declared. They were impelled
by an instinct rather than by a passion; as they had formed
no clear notion of a poor man's sufferings, they cared but
little for his fate.

The same feelings animated the lower orders whenever
the feudal tie was broken. The same ages which witnessed
so many heroic acts of self-devotion on the part of vassals
for their lords, were stained with atrocious barbarities practised from time to time by the lower classes on the higher.

It must not be supposed that this mutual insensibility
arose solely from the absence of public order and education,
for traces of it are to be found in the following centuries,
which became tranquil and enlightened whilst they remained aristocratic.

In 1675 the lower classes in Brittany revolted at the im-
position of a new tax. These disturbances were put down
with unexampled severity. Observe the language in which
Madame de Sévigné, a witness of these horrors, relates
them to her daughter:—

"Aux Rochers, October 30, 1675.

"Your letter from Aix, my daughter, is droll enough.
At least, read your letters over again before sending them;
allow yourself to be surprised by the pretty things that
you have put into them, and console yourself by this pleas-

ure for the trouble you have had in writing so many. Then you have kissed all the people of Provence,* have you? There would be no satisfaction in kissing all Brittany, unless one liked to smell of wine. . . . . . Do you wish to hear the news from Rennes? A tax of a hundred thousand crowns has been imposed upon the citizens; and if this sum is not produced within four and twenty hours, it is to be doubled, and collected by the soldiers. They have cleared the houses and sent away the occupants of one of the great streets, and forbidden anybody to receive them on pain of death; so that the poor wretches — old men, women near their confinement, and children included — may be seen wandering round and crying on their departure from this city, without knowing where to go, and without food or a place to lie in. Day before yesterday, a fiddler was broken on the wheel for getting up a dance and stealing some stamped paper. He was quartered after death, and his limbs exposed at the four corners of the city. Sixty citizens have been thrown into prison, and the business of punishing them is to begin to-morrow. This province sets a fine example to the others, teaching them above all things to respect their governors and *gouvernantes*, and not to throw any more stones into their garden.

" Yesterday, a delightful day, Madame de Tarente visited these wilds; there is no question about preparing a chamber or a collation; she comes by the barrier, and returns the same way. . . . . . ."

In another letter she adds: —

" You talk very pleasantly about our miseries; but we are no longer so jaded with capital punishments; only one a week now, just to keep up appearances. It is true that

---

* Madame de Grignan was *Gouvernante* of Provence, and her mother is here joking with her about the official civilities which she was obliged to practise towards the people who were under her charge.

hanging now seems to me quite a cooling entertainment.
I have got a wholly new idea of justice since I have been
in this region.   Your galley-slaves seem to me a society of
good people who have retired from the world in order to
lead a quiet life."

It would be a mistake to suppose that Madame de Sévigné, who wrote these lines, was a selfish or cruel person ;
she was passionately attached to her children, and very
ready to sympathize in the sorrows of her friends ; nay,
her letters show that she treated her vassals and servants
with kindness and indulgence.   But Madame de Sévigné
had no clear notion of suffering in any one who was not a
person of quality.

In our time, the harshest man, writing to the most insensible person of his acquaintance, would not venture to
indulge in the cruel jocularity which I have quoted ; and
even if his own manners allowed him to do so, the manners of society at large would forbid it.   Whence does this
arise ?   Have we more sensibility than our fathers ?   I do
not know that we have ; but I am sure that our sensibility
is extended to many more objects.

When all the ranks of a community are nearly equal, as
all men think and feel in nearly the same manner, each of
them may judge in a moment of the sensations of all the
others : he casts a rapid glance upon himself, and that is
enough.   There is no wretchedness into which he cannot
readily enter, and a secret instinct reveals to him its extent.
It signifies not that strangers or foes be the sufferers ; imagination puts him in their place : something like a personal
feeling is mingled with his pity, and makes himself suffer
whilst the body of his fellow-creature is in torture.

In democratic ages, men rarely sacrifice themselves for
one another ; but they display general compassion for the
members of the human race.   They inflict no useless ills ;

and they are happy to relieve the griefs of others, when they can do so without much hurting themselves; they are not disinterested, but they are humane.

Although the Americans have in a manner reduced self-ishness to a social and philosophical theory, they are nevertheless extremely open to compassion. In no country is criminal justice administered with more mildness than in the United States. Whilst the English seem disposed carefully to retain the bloody traces of the Middle Ages in their penal legislation, the Americans have almost expunged capital punishment from their codes. North America is, I think, the only country upon earth in which the life of no one citizen has been taken for a political offence in the course of the last fifty years.

The circumstance which conclusively shows that this singular mildness of the Americans arises chiefly from their social condition, is the manner in which they treat their slaves. Perhaps there is not, upon the whole, a single European colony in the New World, in which the physical condition of the blacks is less severe than in the United States; yet the slaves still endure frightful misery there, and are constantly exposed to very cruel punishments. It is easy to perceive that the lot of these unhappy beings inspires their masters with but little compassion, and that they look upon slavery not only as an institution which is profitable to them, but as an evil which does not affect them. Thus, the same man who is full of humanity towards his fellow-creatures, when they are at the same time his equals, becomes insensible to their afflictions as soon as that equality ceases. His mildness should therefore be attributed to the equality of conditions, rather than to civilization and education.

What I have here remarked of individuals is to a certain extent applicable to nations. When each nation has its distinct opinions, belief, laws, and customs, it looks upon itself as the whole of mankind, and is moved by no sorrows but its own. Should war break out between two nations animated by this feeling, it is sure to be waged with great cruelty.

At the time of their highest culture, the Romans slaughtered the generals of their enemies, after having dragged them in triumph behind a car; and they flung their prisoners to the beasts of the Circus for the amusement of the people. Cicero, who declaimed so vehemently at the notion of crucifying a Roman citizen, had not a word to say against these horrible abuses of victory. It is evident that, in his eyes, a barbarian did not belong to the same human race as a Roman.

On the contrary, in proportion as nations become more like each other, they become reciprocally more compassionate, and the law of nations is mitigated.

CHAPTER II.

HOW DEMOCRACY RENDERS THE HABITUAL INTERCOURSE OF THE AMERICANS SIMPLE AND EASY.

DEMOCRACY does not attach men strongly to each other; but it places their habitual intercourse upon an easier footing.

If two Englishmen chance to meet at the Antipodes, where they are surrounded by strangers whose language and manners are almost unknown to them, they will first stare at each other with much curiosity, and a kind of secret uneasiness; they will then turn away, or, if one accosts the other, they will take care only to converse with a constrained and absent air, upon very unimportant subjects. Yet there is no enmity between these men; they have never seen each other before, and each believes the other to be a respectable person. Why then should they stand so cautiously apart? We must go back to England to learn the reason.

When it is birth alone, independent of wealth, which classes men in society, every one knows exactly what his own position is upon the social scale; he does not seek to rise, he does not fear to sink. In a community thus organized, men of different castes communicate very little with each other; but if accident brings them together, they are ready to converse without hoping or fearing to lose their own position. Their intercourse is not upon a footing of equality, but it is not constrained.

When a moneyed aristocracy succeeds to an aristocracy of birth, the case is altered. The privileges of some are still extremely great, but the possibility of acquiring those privileges is open to all: whence it follows, that those who possess them are constantly haunted by the apprehension of losing them, or of other men's sharing them; those who do not yet enjoy them long to possess them at any cost, or, if they fail, to appear at least to possess them, — which is not impossible. As the social importance of men is no longer ostensibly and permanently fixed by blood, and is infinitely varied by wealth, ranks still exist, but it is not easy clearly to distinguish at a glance those who respectively belong to them. Secret hostilities then arise in the community; one set of men endeavor by innumerable artifices to penetrate, or to appear to penetrate, amongst those who are above them; another set are constantly in arms against these usurpers of their rights; or, rather, the same individual does both at once, and whilst he seeks to raise himself into a higher circle, he is always on the defensive against the intrusion of those below him.

Such is the condition of England at the present time; and I am of opinion that the peculiarity just adverted to must be attributed principally to this cause. As aristocratic pride is still extremely great amongst the English, and as the limits of aristocracy are ill-defined, everybody lives in constant dread lest advantage should be taken of his familiarity. Unable to judge at once of the social position of those he meets, an Englishman prudently avoids all contact with them. Men are afraid lest some slight service rendered should draw them into an unsuitable acquaintance; they dread civilities, and they avoid the obtrusive gratitude of a stranger quite as much as his hatred.

Many people attribute these singular anti-social propensities, and the reserved and taciturn bearing of the English, to purely physical causes. I may admit that there is something of it in their race, but much more of it is attributable to their social condition, as is proved by the contrast of the Americans.

In America, where the privileges of birth never existed, and where riches confer no peculiar rights on their possessors, men unacquainted with each other are very ready to frequent the same places, and find neither peril nor advantage in the free interchange of their thoughts. If they meet by accident, they neither seek nor avoid intercourse; their manner is therefore natural, frank, and open: it is easy to see that they hardly expect or apprehend anything from each other, and that they do not care to display, any more than to conceal, their position in the world. If their demeanor is often cold and serious, it is never haughty or constrained; and if they do not converse, it is because they are not in a humor to talk, not because they think it their interest to be silent.

In a foreign country two Americans are at once friends, simply because they are Americans. They are repulsed by no prejudice; they are attracted by their common country. For two Englishmen, the same blood is not enough; they must be brought together by the same rank. The Americans remark this unsociable mood of the English as much as the French do, and are not less astonished by it. Yet the Americans are connected with England by their origin, their religion, their language, and partially by their manners: they only differ in their social condition. It may therefore be inferred, that the reserve of the English proceeds from the constitution of their country, much more than from that of its inhabitants.

CHAPTER III.

WHY THE AMERICANS SHOW SO LITTLE SENSITIVENESS IN THEIR OWN COUNTRY, AND ARE SO SENSITIVE IN EUROPE.

THE temper of the Americans is vindictive, like that of all serious and reflecting nations. They hardly ever forget an offence, but it is not easy to offend them; and their resentment is as slow to kindle as it is to abate.

In aristocratic communities, where a small number of persons manage everything, the outward intercourse of men is subject to settled conventional rules. Every one then thinks he knows exactly what marks of respect or of condescension he ought to display, and none are presumed to be ignorant of the science of etiquette. These usages of the first class in society afterwards serve as a model to all the others; besides which, each of the latter lays down a code of its own, to which all its members are bound to conform. Thus the rules of politeness form a complex system of legislation, which it is difficult to be perfectly master of, but from which it is dangerous for any one to deviate; so that men are constantly exposed involuntarily to inflict or to receive bitter affronts.

But as the distinctions of rank are obliterated, as men differing in education and in birth meet and mingle in the same places of resort, it is almost impossible to agree upon the rules of good breeding. As its laws are uncertain, to disobey them is not a crime, even in the eyes of those who know what they are: men attach more importance to intentions than to forms, and they grow less civil, but at the same time less quarrelsome.

There are many little attentions which an American does not care about ; he thinks they are not due to him, or he presumes that they are not known to be due : he therefore either does not perceive a rudeness, or he forgives it ; his manners become less courteous, and his character more plain and masculine.

The mutual indulgence which the Americans display, and the manly confidence with which they treat each other, also result from another deeper and more general cause, which I have already adverted to in the preceding chapter. In the United States, the distinctions of rank in civil society are slight, in political society they are null ; an American, therefore, does not think himself bound to pay particular attentions to any of his fellow-citizens, nor does he require such attentions from them towards himself. As he does not see that it is his interest eagerly to seek the company of any of his countrymen, he is slow to fancy that his own company is declined : despising no one on account of his station, he does not imagine that any one can despise him for that cause ; and until he has clearly perceived an insult, he does not suppose that an affront was intended. The social condition of the Americans naturally accustoms them not to take offence in small matters ; and, on the other hand, the democratic freedom which they enjoy transfuses this same mildness of temper into the character of the nation.

The political institutions of the United States constantly bring citizens of all ranks into contact, and compel them to pursue great undertakings in concert. People thus engaged have scarcely time to attend to the details of etiquette, and they are besides too strongly interested in living harmoniously for them to stick at such things. They therefore soon acquire a habit of considering the feelings and opinions of those whom they meet more than their manners, and they do not allow themselves to be annoyed by trifles.

I have often remarked, in the United States, that it is not easy to make a man understand that his presence may be dispensed with ; hints will not always suffice to shake him off.   I contradict an American at every word he says, to show him that his conversation bores me ; he instantly labors with fresh pertinacity to convince me : I preserve a dogged silence, and he thinks I am meditating deeply on the truths which he is uttering : at last, I rush from his company, and he supposes that some urgent business hurries me elsewhere.   This man will never understand that he wearies me to death, unless I tell him so ; and the only way to get rid of him is to make him my enemy for life.

It appears surprising, at first sight, that the same man, transported to Europe, suddenly becomes so sensitive and captious, that I often find it as difficult to avoid offending him here, as it was there to put him out of countenance. These two opposite effects proceed from the same cause. Democratic institutions generally give men a lofty notion of their country and of themselves.   An American leaves his country with a heart swollen with pride : on arriving in Europe, he at once finds out that we are not so engrossed by the United States and the great people who inhabit them as he had supposed ; and this begins to annoy him.   He has been informed that the conditions of society are not equal in our part of the globe ; and he observes that, among the nations of Europe, the traces of rank are not wholly obliterated, — that wealth and birth still retain some indeterminate privileges, which force themselves upon his notice whilst they elude definition.   He is therefore profoundly ignorant of the place which he ought to occupy in this half-ruined scale of classes, which are sufficiently distinct to hate and despise each other, yet sufficiently alike for him to be always confounding them.   He is afraid of ranging himself too high, still more is he afraid of being ranged too low : this twofold peril keeps his mind constantly on the stretch, and embarrasses all he says and does.

He learns from tradition that in Europe ceremonial observances were infinitely varied according to different ranks; this recollection of former times completes his perplexity, and he is the more afraid of not obtaining those marks of respect which are due to him, as he does not exactly know in what they consist. He is like a man surrounded by traps: society is not a recreation for him, but a serious toil: he weighs your least actions, interrogates your looks, and scrutinizes all you say, lest there should be some hidden allusion to affront him. I doubt whether there was ever a provincial man of quality so punctilious in breeding as he is: he endeavors to attend to the slightest rules of etiquette, and does not allow one of them to be waived towards himself: he is full of scruples, and at the same time of pretensions; he wishes to do enough, but fears to do too much; and as he does not very well know the limits of the one or of the other, he keeps up a haughty and embarrassed air of reserve.

But this is not all: here is yet another double of the human heart. An American is forever talking of the admirable equality which prevails in the United States: aloud, he makes it the boast of his country, but in secret, he deplores it for himself; and he aspires to show that, for his part, he is an exception to the general state of things which he vaunts. There is hardly an American to be met with who does not claim some remote kindred with the first founders of the Colonies; and as for the scions of the noble families of England, America seemed to me to be covered with them. When an opulent American arrives in Europe, his first care is to surround himself with all the luxuries of wealth: he is so afraid of being taken for the plain citizen of a democracy, that he adopts a hundred distorted ways of bringing some new instance of his wealth before you every day. His house will be in the most fashionable part of the town: he will always be surrounded by a host of servants. I have heard an American complain that, in the best houses of Paris, the society was rather mixed ; the taste which prevails there was not pure enough for him ; and he ventured to hint that, in his opinion, there was a want of elegance of manner ; he could not accustom himself to see wit concealed under such unpretending forms.

These contrasts ought not to surprise us. If the vestiges of former aristocratic distinctions were not so completely effaced in the United States, the Americans would be less simple and less tolerant in their own country ; they would require less, and be less fond of borrowed manners, in ours.

CHAPTER IV.

CONSEQUENCES OF THE THREE PRECEDING CHAPTERS.

WHEN men feel a natural compassion for the sufferings of each other, — when they are brought together by easy and frequent intercourse, and no sensitive feelings keep them asunder, — it may readily be supposed that they will lend assistance to one another whenever it is needed. When an American asks for the co-operation of his fellow-citizens, it is seldom refused; and I have often seen it afforded spontaneously, and with great good-will. If an accident happens on the highway, everybody hastens to help the sufferer; if some great and sudden calamity befalls a family, the purses of a thousand strangers are at once willingly opened, and small but numerous donations pour in to relieve their distress.

It often happens, amongst the most civilized nations of the globe, that a poor wretch is as friendless in the midst of a crowd as the savage in his wilds: this is hardly ever the case in the United States. The Americans, who are always cold and often coarse in their manners, seldom show insensibility; and if they do not proffer services eagerly, yet they do not refuse to render them.

All this is not in contradiction to what I have said before on the subject of individualism. The two things are so far from combating each other, that I can see how they agree. Equality of conditions, whilst it makes men feel their independence, shows them their own weakness: they are free, but exposed to a thousand accidents; and experience soon teaches them that, although they do not habitually require the assistance of others, a time almost always comes when they cannot do without it.

We constantly see, in Europe, that men of the same profession are ever ready to assist each other; they are all exposed to the same ills, and that is enough to teach them to seek mutual preservatives, however hard-hearted and selfish they may otherwise be. When one of them falls into danger, from which the others may save him by a slight transient sacrifice or a sudden effort, they do not fail to make the attempt. Not that they are deeply interested in his fate, — for if, by chance, their exertions are unavailing, they immediately forget the object of them, and return to their own business, — but a sort of tacit and almost involuntary agreement has been passed between them, by which each one owes to the others a temporary support, which he may claim for himself in turn.

Extend to a people the remark here applied to a class, and you will understand my meaning. A similar covenant exists, in fact, between all the citizens of a democracy: they all feel themselves subject to the same weakness and the same dangers; and their interest, as well as their sympathy, makes it a rule with them to lend each other mutual assistance when required. The more equal social conditions become, the more do men display this reciprocal disposition to oblige each other. In democracies, no great benefits are conferred, but good offices are constantly rendered; a man seldom displays self-devotion, but all men are ready to be of service to one another.

CHAPTER V.

HOW DEMOCRACY AFFECTS THE RELATIONS OF MASTERS AND SERVANTS.

AN American who had travelled for a long time in Europe once said to me: "The English treat their servants with a stiffness and imperiousness of manner which surprise us; but, on the other hand, the French sometimes treat their attendants with a degree of familiarity or of politeness which we cannot understand. It looks as if they were afraid to give orders; the posture of the superior and the inferior is ill maintained." The remark was a just one, and I have often made it myself. I have always considered England as the country of all the world where, in our time, the bond of domestic service is drawn most tightly, and France as the country where it is most relaxed. Nowhere have I seen masters stand so high or so low as in these two countries. Between these two extremes the Americans are to be placed. Such is the fact, as it appears upon the surface of things: to discover the causes of that fact, it is necessary to search the matter thoroughly.

No communities have ever yet existed in which social conditions have been so equal that there were neither rich nor poor, and, consequently, neither masters nor servants. Democracy does not prevent the existence of these two classes, but it changes their dispositions, and modifies their mutual relations.

Amongst aristocratic nations, servants form a distinct class, not more variously composed than that of their mas-

ters.   A settled order is soon established; in the former as
well as in the latter class a scale is formed, with numerous
distinctions or marked gradations of rank, and generations
succeed each other thus, without any change of position.
These two communities are superposed one above the
other, always distinct, but regulated by analogous principles.   This aristocratic constitution does not exert a less
powerful influence on the notions and manners of servants
than on those of masters; and, although the effects are different, the same cause may easily be traced.

Both classes constitute small communities in the heart of
the nation, and certain permanent notions of right and
wrong are ultimately established amongst them.   The different acts of human life are viewed by one peculiar and
unchanging light.   In the society of servants, as in that
of masters, men exercise a great influence over each other:
they acknowledge settled rules, and, in the absence of law,
they are guided by a sort of public opinion; their habits
are settled, and their conduct is placed under a certain
control.

These men, whose destiny it is to obey, certainly do not
understand fame, virtue, honesty, and honor in the same
manner as their masters; but they have a pride, a virtue,
and an honesty pertaining to their condition; and they
have a notion, if I may use the expression, of a sort of
servile honor.*   Because a class is mean, it must not be
supposed that all who belong to it are mean-hearted; to
think so would be a great mistake.   However lowly it may
be, he who is foremost there, and who has no notion of quit-

---

* If the principal opinions by which men are guided are examined closely
and in detail, the analogy appears still more striking, and one is surprised
to find amongst them, just as much as amongst the haughtiest scions of a
feudal race, pride of birth, respect for their ancestry and their descendants,
disdain of their inferiors, a dread of contact, and a taste for etiquette, precedents, and antiquity.

ting it, occupies an aristocratic position which inspires him with lofty feelings, pride, and self-respect, that fit him for the higher virtues, and for actions above the common.

Amongst aristocratic nations, it was by no means rare to find men of noble and vigorous minds in the service of the great, who felt not the servitude they bore, and who submitted to the will of their masters without any fear of their displeasure.

But this was hardly ever the case amongst the inferior ranks of domestic servants. It may be imagined, that he who occupies the lowest stage of the order of menials stands very low indeed. The French created a word on purpose to designate the servants of the aristocracy, — they called them "lackeys." This word *lackey* served as the strongest expression, when all others were exhausted, to designate human meanness. Under the old French monarchy, to denote by a single expression a low-spirited contemptible fellow, it was usual to say that he had the *soul of a lackey;* the term was enough to convey all that was intended.

The permanent inequality of conditions not only gives servants certain peculiar virtues and vices, but it places them in a peculiar relation with respect to their masters. Amongst aristocratic nations, the poor man is familiarized from his childhood with the notion of being commanded; to whichever side he turns his eyes, the graduated structure of society and the aspect of obedience meet his view. Hence, in those countries, the master readily obtains prompt, complete, respectful, and easy obedience from his servants, because they revere in him, not only their master, but the class of masters. He weighs down their will by the whole weight of the aristocracy. He orders their actions; to a certain extent, he even directs their thoughts. In aristocracies, the master often exercises, even without being aware of it, an amazing sway over the opinions, the habits, and the manners of those who obey him, and his influence extends even further than his authority.

In aristocratic communities, there are not only hereditary families of servants as well as of masters, but the same families of servants adhere for several generations to the same families of masters (like two parallel lines which neither meet nor separate); and this considerably modifies the mutual relations of these two classes of persons. Thus, although in aristocratic society the master and servant have no natural resemblance, — although, on the contrary, they are placed at an immense distance on the scale of human beings by their fortune, education, and opinions, — yet time ultimately binds them together. They are connected by a long series of common reminiscences, and however different they may be, they grow alike; whilst in democracies, where they are naturally almost alike, they always remain strangers to each other. Amongst an aristocratic people, the master gets to look upon his servants as an inferior and secondary part of himself, and he often takes an interest in their lot by a last stretch of selfishness.

Servants, on their part, are not averse to regard themselves in the same light; and they sometimes identify themselves with the person of the master, so that they become an appendage to him in their own eyes as well as in his. In aristocracies, a servant fills a subordinate position which he cannot get out of; above him is another man, holding a superior rank, which he cannot lose. On one side, are obscurity, poverty, obedience for life; on the other, and also for life, fame, wealth, and command. The two conditions are always distinct and always in propinquity; the tie that connects them is as lasting as they are themselves.

In this predicament, the servant ultimately detaches his notion of interest from his own person; he deserts himself as it were, or rather he transports himself into the character of his master, and thus assumes an imaginary personality. He complacently invests himself with the wealth of those who command him; he shares their fame, exalts himself by their rank, and feeds his mind with borrowed greatness, to which he attaches more importance than those who fully and really possess it. There is something touching, and at the same time ridiculous, in this strange confusion of two different states of being. These passions of masters, when they pass into the souls of menials, assume the natural dimensions of the place they occupy; they are contracted and lowered. What was pride in the former becomes puerile vanity and paltry ostentation in the latter. The servants of a great man are commonly most punctilious as to the marks of respect due to him, and they attach more importance to his slightest privileges than he does himself. In France, a few of these old servants of the aristocracy are still to be met with, here and there; they have survived their race, which will soon disappear with them altogether.

In the United States, I never saw any one at all like them. The Americans are not only unacquainted with the kind of man, but it is hardly possible to make them understand that such ever existed. It is scarcely less difficult for them to conceive it, than for us to form a correct notion of what a slave was amongst the Romans, or a serf in the Middle Ages. All these men were, in fact, though in different degrees, results of the same cause: they are all retiring from our sight, and disappearing in the obscurity of the past, together with the social condition to which they owed their origin.

Equality of conditions turns servants and masters into new beings, and places them in new relative positions. When social conditions are nearly equal, men are constantly changing their situations in life: there is still a class of menials and a class of masters, but these classes are not always composed of the same individuals, still less of the same families; and those who command are not more secure of perpetuity than those who obey. As servants do not form a separate people, they have no habits, prejudices, or manners peculiar to themselves: they are not remarkable for any particular turn of mind or moods of feeling. They know no vices or virtues of their condition, but they partake of the education, the opinions, the feelings, the virtues and the vices of their contemporaries; and they are honest men or scoundrels in the same way as their masters are.

The conditions of servants are not less equal than those of masters. As no marked ranks or fixed subordination are to be found amongst them, they will not display either the meanness or the greatness which characterize the aristocracy of menials, as well as all other aristocracies. I never saw a man in the United States who reminded me of that class of confidential servants of which we still retain a reminiscence in Europe, neither did I ever meet with such a thing as a *lackey:* all traces of the one and the other have disappeared.

In democracies, servants are not only equal amongst themselves, but it may be said that they are, in some sort, the equals of their masters. This requires explanation in order to be rightly understood. At any moment, a servant may become a master, and he aspires to rise to that condition: the servant is therefore not a different man from the master. Why then has the former a right to command, and what compels the latter to obey? — the free and temporary consent of both their wills. Neither of them is, by nature, inferior to the other; they only become so for a time, by covenant. Within the terms of this covenant, the one is a servant, the other a master; beyond it, they are two citizens of the commonwealth, — two men.

I beg the reader particularly to observe, that this is not only the notion which servants themselves entertain of their own condition; domestic service is looked upon by masters in the same light; and the precise limits of authority and obedience are as clearly settled in the mind of the one as in that of the other.

When the greater part of the community have long attained a condition nearly alike, and when equality is an old and acknowledged fact, the public mind, which is never affected by exceptions, assigns certain general limits to the value of man, above or below which no man can long remain placed. It is in vain that wealth and poverty, authority and obedience, accidentally interpose great distances between two men; public opinion, founded upon the usual order of things, draws them to a common level, and creates a species of imaginary equality between them, in spite of the real inequality of their conditions. This all-powerful opinion penetrates at length even into the hearts of those whose interest might arm them to resist it; it affects their judgment, whilst it subdues their will.

In their inmost convictions the master and the servant no longer perceive any deep-seated difference between them, and they neither hope nor fear to meet with any such at any time. They are therefore neither subject to disdain nor to anger, and they discern in each other neither humility nor pride. The master holds the contract of service to be the only source of his power, and the servant regards it as the only cause of his obedience. They do not quarrel about their reciprocal situations, but each knows his own and keeps it.

In the French army, the common soldier is taken from nearly the same class as the officer, and may hold the same commissions: out of the ranks, he considers himself entirely equal to his military superiors, and, in point of fact, he is so; but when under arms, he does not hesitate to obey, and his obedience is not the less prompt, precise, and ready, for being voluntary and defined. This example may give a notion of what takes place between masters and servants in democratic communities.

It would be preposterous to suppose that those warm and deep-seated affections which are sometimes kindled in the domestic service of aristocracy will ever spring up between these two men, or that they will exhibit strong instances of self-sacrifice. In aristocracies, masters and servants live apart, and frequently their only intercourse is through a third person ; yet they commonly stand firmly by one another. In democratic countries, the master and the servant are close together : they are in daily personal contact, but their minds do not intermingle ; they have common occupations, hardly ever common interests.

Amongst such a people, the servant always considers himself as a sojourner in the dwelling of his masters. He knew nothing of their forefathers ; he will see nothing of their descendants ; he has nothing lasting to expect from them. Why, then, should he confound his life with theirs, and whence should so strange a surrender of himself proceed ? The reciprocal position of the two men is changed ; their mutual relations must be so, too.

I would fain illustrate all these reflections by the example of the Americans ; but, for this purpose, the distinctions of persons and places must be accurately traced. In the South of the Union, slavery exists ; all that I have just said is consequently inapplicable there. In the North, the majority of servants are either freedmen, or the children of freedmen : * these persons occupy a contested position in the public estimation ; by the laws, they are brought up to

---

* This is a natural mistake for a stranger to make. In hotels, and other large public establishments, it may be true that a majority of the servants are free blacks ; but very few such persons are employed as servants in private families at the North. — AM. ED.

the level of their masters ; by the manners of the country, they are obstinately detruded from it. They do not themselves clearly know their proper place, and are almost always either insolent or craven.

But in the Northern States, especially in New England, there are a certain number of whites who agree, for wages, to yield a temporary obedience to the will of their fellow-citizens. I have heard that these servants commonly perform the duties of their situations with punctuality and intelligence ; and that, without thinking themselves naturally inferior to the person who orders them, they submit without reluctance to obey him. They appeared to me to carry into service some of those manly habits which independence and equality create. Having once selected a hard way of life, they do not seek to escape from it by indirect means ; and they have sufficient respect for themselves not to refuse to their masters that obedience which they have freely promised. On their part, masters require nothing of their servants but the faithful and rigorous performance of the covenant : they do not ask for marks of respect, they do not claim their love, or devoted attachment ; it is enough that, as servants, they are exact and honest.

It would not, then, be true to assert that, in democratic society, the relation of servants and masters is disorganized : it is organized on another footing ; the rule is different, but there is a rule.

It is not my purpose to inquire whether the new state of things which I have just described is inferior to that which preceded it, or simply different. Enough for me that it is fixed and determined ; for what is most important to meet with among men is not any given ordering, but order.

But what shall I say of those sad and troubled times at which equality is established in the midst of the tumult of revolution, — when democracy, after having been introduced into the state of society, still struggles with difficulty against the prejudices and manners of the country ? The laws, and partially public opinion, already declare that no natural or permanent inferiority exists between the servant and the master. But this new belief has not yet reached the innermost convictions of the latter, or rather his heart rejects it : in the secret persuasion of his mind, the master thinks that he belongs to a peculiar and superior race; he dares not say so, but he shudders at allowing himself to be dragged to the same level. His authority over his servants becomes timid, and at the same time harsh ; he has already ceased to entertain for them the feelings of patronizing kindness which long uncontested power always produces, and he is surprised that, being changed himself, his servant changes also. He wants his attendants to form regular and permanent habits, in a condition of domestic service which is only temporary ; he requires that they should appear contented with and proud of a servile condition, which they will one day shake off, — that they should sacrifice themselves to a man who can neither protect nor ruin them ; and, in short, that they should contract an indissoluble engagement to a being like themselves, and one who will last no longer than they will.

Amongst aristocratic nations, it often happens that the condition of domestic service does not degrade the character of those who enter upon it, because they neither know nor imagine any other ; and the amazing inequality which is manifest between them and their master appears to be the necessary and unavoidable consequence of some hidden law of Providence.

In democracies, the condition of domestic service does not degrade the character of those who enter upon it, because it is freely chosen, and adopted for a time only, — because it is not stigmatized by public opinion, and creates no permanent inequality between the servant and the master.

But whilst the transition from one social condition to another is going on, there is almost always a time when

men's minds fluctuate between the aristocratic notion of
subjection and the democratic notion of obedience. Obedience then loses its moral importance in the eyes of him
who obeys; he no longer considers it as a species of divine
obligation, and he does not yet view it under its purely
human aspect; it has to him no character of sanctity or
of justice, and he submits to it as to a degrading but profitable condition.

At that period, a confused and imperfect phantom of
equality haunts the minds of servants; they do not at once
perceive whether the equality to which they are entitled is
to be found within or without the pale of domestic service;
and they rebel in their hearts against a subordination to
which they have subjected themselves, and from which
they derive actual profit. They consent to serve, and they
blush to obey: they like the advantages of service, but not
the master; or, rather, they are not sure that they ought
not themselves to be masters, and they are inclined to consider him who orders them as an unjust usurper of their
own rights.

Then it is that the dwelling of every citizen offers a
spectacle somewhat analogous to the gloomy aspect of political society. A secret and intestine warfare is going on
there between powers ever rivals and suspicious of one
another: the master is ill-natured and weak, the servant
ill-natured and intractable; the one constantly attempts to
evade by unfair restrictions his obligation to protect and
to remunerate, — the other, his obligation to obey. The
reins of domestic government dangle between them, to be
snatched at by one or the other. The lines which divide
authority from oppression, liberty from license, and right
from might, are to their eyes so jumbled together and confused, that no one knows exactly what he is, or what he
may be, or what he ought to be. Such a condition is not
democracy, but revolution.

CHAPTER VI.

HOW DEMOCRATIC INSTITUTIONS AND MANNERS TEND TO RAISE RENTS AND SHORTEN THE TERMS OF LEASES.

WHAT has been said of servants and masters is applicable, to a certain extent, to land-owners and farming tenants; but this subject deserves to be considered by itself.

In America there are, properly speaking, no farming tenants; every man owns the ground he tills. It must be admitted that democratic laws tend greatly to increase the number of land-owners, and to diminish that of farming tenants. Yet what takes place in the United States is much less attributable to the institutions of the country, than to the country itself. In America land is cheap, and any one may easily become a land-owner; its returns are small, and its produce cannot well be divided between a land-owner and a farmer. America therefore stands alone in this respect, as well as in many others, and it would be a mistake to take it as an example.

I believe that, in democratic as well as in aristocratic countries, there will be land-owners and tenants, but the connection existing between them will be of a different kind. In aristocracies, the hire of a farm is paid to the landlord, not only in rent, but in respect, regard, and duty; in democracies, the whole is paid in cash. When estates are divided and passed from hand to hand, and the permanent connection which existed between families and the soil is dissolved, the land-owner and the tenant are only casually brought into contact. They meet for a moment to settle the conditions of the agreement, and then lose sight of each other; they are two strangers brought together by a common interest, and who keenly talk over a matter of business, the sole object of which is to make money.

In proportion as property is subdivided and wealth distributed over the country, the community is filled with people whose former opulence is declining, and with others whose fortunes are of recent growth, and whose wants increase more rapidly than their resources. For all such persons the smallest pecuniary profit is a matter of importance, and none of them feel disposed to waive any of their claims, or to lose any portion of their income.

As ranks are intermingled, and as very large as well as very scanty fortunes become more rare, every day brings the social condition of the land-owner nearer to that of the farmer: the one has not naturally any uncontested superiority over the other; between two men who are equal, and not at ease in their circumstances, the contract of hire is exclusively an affair of money.

A man whose estate extends over a whole district, and who owns a hundred farms, is well aware of the importance of gaining at the same time the affections of some thousands of men; this object appears to call for his exertions, and to attain it he will readily make considerable sacrifices. But he who owns a hundred acres is insensible to similar considerations, and cares but little to win the private regard of his tenant.

An aristocracy does not expire, like a man, in a single day; the aristocratic principle is slowly undermined in men's opinion, before it is attacked in their laws. Long before open war is declared against it, the tie which had hitherto united the higher classes to the lower may be seen to be gradually relaxed. Indifference and contempt are betrayed by one class, jealousy and hatred by the others: the intercourse between rich and poor becomes less frequent and less kind, and rents are raised. This is not the consequence of a democratic revolution, but its certain harbinger: for an aristocracy which has lost the affections of the people, once and forever, is like a tree dead at the root, which is the more easily torn up by the winds the higher its branches have spread.

In the course of the last fifty years the rents of farms have amazingly increased, not only in France, but throughout the greater part of Europe. The remarkable improvements which have taken place in agriculture and manufactures within the same period do not suffice, in my opinion, to explain this fact: recourse must be had to another cause, more powerful and more concealed. I believe that cause is to be found in the democratic institutions which several European nations have adopted, and in the democratic passions which more or less agitate all the rest.

I have frequently heard great English land-owners congratulate themselves that, at the present day, they derive a much larger income from their estates than their fathers did. They have perhaps good reason to be glad; but most assuredly they know not what they are glad of. They think they are making a clear gain, when it is in reality only an exchange: their influence is what they are parting with for cash; and what they gain in money will erelong be lost in power.

There is yet another sign by which it is easy to know that a great democratic revolution is going on or approaching. In the Middle Ages, almost all lands were leased for lives, or for very long terms: the domestic economy of that period shows that leases for ninety-nine years were more frequent then than leases for twelve years are now. Men then believed that families were immortal; men's conditions seemed settled forever, and the whole of society appeared to be so fixed, that it was not supposed anything would ever be stirred or shaken in its structure. In ages of

equality, the human mind takes a different bent: the prevailing notion is that nothing abides, and man is haunted
by the thought of mutability. Under this impression, the
land-owner and the tenant himself are instinctively averse
to protracted terms of obligation: they are afraid of being
tied up to-morrow by the contract which benefits them
to-day. They have vague anticipations of some sudden
and unforeseen change in their conditions; they mistrust
themselves; they fear lest their taste should change, and
lest they should lament that they cannot rid themselves of
what they coveted. Nor are such fears unfounded; for, in
democratic times, that which is most fluctuating amidst the
fluctuation of all around is the heart of man.

CHAPTER VII.

INFLUENCE OF DEMOCRACY ON WAGES.

MOST of the remarks which I have already made in speaking of masters and servants may be applied to masters and workmen. As the gradations of the social scale come to be less observed, whilst the great sink and the humble rise, and poverty as well as opulence ceases to be hereditary, the distance, both in reality and in opinion, which heretofore separated the workman from the master, is lessened every day. The workman conceives a more lofty opinion of his rights, of his future, of himself; he is filled with new ambition and new desires, he is harassed by new wants. Every instant he views with longing eyes the profits of his employer; and in order to share them, he strives to dispose of his labor at a higher rate, and he generally succeeds at length in the attempt.

In democratic countries, as well as elsewhere, most of the branches of productive industry are carried on at a small cost, by men little removed by their wealth or education above the level of those whom they employ. These manufacturing speculators are extremely numerous; their interests differ; they cannot therefore easily concert or combine their exertions. On the other hand, the workmen have always some sure resources, which enable them to refuse to work when they cannot get what they conceive to be the fair price of their labor. In the constant struggle for wages which is going on between these two classes, their strength is divided, and success alternates from one to the other.

It is even probable that, in the end, the interest of the working class will prevail; for the high wages which they have already obtained make them every day less dependent on their masters; and as they grow more independent, they have greater facilities for obtaining a further increase of wages.

I shall take for example that branch of productive industry which is still, at the present day, the most generally followed in France, and in almost all the countries of the world;— I mean the cultivation of the soil. In France, most of those who labor for hire in agriculture are themselves owners of certain plots of ground, which just enable them to subsist without working for any one else. When these laborers come to offer their services to a neighboring land-owner or farmer, if he refuses them a certain rate of wages, they retire to their own small property and await another opportunity.

I think that, upon the whole, it may be asserted that a slow and gradual rise of wages is one of the general laws of democratic communities. In proportion as social conditions become more equal, wages rise; and as wages are higher, social conditions become more equal.

But a great and gloomy exception occurs in our own time. I have shown, in a preceding chapter, that aristocracy, expelled from political society, has taken refuge in certain departments of productive industry, and has established its sway there under another form; this powerfully affects the rate of wages.

As a large capital is required to embark in the great manufacturing speculations to which I allude, the number of persons who enter upon them is exceedingly limited: as their number is small, they can easily concert together, and fix the rate of wages as they please.

Their workmen, on the contrary, are exceedingly numerous, and the number of them is always increasing; for, from time to time, an extraordinary run of business takes place, during which wages are inordinately high, and they attract the surrounding population to the factories. But, when men have once embraced that line of life, we have already seen that they cannot quit it again, because they soon contract habits of body and mind which unfit them for any other sort of toil. These men have generally but little education and industry, with but few resources; they stand, therefore, almost at the mercy of the master.

When competition, or other fortuitous circumstances, lessen his profits, he can reduce the wages of his workmen almost at pleasure, and make from them what he loses by the chances of business. Should the workmen strike, the master, who is a rich man, can very well wait, without being ruined, until necessity brings them back to him; but they must work day by day or they die, for their only property is in their hands. They have long been impoverished by oppression, and the poorer they become, the more easily may they be oppressed: they can never escape from this fatal circle of cause and consequence.

It is not surprising then that wages, after having sometimes suddenly risen, are permanently lowered in this branch of industry; whereas, in other callings, the price of labor, which generally increases but little, is nevertheless constantly augmented.

This state of dependence and wretchedness, in which a part of the manufacturing population of our time live, forms an exception to the general rule, contrary to the state of all the rest of the community; but, for this very reason, no circumstance is more important or more deserving of the especial consideration of the legislator; for when the whole of society is in motion, it is difficult to keep any one class stationary; and when the greater number of men are opening new paths to fortune, it is no less difficult to make the few support in peace their wants and their desires.

CHAPTER VIII.

INFLUENCE OF DEMOCRACY ON THE FAMILY.

I HAVE just examined the changes which the equality of conditions produces in the mutual relations of the several members of the community amongst democratic nations, and amongst the Americans in particular. I would now go deeper, and inquire into the closer ties of family: my object here is not to seek for new truths, but to show in what manner facts already known are connected with my subject.

It has been universally remarked, that, in our time, the several members of a family stand upon an entirely new footing towards each other; that the distance which formerly separated a father from his sons has been lessened; and that paternal authority, if not destroyed, is at least impaired.

Something analogous to this, but even more striking, may be observed in the United States. In America, the family, in the Roman and aristocratic signification of the word, does not exist. All that remains of it are a few vestiges in the first years of childhood, when the father exercises, without opposition, that absolute domestic authority which the feebleness of his children renders necessary, and which their interest, as well as his own incontestable superiority, warrants. But as soon as the young American approaches manhood, the ties of filial obedience are relaxed day by day: master of his thoughts, he is soon master of his conduct. In America, there is, strictly speaking, no adolescence: at the close of boyhood, the man appears, and begins to trace out his own path.

It would be an error to suppose that this is preceded by a domestic struggle, in which the son has obtained by a sort of moral violence the liberty that his father refused him. The same habits, the same principles, which impel the one to assert his independence, predispose the other to consider the use of that independence as an incontestable right. The former does not exhibit any of those rancorous or irregular passions which disturb men long after they have shaken off an established authority; the latter feels none of that bitter and angry regret which is apt to survive a by-gone power. The father foresees the limits of his authority long beforehand, and when the time arrives, he surrenders it without a struggle: the son looks forward to the exact period at which he will be his own master; and he enters upon his freedom without precipitation and without effort, as a possession which is his own, and which no one seeks to wrest from him.*

It may, perhaps, be useful to show how these changes

* The Americans, however, have not yet thought fit to strip the parent, as has been done in France, of one of the chief elements of parental author-ity, by depriving him of the power of disposing of his property at his death. In the United States, there are no restrictions on the powers of a testator.

In this respect, as in almost all others, it is easy to perceive that, if the political legislation of the Americans is much more democratic than that of the French, the civil legislation of the latter is infinitely more democratic than that of the former. This may easily be accounted for. The civil legislation of France was the work of a man who saw that it was his inter-est to satisfy the democratic passions of his contemporaries in all that was not directly and immediately hostile to his own power. He was willing to allow some popular principles to regulate the distribution of property and the government of families, provided they were not to be introduced into the administration of public affairs. Whilst the torrent of democracy over-whelmed the civil laws of the country, he hoped to find an easy shelter behind its political institutions. This policy was at once both adroit and selfish: but a compromise of this kind could not last; for in the end, po-litical institutions never fail to become the image and expression of civil society; and in this sense it may be said, that nothing is more political in a nation than its civil legislation.

which take place in family relations are closely connected
with the social and political revolution which is approaching its consummation under our own eyes.

There are certain great social principles which a people
either introduces everywhere or tolerates nowhere.   In
countries which are aristocratically constituted with all the
gradations of rank, the government never makes a direct
appeal to the mass of the governed : as men are united
together, it is enough to lead the foremost ; the rest will
follow.   This is applicable to the family, as well as to all
aristocracies which have a head.   Amongst aristocratic nations, social institutions recognize, in truth, no one in the
family but the father ; children are received by society at
his hands ; society governs him, he governs them.   Thus,
the parent has not only a natural right, but he acquires a
political right, to command them : he is the author and the
support of his family ; but he is also its constituted ruler.

In democracies, where the government picks out every
individual singly from the mass to make him subservient to
the general laws of the community, no such intermediate
person is required : a father is there, in the eye of the
law, only a member of the community, older and richer
than his sons.

When most of the conditions of life are extremely unequal, and the inequality of these conditions is permanent,
the notion of a superior grows upon the imaginations of
men : if the law invested him with no privileges, custom
and public opinion would concede them.   When, on the
contrary, men differ but little from each other, and do not
always remain in dissimilar conditions of life, the general
notion of a superior becomes weaker and less distinct : it is
vain for legislation to strive to place him who obeys very
much beneath him who commands ; the manners of the
time bring the two men nearer to one another, and draw
them daily towards the same level.

Although the legislation of an aristocratic people should grant no peculiar privileges to the heads of families, I shall not be the less convinced that their power is more respected and more extensive than in a democracy; for I know that, whatsoever the laws may be, superiors always appear higher, and inferiors lower, in aristocracies than amongst democratic nations.

When men live more for the remembrance of what has been than for the care of what is, and when they are more given to attend to what their ancestors thought than to think themselves, the father is the natural and necessary tie between the past and the present, — the link by which the ends of these two chains are connected. In aristocracies, then, the father is not only the civil head of the family, but the organ of its traditions, the expounder of its customs, the arbiter of its manners. He is listened to with deference, he is addressed with respect, and the love which is felt for him is always tempered with fear.

When the condition of society becomes democratic, and men adopt as their general principle that it is good and lawful to judge of all things for one's self, using former points of belief not as a rule of faith, but simply as a means of information, the power which the opinions of a father exercise over those of his sons diminishes, as well as his legal power.

Perhaps the subdivision of estates which democracy brings about contributes more than anything else to change the relations existing between a father and his children. When the property of the father of a family is scanty, his son and himself constantly live in the same place, and share the same occupations: habit and necessity bring them together, and force them to hold constant communication: the inevitable consequence is a sort of familiar intimacy, which renders authority less absolute, and which can ill be reconciled with the external forms of respect.

Now, in democratic countries, the class of those who are possessed of small fortunes is precisely that which gives strength to the notions and a particular direction to the manners of the community. That class makes its opinions preponderate as universally as its will; and even those who are most inclined to resist its commands are carried away in the end by its example. I have known eager opponents of democracy, who allowed their children to address them with perfect colloquial equality.

Thus, at the same time that the power of aristocracy is declining, the austere, the conventional, and the legal part of parental authority vanishes, and a species of equality prevails around the domestic hearth. I know not, upon the whole, whether society loses by the change, but I am inclined to believe that man individually is a gainer by it. I think that, in proportion as manners and laws become more democratic, the relation of father and son becomes more intimate and more affectionate; rules and authority are less talked of, confidence and tenderness are oftentimes increased, and it would seem that the natural bond is drawn closer in proportion as the social bond is loosened.

In a democratic family, the father exercises no other power than that which is granted to the affection and the experience of age; his orders would perhaps be disobeyed, but his advice is for the most part authoritative. Though he be not hedged in with ceremonial respect, his sons at least accost him with confidence; they have no settled form of addressing him, but they speak to him constantly, and are ready to consult him every day: the master and the constituted ruler have vanished; the father remains.

Nothing more is needed in order to judge of the difference between the two states of society in this respect, than to peruse the family correspondence of aristocratic ages. The style is always correct, ceremonious, stiff, and so cold that the natural warmth of the heart can hardly be felt in the language. In democratic countries, on the contrary, the language addressed by a son to his father is always marked by mingled freedom, familiarity, and affection, which at once show that new relations have sprung up in the bosom of the family.

A similar revolution takes place in the mutual relations of children. In aristocratic families, as well as in aristo cratic society, every place is marked out beforehand. Not only does the father occupy a separate rank, in which he enjoys extensive privileges, but even the children are not equal amongst themselves. The age and sex of each irrevocably determine his rank, and secure to him certain privileges: most of these distinctions are abolished or diminished by democracy.

In aristocratic families, the eldest son, inheriting the greater part of the property, and almost all the rights of the family, becomes the chief, and, to a certain extent, the master, of his brothers. Greatness and power are for him; for them, mediocrity and dependence. But it would be wrong to suppose that, amongst aristocratic nations, the privileges of the eldest son are advantageous to himself alone, or that they excite nothing but envy and hatred around him. The eldest son commonly endeavors to procure wealth and power for his brothers, because the general splendor of the house is reflected back on him who represents it; the younger sons seek to back the elder brother in all his undertakings, because the greatness and power of the head of the family better enable him to provide for all its branches. The different members of an aristocratic family are therefore very closely bound together; their interests are connected, their minds agree, but their hearts are seldom in harmony.

Democracy also binds brothers to each other, but by very different means. Under democratic laws, all the children are perfectly equal, and consequently independent: noth ing brings them forcibly together, but nothing keeps them apart ; and as they have the same origin, as they are trained under the same roof, as they are treated with the same care, and as no peculiar privilege distinguishes or divides them, the affectionate and frank intimacy of early years easily springs up between them. Scarcely anything can occur to break the tie thus formed at the outset of life, for brotherhood brings them daily together, without embarrassing them. It is not then by interest, but by common associations and by the free sympathy of opinion and of taste, that democracy unites brothers to each other. It divides their inheritance, but allows their hearts and minds to unite.

Such is the charm of these democratic manners, that even the partisans of aristocracy are attracted by it ; and after having experienced it for some time, they are by no means tempted to revert to the respectful and frigid observances of aristocratic families. They would be glad to retain the domestic habits of democracy, if they might throw off its social conditions and its laws ; but these elements are indissolubly united, and it is impossible to enjoy the former without enduring the latter.

The remarks I have made on filial love and fraternal affection are applicable to all the passions which emanate spontaneously from human nature itself.

If a certain mode of thought or feeling is the result of some peculiar condition of life, when that condition is altered nothing whatever remains of the thought or feeling. Thus, a law may bind two members of the community very closely to one another ; but that law being abolished, they stand asunder. Nothing was more strict than the tie which united the vassal to the lord under the feudal system : at the present day, the two men know not each other ; the fear, the gratitude, and the affection which formerly connected them have vanished, and not a vestige of the tie remains.

Such, however, is not the case with those feelings which are natural to mankind. Whenever a law attempts to tutor these feelings in any particular manner, it seldom fails to weaken them; by attempting to add to their intensity, it robs them of some of their elements, for they are never stronger than when left to themselves.

Democracy, which destroys or obscures almost all the old conventional rules of society, and which prevents men from readily assenting to new ones, entirely effaces most of the feelings to which these conventional rules have given rise; but it only modifies some others, and frequently imparts to them a degree of energy and sweetness unknown before.

Perhaps it is not impossible to condense into a single proposition the whole purport of this chapter, and of several others that preceded it. Democracy loosens social ties, but tightens natural ones; it brings kindred more closely together, whilst it throws citizens more apart.

CHAPTER IX.

EDUCATION OF YOUNG WOMEN IN THE UNITED STATES.

NO free communities ever existed without morals; and, as I observed in the former part of this work, morals are the work of woman. Consequently, whatever affects the condition of women, their habits and their opinions, has great political importance in my eyes.

Amongst almost all Protestant nations, young women are far more the mistresses of their own actions than they are in Catholic countries. This independence is still greater in Protestant countries like England, which have retained or acquired the right of self-government; freedom is then infused into the domestic circle by political habits and by religious opinions. In the United States, the doctrines of Protestantism are combined with great political liberty and a most democratic state of society; and nowhere are young women surrendered so early or so completely to their own guidance.

Long before an American girl arrives at the marriageable age, her emancipation from maternal control begins: she has scarcely ceased to be a child, when she already thinks for herself, speaks with freedom, and acts on her own impulse. The great scene of the world is constantly open to her view: far from seeking to conceal it from her, it is every day disclosed more completely, and she is taught to survey it with a firm and calm gaze. Thus the vices and dangers of society are early revealed to her; as she sees them clearly, she views them without illusion, and braves them without fear; for she is full of reliance on her own strength, and her confidence seems to be shared by all around her.

An American girl scarcely ever displays that virginal softness in the midst of young desires, or that innocent and ingenuous grace, which usually attend the European woman in the transition from girlhood to youth. It is rare that an American woman, at any age, displays childish timidity or ignorance. Like the young women of Europe, she seeks to please, but she knows precisely the cost of pleasing. If she does not abandon herself to evil, at least she knows that it exists; and she is remarkable rather for purity of manners than for chastity of mind.

I have been frequently surprised, and almost frightened, at the singular address and happy boldness with which young women in America contrive to manage their thoughts and their language, amidst all the difficulties of free conversation; a philosopher would have stumbled at every step along the narrow path which they trod without accident and without effort. It is easy, indeed, to perceive that, even amidst the independence of early youth, an American woman is always mistress of herself: she indulges in all permitted pleasures, without yielding herself up to any of them; and her reason never allows the reins of self-guidance to drop, though it often seems to hold them loosely.

In France, where traditions of every age are still so strangely mingled in the opinions and tastes of the people, women commonly receive a reserved, retired, and almost conventual education, as they did in aristocratic times; and then they are suddenly abandoned, without a guide and without assistance, in the midst of all the irregularities inseparable from democratic society.

The Americans are more consistent. They have found out that, in a democracy, the independence of individuals cannot fail to be very great, youth premature, tastes ill-restrained, customs fleeting, public opinion often unsettled and powerless, paternal authority weak, and marital authority contested. Under these circumstances, believing that they had little chance of repressing in woman the most vehement passions of the human heart, they held that the surer way was to teach her the art of combating those passions for herself. As they could not prevent her virtue from being exposed to frequent danger, they determined that she should know how best to defend it; and more reliance was placed on the free vigor of her will than on safeguards which have been shaken or overthrown. Instead then of inculcating mistrust of herself, they constantly seek to enhance her confidence in her own strength of character. As it is neither possible nor desirable to keep a young woman in perpetual and complete ignorance, they hasten to give her a precocious knowledge on all subjects. Far from hiding the corruptions of the world from her, they prefer that she should see them at once, and train herself to shun them; and they hold it of more importance to protect her conduct, than to be over-scrupulous of the innocence of her thoughts.

Although the Americans are a very religious people, they do not rely on religion alone to defend the virtue of woman; they seek to arm her reason also. In this respect they have followed the same method as in several others: they first make vigorous efforts to cause individual independence to control itself, and they do not call in the aid of religion until they have reached the utmost limits of human strength.

I am aware that an education of this kind is not without danger; I am sensible that it tends to invigorate the judgment at the expense of the imagination, and to make cold and virtuous women instead of affectionate wives and agreeable companions to man. Society may be more tranquil and better regulated, but domestic life has often fewer charms. These, however, are secondary evils, which may be braved for the sake of higher interests. At the stage at which we are now arrived, the choice is no longer left to us; a democratic education is indispensable to protect women from the dangers with which democratic institutions and manners surround them.

CHAPTER X.

THE YOUNG WOMAN IN THE CHARACTER OF A WIFE.

IN America, the independence of woman is irrecoverably lost in the bonds of matrimony. If an unmarried woman is less constrained there than elsewhere, a wife is subjected to stricter obligations. The former makes her father's house an abode of freedom and of pleasure; the latter lives in the home of her husband as if it were a cloister. Yet these two different conditions of life are perhaps not so contrary as may be supposed, and it is natural that the American women should pass through the one to arrive at the other.

Religious communities and trading nations entertain peculiarly serious notions of marriage : the former consider the regularity of woman's life as the best pledge and most certain sign of the purity of her morals ; the latter regard it as the highest security for the order and prosperity of the household. The Americans are, at the same time, a puritanical people and a commercial nation ; their religious opinions, as well as their trading habits, consequently lead them to require much abnegation on the part of women, and a constant sacrifice of her pleasures to her duties, which is seldom demanded of her in Europe. Thus, in the United States, the inexorable opinion of the public carefully circumscribes woman within the narrow circle of domestic interests and duties, and forbids her to step beyond it.

Upon her entrance into the world, a young American woman finds these notions firmly established ; she sees the rules which are derived from them ; she is not slow to perceive that she cannot depart for an instant from the established usages of her contemporaries, without putting in jeopardy her peace of mind, her honor, nay, even her social existence ; and she finds the energy required for such an act of submission in the firmness of her understanding, and in the virile habits which her education has given her. It may be said that she has learned, by the use of her independence, to surrender it without a struggle and without a murmur when the time comes for making the sacrifice.

But no American woman falls into the toils of matrimony as into a snare held out to her simplicity and ignorance. She has been taught beforehand what is expected of her, and voluntarily and freely enters upon this engagement. She supports her new condition with courage, because she chose it. As, in America, paternal discipline is very relaxed and the conjugal tie very strict, a young woman does not contract the latter without considerable circumspection and apprehension. Precocious marriages are rare. American women do not marry until their understandings are exercised and ripened ; whereas, in other countries, most women generally only begin to exercise and ripen their understandings after marriage.

I by no means suppose, however, that the great change which takes place in all the habits of women in the United States, as soon as they are married, ought solely to be attributed to the constraint of public opinion ; it is frequently imposed upon themselves by the sole effort of their own will. When the time for choosing a husband is arrived, that cold and stern reasoning power which has been educated and invigorated by the free observation of the world teaches an American woman that a spirit of levity and independence in the bonds of marriage is a constant subject of annoyance, not of pleasure ; it tells her that the amusements of the girl cannot become the recreations of the wife, and that the sources of a married woman's happiness are in the home of her husband. As she clearly discerns beforehand the only road which can lead to domestic happiness, she enters upon it at once, and follows it to the end without seeking to turn back.

The same strength of purpose which the young wives of America display, in bending themselves at once and without repining to the austere duties of their new condition, is no less manifest in all the great trials of their lives. In no country in the world are private fortunes more precarious than in the United States. It is not uncommon for the same man, in the course of his life, to rise and sink again through all the grades which lead from opulence to poverty. American women support these vicissitudes with calm and unquenchable energy: it would seem that their desires contract as easily as they expand with their fortunes.

The greater part of the adventurers who migrate every year to people the Western wilds belong, as I observed in the former part of this work, to the old Anglo-American race of the Northern States. Many of these men, who rush so boldly onwards in pursuit of wealth, were already in the enjoyment of a competency in their own part of the country. They take their wives along with them, and make them share the countless perils and privations which always attend the commencement of these expeditions. I have often met, even on the verge of the wilderness, with young women who, after having been brought up amidst all the comforts of the large towns of New England, had passed, almost without any intermediate stage, from the wealthy abode of their parents to a comfortless hovel in a forest. Fever, solitude, and a tedious life had not broken the springs of their courage. Their features were impaired and faded, but their looks were firm; they appeared to be

at once sad and resolute.*   I do not doubt that these
young American women had amassed, in the education
of their early years, that inward strength which they displayed under these circumstances.   The early culture of
the girl may still, therefore, be traced, in the United States,
under the aspect of marriage ; her part is changed, her
habits are different, but her character is the same.

* See Appendix S.

CHAPTER XI.

HOW EQUALITY OF CONDITION CONTRIBUTES TO MAINTAIN GOOD MORALS IN AMERICA.

SOME philosophers and historians have said or hinted that the strictness of female morality was increased or diminished simply by the distance of a country from the equator. This solution of the difficulty was an easy one; and nothing was required but a globe and a pair of compasses to settle in an instant one of the most difficult problems in the condition of mankind. But I am not sure that this principle of the materialists is supported by facts. The same nations have been chaste or dissolute, at different periods of their history; the strictness or the laxity of their morals depended, therefore, on some variable cause, and not alone on the natural qualities of their country, which were invariable. I do not deny that, in certain climates, the passions which are occasioned by the mutual attraction of the sexes are peculiarly intense; but I believe that this natural intensity may always be excited or restrained by the condition of society, and by political institutions.

Although the travellers who have visited North America differ on many points, they all agree in remarking that morals are far more strict there than elsewhere. It is evident that, on this point, the Americans are very superior to their progenitors, the English. A superficial glance at the two nations will establish the fact.

In England, as in all other countries of Europe, public malice is constantly attacking the frailties of women. Phi-

losophers and statesmen are heard to deplore that morals
are not sufficiently strict, and the literary productions of
the country constantly lead one to suppose so.   In America, all books, novels not excepted, suppose women to be
chaste, and no one thinks of relating affairs of gallantry.

No doubt, this great regularity of American morals is
due in part to qualities of country, race, and religion ; but
all these causes, which operate elsewhere, do not suffice
to account for it : recourse must be had to some special
reason.   This reason appears to me to be the principle of
equality, and the institutions derived from it.   Equality of
condition does not of itself produce regularity of morals,
but it unquestionably facilitates and increases it.*

Amongst aristocratic nations, birth and fortune frequently make two such different beings of man and woman, that
they can never be united to each other.   Their passions
draw them together, but the condition of society, and the
notions suggested by it, prevent them from contracting a
permanent and ostensible tie.   The necessary consequence
is a great number of transient and clandestine connections.
Nature secretly avenges herself for the constraint imposed
upon her by the laws of man.

This is not so much the case when the equality of conditions has swept away all the imaginary or the real barriers
which separated man from woman.   No girl then believes
that she cannot become the wife of the man who loves her ;
and this renders all breaches of morality before marriage
very uncommon : for, whatever be the credulity of the passions, a woman will hardly be able to persuade herself that

* It is not the equality of condition which makes men immoral and irreligious ; but when men, being equal, are also immoral and irreligious, the
effects of immorality and irreligion more easily manifest themselves, because
men have but little influence over each other, and no class exists which can
undertake to keep society in order.   Equality of condition never creates
profligacy of morals, but it sometimes allows that profligacy to show itself.

she is beloved, when her lover is perfectly free to marry her and does not.

The same cause operates, though more indirectly, on married life. Nothing better serves to justify an illicit passion, either to the minds of those who have conceived it or to the world which looks on, than marriages made by compulsion or chance.*

In a country in which a woman is always free to exercise her choice, and where education has prepared her to choose rightly, public opinion is inexorable to her faults. The rigor of the Americans arises in part from this cause. They consider marriages as a covenant which is often oner-ous, but every condition of which the parties are strictly bound to fulfil, because they knew all those conditions be-forehand, and were perfectly free not to have contracted them.

The very circumstances which render matrimonial fidel-ity more obligatory, also render it more easy.

In aristocratic countries, the object of marriage is rather to unite property than persons; hence the husband is some-times at school and the wife at nurse when they are be-trothed. It cannot be wondered at if the conjugal tie which holds the fortunes of the pair united allows their

---

* The literature of Europe sufficiently corroborates this remark. When a European author wishes to depict in a work of fiction any of those great ca-tastrophes in matrimony which so frequently occur amongst us, he takes care to bespeak the compassion of the reader by bringing before him ill-assorted or compulsory marriages. Although habitual tolerance has long since relaxed our morals, an author could hardly succeed in interesting us in the misfortunes of his characters, if he did not first palliate their faults. This artifice seldom fails: the daily scenes we witness prepare us beforehand to be indulgent. But American writers could never render these palliations probable to their readers; their customs and laws are opposed to it; and as they despair of rendering levity of conduct pleasing, they cease to depict it. This is one of the causes to which must be attributed the small number of novels published in the United States.

hearts to rove ; this is the result of the nature of the contract. When, on the contrary, a man always chooses a wife for himself, without any exernal coercion, or even guidance, it is generally a conformity of tastes and opinions which brings a man and a woman together, and this same conformity keeps and fixes them in close habits of intimacy.

Our forefathers had conceived a strange opinion on the subject of marriage ; as they had remarked that the small number of love-matches which occurred in their time almost always turned out ill, they resolutely inferred that it was dangerous to listen to the dictates of the heart on the subject. Accident appeared to them a better guide than choice.

Yet it was not difficult to perceive that the examples which they witnessed in fact proved nothing at all. For, in the first place, if democratic nations leave a woman at liberty to choose her husband, they take care to give her mind sufficient knowledge, and her will sufficient strength, to make so important a choice ; whereas the young women who, amongst aristocratic nations, furtively elope from the authority of their parents to throw themselves of their own accord into the arms of men whom they have had neither time to know, nor ability to judge of, are totally without those securities. It is not surprising that they make a bad use of their freedom of action the first time they avail themselves of it ; nor that they fall into such cruel mistakes when, not having received a democratic education, they choose to marry in conformity to democratic customs. But this is not all. When a man and woman are bent upon marriage in spite of the differences of an aristocratic state of society, the difficulties to be overcome are enormous. Having broken or relaxed the bonds of filial obedience, they have then to emancipate themselves by a final effort from the sway of custom and the tyranny of opinion ;

and when at length they have succeeded in this arduous task, they stand estranged from their natural friends and kinsmen: the prejudice they have crossed separates them from all, and places them in a situation which soon breaks their courage and sours their hearts.

If, then, a couple married in this manner are first unhappy and afterwards criminal, it ought not to be attributed to the freedom of their choice, but rather to their living in a community in which this freedom of choice is not admitted.

Moreover, it should not be forgotten that the same effort which makes a man violently shake off a prevailing error, commonly impels him beyond the bounds of reason; that, to dare to declare war, in however just a cause, against the opinion of one's age and country, a violent and adventurous spirit is required, and that men of this character seldom arrive at happiness or virtue, whatever be the path they follow. And this, it may be observed by the way, is the reason why, in the most necessary and righteous revolutions, it is so rare to meet with virtuous or moderate revolutionary characters. There is, then, no just ground for surprise if a man who, in an age of aristocracy, chooses to consult nothing but his own opinion and his own taste in the choice of a wife, soon finds that infractions of morality and domestic wretchedness invade his household; but when this same line of action is in the natural and ordinary course of things, — when it is sanctioned by parental authority, and backed by public opinion, — it cannot be doubted that the internal peace of families will be increased by it, and conjugal fidelity more rigidly observed.

Almost all men in democracies are engaged in public or professional life; and on the other hand, the limited income obliges a wife to confine herself to the house, in order to watch in person, and very closely, over the details of domestic economy. All these distinct and compulsory occupations are so many natural barriers, which, by keeping the two sexes asunder, render the solicitations of the one less frequent and less ardent, the resistance of the other more easy.

The equality of conditions cannot, it is true, ever succeed in making men chaste, but it may impart a less dangerous character to their breaches of morality. As no one has then either sufficient time or opportunity to assail a virtue armed in self-defence, there will be at the same time a great number of courtesans and a great number of virtuous women. This state of things causes lamentable cases of individual hardship, but it does not prevent the body of society from being strong and alert: it does not destroy family ties, or enervate the morals of the nation. Society is endangered, not by the great profligacy of a few, but by laxity of morals amongst all. In the eyes of a legislator, prostitution is less to be dreaded than intrigue.

The tumultuous and constantly harassed life which equality makes men lead, not only distracts them from the passion of love, by denying them time to indulge it, but it diverts them from it by another more secret but more certain road. All men who live in democratic times more or less contract the ways of thinking of the manufacturing and trading classes; their minds take a serious, deliberate, and positive turn; they are apt to relinquish the ideal, in order to pursue some visible and proximate object, which appears to be the natural and necessary aim of their desires. Thus, the principle of equality does not destroy the imagination, but lowers its flight to the level of the earth.

No men are less addicted to reverie than the citizens of a democracy; and few of them are ever known to give way to those idle and solitary meditations which commonly precede and produce the great emotions of the heart. It is true they attach great importance to procuring for themselves that sort of deep, regular, and quiet affection, which constitutes the charm and safeguard of life; but they are not apt to run after those violent and capricious sources of excitement which disturb and abridge it.

I am aware that all this is applicable in its full extent only to America, and cannot at present be extended to Europe. In the course of the last half-century, whilst laws and customs have impelled several European nations with unexampled force towards democracy, we have not had occasion to observe that the relations of man and woman have become more orderly or more chaste. In some places, the very reverse may be detected: some classes are more strict, the general morality of the people appears to be more lax. I do not hesitate to make the remark, for I am as little disposed to flatter my contemporaries as to malign them.

This fact must distress, but it ought not to surprise us. The propitious influence which a democratic state of society may exercise upon orderly habits is one of those tendencies which can only be discovered after a time. If equality of condition is favorable to purity of morals, the social commotion by which conditions are rendered equal is adverse to it. In the last fifty years, during which France has been undergoing this transformation, it has rarely had freedom, always disturbance. Amidst this universal confusion of notions and this general stir of opinions, — amidst this incoherent mixture of the just and the unjust, of truth and falsehood, of right and might, — public virtue has become doubtful, and private morality wavering. But all revolutions, whatever may have been their object or their agents, have at first produced similar consequences; even those which have in the end drawn tighter the bonds of morality, began by loosening them. The violations of morality which the French frequently witness do not appear to me to have a permanent character; and this is already betokened by some curious signs of the times.

Nothing is more wretchedly corrupt than an aristocracy which retains its wealth when it has lost its power, and which still enjoys a vast deal of leisure after it is reduced to mere vulgar pastimes. The energetic passions and great conceptions which animated it heretofore leave it then; and nothing remains to it but a host of petty consuming vices, which cling about it like worms upon a carcass.

No one denies that the French aristocracy of the last century was extremely dissolute; yet established habits and ancient belief still preserved some respect for morality amongst the other classes of society. Nor will it be denied that, at the present day, the remnants of that same aristocracy exhibit a certain severity of morals; whilst laxity of morals appears to have spread amongst the middle and lower ranks. Thus the same families which were most profligate fifty years ago are now-a-days the most exemplary, and democracy seems only to have strengthened the morality of the aristocratic classes. The French Revolution, by dividing the fortunes of the nobility, by forcing them to attend assiduously to their affairs and to their families, by making them live under the same roof with their children, and, in short, by giving a more rational and serious turn to their minds, has imparted to them, almost without their being aware of it, a reverence for religious belief, a love of order, of tranquil pleasures, of domestic endearments, and of comfort; whereas the rest of the nation, which had naturally these same tastes, was carried away into excesses by the effort which was required to overthrow the laws and political habits of the country.

The old French aristocracy has undergone the consequences of the revolution, but it neither felt the revolutionary passions, nor shared the anarchical excitement which produced it; it may easily be conceived that this aristocracy feels the salutary influence of the revolution on its manners, before those who achieved it. It may there-

fore be said, though at first it seems paradoxical, that, at
the present day, the most anti-democratic classes of the
nation principally exhibit the kind of morality which may
reasonably be anticipated from democracy. I cannot but
think that, when we shall have obtained all the effects of
this democratic revolution, after having got rid of the
tumult it has caused, the observations which are now only
applicable to the few will gradually become true of the
whole community.

CHAPTER XII.

HOW THE AMERICANS UNDERSTAND THE EQUALITY OF THE SEXES.

I HAVE shown how democracy destroys or modifies the different inequalities which originate in society; but is this all? or does it not ultimately affect that great inequality of man and woman which has seemed, up to the present day, to be eternally based in human nature? I believe that the social changes which bring nearer to the same level the father and son, the master and servant, and, in general, superiors and inferiors, will raise woman, and make her more and more the equal of man. But here, more than ever, I feel the necessity of making myself clearly understood; for there is no subject on which the coarse and lawless fancies of our age have taken a freer range.

There are people in Europe who, confounding together the different characteristics of the sexes, would make man and woman into beings not only equal, but alike. They would give to both the same functions, impose on both the same duties, and grant to both the same rights; they would mix them in all things, — their occupations, their pleasures, their business. It may readily be conceived, that, by thus attempting to make one sex equal to the other, both are degraded; and from so preposterous a medley of the works of nature, nothing could ever result but weak men and disorderly women.

It is not thus that the Americans understand that species of democratic equality which may be established between the sexes. They admit that, as nature has appointed such wide differences between the physical and moral constitution of man and woman, her manifest design was to give a distinct employment to their various faculties ; and they hold that improvement does not consist in making beings so dissimilar do pretty nearly the same things, but in causing each of them to fulfil their respective tasks in the best possible manner. The Americans have applied to the sexes the great principle of political economy which governs the manufactures of our age, by carefully dividing the duties of man from those of woman, in order that the great work of society may be the better carried on.

In no country has such constant care been taken as in America to trace two clearly distinct lines of action for the two sexes, and to make them keep pace one with the other, but in two pathways which are always different. American women never manage the outward concerns of the family, or conduct a business, or take a part in political life ; nor are they, on the other hand, ever compelled to perform the rough labor of the fields, or to make any of those laborious exertions which demand the exertion of physical strength. No families are so poor as to form an exception to this rule. If, on the one hand, an American woman cannot escape from the quiet circle of domestic employments, she is never forced, on the other, to go beyond it. Hence it is, that the women of America, who often exhibit a masculine strength of understanding and a manly energy, generally preserve great delicacy of personal appearance, and always retain the manners of women, although they sometimes show that they have the hearts and minds of men.

Nor have the Americans ever supposed that one consequence of democratic principles is the subversion of marital power, or the confusion of the natural authorities in families. They hold that every association must have a head in order to accomplish its object, and that the natural head

of the conjugal association is man. They do not therefore
deny him the right of directing his partner; and they maintain that, in the smaller association of husband and wife,
as well as in the great social community, the object of democracy is to regulate and legalize the powers which are
necessary, and not to subvert all power.

This opinion is not peculiar to one sex, and contested by
the other: I never observed that the women of America
consider conjugal authority as a fortunate usurpation of
their rights, nor that they thought themselves degraded by
submitting to it. It appeared to me, on the contrary, that
they attach a sort of pride to the voluntary surrender of
their own will, and make it their boast to bend themselves
to the yoke, — not to shake it off. Such, at least, is the
feeling expressed by the most virtuous of their sex; the
others are silent; and, in the United States, it is not the
practice for a guilty wife to clamor for the rights of women,
whilst she is trampling on her own holiest duties.

It has often been remarked, that in Europe a certain degree of contempt lurks even in the flattery which men lavish upon women: although a European frequently affects
to be the slave of woman, it may be seen that he never
sincerely thinks her his equal. In the United States, men
seldom compliment women, but they daily show how much
they esteem them. They constantly display an entire confidence in the understanding of a wife, and a profound respect for her freedom; they have decided that her mind is
just as fitted as that of a man to discover the plain truth,
and her heart as firm to embrace it; and they have never
sought to place her virtue, any more than his, under the
shelter of prejudice, ignorance, and fear.

It would seem that, in Europe, where man so easily submits to the despotic sway of women, they are nevertheless
deprived of some of the greatest attributes of the human
species, and considered as seductive but imperfect beings;

and (what may well provoke astonishment) women ultimately look upon themselves in the same light, and almost
consider it as a privilege that they are entitled to show
themselves futile, feeble, and timid. The women of America claim no such privileges.

Again, it may be said that in our morals we have reserved strange immunities to man; so that there is, as it
were, one virtue for his use, and another for the guidance
of his partner; and that, according to the opinion of the
public, the very same act may be punished alternately as a
crime, or only as a fault. The Americans know not this
iniquitous division of duties and rights; amongst them, the
seducer is as much dishonored as his victim.

It is true that the Americans rarely lavish upon women
those eager attentions which are commonly paid them in
Europe; but their conduct to women always implies that
they suppose them to be virtuous and refined; and such is
the respect entertained for the moral freedom of the sex,
that in the presence of a woman the most guarded language is used, lest her ear should be offended by an expression. In America, a young unmarried woman may, alone
and without fear, undertake a long journey.

The legislators of the United States, who have mitigated
almost all the penalties of criminal law, still make rape a
capital offence, and no crime is visited with more inexorable
severity by public opinion. This may be accounted for;
as the Americans can conceive nothing more precious than
a woman's honor, and nothing which ought so much to be
respected as her independence, they hold that no punishment is too severe for the man who deprives her of them
against her will. In France, where the same offence is
visited with far milder penalties, it is frequently difficult to
get a verdict from a jury against the prisoner. Is this a
consequence of contempt of decency, or contempt of women? I cannot but believe that it is a contempt of both.

Thus, the Americans do not think that man and woman have either the duty or the right to perform the same offices, but they show an equal regard for both their respective parts; and though their lot is different, they consider both of them as beings of equal value. They do not give to the courage of woman the same form or the same direction as to that of man; but they never doubt her courage: and if they hold that man and his partner ought not always to exercise their intellect and understanding in the same manner, they at least believe the understanding of the one to be as sound as that of the other, and her intellect to be as clear. Thus, then, whilst they have allowed the social inferiority of woman to subsist, they have done all they could to raise her morally and intellectually to the level of man; and in this respect they appear to me to have excellently understood the true principle of democratic improvement.

As for myself, I do not hesitate to avow, that, although the women of the United States are confined within the narrow circle of domestic life, and their situation is, in some respects, one of extreme dependence, I have nowhere seen woman occupying a loftier position; and if I were asked, now that I am drawing to the close of this work, in which I have spoken of so many important things done by the Americans, to what the singular prosperity and growing strength of that people ought mainly to be attributed, I should reply, To the superiority of their women.

CHAPTER XIII.

HOW THE PRINCIPLE OF EQUALITY NATURALLY DIVIDES THE AMERICANS INTO A MULTITUDE OF SMALL PRIVATE CIRCLES.

IT might be supposed that the final and necessary effect of democratic institutions would be to confound together all the members of the community in private as well as in public life, and to compel them all to live alike; but this would be to ascribe a very coarse and oppressive form to the equality which originates in democracy. No state of society or laws can render men so much alike, but that education, fortune, and tastes will interpose some differences between them; and, though different men may sometimes find it their interest to combine for the same purposes, they will never make it their pleasure. They will therefore always tend to evade the provisions of law, whatever they may be; and, escaping in some respect from the circle in which the legislator sought to confine them, they will set up, close by the great political community, small private societies, united together by similitude of conditions, habits, and manners.

In the United States, the citizens have no sort of pre-eminence over each other; they owe each other no mutual obedience or respect; they all meet for the administration of justice, for the government of the state, and, in general, to treat of the affairs which concern their common welfare; but I never heard that attempts have been made to bring them all to follow the same diversions, or to amuse themselves promiscuously in the same places of recreation.

The Americans, who mingle so readily in their political

assemblies and courts of justice, are wont carefully to separate into small distinct circles, in order to indulge by themselves in the enjoyments of private life. Each of them willingly acknowledges all his fellow-citizens as his equals, but will only receive a very limited number of them as his friends or his guests. This appears to me to be very natural. In proportion as the circle of public society is extended, it may be anticipated that the sphere of private intercourse will be contracted; far from supposing that the members of modern society will ultimately live in common, I am afraid they will end by forming only small coteries.

Amongst aristocratic nations, the different classes are like vast enclosures, out of which it is impossible to get, into which it is impossible to enter. These classes have no communication with each other, but within them men necessarily live in daily contact; even though they would not naturally suit, the general conformity of a similar condition brings them near together.

But when neither law nor custom professes to establish frequent and habitual relations between certain men, their intercourse originates in the accidental similarity of opinions and tastes; hence private society is infinitely varied. In democracies, where the members of the community never differ much from each other, and naturally stand so near that they may all at any time be confounded in one general mass, numerous artificial and arbitrary distinctions spring up, by means of which every man hopes to keep himself aloof, lest he should be carried away against his will in the crowd.

This can never fail to be the case; for human institutions can be changed, but man cannot: whatever may be the general endeavor of a community to render its members equal and alike, the personal pride of individuals will always seek to rise above the line, and to form somewhere an inequality to their own advantage.

In aristocracies, men are separated from each other by lofty stationary barriers: in democracies, they are divided by many small and almost invisible threads, which are constantly broken or moved from place to place. Thus, whatever may be the progress of equality, in democratic nations a great number of small private associations will always be formed within the general pale of political society; but none of them will bear any resemblance in its manners to the higher class in aristocracies.

CHAPTER XIV.

SOME REFLECTIONS ON AMERICAN MANNERS.

NOTHING seems at first sight less important than the outward form of human actions, yet there is nothing upon which men set more store: they grow used to everything except to living in a society which has not their own manners. The influence of the social and political state of a country upon manners is therefore deserving of serious examination.

Manners are generally the product of the very basis of character, but they are also sometimes the result of an arbitrary convention between certain men; thus they are at once natural and acquired.

When some men perceive that they are the foremost persons in society, without contest and without effort, — when they are constantly engaged on large objects, leaving the more minute details to others, — and when they live in the enjoyment of wealth which they did not amass and do not fear to lose, — it may be supposed that they feel a kind of haughty disdain of the petty interests and practical cares of life, and that their thoughts assume a natural greatness, which their language and their manners denote. In democratic countries, manners are generally devoid of dignity, because private life is there extremely petty in its character; and they are frequently low, because the mind has few opportunities of rising above the engrossing cares of domestic interests.

True dignity in manners consists in always taking one's proper station, neither too high nor too low; and this is as much within the reach of a peasant as of a prince. In democracies, all stations appear doubtful; hence it is that the manners of democracies, though often full of arrogance, are commonly wanting in dignity, and, moreover, they are never either well-trained or accomplished.

The men who live in democracies are too fluctuating for a certain number of them ever to succeed in laying down a code of good breeding, and in forcing people to follow it. Every man therefore behaves after his own fashion, and there is always a certain incoherence in the manners of such times, because they are moulded upon the feelings and notions of each individual, rather than upon an ideal model proposed for general imitation. This, however, is much more perceptible when an aristocracy has just been overthrown, than after it has long been destroyed. New political institutions and new social elements then bring to the same places of resort, and frequently compel to live in common, men whose education and habits are still amazingly dissimilar, and this renders the motley composition of society peculiarly visible. The existence of a former strict code of good breeding is still remembered, but what it contained, or where it is to be found, is already forgotten. Men have lost the common law of manners, and they have not yet made up their minds to do without it; but every one endeavors to make to himself some sort of arbitrary and variable rule, from the remnant of former usages; so that manners have neither the regularity and the dignity which they often display amongst aristocratic nations, nor the simplicity and freedom which they sometimes assume in democracies; they are at once constrained and without constraint.

This, however, is not the normal state of things. When the equality of conditions is long established and complete, as all men entertain nearly the same notions and do nearly the same things, they do not require to agree, or to copy from one another, in order to speak or act in the same manner; their manners are constantly characterized by a number of lesser diversities, but not by any great differences. They are never perfectly alike, because they do not copy from the same pattern; they are never very unlike, because their social condition is the same. At first sight, a traveller would say that the manners of all Americans are exactly similar; it is only upon close examination that the peculiarities in which they differ may be detected.

The English make game of the manners of the Americans; but it is singular that most of the writers who have drawn these ludicrous delineations belonged themselves to the middle classes in England, to whom the same delineations are exceedingly applicable; so that these pitiless censors furnish, for the most part, an example of the very thing they blame in the United States: they do not perceive that they are deriding themselves, to the great amusement of the aristocracy of their own country.

Nothing is more prejudicial to democracy than its outward forms of behavior; many men would willingly endure its vices, who cannot support its manners. I cannot, however, admit that there is nothing commendable in the manners of a democratic people.

Amongst aristocratic nations, all who live within reach of the first class in society commonly strain to be like it, which gives rise to ridiculous and insipid imitations. As a democratic people do not possess any models of high breeding, at least they escape the daily necessity of seeing wretched copies of them. In democracies, manners are never so refined as amongst aristocratic nations, but, on the other hand, they are never so coarse. Neither the coarse oaths of the populace, nor the elegant and choice expressions of the nobility, are to be heard there: the manners of such a people are often vulgar, but they are neither brutal nor mean.

I have already observed that, in democracies, no such thing as a regular code of good breeding can be laid down ; this has some inconveniences and some advantages. In aristocracies, the rules of propriety impose the same demeanor on every one ; they make all the members of the same class appear alike, in spite of their private inclinations ; they adorn and they conceal the natural man. Amongst a democratic people, manners are neither so tutored nor so uniform, but they are frequently more sincere. They form, as it were, a light and loosely-woven veil, through which the real feelings and private opinions of each individual are easily discernible. The form and the substance of human actions, therefore, often stand there in closer relation ; and if the great picture of human life be less embellished, it is more true. Thus it may be said, in one sense, that the effect of democracy is not exactly to give men any particular manners, but to prevent them from having manners at all.

The feelings, the passions, the virtues, and the vices of an aristocracy may sometimes reappear in a democracy, but not its manners ; they are lost, and vanish forever, as soon as the democratic revolution is completed. It would seem that nothing is more lasting than the manners of an aristocratic class, for they are preserved by that class for some time after it has lost its wealth and its power, — nor so fleeting, for no sooner have they disappeared, than not a trace of them is to be found ; and it is scarcely possible to say what they have been, as soon as they have ceased to be. A change in the state of society works this miracle, and a few generations suffice to consummate it. The principal characteristics of aristocracy are handed down by history after an aristocracy is destroyed ; but the light and exquisite touches of manners are effaced from men's memories almost immediately after its fall. Men can no longer conceive what these manners were, when they have ceased to witness them; they are gone, and their departure was unseen, unfelt; for in order to feel that refined enjoyment which is derived from choice and distinguished manners, habit and education must have prepared the heart, and the taste for them is lost almost as easily as the practice of them. Thus, not only a democratic people cannot have aristocratic manners, but they neither comprehend nor desire them; and as they never have thought of them, it is to their minds as if such things had never been. Too much importance should not be attached to this loss, but it may well be regretted.

I am aware that it has not unfrequently happened that the same men have had very high-bred manners and very low-born feelings: the interior of courts has sufficiently shown what imposing externals may conceal the meanest hearts. But though the manners of aristocracy do not constitute virtue, they sometimes embellish virtue itself. It was no ordinary sight to see a numerous and powerful class of men, whose every outward action seemed constantly to be dictated by a natural elevation of thought and feeling, by delicacy and regularity of taste, and by urbanity of manners. Those manners threw a pleasing illusory charm over human nature; and though the picture was often a false one, it could not be viewed without a noble satisfaction.

CHAPTER XV.

OF THE GRAVITY OF THE AMERICANS, AND WHY IT DOES
NOT PREVENT THEM FROM OFTEN DOING INCONSIDERATE
THINGS.

MEN who live in democratic countries do not value the
simple, turbulent, or coarse diversions in which the
people in aristocratic communities indulge: such diversions
are thought by them to be puerile or insipid. Nor have
they a greater inclination for the intellectual and refined
amusements of the aristocratic classes. They want something productive and substantial in their pleasures; they
want to mix actual fruition with their joy.

In aristocratic communities, the people readily give themselves up to bursts of tumultuous and boisterous gayety,
which shake off at once the recollection of their privations: the inhabitants of democracies are not fond of being
thus violently broken in upon, and they never lose sight of
themselves without regret. Instead of these frivolous delights, they prefer those more serious and silent amusements which are like business, and which do not drive
business wholly out of their minds.

An American, instead of going in a leisure hour to dance
merrily at some place of public resort, as the fellows of his
class continue to do throughout the greater part of Europe,
shuts himself up at home to drink. He thus enjoys two
pleasures; he can go on thinking of his business, and can
get drunk decently by his own fireside.

I thought that the English constituted the most serious
nation on the face of the earth; but I have since seen the

Americans and have changed my opinion. I do not mean to say that temperament has not a great deal to do with the character of the inhabitants of the United States, but I think that their political institutions are a still more influential cause.

I believe the seriousness of the Americans arises partly from their pride. In democratic countries, even poor men entertain a lofty notion of their personal importance: they look upon themselves with complacency, and are apt to suppose that others are looking at them too. With this disposition, they watch their language and their actions with care, and do not lay themselves open so as to betray their deficiencies; to preserve their dignity, they think it necessary to retain their gravity.

But I detect another more deep-seated and powerful cause, which instinctively produces amongst the Americans this astonishing gravity. Under a despotism, communities give way at times to bursts of vehement joy; but they are generally gloomy and moody, because they are afraid. Under absolute monarchies tempered by the customs and manners of the country, their spirits are often cheerful and even, because, as they have some freedom and a good deal of security, they are exempted from the most important cares of life; but all free nations are serious, because their minds are habitually absorbed by the contemplation of some dangerous or difficult purpose. This is more especially the case amongst those free nations which form democratic communities. Then there are, in all classes, a large number of men constantly occupied with the serious affairs of the government; and those whose thoughts are not engaged in the matters of the commonwealth, are wholly engrossed by the acquisition of a private fortune. Amongst such a people, a serious demeanor ceases to be peculiar to certain men, and becomes a habit of the nation.

We are told of small democracies in the days of antiquity, in which the citizens met upon the public places with garlands of roses, and spent almost all their time in dancing and theatrical amusements. I do not believe in such republics, any more than in that of Plato; or, if the things we read of really happened, I do not hesitate to affirm that these supposed democracies were composed of very different elements from ours, and that they had nothing in common with the latter except their name.

But it must not be supposed that, in the midst of all their toils, the people who live in democracies think themselves to be pitied; the contrary is remarked to be the case. No men are fonder of their own condition. Life would have no relish for them, if they were delivered from the anxieties which harass them, and they show more attachment to their cares than aristocratic nations to their pleasures.

I am next led to inquire how it is that these same democratic nations which are so serious, sometimes act in so inconsiderate a manner. The Americans, who almost always preserve a staid demeanor and a frigid air, nevertheless frequently allow themselves to be borne away, far beyond the bounds of reason, by a sudden passion or a hasty opinion, and sometimes gravely commit strange absurdities.

This contrast ought not to surprise us. There is one sort of ignorance which originates in extreme publicity. In despotic states, men know not how to act, because they are told nothing: in democratic nations, they often act at random, because nothing is to be left untold. The former do not know, the latter forget; and the chief features of each picture are lost to them in a bewilderment of details.

It is astonishing what imprudent language a public man may sometimes use in free countries, and especially in democratic states, without being compromised; whereas, in absolute monarchies, a few words dropped by accident are enough to unmask him forever, and ruin him without

hope of redemption. This is explained by what goes before. When a man speaks in the midst of a great crowd,
many of his words are not heard, or are forthwith obliterated from the memories of those who hear them; but
amidst the silence of a mute and motionless throng, the
slightest whisper strikes the ear.

In democracies men are never stationary; a thousand
chances waft them to and fro, and their life is always the
sport of unforeseen or (so to speak) extemporaneous circumstances. Thus, they are often obliged to do things
which they have imperfectly learned, to say things which
they imperfectly understand, and to devote themselves to
work for which they are unprepared by long apprenticeship. In aristocracies, every man has one sole object, which
he unceasingly pursues; but amongst democratic nations
the existence of man is more complex; the same mind will
almost always embrace several objects at once, and these
objects are frequently wholly foreign to each other: as it
cannot know them all well, the mind is readily satisfied
with imperfect notions of each.

When the inhabitant of a democracy is not urged by his
wants, he is so at least by his desires; for of all the possessions which he sees around him, none are wholly beyond
his reach. He therefore does everything in a hurry, he is
always satisfied with " pretty well," and never pauses more
than an instant to consider what he has been doing. His
curiosity is at once insatiable and cheaply satisfied; for he
cares more to know a great deal quickly, than to know anything well: he has no time and but little taste to search
things to the bottom.

Thus, then, a democratic people are grave, because their
social and political condition constantly leads them to engage in serious occupations; and they act inconsiderately,
because they give but little time and attention to each of
these occupations. The habit of inattention must be considered as the greatest defect of the democratic character.

CHAPTER XVI.

WHY THE NATIONAL VANITY OF THE AMERICANS IS MORE
RESTLESS AND CAPTIOUS THAN THAT OF THE ENGLISH.

ALL free nations are vainglorious, but national pride
is not displayed by all in the same manner. The
Americans, in their intercourse with strangers, appear impatient of the smallest censure, and insatiable of praise.
The most slender eulogium is acceptable to them, the most
exalted seldom contents them; they unceasingly harass you
to extort praise, and if you resist their entreaties, they fall
to praising themselves. It would seem as if, doubting their
own merit, they wished to have it constantly exhibited
before their eyes. Their vanity is not only greedy, but
restless and jealous; it will grant nothing, whilst it demands everything, but is ready to beg and to quarrel at
the same time.

If I say to an American that the country he lives in is a
fine one, " Ay," he replies, " there is not its equal in the
world." If I applaud the freedom which its inhabitants
enjoy, he answers, " Freedom is a fine thing, but few nations are worthy to enjoy it." If I remark the purity of
morals which distinguishes the United States, " I can imagine," says he, " that a stranger, who has witnessed the
corruption that prevails in other nations, should be astonished at the difference." At length, I leave him to the
contemplation of himself; but he returns to the charge,
and does not desist till he has got me to repeat all I
had just been saying. It is impossible to conceive a more

troublesome or more garrulous patriotism; it wearies even those who are disposed to respect it.*

Such is not the case with the English. An Englishman calmly enjoys the real or imaginary advantages which, in his opinion, his country possesses. If he grants nothing to other nations, neither does he solicit anything for his own. The censure of foreigners does not affect him, and their praise hardly flatters him; his position with regard to the rest of the world is one of disdainful and ignorant reserve: his pride requires no sustenance, — it nourishes itself. It is remarkable that two nations, so recently sprung from the same stock, should be so opposite to one another in their manner of feeling and conversing.

In aristocratic countries the great possess immense privileges, upon which their pride rests, without seeking to rely upon the lesser advantages which accrue to them. As these privileges came to them by inheritance, they regard them in some sort as a portion of themselves, or at least as a natural right inherent in their own persons. They therefore entertain a calm sense of their own superiority; they do not dream of vaunting privileges which every one perceives and no one contests, and these things are not sufficiently new to be made topics of conversation. They stand unmoved in their solitary greatness, well assured that they are seen of all the world without any effort to show themselves off, and that no one will attempt to drive them from that position. When an aristocracy carries on the public affairs, its national pride naturally assumes this reserved, indifferent, and haughty form, which is imitated by all the other classes of the nation.

When, on the contrary, social conditions differ but little, the slightest privileges are of some importance; as every man sees around himself a million of people enjoying precisely similar or analogous advantages, his pride becomes

* See Appendix T.

craving and jealous, he clings to mere trifles, and doggedly defends them. In democracies, as the conditions of life are very fluctuating, men have almost always recently acquired the advantages which they possess ; the consequence is, that they feel extreme pleasure in exhibiting them, to show others and convince themselves that they really enjoy them. As at any instant these same advantages may be lost, their possessors are constantly on the alert, and make a point of showing that they still retain them. Men living in democracies love their country just as they love themselves, and they transfer the habits of their private vanity to their vanity as a nation.

The restless and insatiable vanity of a democratic people originates so entirely in the equality and precariousness of their social condition, that the members of the haughtiest nobility display the very same passion in those lesser portions of their existence in which there is anything fluctuating or contested. An aristocratic class always differs greatly from the other classes of the nation, by the extent and perpetuity of its privileges ; but it often happens that the only differences between the members who belong to it consist in small, transient advantages, which may any day be lost or acquired. The members of a powerful aristocracy, collected in a capital or a court, have been known to contest with virulence those frivolous privileges which depend on the caprice of fashion or the will of their master. These persons then displayed towards each other precisely the same puerile jealousies which animate the men of democracies, the same eagerness to snatch the smallest advantages which their equals contested, and the same desire to parade ostentatiously those of which they were in possession.

If national pride ever entered into the minds of courtiers, I do not question that they would display it in the same manner as the members of a democratic community.

CHAPTER XVII.

HOW THE ASPECT OF SOCIETY IN THE UNITED STATES IS AT ONCE EXCITED AND MONOTONOUS.

IT would seem that nothing could be more adapted to stimulate and to feed curiosity than the aspect of the United States. Fortunes, opinions, and laws are there in ceaseless variation : it is as if immutable Nature herself were mutable, such are the changes worked upon her by the hand of man. Yet, in the end, the spectacle of this excited community becomes monotonous, and, after having watched the moving pageant for a time, the spectator is tired of it.

Amongst aristocratic nations, every man is pretty nearly stationary in his own sphere; but men are astonishingly unlike each other, — their passions, their notions, their habits, and their tastes are essentially different: nothing changes, but everything differs. In democracies, on the contrary, all men are alike, and do things pretty nearly alike. It is true that they are subject to great and frequent vicissitudes; but as the same events of good or adverse fortune are continually recurring, the name of the actors only is changed, the piece is always the same. The aspect of American society is animated, because men and things are always changing; but it is monotonous, because all these changes are alike.

Men living in democratic times have many passions, but most of their passions either end in the love of riches, or proceed from it. The cause of this is, not that their souls are narrower, but that the importance of money is really greater at such times. When all the members of a community are independent of or indifferent to each other, the co-operation of each of them can be obtained only by paying for it: this infinitely multiplies the purposes to which wealth may be applied, and increases its value. When the reverence which belonged to what is old has vanished, birth, condition, and profession no longer distinguish men, or scarcely distinguish them: hardly anything but money remains to create strongly marked differences between them, and to raise some of them above the common level. The distinction originating in wealth is increased by the disappearance or diminution of all other distinctions. Amongst aristocratic nations, money reaches only to a few points on the vast circle of man's desires: in democracies, it seems to lead to all.

The love of wealth is therefore to be traced, either as a principal or an accessory motive, at the bottom of all that the Americans do: this gives to all their passions a sort of family likeness, and soon renders the survey of them exceedingly wearisome. This perpetual recurrence of the same passion is monotonous; the peculiar methods by which this passion seeks its own gratification are no less so.

In an orderly and peaceable democracy like the United States, where men cannot enrich themselves by war, by public office, or by political confiscation, the love of wealth mainly drives them into business and manufactures. Although these pursuits often bring about great commotions and disasters, they cannot prosper without strictly regular habits and a long routine of petty uniform acts. The stronger the passion is, the more regular are these habits, and the more uniform are these acts. It may be said that it is the vehemence of their desires which makes the Americans so methodical; it perturbs their minds, but it disciplines their lives.

The remark I here apply to America may indeed be

addressed to almost all our contemporaries.   Variety is disappearing from the human race; the same ways of acting, thinking, and feeling are to be met with all over the world.   This is not only because nations work more upon each other, and copy each other more faithfully; but as the men of each country relinquish more and more the peculiar opinions and feelings of a caste, a profession, or a family, they simultaneously arrive at something nearer to the constitution of man, which is everywhere the same. Thus they become more alike, even without having imitated each other.   Like travellers scattered about some large wood, intersected by paths converging to one point, if all of them keep their eyes fixed upon that point, and advance towards it, they insensibly draw nearer together, — though they seek not, though they see not and know not each other; and they will be surprised at length to find themselves all collected on the same spot.   All the nations which take, not any particular man, but Man himself, as the object of their researches and their imitations, are tending in the end to a similar state of society, like these travellers converging to the central plot of the forest.

CHAPTER XVIII.

OF HONOR[*] IN THE UNITED STATES AND IN DEMOCRATIC COMMUNITIES.

IT would seem that men employ two very distinct methods in the judgment which they pass upon the actions of their fellow-men; at one time, they judge them by those simple notions of right and wrong which are diffused all over the world; at another, they appreciate them by a few very special rules which belong exclusively to some particular age and country. It often happens that these two standards differ; they sometimes conflict: but they are never either entirely identified or entirely annulled by one another.

Honor, at the periods of its greatest power, sways the will more than the belief of men; and even whilst they yield without hesitation and without a murmur to its dictates, they feel notwithstanding, by a dim but mighty instinct, the existence of a more general, more ancient, and more holy law, which they sometimes disobey, although they cease not to acknowledge it. Some actions have been held to be at the same time virtuous and dishonorable; — a refusal to fight a duel is an instance.

---

[*] The word Honor is not always used in the same sense either in French or English. 1. It first signifies the esteem, glory, or reverence which a man receives from his kind; and in this sense, a man is said *to acquire honor*. 2. Honor signifies the aggregate of those rules by the aid of which this esteem, glory, or reverence is obtained. Thus we say that *a man has always strictly obeyed the laws of honor*; or *a man has violated his honor*. In this chapter, the word is always used in the latter sense.

I think these peculiarities may be otherwise explained than by the mere caprices of certain individuals and nations, as has hitherto been customary. Mankind are subject to general and permanent wants that have created moral laws, to the neglect of which men have ever and in all places attached the notion of censure and shame: to infringe them was *to do ill*, — *to do well* was to conform to them.

Within this vast association of the human race, lesser associations have been formed, which are called nations; and amidst these nations, further subdivisions have assumed the names of classes or castes. Each of these associations forms, as it were, a separate species of the human race; and though it has no essential difference from the mass of mankind, to a certain extent it stands apart, and has certain wants peculiar to itself. To these special wants must be attributed the modifications which affect, in various degrees and in different countries, the mode of considering human actions, and the estimate which is formed of them. It is the general and permanent interest of mankind that men should not kill each other; but it may happen to be the peculiar and temporary interest of a people or a class to justify, or even to honor, homicide.

Honor is simply that peculiar rule founded upon a peculiar state of society, by the application of which a people or a class allot praise or blame. Nothing is more unproductive to the mind than an abstract idea; I therefore hasten to call in the aid of facts and examples to illustrate my meaning.

I select the most extraordinary kind of honor which has ever been known in the world, and that which we are best acquainted with, — viz. aristocratic honor springing out of feudal society. I shall explain it by means of the principle already laid down, and explain the principle by means of this illustration.

I am not here led to inquire when and how the aristocracy of the Middle Ages came into existence, why it was so deeply severed from the remainder of the nation, or what founded and consolidated its power. I take its existence as an established fact, and I am endeavoring to account for the peculiar view which it took of the greater part of human actions.

The first thing that strikes me is, that, in the feudal world, actions were not always praised or blamed with reference to their intrinsic worth, but were sometimes appreciated exclusively with reference to the person who was the actor or the object of them, which is repugnant to the general conscience of mankind. Thus, some of the actions which were indifferent on the part of a man in humble life, dishonored a noble; others changed their whole character according as the person aggrieved by them belonged, or did not belong, to the aristocracy.

When these different notions first arose, the nobility formed a distinct body amidst the people, which it commanded from the inaccessible heights where it was ensconced. To maintain this peculiar position, which constituted its strength, it not only required political privileges, but it required a standard of right and wrong for its own special use.

That some particular virtue or vice belonged to the nobility rather than to the humble classes, — that certain actions were guiltless when they affected the villain, which were criminal when they touched the noble, — these were often arbitrary matters; but that honor or shame should be attached to a man's actions according to his condition, was a result of the internal constitution of an aristocratic community. This has been actually the case in all the countries which have had an aristocracy; as long as a trace of the principle remains, these peculiarities will still exist: to debauch a woman of color scarcely injures the reputation of an American, — to marry her dishonors him.

In some cases, feudal honor enjoined revenge, and stigmatized the forgiveness of insults; in others, it imperiously commanded men to conquer their own passions, and required forgetfulness of self. It did not make humanity or kindness its law, but it extolled generosity; it set more store on liberality than on benevolence; it allowed men to enrich themselves by gambling or by war, but not by labor; it preferred great crimes to small earnings; cupidity was less distasteful to it than avarice; violence it often sanctioned, but cunning and treachery it invariably reprobated as contemptible.

These fantastical notions did not proceed exclusively from the caprice of those who entertained them. A class which has succeeded in placing itself above all others, and which makes perpetual exertions to maintain this lofty position, must especially honor those virtues which are conspicuous for their dignity and splendor, and which may be easily combined with pride and the love of power. Such men would not hesitate to invert the natural order of conscience in order to give these virtues precedence over all others. It may even be conceived that some of the more bold and brilliant vices would readily be set above the quiet, unpretending virtues. The very existence of such a class in society renders these things unavoidable.

The nobles of the Middle Ages placed military courage foremost amongst virtues, and in lieu of many of them. This, again, was a peculiar opinion, which arose necessarily from the peculiar state of society. Feudal aristocracy existed by war and for war; its power had been founded by arms, and by arms that power was maintained: it therefore required nothing more than military courage, and that quality was naturally exalted above all others; whatever denoted it, even at the expense of reason and humanity, was therefore approved and frequently enjoined by the manners of the time. Such was the main principle; the caprice of man was to be traced only in minuter details. That a man should regard a tap on the cheek as an unbearable insult, and should be obliged to kill in single combat the person who struck him thus lightly, is an arbitrary rule ; but that a noble could not tranquilly receive an insult, and was dishonored if he allowed himself to take a blow without fighting, were direct consequences of the fundamental principles and the wants of a military aristocracy.

Thus it was true, to a certain extent, that the laws of honor were capricious ; but these caprices of honor were always confined within certain necessary limits. The peculiar rule which was called honor by our forefathers is so far from being an arbitrary law in my eyes, that I would readily engage to ascribe its most incoherent and fantastical injunctions to a small number of fixed and invariable wants inherent in feudal society.

If I were to trace the notion of feudal honor into the domain of politics, I should not find it more difficult to explain its dictates. The state of society and the political institutions of the Middle Ages were such, that the supreme power of the nation never governed the community directly. That power did not exist in the eyes of the people : every man looked up to a certain individual whom he was bound to obey ; by that intermediate personage he was connected with all the others. Thus, in feudal society, the whole system of the commonwealth rested upon the sentiment of fidelity to the person of the lord ; to destroy that sentiment was to fall into anarchy. Fidelity to a political superior was, moreover, a sentiment of which all the members of the aristocracy had constant opportunities of estimating the importance ; for every one of them was a vassal as well as a lord, and had to command as well as to obey. To remain faithful to the lord, to sacrifice one's self for him if called upon, to share his good or evil fortunes, to stand by him in his undertakings whatever they might be, — such were the first injunctions of feudal honor in relation to the political institutions of those times. The treachery of a vassal was branded with extraordinary severity by public opinion, and a name of peculiar infamy was invented for the offence ; it was called *felony*.

On the contrary, few traces are to be found in the Middle Ages of the passion which constituted the life of the nations of antiquity, — I mean patriotism ; the word itself is not of very ancient date in the language.* Feudal institutions concealed the country at large from men's sight, and rendered the love of it less necessary. The nation was forgotten in the passions which attached men to persons. Hence it was no part of the strict law of feudal honor to remain faithful to one's country. Not indeed that the love of their country did not exist in the hearts of our forefathers ; but it constituted a dim and feeble instinct, which has grown more clear and strong in proportion as aristocratic classes have been abolished, and the supreme power of the nation centralized.

This may be clearly seen from the contrary judgments which European nations have passed upon the various events of their histories, according to the generations by which such judgments were formed. The circumstance which most dishonored the Constable de Bourbon in the eyes of his contemporaries was, that he bore arms against his king : that which most dishonors him in our eyes is, that he made war against his country. We brand him as deeply as our forefathers did, but for different reasons.

I have chosen the honor of feudal times by way of illustration of my meaning, because its characteristics are more distinctly marked and more familiar to us than those of any other period ; but I might have taken an example else-

* Even the word *patrie* was not used by the French writers until the sixteenth century.

where, and I should have reached the same conclusion by a different road.

Although we are less perfectly acquainted with the Romans than with our own ancestors, yet we know that certain peculiar notions of glory and disgrace obtained amongst them, which were not derived solely from the general principles of right and wrong. Many human actions were judged differently, according as they affected a Roman citizen or a stranger, a freeman or a slave; certain vices were blazoned abroad, certain virtues were extolled above all others. "In that age," says Plutarch, in the Life of Coriolanus, "martial prowess was more honored and prized in Rome than all the other virtues, insomuch that it was called *virtus*, the name of virtue itself, by applying the name of the kind to this particular species; so that *virtue* in Latin was as much as to say *valor*." Can any one fail to recognize the peculiar want of that singular community which was formed for the conquest of the world?

Any nation would furnish us with similar grounds of observation; for, as I have already remarked, whenever men collect together as a distinct community, the notion of honor instantly grows up amongst them; that is to say, a system of opinions peculiar to themselves as to what is blamable or commendable; and these peculiar rules always originate in the special habits and special interests of the community.

This is applicable to a certain extent to democratic communities as well as to others, as we shall now proceed to prove by the example of the Americans.*

Some loose notions of the old aristocratic honor of Europe are still to be found scattered amongst the opinions of the Americans; but these traditional opinions are few in

---

* I speak here of the Americans inhabiting those States where slavery does not exist; they alone can be said to present a complete picture of democratic society.

number, they have but little root in the country, and but little power. They are like a religion which has still some temples left standing, though men have ceased to believe in it. But amidst these half-obliterated notions of exotic honor some new opinions have sprung up, which constitute what may be termed in our days American honor.

I have shown how the Americans are constantly driven to engage in commerce and industry. Their origin, their social condition, their political institutions, and even the region they inhabit, urge them irresistibly in this direction. Their present condition, then, is that of an almost exclusively manufacturing and commercial association, placed in the midst of a new and boundless country, which their principal object is to explore for purposes of profit. This is the characteristic which most distinguishes the American people from all others at the present time.

All those quiet virtues which tend to give a regular movement to the community, and to encourage business, will therefore be held in peculiar honor by that people, and to neglect those virtues will be to incur public contempt. All the more turbulent virtues, which often dazzle, but more frequently disturb society, will, on the contrary, occupy a subordinate rank in the estimation of this same people; they may be neglected without forfeiting the esteem of the community; to acquire them would perhaps be to run a risk of losing it.

The Americans make a no less arbitrary classification of men's vices. There are certain propensities which appear censurable to the general reason and the universal conscience of mankind, but which happen to agree with the peculiar and temporary wants of the American community: these propensities are lightly reproved, sometimes even encouraged; for instance, the love of wealth and the secondary propensities connected with it may be more particularly cited. To clear, to till, and to transform the vast uninhabited continent which is his domain, the American requires the daily support of an energetic passion; that passion can only be the love of wealth; the passion for wealth is therefore not reprobated in America, and, provided it does not go beyond the bounds assigned to it for public security, it is held in honor. The American lauds as a noble and praiseworthy ambition what our own forefathers, in the Middle Ages, stigmatized as servile cupidity, just as he treats as a blind and barbarous frenzy that ardor of conquest and martial temper which bore them to battle.

In the United States, fortunes are lost and regained without difficulty; the country is boundless, and its resources inexhaustible. The people have all the wants and cravings of a growing creature; and, whatever be their efforts, they are always surrounded by more than they can appropriate. It is not the ruin of a few individuals, which may be soon repaired, but the inactivity and sloth of the community at large, which would be fatal to such a people. Boldness of enterprise is the foremost cause of its rapid progress, its strength, and its greatness. Commercial business is there like a vast lottery, by which a small number of men continually lose, but the state is always a gainer; such a people ought therefore to encourage and do honor to boldness in commercial speculations. But any bold speculation risks the fortune of the speculator and of all those who put their trust in him. The Americans, who make a virtue of commercial temerity, have no right in any case to brand with disgrace those who practise it. Hence arises the strange indulgence which is shown to bankrupts in the United States; their honor does not suffer by such an accident. In this respect the Americans differ, not only from the nations of Europe, but from all the commercial nations of our time; and accordingly they resemble none of them in their position or their wants.

In America, all those vices which tend to impair the purity of morals, and to destroy the conjugal tie, are treated with a degree of severity which is unknown in the rest of the world. At first sight, this seems strangely at variance with the tolerance shown there on other subjects, and one is surprised to meet with a morality so relaxed and also so austere amongst the self-same people. But these things are less incoherent than they seem to be. Public opinion in the United States very gently represses that love of wealth which promotes the commercial greatness and the prosperity of the nation, and it especially condemns that laxity of morals which diverts the human mind from the pursuit of well-being, and disturbs the internal order of domestic life which is so necessary to success in business. To earn the esteem of their countrymen, the Americans are therefore constrained to adapt themselves to orderly habits; and it may be said in this sense that they make it a matter of honor to live chastely.

On one point, American honor accords with the notions of honor acknowledged in Europe; it places courage as the highest virtue, and treats it as the greatest of the moral necessities of man; but the notion of courage itself assumes a different aspect. In the United States, martial valor is but little prized; the courage which is best known and most esteemed is that which emboldens men to brave the dangers of the ocean, in order to arrive earlier in port, — to support the privations of the wilderness without complaint, and solitude more cruel than privations, — the courage which renders them almost insensible to the loss of a fortune laboriously acquired, and instantly prompts to fresh exertions to make another. Courage of this kind is peculiarly necessary to the maintenance and prosperity of the American communities, and it is held by them in peculiar honor and estimation; to betray a want of it is to incur certain disgrace.

I have yet another characteristic point which may serve

to place the idea of this chapter in stronger relief. In a democratic society like that of the United States, where fortunes are scanty and insecure, everybody works, and work opens a way to everything: this has changed the point of honor quite round, and has turned it against idleness. I have sometimes met in America with young men of wealth, personally disinclined to all laborious exertion, but who had been compelled to embrace a profession. Their disposition and their fortune allowed them to remain without employment: public opinion forbade it, too imperiously to be disobeyed. In the European countries, on the contrary, where aristocracy is still struggling with the flood which overwhelms it, I have often seen men, constantly spurred on by their wants and desires, remain in idleness, in order not to lose the esteem of their equals; and I have known them submit to ennui and privations rather than to work. No one can fail to perceive that these opposite obligations are two different rules of conduct, both nevertheless originating in the notion of honor.

What our forefathers designated as honor absolutely was in reality only one of its forms; they gave a generic name to what was only a species. Honor, therefore, is to be found in democratic as well as in aristocratic ages, but it will not be difficult to show that it assumes a different aspect in the former. Not only are its injunctions different, but we shall shortly see that they are less numerous, less precise, and that its dictates are less rigorously obeyed.

The position of a caste is always much more peculiar than that of a people. Nothing is so exceptional in the world as a small community invariably composed of the same families, (as was, for instance, the aristocracy of the Middle Ages,) whose object is to concentrate and to retain, exclusively and hereditarily, education, wealth, and power amongst its own members. But the more exceptional the position of a community happens to be, the more numerous are its special wants, and the more extensive are its notions of honor corresponding to those wants.

The rules of honor will therefore always be less numerous amongst a people not divided into castes than amongst any other. If ever any nations are constituted in which it may even be difficult to find any peculiar classes of society, the notion of honor will be confined to a small number of precepts, which will be more and more in accordance with the moral laws adopted by the mass of mankind.

Thus the laws of honor will be less peculiar and less multifarious amongst a democratic people than in an aristocracy. They will also be more obscure; and this is a necessary consequence of what goes before; for as the distinguishing marks of honor are less numerous and less peculiar, it must often be difficult to distinguish them. To this other reasons may be added. Amongst the aristocratic nations of the Middle Ages, generation succeeded generation in vain; each family was like a never-dying, ever-stationary man, and the state of opinions was hardly more changeable than that of conditions. Every one then had the same objects always before his eyes, which he contemplated from the same point; his eyes gradually detected the smallest details, and his discernment could not fail to become in the end clear and accurate. Thus, not only had the men of feudal times very extraordinary opinions in matters of honor, but each of those opinions was present to their minds under a clear and precise form.

This can never be the case in America, where all men are in constant motion, and where society, transformed daily by its own operations, changes its opinions together with its wants. In such a country, men have glimpses of the rules of honor, but they seldom have time to fix attention upon them.

But even if society were motionless, it would still be difficult to determine the meaning which ought to be attached to the word honor. In the Middle Ages, as each class had its own honor, the same opinion was never received at the same time by a large number of men; and this rendered it possible to give it a determined and accurate form, which was the more easy, as all those by whom it was received, having a perfectly identical and most peculiar position, were naturally disposed to agree upon the points of a law which was made for themselves alone.

Thus the code of honor became a complete and detailed system, in which everything was anticipated and provided for beforehand, and a fixed and always palpable standard was applied to human actions. Amongst a democratic nation, like the Americans, in which ranks are confounded, and the whole of society forms one single mass, composed of elements which are all analogous though not entirely similar, it is impossible ever to agree beforehand on what shall or shall not be allowed by the laws of honor.

Amongst that people, indeed, some national wants exist, which give rise to opinions common to the whole nation on points of honor: but these opinions never occur at the same time, in the same manner, or with the same intensity, to the minds of the whole community; the law of honor exists, but it has no organs to promulgate it.

The confusion is far greater still in a democratic country like France, where the different classes of which the former fabric of society was composed, being brought together but not yet mingled, import day by day into each other's circles various and sometimes conflicting notions of honor, — where every man, at his own will and pleasure, forsakes one portion of his forefathers' creed, and retains another; so that, amidst so many arbitrary measures, no common rule can ever be established, and it is almost impossible to predict which actions will be held in honor and which will be thought disgraceful. Such times are wretched, but they are of short duration.

As honor, amongst democratic nations, is imperfectly defined, its influence is of course less powerful; for it is difficult to apply with certainty and firmness a law which is not distinctly known. Public opinion, the natural and supreme interpreter of the laws of honor, not clearly discerning to which side censure or approval ought to lean, can only pronounce a hesitating judgment. Sometimes the opinion of the public may contradict itself; more frequently it does not act, and lets things pass.

The weakness of the sense of honor in democracies also arises from several other causes. In aristocratic countries, the same notions of honor are always entertained by only a few persons, always limited in number, often separated from the rest of their fellow-citizens. Honor is easily mingled and identified in their minds with the idea of all that distinguishes their own position; it appears to them as the chief characteristic of their own rank; they apply its different rules with all the warmth of personal interest, and they feel (if I may use the expression) a passion for complying with its dictates.

This truth is extremely obvious in the old black-letter law-books on the subject of trial by battel. The nobles, in their disputes, were bound to use the lance and sword; whereas the villains amongst themselves used only sticks, " inasmuch as," to use the words of the old books, " villains have no honor." This did not mean, as it may be imagined at the present day, that these people were contemptible ; but simply that their actions were not to be judged by the same rules which were applied to the actions of the aristocracy.

It is surprising, at first sight, that, when the sense of honor is most predominant, its injunctions are usually most strange; so that, the further it is removed from common reason, the better it is obeyed; whence it has sometimes been inferred that the laws of honor were strengthened by their own extravagance. The two things, indeed, originate from the same source, but the one is not derived from the other. Honor becomes fantastical in proportion to the peculiarity of the wants which it denotes, and the paucity of the men by whom those wants are felt; and it is because it denotes wants of this kind that its influence is great. Thus, the notion of honor is not the stronger for being fantastical, but it is fantastical and strong from the self-same cause.

Further, amongst aristocratic nations each rank is different, but all ranks are fixed; every man occupies a place in his own sphere which he cannot relinquish, and he lives there amidst other men who are bound by the same ties. Amongst these nations, no man can either hope or fear to escape being seen; no man is placed so low but that he has a stage of his own, and none can avoid censure or applause by his obscurity.

In democratic states, on the contrary, where all the members of the community are mingled in the same crowd and in constant agitation, public opinion has no hold on men; they disappear at every instant, and elude its power. Consequently, the dictates of honor will be there less imperious and less stringent; for honor acts solely for the public eye, — differing in this respect from mere virtue, which lives upon itself, contented with its own approval.

If the reader has distinctly apprehended all that goes before, he will understand that there is a close and necessary relation between the inequality of social conditions and what has here been styled honor, — a relation which, if I am not mistaken, had not before been clearly pointed out. I shall therefore make one more attempt to illustrate it satisfactorily.

Suppose a nation stands apart from the rest of mankind: independently of certain general wants inherent in the human race, it will also have wants and interests peculiar to itself: certain opinions in respect to censure or approbation forthwith arise in the community, which are peculiar to

itself, and which are styled honor by the members of that
community. Now suppose that in this same nation a caste
arises, which, in its turn, stands apart from all the other
classes, and contracts certain peculiar wants, which give
rise in their turn to special opinions. The honor of this
caste, composed of a medley of the peculiar notions of the
nation, and the still more peculiar notions of the caste, will
be as remote as it is possible to conceive from the simple
and general opinions of men.

Having reached this extreme point of the argument, I
now return.

When ranks are commingled and privileges abolished,
the men of whom a nation is composed being once more
equal and alike, their interests and wants become identical,
and all the peculiar notions which each caste styled honor
successively disappear: the notion of honor no longer proceeds from any other source than the wants peculiar to the
nation at large, and it denotes the individual character of
that nation to the world.

Lastly, if it were allowable to suppose that all the races
of mankind should be commingled, and that all the nations
of earth should ultimately come to have the same interests,
the same wants, undistinguished from each other by any
characteristic peculiarities, no conventional value whatever
would then be attached to men's actions; they would all
be regarded by all in the same light; the general necessities
of mankind, revealed by conscience to every man, would
become the common standard. The simple and general
notions of right and wrong only would then be recognized
in the world, to which, by a natural and necessary tie, the
idea of censure or approbation would be attached.

Thus, to comprise all my meaning in a single proposition, the dissimilarities and inequalities of men gave rise
to the notion of honor; that notion is weakened in proportion as these differences are obliterated, and with them it
would disappear.

CHAPTER XIX.

WHY SO MANY AMBITIOUS MEN AND SO LITTLE LOFTY AMBI-
TION ARE TO BE FOUND IN THE UNITED STATES.

THE first thing which strikes a traveller in the United
States is the innumerable multitude of those who seek
to emerge from their original condition; and the second is
the rarity of lofty ambition to be observed in the midst of
the universally ambitious stir of society. No Americans
are devoid of a yearning desire to rise; but hardly any
appear to entertain hopes of great magnitude, or to pursue
very lofty aims. All are constantly seeking to acquire
property, power, and reputation; few contemplate these
things upon a great scale; and this is the more surprising,
as nothing is to be discerned in the manners or laws of
America to limit desire, or to prevent it from spreading its
impulses in every direction. It seems difficult to attribute
this singular state of things to the equality of social condition; for as soon as that same equality was established in
France, the flight of ambition became unbounded. Nevertheless, I think that we may find the principal cause of this
fact in the social condition and democratic manners of the
Americans.

All revolutions enlarge the ambition of men: this is
more peculiarly true of those revolutions which overthrow
an aristocracy. When the former barriers which kept back
the multitude from fame and power are suddenly thrown
down, a violent and universal movement takes place towards that eminence so long coveted and at length to be
enjoyed. In this first burst of triumph, nothing seems

impossible to any one : not only are desires boundless, but the power of satisfying them seems almost boundless too.   Amidst the general and sudden change of laws and customs, in this vast confusion of all men and all ordinances, the various members of the community rise and sink again with excessive rapidity, and power passes so quickly from hand to hand that none need despair of catching it in turn.

It must be recollected, moreover, that the people who destroy an aristocracy have lived under its laws ; they have witnessed its splendor, and they have unconsciously imbibed the feelings and notions which it entertained.   Thus, at the moment when an aristocracy is dissolved, its spirit still pervades the mass of the community, and its tendencies are retained long after it has been defeated.   Ambition is therefore always extremely great as long as a democratic revolution lasts, and it will remain so for some time after the revolution is consummated.

The reminiscence of the extraordinary events which men have witnessed is not obliterated from their memory in a day.   The passions which a revolution has roused do not disappear at its close.   A sense of instability remains in the midst of re-established order ; a notion of easy success survives the strange vicissitudes which gave it birth ; desires still remain extremely enlarged, while the means of satisfying them are diminished day by day.   The taste for large fortunes subsists, though large fortunes are rare ; and on every side we trace the ravages of inordinate and unsuccessful ambition kindled in hearts which it consumes in secret and in vain.

At length, however, the last vestiges of the struggle are effaced ; the remains of aristocracy completely disappear ; the great events by which its fall was attended are forgotten ; peace succeeds to war, and the sway of order is restored in the new realm ; desires are again adapted to the means by which they may be fulfilled ; the wants, the opinions, and the feelings of men cohere once more; the level of the community is permanently determined, and democratic society established.

A democratic nation, arrived at this permanent and regular state of things, will present a very different spectacle from that which we have just described; and we may readily conclude that, if ambition becomes great whilst the conditions of society are growing equal, it loses that quality when they have grown so.

As wealth is subdivided and knowledge diffused, no one is entirely destitute of education or of property; the privileges and disqualifications of caste being abolished, and men having shattered the bonds which once held them fixed, the notion of advancement suggests itself to every mind, the desire to rise swells in every heart, and all men want to mount above their station; ambition is the universal feeling.

But if the equality of conditions gives some resources to all the members of the community, it also prevents any of them from having resources of great extent, which necessarily circumscribes their desires within somewhat narrow limits. Thus, amongst democratic nations, ambition is ardent and continual, but its aim is not habitually lofty; and life is generally spent in eagerly coveting small objects which are within reach.

What chiefly diverts the men of democracies from lofty ambition is not the scantiness of their fortunes, but the vehemence of the exertions they daily make to improve them. They strain their faculties to the utmost to achieve paltry results, and this cannot fail speedily to limit their range of view, and to circumscribe their powers. They might be much poorer, and still be greater.

The small number of opulent citizens who are to be found amidst a democracy do not constitute an exception to this rule. A man who raises himself by degrees to wealth and power, contracts, in the course of this protracted labor, habits of prudence and restraint which he cannot afterwards shake off. A man cannot gradually enlarge his mind as he does his house.

The same observation is applicable to the sons of such a man : they are born, it is true, in a lofty position, but their parents were humble ; they have grown up amidst feelings and notions which they cannot afterwards easily get rid of; and it may be presumed that they will inherit the propensities of their father, as well as his wealth.

It may happen, on the contrary, that the poorest scion of a powerful aristocracy may display vast ambition, because the traditional opinions of his race and the general spirit of his order still buoy him up for some time above his fortune.

Another thing which prevents the men of democratic periods from easily indulging in the pursuit of lofty objects, is the lapse of time which they foresee must take place before they can be ready to struggle for them. " It is a great advantage," says Pascal, " to be a man of quality, since it brings one man as forward at eighteen or twenty, as another man would be at fifty, which is a clear gain of thirty years." Those thirty years are commonly wanting to the ambitious characters of democracies. The principle of equality, which allows every man to arrive at everything, prevents all men from rapid advancement.

In a democratic society, as well as elsewhere, there are only a certain number of great fortunes to be made ; and as the paths which lead to them are indiscriminately open to all, the progress of all must necessarily be slackened. As the candidates appear to be nearly alike, and as it is difficult to make a selection without infringing the principle of equality, which is the supreme law of democratic societies, the first idea which suggests itself is to make them all advance at the same rate, and submit to the same trials. Thus, in proportion as men become more alike, and the principle of equality is more peaceably and deeply infused into the institutions and manners of the country, the rules for advancement become more inflexible, advancement itself slower, the difficulty of arriving quickly at a certain height far greater. From hatred of privilege and from the embarrassment of choosing, all men are at last constrained, whatever may be their standard, to pass the same ordeal ; all are indiscriminately subjected to a multitude of petty preliminary exercises, in which their youth is wasted and their imagination quenched, so that they despair of ever fully attaining what is held out to them ; and when at length they are in a condition to perform any extraordinary acts, the taste for such things has forsaken them.

In China, where the equality of conditions is very great and very ancient, no man passes from one public office to another without undergoing a competitive trial. This probation occurs afresh at every stage of his career; and the notion is now so rooted in the manners of the people, that I remember to have read a Chinese novel in which the hero, after numberless crosses, succeeds at length in touching the heart of his mistress by taking honors. A lofty ambition breathes with difficulty in such an atmosphere.

The remark I apply to politics extends to everything : equality everywhere produces the same effects ; where the laws of a country do not regulate and retard the advancement of men by positive enactment, competition attains the same end.

In a well-established democratic community, great and rapid elevation is therefore rare ; it forms an exception to the common rule ; and it is the singularity of such occurrences that makes men forget how rarely they happen.

Men living in democracies ultimately discover these things ; they find out at last that the laws of their country open a boundless field of action before them, but that no one can hope to hasten across it. Between them and the final object of their desires they perceive a multitude of small intermediate impediments, which must be slowly surmounted : this prospect wearies and discourages their ambition at once. They therefore give up hopes so doubtful and remote, to search nearer to themselves for less lofty and more easy enjoyments. Their horizon is not bounded by the laws, but narrowed by themselves.

I have remarked that lofty ambitions are more rare in the ages of democracy than in times of aristocracy : I may add, that when, in spite of these natural obstacles, they do spring into existence, their character is different. In aristocracies, the career of ambition is often wide, but its boundaries are determined. In democracies, ambition commonly ranges in a narrower field, but, if once it gets beyond that, hardly any limits can be assigned to it. As men are individually weak, — as they live asunder, and in constant motion, — as precedents are of little authority, and laws but of short duration, — resistance to novelty is languid, and the fabric of society never appears perfectly erect or firmly consolidated. So that, when once an ambitious man has the power in his grasp, there is nothing he may not dare ; and when it is gone from him, he meditates the overthrow of the state to regain it. This gives to great political ambition a character of revolutionary violence, which it seldom exhibits to an equal degree in aristocratic communities. The common aspect of democratic nations will present a great number of small and very rational objects of ambition, from amongst which a few ill-controlled desires of a larger growth will at intervals break out ; but no such a thing as ambition, conceived and regulated on a vast scale, is to be met with there.

I have shown elsewhere by what secret influence the principle of equality makes the passion for physical gratification and the exclusive love of the present predominate in the human heart: these different propensities mingle with the sentiment of ambition, and tinge it, as it were, with their hues.

I believe that ambitious men in democracies are less engrossed than any others with the interests and the judgment of posterity; the present moment alone engages and absorbs them. They are more apt to complete a number of undertakings with rapidity, than to raise lasting monuments of their achievements; and they care much more for success than for fame. What they most ask of men is obedience, what they most covet is empire. Their manners have, in almost all cases, remained below their station; the consequence is, that they frequently carry very low tastes into their extraordinary fortunes, and that they seem to have acquired the supreme power only to minister to their coarse or paltry pleasures.

I think that, in our time, it is very necessary to purify, to regulate, and to proportion the feeling of ambition, but that it would be extremely dangerous to seek to impoverish and to repress it over much. We should attempt to lay down certain extreme limits, which it should never be allowed to outstep; but its range within those established limits should not be too much checked.

I confess that I apprehend much less for democratic society from the boldness than from the mediocrity of desires. What appears to me most to be dreaded is, that, in the midst of the small, incessant occupations of private life, ambition should lose its vigor and its greatness; that the passions of man should abate, but at the same time be lowered; so that the march of society should every day become more tranquil and less aspiring.

I think, then, that the leaders of modern society would be wrong to seek to lull the community by a state of too uniform and too peaceful happiness; and that it is well to expose it from time to time to matters of difficulty and danger, in order to raise ambition, and to give it a field of action.

Moralists are constantly complaining that the ruling vice of the present time is pride. This is true in one sense, for indeed every one thinks that he is better than his neighbor, or refuses to obey his superior; but it is extremely false in another, for the same man who cannot endure subordination or equality, has so contemptible an opinion of himself that he thinks he is born only to indulge in vulgar pleasures. He willingly takes up with low desires, without daring to embark in lofty enterprises, of which he scarcely dreams.

Thus, far from thinking that humility ought to be preached to our contemporaries, I would have endeavors made to give them a more enlarged idea of themselves and of their kind. Humility is unwholesome to them; what they most want is, in my opinion, pride. I would willingly exchange several of our small virtues for this one vice.

CHAPTER XX.

THE TRADE OF PLACE-HUNTING IN CERTAIN DEMOCRATIC COUNTRIES.

IN the United States, as soon as a man has acquired some education and pecuniary resources, he either endeavors to get rich by commerce or industry, or he buys land in the bush and turns pioneer. All that he asks of the state is, not to be disturbed in his toil, and to be secure of his earnings. Amongst most European nations, when a man begins to feel his strength and to extend his desires, the first thing that occurs to him is to get some public employment. These opposite effects, originating in the same cause, deserve our passing notice.

When public employments are few in number, ill-paid, and precarious, whilst the different kinds of business are numerous and lucrative, it is to business, and not to official duties, that the new and eager desires created by the principle of equality turn from every side. But if, whilst the ranks of society are becoming more equal, the education of the people remains incomplete, or their spirit the reverse of bold, — if commerce and industry, checked in their growth, afford only slow and arduous means of making a fortune, — the various members of the community, despairing of ameliorating their own condition, rush to the head of the state and demand its assistance. To relieve their own necessities at the cost of the public treasury appears to them the easiest and most open, if not the only, way of rising above a condition which no longer contents them; place-hunting becomes the most generally followed of all trades.

This must especially be the case in those great centralized monarchies, in which the number of paid offices is immense, and the tenure of them tolerably secure, so that no one despairs of obtaining a place, and of enjoying it as undisturbedly as an hereditary fortune.

I shall not remark that the universal and inordinate desire for place is a great social evil; that it destroys the spirit of independence in the citizen, and diffuses a venal and servile humor throughout the frame of society; that it stifles the manlier virtues: nor shall I be at the pains to demonstrate that this kind of traffic only creates an unproductive activity, which agitates the country without adding to its resources: all these things are obvious. But I would observe, that a government which encourages this tendency risks its own tranquillity, and places its very existence in great jeopardy.

I am aware that, at a time like our own, when the love and respect which formerly clung to authority are seen gradually to decline, it may appear necessary to those in power to lay a closer hold on every man by his own interest, and it may seem convenient to use his own passions to keep him in order and in silence; but this cannot be so long, and what may appear to be a source of strength for a certain time will assuredly become, in the end, a great cause of embarrassment and weakness.

Amongst democratic nations, as well as elsewhere, the number of official appointments has, in the end, some limits; but amongst those nations, the number of aspirants is unlimited; it perpetually increases, with a gradual and irresistible rise, in proportion as social conditions become more equal, and is only checked by the limits of the population.

Thus, when public employments afford the only outlet for ambition, the government necessarily meets with a permanent opposition at last; for it is tasked to satisfy with limited means unlimited desires. It is very certain that, of all people in the world, the most difficult to restrain and to manage are a people of office-hunters. Whatever endeavors are made by rulers, such a people can never be contented; and it is always to be apprehended that they will ultimately overturn the constitution of the country, and change the aspect of the state, for the sole purpose of making a clearance of places.

The sovereigns of the present age, who strive to fix upon themselves alone all those novel desires which are aroused by equality, and to satisfy them, will repent in the end, if I am not mistaken, that ever they embarked in this policy : they will one day discover that they have hazarded their own power by making it so necessary, and that the more safe and honest course would have been to teach their subjects the art of providing for themselves.

CHAPTER XXI.

WHY GREAT REVOLUTIONS WILL BECOME MORE RARE.

A PEOPLE who have existed for centuries under a system of castes and classes, can only arrive at a democratic state of society by passing through a long series of more or less critical transformations, accomplished by violent efforts, and after numerous vicissitudes; in the course of which, property, opinions, and power are rapidly transferred from one to another. Even after this great revolution is consummated, the revolutionary habits produced by it may long be traced, and it will be followed by deep commotion. As all this takes place at the very time when social conditions are becoming more equal, it is inferred that some concealed relation and secret tie exists between the principle of equality itself and revolution, insomuch that the one cannot exist without giving rise to the other.

On this point, reasoning may seem to lead to the same result as experience. Amongst a people whose ranks are nearly equal, no ostensible bond connects men together, or keeps them settled in their station. None of them have either a permanent right or power to command, none are forced by their condition to obey; but every man, finding himself possessed of some education and some resources, may choose his own path, and proceed apart from all his fellow-men. The same causes which make the members of the community independent of each other, continually impel them to new and restless desires, and constantly spur them onwards. It therefore seems natural that, in a democratic community, men, things, and opinions should be forever changing their form and place, and that democratic ages should be times of rapid and incessant transformation.

But is this really the case? Does the equality of social conditions habitually and permanently lead men to revolution? Does that state of society contain some perturbing principle, which prevents the community from ever subsiding into calm, and disposes the citizens to alter incessantly their laws, their principles, and their manners? I do not believe it; and as the subject is important, I beg for the reader's close attention.

Almost all the revolutions which have changed the aspect of nations have been made to consolidate or to destroy social inequality. Remove the secondary causes which have produced the great convulsions of the world, and you will almost always find the principle of inequality at the bottom. Either the poor have attempted to plunder the rich, or the rich to enslave the poor. If, then, a state of society can ever be founded in which every man shall have something to keep, and little to take from others, much will have been done for the peace of the world.

I am aware that, amongst a great democratic people, there will always be some members of the community in great poverty, and others in great opulence; but the poor, instead of forming the immense majority of the nation, as is always the case in aristocratic communities, are comparatively few in number, and the laws do not bind them together by the ties of irremediable and hereditary penury.

The wealthy, on their side, are few and powerless; they have no privileges which attract public observation; even their wealth, as it is no longer incorporated and bound up with the soil, is impalpable, and, as it were, invisible. As there is no longer a race of poor men, so there is no longer a race of rich men; the latter spring up daily from the multitude, and relapse into it again. Hence they do not form a distinct class, which may be easily marked out and plundered ; and, moreover, as they are connected with the mass of their fellow-citizens by a thousand secret ties, the people cannot assail them without inflicting an injury upon themselves.

Between these two extremes of democratic communities stand an innumerable multitude of men almost alike, who, without being exactly either rich or poor, are possessed of sufficient property to desire the maintenance of order, yet not enough to excite envy. Such men are the natural enemies of violent commotions ; their stillness keeps all beneath them and above them still, and secures the balance of the fabric of society.

Not, indeed, that even these men are contented with what they have gotten, or that they feel a natural abhorrence for a revolution in which they might share the spoil without sharing the calamity ; on the contrary, they desire, with unexampled ardor, to get rich, but the difficulty is to know from whom riches can be taken. The same state of society which constantly prompts desires, restrains these desires within necessary limits ; it gives men more liberty of changing, and less interest in change.

Not only are the men of democracies not naturally desirous of revolutions, but they are afraid of them. All revolutions more or less threaten the tenure of property : but most of those who live in democratic countries are possessed of property ; not only are they possessed of property, but they live in the condition where men set the greatest store upon their property.

If we attentively consider each of the classes of which society is composed, it is easy to see that the passions created by property are keenest and most tenacious amongst the middle classes. The poor often care but little for what they possess, because they suffer much more from the want of what they have not, than they enjoy the little they have. The rich have many other passions besides that of riches to satisfy; and, besides, the long and arduous enjoyment of a great fortune sometimes makes them in the end insensible to its charms. But the men who have a competency, alike removed from opulence and from penury, attach an enormous value to their possessions. As they are still almost within the reach of poverty, they see its privations near at hand, and dread them; between poverty and themselves there is nothing but a scanty fortune, upon which they immediately fix their apprehensions and their hopes. Every day increases the interest they take in it, by the constant cares which it occasions; and they are the more attached to it by their continual exertions to increase the amount. The notion of surrendering the smallest part of it is insupportable to them, and they consider its total loss as the worst of misfortunes.

Now, these eager and apprehensive men of small property constitute the class which is constantly increased by the equality of conditions. Hence, in democratic communities, the majority of the people do not clearly see what they have to gain by a revolution, but they continually and in a thousand ways feel that they might lose by one.

I have shown, in another part of this work, that the equality of conditions naturally urges men to embark in commercial and industrial pursuits, and that it tends to increase and to distribute real property: I have also pointed out the means by which it inspires every man with an eager and constant desire to increase his welfare. Nothing is more opposed to revolutionary passions than these things. It may happen that the final result of a revolution is favorable to commerce and manufactures; but its first consequence will almost always be the ruin of manufactures and mercantile men, because it must always change at once the general principles of consumption, and temporarily upset the existing proportion between supply and demand.

I know of nothing more opposite to revolutionary man-

ners than commercial manners. Commerce is naturally
adverse to all the violent passions; it loves to temporize,
takes delight in compromise, and studiously avoids irritation. It is patient, insinuating, flexible, and never has
recourse to extreme measures until obliged by the most
absolute necessity. Commerce renders men independent
of each other, gives them a lofty notion of their personal
importance, leads them to seek to conduct their own affairs,
and teaches how to conduct them well; it therefore prepares
men for freedom, but preserves them from revolutions.

In a revolution, the owners of personal property have
more to fear than all others; for, on the one hand, their
property is often easy to seize; and, on the other, it may
totally disappear at any moment, — a subject of alarm to
which the owners of real property are less exposed, since,
although they may lose the income of their estates, they
may hope to preserve the land itself through the greatest
vicissitudes. Hence the former are much more alarmed at
the symptoms of revolutionary commotion than the latter.
Thus, nations are less disposed to make revolutions in proportion as personal property is augmented and distributed
amongst them, and as the number of those possessing it is
increased.

Moreover, whatever profession men may embrace, and
whatever species of property they may possess, one characteristic is common to them all. No one is fully contented
with his present fortune; all are perpetually striving, in a
thousand ways, to improve it. Consider any one of them
at any period of his life, and he will be found engaged with
some new project for the purpose of increasing what he
has; talk not to him of the interests and the rights of mankind, this small domestic concern absorbs for the time all
his thoughts, and inclines him to defer political agitations
to some other season. This not only prevents men from
making revolutions, but deters men from desiring them.

Violent political passions have but little hold on those who have devoted all their faculties to the pursuit of their well-being. The ardor which they display in small matters calms their zeal for momentous undertakings.

From time to time, indeed, enterprising and ambitious men will arise in democratic communities, whose unbounded aspirations cannot be contented by following the beaten track. Such men like revolutions, and hail their approach; but they have great difficulty in bringing them about, unless extraordinary events come to their assistance. No man can struggle with advantage against the spirit of his age and country; and, however powerful he may be supposed to be, he will find it difficult to make his contemporaries share in feelings and opinions which are repugnant to all their feelings and desires.

It is a mistake to believe that, when once the equality of condition has become the old and uncontested state of society, and has imparted its characteristics to the manners of a nation, men will easily allow themselves to be thrust into perilous risks by an imprudent leader or a bold innovator. Not indeed that they will resist him openly, by well-contrived schemes, or even by a premeditated plan of resistance. They will not struggle energetically against him, — sometimes they will even applaud him; but they do not follow him. To his vehemence they secretly oppose their inertia, to his revolutionary tendencies their conservative interests, their homely tastes to his adventurous passions, their good sense to the flights of his genius, to his poetry their prose. With immense exertion he raises them for an instant, but they speedily escape from him, and fall back, as it were, by their own weight. He strains himself to rouse the indifferent and distracted multitude, and finds at last that he is reduced to impotence, not because he is conquered, but because he is alone.

I do not assert that men living in democratic communities are naturally stationary; I think, on the contrary, that a perpetual stir prevails in the bosom of those societies, and that rest is unknown there; but I think that men bestir themselves within certain limits, beyond which they hardly ever go. They are forever varying, altering, and restoring secondary matters; but they carefully abstain from touching what is fundamental. They love change, but they dread revolutions.

Although the Americans are constantly modifying or abrogating some of their laws, they by no means display revolutionary passions. It may be easily seen, from the promptitude with which they check and calm themselves when public excitement begins to grow alarming, and at the very moment when passions seem most roused, that they dread a revolution as the worst of misfortunes, and that every one of them is inwardly resolved to make great sacrifices to avoid such a catastrophe. In no country in the world is the love of property more active and more anxious than in the United States; nowhere does the majority display less inclination for those principles which threaten to alter, in whatever manner, the laws of property.

I have often remarked, that theories which are of a revolutionary nature, since they cannot be put in practice without a complete and sometimes a sudden change in the state of property and persons, are much less favorably viewed in the United States than in the great monarchical countries of Europe: if some men profess them, the bulk of the people reject them with instinctive abhorrence. I do not hesitate to say, that most of the maxims commonly called democratic in France would be proscribed by the democracy of the United States. This may easily be understood; in America, men have the opinions and passions of democracy; in Europe, we have still the passions and opinions of revolution.

If ever America undergoes great revolutions, they will

be brought about by the presence of the black race on the soil of the United States; that is to say, they will owe their origin, not to the equality, but to the inequality of condition.

When social conditions are equal, every man is apt to live apart, centred in himself and forgetful of the public. If the rulers of democratic nations were either to neglect to correct this fatal tendency, or to encourage it from a notion that it weans men from political passions and thus wards off revolutions, they might eventually produce the evil they seek to avoid, and a time might come when the inordinate passions of a few men, aided by the unintelligent selfishness or the pusillanimity of the greater number, would ultimately compel society to pass through strange vicissitudes. In democratic communities, revolutions are seldom desired except by a minority; but a minority may sometimes effect them.

I do not assert that democratic nations are secure from revolutions; I merely say that the state of society in those nations does not lead to revolutions, but rather wards them off. A democratic people left to itself will not easily embark in great hazards; it is only led to revolutions unawares; it may sometimes undergo them, but it does not make them: and I will add, that, when such a people has been allowed to acquire sufficient knowledge and experience, it will not suffer them to be made.

I am well aware that, in this respect, public institutions may themselves do much; they may encourage or repress the tendencies which originate in the state of society. I therefore do not maintain, I repeat, that a people is secure from revolutions simply because conditions are equal in the community; but I think that, whatever the institutions of such a people may be, great revolutions will always be far less violent and less frequent than is supposed; and I can easily discern a state of polity which, when combined with

the principle of equality, would render society more stationary than it has ever been in our western part of the world.

The observations I have here made on events may also
be applied in part to opinions.   Two things are surprising
in the United States, — the mutability of the greater part
of human actions, and the singular stability of certain principles.   Men are in constant motion ; the mind of man appears almost unmoved.   When once an opinion has spread
over the country and struck root there, it would seem that
no power on earth is strong enough to eradicate it.   In the
United States, general principles in religion, philosophy,
morality, and even politics, do not vary, or at least are only
modified by a hidden and often an imperceptible process :
even the grossest prejudices are obliterated with incredible
slowness, amidst the continual friction of men and things.

I hear it said that it is in the nature and the habits of
democracies to be constantly changing their opinions and
feelings.   This may be true of small democratic nations,
like those of the ancient world, in which the whole community could be assembled in a public place, and then
excited at will by an orator.   But I saw nothing of the
kind amongst the great democratic people which dwells
upon the opposite shores of the Atlantic Ocean.   What
struck me in the United States was, the difficulty of shak-
ing the majority in an opinion once conceived, or of drawing it off from a leader once adopted.   Neither speaking
nor writing can accomplish it ; nothing but experience will
avail, and even experience must be repeated.

This is surprising at first sight, but a more attentive investigation explains the fact.   I do not think that it is as
easy as is supposed to uproot the prejudices of a democratic
people, to change its belief, to supersede principles once established by new principles in religion, politics, and morals,
— in a word, to make great and frequent changes in men's
minds.   Not that the human mind is there at rest, — it is

in constant agitation ; but it is engaged in infinitely varying the consequences of known principles, and in seeking
for new consequences, rather than in seeking for new principles. Its motion is one of rapid circumvolution, rather
than of straightforward impulse by rapid and direct effort ;
it extends its orbit by small continual and hasty movements, but it does not suddenly alter its position.

Men who are equal in rights, in education, in fortune, or,
to comprise all in one word, in their social condition, have
necessarily wants, habits, and tastes which are hardly dissimilar. As they look at objects under the same aspect,
their minds naturally tend to similar conclusions ; and,
though each of them may deviate from his contemporaries
and form opinions of his own, they will involuntarily and
unconsciously concur in a certain number of received opinions. The more attentively I consider the effects of equality
upon the mind, the more am I persuaded that the intellectual anarchy which we witness about us is not, as many men
suppose, the natural state of democratic nations. I think it
is rather to be regarded as an accident peculiar to their
youth, and that it only breaks out at that period of transition when men have already snapped the former ties which
bound them together, but are still amazingly different in
origin, education, and manners ; so that, having retained
opinions, propensities, and tastes of great diversity, nothing
any longer prevents men from avowing them openly. The
leading opinions of men become similar in proportion as
their conditions assimilate : such appears to me to be the
general and permanent law ; the rest is casual and transient.

I believe that it will rarely happen to any man, in a democratic community, suddenly to frame a system of notions
very remote from that which his contemporaries have
adopted ; and if some such innovator appeared, I apprehend that he would have great difficulty in finding listen-
ers, still more in finding believers. When the conditions

of men are almost equal, they do not easily allow themselves to be persuaded by each other. As they all live in close intercourse, as they have learned the same things together, and as they lead the same life, they are not naturally disposed to take one of themselves for a guide, and to follow him implicitly. Men seldom take the opinion of their equal, or of a man like themselves, upon trust.

Not only is confidence in the superior attainments of certain individuals weakened amongst democratic nations, as I have elsewhere remarked, but the general notion of the intellectual superiority which any man whatsoever may acquire in relation to the rest of the community is soon overshadowed. As men grow more like each other, the doctrine of the equality of the intellect gradually infuses itself into their opinions; and it becomes more difficult for any innovator to acquire or to exert much influence over the minds of a people. In such communities, sudden intellectual revolutions will therefore be rare; for, if we read aright the history of the world, we shall find that great and rapid changes in human opinions have been produced far less by the force of reasoning than by the authority of a name.

Observe, too, that, as the men who live in democratic societies are not connected with each other by any tie, each of them must be convinced individually; whilst, in aristocratic society, it is enough to convince a few, the rest follow. If Luther had lived in an age of equality, and had not had princes and potentates for his audience, he would perhaps have found it more difficult to change the aspect of Europe.

Not, indeed, that the men of democracies are naturally strongly persuaded of the certainty of their opinions, or are unwavering in belief; they frequently entertain doubts which no one, in their eyes, can remove. It sometimes happens, at such times, that the human mind would willingly

change its position ; but as nothing urges or guides it forward, it oscillates to and fro without progressive motion.*

Even when the confidence of a democratic people has
been won, it is still no easy matter to gain their attention.
It is extremely difficult to obtain a hearing from men living
in democracies, unless it be to speak to them of themselves.
They do not attend to the things said to them, because they
are always fully engrossed with the things they are doing.
For, indeed, few men are idle in democratic nations ; life
is passed in the midst of noise and excitement, and men
are so engaged in acting that little time remains to them
for thinking. I would especially remark, that they are not
only employed, but that they are passionately devoted to
their employments. They are always in action, and each
of their actions absorbs their faculties : the zeal which they
display in business puts out the enthusiasm they might
otherwise entertain for ideas.

I think that it is extremely difficult to excite the enthu-

* If I inquire what state of society is most favorable to the great revolutions of the mind, I find that it occurs somewhere between the complete
equality of the whole community and the absolute separation of ranks.
Under a system of castes, generations succeed each other without altering
men's positions : some have nothing more, others nothing better, to hope
for. The imagination slumbers amidst this universal silence and stillness,
and the very idea of change fades from the human mind.

When ranks have been abolished and social conditions are almost equalized, all men are in ceaseless excitement, but each of them stands alone,
independent and weak. This latter state of things is excessively different
from the former one ; yet it has one point of analogy, — great revolutions
of the human mind seldom occur in it.

But between these two extremes of the history of nations is an intermediate period, — a period as glorious as it is agitated, — when the conditions
of men are not sufficiently settled for the mind to be lulled in torpor, when
they are sufficiently unequal for men to exercise a vast power on the minds
of one another, and when some few may modify the convictions of all. It
is at such times that great reformers start up, and new opinions suddenly
change the face of the world.

siasm of a democratic people for any theory which has not a palpable, direct, and immediate connection with the daily occupations of life : therefore they will not easily forsake their old opinions ; for it is enthusiasm which flings the minds of men out of the beaten track, and effects the great revolutions of the intellect, as well as the great revolutions of the political world.

Thus, democratic nations have neither time nor taste to go in search of novel opinions. Even when those they possess become doubtful, they still retain them, because it would take too much time and inquiry to change them ; they retain them, not as certain, but as established.

There are yet other and more cogent reasons which prevent any great change from being easily effected in the principles of a democratic people. I have already adverted to them in the nineteenth chapter.

If the influence of individuals is weak and hardly perceptible amongst such a people, the power exercised by the mass upon the mind of each individual is extremely great, — I have already shown for what reasons. I would now observe, that it is wrong to suppose that this depends solely upon the form of government, and that the majority would lose its intellectual supremacy if it were to lose its political power.

In aristocracies, men have often much greatness and strength of their own : when they find themselves at variance with the greater number of their fellow-countrymen, they withdraw to their own circle, where they support and console themselves. Such is not the case in a democratic country ; there, public favor seems as necessary as the air we breathe, and to live at variance with the multitude is, as it were, not to live. The multitude require no laws to coerce those who think not like themselves : public disapprobation is enough ; a sense of their loneliness and impotence overtakes them and drives them to despair.

Whenever social conditions are equal, public opinion presses with enormous weight upon the minds of each individual; it surrounds, directs, and oppresses him; and this arises from the very constitution of society, much more than from its political laws. As men grow more alike, each man feels himself weaker in regard to all the rest; as he discerns nothing by which he is considerably raised above them, or distinguished from them, he mistrusts himself as soon as they assail him. Not only does he mistrust his strength, but he even doubts of his right; and he is very near acknowledging that he is in the wrong, when the greater number of his countrymen assert that he is so. The majority do not need to constrain him; they convince him. In whatever way, then, the powers of a democratic community may be organized and balanced, it will always be extremely difficult to believe what the bulk of the people reject, or to profess what they condemn.

This circumstance is extraordinarily favorable to the stability of opinions. When an opinion has taken root amongst a democratic people, and established itself in the minds of the bulk of the community, it afterwards subsists by itself and is maintained without effort, because no one attacks it. Those who at first rejected it as false, ultimately receive it as the general impression; and those who still dispute it in their hearts, conceal their dissent; they are careful not to engage in a dangerous and useless conflict.

It is true, that, when the majority of a democratic people change their opinions, they may suddenly and arbitrarily effect strange revolutions in men's minds; but their opinions do not change without much difficulty, and it is almost as difficult to show that they are changed.

Time, events, or the unaided individual action of the mind, will sometimes undermine or destroy an opinion, without any outward sign of the change. It has not been openly assailed, no conspiracy has been formed to make

war on it, but its followers one by one noiselessly secede;
day by day a few of them abandon it, until at last it is only
professed by a minority. In this state it will still continue
to prevail. As its enemies remain mute, or only interchange their thoughts by stealth, they are themselves un-
aware for a long period that a great revolution has actually
been effected; and in this state of uncertainty they take no
steps; they observe each other and are silent. The majority have ceased to believe what they believed before; but
they still affect to believe, and this empty phantom of public
opinion is strong enough to chill innovators, and to keep
them silent and at a respectful distance.

We live at a time which has witnessed the most rapid
changes of opinion in the minds of men; nevertheless it
may be that the leading opinions of society will erelong be
more settled than they have been for several centuries in
our history: that time is not yet come, but it may perhaps
be approaching. As I examine more closely the natural
wants and tendencies of democratic nations, I grow persuaded that, if ever social equality is generally and permanently established in the world, great intellectual and
political revolutions will become more difficult and less
frequent than is supposed. Because the men of democracies appear always excited, uncertain, eager, changeable in
their wills and in their positions, it is imagined that they
are suddenly to abrogate their laws, to adopt new opinions,
and to assume new manners. But if the principle of equality predisposes men to change, it also suggests to them
certain interests and tastes which cannot be satisfied without a settled order of things; equality urges them on, but
at the same time it holds them back; it spurs them, but
fastens them to earth; it kindles their desires, but limits
their powers.

This, however, is not perceived at first; the passions
which tend to sever the citizens of a democracy are obvi-

ous enough; but the hidden force which restrains and unites them is not discernible at a glance.

Amidst the ruins which surround me, shall I dare to say that revolutions are not what I most fear for coming generations? If men continue to shut themselves more closely within the narrow circle of domestic interests, and to live upon that kind of excitement, it is to be apprehended that they may ultimately become inaccessible to those great and powerful public emotions which perturb nations, but which develop them and recruit them. When property becomes so fluctuating, and the love of property so restless and so ardent, I cannot but fear that men may arrive at such a state as to regard every new theory as a peril, every innovation as an irksome toil, every social improvement as a stepping-stone to revolution, and so refuse to move altogether for fear of being moved too far. I dread, and I confess it, lest they should at last so entirely give way to a cowardly love of present enjoyment, as to lose sight of the interests of their future selves and those of their descendants; and prefer to glide along the easy current of life, rather than to make, when it is necessary, a strong and sudden effort to a higher purpose.

It is believed by some that modern society will be ever changing its aspect; for myself, I fear that it will ultimately be too invariably fixed in the same institutions, the same prejudices, the same manners, so that mankind will be stopped and circumscribed; that the mind will swing backwards and forwards forever, without begetting fresh ideas; that man will waste his strength in bootless and solitary trifling; and, though in continual motion, that humanity will cease to advance.

CHAPTER XXII.

WHY DEMOCRATIC NATIONS ARE NATURALLY DESIROUS OF PEACE, AND DEMOCRATIC ARMIES OF WAR.

THE same interests, the same fears, the same passions, which deter democratic nations from revolutions, deter them also from war; the spirit of military glory and the spirit of revolution are weakened at the same time and by the same causes. The ever-increasing numbers of men of property who are lovers of peace, the growth of personal wealth which war so rapidly consumes, the mildness of manners, the gentleness of heart, those tendencies to pity which are produced by the equality of conditions, that coolness of understanding which renders men comparatively insensible to the violent and poetical excitement of arms, — all these causes concur to quench the military spirit. I think it may be admitted as a general and constant rule, that, amongst civilized nations, the warlike passions will become more rare and less intense in proportion as social conditions shall be more equal.

War is nevertheless an occurrence to which all nations are subject, democratic nations as well as others. Whatever taste they may have for peace, they must hold themselves in readiness to repel aggression, or, in other words, they must have an army. Fortune, which has conferred so many peculiar benefits upon the inhabitants of the United States, has placed them in the midst of a wilderness, where they have, so to speak, no neighbors: a few thousand soldiers are sufficient for their wants; but this is peculiar to America, not to democracy.

The equality of conditions, and the manners as well as the institutions resulting from it, do not exempt a democratic people from the necessity of standing armies, and their armies always exercise a powerful influence over their fate. It is therefore of singular importance to inquire what are the natural propensities of the men of whom these armies are composed.

Amongst aristocratic nations, especially amongst those in which birth is the only source of rank, the same inequality exists in the army as in the nation; the officer is noble, the soldier is a serf; the one is naturally called upon to command, the other to obey. In aristocratic armies, the private soldier's ambition is therefore circumscribed within very narrow limits. Nor has the ambition of the officer an unlimited range. An aristocratic body not only forms a part of the scale of ranks in the nation, but it contains a scale of ranks within itself: the members of whom it is composed are placed one above another, in a particular and unvarying manner. Thus, one man is born to the command of a regiment, another to that of a company; when once they have reached the utmost object of their hopes, they stop of their own accord, and remain contented with their lot.

There is, besides, a strong cause, which, in aristocracies, weakens the officer's desire of promotion. Amongst aristocratic nations, an officer, independently of his rank in the army, also occupies an elevated rank in society; the former is almost always, in his eyes, only an appendage to the latter. A nobleman who embraces the profession of arms follows it less from motives of ambition than from a sense of the duties imposed on him by his birth. He enters the army in order to find an honorable employment for the idle years of his youth, and to be able to bring back to his home and his peers some honorable recollections of military life; but his principal object is not to obtain by that profession either property, distinction, or power, for he possesses these advantages in his own right, and enjoys them without leaving his home.

In democratic armies, all the soldiers may become officers, which makes the desire of promotion general, and immeasurably extends the bounds of military ambition. The officer, on his part, sees nothing which naturally and necessarily stops him at one grade more than at another; and each grade has immense importance in his eyes, because his rank in society almost always depends on his rank in the army. Amongst democratic nations, it often happens that an officer has no property but his pay, and no distinction but that of military honors: consequently, as often as his duties change his fortune changes, and he becomes, as it were, a new man. What was only an appendage to his position in aristocratic armies, has thus become the main point, the basis of his whole condition.

Under the old French monarchy, officers were always called by their titles of nobility; they are now always called by the title of their military rank. This little change in the forms of language suffices to show that a great revolution has taken place in the constitution of society and in that of the army.

In democratic armies, the desire of advancement is almost universal: it is ardent, tenacious, perpetual; it is strengthened by all other desires, and only extinguished with life itself. But it is easy to see, that, of all armies in the world, those in which advancement must be slowest in time of peace are the armies of democratic countries. As the number of commissions is naturally limited, whilst the number of competitors is almost unlimited, and as the strict law of equality is over all alike, none can make rapid progress, — many can make no progress at all. Thus, the desire of advancement is greater, and the opportunities of advancement fewer there than elsewhere. All the ambitious spirits of a democratic army are consequently ardently desirous of war, because war makes vacancies, and warrants the violation of that law of seniority which is the sole privilege natural to democracy.

We thus arrive at this singular consequence, that, of all armies, those most ardently desirous of war are democratic armies, and of all nations, those most fond of peace are democratic nations; and what makes these facts still more extraordinary is, that these contrary effects are produced at the same time by the principle of equality.

All the members of the community, being alike, constantly harbor the wish and discover the possibility of changing their condition and improving their welfare: this makes them fond of peace, which is favorable to industry, and allows every man to pursue his own little undertakings to their completion. On the other hand, this same equality makes soldiers dream of fields of battle, by increasing the value of military honors in the eyes of those who follow the profession of arms, and by rendering those honors accessible to all. In either case, the inquietude of the heart is the same, the taste for enjoyment as insatiable, the ambition of success as great, — the means of gratifying it alone are different.

These opposite tendencies of the nation and the army expose democratic communities to great dangers. When a military spirit forsakes a people, the profession of arms immediately ceases to be held in honor, and military men fall to the lowest rank of the public servants: they are little esteemed, and no longer understood. The reverse of what takes place in aristocratic ages then occurs; the men who enter the army are no longer those of the highest, but of the lowest rank. Military ambition is only indulged when no other is possible. Hence arises a circle of cause and consequence from which it is difficult to escape: the best part of the nation shuns the military profession because that profession is not honored, and the profession is not honored because the best part of the nation has ceased to follow it.

It is then no matter of surprise that democratic armies are often restless, ill-tempered, and dissatisfied with their lot, although their physical condition is commonly far better, and their discipline less strict, than in other countries. The soldier feels that he occupies an inferior position, and his wounded pride either stimulates his taste for hostilities which would render his services necessary, or gives him a desire for revolution, during which he may hope to win by force of arms the political influence and personal importance now denied him.

The composition of democratic armies makes this last-mentioned danger much to be feared. In democratic communities, almost every man has some property to preserve ; but democratic armies are generally led by men without property, most of whom have little to lose in civil broils. The bulk of the nation is naturally much more afraid of revolutions than in the ages of aristocracy, but the leaders of the army much less so.

Moreover, as amongst democratic nations (to repeat what I have just remarked) the wealthiest, best educated, and ablest men seldom adopt the military profession, the army, taken collectively, eventually forms a small nation by itself, where the mind is less enlarged, and habits are more rude, than in the nation at large. Now, this small uncivilized nation has arms in its possession, and alone knows how to use them ; for, indeed, the pacific temper of the community increases the danger to which a democratic people is exposed from the ·military and turbulent spirit of the army. Nothing is so dangerous as an army amidst an unwarlike nation ; the excessive love of the whole community for quiet continually puts the constitution at the mercy of the soldiery.

It may therefore be asserted, generally speaking, that, if democratic nations are naturally prone to peace from their interests and their propensities, they are constantly drawn to war and revolutions by their armies. Military revolutions, which are scarcely ever to be apprehended in aristocracies, are always to be dreaded amongst democratic nations. These perils must be reckoned amongst the most formidable which beset their future fate, and the attention of statesmen should be sedulously applied to find a remedy for the evil.

When a nation perceives that it is inwardly affected by the restless ambition of its army, the first thought which occurs is to give this inconvenient ambition an object by going to war. I do not wish to speak ill of war: war almost always enlarges the mind of a people, and raises their character. In some cases, it is the only check to the excessive growth of certain propensities which naturally spring out of the equality of conditions, and it must be considered as a necessary corrective to certain inveterate diseases to which democratic communities are liable.

War has great advantages, but we must not flatter ourselves that it can diminish the danger I have just pointed out. That peril is only suspended by it, to return more fiercely when the war is over; for armies are much more impatient of peace after having tasted military exploits. War could only be a remedy for a people who should always be athirst for military glory.

I foresee that all the military rulers who may rise up in great democratic nations will find it easier to conquer with their armies, than to make their armies live at peace after conquest. There are two things which a democratic people will always find very difficult, — to begin a war and to end it.

Again, if war has some peculiar advantages for democratic nations, on the other hand, it exposes them to certain dangers, which aristocracies have no cause to dread to an equal extent. I shall point out only two of these.

Although war gratifies the army, it embarrasses and often exasperates that countless multitude of men whose minor passions every day require peace in order to be satisfied. Thus there is some risk of its causing, under another form, the very disturbance it is intended to prevent.

No protracted war can fail to endanger the freedom of a democratic country. Not indeed that, after every victory, it is to be apprehended that the victorious generals will possess themselves by force of the supreme power, after the manner of Sylla and Cæsar: the danger is of another kind. War does not always give over democratic communities to military government, but it must invariably and immeasurably increase the powers of civil government; it must almost compulsorily concentrate the direction of all men and the management of all things in the hands of the administration. If it lead not to despotism by sudden violence, it prepares men for it more gently by their habits. All those who seek to destroy the liberties of a democratic nation ought to know that war is the surest and the shortest means to accomplish it. This is the first axiom of the science.

One remedy, which appears to be obvious when the ambition of soldiers and officers becomes the subject of alarm, is to augment the number of commissions to be distributed by increasing the army. This affords temporary relief, but it plunges the country into deeper difficulties at some future period. To increase the army may produce a lasting effect in an aristocratic community, because military ambition is there confined to one class of men, and the ambition of each individual stops, as it were, at a certain limit; so that it may be possible to satisfy all who feel its influence. But nothing is gained by increasing the army amongst a democratic people, because the number of aspirants always rises ın exactly the same ratio as the army itself. Those whose claims have been satisfied by the creation of new commissions are instantly succeeded by a fresh multitude beyond all power of satisfaction; and even those who were but now satisfied soon begin to crave more advancement; for the same excitement prevails in the ranks of the army as in the civil classes of democratic society, and what men want is, not to reach a certain grade, but to have constant promotion. Though these wants may not be very vast, they are perpetually recurring. Thus a democratic nation, by augmenting its army, only allays for a time the ambition of the military profession, which soon becomes even more formidable, because the number of those who feel it is increased.

I am of opinion that a restless and turbulent spirit is an evil inherent in the very constitution of democratic armies, and beyond hope of cure. The legislators of democracies, must not expect to devise any military organization capable by its influence of calming and restraining the military profession: their efforts would exhaust their powers, before the object could be attained.

The remedy for the vices of the army is not to be found in the army itself, but in the country. Democratic nations are naturally afraid of disturbance and of despotism; the object is to turn these natural instincts into intelligent, deliberate, and lasting tastes. When men have at last learned to make a peaceful and profitable use of freedom, and have felt its blessings, — when they have conceived a manly love of order, and have freely submitted themselves to discipline, — these same men, if they follow the profession of arms, bring into it, unconsciously and almost against their will, these same habits and manners. The general spirit of the nation being infused into the spirit peculiar to the army, tempers the opinions and desires engendered by military life, or represses them by the mighty force of public opinion. Teach but the citizens to be educated, orderly, firm, and free, and the soldiers will be disciplined and obedient.

Any law which, in repressing the turbulent spirit of the army, should tend to diminish the spirit of freedom in the nation, and to overshadow the notion of law and right, would defeat its object: it would do much more to favor, than to defeat the establishment of military tyranny.

After all, and in spite of all precautions, a large army amidst a democratic people will always be a source of great danger; the most effectual means of diminishing that danger would be to reduce the army, but this is a remedy which all nations are not able to apply.

CHAPTER XXIII.

WHICH IS THE MOST WARLIKE AND MOST REVOLUTIONARY CLASS IN DEMOCRATIC ARMIES.

IT is of the essence of a democratic army to be very numerous in proportion to the people to which it belongs, as I shall hereafter show. On the other hand, men living in democratic times seldom choose a military life. Democratic nations are therefore soon led to give up the system of voluntary recruiting for that of compulsory enlistment. The necessity of their social condition compels them to resort to the latter means, and it may easily be foreseen that they will all eventually adopt it.

When military service is compulsory, the burden is indiscriminately and equally borne by the whole community. This is another necessary consequence of the social condition of these nations, and of their notions. The government may do almost whatever it pleases, provided it appeals to the whole community at once : it is the unequal distribution of the weight, not the weight itself, which commonly occasions resistance. But as military service is common to all the citizens, the evident consequence is, that each of them remains but for a few years on active duty. Thus it is in the nature of things that the soldier in democracies only passes through the army, whilst, among most aristocratic nations, the military profession is one which the soldier adopts, or which is imposed upon him, for life.

This has important consequences. Amongst the soldiers of a democratic army, some acquire a taste for military life ; but the majority, being enlisted against their will, and ever

ready to go back to their homes, do not consider themselves
as seriously engaged in the military profession, and are always thinking of quitting it. Such men do not contract
the wants, and only half partake in the passions, which
that mode of life engenders. They adapt themselves to
their military duties, but their minds are still attached to
the interests and the duties which engaged them in civil
life. They do not therefore imbibe the spirit of the army,
or, rather, they infuse the spirit of the community at large
into the army, and retain it there. Amongst democratic
nations, the private soldiers remain most like civilians :
upon them the habits of the nation have the firmest hold,
and public opinion has most influence. It is through the
private soldiers, especially, that it may be possible to infuse
into a democratic army the love of freedom and the respect
for rights, if these principles have once been successfully inculcated on the people at large. The reverse happens amongst aristocratic nations, where the soldiery have
eventually nothing in common with their fellow-citizens,
and where they live amongst them as strangers, and often
as enemies.

In aristocratic armies, the officers are the conservative
element, because the officers alone have retained a strict
connection with civil society, and never forego their purpose of resuming their place in it sooner or later : in democratic armies, the private soldiers stand in this position, and
from the same cause.

It often happens, on the contrary, that, in these same
democratic armies, the officers contract tastes and wants
wholly distinct from those of the nation, — a fact which
may be thus accounted for. Amongst democratic nations,
the man who becomes an officer severs all the ties which
bound him to civil life ; he leaves it forever, and no interest urges him to return to it. His true country is the
army, since he owes all he has to the rank he has attained

in it ; he therefore follows the fortunes of the army, rises or sinks with it, and henceforward directs all his hopes to that quarter only. As the wants of an officer are distinct from those of the country, he may, perhaps, ardently desire war, or labor to bring about a revolution, at the very moment when the nation is most desirous of stability and peace.

There are, nevertheless, some causes which allay this restless and warlike spirit. Though ambition is universal and continual amongst democratic nations, we have seen that it is seldom great. A man who, being born in the lower classes of the community, has risen from the ranks to be an officer, has already taken a prodigious step. He has gained a footing in a sphere above that which he filled in civil life, and has acquired rights which most democratic nations will ever consider as inalienable.* He is willing to pause after so great an effort, and to enjoy what he has won. The fear of risking what he has already obtained damps the desire of acquiring what he has not got. Having conquered the first and greatest impediment which opposed his advancement, he resigns himself with less impatience to the slowness of his progress. His ambition will be more and more cooled in proportion as the increasing distinction of his rank teaches him that he has more to put in jeopardy. If I am not mistaken, the least warlike, and also the least revolutionary, part of a democratic army will always be its chief commanders.

But the remarks I have just made on officers and soldiers are not applicable to a numerous class which, in all armies, fills the intermediate space between them; I mean the class of non-commissioned officers. This class of non-

---

* The position of officers is indeed much more secure amongst democratic nations than elsewhere ; the lower the personal standing of the man, the greater is the comparative importance of his military grade, and the more just and necessary is it that the enjoyment of that rank should be secured by the laws.

commissioned officers, which had never acted a part in history until the present century, is henceforward destined, I think, to play one of some importance. Like the officers, non-commissioned officers have broken, in their minds, all the ties which bound them to civil life; like the former, they devote themselves permanently to the service, and perhaps make it even more exclusively the object of all their desires; but non-commissioned officers are men who have not yet reached a firm and lofty post, at which they may pause and breathe more freely, ere they can attain further promotion.

By the very nature of his duties, which are invariable, a non-commissioned officer is doomed to lead an obscure, confined, comfortless, and precarious existence; as yet, he sees nothing of military life but its dangers; he knows nothing but its privations and its discipline, — more difficult to support than dangers: he suffers the more from his present miseries, from knowing that the constitution of society and of the army allow him to rise above them; he may, indeed, at any time, obtain his commission, and enter at once upon command, honors, independence, rights, and enjoyments. Not only does this object of his hopes appear to him of immense importance, but he is never sure of reaching it till it is actually his own; the grade he fills is by no means irrevocable; he is always entirely abandoned to the arbitrary pleasure of his commanding officer, for this is imperiously required by the necessity of discipline: a slight fault, a whim, may always deprive him in an instant of the fruits of many years of toil and endeavor; until he has reached the grade to which he aspires, he has accomplished nothing; not till he reaches that grade does his career seem to begin. A desperate ambition cannot fail to be kindled in a man thus incessantly goaded on by his youth, his wants, his passions, the spirit of his age, his hopes, and his fears.

Non-commissioned officers are therefore bent on war, — on war always, and at any cost; but if war be denied them, then they desire revolutions, to suspend the authority of established regulations, and to enable them, aided by the general confusion and the political passions of the time, to get rid of their superior officers, and to take their places. Nor is it impossible for them to bring about such a crisis, because their common origin and habits give them much influence over the soldiers, however different may be their passions and their desires.

It would be an error to suppose that these various characteristics of officers, non-commissioned officers, and men belong to any particular time or country; they will always occur at all times, and amongst all democratic nations. In every democratic army the non-commissioned officers will be the worst representatives of the pacific and orderly spirit of the country, and the private soldiers will be the best. The latter will carry with them into military life the strength or weakness of the manners of the nation; they will display a faithful reflection of the community: if that community is ignorant and weak, they will allow themselves to be drawn by their leaders into disturbances, either unconsciously or against their will; if it is enlightened and energetic, the community will itself keep them within the bounds of order.

CHAPTER XXIV.

CAUSES WHICH RENDER DEMOCRATIC ARMIES WEAKER THAN
OTHER ARMIES AT THE OUTSET OF A CAMPAIGN, AND MORE
FORMIDABLE IN PROTRACTED WARFARE.

ANY army is in danger of being conquered at the outset of a campaign, after a long peace; any army
which has long been engaged in warfare has strong chances
of victory : this truth is peculiarly applicable to democratic
armies. In aristocracies, the military profession, being a
privileged career, is held in honor even in time of peace.
Men of great talents, great attainments, and great ambition embrace it; the army is in all respects on a level with
the nation, and frequently above it.

. We have seen, on the contrary, that, amongst a democratic people, the choicer minds of the nation are gradually
drawn away from the military profession, to seek by other
paths distinction, power, and especially wealth. After a
long peace, — and in democratic times the periods of peace
are long, — the army is always inferior to the country itself.
In this state, it is called into active service; and, until war
has altered it, there is danger for the country as well as for
the army.

I have shown that, in democratic armies, and in time of
peace, the rule of seniority is the supreme and inflexible
law of promotion. This is a consequence, as I have before
observed, not only of the constitution of these armies, but
of the constitution of the people; and it will always occur.

Again, as amongst these nations, the officer derives his
position in the country solely from his position in the army,

and as he draws all the distinction and the competency he enjoys from the same source, he does not retire from his profession, or is not superannuated, till very near the close of life. The consequence of these two causes is, that, when a democratic people goes to war after a long interval of peace, all the leading officers of the army are old men. I speak not only of the generals, but of the non-commissioned officers, who have most of them been stationary, or have advanced only step by step. It may be remarked with surprise, that, in a democratic army, after a long peace, all the soldiers are mere boys, and all the superior officers in declining years; so that the former are wanting in experience, the latter in vigor. This is a leading cause of defeat, for the first condition of successful generalship is youth: I should not have ventured to say so, if the greatest captain of modern times had not made the observation.

These two causes do not act in the same manner upon aristocratic armies: as men are promoted in them by right of birth much more than by right of seniority, there are in all ranks a certain number of young men who bring to their profession all the early vigor of body and mind. Again, as the men who seek for military honors amongst an aristocratic people enjoy a settled position in civil society, they seldom continue in the army until old age overtakes them. After having devoted the most vigorous years of youth to the career of arms, they voluntarily retire, and spend at home the remainder of their maturer years.

A long peace not only fills democratic armies with elderly officers, but it also gives to all the officers habits both of body and mind which render them unfit for actual service. The man who has long lived amidst the calm and lukewarm atmosphere of democratic manners, can at first ill adapt himself to the harder toils and sterner duties of warfare; and if he has not absolutely lost the taste for arms, at least he has assumed a mode of life which unfits him for conquest.

Amongst aristocratic nations, the enjoyments of civil life exercise less influence on the manners of the army, because, amongst those nations, the aristocracy commands the army; and an aristocracy, however plunged in luxurious pleasures, has always many other passions besides that of its own well-being, and to satisfy those passions more thoroughly its well-being will be readily sacrificed.*

I have shown that, in democratic armies, in time of peace, promotion is extremely slow. The officers at first support this state of things with impatience; they grow excited, restless, exasperated; but in the end most of them make up their minds to it. Those who have the largest share of ambition and of resources quit the army; others, adapting their tastes and their desires to their scanty fortunes, ultimately look upon the military profession in a civil point of view. The quality they value most in it is the competency and security which attend it: their whole notion of the future rests upon the certainty of this little provision, and all they require is peaceably to enjoy it. Thus, not only does a long peace fill an army with old men, but it frequently imparts the views of old men to those who are still in the prime of life.

I have also shown that, amongst democratic nations, in time of peace, the military profession is held in little honor and practised with little spirit. This want of public favor is a heavy discouragement to the army; it weighs down the minds of the troops, and when war breaks out at last, they cannot immediately resume their spring and vigor. No similar cause of moral weakness exists in aristocratic armies: there, the officers are never lowered, either in their own eyes or in those of their countrymen; because, independently of their military greatness, they are personally great. But, even if the influence of peace operated on the

* See Appendix U.

two kinds of armies in the same manner, the results would still be different.

When the officers of an aristocratic army have lost their warlike spirit and the desire of raising themselves by service, they still retain a certain respect for the honor of their class, and an old habit of being foremost to set an example. But when the officers of a democratic army have no longer the love of war and the ambition of arms, nothing whatever remains to them.

I am therefore of opinion, that, when a democratic people engages in a war after a long peace, it incurs much more risk of defeat than any other nation ; but it ought not easily to be cast down by its reverses, for the chances of success for such an army are increased by the duration of the war. When a war has at length, by its long continuance, roused the whole community from their peaceful occupations, and ruined their minor undertakings, the same passions which made them attach so much importance to the maintenance of peace will be turned to arms. War, after it has destroyed all modes of speculation, becomes itself the great and sole speculation, to which all the ardent and ambitious desires that equality engenders are exclusively directed. Hence it is, that the selfsame democratic nations which are so reluctant to engage in hostilities, sometimes perform prodigious achievements when once they have taken the field.

As the war attracts more and more of public attention, and is seen to create high reputations and great fortunes in a short space of time, the choicest spirits of the nation enter the military profession : all the enterprising, proud, and martial minds, no longer of the aristocracy solely, but of the whole country, are drawn in this direction. As the number of competitors for military honors is immense, and war drives every man to his proper level, great generals are always sure to spring up. A long war produces upon a democratic army the same effects that a revolution produces upon a people; it breaks through regulations, and allows extraordinary men to rise above the common level. Those officers whose bodies and minds have grown old in peace, are removed, or superannuated, or they die. In their stead, a host of young men are pressing on, whose frames are already hardened, whose desires are extended and inflamed by active service. They are bent on advancement at all hazards, and perpetual advancement; they are followed by others with the same passions and desires, and after these are others, yet unlimited by aught but the size of the army. The principle of equality opens the door of ambition to all, and death provides chances for ambition. Death is constantly thinning the ranks, making vacancies, closing and opening the career of arms.

There is, moreover, a secret connection between the military character and the character of democracies, which war brings to light. The men of democracies are naturally passionately eager to acquire what they covet, and to enjoy it on easy conditions. They for the most part worship chance, and are much less afraid of death than of difficulty. This is the spirit which they bring to commerce and manufactures; and this same spirit, carried with them to the field of battle, induces them willingly to expose their lives in order to secure in a moment the rewards of victory. No kind of greatness is more pleasing to the imagination of a democratic people than military greatness, — a greatness of vivid and sudden lustre, obtained without toil, by nothing but the risk of life.

Thus, whilst the interest and the tastes of the members of a democratic community divert them from war, their habits of mind fit them for carrying on war well: they soon make good soldiers, when they are aroused from their business and their enjoyments.

If peace is peculiarly hurtful to democratic armies, war

secures to them advantages which no other armies ever possess; and these advantages, however little felt at first, cannot fail in the end to give them the victory. An aristocratic nation, which, in a contest with a democratic people, does not succeed in ruining the latter at the outset of the war, always runs a great risk of being conquered by it.

CHAPTER XXV.

OF DISCIPLINE IN DEMOCRATIC ARMIES.

IT is a very common opinion, especially in aristocratic countries, that the great social equality which prevails in democracies ultimately renders the private soldier independent of the officer, and thus destroys the bond of discipline. This is a mistake, for there are two kinds of discipline, which it is important not to confound.

When the officer is noble and the soldier a serf, — one rich, the other poor, — the one educated and strong, the other ignorant and weak, — the strictest bond of obedience may easily be established between the two men. The soldier is broken in to military discipline, as it were, before he enters the army; or rather, military discipline is nothing but an enhancement of social servitude. In aristocratic armies, the soldier will soon become insensible to everything but the orders of his superior officers; he acts without reflection, triumphs without enthusiasm, and dies without complaint: in this state, he is no longer a man, but he is still a most formidable animal trained for war.

A democratic people must despair of ever obtaining from soldiers that blind, minute, submissive, and invariable obedience, which an aristocratic people may impose on them without difficulty. The state of society does not prepare them for it, and the nation might be in danger of losing its natural advantages, if it sought artificially to acquire advantages of this particular kind. Amongst democratic communities, military discipline ought not to attempt to annihilate the free action of the faculties; all that can be

done by discipline is to direct it; the obedience thus inculcated is less exact, but it is more eager and more intelligent.
It has its root in the will of him who obeys: it rests not
only on his instinct, but on his reason; and consequently,
it will often spontaneously become more strict as danger
requires. The discipline of an aristocratic army is apt to
be relaxed in war, because that discipline is founded upon
habits, and war disturbs those habits. The discipline of a
democratic army, on the contrary, is strengthened in sight
of the enemy, because every soldier then clearly perceives
that he must be silent and obedient in order to conquer.

The nations which have performed the greatest warlike
achievements knew no other discipline than that which I
speak of. Amongst the ancients, none were admitted into
the armies but freemen and citizens, who differed but little
from one another, and were accustomed to treat each other
as equals. In this respect, it may be said that the armies
of antiquity were democratic, although they came out of
the bosom of aristocracy; the consequence was, that in
those armies a sort of fraternal familiarity prevailed between the officers and the men. Plutarch's lives of great
commanders furnish convincing instances of the fact: the
soldiers were in the constant habit of freely addressing their
general, and the general listened to and answered whatever
the soldiers had to say; they were kept in order by language and by example, far more than by constraint or punishment; the general was as much their companion as their
chief. I know not whether the soldiers of Greece and
Rome ever carried the minutiæ of military discipline to the
same degree of perfection as the Russians have done; but
this did not prevent Alexander from conquering Asia, —
and Rome, the world.

CHAPTER XXVI.

SOME CONSIDERATIONS ON WAR IN DEMOCRATIC COMMUNITIES.

WHEN the principle of equality is spreading, not only amongst a single nation, but amongst several neighboring nations at the same time, as is now the case in Europe, the inhabitants of these different countries, notwithstanding the dissimilarity of language, of customs, and of laws, still resemble each other in their equal dread of war and their common love of peace.* It is in vain that ambition or anger puts arms in the hands of princes; they are appeased in spite of themselves by a species of general apathy and good-will, which makes the sword drop from their grasp, and wars become more rare.

As the spread of equality, taking place in several countries at once, simultaneously impels their various inhabitants to follow manufactures and commerce, not only do their tastes become similar, but their interests are so mixed and entangled with one another, that no nation can inflict evils on other nations without those evils falling back upon itself; and all nations ultimately regard war as a calamity almost as severe to the conqueror as to the conquered.

Thus, on the one hand, it is extremely difficult in democratic times to draw nations into hostilities; but, on the

---

* It is scarcely necessary for me to observe, that the dread of war displayed by the nations of Europe is not attributable solely to the progress made by the principle of equality amongst them; independently of this permanent cause, several other accidental causes of great weight might be pointed out, and I may mention, before all the rest, the extreme lassitude which the wars of the Revolution and the Empire have left behind them.

other, it is almost impossible that any two of them should go to war without embroiling the rest. The interests of all are so interlaced, their opinions and their wants so much alike, that none can remain quiet when the others stir. Wars therefore become more rare, but when they break out, they spread over a larger field.

Neighboring democratic nations not only become alike in some respects, but they eventually grow to resemble each other in almost all.* This similitude of nations has consequences of great importance in relation to war.

* This is not only because these nations have the same social condition, but it arises from the very nature of that social condition, which leads men to imitate and identify themselves with each other.

When the members of a community are divided into castes and classes, they not only differ from one another, but they have no taste and no desire to be alike; on the contrary, every one endeavors, more and more, to keep his own opinions undisturbed, to retain his own peculiar habits, and to remain himself. The characteristics of individuals are very strongly marked.

When the state of society amongst a people is democratic, — that is to say, when there are no longer any castes or classes in the community, and all its members are nearly equal in education and in property, — the human mind follows the opposite direction. Men are much alike, and they are annoyed, as it were, by any deviation from that likeness: far from seeking to preserve their own distinguishing singularities, they endeavor to shake them off, in order to identify themselves with the general mass of the people, which is the sole representative of right and of might to their eyes. The characteristics of individuals are nearly obliterated.

In the ages of aristocracy, even those who are naturally alike strive to create imaginary differences between themselves: in the ages of democracy, even those who are not alike seek nothing more than to become so, and to copy each other, so strongly is the mind of every man always carried away by the general impulse of mankind.

Something of the same kind may be observed between nations: two nations, having the same aristocratic social condition, might remain thoroughly distinct and extremely different, because the spirit of aristocracy is to retain strong individual characteristics; but if two neighboring nations have the same democratic social condition, they cannot fail to adopt similar opinions and manners, because the spirit of democracy tends to assimilate men to each other.

If I inquire why it is that the Helvetic Confederacy made the greatest and most powerful nations of Europe tremble in the fifteenth century, whilst, at the present day, the power of that country is exactly proportioned to its population, I perceive that the Swiss are become like all the surrounding communities, and those surrounding communities like the Swiss : so that, as numerical strength now forms the only difference between them, victory necessarily attends the largest army.   Thus, one of the consequences of the democratic revolution which is going on in Europe is to make numerical strength preponderate on all fields of battle, and to constrain all small nations to incorporate themselves with large states, or at least to adopt the policy of the latter.

As numbers are the determining cause of victory, each people ought of course to strive by all the means in its power to bring the greatest possible number of men into the field.   When it was possible to enlist a kind of troops superior to all others, such as the Swiss infantry or the French horse of the sixteenth century, it was not thought necessary to raise very large armies ; but the case is altered when one soldier is as efficient as another.

The same cause which begets this new want also supplies means of satisfying it ; for, as I have already observed, when men are all alike they are all weak, and the supreme power of the state is naturally much stronger amongst democratic nations than elsewhere.   Hence, whilst these nations are desirous of enrolling the whole male population in the ranks of the army, they have the power of effecting this object : the consequence is, that, in democratic ages, armies seem to grow larger in proportion as the love of war declines.

In the same ages, too, the manner of carrying on war is likewise altered by the same causes.   Machiavelli observes, in " The Prince," " that it is much more difficult to subdue a people who have a prince and his barons for their leaders, than a nation which is commanded by a prince and his slaves." To avoid offence, let us read "public function-aries" for "slaves," and this important truth will be strictly applicable to our own time.

A great aristocratic people cannot either conquer its neighbors or be conquered by them, without great difficulty. It cannot conquer them, because all its forces can never be collected and held together for a considerable period: it cannot be conquered, because an enemy meets at every step small centres of resistance, by which invasion is arrested. War against an aristocracy may be compared to war in a mountainous country, — the defeated party has constant opportunities of rallying its forces to make a stand in a new position.

Exactly the reverse occurs amongst democratic nations: they easily bring their whole disposable force into the field, and when the nation is wealthy and populous it soon becomes victorious; but if ever it is conquered, and its territory invaded, it has few resources at command; and if the enemy takes the capital, the nation is lost. This may very well be explained: as each member of the community is individually isolated and extremely powerless, no one of the whole body can either defend himself or present a rallying-point to others. Nothing is strong in a democratic country except the state; as the military strength of the state is destroyed by the destruction of the army, and its civil power paralyzed by the capture of the chief city, all that remains is only a multitude without strength or government, unable to resist the organized power by which it is assailed. I am aware that this danger may be lessened by the creation of local liberties, and consequently of local powers; but this remedy will always be insufficient. For after such a catastrophe, not only is the population unable to carry on hostilities, but it may be apprehended that they will not be inclined to attempt it.

According to the law of nations adopted in civilized countries, the object of war is, not to seize the property of private individuals, but simply to get possession of political power. The destruction of private property is only occasionally resorted to, for the purpose of attaining the latter object.

When an aristocratic country is invaded after the defeat of its army, the nobles, although they are at the same time the wealthiest members of the community, will continue to defend themselves individually rather than submit; for if the conqueror remained master of the country he would deprive them of their political power, to which they cling even more closely than to their property. They therefore prefer fighting to submission, which is to them the greatest of all misfortunes; and they readily carry the people along with them, because the people have long been used to follow and obey them, and besides have but little to risk in the war.

Amongst a nation in which equality of condition prevails, on the contrary, each citizen has but a slender share of political power, and often has no share at all: on the other hand, all are independent, and all have something to lose; so that they are much less afraid of being conquered, and much more afraid of war, than an aristocratic people. It will always be extremely difficult to decide a democratic population to take up arms when hostilities have reached its own territory. Hence the necessity of giving to such a people the rights and the political character which may impart to every citizen some of those interests that cause the nobles to act for the public welfare in aristocratic countries.

It should never be forgotten by the princes and other leaders of democratic nations, that nothing but the love and the habit of freedom can maintain an advantageous contest with the love and the habit of physical well-being.

I can conceive nothing better prepared for subjection, in case of defeat, than a democratic people without free institutions.

Formerly, it was customary to take the field with a small body of troops, to fight in small engagements, and to make long regular sieges : modern tactics consist in fighting decisive battles, and, as soon as a line of march is open before the army, in rushing upon the capital city, in order to terminate the war at a single blow. Napoleon, it is said, was the inventor of this new system ; but the invention of such a system did not depend on any individual man, whoever he might be. The mode in which Napoleon carried on war was suggested to him by the state of society in his time ; that mode was successful, because it was eminently adapted to that state of society, and because he was the first to employ it. Napoleon was the first commander who marched at the head of an army from capital to capital ; but the road was opened for him by the ruin of feudal society. It may fairly be believed that, if that extraordinary man had been born three hundred years ago, he would not have derived the same results from his method of warfare, or, rather, that he would have had a different method.

I shall add but a few words on civil wars, for fear of exhausting the patience of the reader. Most of the remarks which I have made respecting foreign wars are applicable *a fortiori* to civil wars. Men living in democracies have not naturally the military spirit ; they sometimes acquire it, when they have been dragged by compulsion to the field ; but to rise in a body, and voluntarily to expose themselves to the horrors of war, and especially of civil war, is a course which the men of democracies are not apt to adopt. None but the most adventurous members of the community consent to run into such risks ; the bulk of the population remain motionless.

But even if the population were inclined to act, considerable obstacles would stand in their way; for they can resort to no old and well-established influence which they are willing to obey, — no well-known leaders to rally the discontented, as well as to discipline and to lead them, — no political powers subordinate to the supreme power of the nation, which afford an effectual support to the resistance directed against the government.

In democratic countries, the moral power of the majority is immense, and the physical resources which it has at its command are out of all proportion to the physical resources which may be combined against it. Therefore, the party which occupies the seat of the majority, which speaks in its name and wields its power, triumphs instantaneously and irresistibly over all private resistance; it does not even give such opposition time to exist, but nips it in the bud.

Those who, in such nations, seek to effect a revolution by force of arms, have no other resource than suddenly to seize upon the whole engine of government as it stands, which can better be done by a single blow than by a war; for as soon as there is a regular war, the party which represents the state is always certain to conquer.

The only case in which a civil war could arise is, if the army should divide itself into two factions, the one raising the standard of rebellion, the other remaining true to its allegiance. An army constitutes a small community, very closely united together, endowed with great powers of vitality, and able to supply its own wants for some time. Such a war might be bloody, but it could not be long; for either the rebellious army would gain over the government by the sole display of its resources, or by its first victory, and then the war would be over; or the struggle would take place, and then that portion of the army which should not be supported by the organized powers of the state would speedily either disband itself, or be destroyed. It may therefore be admitted as a general truth, that, in ages of equality, civil wars will become much less frequent and less protracted.*

* It should be borne in mind that I speak here of sovereign and independent democratic nations, not of confederate democracies; in confederacies, as the preponderating power always resides, in spite of all political fictions, in the state governments, and not in the federal government, civil wars are, in fact, nothing but foreign wars in disguise.

FOURTH BOOK.

INFLUENCE OF DEMOCRATIC IDEAS AND FEELINGS ON POLITICAL SOCIETY.

I SHOULD imperfectly fulfil the purpose of this book, if, after having shown what ideas and feelings are suggested by the principle of equality, I did not point out, ere I conclude, the general influence which these same ideas and feelings may exercise upon the government of human societies. To succeed in this object, I shall frequently have to retrace my steps; but I trust the reader will not refuse to follow me through paths already known to him, which may lead to some new truth.

CHAPTER I.

EQUALITY NATURALLY GIVES MEN A TASTE FOR FREE INSTITUTIONS.

THE principle of equality, which makes men independent of each other, gives them a habit and a taste for following, in their private actions, no other guide than their own will. This complete independence, which they constantly enjoy in regard to their equals and in the intercourse of private life, tends to make them look upon all authority with a jealous eye, and speedily suggests to them the notion and the love of political freedom. Men living at such times have a natural bias to free institutions. Take any one of them at a venture, and search if you can his most deep-seated instincts; and you will find that, of all governments, he will soonest conceive and most highly value that government whose head he has himself elected, and whose administration he may control.

Of all the political effects produced by the equality of conditions, this love of independence is the first to strike the observing, and to alarm the timid; nor can it be said that their alarm is wholly misplaced, for anarchy has a more formidable aspect in democratic countries than elsewhere. As the citizens have no direct influence on each other, as soon as the supreme power of the nation fails, which kept them all in their several stations, it would seem that disorder must instantly reach its utmost pitch, and that, every man drawing aside in a different direction, the fabric of society must at once crumble away.

I am persuaded, however, that anarchy is not the principal evil which democratic ages have to fear, but the least. For the principle of equality begets two tendencies: the one leads men straight to independence, and may suddenly drive them into anarchy; the other conducts them by a longer, more secret, but more certain road, to servitude. Nations readily discern the former tendency, and are prepared to resist it; they are led away by the latter, without perceiving its drift; hence it is peculiarly important to point it out.

For myself, I am so far from urging it as a reproach to the principle of equality that it renders men intractable, that this very circumstance principally calls forth my approbation. I admire to see how it deposits in the mind and heart of man the dim conception and instinctive love of political independence, thus preparing the remedy for the evil which it produces: it is on this very account that I am attached to it.

CHAPTER II.

THAT THE OPINIONS OF DEMOCRATIC NATIONS ABOUT GOV-
ERNMENT ARE NATURALLY FAVORABLE TO THE CONCEN-
TRATION OF POWER.

THE notion of secondary powers, placed between the
sovereign and his subjects, occurred naturally to the
imagination of aristocratic nations, because those communities contained individuals or families raised above the
common level, and apparently destined to command by
their birth, their education, and their wealth. This same
notion is naturally wanting in the minds of men in democratic ages, for converse reasons; it can only be introduced
artificially, it can only be kept there with difficulty; whereas they conceive, as it were without thinking upon the
subject, the notion of a single and central power, which
governs the whole community by its direct influence.
Moreover, in politics as well as in philosophy and in religion, the intellect of democratic nations is peculiarly open
to simple and general notions. Complicated systems are
repugnant to it, and its favorite conception is that of a
great nation composed of citizens all formed upon one
pattern, and all governed by a single power.

The very next notion to that of a single and central
power, which presents itself to the minds of men in the
ages of equality, is the notion of uniformity of legislation.
As every man sees that he differs but little from those
about him, he cannot understand why a rule which is applicable to one man should not be equally applicable to all
others. Hence the slightest privileges are repugnant to

his reason; the faintest dissimilarities in the political institutions of the same people offend him, and uniformity of legislation appears to him to be the first condition of good government.

I find, on the contrary, that this notion of a uniform rule, equally binding on all the members of the community, was almost unknown to the human mind in aristocratic ages; it was either never broached, or it was rejected. These contrary tendencies of opinion ultimately turn on both sides to such blind instincts and ungovernable habits, that they still direct the actions of men, in spite of particular exceptions. Notwithstanding the immense variety of conditions in the Middle Ages, a certain number of persons existed at that period in precisely similar circumstances; but this did not prevent the laws then in force from assigning to each of them distinct duties and different rights. On the contrary, at the present time, all the powers of government are exerted to impose the same customs and the same laws on populations which have as yet but few points of resemblance.

As the conditions of men become equal amongst a people, individuals seem of less, and society of greater importance; or rather, every citizen, being assimilated to all the rest, is lost in the crowd, and nothing stands conspicuous but the great and imposing image of the people at large. This naturally gives the men of democratic periods a lofty opinion of the privileges of society, and a very humble notion of the rights of individuals; they are ready to admit that the interests of the former are everything, and those of the latter nothing. They are willing to acknowledge that the power which represents the community has far more information and wisdom than any of the members of that community; and that it is the duty, as well as the right, of that power, to guide as well as govern each private citizen.

If we closely scrutinize our contemporaries, and penetrate to the root of their political opinions, we shall detect some of the notions which I have just pointed out, and we shall perhaps be surprised to find so much accordance between men who are so often at variance.

The Americans hold, that, in every state, the supreme power ought to emanate from the people; but when once that power is constituted, they can conceive, as it were, no limits to it, and they are ready to admit that it has the right to do whatever it pleases. They have not the slightest notion of peculiar privileges granted to cities, families, or persons: their minds appear never to have foreseen that it might be possible not to apply with strict uniformity the same laws to every part of the state, and to all its inhabitants.

These same opinions are more and more diffused in Europe; they even insinuate themselves amongst those nations which most vehemently reject the principle of the sovereignty of the people. Such nations assign a different origin to the supreme power, but they ascribe to that power the same characteristics. Amongst them all, the idea of intermediate powers is weakened and obliterated; the idea of rights inherent in certain individuals is rapidly disappearing from the minds of men; the idea of the omnipotence and sole authority of society at large rises to fill its place. These ideas take root and spread in proportion as social conditions become more equal, and men more alike; they are produced by equality, and in turn they hasten the progress of equality.

In France, where the revolution of which I am speaking has gone further than in any other European country, these opinions have got complete hold of the public mind. If we listen attentively to the language of the various parties in France, we shall find that there is not one which has not adopted them. Most of these parties censure the conduct of the government, but they all hold that the government ought perpetually to act and interfere in everything that is done. Even those which are most at variance are nevertheless agreed upon this head. The unity, the ubiquity, the omnipotence of the supreme power, and the uniformity of its rules, constitute the principal characteristics of all the political systems which have been put forward in our age. They recur even in the wildest visions of political regeneration : the human mind pursues them in its dreams.

If these notions spontaneously arise in the minds of private individuals, they suggest themselves still more forcibly to the minds of princes. Whilst the ancient fabric of European society is altered and dissolved, sovereigns acquire new conceptions of their opportunities and their duties ; they learn for the first time that the central power which they represent may and ought to administer, by its own agency and on a uniform plan, all the concerns of the whole community. This opinion, which, I will venture to say, was never conceived before our time by the monarchs of Europe, now sinks deeply into the minds of kings, and abides there amidst all the agitation of more unsettled thoughts.

Our contemporaries are therefore much less divided than is commonly supposed ; they are constantly disputing as to the hands in which supremacy is to be vested, but they readily agree upon the duties and the rights of that supremacy. The notion they all form of government is that of a sole, simple, providential, and creative power.

All secondary opinions in politics are unsettled ; this one remains fixed, invariable, and consistent. It is adopted by statesmen and political philosophers ; it is eagerly laid hold of by the multitude ; those who govern and those who are governed agree to pursue it with equal ardor ; it is the earliest notion of their minds, it seems innate. It originates, therefore, in no caprice of the human intellect, but it is a necessary condition of the present state of mankind.

CHAPTER III.

THAT THE SENTIMENTS OF DEMOCRATIC NATIONS ACCORD
WITH THEIR OPINIONS IN LEADING THEM TO CONCEN-
TRATE POLITICAL POWER.

IF it be true that, in ages of equality, men readily adopt
the notion of a great central power, it cannot be doubted,
on the other hand, that their habits and sentiments predispose them to recognize such a power, and to give it their
support.   This may be demonstrated in a few words, as the
greater part of the reasons to which the fact may be attributed have been previously stated.*

As the men who inhabit democratic countries have no
superiors, no inferiors, and no habitual or necessary part-
ners in their undertakings, they readily fall back upon themselves, and consider themselves as beings apart.   I had
occasion to point this out at considerable length in treating
of individualism.   Hence such men can never, without an
effort, tear themselves from their private affairs to engage
in public business ; their natural bias leads them to abandon
the latter to the sole visible and permanent representative
of the interests of the community, that is to say, to the
state.   Not only are they naturally wanting in a taste for
public business, but they have frequently no time to attend
to it.   Private life in democratic times is so busy, so excited, so full of wishes and of work, that hardly any energy
or leisure remains to each individual for public life.   I am
the last man to contend that these propensities are unconquerable, since my chief object in writing this book has

* See Appendix V.

been to combat them. I only maintain that, at the present day, a secret power is fostering them in the human heart, and that, if they are not checked, they will wholly overgrow it.

I have also had occasion to show how the increasing love of well-being and the fluctuating character of property cause democratic nations to dread all violent disturbances. The love of public tranquillity is frequently the only passion which these nations retain, and it becomes more active and powerful amongst them in proportion as all other passions droop and die. This naturally disposes the members of the community constantly to give or to surrender additional rights to the central power, which alone seems to be interested in defending them by the same means that it uses to defend itself.

As in periods of equality, no man is compelled to lend his assistance to his fellow-men, and none has any right to expect much support from them, every one is at once independent and powerless. These two conditions, which must never be either separately considered or confounded together, inspire the citizen of a democratic country with very contrary propensities. His independence fills him with self-reliance and pride amongst his equals; his debility makes him feel from time to time the want of some outward assistance, which he cannot expect from any of them, because they are all impotent and unsympathizing. In this predicament, he naturally turns his eyes to that imposing power which alone rises above the level of universal depression. Of that power his wants and especially his desires continually remind him, until he ultimately views it as the sole and necessary support of his own weakness.*

* In democratic communities, nothing but the central power has any stability in its position or any permanence in its undertakings. All the members of society are in ceaseless stir and transformation. Now it is in the nature of all governments to seek constantly to enlarge their sphere of

This may more completely explain what frequently takes place in democratic countries, where the very men who are so impatient of superiors patiently submit to a master, exhibiting at once their pride and their servility.

The hatred which men bear to privilege increases in proportion as privileges become fewer and less considerable, so that democratic passions would seem to burn most fiercely just when they have least fuel. I have already given the reason of this phenomenon. When all conditions are unequal, no inequality is so great as to offend the eye; whereas the slightest dissimilarity is odious in the midst of general uniformity: the more complete this uniformity is, the more insupportable does the sight of such a difference become. Hence it is natural that the love of equality should constantly increase together with equality itself, and that it should grow by what it feeds on.

action; hence it is almost impossible that such a government should not ultimately succeed, because it acts with a fixed principle and a constant will, upon men whose position, whose notions, and whose desires are in continual vacillation.

It frequently happens that the members of the community promote the influence of the central power without intending it. Democratic ages are periods of experiment, innovation, and adventure. At such times, there are always a multitude of men engaged in difficult or novel undertakings, which they follow alone, without caring for their fellow-men. Such persons may be ready to admit, as a general principle, that the public authority ought not to interfere in private concerns; but, by an exception to that rule, each of them craves its assistance in the particular concern on which he is engaged, and seeks to draw upon the influence of the government for his own benefit, though he would restrict it on all other occasions. If a large number of men apply this particular exception to a great variety of different purposes, the sphere of the central power extends itself insensibly in all directions, although each of them wishes it to be circumscribed.

Thus a democratic government increases its power simply by the fact of its permanence. Time is on its side; every incident befriends it; the passions of individuals unconsciously promote it; and it may be asserted, that, the older a democratic community is, the more centralized will its government become.

This never-dying, ever-kindling hatred, which sets a democratic people against the smallest privileges, is peculiarly favorable to the gradual concentration of all political rights in the hands of the representative of the state alone. The sovereign, being necessarily and incontestably above all the citizens, excites not their envy, and each of them thinks that he strips his equals of the prerogative which he concedes to the crown. The man of a democratic age is extremely reluctant to obey his neighbor who is his equal; he refuses to acknowledge superior ability in such a person; he mistrusts his justice, and is jealous of his power; he fears and he contemns him; and he loves continually to remind him of the common dependence in which both of them stand to the same master.

Every central power, which follows its natural tendencies, courts and encourages the principle of equality; for equality singularly facilitates, extends, and secures the influence of a central power.

In like manner, it may be said that every central government worships uniformity: uniformity relieves it from inquiry into an infinity of details, which must be attended to if rules have to be adapted to different men, instead of indiscriminately subjecting all men to the same rule. Thus the government likes what the citizens like, and naturally hates what they hate. These common sentiments, which, in democratic nations, constantly unite the sovereign and every member of the community in one and the same conviction, establish a secret and lasting sympathy between them. The faults of the government are pardoned for the sake of its tastes; public confidence is only reluctantly withdrawn in the midst even of its excesses and its errors; and it is restored at the first call. Democratic nations often hate those in whose hands the central power is vested; but they always love that power itself.

Thus, by two separate paths, I have reached the same

conclusion. I have shown that the principle of equality suggests to men the notion of a sole, uniform, and strong government: I have now shown that the principle of equality imparts to them a taste for it. To governments of this kind the nations of our age are therefore tending. They are drawn thither by the natural inclination of mind and heart; and in order to reach that result, it is enough that they do not check themselves in their course.

I am of opinion, that, in the democratic ages which are opening upon us, individual independence and local liberties will ever be the products of art; that centralization will be the natural government.*

*See Appendix W.

CHAPTER IV.

OF CERTAIN PECULIAR AND ACCIDENTAL CAUSES, WHICH
EITHER LEAD A PEOPLE TO COMPLETE THE CENTRALIZA-
TION OF GOVERNMENT, OR WHICH DIVERT THEM FROM IT.

IF all democratic nations are instinctively led to the centralization of government, they tend to this result in an
unequal manner. This depends on the particular circumstances which may promote or prevent the natural consequences of that state of society, — circumstances which are
exceedingly numerous, but of which I shall mention only a
few.

Amongst men who have lived free long before they became equal, the tendencies derived from free institutions
combat, to a certain extent, the propensities superinduced
by the principle of equality; and although the central
power may increase its privileges amongst such a people,
the private members of such a community will never entirely forfeit their independence. But when the equality
of conditions grows up amongst a people who have never
known, or have long ceased to know, what freedom is, (and
such is the case upon the continent of Europe,) as the former habits of the nation are suddenly combined, by some
sort of natural attraction, with the new habits and principles engendered by the state of society, all powers seem
spontaneously to rush to the centre. These powers accumulate there with astonishing rapidity, and the state instantly attains the utmost limits of its strength, whilst
private persons allow themselves to sink as suddenly to
the lowest degree of weakness.

The English who emigrated three hundred years ago to found a democratic commonwealth on the shores of the New World had all learned to take a part in public affairs in their mother country ; they were conversant with trial by jury ; they were accustomed to liberty of speech and of the press, — to personal freedom, to the notion of rights and the practice of asserting them. They carried with them to America these free institutions and manly customs, and these institutions preserved them against the encroachments of the state. Thus, amongst the Americans, it is freedom which is old, — equality is of comparatively modern date. The reverse is occurring in Europe, where equality, introduced by absolute power and under the rule of kings, was already infused into the habits of nations long before freedom had entered into their thoughts.

I have said that, amongst democratic nations, the notion of government naturally presents itself to the mind under the form of a sole and central power, and that the notion of intermediate powers is not familiar to them. This is peculiarly applicable to the democratic nations which have witnessed the triumph of the principle of equality by means of a violent revolution. As the classes which managed local affairs have been suddenly swept away by the storm, and as the confused mass which remains has as yet neither the organization nor the habits which fit it to assume the administration of these affairs, the state alone seems capable of taking upon itself all the details of government, and centralization becomes, as it were, the unavoidable state of the country.

Napoleon deserves neither praise nor censure for having centred in his own hands almost all the administrative power of France ; for, after the abrupt disappearance of the nobility and the higher rank of the middle classes, these powers devolved on him of course : it would have been almost as difficult for him to reject as to assume them.

But a similar necessity has never been felt by the Americans, who, having passed through no revolution, and having governed themselves from the first, never had to call upon the state to act for a time as their guardian.   Thus, the progress of centralization amongst a democratic people depends not only on the progress of equality, but on the manner in which this equality has been established.

At the commencement of a great democratic revolution, when hostilities have but just broken out between the different classes of society, the people endeavor to centralize the public administration in the hands of the government, in order to wrest the management of local affairs from the aristocracy.   Towards the close of such a revolution, on the contrary, it is usually the conquered aristocracy who endeavor to make over the management of all affairs to the state, because such an aristocracy dread the tyranny of a people who have become their equal, and not unfrequently their master.   Thus, it is not always the same class of the community which strives to increase the prerogative of the government ; but as long as the democratic revolution lasts, there is always one class in the nation, powerful in numbers or in wealth, who are induced, by peculiar passions or interests, to centralize the public administration, independently of that hatred of being governed by one's neighbor which is a general and permanent feeling amongst democratic nations.

It may be remarked, that, at the present day, the lower orders in England are striving with all their might to destroy local independence, and to transfer the administration from all the points of the circumference to the centre ; whereas the higher classes are endeavoring to retain this administration within its ancient boundaries.   I venture to predict that a time will come when the very reverse will happen.

These observations explain why the supreme power is

always stronger, and private individuals weaker, amongst a democratic people, who have passed through a long and arduous struggle to reach a state of equality, than amongst a democratic community in which the citizens have been equal from the first. The example of the Americans completely demonstrates the fact. The inhabitants of the United States were never divided by any privileges; they have never known the mutual relation of master and inferior; and as they neither dread nor hate each other, they have never known the necessity of calling in the supreme power to manage their affairs. The lot of the Americans is singular: they have derived from the aristocracy of England the notion of private rights and the taste for local freedom; and they have been able to retain both, because they have had no aristocracy to combat.

If education enables men at all times to defend their independence, this is most especially true in democratic times. When all men are alike, it is easy to found a sole and all-powerful government by the aid of mere instinct. But men require much intelligence, knowledge, and art to organize and to maintain secondary powers under similar circumstances, and to create, amidst the independence and individual weakness of the citizens, such free associations as may be able to struggle against tyranny without destroying public order.

Hence the concentration of power and the subjection of individuals will increase amongst democratic nations, not only in the same proportion as their equality, but in the same proportion as their ignorance. It is true that, in ages of imperfect civilization, the government is frequently as wanting in the knowledge required to impose a despotism upon the people, as the people are wanting in the knowledge required to shake it off; but the effect is not the same on both sides. However rude a democratic people may be, the central power which rules them is never completely devoid of cultivation, because it readily draws to its own uses what little cultivation is to be found in the country, and, if necessary, may seek assistance elsewhere. Hence, amongst a nation which is ignorant as well as democratic, an amazing difference cannot fail speedily to arise between the intellectual capacity of the ruler and that of each of his subjects. This completes the easy concentration of all power in his hands : the administrative function of the state is perpetually extended, because the state alone is competent to administer the affairs of the country.

Aristocratic nations, however unenlightened they may be, never afford the same spectacle, because, in them, instruction is nearly equally diffused between the monarch and the leading members of the community.

The Pacha who now rules in Egypt found the population of that country composed of men exceedingly ignorant and equal, and he has borrowed the science and ability of Europe to govern that people. As the personal attainments of the sovereign are thus combined with the ignorance and democratic weakness of his subjects, the utmost centralization has been established without impediment, and the Pacha has made the country his manufactory, and the inhabitants his workmen.

I think that extreme centralization of government ultimately enervates society, and thus, after a length of time, weakens the government itself; but I do not deny that a centralized social power may be able to execute great undertakings with facility in a given time and on a particular point. This is more especially true of war, in which success depends much more on the means of transferring all the resources of a nation to one single point, than on the extent of those resources. Hence it is chiefly in war that nations desire, and frequently need, to increase the powers of the central government. All men of military genius are fond of centralization, which increases their strength ; and all men of centralizing genius are fond of war, which compels nations to combine all their powers in the hands of the government. Thus, the democratic tendency which leads men unceasingly to multiply the privileges of the state, and to circumscribe the rights of private persons, is much more rapid and constant amongst those democratic nations which are exposed by their position to great and frequent wars, than amongst all others.

I have shown how the dread of disturbance and the love of well-being insensibly lead democratic nations to increase the functions of central government, as the only power which appears to be intrinsically sufficiently strong, enlightened, and secure to protect them from anarchy. I would now add, that all the particular circumstances which tend to make the state of a democratic community agitated and precarious, enhance this general propensity, and lead private persons more and more to sacrifice their rights to their tranquillity.

A people are therefore never so disposed to increase the functions of central government as at the close of a long and bloody revolution, which, after having wrested property from the hands of its former possessors, has shaken all belief, and filled the nation with fierce hatreds, conflicting interests, and contending factions. The love of public tranquillity becomes at such times an indiscriminate passion, and the members of the community are apt to conceive a most inordinate devotion to order.

I have already examined several of the incidents which may concur to promote the centralization of power, but the principal cause still remains to be noticed. The foremost of the incidental causes which may draw the management of all affairs into the hands of the ruler in democratic countries, is the origin of that ruler himself, and his own propensities. Men who live in the ages of equality are naturally fond of central power, and are willing to extend its privileges ; but if it happens that this same power faithfully represents their own interests, and exactly copies their own inclinations, the confidence they place in it knows no bounds, and they think that whatever they bestow upon it is bestowed upon themselves.

The attraction of administrative powers to the centre will always be less easy and less rapid under the reign of kings who are still in some way connected with the old aristocratic order, than under new princes, the children of their own achievements, whose birth, prejudices, propensities, and habits appear to bind them indissolubly to the cause of equality. I do not mean that princes of aristocratic origin who live in democratic ages do not attempt to centralize ; I believe they apply themselves as diligently as any others to that object. For them, the sole advantages of equality lie in that direction ; but their opportunities are less great, because the community, instead of volunteering compliance with their desires, frequently obey them with reluctance. In democratic communities, the rule is, that centralization must increase in proportion as the sovereign is less aristocratic.

When an ancient race of kings stands at the head of an aristocracy, as the natural prejudices of the sovereign perfectly accord with the natural prejudices of the nobility, the vices inherent in aristocratic communities have a free course, and meet with no corrective. The reverse is the case when the scion of a feudal stock is placed at the head of a democratic people. The sovereign is constantly led, by his education, his habits, and his associations, to adopt sentiments suggested by the inequality of conditions, and the people tend as constantly, by their social condition, to those manners which are engendered by equality. At such times, it often happens that the citizens seek to control the central power far less as a tyrannical than as an aristocratical power, and that they persist in the firm defence of their independence, not only because they would remain free, but especially because they are determined to remain equal.

A revolution which overthrows an ancient regal family in order to place new men at the head of a democratic people may temporarily weaken the central power ; but, however anarchical such a revolution may appear at first, we need not hesitate to predict that its final and certain consequence will be to extend and to secure the prerogatives of that power.

The foremost, or indeed the sole condition, which is required in order to succeed in centralizing the supreme power in a democratic community, is to love equality, or to get men to believe you love it. Thus, the science of despotism, which was once so complex, is simplified, and reduced, as it were, to a single principle.

CHAPTER V.

THAT AMONGST THE EUROPEAN NATIONS OF OUR TIME THE SOVEREIGN POWER IS INCREASING, ALTHOUGH THE SOVER-EIGNS ARE LESS STABLE.

ON reflecting upon what has already been said, the reader will be startled and alarmed to find that in Europe everything seems to conduce to the indefinite extension of the prerogatives of government, and to render every day private independence more weak, more subordinate, and more precarious.

The democratic nations of Europe have all the general and permanent tendencies which urge the Americans to the centralization of government, and they are moreover exposed to a number of secondary and incidental causes with which the Americans are unacquainted. It would seem as if every step they make towards equality brings them nearer to despotism.

And, indeed, if we do but cast our looks around, we shall be convinced that such is the fact. During the aristocratic ages which preceded the present time, the sovereigns of Europe had been deprived of, or had relinquished, many of the rights inherent in their power. Not a hundred years ago, amongst the greater part of European nations, numerous private persons and corporations were sufficiently independent to administer justice, to raise and maintain troops, to levy taxes, and frequently even to make or interpret the law. The state has everywhere resumed to itself alone these natural attributes of sovereign power; in all matters of government, the state tolerates no intermediate agent between itself and the people, and it directs them by itself in general affairs. I am far from blaming this concentration of power, — I simply point it out.

At the same period a great number of secondary powers existed in Europe, which represented local interests and administered local affairs. Most of these local authorities have already disappeared; all are speedily tending to disappear, or to fall into the most complete dependence. From one end of Europe to the other the privileges of the nobility, the liberties of cities, and the powers of provincial bodies are either destroyed or are upon the verge of destruction.

Europe has endured, in the course of the last half-century, many revolutions and counter revolutions, which have agitated it in opposite directions; but all these perturbations resemble each other in one respect, — they have all shaken or destroyed the secondary powers of government. The local privileges which the French did not abolish in the countries they conquered, have finally succumbed to the policy of the princes who conquered the French. Those princes rejected all the innovations of the French Revolution except centralization : that is the only principle they consented to receive from such a source.

My object is to remark, that all these various rights, which have been successively wrested, in our time, from classes, corporations, and individuals, have not served to raise new secondary powers on a more democratic basis, but have uniformly been concentrated in the hands of the sovereign. Everywhere the state acquires more and more direct control over the humblest members of the community, and a more exclusive power of governing each of them in his smallest concerns.*

---

* This gradual weakening of individuals in relation to society at large may be traced in a thousand things. I shall select from amongst these examples one derived from the law of wills.

In aristocracies, it is common to profess the greatest reverence for the last

Almost all the charitable establishments of Europe were formerly in the hands of private persons or of corporations; they are now almost all dependent on the supreme government, and in many countries are actually administered by that power. The state almost exclusively undertakes to supply bread to the hungry, assistance and shelter to the sick, work to the idle, and to act as the sole reliever of all kinds of misery.

Education, as well as charity, is become in most countries, at the present day, a national concern. The state receives, and often takes, the child from the arms of the mother, to hand it over to official agents: the state undertakes to train the heart and to instruct the mind of each generation. Uniformity prevails in the courses of public instruction as in everything else; diversity, as well as freedom, are disappearing day by day.

Nor do I hesitate to affirm, that, amongst almost all the Christian nations of our days, Catholic as well as Protestant, religion is in danger of falling into the hands of the government. Not that rulers are over-jealous of the right of settling points of doctrine, but they get more and more hold upon the will of those by whom doctrines are expounded; they deprive the clergy of their property, and pay them by salaries; they divert to their own use the influence of the priesthood, they make them their own minis-

testamentary dispositions of a man; this feeling sometimes even became superstitious amongst the elder nations of Europe: the power of the state, far from interfering with the caprices of a dying man, gave full force to the very least of them, and insured to him a perpetual power.

When all living men are enfeebled, the will of the dead is less respected; it is circumscribed within a narrow range, beyond which it is annulled or checked by the supreme power of the laws. In the Middle Ages, testamentary power had, so to speak, no limits: amongst the French, at the present day, a man cannot distribute his fortune amongst his children without the interference of the state; after having domineered over a whole life, the law insists upon regulating the very last act of it.

ters, — often their own servants, — and by this alliance with religion they reach the inner depths of the soul of man.*

But this is as yet only one side of the picture. The authority of government has not only spread, as we have just seen, throughout the sphere of all existing powers, till that sphere can no longer contain it, but it goes further, and invades the domain heretofore reserved to private independence. A multitude of actions, which were formerly entirely beyond the control of the public administration, have been subjected to that control in our time, and the number of them is constantly increasing.

Amongst aristocratic nations, the supreme government usually contented itself with managing and superintending the community in whatever directly and ostensibly concerned the national honor; but in all other respects, the people were left to work out their own free will. Amongst these nations, the government often seemed to forget that there is a point at which the faults and the sufferings of private persons involved the general prosperity, and that to prevent the ruin of a private individual must sometimes be a matter of public importance.

The democratic nations of our time lean to the opposite extreme. It is evident that most of our rulers will not content themselves with governing the people collectively; it would seem as if they thought themselves responsible for the actions and private condition of their subjects, — as if they had undertaken to guide and to instruct each of them in the various incidents of life, and to secure their happiness quite independently of their own consent. On the

---

* In proportion as the duties of the central power are augmented, the number of public officers by whom that power is represented must increase also. They form a nation in each nation; and as they share the stability of the government, they more and more fill up the place of an aristocracy.

In almost every part of Europe, the government rules in two ways; it rules one portion of the community by the fear which they entertain of its agents, and the other by the hope they have of becoming its agents.

other hand, private individuals grow more and more apt to look upon the supreme power in the same light; they invoke its assistance in all their necessities, and they fix their eyes upon the administration as their mentor or their guide.

I assert that there is no country in Europe in which the public administration has not become, not only more centralized, but more inquisitive and more minute: it everywhere interferes in private concerns more than it did; it regulates more undertakings, and undertakings of a lesser kind; and it gains a firmer footing every day about, above, and around all private persons, to assist, to advise, and to coerce them.

Formerly, a sovereign lived upon the income of his lands, or the revenue of his taxes; this is no longer the case now that his wants have increased as well as his power. Under the same circumstances which formerly compelled a prince to put on a new tax, he now has recourse to a loan. Thus the state gradually becomes the debtor of most of the wealthier members of the community, and centralizes the largest amounts of capital in its own hands.

Small capital is drawn into its keeping by another method. As men are intermingled and conditions become more equal, the poor have more resources, more education, and more desires; they conceive the notion of bettering their condition, and this teaches them to save. These savings are daily producing an infinite number of small capitals, the slow and gradual produce of labor, which are always increasing. But the greater part of this money would be unproductive, if it remained scattered in the hands of its owners. This circumstance has given rise to a philanthropic institution, which will soon become, if I am not mistaken, one of our most important political institutions. Some charitable persons conceived the notion of collecting the savings of the poor and placing them out at interest. In some countries, these benevolent associations are still completely distinct from the state; but in almost all, they manifestly tend to identify themselves with the government; and in some of them, the government has superseded them, taking upon itself the enormous task of centralizing in one place, and putting out at interest, on its own responsibility, the daily savings of many millions of the working classes.

Thus the state draws to itself the wealth of the rich by loans, and has the poor man's mite at its disposal in the savings banks. The wealth of the country is perpetually flowing around the government, and passing through its hands; the accumulation increases in the same proportion as the equality of conditions; for in a democratic country, the state alone inspires private individuals with confidence, because the state alone appears to be endowed with strength and durability.*

Thus the sovereign does not confine himself to the management of the public treasury; he interferes in private money matters; he is the superior, and often the master, of all the members of the community; and, in addition to this, he assumes the part of their steward and paymaster.

The central power not only fulfils of itself the whole of the duties formerly discharged by various authorities, — extending those duties, and surpassing those authorities, — but it performs them with more alertness, strength, and independence than it displayed before. All the governments of Europe have, in our time, singularly improved the science of administration: they do more things, and they do everything with more order, more celerity, and at

---

* On the one hand, the taste for worldly welfare is perpetually increasing; and, on the other, the government gets more and more complete possession of the sources of that welfare.

Thus men are following two separate roads to servitude; the taste for their own welfare withholds them from taking a part in the government, and their love of that welfare places them in closer dependence upon those who govern.

less expense; they seem to be constantly enriched by all
the experience of which they have stripped private persons.
From day to day, the princes of Europe hold their subordinate officers under stricter control, and invent new methods
for guiding them more closely, and inspecting them with
less trouble. Not content with managing everything by
their agents, they undertake to manage the conduct of their
agents in everything: so that the public administration not
only depends upon one and the same power, but it is more
and more confined to one spot and concentrated in the
same hands. The government centralizes its agency whilst
it increases its prerogative; — hence a twofold increase of
strength.

In examining the ancient constitution of the judicial
power, amongst most European nations, two things strike
the mind, — the independence of that power, and the extent of its functions. Not only did the courts of justice
decide almost all differences between private persons, but
in very many cases they acted as arbiters between private
persons and the state.

I do not here allude to the political and administrative
functions which courts of judicature had in some countries
usurped, but to the judicial duties common to them all. In
most of the countries of Europe, there were, and there still
are, many private rights, connected for the most part with
the general right of property, which stood under the protection of the courts of justice, and which the state could
not violate without their sanction. It was this semi-politi-
cal power which mainly distinguished the European courts
of judicature from all others; for all nations have had
judges, but all have not invested their judges with the
same privileges.

Upon examining what is now occurring amongst the
democratic nations of Europe which are called free, as well
as amongst the others, it will be observed that new and

more dependent courts are everywhere springing up by the
side of the old ones, for the express purpose of deciding, by
an extraordinary jurisdiction, such litigated matters as may
arise between the government and private persons.   The
elder judicial power retains its independence, but its jurisdiction is narrowed ; and there is a growing tendency to
reduce it to be exclusively the arbiter between private interests.

The number of these special courts of justice is continually increasing, and their functions increase likewise.   Thus,
the government is more and more absolved from the necessity of subjecting its policy and its rights to the sanction of
another power.   As judges cannot be dispensed with, at
least the state is to select them, and always to hold them
under its control ; so that between the government and
private individuals they place the effigy of justice rather
than justice itself.   The state is not satisfied with drawing
all concerns to itself, but it acquires an ever-increasing
power of deciding on them all, without restriction and
without appeal.*

There exists amongst the modern nations of Europe one
great cause, independent of all those which have already
been pointed out, which perpetually contributes to extend
the agency or to strengthen the prerogative of the supreme
power, though it has not been sufficiently attended to: I
mean the growth of manufactures, which is fostered by the
progress of social equality.   Manufacturers generally collect
a multitude of men on the same spot, amongst whom new
and complex relations spring up.   These men are exposed

* A strange sophism has been uttered on this head in France.   When a
suit arises between the government and a private person, it is not to be tried
before an ordinary judge, — in order, they say, not to mix the administrative
and the judicial powers; as if it were not to mix those powers, and to mix
them in the most dangerous and oppressive manner, to invest the government with the office of judging and administering at the same time.

by their calling to great and sudden alternations of plenty and want, during which public tranquillity is endangered. It may also happen that these employments sacrifice the health, and even the life, of those who gain by them, or of those who live by them. Thus, the manufacturing classes require more regulation, superintendence, and restraint than the other classes of society, and it is natural that the powers of government should increase in the same proportion as those classes.

This is a truth of general application; what follows more especially concerns the nations of Europe. In the centuries which preceded that in which we live, the aristocracy was in possession of the soil, and was competent to defend it: landed property was therefore surrounded by ample securities, and its possessors enjoyed great independence. This gave rise to laws and customs which have been perpetuated, notwithstanding the subdivision of lands and the ruin of the nobility; and, at the present time, land-owners and agriculturists are still those amongst the community who most easily escape from the control of the supreme power.

In these same aristocratic ages, in which all the sources of our history are to be traced, personal property was of small importance, and those who possessed it were despised and weak: the manufacturing class formed an exception in the midst of those aristocratic communities; as it had no certain patronage, it was not outwardly protected, and was often unable to protect itself. Hence a habit sprang up of considering manufacturing property as something of a peculiar nature, not entitled to the same deference, and not worthy of the same securities, as property in general; and manufacturers were looked upon as a small class in the social hierarchy, whose independence was of small importance, and who might with propriety be abandoned to the disciplinary passions of princes. On glancing over the codes of the Middle Ages, one is surprised to see, in those periods of personal independence, with what incessant royal regulations manufactures were hampered, even in their smallest details: on this point, centralization was as active and as minute as it can ever be.

Since that time, a great revolution has taken place in the world; manufacturing property, which was then only in the germ, has spread till it covers Europe: the manufacturing class has been multiplied and enriched by the remnants of all other ranks: it has grown, and is still perpetually growing, in number, in importance, in wealth. Almost all those who do not belong to it are connected with it at least on some one point: after having been an exception in society, it threatens to become the chief, if not the only class; nevertheless, the notions and political habits created by it of old still continue. These notions and habits remain unchanged, because they are old, and also because they happen to be in perfect accordance with the new notions and general habits of our contemporaries.

Manufacturing property, then, does not extend its rights in the same ratio as its importance. The manufacturing classes do not become less dependent, whilst they become more numerous; but, on the contrary, it would seem as if despotism lurked within them, and naturally grew with their growth.*

* I shall quote a few facts in corroboration of this remark.

Mines are the natural sources of manufacturing wealth: as manufactures have grown up in Europe, as the produce of mines has become of more general importance, and good mining more difficult from the subdivision of property which is a consequence of the equality of conditions, most governments have asserted a right of owning the soil in which the mines lie, and of inspecting the works, which has never been the case with any other kind of property.

Thus, mines, which were private property, liable to the same obligations and sheltered by the same guaranties as all other landed property, have fallen under the control of the state. The state either works them or farms them; the owners of them are mere tenants, deriving their rights from the

As a nation becomes more engaged in manufactures, the want of roads, canals, harbors, and other works of a semi-public nature, which facilitate the acquisition of wealth, is more strongly felt; and as a nation becomes more democratic, private individuals are less able, and the state more able, to execute works of such magnitude. I do not hesitate to assert, that the manifest tendency of all governments at the present time is to take upon themselves alone the execution of these undertakings, by which means they daily hold in closer dependence the population which they govern.

On the other hand, in proportion as the power of a state increases, and its necessities are augmented, the state consumption of manufactured produce is always growing larger; and these commodities are generally made in the arsenals or establishments of the government. Thus, in every kingdom, the ruler becomes the principal manufacturer: he collects and retains in his service a vast number of engineers, architects, mechanics, and handicraftsmen.

Not only is he the principal manufacturer, but he tends more and more to become the chief, or rather the master, of all other manufacturers. As private persons become powerless by becoming more equal, they can effect nothing in manufactures without combination; but the government naturally seeks to place these combinations under its own control.

state; and, moreover, the state almost everywhere claims the power of directing their operations : it lays down rules, enforces the adoption of particular methods, subjects the mining adventurers to constant superintendence, and, if refractory, they are ousted by a government court of justice, and the government transfers their contract to other hands; so that the government not only possesses the mines, but has all the adventurers in its power. Nevertheless, as manufactures increase, the working of old mines increases also; new ones are opened; the mining population extends and grows up; day by day, governments augment their subterranean dominions, and people them with their agents.

It must be admitted that these collective beings, which are called companies, are stronger and more formidable than a private individual can ever be, and that they have less of the responsibility of their own actions; whence it seems reasonable that they should not be allowed to retain so great an independence of the supreme government as might be conceded to a private individual.

Rulers are the more apt to follow this line of policy, as their own inclinations invite them to it. Amongst democratic nations it is only by association that the resistance of the people to the government can ever display itself: hence the latter always looks with ill-favor on those associations which are not in its own power; and it is well worthy of remark, that, amongst democratic nations, the people themselves often entertain against these very associations a secret feeling of fear and jealousy, which prevents the citizens from defending the institutions of which they stand so much in need. The power and the duration of these small private bodies, in the midst of the weakness and instability of the whole community, astonish and alarm the people; and the free use which each association makes of its natural powers is almost regarded as a dangerous privilege. All the associations which spring up in our age are, moreover, new corporate powers, whose rights have not been sanctioned by time; they come into existence at a time when the notion of private rights is weak, and when the power of government is unbounded; hence it is not surprising that they lose their freedom at their birth.

Amongst all European nations there are some kinds of associations or companies which cannot be formed until the state has examined their by-laws and authorized their existence. In several others, attempts are made to extend this rule to all associations; the consequences of such a policy, if it were successful, may easily be foreseen.

If once the sovereign had a general right of authorizing

associations of all kinds upon certain conditions, he would not be long without claiming the right of superintending and managing them, in order to prevent them from departing from the rules laid down by himself. In this manner, the state, after having reduced all who are desirous of forming associations into dependence, would proceed to reduce into the same condition all who belong to associations already formed, — that is to say, almost all the men who are now in existence.

Governments thus appropriate to themselves and convert to their own purposes the greater part of this new power which manufacturing interests have in our time brought into the world. Manufactures govern us, they govern manufactures.

I attach so much importance to all that I have just been saying, that I am tormented by the fear of having impaired my meaning in seeking to render it more clear. If the reader thinks that the examples I have adduced to support my observations are insufficient or ill-chosen, — if he imagines that I have anywhere exaggerated the encroachments of the supreme power, and, on the other hand, that I have underrated the extent of the sphere which still remains open to the exertions of individual independence, — I entreat him to lay down the book for a moment, and to turn his mind to reflect upon the subjects I have attempted to explain. Let him attentively examine what is taking place in France and in other countries, let him inquire of those about him, let him search himself, and I am much mistaken if he does not arrive, without my guidance, and by other paths, at the point to which I have sought to lead him.

He will perceive that, for the last half-century, centralization has everywhere been growing up in a thousand different ways. Wars, revolutions, conquests, have served to promote it; all men have labored to increase it. In the course of the same period, during which men have succeeded each other with singular rapidity at the head of affairs, their notions, interests, and passions have been infinitely diversified; but all have, by some means or other, sought to centralize. This instinctive centralization has been the only settled point amidst the extreme mutability of their lives and their thoughts.

If the reader, after having investigated these details of human affairs, will seek to survey the wide prospect as a whole, he will be struck by the result. On the one hand, the most settled dynasties shaken or overthrown; the people everywhere escaping by violence from the sway of their laws, — abolishing or limiting the authority of their rulers or their princes; the nations which are not in open revolution restless at least, and excited, — all of them animated by the same spirit of revolt: and, on the other hand, at this very period of anarchy, and amongst these untractable nations, the incessant increase of the prerogative of the supreme government, becoming more centralized, more adventurous, more absolute, more extensive, — the people perpetually falling under the control of the public administration, — led insensibly to surrender to it some further portion of their individual independence, till the very men who from time to time upset a throne and trample on a race of kings, bend more and more obsequiously to the slightest dictate of a clerk. Thus, two contrary revolutions appear, in our days, to be going on; the one continually weakening the supreme power, the other as continually strengthening it: at no other period in our history has it appeared so weak or so strong.

But, upon a more attentive examination of the state of the world, it appears that these two revolutions are intimately connected together, that they originate in the same source, and that, after having followed a separate course, they lead men at last to the same result.

I may venture once more to repeat what I have already said or implied in several parts of this book : great care must be taken not to confound the principle of equality itself with the revolution which finally establishes that principle in the social condition and the laws of a nation : here lies the reason of almost all the phenomena which occasion our astonishment.

All the old political powers of Europe, the greatest as well as the least, were founded in ages of aristocracy, and they more or less represented or defended the principles of inequality and of privilege.   To make the novel wants and interests which the growing principle of equality introduced preponderate in government, our contemporaries had to overturn or to coerce the established powers.   This led men to make revolutions, and breathed into many of them that fierce love of disturbance and independence, which all revolutions, whatever be their object, always engender.

I do not believe that there is a single country in Europe in which the progress of equality has not been preceded or followed by some violent changes in the state of property and persons ; and almost all these changes have been attended with much anarchy and license, because they have been made by the least civilized portion of the nation against that which is most civilized.

Hence proceeded the twofold contrary tendencies which I have just pointed out.   As long as the democratic revolution was glowing with heat, the men who were bent upon the destruction of old aristocratic powers hostile to that revolution displayed a strong spirit of independence ; but as the victory of the principle of equality became more complete, they gradually surrendered themselves to the propensities natural to that condition of equality, and they strengthened and centralized their governments.   They had sought to be free in order to make themselves equal ;

but in proportion as equality was more established by the aid of freedom, freedom itself was thereby rendered of more difficult attainment.

These two states of a nation have sometimes been contemporaneous: the last generation in France showed how a people might organize a stupendous tyranny in the community, at the very time when they were baffling the authority of the nobility and braving the power of all kings, — at once teaching the world the way to win freedom, and the way to lose it.

In our days, men see that constituted powers are crumbling down on every side, — they see all ancient authority dying out, all ancient barriers tottering to their fall, and the judgment of the wisest is troubled at the sight: they attend only to the amazing revolution which is taking place before their eyes, and they imagine that mankind is about to fall into perpetual anarchy: if they looked to the final consequences of this revolution, their fears would perhaps assume a different shape. For myself, I confess that I put no trust in the spirit of freedom which appears to animate my contemporaries. I see well enough that the nations of this age are turbulent, but I do not clearly perceive that they are liberal; and I fear lest, at the close of those perturbations which rock the base of thrones, the dominion of sovereigns may prove more powerful than it ever was before.

CHAPTER VI.

WHAT SORT OF DESPOTISM DEMOCRATIC NATIONS HAVE TO FEAR.

I HAD remarked during my stay in the United States, that a democratic state of society, similar to that of the Americans, might offer singular facilities for the establishment of despotism; and I perceived, upon my return to Europe, how much use had already been made, by most of our rulers, of the notions, the sentiments, and the wants created by this same social condition, for the purpose of extending the circle of their power. This led me to think that the nations of Christendom would perhaps eventually undergo some oppression like that which hung over several of the nations of the ancient world.

A more accurate examination of the subject, and five years of further meditation, have not diminished my fears, but have changed the object of them.

No sovereign ever lived in former ages so absolute or so powerful as to undertake to administer by his own agency, and without the assistance of intermediate powers, all the parts of a great empire : none ever attempted to subject all his subjects indiscriminately to strict uniformity of regulation, and personally to tutor and direct every member of the community. The notion of such an undertaking never occurred to the human mind; and if any man had conceived it, the want of information, the imperfection of the administrative system, and, above all, the natural obstacles caused by the inequality of conditions, would speedily have checked the execution of so vast a design.

When the Roman Emperors were at the height of their power, the different nations of the empire still preserved manners and customs of great diversity; although they were subject to the same monarch, most of the provinces were separately administered; they abounded in powerful and active municipalities; and although the whole government of the empire was centred in the hands of the Emperor alone, and he always remained, in case of need, the supreme arbiter in all matters, yet the details of social life and private occupations lay for the most part beyond his control. The Emperors possessed, it is true, an immense and unchecked power, which allowed them to gratify all their whimsical tastes, and to employ for that purpose the whole strength of the state. They frequently abused that power arbitrarily to deprive their subjects of property or of life: their tyranny was extremely onerous to the few, but it did not reach the many; it was fixed to some few main objects, and neglected the rest; it was violent, but its range was limited.

It would seem that, if despotism were to be established amongst the democratic nations of our days, it might assume a different character; it would be more extensive and more mild; it would degrade men without tormenting them. I do not question, that, in an age of instruction and equality like our own, sovereigns might more easily succeed in collecting all political power into their own hands, and might interfere more habitually and decidedly with the circle of private interests, than any sovereign of antiquity could ever do. But this same principle of equality which facilitates despotism, tempers its rigor. We have seen how the manners of society become more humane and gentle, in proportion as men become more equal and alike. When no member of the community has much power or much wealth, tyranny is, as it were, without opportunities and a field of action. As all fortunes are scanty, the passions of men are naturally circumscribed, their imagination limited, their pleasures simple. This universal moderation moderates the sovereign himself, and checks within certain limits the inordinate stretch of his desires.

Independently of these reasons, drawn from the nature of the state of society itself, I might add many others arising from causes beyond my subject; but I shall keep within the limits I have laid down.

Democratic governments may become violent, and even cruel, at certain periods of extreme effervescence or of great danger; but these crises will be rare and brief. When I consider the petty passions of our contemporaries, the mildness of their manners, the extent of their education, the purity of their religion, the gentleness of their morality, their regular and industrious habits, and the restraint which they almost all observe in their vices no less than in their virtues, I have no fear that they will meet with tyrants in their rulers, but rather with guardians.*

I think, then, that the species of oppression by which democratic nations are menaced is unlike anything which ever before existed in the world: our contemporaries will find no prototype of it in their memories. I seek in vain for an expression which will accurately convey the whole of the idea I have formed of it, the old words despotism and tyranny are inappropriate: the thing itself is new, and since I cannot name, I must attempt to define it.

I seek to trace the novel features under which despotism may appear in the world. The first thing that strikes the observation is an innumerable multitude of men, all equal and alike, incessantly endeavoring to procure the petty and paltry pleasures with which they glut their lives. Each of them, living apart, is as a stranger to the fate of all the rest, — his children and his private friends constitute to him the whole of mankind; as for the rest of his fellow-

* See Appendix X.

citizens, he is close to them, but he sees them not;—he touches them, but he feels them not; he exists but in himself and for himself alone; and if his kindred still remain to him, he may be said at any rate to have lost his country.

Above this race of men stands an immense and tutelary power, which takes upon itself alone to secure their gratifications, and to watch over their fate. That power is absolute, minute, regular, provident, and mild. It would be like the authority of a parent, if, like that authority, its object was to prepare men for manhood; but it seeks, on the contrary, to keep them in perpetual childhood: it is well content that the people should rejoice, provided they think of nothing but rejoicing. For their happiness such a government willingly labors, but it chooses to be the sole agent and the only arbiter of that happiness; it provides for their security, foresees and supplies their necessities, facilitates their pleasures, manages their principal concerns, directs their industry, regulates the descent of property, and subdivides their inheritances: what remains, but to spare them all the care of thinking and all the trouble of living?

Thus, it every day renders the exercise of the free agency of man less useful and less frequent; it circumscribes the will within a narrower range, and gradually robs a man of all the uses of himself. The principle of equality has prepared men for these things; it has predisposed men to endure them, and oftentimes to look on them as benefits.

After having thus successively taken each member of the community in its powerful grasp, and fashioned him at will, the supreme power then extends its arm over the whole community. It covers the surface of society with a network of small complicated rules, minute and uniform, through which the most original minds and the most energetic characters cannot penetrate, to rise above the crowd.

The will of man is not shattered, but softened, bent, and guided ; men are seldom forced by it to act, but they are constantly restrained from acting : such a power does not destroy, but it prevents existence ; it does not tyrannize, but it compresses, enervates, extinguishes, and stupefies a people, till each nation is reduced to be nothing better than a flock of timid and industrious animals, of which the government is the shepherd.

I have always thought that servitude of the regular, quiet, and gentle kind which I have just described might be combined more easily than is commonly believed with some of the outward forms of freedom, and that it might even establish itself under the wing of the sovereignty of the people.

Our contemporaries are constantly excited by two conflicting passions ; they want to be led, and they wish to remain free : as they cannot destroy either the one or the other of these contrary propensities, they strive to satisfy them both at once. They devise a sole, tutelary, and all-powerful form of government, but elected by the people. They combine the principle of centralization and that of popular sovereignty ; this gives them a respite : they console themselves for being in tutelage by the reflection that they have chosen their own guardians. Every man allows himself to be put in leading-strings, because he sees that it is not a person or a class of persons, but the people at large, who hold the end of his chain.

By this system, the people shake off their state of dependence just long enough to select their master, and then relapse into it again. A great many persons at the present day are quite contented with this sort of compromise between administrative despotism and the sovereignty of the people ; and they think they have done enough for the protection of individual freedom when they have surrendered it to the power of the nation at large. This does

not satisfy me : the nature of him I am to obey signifies
less to me than the fact of extorted obedience.

I do not, however, deny that a constitution of this kind
appears to me to be infinitely preferable to one which, after
having concentrated all the powers of government, should
vest them in the hands of an irresponsible person or body
of persons. Of all the forms which democratic despotism
could assume, the latter would assuredly be the worst.

When the sovereign is elective, or narrowly watched by
a legislature which is really elective and independent, the
oppression which he exercises over individuals is sometimes
greater, but it is always less degrading ; because every man,
when he is oppressed and disarmed, may still imagine that,
whilst he yields obedience, it is to himself he yields it, and
that it is to one of his own inclinations that all the rest
give way. In like manner, I can understand that, when
the sovereign represents the nation, and is dependent upon
the people, the rights and the power of which every citizen
is deprived not only serve the head of the state, but the
state itself ; and that private persons derive some return
from the sacrifice of their independence which they have
made to the public. To create a representation of the people in every centralized country is, therefore, to diminish
the evil which extreme centralization may produce, but not
to get rid of it.

I admit that, by this means, room is left for the intervention of individuals in the more important affairs ; but it is
not the less suppressed in the smaller and more private
ones. It must not be forgotten that it is especially dangerous to enslave men in the minor details of life. For my
own part, I should be inclined to think freedom less necessary in great things than in little ones, if it were possible
to be secure of the one without possessing the other.

Subjection in minor affairs breaks out every day, and is
felt by the whole community indiscriminately. It does not

drive men to resistance, but it crosses them at every turn, till they are led to surrender the exercise of their own will. Thus their spirit is gradually broken and their character enervated ; whereas that obedience which is exacted on a few important but rare occasions, only exhibits servitude at certain intervals, and throws the burden of it upon a small number of men. It is in vain to summon a people, who have been rendered so dependent on the central power, to choose from time to time the representatives of that power ; this rare and brief exercise of their free choice, however important it may be, will not prevent them from gradually losing the faculties of thinking, feeling, and acting for themselves, and thus gradually falling below the level of humanity.*

I add, that they will soon become incapable of exercising the great and only privilege which remains to them. The democratic nations which have introduced freedom into their political constitution, at the very time when they were augmenting the despotism of their administrative constitution, have been led into strange paradoxes. To manage those minor affairs in which good sense is all that is wanted, — the people are held to be unequal to the task ; but when the government of the country is at stake, the people are invested with immense powers ; they are alternately made the playthings of their ruler, and his masters, — more than kings, and less than men. After having exhausted all the different modes of election, without finding one to suit their purpose, they are still amazed, and still bent on seeking further ; as if the evil they remark did not originate in the constitution of the country, far more than in that of the electoral body.

It is, indeed, difficult to conceive how men who have entirely given up the habit of self-government should succeed in making a proper choice of those by whom they are

* See Appendix Y.

to be governed; and no one will ever believe that a liberal, wise, and energetic government can spring from the suffrages of a subservient people.

A constitution which should be republican in its head, and ultra-monarchical in all its other parts, has ever appeared to me to be a short-lived monster. The vices of rulers and the inaptitude of the people would speedily bring about its ruin; and the nation, weary of its representatives and of itself, would create freer institutions, or soon return to stretch itself at the feet of a single master.

CHAPTER VII.

CONTINUATION OF THE PRECEDING CHAPTERS.

I BELIEVE that it is easier to establish an absolute and despotic government amongst a people in which the conditions of society are equal, than amongst any other; and I think that, if such a government were once established amongst such a people, it would not only oppress men, but would eventually strip each of them of several of the highest qualities of humanity. Despotism, therefore, appears to me peculiarly to be dreaded in democratic times. I should have loved freedom, I believe, at all times, but in the time in which we live I am ready to worship it.

On the other hand, I am persuaded that all who shall attempt, in the ages upon which we are entering, to base freedom upon aristocratic privilege, will fail; that all who shall attempt to draw and to retain authority within a single class, will fail. At the present day, no ruler is skilful or strong enough to found a despotism by re-establishing permanent distinctions of rank amongst his subjects: no legislator is wise or powerful enough to preserve free institutions, if he does not take equality for his first principle and his watchword. All of our contemporaries who would establish or secure the independence and the dignity of their fellow-men, must show themselves the friends of equality; and the only worthy means of showing themselves as such is to be so: upon this depends the success of their holy enterprise. Thus, the question is not how to reconstruct aristocratic society, but how to make liberty proceed out of that democratic state of society in which God has placed us.

These two truths appear to me simple, clear, and fertile in consequences ; and they naturally lead me to consider what kind of free government can be established amongst a people in which social conditions are equal.

It results, from the very constitution of democratic nations and from their necessities, that the power of government amongst them must be more uniform, more centralized, more extensive, more searching, and more efficient than in other countries. Society at large is naturally stronger and more active, the individual more subordinate and weak ; the former does more, the latter less ; and this is inevitably the case.

It is not, therefore, to be expected that the range of private independence will ever be as extensive in democratic as in aristocratic countries ; — nor is this to be desired ; for, amongst aristocratic nations, the mass is often sacrificed to the individual, and the prosperity of the greater number to the greatness of the few. It is both necessary and desirable that the government of a democratic people should be active and powerful : and our object should not be to render it weak or indolent, but solely to prevent it from abusing its aptitude and its strength.

The circumstance which most contributed to secure the independence of private persons in aristocratic ages was, that the supreme power did not affect to take upon itself alone the government and administration of the community ; those functions were necessarily partially left to the members of the aristocracy : so that, as the supreme power was always divided, it never weighed with its whole weight and in the same manner on each individual.

Not only did the government not perform everything by its immediate agency ; but, as most of the agents who discharged its duties derived their power, not from the state, but from the circumstance of their birth, they were not perpetually under its control. The government could not make or unmake them in an instant, at pleasure, or bend them in strict uniformity to its slightest caprice; — this was an additional guaranty of private independence.

I readily admit that recourse cannot be had to the same means at the present time; but I discover certain democratic expedients which may be substituted for them. Instead of vesting in the government alone all the administrative powers of which corporations and nobles have been deprived, a portion of them may be intrusted to secondary public bodies temporarily composed of private citizens: thus the liberty of private persons will be more secure, and their equality will not be diminished.

The Americans, who care less for words than the French, still designate by the name of County the largest of their administrative districts; but the duties of the count or lord-lieutenant are in part performed by a provincial assembly.

At a period of equality like our own, it would be unjust and unreasonable to institute hereditary officers; but there is nothing to prevent us from substituting elective public officers to a certain extent. Election is a democratic expedient, which insures the independence of the public officer in relation to the government as much as hereditary rank can insure it amongst aristocratic nations, and even more so.

Aristocratic countries abound in wealthy and influential persons who are competent to provide for themselves, and who cannot be easily or secretly oppressed: such persons restrain a government within general habits of moderation and reserve. I am well aware that democratic countries contain no such persons naturally; but something analogous to them may be created by artificial means. I firmly believe that an aristocracy cannot again be founded in the world; but I think that private citizens, by combining together, may constitute bodies of great wealth, influence, and strength, corresponding to the persons of an aristocracy. By this means, many of the greatest political advantages of aristocracy would be obtained, without its injustice or its dangers.   An association for political, commercial, or manufacturing purposes, or even for those of science and literature, is a powerful and enlightened member of the community, which cannot be disposed of at pleasure, or oppressed without remonstrance ; and which, by defending its own rights against the encroachments of the government, saves the common liberties of the country.

In periods of aristocracy, every man is always bound so closely to many of his fellow-citizens that he cannot be assailed without their coming to his assistance.   In ages of equality, every man naturally stands alone ; he has no hereditary friends whose co-operation he may demand ; no class upon whose sympathy he may rely : he is easily got rid of, and he is trampled on with impunity.   At the present time, an oppressed member of the community has therefore only one method of self-defence, — he may appeal to the whole nation ; and if the whole nation is deaf to his complaint, he may appeal to mankind : the only means he has of making this appeal is by the press.   Thus, the liberty of the press is infinitely more valuable amongst democratic nations than amongst all others ; it is the only cure for the evils which equality may produce.   Equality sets men apart and weakens them ; but the press places a powerful weapon within every man's reach, which the weakest and loneliest of them all may use.   Equality deprives a man of the support of his connections ; but the press enables him to summon all his fellow-countrymen and all his fellow-men to his assistance.   Printing has accelerated the progress of equality, and it is also one of its best correctives.

I think that men living in aristocracies may, strictly speaking, do without the liberty of the press : but such is not the case with those who live in democratic countries. To protect their personal independence I trust not to great political assemblies, to parliamentary privilege, or to the assertion of popular sovereignty. All these things may, to a certain extent, be reconciled with personal servitude. But that servitude cannot be complete if the press is free: the press is the chief democratic instrument of freedom.

Something analogous may be said of the judicial power. It is a part of the essence of judicial power to attend to private interests, and to fix itself with predilection on minute objects submitted to its observation: another essential quality of judicial power is never to volunteer its assistance to the oppressed, but always to be at the disposal of the humblest of those who solicit it; their complaint, however feeble they may themselves be, will force itself upon the ear of justice and claim redress, for this is inherent in the very constitution of courts of justice.

A power of this kind is therefore peculiarly adapted to the wants of freedom, at a time when the eye and finger of the government are constantly intruding into the minutest details of human actions, and when private persons are at once too weak to protect themselves, and too much isolated for them to reckon upon the assistance of their fellows. The strength of the courts of law has ever been the greatest security which can be offered to personal independence; but this is more especially the case in democratic ages: private rights and interests are in constant danger, if the judicial power does not grow more extensive and more strong to keep pace with the growing equality of conditions.

Equality awakens in men several propensities extremely dangerous to freedom, to which the attention of the legislator ought constantly to be directed. I shall only remind the reader of the most important amongst them.

Men living in democratic ages do not readily comprehend the utility of forms: they feel an instinctive contempt for them, — I have elsewhere shown for what reasons. Forms excite their contempt, and often their hatred; as they commonly aspire to none but easy and present gratifications, they rush onwards to the object of their desires, and the slightest delay exasperates them. This same temper, carried with them into political life, renders them hostile to forms, which perpetually retard or arrest them in some of their projects.

Yet this objection, which the men of democracies make to forms, is the very thing which renders forms so useful to freedom; for their chief merit is to serve as a barrier between the strong and the weak, the ruler and the people, to retard the one, and give the other time to look about him. Forms become more necessary in proportion as the government becomes more active and more powerful, whilst private persons are becoming more indolent and more feeble. Thus democratic nations naturally stand more in need of forms than other nations, and they naturally respect them less. This deserves most serious attention.

Nothing is more pitiful than the arrogant disdain of most of our contemporaries for questions of form; for the smallest questions of form have acquired in our time an importance which they never had before: many of the greatest interests of mankind depend upon them. I think, that, if the statesmen of aristocratic ages could sometimes contemn forms with impunity, and frequently rise above them, the statesmen to whom the government of nations is now confided ought to treat the very least among them with respect, and not neglect them without imperious necessity. In aristocracies, the observance of forms was superstitious; amongst us, they ought to be kept up with a deliberate and enlightened deference.

Another tendency, which is extremely natural to democratic nations and extremely dangerous, is that which leads them to despise and undervalue the rights of private persons. The attachment which men feel to a right, and the respect which they display for it, is generally proportioned to its importance, or to the length of time during which they have enjoyed it. The rights of private persons amongst democratic nations are commonly of small importance, of recent growth, and extremely precarious; the consequence is, that they are often sacrificed without regret, and almost always violated without remorse.

But it happens that, at the same period and amongst the same nations in which men conceive a natural contempt for the rights of private persons, the rights of society at large are naturally extended and consolidated: in other words, men become less attached to private rights just when it is most necessary to retain and defend what little remains of them. It is therefore most especially in the present democratic times, that the true friends of the liberty and the greatness of man ought constantly to be on the alert, to prevent the power of government from lightly sacrificing the private rights of individuals to the general execution of its designs. At such times, no citizen is so obscure that it is not very dangerous to allow him to be oppressed; no private rights are so unimportant that they can be surrendered with impunity to the caprices of a government. The reason is plain: — if the private right of an individual is violated at a time when the human mind is fully impressed with the importance and the sanctity of such rights, the injury done is confined to the individual whose right is infringed; but to violate such a right at the present day is deeply to corrupt the manners of the nation, and to put the whole community in jeopardy, because the very notion of this kind of right constantly tends amongst us to be impaired and lost.

There are certain habits, certain notions, and certain vices which are peculiar to a state of revolution, and which a protracted revolution cannot fail to create and to propagate, whatever be, in other respects, its character, its purpose, and the scene on which it takes place. When any nation has, within a short space of time, repeatedly varied its rulers, its opinions, and its laws, the men of whom it is composed eventually contract a taste for change, and grow accustomed to see all changes effected by sudden violence. Thus they naturally conceive a contempt for forms which daily prove ineffectual; and they do not support, without impatience, the dominion of rules which they have so often seen infringed.

As the ordinary notions of equity and morality no longer suffice to explain and justify all the innovations daily begotten by a revolution, the principle of public utility is called in, the doctrine of political necessity is conjured up, and men accustom themselves to sacrifice private interests without scruple, and to trample on the rights of individuals in order more speedily to accomplish any public purpose.

These habits and notions, which I shall call revolutionary, because all revolutions produce them, occur in aristocracies just as much as amongst democratic nations; but amongst the former they are often less powerful and always less lasting, because there they meet with habits, notions, defects, and impediments, which counteract them: they consequently disappear as soon as the revolution is terminated, and the nation reverts to its former political courses. This is not always the case in democratic countries, in which it is ever to be feared that revolutionary tendencies, becoming more gentle and more regular, without entirely disappearing from society, will be gradually transformed into habits of subjection to the administrative authority of the government. I know of no countries in which revolutions are more dangerous than in democratic countries; because, independently of the accidental and transient evils which must always attend them, they may always create some evils which are permanent and unending.

I believe that there are such things as justifiable resistance and legitimate rebellion: I do not therefore assert, as an absolute proposition, that the men of democratic ages ought never to make revolutions; but I think that they have especial reason to hesitate before they embark in them, and that it is far better to endure many grievances in their present condition, than to have recourse to so perilous a remedy.

I shall conclude by one general idea, which comprises not only all the particular ideas which have been expressed in the present chapter, but also most of those which it is the object of this book to treat of. In the ages of aristocracy which preceded our own, there were private persons of great power, and a social authority of extreme weakness. The outline of society itself was not easily discernible, and constantly confounded with the different powers by which the community was ruled. The principal efforts of the men of those times were required to strengthen, aggrandize, and secure the supreme power; and, on the other hand, to circumscribe individual independence within narrower limits, and to subject private interests to the interests of the public. Other perils and other cares await the men of our age. Amongst the greater part of modern nations, the government, whatever may be its origin, its constitution, or its name, has become almost omnipotent, and private persons are falling, more and more, into the lowest stage of weakness and dependence.

In olden society, everything was different; unity and uniformity were nowhere to be met with. In modern society, everything threatens to become so much alike, that the peculiar characteristics of each individual will soon be entirely lost in the general aspect of the world. Our forefathers were ever prone to make an improper use of the notion that private rights ought to be respected; and we are naturally prone, on the other hand, to exaggerate the idea that the interest of a private individual ought always to bend to the interest of the many.

The political world is metamorphosed: new remedies must henceforth be sought for new disorders. To lay down extensive but distinct and settled limits to the action of the government; to confer certain rights on private persons, and to secure to them the undisputed enjoyment of those rights; to enable individual man to maintain whatever independence, strength, and original power he still possesses; to raise him by the side of society at large, and uphold him in that position, — these appear to me the main objects of legislators in the ages upon which we are now entering.

It would seem as if the rulers of our time sought only to use men in order to make things great; I wish that they would try a little more to make great men; that they would set less value on the work, and more upon the workman; that they would never forget that a nation cannot long remain strong when every man belonging to it is individually weak; and that no form or combination of social polity has yet been devised to make an energetic people out of a community of pusillanimous and enfeebled citizens.

I trace amongst our contemporaries two contrary notions which are equally injurious. One set of men can perceive nothing in the principle of equality but the anarchical tendencies which it engenders: they dread their own free agency, they fear themselves. Other thinkers, less numerous but more enlightened, take a different view: beside that track which starts from the principle of equality to terminate in anarchy, they have at last discovered the road which seems to lead men to inevitable servitude. They shape their souls beforehand to this necessary condition; and, despairing of remaining free, they already do obeisance in their hearts to the master who is soon to appear. The former abandon freedom because they think it dangerous; the latter, because they hold it to be impossible.

If I had entertained the latter conviction, I should not

have written this book, but I should have confined myself to deploring in secret the destiny of mankind. I have sought to point out the dangers to which the principle of equality exposes the independence of man, because I firmly believe that these dangers are the most formidable, as well as the least foreseen, of all those which futurity holds in store; but I do not think that they are insurmountable.

The men who live in the democratic ages upon which we are entering have naturally a taste for independence; they are naturally impatient of regulation, and they are wearied by the permanence even of the condition they themselves prefer. They are fond of power; but they are prone to despise and hate those who wield it, and they easily elude its grasp by their own mobility and insignificance.

These propensities will always manifest themselves, because they originate in the groundwork of society, which will undergo no change: for a long time they will prevent the establishment of any despotism, and they will furnish fresh weapons to each succeeding generation which shall struggle in favor of the liberty of mankind. Let us, then, look forward to the future with that salutary fear which makes men keep watch and ward for freedom, not with that faint and idle terror which depresses and enervates the heart.

CHAPTER VIII.

GENERAL SURVEY OF THE SUBJECT.

BEFORE closing forever the subject that I have now discussed, I would fain take a parting survey of all the different characteristics of modern society, and appreciate at last the general influence to be exercised by the principle of equality upon the fate of mankind ; but I am stopped by the difficulty of the task, and, in presence of so great a theme, my sight is troubled, and my reason fails.

The society of the modern world, which I have sought to delineate, and which I seek to judge, has but just come into existence. Time has not yet shaped it into perfect form ; the great revolution by which it has been created is not yet over ; and, amidst the occurrences of our time, it is almost impossible to discern what will pass away with the revolution itself, and what will survive its close. The world which is rising into existence is still half encumbered by the remains of the world which is waning into decay ; and, amidst the vast perplexity of human affairs, none can say how much of ancient institutions and former manners will remain, or how much will completely disappear.

Although the revolution which is taking place in the social condition, the laws, the opinions, and the feelings of men is still very far from being terminated, yet its results already admit of no comparison with anything that the world has ever before witnessed. I go back from age to age up to the remotest antiquity, but I find no parallel to what is occurring before my eyes : as the past has ceased to throw its light upon the future, the mind of man wanders in obscurity.

Nevertheless, in the midst of a prospect so wide, so novel, and so confused, some of the more prominent characteristics may already be discerned and pointed out. The good things and the evils of life are more equally distributed in the world: great wealth tends to disappear, the number of small fortunes to increase; desires and gratifications are multiplied, but extraordinary prosperity and irremediable penury are alike unknown. The sentiment of ambition is universal, but the scope of ambition is seldom vast. Each individual stands apart in solitary weakness; but society at large is active, provident, and powerful: the performances of private persons are insignificant, those of the state immense.

There is little energy of character, but manners are mild, and laws humane. If there be few instances of exalted heroism or of virtues of the highest, brightest, and purest temper, men's habits are regular, violence is rare, and cruelty almost unknown. Human existence becomes longer, and property more secure: life is not adorned with brilliant trophies, but it is extremely easy and tranquil. Few pleasures are either very refined or very coarse; and highly polished manners are as uncommon as great brutality of tastes. Neither men of great learning, nor extremely ignorant communities, are to be met with; genius becomes more rare, information more diffused. The human mind is impelled by the small efforts of all mankind combined together, not by the strenuous activity of a few men. There is less perfection, but more abundance, in all the productions of the arts. The ties of race, of rank, and of country are relaxed; the great bond of humanity is strengthened.

If I endeavor to find out the most general and most prominent of all these different characteristics, I perceive that what is taking place in men's fortunes manifests itself under a thousand other forms. Almost all extremes are

softened or blunted: all that was most prominent is superseded by some middle term, at once less lofty and less low,
less brilliant and less obscure, than what before existed in
the world.

When I survey this countless multitude of beings, shaped
in each other's likeness, amidst whom nothing rises and
nothing falls, the sight of such universal uniformity sad-
dens and chills me, and I am tempted to regret that state
of society which has ceased to be. When the world was
full of men of great importance and extreme insignificance,
of great wealth and extreme poverty, of great learning and
extreme ignorance, I turned aside from the latter to fix my
observation on the former alone, who gratified my sympathies. But I admit that this gratification arose from my
own weakness: it is because I am unable to see at once all
that is around me, that I am allowed thus to select and
separate the objects of my predilection from among so
many others. Such is not the case with that Almighty
and Eternal Being, whose gaze necessarily includes the
whole of created things, and who surveys distinctly, though
at once, mankind and man.

We may naturally believe that it is not the singular prosperity of the few, but the greater well-being of all, which
is most pleasing in the sight of the Creator and Preserver
of men. What appears to me to be man's decline is, to
His eye, advancement; what afflicts me is acceptable to
Him. A state of equality is perhaps less elevated, but it
is more just: and its justice constitutes its greatness and
its beauty. I would strive, then, to raise myself to this
point of the Divine contemplation, and thence to view and
to judge the concerns of men.

No man, upon the earth, can as yet affirm, absolutely and
generally, that the new state of the world is better than its
former one; but it is already easy to perceive that this state
is different. Some vices and some virtues were so inherent

in the constitution of an aristocratic nation, and are so opposite to the character of a modern people, that they can
never be infused into it; some good tendencies and some
bad propensities which were unknown to the former, are
natural to the latter; some ideas suggest themselves spontaneously to the imagination of the one, which are utterly
repugnant to the mind of the other. They are like two
distinct orders of human beings, each of which has its own
merits and defects, its own advantages and its own evils.
Care must therefore be taken not to judge the state of
society which is now coming into existence, by notions
derived from a state of society which no longer exists;
for, as these states of society are exceedingly different in
their structure, they cannot be submitted to a just or fair
comparison. It would be scarcely more reasonable to require of our contemporaries the peculiar virtues which
originated in the social condition of their forefathers, since
that social condition is itself fallen, and has drawn into one
promiscuous ruin the good and evil which belonged to it.

But as yet these things are imperfectly understood. I
find that a great number of my contemporaries undertake
to make a selection from amongst the institutions, the opinions, and the ideas which originated in the aristocratic constitution of society as it was: a portion of these elements
they would willingly relinquish, but they would keep the
remainder and transplant them into their new world. I
apprehend that such men are wasting their time and their
strength in virtuous but unprofitable efforts. The object
is, not to retain the peculiar advantages which the inequality of conditions bestows upon mankind, but to secure the
new benefits which equality may supply. We have not to
seek to make ourselves like our progenitors, but to strive
to work out that species of greatness and happiness which
is our own.

For myself, who now look back from this extreme limit

of my task, and discover from afar, but at once, the various objects which have attracted my more attentive investigation upon my way, I am full of apprehensions and of hopes. I perceive mighty dangers which it is possible to ward off, — mighty evils which may be avoided or alleviated; and I cling with a firmer hold to the belief, that, for democratic nations to be virtuous and prosperous, they require but to will it.

I am aware that many of my contemporaries maintain that nations are never their own masters here below, and that they necessarily obey some insurmountable and unintelligent power, arising from anterior events, from their race, or from the soil and climate of their country. Such principles are false and cowardly; such principles can never produce aught but feeble men and pusillanimous nations. Providence has not created mankind entirely independent or entirely free. It is true, that around every man a fatal circle is traced, beyond which he cannot pass; but within the wide verge of that circle he is powerful and free: as it is with man, so with communities. The nations of our time cannot prevent the conditions of men from becoming equal; but it depends upon themselves whether the principle of equality is to lead them to servitude or freedom, to knowledge or barbarism, to prosperity or wretchedness.

APPENDIX.

APPENDIX A. — Vol. I. p. 22.

FOR information concerning all the countries of the West which have not yet been visited by Europeans, consult the account of two expeditions undertaken at the expense of Congress by Major Long. This traveller particularly mentions, on the subject of the great American desert, that a line may be drawn nearly parallel to the 20th degree of longitude (meridian of Washington, 97° of Greenwich), beginning from the Red River, and ending at the River Platte. From this imaginary line to the Rocky Mountains, which bound the valley of the Mississippi on the west, lie immense plains, which are generally covered with sand incapable of cultivation, or scattered over with masses of granite. In summer, these plains are destitute of water, and nothing is to be seen on them but herds of buffaloes and wild horses. Some hordes of Indians are also found there, but in no great numbers.

Major Long was told that, in travelling northwards from the River Platte, you find the same desert lying constantly on the left; but he was unable to ascertain the truth of this report. (Long's Expedition, Vol. II. p. 361.)

However worthy of confidence may be the narrative of Major Long, it must be remembered that he only passed through the country of which he speaks, without deviating widely from the line which he had traced out for his journey.

Appendix B. — Vol. I. p. 24.

SOUTH America, in the regions between the tropics, produces an incredible profusion of climbing plants, of which
the Flora of the Antilles alone furnishes forty different species.

Among the most graceful of these shrubs is the Passion-flower,
which, according to Descourtiz, climbs trees by means of the ten-
drils with which it is provided, and forms moving bowers of rich
and elegant festoons, decorated with blue and purple flowers, and
fragrant with perfume.   (Vol. I. p. 265.)

The *Mimosa scandens* (*Acacia à grandes gousses*) is a creeper
of enormous and rapid growth, which climbs from tree to tree, and
sometimes covers more than half a league.   (Vol. III. p. 227.)

———————

Appendix C. — Vol. I. p. 26.

THE languages which are spoken by the Indians of America,
from the Pole to Cape Horn, are said to be all formed upon
the same model, and subject to the same grammatical rules;
whence it may fairly be concluded that all the Indian nations
sprang from the same stock.

Each tribe of the American continent speaks a different dialect; but the number of languages, properly so called, is very
small, — a fact which tends to prove that the nations of the New
World had not a very remote origin.

Moreover, the languages of America have a great degree of
regularity, from which it seems probable that the tribes which
employ them had not undergone any great revolutions, or been
incorporated, voluntarily or by constraint, with foreign nations;
for it is generally the union of several languages into one which
produces grammatical irregularities.

It is not long since the American languages, especially those
of the North, first attracted the serious attention of philologists,
when the discovery was made, that this idiom of a barbarous

people was the product of a complicated system of ideas and very learned combinations. These languages were found to be very rich, and great pains had been taken at their formation to render them agreeable to the ear.

The grammatical system of the Americans differs from all others in several points, but especially in the following: —

Some nations of Europe, amongst others the Germans, have the power of combining at pleasure different expressions, and thus giving a complex sense to certain words. The Indians have given a most surprising extension to this power, so as to connect a great number of ideas with a single term. This will be easily understood with the help of an example quoted by Mr. Duponceau, in the Memoirs of the Philosophical Society of America.

"A Delaware woman playing with a cat or a young dog," says this writer, "is heard to pronounce the word *kuligatschis*, which is thus composed: *k* is the sign of the second person, and signifies 'thou' or 'thy'; *uli* is a part of the word *wulit*, which signifies 'beautiful,' 'pretty'; *gat* is another fragment of the word *wichgat*, which means 'paw'; and, lastly, *schis* is a diminutive giving the idea of smallness. Thus, in one word, the Indian woman has expressed, 'Thy pretty little paw.'"

Take another example of the felicity with which the savages of America have composed their words. A young man, in the Delaware tongue, is called *pilapé*. This word is formed from *pilsit*, chaste, innocent; and *lenapé*, man; — viz. man in his purity and innocence.

This facility of combining words is most remarkable in the strange formation of their verbs. The most complex action is often expressed by a single verb, which serves to convey all the shades of an idea by the modification of its construction.

Those who may wish to examine more in detail this subject, which I have only glanced at superficially, should read, —

1. The correspondence of Mr. Duponceau and the Rev. Mr. Heckewelder relative to the Indian languages, found in the first volume of the Memoirs of the Philosophical Society of America, published at Philadelphia, 1819.

2. The grammar of the Delaware or Lenape language by

Geiberger, and the Preface of Mr. Duponceau. All these are in the same collection, Vol. III.

3. An excellent account of these works, which is at the end of the sixth volume of the American Encyclopædia.

———•———

Appendix D. — Vol. I. p. 28.

SEE, in Charlevoix, Vol. I. p. 235, the history of the first war which the French inhabitants of Canada carried on, in 1610, against the Iroquois. The latter, armed with bows and arrows, offered a desperate resistance to the French and their allies. Charlevoix is not a great painter, yet he exhibits clearly enough in this narrative the contrast between the European manners and those of savages, as well as the different sense which the two races had of honor.

When the French, says he, seized upon the beaver-skins which covered the Indians who had fallen, the Hurons, their allies, were greatly offended at this proceeding; but they set to work in their usual manner, inflicting horrid cruelties upon the prisoners, and devouring one of those who had been killed, which made the Frenchmen shudder. Thus the barbarians prided themselves upon a disinterestedness which they were surprised at not finding in our nation, and could not understand that there was less to reprehend in stripping dead bodies than in devouring their flesh like wild beasts.

Charlevoix, in another place (Vol. I. p. 230), thus describes the first torture of which Champlain was an eyewitness, and the return of the Hurons into their own village.

"Having proceeded about eight leagues," says he, "our allies halted; and having singled out one of their captives, they reproached him with all the cruelties which he had practised upon the warriors of their nation who had fallen into his hands, and told him that he might expect to be treated in like manner, adding, that, if he had any spirit, he would prove it by singing. He immediately chanted forth his death-song, and then his war-song, and all the songs he knew, but in a very mournful strain," says Champlain, who was not then aware that all savage music has a melancholy character. The tortures which succeeded, accompanied by all the horrors which we shall mention hereafter, terrified the French, who made every effort to put a stop to them, but in vain. The following night, one of the Hurons having dreamt that they were pursued, the retreat was changed to a real flight, and the savages never stopped until they were out of the reach of danger.

" The moment they perceived the cabins of their own village, they cut themselves long sticks, to which they fastened the scalps which had fallen to their share, and carried them in triumph. At this sight, the women swam to the canoes, where they received the bloody scalps from the hands of their husbands, and tied them round their necks."

The warriors offered one of these horrible trophies to Champlain; they also presented him with some bows and arrows, — the only spoils of the Iroquois which they had ventured to seize, — entreating him to show them to the King of France.

Champlain lived a whole winter quite alone among these barbarians, without being under any alarm for his person or property.

APPENDIX E. — Vol. I. p. 48.

ALTHOUGH the puritanical strictness which presided over the establishment of the English colonies in America is now much relaxed, remarkable traces of it are still found in their habits and laws. In 1792, at the very time when the Antichristian republic of France began its ephemeral existence, the legislative body of Massachusetts promulgated the following law, to compel the citizens to observe the Sabbath. We give the preamble and a few articles of this law, which is worthy of the reader's attention.

" Whereas," says the legislator, "the observation of the Sunday is an affair of public interest; inasmuch as it produces a necessary suspension of labor, leads men to reflect upon the duties of life and the errors to which human nature is liable, and provides for the public and private worship of God, the Creator and Governor of the universe, and for the performance of such acts of charity as are the ornament and comfort of Christian societies: —

" Whereas irreligious or light-minded persons, forgetting the duties which the Sabbath imposes, and the benefits which these duties confer on society, are known to profane its sanctity, by following their pleasures or their affairs; this way of acting being contrary to their own interest as Christians, and calculated to annoy those who do not follow their example; being also of great injury to society at large, by spreading a taste for dissipation and dissolute manners;

" Be it enacted and ordained by the Governor, Council, and Representatives convened in General Court of Assembly, that all and every person and persons shall on that day carefully apply themselves to the duties of religion and piety, that no tradesman or laborer shall exercise his ordinary calling, and that no game or recreation shall be used on the Lord's day, upon pain of forfeiting ten shillings.

" That no one shall travel on that day, or any part thereof, under pain of forfeiting twenty shillings; that no vessel shall leave a harbor of the colony; that no person shall keep outside the meeting-house during the time of public worship, or profane the time by playing or talking, on penalty of five shillings." (Law of the 8th March, 1792; *General Laws of Massachusetts*, Vol. I. p. 410.)

On the 11th of March, 1797, a new law increased the amount of fines, half of which was to be given to the informer. (Same collection, Vol. I. p. 525.)

On the 16th of February, 1816, a new law confirmed these same measures. (Same collection, Vol. II. p. 405.)

Similar enactments exist in the laws of the State of New York, revised in 1827 and 1828. (See *Revised Statutes*, Part I. chapter 20, p. 675.) In these it is declared that no one is allowed on the Sabbath to sport, to fish, to play at games, or to frequent houses where liquor is sold. No one can travel, except in case of necessity.

And this is not the only trace which the religious strictness and austere manners of the first emigrants have left behind them in the American laws.

In the Revised Statutes of the State of New York, Vol. I. p. 662, is the following clause: —

"Whoever shall win or lose in the space of twenty-four hours, by gaming or betting, the sum of twenty-five dollars, shall be found guilty of a misdemeanor, and, upon conviction, shall be condemned to pay a fine equal to at least five times the value of the sum lost or won ; which shall be paid to the inspector of the poor of the township. He that loses twenty-five dollars or more may bring an action to recover them ; and if he neglects to do so, the inspector of the poor may prosecute the winner, and oblige him to pay into the poor's box both the sum he has gained and three times as much besides."

The laws we quote from are of recent date ; but they are un-intelligible without going back to the very origin of the Colonies. I have no doubt that, in our days, the penal part of these laws is very rarely applied. Laws preserve their inflexibility long after the manners of a nation have yielded to the influence of time. It is still true, however, that nothing strikes a foreigner on his arrival in America more forcibly than the regard paid to the Sabbath.

There is one, in particular, of the large American cities, in which all social movements begin to be suspended even on Saturday evening. You traverse its streets at the hour when you expect men in the middle of life to be engaged in business, and young people in pleasure ; and you meet with solitude and silence. Not only have all ceased to work, but they appear to have ceased to exist. Neither the movements of industry are heard, nor the accents of joy, nor even the confused murmur which arises from the midst of a great city. Chains are hung across the streets in the neighborhood of the churches ; the half-closed shutters of the houses scarcely admit a ray of sun into the dwellings of the citizens. Now and then you perceive a solitary individual, who glides silently along the deserted streets and lanes.

But on Monday, at early dawn, the rolling of carriages, the noise of hammers, the cries of the population, begin to make themselves heard again. The city is awake. An eager crowd hastens towards the resort of commerce and industry; everything around you bespeaks motion, bustle, hurry. A feverish activity succeeds to the lethargic stupor of yesterday; you might almost suppose that they had but one day to acquire wealth and to enjoy it.

Appendix F. — Vol. I. p. 55.

IT is unnecessary to say, that, in the chapter which has just been read, I have not pretended to give a history of America. My only object has been to enable the reader to appreciate the influence which the opinions and manners of the first emigrants had exercised upon the fate of the different colonies, and of the Union in general. I have therefore cited only a few detached fragments.

I do not know whether I am deceived, but it appears to me that, by pursuing the path which I have merely pointed out, it would be easy to present such pictures of the American republics as would not be unworthy the attention of the public, and could not fail to suggest to the statesman matter for reflection. Not being able to devote myself to this labor, I am anxious to render it easy to others; and, for this purpose, I subjoin a short catalogue and analysis of the works which seem to me the most important to consult.*

At the head of the general documents which it would be advantageous to examine, I place the work entitled *An Historical Collection of State Papers, and other authentic Documents, intended as Materials for a History of the United States of America;*

---

* As this catalogue, though novel and interesting for many readers in France, contains little that is new or important for persons in this country, and has also in great part been superseded by later publications, I have considerably abridged it. — AM. ED.

by Ebenezer Hasard. The first volume of this compilation, which was printed at Philadelphia in 1792, contains a literal copy of all the charters granted by the Crown of England to the emigrants, as well as the principal acts of the colonial governments, during the commencement of their existence. The second volume is almost entirely devoted to the acts of the Confederation of 1643. This federal compact, which was entered into by the Colonies of New England with the view of resisting the Indians, was the first instance of union afforded by the Anglo-Americans.

Each colony has, besides, its own historic monuments, some of which are extremely curious; beginning with Virginia, the State which was first peopled. The earliest historian of Virginia was its founder, Captain John Smith. Captain Smith has left us an octavo volume, entitled *The generall Historie of Virginia and New England, by Captain John Smith, sometymes Governor in those Countryes, and Admirall of New England; printed at London in* 1627. The work is adorned with curious maps and engravings of the time when it appeared; the narrative extends from the year 1584 to 1626.

The second historian to consult is Beverley, who commences his narrative with the year 1585, and ends it with 1700. The first part of his book contains historical documents, properly so called, relative to the infancy of the Colony. The second affords a most curious picture of the state of the Indians at this remote period. The third conveys very clear ideas concerning the manners, social condition, laws, and political customs of the Virginians in the author's lifetime.

I saw in America another work which ought to be consulted, entitled *The History of Virginia, by William Stith.* This book affords some curious details, but I thought it long and diffuse.

The most ancient, as well as the best document to be consulted on the history of Carolina, is a work in small quarto, entitled *The History of Carolina, by John Lawson, printed at London in* 1718. This work contains, in the first part, a journey of discovery in the west of Carolina; the account of which, given in the form of a journal, is in general confused and superficial; but it contains a very striking description of the mortality caused among the savages of that time both by the small-pox and the immoderate use of brandy; with a curious picture of the corruption of manners prevalent amongst them, which was increased by the presence of Europeans. The second part of Lawson's book is taken up with a description of the physical condition of Carolina and its productions.

From the southern I pass at once to the northern extremity of the United States, as the intermediate space was not peopled till a later period.

I would first mention a very curious compilation, entitled *Collections of the Massachusetts Historical Society, printed for the first time at Boston in* 1792, *and reprinted in* 1806. This Collection, which is continued to the present day, contains a great number of very valuable documents relating to the history of the different States of New England. Among them are letters which have never been published, and authentic pieces which had been buried in provincial archives. The whole work of Gookin, concerning the Indians, is inserted there.

I have mentioned several times, in the chapter to which this note relates, the work of Nathaniel Morton, entitled *New England's Memorial;* sufficiently, perhaps, to prove that it deserves the attention of those who would be conversant with the history of New England.

The most valuable and important authority which exists upon the history of New England is the work of the Rev. Cotton Mather, entitled *Magnalia Christi Americana, or the Ecclesiastical History of New England,* 1620 – 1698, 2 vols. 8vo, *reprinted at Hartford, United States, in* 1820. The author divided his work into seven books. The first presents the history of the events which prepared and brought about the establishment of New England. The second contains the lives of the first governors and chief magistrates who presided over the country. The third is devoted to the lives and labors of the evangelical ministers who, during the same period, had the care of souls. In the fourth, the author relates the institution and progress of the University of Cambridge (Massachusetts). In the fifth, he describes the principles and the discipline of the Church of New England. The sixth is taken up in retracing certain facts, which, in the opinion of Mather, prove the merciful interposition of

Providence in behalf of the inhabitants of New England. Lastly, in the seventh, the author gives an account of the heresies and the troubles to which the Church of New England was exposed. Cotton Mather was an evangelical minister, who was born at Boston, and passed his life there. His narratives are distinguished by the same ardor and religious zeal which led to the foundation of the colonies of New England. Traces of bad taste often occur in his manner of writing; but he interests, because he is full of enthusiasm. He is often intolerant, still oftener credulous, but he never betrays an intention to deceive.

When he declares the principles of the Church of New England with respect to morals, Mather inveighs with violence against the custom of drinking healths at table, which he denounces as a pagan and abominable practice. He proscribes with the same rigor all ornaments for the hair used by the female sex, as well as their custom of having the arms and neck uncovered. In another part of his work, he relates several instances of witchcraft which had alarmed New England. It is plain that the visible action of the Devil in the affairs of this world appeared to him an incontestable and evident fact.

In passing from the general documents relative to the history of New England to those which describe the several States comprised within its limits, I ought first to notice *The History of the Colony of Massachusetts, by Thomas Hutchinson, Lieutenant-Governor of the Massachusetts Province,* 2 vols. 8vo. The History by Hutchinson, which I have several times quoted in the chapter to which this note relates, commences in the year 1628, and ends in 1750. Throughout the work there is a striking air of truth and the greatest simplicity of style : it is full of minute details.

The best History to consult concerning Connecticut is that of Benjamin Trumbull, entitled *A Complete History of Connecticut, Civil and Ecclesiastical,* 1630–1764, 2 vols. 8vo, *printed in* 1818, *at New Haven.* This History contains a clear and calm account of all the events which happened in Connecticut during the period given in the title. The author drew from the best sources, and his narrative bears the stamp of truth.

The History of New Hampshire, by Jeremy Belknap, is a work held in merited estimation. It was printed at Boston in 1792, in 2 vols. 8vo. The third chapter of the first volume is particularly worthy of attention for the valuable details it affords on the political and religious principles of the Puritans, on the causes of their emigration, and on their laws. The reader of Belknap will find in his work more general ideas, and more strength of thought, than are to be met with in the American historians even to the present day.

Among the Central States which deserve our attention for their remote origin, New York and Pennsylvania are the foremost. The best History we have of the former is entitled, *A History of New York, by William Smith, printed at London in* 1757. Smith gives us important details of the wars between the French and English in America. His is the best acccount of the famous confederation of the Iroquois.

With respect to Pennsylvania, I cannot do better than point out the work of Proud, entitled the *History of Pennsylvania, from the original Institution and Settlement of that Province, under the first Proprietor and Governor, William Penn, in* 1681, *till after the Year* 1742, *by Robert Proud,* 2 vols. 8vo, *printed at Philadelphia in* 1797. This work is deserving of the especial attention of the reader ; it contains a mass of curious documents concerning Penn, the doctrine of the Quakers, and the character, manners, and customs of the first inhabitants of Pennsylvania.

I need not add, that among the most important documents relating to this State are the works of Penn himself, and those of Franklin.

———◆———

Appendix G. — Vol. I. p. 63.

WE read in Jefferson's Memoirs as follows : —
"At the time of the first settlement of the English in Virginia, when land was to be had for little or nothing, some provident persons having obtained large grants of it, and being desirous of maintaining the splendor of their families, entailed their

property upon their descendants. The transmission of these estates from generation to generation, to men who bore the same name, had the effect of raising up a distinct class of families, who, possessing by law the privilege of perpetuating their wealth, formed by these means a sort of patrician order, distinguished by the grandeur and luxury of their establishments. From this order it was that the King usually chose his councillors of state."

In the United States, the principal provisions of English law respecting inheritance have been universally rejected. "The first rule that we follow," says Chancellor Kent, "touching inheritance, is the following : — If a man dies intestate, his property goes to his heirs in a direct line. If he has but one heir or heiress, he or she succeeds to the whole. If there are several heirs of the same degree, they divide the inheritance equally amongst them, without distinction of sex."

This rule was prescribed for the first time in the State of New York, by a statute of the 23d of February, 1786. At the present day, this law holds good throughout the whole of the United States, with the exception of the State of Vermont, where the male heir inherits a double portion. (Kent's *Commentaries*, Vol. IV. p. 370.) Chancellor Kent, in the same work, Vol. IV. pp. 1 – 22, gives an historical account of American legislation on the subject of entail : by this we learn that, previous to the Revolution, the Colonies followed the English law of entail. Estates tail were abolished in Virginia in 1776, on motion of Mr. Jefferson. They were suppressed in New York in 1786, and have since been abolished in North Carolina, Kentucky, Tennessee, Georgia, and Missouri. In Vermont, Indiana, Illinois, South Carolina, and Louisiana, entail was never introduced. Those States which thought proper to preserve the English law of entail, modified it in such a way as to deprive it of its most aristocratic tendencies. "Our general principles on the subject of government," says Kent, "tend to favor the free circulation of property."

It cannot fail to strike the French reader who studies the law of inheritance, that on these questions the French legislation is infinitely more democratic even than the American.

The American law makes an equal division of the father's property, but only in the case of his will not being known ; "for

every man," says the law, " in the State of New York, has entire
liberty, power, and authority to dispose of his property by will,
to leave it entire, or divided in favor of any persons he chooses
as his heirs, provided he do not leave it to a political body or any
corporation." The French law obliges the testator to divide his
property equally, or nearly so, among his heirs.

Most of the American republics still admit of entails, under
certain restrictions ; but the French law prohibits entail in all
cases.

If the social condition of the Americans is more democratic
than that of the French, the laws of the latter are the more
democratic of the two. This may be explained more easily
than at first appears to be possible. In France, democracy is
still occupied in the work of destruction ; in America, it reigns
quietly over the ruins it has made.

Appendix H. — Vol. I. p. 71.

SUMMARY OF THE QUALIFICATIONS OF VOTERS IN THE UNITED STATES.*

ALL the States agree in granting the right of voting at the
age of twenty-one. In all of them, it is necessary to have
resided for a certain time in the district where the vote is given.
This period varies from three months to two years.

As to the qualification, — in the State of Massachusetts, it is

---

* I retain this note only as a curious illustration of the rapid progress of
democracy in the United States, which, in the thirty years since this book
was written, has swept away nearly every one of the limitations of the right
of suffrage that are here enumerated by M. de Tocqueville. Generally it
may be said, that, to be a voter now in any of the States, it is only necessary
to be twenty-one years of age, to have resided a short time in the district
where the vote is given, and to have paid a tax which may not amount
to more than one or two dollars. Several of the States do not require even
this payment of a tax. — AM. ED.

necessary to have an income of three pounds sterling, or a capital of sixty pounds.

In Rhode Island, a man must possess landed property to the amount of 100 dollars.

In Connecticut, he must have a property which gives an income of seventeen dollars. A year of service in the militia also gives the elective privilege.

In New Jersey, an elector must have a property of fifty pounds a year.

In South Carolina and Maryland, the elector must possess fifty acres of land.

In Tennessee, he must possess some property.

In the States of Mississippi, Ohio, Georgia, Virginia, Pennsylvania, Delaware, New York, the only necessary qualification for voting is that of paying the taxes; and in most of the States, to serve in the militia is equivalent to the payment of taxes.

In Maine and New Hampshire, any man can vote who is not on the pauper list.

Lastly, in the States of Missouri, Alabama, Illinois, Louisiana, Indiana, Kentucky, and Vermont, the conditions of voting have no reference to the property of the elector.

I believe there is no other State beside that of North Carolina in which different conditions are applied to voting for the Senate and electing the House of Representatives. The electors of the former, in this case, should possess in property fifty acres of land; to vote for the latter, nothing more is required than to pay taxes.

———◆———

APPENDIX I. — Vol. I. p. 119.

THE small number of custom-house officers employed in the United States, and the great extent of the coast, render smuggling very easy; notwithstanding, it is less practised than elsewhere, because everybody endeavors to repress it. In America, there is no police for the prevention of fires, and such accidents are more frequent than in Europe; but, in general, they are more speedily extinguished, because the surrounding population is prompt to lend assistance.

---*---

Appendix K. — Vol. I. p. 121.

IT is incorrect to say that centralization was produced by the French Revolution: the Revolution brought it to perfection, but did not create it. The mania for centralization and government regulations dates from the period when jurists began to take a share in the government, in the time of Philippe-le-Bel; ever since this period, they have been on the increase. In the year 1775, M. de Malesherbes, speaking in the name of the *Cour des Aides,* said to Louis XIV.: —

"Every corporation and every community of citizens retained the right of administering its own affairs, — a right which not only forms part of the primitive constitution of the kingdom, but has a still higher origin; for it is the right of nature and of reason. Nevertheless, your subjects, Sire, have been deprived of it; and we do not fear to say that, in this respect, your government has fallen into puerile extremes. From the time when powerful ministers made it a political principle to prevent the convocation of a national assembly, one consequence has succeeded another, until the deliberations of the inhabitants of a village are declared null if they have not been authorized by the Intendant. Of course, if the community has an expensive undertaking to carry through, it must remain under the control of the sub-delegate of the Intendant, and, consequently, follow the plan he proposes, employ his favorite workmen, pay them according to his pleasure; and if an action at law is deemed necessary, the Intendant's permission must be obtained. The cause must be pleaded before this first tribunal, previous to its being carried into a public court; and if the opinion of the Intendant is opposed to that of the inhabitants, or if their adversary enjoys his favor, the community is deprived of the power of defending its rights. Such are the means, Sire, which have been exerted to extinguish the municipal spirit in France, and to stifle, if possible, the opinions of the citizens. The nation may be said to lie under an interdict, and to be in wardship under guardians."

What could be said more to the purpose at the present day, when the Revolution has achieved what are called *its victories* in centralization ?

In 1789, Jefferson wrote from Paris to one of his friends : " There is no country where the mania for over-governing has taken deeper root than in France, or been the source of greater mischief." Letter to Madison, 28th August, 1789.

The fact is, that, for several centuries, the central power of France has done everything it could to extend central administration ; it has acknowledged no other limits than its own strength. The central power to which the Revolution gave birth made more rapid advances than any of its predecessors, because it was stronger and wiser than they had been. Louis XIV. committed the welfare of the municipal communities to the caprice of an Intendant ; Napoleon left them to that of the Minister. The same principle governed both, though its consequences were more or less remote.

◆

APPENDIX L. — Vol. I. p. 126.

THIS immutability of the Constitution in France is a necessary consequence of the laws.

To begin with the most important of all the laws, — that which decides the order of succession to the throne ; what can be more immutable in its principle than a political order founded upon the natural succession of father to son ? In 1814, Louis XVIII. established the perpetual law of hereditary succession in favor of his own family. Those who regulated the consequences of the Revolution of 1830 followed his example ; they merely established the perpetuity of the law in favor of another family. In this respect, they imitated the Chancellor Maupeou, who, when he erected the new Parliament upon the ruins of the old, took care to declare in the same ordinance, that the rights of the new magistrates should be as inalienable as those of their predecessors had been.

The laws of 1830, like those of 1814, point out no way of changing the Constitution; and it is evident that the ordinary means of legislation are insufficient for this purpose. As the King, the Peers, and the Deputies, all derive their authority from the Constitution, these three powers united cannot alter a law by virtue of which alone they govern. Out of the Constitution, they are nothing: where, then, could they take their stand to effect a change in its provisions? The alternative is clear: either their efforts are powerless against the Charter, which continues to exist in spite of them, in which case they only reign in the name of the Charter; or, they succeed in changing the Charter, and then the law by which they existed being annulled, they themselves cease to exist. By destroying the Charter, they destroy themselves.

This is much more evident in the laws of 1830 than in those of 1814. In 1814, the royal prerogative took its stand above and beyond the Constitution; but in 1830, it was avowedly created by, and dependent on, the Constitution.

A part, therefore, of the French Constitution is immutable, because it is united to the destiny of a family; and the body of the Constitution is equally immutable, because there appear to be no legal means of changing it.

These remarks are not applicable to England. That country having no written Constitution, who can tell when its Constitution is changed?

APPENDIX M. — Vol. I. p. 126.

THE most esteemed authors who have written upon the English Constitution agree with each other in establishing the omnipotence of Parliament.

Delolme says, " It is a fundamental principle with the English lawyers, that Parliament can do everything except making a woman a man, or a man a woman."

Blackstone expresses himself more in detail, if not more energetically, than Delolme, in the following terms : —

" The power and jurisdiction of Parliament, says Sir Edward Coke (4 Inst. 36), is so transcendent and absolute, that it cannot be confined, either for causes or persons, within any bounds. And of this high Court, he adds, may truly be said, ' *Si antiquitatem spectes, est vetustissima ; si dignitatem, est honoratissima ; si jurisdictionem, est capacissima.*' It hath sovereign and uncontrollable authority in the making, confirming, enlarging, restraining, abrogating, repealing, reviving, and expounding of laws, concerning matters of all possible denominations ; ecclesiastical or temporal ; civil, military, maritime, or criminal ; this being the place where that absolute despotic power which must, in all governments, reside somewhere, is intrusted by the Constitution of these kingdoms. All mischiefs and grievances, operations and remedies, that transcend the ordinary course of the laws, are within the reach of this extraordinary tribunal. It can regulate or new-model the succession to the Crown ; as was done in the reign of Henry VIII. and William III. It can alter the established religion of the land ; as was done in a variety of instances in the reigns of King Henry VIII. and his three children. It can *change and create afresh even the Constitution of the kingdom*, and of parliaments themselves ; as was done by the Act of Union and the several statutes for triennial and septennial elections. It can, in short, do everything that is not naturally impossible to be done ; and, therefore, some have not scrupled to call its power, by a figure rather too bold, the omnipotence of Parliament."

Appendix N. — Vol. I. p. 139.

THERE is no question upon which the American Constitutions agree more fully than upon that of political jurisdiction. All the Constitutions which take cognizance of this matter give to the

House of Representatives the exclusive right of impeachment; excepting only the Constitution of North Carolina, which grants the same privilege to grand juries. (Article 23.)

Almost all the Constitutions give to the Senate, or to the legislative body which occupies its place, the exclusive right of trying the impeachment and pronouncing judgment.

The only punishments which the political tribunals can inflict are removal from office, and the interdiction of public functions for the future. The Constitution of Virginia alone enables them to inflict any kind of punishment.

The crimes which are subject to political jurisdiction are, — in the Federal Constitution (Section 4, Art. 1); in that of Indiana (Art. 3, paragraphs 23 and 24); of New York (Art. 5); of Delaware (Art. 5), — high treason, bribery, and other high crimes or misdemeanors.

In the Constitution of Massachusetts (Chap. 1, Section 2); that of North Carolina (Art. 23); of Virginia (p. 252), — misconduct and maladministration.

In the Constitution of New Hampshire (p. 105), corruption, intrigue, and maladministration.

In Vermont (Chap. 2, Art. 24), maladministration.

In South Carolina (Art. 5); Kentucky (Art. 5); Tennessee (Art. 4); Ohio (Art. 1, §§ 23, 24); Louisiana (Art. 5); Mississippi (Art. 5); Alabama (Art. 6); Pennsylvania (Art. 4), — crimes committed in the performance of official duties.

In the States of Illinois, Georgia, Maine, and Connecticut, no particular offences are specified.

———◆———

Appendix O. — Vol. I. p. 218.

IT is true that the powers of Europe may carry on maritime wars against the Union; but there is always greater facility and less danger in supporting a maritime than a continental war. Maritime warfare only requires one species of effort. A commercial people which consents to furnish its government with the necessary funds, is sure to possess a fleet. And it is far easier to induce a nation to part with its money, almost unconsciously, than to reconcile it to sacrifices of men and personal efforts. Moreover, defeat by sea rarely compromises the existence or independence of the people which endures it.

As for continental wars, it is evident that the nations of Europe cannot be formidable in this way to the American Union. It would be very difficult to transport and maintain in America more than 25,000 soldiers, — an army which may be considered to represent a nation of about 2,000,000 of men. The most populous nation of Europe, contending in this way against the Union, is in the position of a nation of 2,000,000 of inhabitants at war with one of 12,000,000. Add to this, that America has all its resources within reach, whilst the European is at 4,000 miles distance from his; and that the immensity of the American continent would of itself present an insurmountable obstacle to its conquest.

APPENDIX P. — Vol. I. p. 239.

THE first American journal appeared in April, 1704, and was published at Boston. See *Collections of the Historical Society of Massachusetts*, Vol. VI. p. 66.

It would be a mistake to suppose that the periodical press has always been entirely free in the American Colonies : an attempt was made to establish something like a censorship and preliminary security. Consult the Legislative Documents of Massachusetts for the 14th of January, 1722.

The Committee appointed by the General Assembly (the legislative body of the Province), for the purpose of examining an affair relative to a paper entitled " The New England Courant," expresses its opinion that " the tendency of the said journal is to turn religion into derision, and bring it into contempt; that it mentions the sacred writers in a profane and irreligious manner : that it puts malicious interpretations upon the conduct of the ministers of the Gospel; and that the government of His Majesty is insulted, and the peace and tranquillity of the Province disturbed, by the said journal. The Committee is consequently of opinion that the printer and publisher, James Franklin, should be forbidden to print and publish the said journal or any other work in future, without having previously submitted it to the Secretary of the Province; and that the justices of the peace for the county of Suffolk should be commissioned to require bail of the said James Franklin for his good conduct during the ensuing year."

The suggestion of the Committee was adopted, and passed into a law; but the effect was null, for the journal eluded the prohibition by putting the name of Benjamin Franklin, instead of James Franklin, at the bottom of its columns, and this manœuvre was supported by public opinion.

——◆——

Appendix Q. — Vol. I. p. 362.

THE Federal Constitution has introduced the jury into the tribunals of the Union, just as the States had introduced it into their own several courts; but as it has not established any fixed rules for the choice of jurors, the Federal Courts select them from the ordinary jury-list which each State makes for itself. The laws of the States must therefore be examined for the theory of the formation of juries.

In order thoroughly to understand American principles with respect to the formation of juries, I examined the laws of States at a distance from one another, and the following observations were the result of my inquiries.

In America, all the citizens who exercise the elective franchise have the right of serving upon a jury. The great State of New York, however, has made a slight difference between the two privileges, but in a spirit quite contrary to that of the laws of France; for in the State of New York there are fewer persons eligible as jurymen than there are electors. It may be said, in general, that the right of forming part of a jury, like the right of electing representatives, is open to all the citizens ; the exercise of this right, however, is not put indiscriminately into any hands.

Every year, a body of town or county magistrates — called *selectmen* in New England, *supervisors* in New York, *trustees* in Ohio, and *sheriffs of the parish* in Louisiana — choose for each county a certain number of citizens who have the right of serving as jurymen, and who are supposed to be capable of doing so. These magistrates, being themselves elective, excite no distrust ; their powers, like those of most republican magistrates, are very extensive and very arbitrary, and they frequently make use of them, especially in New England, to remove unworthy or incompetent jurymen.

The names of the jurymen thus chosen are transmitted to the County Court ; and the jury who have to decide any affair are drawn by lot from the whole list of names.

The Americans have endeavored in every way to make the common people eligible to the jury, and to render the service as little onerous as possible. The jurors being very numerous, each one's turn does not come round oftener than once in three years. The sessions are held in the chief town of every county, and the jury are indemnified for their attendance either by the State or the parties concerned. They receive in general a dollar per day, besides their travelling expenses. In America, the being placed upon the jury is looked upon as a burden, but it is a burden which is very supportable.

APPENDIX R. — Vol. I. p. 366.

IF we attentively examine the constitution of the jury in civil proceedings in England, we shall readily perceive that the jurors are under the immediate control of the judge. It is true that the verdict of the jury, in civil as well as in criminal cases, comprises the questions of fact and of law in the same reply. Thus, a house is claimed by Peter as having been purchased by him ; this is the fact to be decided. The defendant puts in a plea of incompetency on the part of the vendor : this is the legal question to be resolved. The jury simply says that the house shall be delivered to Peter, and thus decides both the questions of fact and of law.

But, according to the practice of the English courts, the opinion of the jury is not held to be infallible in civil, as it is in criminal cases. If the judge thinks that their verdict has made a wrong application of the law, he may refuse to receive it, and send back the jury to deliberate over again. Even if the judge allows the verdict to pass without observation, the case is not yet finally determined; there are still many modes of arresting judgment. The principal one consists in asking the court to set aside the verdict, and order a new trial before another jury. It is true that such a request is seldom granted, and never more than twice; yet I have actually known this to happen. See Blackstone's *Commentaries*.

Appendix S. — Vol. II. p. 248.

I FIND in my travelling-journal a passage which may serve to convey a more complete notion of the trials to which the women of America, who consent to follow their husbands into the wilds, are often subjected. This description has nothing to recommend it but its perfect truth.

"From time to time, we come to fresh clearings; all these places are alike: I shall describe the one at which we halted to-night, since it will serve me for a picture of all the others.

"The bell which the pioneers hang round the necks of their cattle, in order to find them again in the woods, announced from afar our approach to a clearing; and we soon afterwards heard the stroke of the axe, hewing down the trees of the forest. As we came nearer, traces of destruction marked the presence of civilized man: the road was strewn with cut boughs; trunks of trees, half consumed by fire, or mutilated by the axe, were still standing in the track. We proceeded till we reached a wood in which all the trees seemed to have been suddenly struck dead; in the middle of summer, their boughs were as leafless as in winter; and, upon closer examination, we found that a deep circle had been cut through the bark, which, by stopping the circulation of the sap, soon kills the tree. We were informed that this is commonly the first thing a pioneer does; as he cannot, in the first year, cut down all the trees which cover his new domain, he sows Indian corn under their branches, and puts the trees to death in order to prevent them from injuring his crop. Beyond this field, at present imperfectly traced out, — the first work of civilization in the desert, — we suddenly came upon the cabin of its owner, situated in the centre of a plot of ground more carefully cultivated than the rest, but where man was still waging unequal warfare with the forest; there the trees were cut down, but their roots were not removed, and the trunks still encumbered the ground which they so recently shaded. Around these dry blocks, wheat, suckers of trees, and plants of every kind, grow and intertwine in all the luxuriance of wild, untutored Nature. Amidst this vigorous and various vegetation stands the house of the pioneer, or, as they call it, the *log-house*. Like the ground about it, this rustic dwelling bore marks of recent and hasty labor: its length seemed not to exceed thirty feet, its height fifteen; the walls as well as the roof were formed of rough trunks of trees, between which a little moss and clay had been inserted to keep out the cold and rain.

"As night was coming on, we determined to ask the master of the log-house for a lodging. At the sound of our footsteps, the children who were playing amongst the scattered branches sprang up, and ran towards the house, as if they were frightened at the sight of man; whilst two large dogs, almost wild, with ears erect and outstretched nose, came growling out of their hut, to cover the retreat of their young masters. The pioneer himself made his appearance at the door of his dwelling; he looked at us with a rapid and inquisitive glance, made a sign to the dogs to go into the house, and set them the example, without betraying either curiosity or apprehension at our arrival.

"We entered the log-house: the inside is quite unlike that of the cottages of the peasantry of Europe: it contains more that is superfluous, less that is necessary. A single window with a muslin blind; on a hearth of trodden clay an immense fire, which lights the whole interior ; above the hearth, a good rifle, a deer's skin, and plumes of eagles' feathers ; on the right hand of the chimney, a map of the United States, raised and shaken by the wind through the crannies in the wall; near the map, upon a shelf formed of a roughly hewn plank, a few volumes of books, — a Bible, the six first books of Milton, and two of Shakespeare's plays ; along the wall, trunks instead of closets ; in the centre of the room, a rude table, with legs of green wood with the bark still upon them, looking as if they grew out of the ground on which they stood ; but on this table a teapot of British ware, silver spoons, cracked tea-cups, and some newspapers.

" The master of this dwelling has the angular features and lank limbs peculiar to the native of New England. It is evident that this man was not born in the solitude in which we have found him : his physical constitution suffices to show that his earlier years were spent in the midst of civilized society, and that he belongs to that restless, calculating, and adventurous race of men, who do with the utmost coolness things only to be accounted for by the ardor of passion, and who endure the life of savages for a time, in order to conquer and civilize the backwoods.

" When the pioneer perceived that we were crossing his threshold, he came to meet us and shake hands, as is their custom ; but his face was quite unmoved ; he opened the conversation by inquiring what was going on in the world; and when his curiosity was satisfied, he held his peace, as if he were tired of the noise and importunity of mankind. When we questioned him in our turn, he gave us all the information we asked ; he then attended sedulously, but without eagerness, to our wants. Whilst he was engaged in providing thus kindly for us, how came it that, in spite of ourselves, we felt our gratitude die upon our lips ? It is, that our host, whilst he performs the duties of hospitality, seems to be obeying an irksome necessity of his condition : he treats it as a duty imposed upon him by his situation, not as a pleasure.

" By the side of the hearth sits a woman with a baby on her lap; she nods to us without disturbing herself. Like the pioneer, this woman is in the prime of life; her appearance seems superior to her condition, and her apparel even betrays a lingering taste for dress; but her delicate limbs appear shrunken, her features are drawn in, her eye is mild and melancholy; her whole physiognomy bears marks of religious resignation, a deep quiet of all passions, and some sort of natural and tranquil firmness, ready to meet all the ills of life without fearing and without braving them.

"Her children cluster about her, full of health, turbulence, and energy: they are true children of the wilderness; their mother watches them from time to time with mingled melancholy and joy: to look at their strength and her languor, one might imagine that the life she has given them has exhausted her own, and still she regrets not what they have cost her.

"The house inhabited by these emigrants has no internal partition or loft. In the one chamber of which it consists the whole family is gathered for the night. The dwelling is itself a little world, — an ark of civilization amidst an ocean of foliage : a hundred steps beyond it the primeval forest spreads its shades, and solitude resumes its sway."

Appendix T. — Vol. II. p. 276.

SETTING aside all those who do not think at all, and those who dare not say what they think, the immense majority of the Americans will still be found to appear satisfied with their political institutions; and I believe they really are so. I look upon this state of public opinion as an indication, but not as a proof, of the absolute excellence of American laws. National pride, the gratification of certain ruling passions by the law, a concourse of circumstances, defects which escape notice, and, more than all the rest, the influence of a majority which shuts the mouth of all cavillers, may long perpetuate the delusions of a people as well as those of a man.

Look at England throughout the eighteenth century. No nation was ever more prodigal of self-applause, no people were ever better satisfied with themselves ; then, every part of their constitution was right, — everything, even to its most obvious defects, was irreproachable. At the present day, a vast number of Englishmen seem to be occupied only in proving that this constitution was faulty in a thousand respects. Which was right? — the English people of the last century, or the English people of the present day?

The same thing occurred in France. It is certain that, during the reign of Louis XIV., the great bulk of the nation was devotedly attached to the form of government which then governed the community. It is a vast error to suppose that there was anything degraded in the character of the French of that age. There might be some sort of servitude in France at that time, but assuredly there was no servile spirit among the people. The writers of that age felt a species of genuine enthusiasm in raising the power of their king over all other authority ; and there was no peasant so obscure in his hovel as not to take a pride in the glory of his sovereign, and to die cheerfully with the cry "Vive le Roi !" upon his lips. These same forms of loyalty have now become odious to the French people. Which are wrong? — the French of the age of Louis XIV., or their descendants of the present day?

Our judgment of the laws of a people, then, must not be founded exclusively upon its inclinations, since those inclinations change from age to age ; but upon more elevated principles and a more general experience. The love which a people may show for its laws proves only this, that we should not be in a hurry to change them.

———◆———

APPENDIX U. — Vol. II. p. 340.

IN the chapter to which this note relates I have pointed out one source of danger ; I am now about to point out another, more rare indeed, but more formidable if it were ever to appear.

If the love of physical gratification and the taste for well-being, which are naturally suggested to men by a state of equality, were to possess the mind of a democratic people, and to fill it completely, the manners of the nation would become so totally opposed to military pursuits, that perhaps even the army would eventually acquire a love of peace, in spite of the peculiar interest which leads it to desire war. Living in a state of general relaxation, the troops would ultimately think it better to rise without efforts, by the slow but commodious advancement of a peace establishment, than to purchase more rapid promotion at the cost of all the toils and privations of the field. With these feelings, they would take up arms without enthusiasm, and use them without energy; they would allow themselves to be led to meet the foe, instead of marching to attack him.

It must not be supposed that this pacific state of the army would render it adverse to revolutions; for revolutions, and especially military revolutions, which are generally very rapid, are attended indeed with great dangers, but not with protracted toil; they gratify ambition at less cost than war; life only is at stake, and the men of democracies care less for their lives than for their comfort.

Nothing is more dangerous for the freedom and the tranquillity of a people than an army afraid of war, because, as such an army no longer seeks to maintain its importance and its influence on the field of battle, it seeks to assert them elsewhere. Thus it might happen, that the men of whom a democratic army consists should lose the interests of citizens without acquiring the virtues of soldiers; and that the army should cease to be fit for war without ceasing to be turbulent. I shall here repeat what I have said in the text: the remedy for these dangers is not to be found in the army, but in the country; a democratic people which has preserved the manliness of its character will never be at a loss for military prowess in its soldiers.

Appendix V. — Vol. II. p. 360.

MEN place the greatness of their idea of unity in the means, God in the ends; hence this idea of greatness, as men conceive it, leads us to infinite littleness. To compel all men to follow the same course towards the same object, is a human conception; to introduce infinite variety of action, but so combined that all these acts lead in a thousand different ways to the accomplishment of one great design, is a conception of the Deity.

The human idea of unity is almost always barren; the Divine idea is infinitely fruitful. Men think they manifest their greatness by simplifying the means they use; but it is the purpose of God which is simple, — his means are infinitely varied.

—◆—

Appendix W. — Vol. II. p. 364.

A DEMOCRATIC people is not only led by its own taste to centralize its government, but the passions of all the men by whom it is governed constantly urge it in the same direction. It may easily be foreseen that almost all the able and ambitious members of a democratic community will labor unceasingly to extend the powers of government, because they all hope at some time or other to wield those powers. It would be a waste of time to attempt to prove to them that extreme centralization may be injurious to the state, since they are centralizing it for their own benefit. Amongst the public men of democracies, there are hardly any but men of great disinterestedness or extreme mediocrity who seek to oppose the centralization of government: the former are scarce, the latter powerless.

Appendix X. — Vol. II. p. 391.

I HAVE often asked myself what would happen if, amidst the relaxation of democratic manners, and as a consequence of the restless spirit of the army, a military government were ever to be founded amongst any of the nations of our times. I think that such a government would not differ much from the outline I have drawn in the chapter to which this note belongs, and that it would retain none of the fierce characteristics of a military oligarchy. I am persuaded that, in such a case, a sort of fusion would take place between the habits of official men and those of the military service. The administration would assume something of a military character, and the army some of the usages of the civil administration. The result would be a regular, clear, exact, and absolute system of government; the people would become the reflection of the army, and the community be drilled like a garrison.

—◆—

Appendix Y. — Vol. II. p. 395.

IT cannot be absolutely or generally affirmed that the greatest danger of the present age is license or tyranny, anarchy or despotism. Both are equally to be feared; and the one may as easily proceed as the other from the self-same cause, namely, that *general apathy*, which is the consequence of what I have termed *individualism*: it is because this apathy exists, that the executive government, having mustered a few troops, is able to commit acts of oppression one day; and the next day, a party which has mustered some thirty men in its ranks can also commit acts of oppression. Neither the one nor the other can found anything to last; and the causes which enable them to succeed easily prevent them from succeeding long: they rise because nothing opposes them, and they sink because nothing supports them. The proper object, therefore, of our most strenuous resistance, is far less either anarchy or despotism, than that apathy which may almost indifferently beget either the one or the other.

DEMOCRACY IN SWITZERLAND.

A REPORT MADE TO THE ACADEMY OF THE MORAL AND POLITICAL
SCIENCES IN 1847, BY M. DE TOCQUEVILLE.

M. CHERBULIEZ, Professor of Law in the University of Geneva, has published a work upon the political institutions and manners of his countrymen, entitled "Democracy in Switzerland," and has presented a copy of this book to the Academy of the Moral Sciences. I have thought that the importance of the subject treated by him required a special examination of his work; and I have undertaken it, believing that such an examination might be useful.

My intention is, to take my stand entirely beyond the range of the prejudices of the passing hour, as it is proper to do in this assembly, to pass in silence over present occurrences which do not concern us, and to regard, in Switzerland, not so much what the political society is now doing, as this society itself, the laws which constitute it, their origin, their tendencies, and their character. I hope that the picture, though thus limited, will yet be worthy of interest. What is now passing in Switzerland * is not an isolated fact; it is but one step in the general movement which is overturning the whole edifice of the old institu-

---

* The author here alludes to the warlike agitation which then pervaded Switzerland, consequent upon the proceedings of the Sonderbund, or League of the Seven Cantons. — AM. ED.

tions of Europe.   The spectacle has some grandeur, then, though the theatre is a small one; above all, it has a singular originality.   The democratic revolution which is now agitating the world has nowhere appeared under circumstances at once so strange and so complicated.   One people, composed of several races, speaking different languages, professing various beliefs, many opposing sects, two equally established and privileged churches, all political questions now turning upon religious disputes, then all theological controversies ending in political movements, and, finally, two communities, the one very old and the other very young, but indissolubly united in spite of the difference in their ages, — such is the spectacle which we now behold in Switzerland.   To make a faithful picture of it, I think we should take a higher point of view than our author has chosen.   M. Cherbuliez declares in his Preface, and I believe the assertion is a very sincere one, that he has aimed at strict impartiality.   He even fears that the completely impartial character of his work has made the treatment of the subject somewhat monotonous.   This apprehension is certainly unfounded.   In fact, the author wishes to be impartial, but has not succeeded in his wish.   His book manifests learning, clear-sightedness, real talent, and unmistakable good faith, which shines forth even in the midst of passionate judgments.   The very quality in which it is most deficient is impartiality.   We find in it much intellect, and very little liberty of intellect.

What forms of political association does the author prefer?   At first, it seems difficult to tell.   He approves, to a certain extent, the conduct of the most zealous Catholics in Switzerland; yet he is a decided opponent of Catholicism, and even wishes to prohibit by law the Catholic religion from extending into districts where it is not already established.   On the other hand, he is a determined adversary of the various Protestant sects.   Opposed to the government of the people, he also dislikes the dominion of the nobility. In religion, a Protestant church controlled by the state; in politics, a state governed by an aristocracy among the citizens, — such is the ideal which our author contemplates. This was the condition of Geneva before its latest revolution.

But if we cannot always clearly perceive what it is that he prefers, it is easy to see what he thoroughly dislikes. What he hates is democracy. Wounded in his opinions, in his friendships, perhaps in his interests, by the democratic revolution which he describes, he never speaks of it but as an adversary. Democracy is attacked by him, not only in some of its consequences, but even in its principle. He is blind to its good qualities and implacable to its faults. Among the evils which may result from it, he does not distinguish those which are radical and permanent from those which are accidental and transitory, — what must be borne with because inevitable, from what is within our power and capable of amendment. Perhaps the subject could not but be viewed in this manner by a man as deeply concerned as M. Cherbuliez has been in the agitations of his country. This we must be permitted to regret. We shall see, in the course of this analysis, that Swiss democracy has great need to be enlightened upon the imperfection of its laws. But to do this to any good purpose, the first condition is, not to be a hater of democracy.

"Democracy in Switzerland" is the title that M. Cherbuliez has given to his work. This would lead one to believe that, in his opinion, Switzerland is a country in which we can study the theory of democracy, and where democratic institutions are exhibited as they really are, or in their natural state. This opinion I hold to be the chief source of almost all the errors of his book. In fact, Switzerland has been for fifteen years in a revolutionary state. Democracy there is not so much a regular form of government, as a weapon which is habitually used to destroy, and sometimes to defend, the old forms of society. We find there the particular phenomena resulting from the revolutionary state in the democratic period in which our lot is cast, but not democracy itself in its permanent and tranquil aspect. Whoever does not have this fact as a point of departure constantly present to his mind, will have great difficulty in understanding Swiss institutions as they now appear ; for my own part, I should find it almost impossible to explain my judgment of what is, without saying how I understand what has been.

There is a very common mistake as to the condition of Switzerland at the time of the outbreak of the French Revolution. As the Swiss had then been living for a long time under a republican form of government, it was easy to imagine that they were much nearer than the other nations of Continental Europe to the institutions which constitute, and the spirit which animates, modern liberty. But this is the very opposite of the truth.

Although the independence of the Swiss was born from an insurrection against the aristocracy, the governments which were then established soon borrowed from aristocracy its customs, its laws, and even its opinions and inclinations. Liberty presented itself to them only under the form of privilege, and the idea of a universal and pre-existent right of all men to be free, was as foreign to their apprehension as it could be to that of the princes of the house of Austria whom they had vanquished. All the powers of government, therefore, were drawn without delay into the hands of small, close aristocracies perpetuating themselves, and were retained there. In the north, these aristocracies assumed a commercial or manufacturing character ; in the south, they had a military organization. But in both cases, they were equally narrow and exclusive. In most of the Cantons, three fourths of the inhabitants were excluded from any participation whatever, direct or indirect, in the administration of the country; and moreover, each Canton had subjects, or communities existing entirely under their control.

These small societies, to which a great convulsion had given rise, soon became so firmly established that no movement could take place in them. The aristocracy, finding themselves neither urged forward by the people nor controlled by a king, held society there immovable under the old garb of the Middle Ages. Switzerland remained closed against modern ideas of freedom, long after the progress of the age had introduced them into the most monarchical nations of Europe.

The principle of separating legislative, executive, and judicial powers was admitted by all publicists; but it was not applied in Switzerland. The liberty of the press, which existed, practically at least, in several absolute monarchies on the Continent, had no existence there either *de facto* or *de jure;* the power of forming political associations there was neither acknowledged nor exercised; and even liberty of speech, for the Swiss, was restrained within very narrow limits. The equality of burdens, towards which all enlightened governments were tending, was as unknown to them as the equality of rights. Industry there labored under many fetters; personal liberty there had no legal guaranty. Religious liberty, which was beginning to penetrate even into the most orthodox states, had not yet dawned upon Switzerland. Dissenting churches were entirely prohibited in several Cantons, and loaded with restraints in all. Differences of religious profession were almost everywhere punished by political disfranchisement.

Switzerland was still in this condition in 1798, when the French Revolution by force of arms broke into its territory. There it overturned for a time the old institutions, but put nothing fixed and durable in their place. Some years afterwards, Napoleon, who by the Act of Mediation rescued the Swiss from anarchy, gave them the principle of equality indeed, but not constitutional liberty; the political system which he imposed upon them was so constructed that public life was paralyzed. The government, exercised in the name of the people, but placed far above them, was surrendered entirely into the hands of the executive power.

A few years later, when the Act of Mediation was thrown down together with its author, the Swiss did not gain liberty by the change, but only lost equality. Everywhere the old aristocracies resumed the reins of government, and brought again into force the exclusive and superannuated principles which had prevailed before the revolution. M. Cherbuliez truly says, that things then returned nearly to the same position where they were in 1798. The allied monarchs have been wrongly accused of imposing this restoration upon Switzerland by force. It was done with their consent, but not by their agency. The truth is, that the Swiss, like the other nations on the Continent, were carried away by that short-lived but universal reaction which then suddenly re-established the old institutions of society throughout Europe; and as, in their case, the restoration was not effected by the monarchs, whose interests after all are separate from those of the old privileged classes, but by those privileged classes themselves, it was there more complete, more blind, and more obstinate, than in the other portions of Europe. It did not appear tyrannical, but it was very exclusive. A legislative power entirely under the control of the executive authority; the latter vested exclusively in the hands of an aristocracy by birth; the middle classes shut out of the government entirely; and the whole people deprived of political life altogether; — such was the picture presented in almost every part of Switzerland down to 1830. It was then that the new era of democracy first opened upon the Swiss people.

The object of this brief exposition has been, to cause two things to be clearly understood. The first is, that Switzerland is the country where the revolution was more thorough, and the restoration which followed it more complete, than in any other part of Europe; so that, institutions foreign or hostile to the new demands of the age having there preserved or recovered a strong hold, the tendency to a new revolution must also have been greater there than elsewhere. The second is, that in the greater part of Switzerland, the people, down to our own day, have never had even the smallest share in the government; that the judicial forms which are the safeguards of civil liberty, the liberty of association, the liberty of speech, the liberty of the press, the liberty of religious belief, have also always been, I might almost say, more unknown to the great majority of the citizens of those republics, than they could have been, at the same period, to the subjects of most monarchies.

These are the facts which M. Cherbuliez often loses sight of, but which ought to be unceasingly present to our minds in the careful examination which we are now to make of the institutions which Switzerland has established.

All the world knows that, in Switzerland, the sovereignty is divided into parts; on the one hand is the Federal power, and on the other, the governments of the Cantons. M. Cherbuliez begins with the consideration of what is taking place in the Cantons; and he is right, for in them is the real government of the community. I shall follow him in this respect, and shall first consider the constitutions of the Cantons. All these constitutions, at present, are democratic; but democracy does not show itself in all of them under the same features. In a major-

ity of the Cantons, the exercise of power has been delegated to assemblies which represent the people; in the
others, the people have reserved this power to themselves.
They form themselves into one body, and thus constitute
the government.   The former are denominated by our
author *representative democracies;* the latter he calls *pure
democracies.*

I shall take the liberty not to follow the author in the
very interesting examination which he has made of pure
democracies; and this for several reasons.   Although the
Cantons which live under a pure democracy have played a
great part in history, and may still play a considerable one
in politics, a study of them would be rather curious than
useful.   Pure democracy is a fact almost unique in the
modern world, and very rare even in Switzerland, where
only a thirteenth part of the population are governed in
this manner.   Moreover, it is a transitory form.   It is not
sufficiently known that, even in the Swiss Cantons, where
the people have the best preserved the exercise of power,
a representative body still exists, upon whom devolves in
part the business of government.   Now it is easy to see,
in studying the recent history of Switzerland, that the
affairs which are managed by the whole people are gradually diminishing, while, on the other hand, those which are
directed by their representatives are every day increasing
in number and variety.   Thus the principle of pure democracy is losing ground which the opposite system gains.
The one insensibly becomes the exception, the other the
rule.

Besides, the pure democracies of Switzerland belong to
another age; they can teach us nothing in regard either
to the present or the future.   Although we are obliged, in
order to designate them, to make use of a term borrowed
from modern science, they live only in the past.   Every
age has its dominant spirit, which nothing is able to resist.

If principles should be introduced under its reign which are foreign or hostile to it, very soon it infuses itself into them, and if it cannot shut out their action altogether, it appropriates them and assimilates them to itself. The Middle Ages succeeded at last in shaping democratic liberty itself into an aristocratic form. In the midst of the most republican laws, by the side of universal suffrage itself, were placed religious dogmas, opinions, sentiments, customs, associations, families, which kept the real power beyond the action of the people. The petty governments of the Swiss Cantons must be regarded as the last, though the respectable, relics of an age which has passed away.

On the contrary, the representative democracies of Switzerland are the true progeny of the spirit of modern times. All of them are founded on the ruins of a preceding aristocratic state of society; all emanate from the single principle of the sovereignty of the people; all have made almost the same application of it in their laws. We shall see that these laws are very imperfect, and this fact alone would suffice to indicate, in the silence of history, that democracy, and even liberty, in Switzerland, have neither age nor experience in their favor.

It is first to be observed that, even in the representative democracies of Switzerland, the people have kept in their own hands the direct exercise of a portion of their power. In some Cantons, after the principal laws have received the assent of the legislature, they must still be submitted to the approval or disapproval of the people. Hence, in these special cases, the representative degenerates into the pure form of democracy. In almost all the Cantons, the people must be consulted from time to time, usually at short intervals, to know whether they wish to modify or to maintain the constitution. All the laws are thus made to waver at once, and at frequently recurring periods.

All legislative authority which the people have not retained in their own hands is confided to a single assembly, which acts in their name and under their observation. In no Canton is the legislature divided into two branches, everywhere it consists of a single body; not only its movements are not delayed by the necessity of coming to an agreement with another assembly, but its wishes do not find even the hinderance of a prolonged deliberation. The discussion of the general laws is subject to certain formalities, which require time; but the most important resolutions, under the name of decrees, may be proposed, discussed, and enacted in a moment. The decrees cause the secondary laws to be as unforeseen, as rapid, and as irresistible in their operation, as the passions of a multitude.

Outside of the legislature, there is no resisting power. The separation, and, above all, the relative independence, of the legislative, administrative, and judicial authorities have never been established. In none of the Cantons are the representatives of the executive power chosen directly by the people; it is the legislature that elects them. The executive power, consequently, has no strength which is peculiar to it; it is only the creature, and it may be only the servile agent, of another power. To this cause of weakness several others are added. Nowhere is the executive power delegated to a single person. It is vested in a small assembly, where its responsibility is divided and its action debilitated. Moreover, several of the prerogatives which properly belong to executive authority are taken away. It exercises no veto, or only an insignificant one, on the enactment of laws. It has not the pardoning power, it does not appoint its own agents, and cannot deprive them of office. It may even be said that it has no agents, as it is generally obliged to make use only of the municipal magistrates.

But, above all, it is through the bad constitution and bad

materials of the judicial power that the Swiss democracy suffers. M. Cherbuliez remarks this defect, but does not place stress enough upon it in my opinion. He does not seem perfectly to understand, that it is the judicial power in democracies which is destined to be at the same time a barrier and a safeguard for the power of the people.

The independence of the judiciary is a modern idea. The Middle Ages had never thought of such a thing, or, at most, had formed only a very obscure conception of it. It may be said, that, in all the nations of Europe, executive and judicial functions were at first joined together; even in France, where, by a happy exception, the administration of justice had at an early period a very vigorous separate existence, we are still able to affirm that the division of the two powers remained very incomplete. It was not, it is true, the administration which retained judicial power in its own hands, but it was the judiciary which exercised in part administrative functions. Switzerland, on the other hand, of all the countries of Europe, has most completely confounded judicial with political authority, making the former one of the attributes of the latter. It may be said that the very idea which we have of the judiciary, that free impartial power which is interposed between all interests and all authorities, in order to enforce upon all a respect for the law, has never been present to the minds of the Swiss, and, even at the present day, is but very imperfectly understood by them.

The new constitutions have undoubtedly given to the legal tribunals a more distinct place than that which they occupied in the old division of power, but not a more independent position. The inferior judges are elected by the people, and subject to a re-election. The supreme court of each Canton is appointed, not by the executive, but by the legislative power, and thus its members have no security against the daily caprices of the majority. Not only do the people, or the assembly which represents the people, choose the judges, but no restraint is imposed upon their choice. In general, no qualifications are required. The judge, moreover, a simple executor of the law, has no right to inquire whether this law is conformable to the constitution. In truth, it is the majority itself which judges, employing the judiciary only as its organ. In Switzerland, too, the judicial authority, even if it had received from the law the independence and the rights which are essential to it, would still find great difficulty in exercising its functions, for it is a power resting upon tradition and opinion, and needing to be fortified by judicial ideas and manners.

I could easily expose the defects which are found in the institutions that I have just described, and prove that they all tend to render the government of the people irregular in its action, precipitate in its resolutions, and tyrannical in its acts. But this would carry me too far. I shall confine myself to bringing out the contrast between these laws and those which have been established in a democratic society which is older, more peaceable, and more prosperous. M. Cherbuliez thinks that the imperfect institutions which the Swiss Cantons possess are the only ones which are natural to a democracy, or are even compatible with it. The comparison which I am about to make will prove the contrary, and will show how it has been possible elsewhere, aided by more experience, more art, and greater wisdom, to deduce different results from the principle of the sovereignty of the people. I shall take for an example the State of New York, which alone contains as many inhabitants as the whole of Switzerland.

In the State of New York, as in the Swiss Cantons, the principle of government is the sovereignty of the people, exercised through universal suffrage. But the people there exercise their authority only for a single day, in the choice of their delegates. In no case do they habitually

keep in their own hands any portion whatever of the legislative, executive, or judicial authority. They make choice
of those who are to govern in their name, and then abdicate their power till the next election.

Although the laws are subject to change, their foundation
is fixed. The idea has never been entertained of subjecting the constitution, as in Switzerland, to successive and
periodical revisions, which, as they come round or are
looked forward to, keep the community in constant suspense. When a new want is felt, the legislature decide
that a modification of the constitution has become necessary, and the following legislature effects it.

Although the legislative authority cannot, any more than
in Switzerland, shake off the directing power of public
opinion, it is so constituted as to resist its caprices. No
proposition can become a law till it has been subjected to
examination by two legislative bodies. These two portions
of the legislature are chosen in the same manner and composed of the same elements; both emanate equally from the
people, but do not represent the people exactly in the same
manner; the office of the one is to follow the daily impressions, that of the other to obey the habitual instincts and
permanent inclinations, of the community.

In New York, the division of the powers of government
exists not only in appearance, but in reality. The executive authority is exercised, not by a number of persons, but
by one man, who alone is responsible for it, and exercises
with decision and firmness its rights and prerogatives.
Chosen by the people, he is not, as in Switzerland, the
creature and the agent of the legislature; he stands beside
it as its equal, representing equally, though in a different
sphere, the sovereign in whose name they both act. He
draws his strength from the same source whence they
derive theirs. He has not only the name of the executive
power, but he exercises its natural and legitimate preroga-

tives. He is the commander-in-chief of the military force, and appoints its principal officers; he nominates several of the higher functionaries of the State; he exercises the right of pardon; the veto which he can oppose to the decisions of the legislature, though not absolute, is still efficacious. Though the Governor of the State of New York is undoubtedly much less powerful than a constitutional king in Europe, at least he is infinitely more so than a petty Council in Switzerland.

But it is especially in the organization of the judicial power that the difference becomes striking.

The judge, although he emanates from the people and is dependent upon them, is still a power to which the people themselves are subject. The judiciary there occupies this exceptional position in respect to its origin, its permanence, its competency, and especially in relation to public manners and public opinion.

The members of the higher tribunals are not chosen, as in Switzerland, by the legislature, a collective power which is often passionate, sometimes blind, and always irresponsible, but by the Governor of the State.* The legal magistrate, when once inducted into office, is regarded as irremovable. No litigation can be determined, no penalty inflicted, except by his agency. Not only does he interpret the law, it may even be said that he judges it. When the legislators, drawn by the manœuvres of contending factions, depart from the spirit or the letter of the constitution, the legal tribunals bring them back to it by refusing to apply their enactments; so that, if the judge cannot compel the people to preserve their constitution, he obliges them, at

* Unfortunately, since M. de Tocqueville wrote, the constitution of the New York judiciary in this respect has been altered. The judges are now elected directly by the people, and only for a limited period of years. This is a change pregnant with disastrous results, though as yet these are but imperfectly developed. — Am. Ed.

least, to respect it so long as it exists. He does not guide, but he restrains and keeps within certain bounds, the action of the community. The judiciary, which hardly exists in Switzerland, is the true moderator of the American democracy.

Now let us examine this constitution, even in its smallest details, and we shall not find in it an atom of aristocracy; — nothing that resembles a class or a privilege, but everywhere the same rights, one spirit animating all the institutions, and no conflicting tendencies; the principle of democracy pervades and governs all things. And yet these governments, so completely democratic, have a far more solid foundation, a more peaceable aspect, and much more regular movements, than the democratic governments of Switzerland.

It is allowable to say, that this comes in part from the difference of the laws. The laws of the State of New York, which I have just described, are so contrived as to balance and remedy the natural defects of democracy, while the Swiss institutions which I have portrayed seem made for the very purpose of enhancing them. Here they restrain the people, there they incite them. In America, the fear was lest they should be tyrannical; while in Switzerland, the only desire seems to have been to render them irresistible.

I would not exaggerate the influence which the mechanism of the laws may exert upon the destiny of a nation. I know that there are other causes, more general and more deeply-seated, to which must chiefly be attributed the great events of this world. But it cannot be denied that the institutions of government have a certain virtue which is peculiar to them, and that, in themselves alone, they contribute largely to the prosperity or the misery of society.

If, instead of absolutely condemning almost all the laws of his country, M. Cherbuliez had pointed out wherein they are faulty, and how they might be improved without altering the principle on which they rest, he would have written a book more worthy of posterity, and more useful to his contemporaries.

After showing how democracy works in the Cantons, the author inquires into the influence which it exerts upon the Confederacy itself. Before following him in this direction, it is necessary to do what he has left undone, and clearly indicate what the Federal government is, how it is organized in theory and in fact, and how it operates.

It will be proper to ask, in the first place, if the legislators of the Swiss Confederation wished to make a federal constitution, or only to establish a league; in other words, if they intended to sacrifice a portion of the sovereignty of the Cantons, or not to alienate any part of it. When it is considered that the Cantons are forbidden to exercise several rights which are inherent in sovereignty, and that these are permanently conceded to the Federal government, and especially if we reflect that they have determined the will of the majority to be the law upon the questions thus surrendered to their government, it cannot be doubted that the legislators of the Swiss Confederation desired to establish a true federal constitution, and not a simple league. But it must be confessed that they have concerted measures very ill for success in this undertaking. I do not hesitate to avow my own opinion, that the Federal constitution of Switzerland is the most imperfect of all the institutions of this sort which have hitherto appeared in the world. One would think, on reading it, that we had gone back quite to the Middle Ages, and we cannot be too much astonished to learn, that this confused and imperfect work is the product of an age so well informed and so rich in experience as our own.*

* It must not be forgotten that all this was written in 1847, and before the reaction from the Revolution of 1848 had brought about a reform of the old Federal compact.

It is often alleged, and not without reason, that the Compact restricted altogether too much the rights of the Confederation ; that it left outside of the action of the Federal government certain objects, essentially national in character, which it would naturally belong to the Diet to regulate, — such, for example, as the administration of the post-office and the mails, the regulation of weights and measures, and the coining of money ; and the weakness of the Federal power has been attributed to the small number of functions which have been confided to its management.

It is very true, that the Compact has denied to the Federal authority several of the powers which naturally, and even necessarily, belong to this government. But it is not here that we are to look for the true cause of the weakness of this authority, since the rights which the Compact has given it would suffice, if it could use them, soon to acquire all those which are now wanting.

The Diet can collect troops, levy money, declare war, make peace, conclude treaties of commerce, and appoint ambassadors. The constitutions of the Cantons, and the great principles of equality before the law, are placed under its protection ; which would enable it, in case of need, to interfere in all local affairs. Duties upon imports, tolls upon roads, &c., are regulated by the Diet, so that it is authorized to direct or control the great public works. Finally, the fourth article of the Compact says, *the Diet takes all measures necessary for the security of Switzerland, both at home and abroad,* — which gives it the power of doing anything.

The strongest federal governments have not had greater prerogatives ; and, far from thinking that the powers of the central government in Switzerland are too restricted, I am inclined to believe that their limits are not carefully enough determined.

How comes it, then, that, with such great privileges, the

government of the Confederation usually has so little
power? The reason is a very simple one: it is because
the Compact has not furnished the means of accomplishing
what has actually been granted to it, namely, the right to
say that certain things ought to be done. Never was a
government more completely reduced to inaction and impotence through the imperfection of its organs.

It belongs to the essence of a federal government to act,
not in the name of the people, but in the name of the
states of which the confederation is composed. If it were
otherwise, the constitution would immediately cease to be
federal. Hence it results, among other necessary and inevitable consequences, that federal governments are habitually less daring in their resolutions, and slower in their
movements, than others.

Most legislators of confederations have endeavored, by
the aid of more or less ingenious contrivances, into an examination of which I do not wish to enter, to correct in
part this natural vice of the federal system. The Swiss
have rendered it vastly more obvious than anywhere else,
through the special forms which they have adopted. In
their case, not merely do the members of the Diet act only
in the name of the different Cantons which they represent,
but, generally speaking, they do not take any resolution
which has not been foreseen or approved by these Cantons.
Hardly anything is left to their free will; every one of them
believes himself bound by an imperative mandate imposed
beforehand; so that the Diet is a deliberative assembly,
where, to say the truth, there is nothing left for deliberation, and where the members speak, not before those who
are to adopt the resolution, but before those who have only
the right of carrying it into effect. The Diet is a government which determines nothing of itself, but only realizes
what twenty-two other governments have separately determined, — a government which, whatever be the nature of

events, can decide nothing, foresee nothing, provide for nothing. No combination could be imagined which would be better fitted to increase the natural inactivity of the Federal government, or to change its weakness into a sort of senile incapacity.

There are yet many other causes which, independently of the vices inherent in all federal constitutions, explain the habitual impotence of the government of the Swiss Confederation.

Not only has the Confederation a weak government, but it may be said that it has no government of its own. The constitution, in this respect, is without a parallel in the world. At its head are rulers who do not represent the Confederation. The members of the Directory, who constitute the executive authority of Switzerland, are not chosen by the Diet, still less by the Helvetic people; it is a government of chance, which the Confederation borrows every two years from Berne, from Zurich, or from Lucerne. This Directory, chosen by the inhabitants of a Canton to direct the affairs of a Canton, becomes, in addition to its main function, the head and the arm of the whole country. Certainly, this may pass for one of the greatest political curiosities which the history of human laws affords. The results of such an arrangement are always deplorable, and often very extraordinary. For example, nothing could be more strange than what happened in 1839. That year the Diet was sitting at Zurich, and the Confederation had for its governing body the Directory of the state of Zurich. A revolution took place in the Canton of Zurich, where a popular insurrection overturned the constituted authorities. The Diet immediately found itself without a President, and the federal life remained suspended, till it pleased the Canton to institute for itself other laws and other rulers. The people of Zurich, by changing their local administration, had decapitated Switzerland without wishing it.

Even if the Confederation had an executive authority of its own, its government would still be powerless to compel obedience, from the want of any direct and immediate action upon the citizens. This cause of weakness is more fertile in itself alone than all the others put together; but in order that it may be well understood, we must do more than merely indicate it.

A federal government may have a very limited sphere of action, and yet be strong. If, in this narrow sphere, it can act of itself, without intervention, as ordinary governments do in the unlimited sphere in which they move; if it has its own functionaries, who address themselves directly to every citizen, its own tribunals, who compel every citizen to submit to its laws, — it easily obtains obedience, because it has never anything to fear but the resistance of individuals, and as all obstacles which are raised against it terminate in lawsuits.

On the other hand, a federal government may have a very large field of action, and yet possess only a very weak and very precarious authority, if, instead of addressing itself individually to the citizens, it is obliged to have recourse to the provincial governments; for if these resist, the federal power immediately finds itself at variance, not so much with a subject, as with a rival, from whom it can obtain redress only by war.

The strength of a federal government, then, consists much less in the extent of the powers conferred upon it, than in the greater or less ability which it has of exercising them through its own agents. It is always strong when it can command the citizens; it is always weak when it can issue its commands only to the local governments. The history of confederations affords examples of both systems. But in no confederation that I know of has the central authority been so entirely deprived of all means of action upon the citizens, as in Switzerland. There is not, so to speak, one of its powers which the Federal government there can exercise of itself; there are no functionaries who are entirely dependent upon it, no tribunals which represent exclusively its sovereignty. One would say it was a being to whom some power had given life, but had deprived it of any organs.

Such is the Federal constitution as it is determined by the Compact. Now let us consider, in a few words, with the author of the book which we are analyzing, what influence is exercised upon it by democracy. It cannot be denied, that the democratic revolutions which have successively changed almost all the constitutions of the Cantons during the last fifteen years, have had a great influence also upon the Federal government; but this influence has been exercised in two entirely opposite directions. It is very necessary to have a complete view of this double phenomenon.

The effect of the democratic revolutions which have taken place in the several Cantons has been, to give to the local authorities more activity and more power. The new governments created by these revolutions, resting upon the people and incited by them, found in themselves, all at once, greater strength and a higher idea of their strength, than could be manifested by the governments which they had overturned. And as a similar renovation was not accomplished at the same time in the Federal government, the result which ought to have been expected, and which actually followed, was, that the latter found itself weaker, in comparison with the former, than it had previously been. Provincial pride, the instinct of local independence, impatience of any control in the internal affairs of each Canton, jealousy of a central and supreme authority, are all feelings which have waxed stronger since the establishment of democracy; and from this point of view, it may be said, that democracy has weakened the already feeble power of the

Confederation, and has rendered its daily and habitual task more laborious and more difficult.

But in other respects, it has given it an energy, and, so to speak, an existence, which it never before possessed.

The establishment of democratic institutions in Switzerland has brought about two things entirely new. Every Canton formerly had its separate interests and separate inclinations. The accession of democracy has divided all the Swiss, to whatever Cantons they belonged, into two parties, the one favorable to democratic principles, the other opposed to them. It has created common interests and common passions, which have felt the need, in order to satisfy themselves, of a general and common power, which should extend at the same time over the whole country. The Federal government thus obtained, for the first time, a great aid which it has always wanted ; it has been able to rest upon a party ; — a source of strength which is dangerous, but indispensable in free countries, where, without it, the government can hardly do anything.

At the same time that democracy divided Switzerland into two parties, it arrayed Switzerland in one of the great parties which divide the world ; it created for it a foreign policy ; as it gave the country natural allies, it also created for it necessary enemies ; it caused the nation to feel the absolute necessity of a government, in order to cultivate and restrain the former, to guard against and repel the latter. It caused a local public spirit to give place to a national public spirit.

Such are the direct effects by which democracy fortified the national government. The indirect influence which it has exercised, and will exercise, in the long run, is not less important. The opposition and the difficulties which a federal government meets with are greater and more various in proportion as the confederate communities are more dissimilar in their institutions, their sentiments, their usages, and their opinions. Similarity of interests is even less important than that resemblance of the laws, the opinions, and the social condition of the people, which makes the task of the government of the American Union so easy. It may even be said, that the strange weakness of the old Federal government in Switzerland was principally due to the prodigious difference and singular opposition which existed between the characters, the opinions, and the laws of the various communities which it had to govern. To keep under the same direction, and to embrace within the same political system, people who are naturally so far apart and so unlike each other, was a most laborious undertaking. A government far better constituted and more skilfully organized would not have succeeded in such an endeavor. The effect of the democratic revolution which is taking place in Switzerland is, to cause certain institutions, certain maxims of government, certain similar ideas, to prevail successively in all the Cantons. If the democratic revolution enhances in the Cantons their spirit of independence of the central power, on the other hand it facilitates the action of that power; it takes away, in a great degree, the causes of opposition, and, without giving the Cantonal governments any stronger desire to obey the Federal government, it makes obedience to its commands infinitely easier.

We ought to study with great care the two contrary effects which I have described, in order to understand the present state, and to foresee the impending condition, of the country. It is by paying attention to only one of these two tendencies, that some have been induced to believe, that the accession of democracy in the governments of the Cantons will produce, as its immediate result, an easy extension of the legislative sphere of the Federal government, and will concentrate in its hands the ordinary direction of local affairs; in a word, that it will modify the whole economy of the Compact by increasing the centralization of affairs. For my own part, I am convinced that, for a long time, such a revolution will meet with far more obstacles than is generally imagined. The present governments of the Cantons will show no more inclination than their predecessors for a revolution of this sort, and they will do all they can to prevent its accomplishment.

And yet I believe that, in spite of this opposition, the Federal government is destined, in the long run, to acquire greater power. In this respect, laws will not favor it so much as other circumstances. It will not, perhaps, very visibly increase its prerogatives, but it will make a different and more frequent use of them. It will become greater in fact, it will remain the same in theory; its power will be developed rather by the interpretation, than by the alteration, of the Compact; and its authority will preponderate over all others, before it has become capable of governing Switzerland.

It may also be foreseen, that the very persons who, up to the present time, have been the most opposed to the regular extension of the Federal authority, will soon be induced to favor it, either to escape the intermittent pressure of a power so ill-organized, or to protect themselves against the heavier and more imminent tyranny of the local governments.

But it is certain that, for the future, whatever modifications may be made in the letter of the Compact, the Federal constitution of Switzerland is thoroughly and irrevocably changed. The Confederation has changed its nature. It has become a new thing in Europe; an energetic policy has succeeded to its former one of inertness and neutrality; its existence, from being purely municipal, has become national, — an existence which is grander, but more laborious, more agitated, and more uncertain.

SPEECH OF M. DE TOCQUEVILLE

IN THE CHAMBER OF DEPUTIES, JANUARY 27, 1848, IN THE DEBATE ON THE
PROPOSED ANSWER TO AN ADDRESS FROM THE THRONE.*

MY intention, gentlemen, is not to continue the particular discussion which has been begun. I think
the subject will be taken up again to better advantage
when we come to consider the bill for the regulation of
prisons. My object in taking the floor is a more general
one.

The fourth paragraph of the Address, which is now
under discussion, naturally invites the Chamber to take a
general view of our whole internal policy, and especially
of that aspect of our home politics which has been pointed
out, and made the subject of an amendment, by my honorable friend, M. Billault. It is this portion of the discussion on the Address which I wish to bring before the
Chamber.

I may be deceived, gentlemen, but it seems to me that

---

* In the advertisement prefixed to the twelfth edition of this work, the
author thought himself entitled to say, that the Revolution of 1848 had not
taken him by surprise. Our readers will thank us, then, for inserting here,
as a proof of this assertion, a report of the speech made by him in the
Chamber of Deputies just one month before the fearful outbreak of the
Revolution of 1848. In this remarkable speech, with great precision and
truly prophetic forecast, qualities for which he was indebted to the thorough
study that he had made of modern democracy, the great publicist foretold,
not only the imminence of the Revolution, but the social and economical,
rather than political, character which it was at once to manifest. — *Note by
the French publisher.*

the present state of things, the present state of opinion, the present state of people's minds in France, is such as to create alarm and distress. For my own part, I sincerely declare that, for the first time for fifteen years, I feel a special dread of the future ; and what proves to me that I am right, is that I am not alone in this impression. I believe I may appeal to all who hear me, and all will answer, that, in the districts which they represent, a similar impression exists ; that a peculiar uneasiness, an undefined dread, pervades the minds of men ; that, for the first time perhaps for sixteen years, the sentiment, the instinct, of instability, that sentiment which is the precursor of revolutions, which often announces and sometimes produces them, that this sentiment exists in the country to a very grave degree.

If I perfectly understood what was said the other day in conclusion by the Minister of Finance, the Cabinet themselves admit the reality of the impression of which I speak ; but he attributes it to certain special causes, to certain recent accidental events in political life which have agitated the minds of men, and to words which have roused their passions.

Gentlemen, by attributing the admitted evil to the causes thus indicated, I fear that they impute it not to the disease itself, but only to its symptoms. For my own part, I am convinced that the malady is not there ; it is more general and more deeply seated. This disease, which must be cured, cost what it may, and which, believe me, will sweep us all away, — understand me ! all, if we do not beware, — is the present condition of the public mind and of public morals. Here lies the complaint ; it is to this point that I wish to draw your attention. I believe that the public morals, the public mind, are in a dangerous condition ; and I believe, too, that the government have contributed, and contributed in the gravest manner, to increase the danger. This is what has made me rise to speak.

Gentlemen, when I attentively consider the class who govern, the class who have political rights, and then turn to those who are governed, I am troubled and appalled by what I see in both. And, to speak first of those whom I have called the class who govern, — (observe that I use these words in their most general acceptation, — I speak not merely of the middle classes, but of all citizens, in whatever position they may be, who possess and exercise political rights,) — I say, then, that I am troubled and appalled by what is manifest in the governing class. What I see there, gentlemen, I can express in a word. Public morals are degraded there, — they are already deeply degraded; they are degraded there more and more every day; common opinions, sentiments, and ideas are there giving place every day, more and more, to individual interests, private aims, and motives borrowed from private life and private ambition.

I do not intend to compel the Chamber to expatiate any more than is necessary upon these sad details; I will only address myself to my opponents themselves, to my fellow-members of the ministerial majority. I entreat them to make for their own use a sort of statistical review of the electoral colleges which have made them their deputies in this place. Let them form a first class of those who have voted for them, not from political opinions, but from sentiments of private friendship or good neighborhood. In a second class let them put those who vote for them, not from any motive of public or common interest, but for purely local purposes. To this second category let them finally add a third, consisting of those who vote for them from motives of exclusively private interest; and I ask them if those who remain are very numerous, — I ask them if those who vote from disinterested public sentiment, led by opinion or public feeling, if these form the majority of the voters who have conferred upon them the office of Deputy. I am sure that they must answer in the negative. I will venture also to ask of them, if, to their certain knowledge, for five years, ten years, fifteen years, the number of those who vote for them from motives of personal and private interest has not been continually increasing, and the number of those who vote from political opinion continually decreasing. Finally, let them say if, around them, under their own eyes, there has not been establishing itself, by degrees, in public opinion a kind of singular toleration for the facts of which I speak; if, by degrees, a kind of low and vulgar morality is not created, according to which the man who possesses political rights owes it to himself, owes it to his children, to his wife, to his relations, to make a personal use of these rights to further their interests; and if this is not gradually rising to be considered as a sort of duty on the part of a father of a family, — if this new morality, unknown in the grander periods of our history, unknown at the beginning of our Revolution, is not developing itself more and more, and every day gaining possession of the minds of men. I ask them this.

Now, what does all this amount to, except a continuous and profound degradation, a depravation more and more complete of the public morals?

And if, turning from public to private life, I consider what is passing, — if I pay attention to all that you have witnessed, especially during the last year, to all those notorious scandals, all those crimes, all those misdemeanors, all those offences, all those extraordinary vices, which every circumstance has seemed to bring to light in all quarters, and which every judicial investigation reveals, — if I attend to all this, have I not cause to be appalled? Am I not entitled to say, that not only our public, but our private morals, are becoming more and more depraved?

And observe that I do not say this from a moralist's point of view, but that I speak from a political motive. Do you know what is the general, efficient, deeply-seated cause, why private morals are degraded? It is because public morals have first become depraved. It is because pure morality does not govern the principal actions of life, that it does not descend to the smaller ones. It is because private interest has taken the place of disinterested sentiment in public action, that selfishness has become the law in private life.

It has been said that there are two sorts of morality, the one for politics, and the other for private life. Certainly, if what is passing around us really is what I see it to be, never was the falsity of such an assertion proved in a more striking and unhappy manner than in our own day. Yes, I believe that a change is taking place in our private morals of such a nature as to trouble and alarm all good citizens, and that this change proceeds in great part from what is coming to pass in our public morals. (*Marks of dissent.*)

Well, gentlemen, if you will not believe me on this point, you will at least believe the general impression of Europe. I think I am as well informed as any person in this Chamber of what is said and published about us in other parts of Europe; and I assure you, in the sincerity of my heart, that I am not only saddened, but profoundly distressed, at what I hear and read every day; I am distressed when I see the advantage which is taken against us from the facts of which I speak, the exaggerated consequences that are deduced from them against the whole nation, against the entire national character. I am distressed when I see how much the power of France is gradually weakened in the world; I am distressed when I see that not only the moral power of France, but the power of her principles, her ideas, and her sentiments, is enfeebled.

France was the first to throw into the world, amid the thunders of her first Revolution, dogmas which have subsequently become the regenerating principles of all modern societies. This has been her glory; it is the most precious portion of her history. Now it is these very principles which our example at the present day is depriving of force. The application which we seem to make of them in our own case leads the world to doubt their truth. Europe, which is watching us, begins to ask if we were right or wrong; she asks if it is true, what we have so often affirmed, that we are leading the nations of the world towards a happier and more prosperous future, or whether we are not dragging them down after us into moral degradation and ruin. This, gentlemen, is what is causing me most grief in the spectacle which we are offering to the world. It not only injures us, but it injures our principles, it injures our cause, it injures this intellectual country to which, for my own part, as a Frenchman, I am more attached than to the material and physical country which is before our eyes.

Gentlemen, if the spectacle which we are offering produces such an effect when seen from afar, when viewed from the confines of Europe, what effect do you think it is producing in France itself, upon those classes who have no political rights, and who, from the midst of the political inaction to which they are condemned by our laws, behold us alone acting upon the grand theatre on which we are placed? What do you think is the effect produced on them by such a spectacle?

For my own part, I am appalled by it. Some say there is no danger, because there is no insurrection; they say that, as there is no material disorder on the surface of society, revolution is still far distant.

Gentlemen, allow me to tell you that I think you are deceived. Undoubtedly the disorder does not yet appear in overt acts, but it has sunk deeply into the minds of the people. Look at what is passing among the working classes, though at present, I own, they are tranquil. It is true that they are not agitated by political passions properly so called, as much as they formerly were; but do you not see that the agitation among them is no longer political, but social? Do you not see that there are gradually diffused among them opinions and ideas, which do not tend merely to overturn such and such laws, this or that ministry, this or that government even, but to subvert society itself, and to shake the very foundations on which it now rests? Do you not know what they are every day talking about? Do you not hear them incessantly declare, that all who are above them are incapable and unworthy to govern, — that the present distribution of wealth is unjust, and that property does not rest upon any equitable basis? And do you not believe that, when such opinions have taken root, when they are almost universally diffused, when they have penetrated deeply into the minds of the multitude, they must bring about sooner or later — I know not when, I know not how — but they must bring about sooner or later the most fearful revolutions?

This, gentlemen, is my profound conviction. I believe we are at the present moment slumbering upon a volcano. (*Murmurs.*) I am thoroughly convinced of it.

Now, permit me to inquire before you, in a few words, but with truth and perfect sincerity, who are the true authors, the principal authors, of the evil which I have just endeavored to describe.

I know very well that evils such as I have just spoken of do not all flow, perhaps do not even principally flow, from the action of governments. I know very well that the long revolutions, which have so often heaved and shaken the ground of this country, must have left a singular instability in the minds of men. I know very well that, in the passions and excitements of party, certain secondary but considerable causes may be found, which may serve to explain the deplorable phenomenon which I have just made known to you; but I have too high an idea of the part which the power of government plays in this world's affairs, not to be convinced that, when a great evil is produced in society, — a great political evil, a great moral evil, — the government is largely responsible for it.

What has the government done, then, to produce the evil which I have just described to you? What has it done to bring about this deeply seated disorder, first in public, and then in private morals? How has it contributed to this result?

I believe it can be said, without wounding anybody, that the government has again, especially during these latter years, seized upon larger rights, a greater influence, more considerable and more various prerogatives, than it had possessed at any other epoch. It has become infinitely greater than could ever have been imagined, not only by those who gave, but by those who received, it in 1830. It may be affirmed, on the other hand, that the principle of liberty has been less developed than any one could then have expected. I pass no judgment on the fact itself; I look only at its consequences. If a result so singular and so unexpected, so strange a turn of human affairs, has baffled some bad passions, some guilty hopes, do you not believe that, on witnessing it, many noble sentiments, many disinterested aspirations, have become extinct, — that there has followed from it, in many honest hearts, an abandonment of all political hopes as illusions, and a real depression of soul?

But it is especially the manner in which this result has been produced, the underhand, and, up to a certain point, the surreptitious manner in which this end has been obtained, which has given a fatal blow to the public morality.

It is by seizing again upon the old prerogatives which were supposed to have been abolished by the Revolution of July, by reviving old powers which seemed to have been annulled, by restoring to vigor old laws which people thought had been abrogated, by applying new laws to purposes for which they were not enacted, — it is by all these underhand means, by this skilful and patient management, that the government has at last obtained more power, more activity and influence, than it ever before possessed in France.

This, gentlemen, is what the government has done, and particularly what the present ministry have done. And think you that this manner, which I have just called underhand and surreptitious, of recovering power by degrees, of taking it as it were by surprise, by using other means than those which the constitution had granted, — think you that this strange spectacle of adroitness and skilful management, held up before the world for several years, on so vast a theatre, to a whole nation which is looking on, — think you that this spectacle has been such as to improve the public morals?

For my own part, I am profoundly convinced of the contrary. I would not attribute to my opponents dishonorable motives which they have not entertained; I will admit, if you wish, that, in making use of the means which I censure, they thought they were submitting to a necessary evil, — that the magnitude of the end concealed from them the danger and the immorality of the means. I am willing to believe all this; but does this make the means any the less dangerous? They believe that the revolution which has taken place during the last fifteen years in the powers of government was necessary; — be it so! that they have not made it to promote their own interests; — I am willing to believe it! But it is not the less true that they have effected it by means which the public morality disavows; it is not the less true that they have effected it by taking men, not by their honest side, but by their bad side, — by their passions, by their weakness, by their interests, often by their vices. Hence it is, that, while having perhaps an honest purpose, they have done things which were not honest. And in order to do these things, it was necessary to call to their side, to honor with their favor, to introduce into their daily company, men who desired from the power that was confided to them only the gross satisfaction of their private interests; they have thus granted a sort of premium to immorality and vice.

I will cite but one example to show what I mean; it is that of the minister, whose name I do not remember, who was called to be a member of the Cabinet, although all France, as well as his colleagues, knew already that he was unworthy to sit there; who left the Cabinet, because this unworthiness became too notorious, and was then placed — where? On the highest bench of the legal tribunals, whence he was soon obliged to descend to take his stand at the bar as a criminal under prosecution.

As for me, gentlemen, I do not regard this as an isolated fact; I consider it as the symptom of a general malady, the most striking example of a whole scheme of policy; by walking in the ways which you had chosen, you had need of such men.

But it is especially through the abuse of government influence, to which the Minister of Foreign Affairs has had recourse, that the moral evil of which I was speaking has been diffused and generalized, and has pervaded the country. It is here that you have acted, directly and without intervention, upon public morality, no longer by examples, but by acts. I do not wish in this respect to place the ministers in a worse position than they really occupy; I know well that they have been exposed to an immense temptation; I know well, that at no time, in no country, has a government ever been exposed to a similar one, — that nowhere has power had in its hands so many means of corruption, nowhere had before it a political class so limited in number, and standing so much in want of many things, that the facility of acting upon it by corruption appeared greater, or the desire of so acting upon it more irresistible. I admit, then, that it is not by a premeditated desire of acting upon men through their private interests only, as if this were the single chord in their hearts which could be made to vibrate, that the ministry have done this great evil; I know well that they have been hurried down an inclined plane, on which it was very difficult to hold their ground; I know all that. The only thing that I reproach them with is, that of having placed themselves there, of having put themselves in a position where, in order to govern, they found it necessary to appeal, not to opinions, to sentiments, to general ideas, but to private interests. Once embarked in this boat, I hold it for certain that, whatever might have been their wishes, whatever their desire to turn back, a fatality urged them, and must have urged them, constantly farther and farther on, to every position which they have since occupied. But one thing was wanting for this result, — that they should continue to live. Just as soon as they reached the point where I just now placed them, it was only necessary to exist eight years, in order to do all which we have seen that they have done, in order not only to use all the immoral means of government of which I have just spoken, but to exhaust them.

It was this fatality which first made them increase beyond bounds the number of offices; which then, when these failed them, induced them to divide, and, so to speak, to break up into fractions, in order to have a larger number, if not the offices, at least the emoluments, as has been done in all the bureaux of the Department of Finance. It was this same necessity which, when, in spite of this management, places and salaries were again wanted, caused them, as we saw the other day in Petit's case, to create vacancies artificially, and by underhand means, in places which had been already filled.

The Minister of Foreign Affairs has told us many times, that the opposition was unjust in its attacks, and that the accusations it had directed against him were violent, unfounded, and false. But I put the question to him directly, has the opposition ever, in its worst moments, accused him of what has this day been proved? The opposition has certainly uttered grave reproaches, — excessive reproaches, perhaps, but I know not; — but it has never accused him of doing what he has recently himself confessed that he had done.

And for my own part, I declare that not only have I never accused the Minister of Foreign Affairs of these things, but never had I even suspected him of them. Never, never would I have believed, on hearing him support from this place, with a marvellous command of language, the claims of morality in politics, — on hearing him hold such language, which made me, in spite of my opposition, proud of my country, — assuredly I would never have believed that what has happened was possible; I should have believed that I was wanting not only to him, but still more to myself, if I had supposed what was nevertheless the truth. Shall I believe, as was said the other day, that, when the Minister of Foreign Affairs held this fine and noble language, he was not saying what he thought? As for me, I will not go so far; I believe that the instinct, the taste, of the Minister was to act differently from what he has done. But he has been pushed on, drawn away in spite of himself, deprived of his own will, so to speak, by that sort of political and ministerial fatality which he has imposed upon himself, and which I just now portrayed.

He asked the other day, what there was so grave in the fact which he called a petty fact. What there is so grave in it is that it should be imputed to you, — that it should be you, you, of all the politicians perhaps in this Chamber, who by your language had given the least cause to think that you had committed acts of this sort, — that it is you who should be convicted of it.

And if this act, if this spectacle is of a nature to make a profound and painful impression, a deplorable one for morality in general, what impression do you not suppose it will make upon the particular morality of the agents of government? There is a comparison which appeared singularly striking to me, as soon as I became acquainted with the facts.

Three years ago, a functionary of the Minister of Foreign Affairs, a high functionary, differed in political opinion from the Minister upon one point. He did not express his dissent in an obtrusive manner, but he silently voted. The Minister of Foreign Affairs declared that it was impossible for him to live in the official company of a man who did not think precisely as he did; he dismisses him, or, to speak plainly, he expels him from office.

And now, behold another agent, placed not so high in the scale, but nearer to the person of the Minister of Foreign Affairs, commits the acts which you know of. At first, the Minister of Foreign Affairs did not deny that he was acquainted with them; he has since denied it; I admit for a moment that he was ignorant of them. But if he can deny any knowledge of these facts when they occurred, at least he cannot deny that they did take place, and that he now knows them; they are certain. Here there is no longer question concerning a difference of political opinion between you and this agent; the question relates to a moral disagreement, to what most intimately concerns the heart and conscience of man; it is not only the Minister who is here compromised, observe it well, it is the man. You, who have not been able to allow a difference of political opinion more or less important between you and an honorable man who had only voted against you, you find no blame — nay, more, you find recompense — for the functionary who, even if he has not carried out your own thought, has unworthily compromised you, has certainly placed you in the most serious and painful position in which you have ever been since you first entered political life. You retain this functionary, — much more, you recompense, you honor him.

What do you wish people should think of it? How do you suppose they can refrain from drawing one of these two conclusions: — either that you have a singular partiality for this class of differences of opinion, or that you are no longer free to punish them? I defy you, in spite of the immense talent which I acknowledge you to possess, I defy you to escape from this alternative. If the man of whom I speak has really acted in spite of you, why do you keep him near you? If you keep him near you, if you reward him, if you refuse to censure him, even in the lightest degree, we must necessarily draw the conclusion that I have just mentioned.

But let us admit that I am mistaken concerning the causes of the great evil of which I was speaking; let us admit, for a moment, that, in fact, the government in general and the cabinet in particular are in no wise responsible for it. The evil itself, gentlemen, is it any the less immense? Do we not owe it to our country, to ourselves, to make the most energetic and persevering efforts to overcome it? I was just now telling you that this evil would bring about, sooner or later, — I know not how, I know not whence it will come, — but, sooner or later, it will produce a most serious revolution in the country. Be sure of it.

When I begin to inquire what was the real efficient cause, which, at various times, at different epochs, among different nations, has brought about the ruin of the classes which held the government, I find indeed this or that event, this or that man, this or that accident or superficial cause; but believe me, the real cause, the efficient cause, which has made men lose power, is that they had become unworthy to hold it.

Consider, gentlemen, the old French monarchy; it was stronger than you are, stronger by its origin; it was supported better than you are by ancient usages, by ancestral manners, by venerable creeds; it was stronger than you are, and yet it was prostrated in the dust. And why did it fall? Think you that it was the action of this or that man, the deficit in the finances, the oath in the tennis-court, Lafayette, Mirabeau? No, gentlemen. There was a more real and deeply-seated cause, and this cause was, that the class which then formed the government, through its indifference, its selfishness, and its vices, had become unable and unworthy to govern. This was the true cause.

Oh! if it is right to have our minds engrossed by patriotic solicitude at all times, how much more incumbent is it upon us to be thus anxious at the present hour! Are you not aware, by a sort of instinctive intuition that you cannot analyze, but which is certain, that the ground is heaving anew in Europe? Do you not feel that the air is already stirred by the coming gust of a revolution? This movement in the air, one knows not what produces it, or whence it comes, or what it will sweep away; but is it at such a moment that you remain passive spectators of what it is not too strong a phrase to call the degradation of the public morals?

I speak without bitterness; I speak even, as I believe, without party spirit; I am attacking men against whom I have no personal animosity; but I am obliged to tell the country what is my profound and settled conviction. My profound and settled conviction is, that the public morals are becoming corrupt, and that this public corruption will bring upon you, in a short time, perhaps at an hour which is already at hand, a new revolution. Does the life of kings hang by a thread which is thicker or more difficult to break than that of other men? Do you know what may happen in France within a year, within a month, perhaps within a day. You know not; but what you do know is, that the tempest is on the horizon, that it is mounting over your heads. Will you allow it to burst upon you unawares?

Gentlemen, I beg you not to do so; I do not demand, I entreat; I would willingly bend my knees before you, so real and serious do I hold the danger to be, so truly do I believe that pointing it out is not having recourse to an empty rhetorical form. Yes, the danger is great! Guard against it, whilst there is yet time; avert the calamity by energetic measures; attack not merely its symptoms, but the malady itself.

Changes in our system of laws have been mentioned. I am much inclined to believe that these changes are not only useful, but necessary; thus, I believe in the utility of electoral reform, in the urgency of parliamentary reform. But, gentlemen, I am not foolish enough not to know, that it is not laws alone which shape the destiny of nations. No, it is not the mechanism of the laws which produces the great events of this world; that which regulates events is the spirit of the government. Keep the laws, if you will; although I believe it will be very wrong in you to do so, yet keep them; retain even the men, if that pleases you, and, for my own part, I will offer no opposition to your doing so; but for God's sake, change the spirit of the government, for I repeat it, that spirit is leading you to destruction.

BIOGRAPHICAL NOTICE OF DE TOCQUEVILLE.

THE family of Clerel, from which M. de Tocqueville was descended, belongs to the nobility of France, and has been established for centuries in that peninsula, forming the modern department of La Manche, which projects from the coast of Normandy into the English Channel, and has Cherbourg at its extremity. Here they possessed with seignorial rights the village and lands of Tocqueville, whence they derived their territorial designation. The title of Count, formally bestowed by Louis XVIII. on the father of Alexis, was only the acknowledgment of an ancient distinction. The chateau that formed the family residence consisted at first of a huge stone tower, now of great antiquity, which was enlarged in the seventeenth century by appending to it a quadrangle, that served both for the residence of the family and for farm buildings. An old " feudal weathercock " surmounted the great tower; and a large dove-cot, now tenantless, still marks the ancient right of the lord of the manor to keep his pigeons at the expense of his peasantry. " A stain over the door indicates the spot from which the Revolution of '93 tore the escutcheon of the family."

Count de Tocqueville, the father of Alexis, came into possession of this estate at an early age, and married Mademoiselle de Rosambo, a granddaughter of the celebrated M. de Malesherbes. This marriage took place in 1793, shortly after the execution of Louis XVI. had caused M. de Malesherbes to retire to his country-seat, at which place the wedding was celebrated. Only six months afterwards, the illustrious old man himself, — for so he is entitled to be called after his courageous defence of his king, — and his whole family, consisting of his daughter, his granddaughter, Madame de Chateaubriand, and her husband, a brother of the celebrated statesman and author, were seized and sent as prisoners to Paris; where, on the 22d of April, 1794, they were all guillotined together. Count de Tocqueville and his wife were arrested at about the same time; but after remaining a long time in prison, they were at length liberated by the fall of Robespierre. They then returned to his family mansion, and as they never emigrated, they were allowed to retain their estate, where they lived in dignified seclusion most of the time till the restoration of the Bourbons. Then the Count reaped some reward for his consistent and uncompromising conduct and opinions as an ardent royalist, being appointed successively Prefect at Metz, at Amiens, and at Versailles, and finally created a peer of France. Late in life, stimulated perhaps by the success of his son, the Count became an author, and achieved no small distinction, his "Philosophical History of the Reign of Louis XV." being one of the most valuable productions of the modern school of French historians.

These particulars respecting the parentage and family of De Tocqueville are interesting, as they show what were the influences under which he received his early training, and which undoubtedly colored his sentiments and opinions throughout life. He was, so to speak, born and bred an aristocrat and a loyalist, and as such he witnessed with mournful but dignified composure the rapid and overwhelming development of democracy in his day, which he knew full well would finally sweep away every vestige of those distinctions which had constituted the local grandeur of his house. What others would merely have brooded over as a misfortune, became to him an object of philosophical study ; and, far from seeking to limit or repress, he sought only to direct and chasten, that irresistible growth of opinion and march of public affairs which are so swiftly levelling all inequalities of condition, and establishing the principle of the sovereignty of the people as the sole element in the government of this world's affairs. He came to America in order to study the phenomenon where it had existed the longest, and had been most freely developed under favorable circumstances. In the Introduction to his work, he says : " The whole book has been written under the impression of a kind of religious terror, produced in the author's mind by the view of that irresistible revolution which has advanced for centuries in spite of every obstacle, and which is still advancing in the midst of the ruins it has caused." This personal interest in his subject was unquestionably one great cause of the ardor and the success with which he studied and analyzed it ; and this interest, as we have seen, arose from the circumstances of his birth and the position and history of his family.

Alexis Charles Henri Clerel de Tocqueville, the third son of his parents, was born at Paris, whither the family had gone upon a visit, on the 29th of July, 1805. While yet an infant, he was carried home to Tocqueville in a pannier slung across a horse, with his nurse on a pillion, the facilities for travelling in those days, in districts at any considerable distance from the capital, being of a very primitive character. He does not seem to have received a very regular or finished education, being trained chiefly at home, under the instruction of an Abbé Lesueur, to whom he was much attached, and afterwards at the College of Metz, where he began his classical studies while his father was Prefect of that city. There he did not acquire any distinction in the classics, but paid great attention to writing French prose, and in 1822 gained the first prize in rhetoric. But the most effective education which he had was an unconscious one under the quiet influences of home, where the counsels and example of his parents formed his manners, and developed in him a nice sense of honor and strong religious sentiment and conviction. On his father's death, in 1856, he wrote to one of his intimate friends, " If I am worth anything, I owe it above all to my education, to those examples of uprightness, simplicity, and honor which I found about me in coming into the world and as I advanced in life. I owe my parents much more than mere existence."

Having determined to enter the legal profession, he completed the study of law at Paris in 1826, and then set out upon a tour through Italy and Sicily, accompanied by his next elder brother, the Baron Edward de Tocqueville. A small portion of the copious memoranda which he made during this journey has been published in his Memoirs ; it relates to the island of Sicily and its inhabitants, and is chiefly curious as showing how the philosophical bent of his mind turned, even in early manhood, to observation of the social and intellectual state of a people, as affected by their laws and political institutions.

From this delightful experience of Italian travel he was recalled by a letter from home, in April, 1827, announcing that he had been appointed *Juge Auditeur*, a sort of deputy or assistant prosecuting officer, attached to the lower courts at Versailles, of which town his father was then Prefect. It was the first round on the ladder of advancement in the legal magistracy, the higher steps remaining to be taken according as self-achieved distinction or interest with the ministry might in time secure his promotion. The office was one which might be held nearly as a sinecure, or to which the incumbent could cause regular duties to be attached. De Tocqueville was industrious and ambitious, and therefore solicited and obtained active employment. He soon displayed solid rather than brilliant talents, which, with his grave manner of speaking, caused more than one of the presiding judges to foretell his high advancement in the profession. But the strong tendency to generalization which he even then betrayed, and his aversion to technicalities and details, rendered it doubtful in the minds of some of his friends whether this prophecy would hold good. Among his colleagues at the bar he found M. Gustave de Beaumont, with whom he soon contracted a close intimacy, that continued throughout life. With this congenial associate, whatever time could be rescued from judicial labors was soon devoted to more attractive studies than that of the law, especially to those connected with general history and politics. Already the young friends aspired to become philosophical statesmen and to guide the helm of state.

These studies and day-dreams were soon broken by an untoward event for De Tocqueville, — the Revolution of 1830. All his philosophy had not overcome his early predilections as a legitimist, and only with great reluctance did he give in his adhesion to the new dynasty. The event contributed further to wean him from his profession, as he could no longer count upon his father's influence at court to facilitate his promotion. "Every day he became more and more convinced that France, in irresistibly drifting into democracy, was also drifting into its perils. He determined to visit the only great country in which those dangers have been conquered, and where perfect equality reigns side by side with liberty. He communicated his scheme to his late colleague at Versailles, then *Substitut du Procureur du Roi* in Paris, who was charmed with the proposal. Obstacles, however, stood in their way: as magistrates they both required leave of absence, and a legitimate cause for obtaining it. At that time, as is always the case immediately after a revolution, all innovation was held in honor, and a reform of real but of secondary importance (that of the prisons) attracted public attention. A penitentiary system, which had proved successful in the United States, was talked of. The two young magistrates presented to the then Minister of the Interior, the Comte de Montalivet, a paper in which, after setting forth the question, they offered to study it on the spot, if they might be sent on an official mission. It was granted to them; and the Minister of Justice having consented, the two friends set out with a leave obtained in due form. It has often been said that this mission was the cause of Alexis de Tocqueville's expedition. It was in truth only the pretext. His real and long premeditated object was to study the customs and institutions of American society."

Having arrived at New York on the 10th of May, 1831, De Tocqueville devoted about a year to travelling in the United States, to observations connected with the subject of his formal mission, and to other inquiries of a more general nature, which were to furnish the material for the great work which he was now meditating. While journeying in the depth of a severe winter through our Southwestern States, he was exposed to unaccustomed privations and hardships, which operated hardly on a constitution originally slender, and probably laid the seeds of a malady which was ultimately to prove fatal. Returning to Europe in the spring of 1832, his attention was necessarily first directed to the preparation of a report to the Minister of the Interior on the subject of his mission. This work, the joint composition of his friend and himself, soon appeared under the title of " The Penitentiary System in the United States, and its Application in France," and had good success. It passed through three editions, was translated both into German and English, and has shaped much of the subsequent legislation of France upon the subject.

Even before this report was completed, De Tocqueville had quitted the legal profession forever. De Beaumont, having refused to speak on an occasion when the official part which he had to play appeared to him discreditable, was summarily dismissed from office; and his friend resented this procedure so highly, that he immediately sent in his own resignation. He was probably glad of an opportunity to break off all connection with a government for which he had never entertained either sympathy or respect, to quit at the same time a profession which he had always disliked, and to give his whole time and effort to the preparation of the work on which his thoughts had so long been deeply engaged. The two years from 1832 to 1834, which were probably the happiest of his life, were devoted to the composition of the First Part, which, after being rejected by one publisher and accepted only with great reluctance by another, appeared in January, 1835. Even if it had not been successful, the labor bestowed upon it would have been its own exceeding great reward. Secluding himself during these two years from society, spending the daytime, in order to avoid interruption, in a lodging the secret of which was known to very few of his friends, sustained by the flattering dreams which always visit a young author and by the attachment which he had already formed to the lady whom he was soon to marry, he gave himself up to the intoxication which generally attends the continuous creative action of mind. The success of the work was great, but it was no more than he had anticipated.

"Since Montesquieu, there has been nothing like it," said Royer-Collard; and on a subsequent occasion, M. de Barante added, "Twenty years later, we repeat the same judgment." It has passed through fourteen editions at Paris, and has been translated into nearly all the languages of modern Europe. In 1836, the French Institute adjudged

to its author the Monthyon prize, which is given annually
for the work of the highest moral utility that has been produced during the year; and in this case, to mark a special
distinction, the prize was increased from 6,000 francs, its
usual amount, to 8,000. A year later, De Tocqueville
was chosen a member of the Academy of the Moral and
Political Sciences; and in 1841, he became one of the
forty members of the French Academy, the highest literary
honor that a Frenchman can attain. This last distinction
was well deserved, for considered only as a specimen of
refined and idiomatic French prose, evincing a careful
study of the inimitable style of Pascal, but betraying also
an imitation of the curt and sententious manner of Montesquieu, the book is fairly entitled to take rank as a classic
in the literature of France. In respect to doctrine, it was
welcomed both by the friends and opponents of democracy; by the former, because it points out so clearly the
rapid development and future universal dominion of democratic principles; by the latter, because it shows with equal
clearness the dangers incident to this progress, and the
ease with which such dominion degenerates into a tyranny
even more hateful than the despotism of one man. Perhaps the greatest merit of the author consists in the resolute impartiality with which he looks at the subject on all
its sides, and shows that the welfare of a nation under
democratic rule can be maintained only on condition of
such a union of general intelligence and religious faith
with submissiveness to constitutional restraint, as is rarely
exemplified in the history of mankind.

In the same year in which his book became so generally
popular, he married Miss Mary Motley, an English lady
without fortune, but who united those qualities of character
and intellect which rendered her, during an unbroken union
of twenty-five years, his best companion, counsellor, and
friend. He often remarked that his marriage, though cen-

sured by those prudent friends who look only to the contribution which a wife is first able to make to her husband's pecuniary or social position in the world, had proved to be the most sensible action of his life. About the same time, he visited England, whither his literary renown had preceded him, and where he consequently received a cordial welcome into the best circles of literary and aristocratic society. The character of De Tocqueville's mind, in several respects, approached more nearly to the English than the French standard of excellence; and he soon contracted an intimate friendship with many eminent Englishmen, on frequent intercourse with whom depended much of the happiness of his subsequent career. His personal qualities, indeed, were such as to make him an object of strong attachment to all his friends. An Englishman who knew him well says of him, that " the extreme delicacy of his physical organization, the fastidious refinement of his tastes, and the charm of his manners, made him the very type of a high-bred gentleman."

His mother died shortly after his return to France, and then, through a family arrangement with his two older brothers, he obtained possession of the paternal estate at Tocqueville, and made it his permanent residence. The old chateau was in bad repair, — "full of associations and ruins," says his French biographer; but the country around is rich and pleasant, and the upper part of the building commands a magnificent view of the sea-coast and the English Channel. Here De Tocqueville devoted himself to the management of the estate, for which his knowledge of agriculture did not very well qualify him, to the preparation of the Second Part of his work, and to cultivating that acquaintance with his country neighbors, on which he was to depend for election to the Chamber of Deputies, and thus for an introduction to political life. To this object his ambition was now directed; he longed for an opportunity to carry out in practice some of the theoretical views which he had so nobly developed; and perhaps his success in abstract speculation made him over-estimate his fitness for the practical management of affairs.

The Second Part of his work, which treats of the influence of democracy upon the action of mind, and upon feelings and manners, was published in 1840, and its success was decided, though not so brilliant and general as that of its predecessor. The subject, of course, had now less of novelty to recommend it, and the treatment of it, though even more elaborate in thought and expression than the First Part, abounded too much in abstract speculation and acute philosophical analysis for the taste of ordinary readers. The year before it was published, its author offered himself as a candidate to his own district for election to the Chamber of Deputies. His relative, Count Molé, then Prime Minister of France, gave orders, without consultation with him, that all the influence of the government should be exerted in his favor. Fearful lest he should be thus committed to a support of the ministerial policy, De Tocqueville wrote back with some haughtiness to decline the proffered · aid. The Minister replied with considerable spirit, but with politeness and good sense, remarking that he had not intended to impose any obligation, that isolation is not independence, that the party of government were acting together, not from interested motives, but from sincere conviction, in defençe of the institutions of the country, and that their assistance, as it was not desired, should be promptly withdrawn. The candidacy of De Tocqueville, thus deprived of government aid, proved unsuccessful; his neighbors could not be made to believe that, although he belonged by birth and social position to the nobility, he did not share the feelings and the prejudices of his order, but was really the friend and the expounder of democracy. The popular opinion respecting him was well expressed by his opponent, a retired manufacturer, who cried out lustily, " Beware!   He is going to bring back his aristocratic pigeons into their old dove-cot." Two years afterwards, when his temper and principles had come to be better understood in the neighborhood, he was elected by a triumphant majority to the Chamber, and he continued to represent his district thoughout his parliamentary career.

That career lasted only twelve years, up to December, 1851, when Louis Napoleon's *coup d'état* destroyed the constitutional liberties of France, and De Tocqueville, unwilling to take an oath of fidelity to one whom he regarded as a usurper, retired altogether to private life.   Up to February, 1848, he was a member of the opposition, and contended strongly, though without personal animosity, against Guizot's ministry ; after the Revolution, he joined the party of the moderate republicans, who, with Cavaignac for a leader, strove gallantly, though with only faint hopes of success, against the mad schemes of the radicals on the one hand, and the intriguing ambition of the future Emperor on the other.   But it must be owned that his mind was of too fine a texture, his principles too pure and unwavering, and his disposition for abstract thought and analytical investigation too strongly marked, to allow him to succeed in the strife of parties or the tournaments of parliamentary debate.   He commanded the confidence of his friends and the respect of his opponents ; but he was not put forward into the front rank in battle, nor elevated to the chief seat in council.   The best portions of his parliamentary labors were his reports on the abolition of colonial slavery, on prison reform, and on the administration of Algeria, a country which he had twice visited, and whose affairs he thoroughly understood.   When the new Republic was settling into a calm, he became a member of the Committee appointed to frame a new Constitution for France, and endeavored in vain to induce his colleagues to adopt the principle of a division of the legislature into two houses. Louis Napoleon understood his value arising from his weight of character, and endeavored to secure his aid by offering him considerable attention. But the bribe of a usurper was coldly declined. After dining with the President on one occasion at the Elysée, De Tocqueville remarked on leaving, " I have been dining with a man who believes in his own hereditary right to the crown as firmly as Charles X. himself."

" One chance remained to avert the final catastrophe. It was possible that the President might still be content to accept a constitutional position; to govern by responsible ministers, who hoped to effect a revision of the constitution by legal means. At any rate, to abandon or to oppose him was to compel him to resort to an immediate *coup d'état.* On this principle, M. Odilon Barrot and the leading liberals formed an administration on the 2d June, 1849, in which M. de Tocqueville took the important office of Minister of Foreign Affairs. It would be inappropriate here to enter upon the political transactions in which he was engaged. As he said, on quitting his office four months later, — ' I have contributed to maintain order on the 13th of June, to preserve the general peace, to improve the relations of France and England. These are recollections which give some value to my passage through affairs. I need hardly say anything to you of the cause which led to the fall of the Cabinet. The President chooses to govern alone, and to have mere agents and creatures in his ministers. Perhaps he is right. I don't examine that question, but we were not the men to serve him on these terms.' "

After leaving the ministry, as his health was considerably impaired, he went to Italy, and spent the winter at Sorrento, engaged in his literary undertakings. On his return, he took little share in the proceedings of the

Assembly, except to draw up the celebrated Report on the Revision of the Constitution, which was presented on the 8th of July, 1851. It was the ablest of his parliamentary productions, and the presentation of it may be regarded as the closing act of his political life.

Yet he was present in the struggle, if it can be called one, of the 2d of December, 1851, and, in company with about 230 other representatives, signed a paper deposing the President from all authority, and requiring the High Court of Justice to proceed to judgment against him and his accomplices. It was a bootless proceeding, except for the purpose of putting on record the protest of the legislature; for Louis Napoleon immediately arrested the whole party, and the High Court of Justice too, and sent them to prison, whence most of them were released after only two days' confinement. De Tocqueville drew up a temperate narrative of the proceeding, which he published in *The Times* newspaper, England being then the only country in Europe where such a document could be printed with impunity. Then, with a sad heart, he went back to his residence in the country, to give the few years of life which remained to intercourse with his friends, to the care of his estate, and to one other literary effort in which he was deeply interested.

This project, as originally conceived, was that of a new history of the first French Revolution, with especial reference to the causes which had produced it in the preceding state of the country and the government. It was not to be so much a narrative of events, as a philosophical inquiry into the nature of the circumstances which precede and originate great changes in the constitution of society. Perhaps it would have been better if he had acted earlier upon the conviction which he expressed in January, 1851, in a letter to a friend. " It has occurred to me a hundred times," he says, " that, if I am to leave any traces of my passage through the world, it will be far more by my writings than by my actions." His subject required much research, not only in the great public libraries of the state, but among the archives of the old provincial administrations, especially in that of Tours; and to facilitate these researches, as well as to benefit his health, he resided for some months in 1854 at St. Cyr, near Tours. The next year, he visited Germany, and learned the language of the country, that he might be able to consult original documents in German. The first part of his work was published in 1856, entitled *L'Ancien Régime et la Revolution*, and was received with decided tokens of general approbation. It was translated into several languages, and commended in all the leading journals of Europe. Yet it was only a fragment, as the whole work would probably have filled three volumes. Two chapters only of the second volume were found at his death in so finished a state as to warrant their publication in his " Memoirs and Correspondence." The manuscript preparations for the remainder of the work were very extensive, but not in a state fit for presentation to the public.

Among his other unfinished works was one of considerable length, on the "Establishment of the English in India." His pen was always active, but he was chary of publication, except of a work which might aid some important object, or add to its author's fame; he could not tolerate bookmaking. Hence, though he left a great amount of manuscript, it is probable that only a small portion of it will ever see the light. One important fragment of contemporary history, however, will probably appear as soon as the French government can tolerate it, and delicacy to surviving individuals will permit; it is entitled " Souvenirs," and relates chiefly to public affairs in France in 1848 – 49. Some very interesting portions of his correspondence, also, are as yet kept back, as their appearance might irritate the government or wound the feelings of persons in private life.

The health of De Tocqueville had never been robust, and ever after 1850, at least, when he was compelled to spend the winter at Sorrento, he was affected by pulmonary disease, though it appears to have escaped the observation both of himself and his medical attendants. But in the summer of 1858 he broke a bloodvessel, and showed other unequivocal symptoms of the fatal malady. In the autumn, as his strength had rapidly declined, his physicians required him to go to the South of France for the winter. Though very reluctant to leave home, he prepared to obey; and having made large provision of books, manuscripts, and other materials for the completion of his work, he set out for Cannes, where he arrived early in November, 1858. He was accompanied by his wife and his brothers, and was visited in Provençe by several of his friends. With others he kept up a frequent correspondence, and even labored at times upon his work during the winter, though it was evident to every eye but his own that he was sinking fast. Christian faith, which had always governed his convictions and regulated his life, supported him in his last moments. Having received the sacraments according to the rites of that Church to which he was strongly attached, he died on the 16th of April, 1859, at the age of fifty-four. In conformity with his own request, his remains were carried to Tocqueville, and in the village cemetery there a plain wooden cross marks his grave.

THE END.